Historical Dictionaries of Ancient Civilizations and Historical Eras
Series editor: Jon Woronoff

1. *Ancient Egypt*, Morris L. Bierbrier, 1999. *Out of Print. See No. 22.*
2. *Ancient Mesoamerica*, Joel W. Palka, 2000.
3. *Pre-Colonial Africa*, Robert O. Collins, 2001.
4. *Byzantium*, John H. Rosser, 2001.
5. *Medieval Russia*, Lawrence N. Langer, 2001.
6. *Napoleonic Era*, George F. Nafziger, 2001.
7. *Ottoman Empire*, Selcuk Aksin Somel, 2003.
8. *Mongol World Empire*, Paul D. Buell, 2003.
9. *Mesopotamia*, Gwendolyn Leick, 2003.
10. *Ancient and Medieval Nubia*, Richard A. Lobban Jr., 2003.
11. *The Vikings*, Katherine Holman, 2003.
12. *The Renaissance*, Charles G. Nauert, 2004.
13. *Ancient Israel*, Niels Peter Lemche, 2004.
14. *The Hittites*, Charles Burney, 2004.
15. *Early North America*, Cameron B. Wesson, 2005.
16. *The Enlightenment*, by Harvey Chisick, 2005.
17. *Cultural Revolution*, by Guo Jian, Yongyi Song, and Yuan Zhou, 2006.
18. *Ancient Southeast Asia*, by John N. Miksic, 2007.
19. *Medieval China*, by Victor Cunrui Xiong, 2008.
20. *Medieval India*, by Iqtidar Alam Khan, 2008.
21. *Ancient South America*, by Martin Giesso, 2008.
22. *Egypt,* 2nd Ed., Morris L. Bierbrier, 2008.

8

Historical Dictionary of Ancient Egypt

Second Edition

Morris L. Bierbrier

Historical Dictionaries of Ancient
Civilizations and Historical Eras, No. 22

The Scarecrow Press, Inc.
Lanham, Maryland • Toronto • Plymouth, UK
2008

SCARECROW PRESS, INC.

Published in the United States of America
by Scarecrow Press, Inc.
A wholly owned subsidary of
The Rowman & Littlefield Publishing Group, Inc.
4501 Forbes Boulevard, Suite 200, Lanham, Maryland 20706
www.scarecrowpress.com

Estover Road
Plymouth PL6 7PY
United Kingdom

British Library Cataloguing in Publication Information Available

Library of Congress Cataloging-in-Publication Data

Bierbrier, M. L.
   Historical dictionary of ancient Egypt / Morris L. Bierbrier. — 2nd ed.
      p. cm. — (Historical dictionaries of ancient civilizations and historical eras ;
no. 22)
   Previously published: 1999.
   Includes bibliographical references.
   ISBN-13: 978-0-8108-5794-0 (hardback : alk. paper)
   ISBN-10: 0-8108-5794-4 (hardback : alk. paper)
   eISBN-13: 978-0-8108-6250-0
   eISBN-10: 0-8108-6250-6
1. Egypt—History—To 640 A.D.—Dictionaries. I. Title.
   DT83.B56 2008
   932.003—dc22

                                                          2008012502

∞™ The paper used in this publication meets the minimum requirements of
American National Standard for Information Sciences—Permanence of Paper
for Printed Library Materials, ANSI/NISO Z39.48-1992.
Manufactured in the United States of America.

To my wife
Lydia Collins

Contents

Editor's Foreword

Historical Dictionary of Ancient Egypt was the first volume in the Historical Dictionaries of Ancient Civilizations and Historical Eras series, and now it is the first to be expanded and updated. This is quite fitting because while the Egyptian civilization is not the oldest, it is certainly the grandest. It stands out for the vast area it covered, the amazing span of its history, and the exceptional works of art and architecture it left behind. The Egyptian civilization is also one of the most topical of the ancient cultures, its achievements studied in classrooms around the globe, major events—or simulations thereof—conveyed in movies and operas, and its vestiges still visited by countless millions of people every year, whether in present-day Egypt or dozens of museums. There are indeed few who do not recognize the pyramids and the Sphinx, Luxor and the Valley of the Kings, and Tutankhamun and Cleopatra.

This series of historical dictionaries, like the others, provides information on significant people, places, and events. In this second edition, both the old and new eras of achievement are presented. Entries provide information on ancient kings and queens, generals and workmen, as well as the archaeologists who brought these important figures to light and the sites that display them. The book also covers such broader subjects as art, language, and religion and aspects of architecture and historical periods. The volume is supported by a chronology of key events, an introduction that places the significant happenings in context, and appendixes containing a dynastic list and museums with Egyptian collections. The extensive bibliography, carefully structured by subject, leads the reader to additional authoritative sources. While this second edition resembles the first, it has been substantially expanded with many new entries and updated with the latest research.

This second edition is written by Morris Leonard Bierbrier who, while providing numerous fine points of Egyptology, has fashioned a book that can also be used by a broader public. The entries are informative yet concise, providing considerable insight into a field that interests generalists and specialists alike. To compile such a handy guide, Bierbrier drew on an impressive accumulation of knowledge and experience. He studied Egyptology at the University of Toronto and the University of Liverpool and joined the Department of Egyptian Antiquities of the British Museum in 1976, where he spent 25 years as assistant keeper until his retirement. He is also author of numerous articles and two books, *The Late New Kingdom in Egypt: A Genealogical and Chronological Investigation* and *The Tomb-Builders of the Pharaohs*. He is also editor of *Who Was Who in Egyptology*.

Jon Woronoff
Series Editor

Acknowledgments

This second edition of *Historical Dictionary of Ancient Egypt* could not have been written without the assistance of Dr. Patricia Spencer, director of the Egypt Exploration Society; Christopher Naunton, deputy director of the Egypt Exploration Society; and the society's staff, Andrew Bednarski, Karen Exell, Tracey Gargetta, Roo Mitcheson, and Alice Stevenson, whom I warmly thank for their encouragement and technical advice. No text of this nature is ever finite, as new discoveries—both archaeological and intellectual—continue to advance and refine the history of ancient Egypt. The selection of topics and entries is my responsibility, but I have benefited from advice from the series editor, Jon Woronoff.

This book could not have been completed without the assistance of my dear wife, Lydia Collins, who has advised and supported me throughout its production. It is a pleasure, once again, to dedicate this volume to her.

Reader's Note

The pronunciation of ancient Egyptian is uncertain as vowels were not written down. Thus the names of Egyptian people and places have been interpreted in different ways by Egyptologists over the years. Some have preferred to use Greek versions of such royal names as Amenophis or Sethos, although Greek versions do not survive for all royal names, and some are obviously garbled. In this text, an Egyptian form is cited for most personal names, although it is not always possible to be completely consistent with well-known names like Ramesses. Place names are given the most commonly known form—Arabic, Greek, and rarely Egyptian.

The names, order, and dates of the rulers of ancient Egypt are not fixed because of gaps in our knowledge. From the New Kingdom, there is a margin of error of about 25 years, but it may be greater in earlier periods. Some dynasties are contemporaneous, which adds to the confusion. New discoveries constantly refine our knowledge, but many problems remain.

Names and terms printed in boldface in the dictionary section indicate that there is a corresponding entry for additional information.

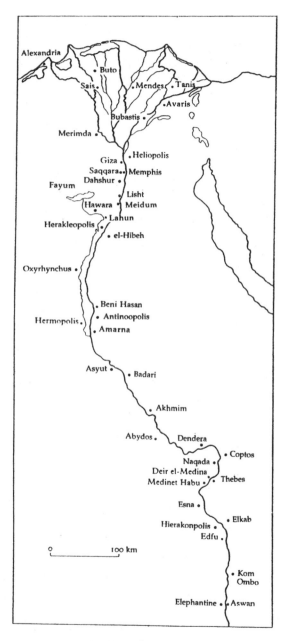

Map of Egypt

Chronology

200000–12000 BC   Palaeolithic Period.

12000–5000 BC   Epipalaeolithic Period.

5000 BC   Beginning of Neolithic Period.

5000–4000 BC   Badarian culture.

4000–3500 BC   Naqada I Period.

3500–3100 BC   Naqada II Period.

3100 BC   Union of Egypt. Dynasty 1.

3100–2686 BC   Early Dynastic Period (Dynasties 1–2).

c. 3100 BC   Reign of Narmer.

c. 3080 BC   Reign of Aha.

c. 3050 BC   Reign of Djer.

c. 3000 BC   Reign of Djet.

c. 2985 BC   Reign of Den. Merneith regent.

c. 2935 BC   Reign of Anedjib.

c. 2925 BC   Reign of Semerkhet.

c. 2915 BC   Reign of Qaa.

2890–2686 BC   Dynasty 2.

c. 2890 BC   Reign of Hotepsekhemwy.

c. 2850 BC   Reign of Raneb.

c. 2810 BC   Reign of Nynetjer.

c. 2760 BC   Reign of Peribsen.

c. 2730 BC   Reign of Khasekhemwy.

2686–2181 BC   Old Kingdom.

2686 BC   Beginning of Dynasty 3.

2686–2667 BC   Reign of Sanakhte.

2667–2648 BC   Reign of Djoser. Construction of step pyramid of Djoser at Saqqara. First stone building.

2648–2640 BC   Reign of Sekhemkhet. Unfinished pyramid at Saqqara.

2640–2637 BC   Reign of Khaba.

2637–2613 BC   Reign of Huni.

2613–2589 BC   Dynasty 4. Reign of Snefru. Construction of first true pyramids at Dahshur and Meidum.

2589–2566 BC   Reign of Khufu. Construction of first pyramid at Giza.

2566–2558 BC   Reign of Djedefre. Construction of pyramid at Abu Roash.

2558–2532 BC   Reign of Khafre. Construction of second pyramid at Giza.

2532–2503 BC   Reign of Menkaure. Construction of third pyramid at Giza.

2494–2345 BC   Dynasty 5. Cult of Re. Construction of pyramids at Abusir.

2494–2487 BC   Reign of Userkaf.

2487–2475 BC   Reign of Sahure.

2475–2455   Reign of Neferirkare.

2455–2448 BC   Reign of Shepsekare.

2448–2445 BC   Reign of Raneferef.

2445–2421 BC   Reign of Niuserre.

2421–2414 BC   Reign of Menkauhor.

2414–2375   Reign of Djedkare.

2375–2345 BC   Reign of Unas. Construction of first inscribed pyramid at Saqqara.

2345–2181 BC   Dynasty 6.

2345–2323 BC   Reign of Teti.

2323–2321 BC   Reign of Userkare.

2321–2287 BC   Reign of Pepy I.

2287–2278 BC   Reign of Merenre Nemtyemsaf I.

2278–2184 BC   Reign of Pepy II.

2184–2183 BC   Reign of Merenre Nemtyemsaf II.

2183–2181   Reign of Nitocris.

2181–2040 BC   First Intermediate Period. Collapse of central authority and onset of civil war. Dynasties 7–11.

c. 2125 BC   Reign of Mentuhotep I. Founding of Dynasty 11 at Thebes.

2055 BC   Accession of Mentuhotep II of Dynasty 11 at Thebes.

2040–1795 BC   Middle Kingdom.

2040–1985 BC   Dynasty 11 of united Egypt.

2040 BC   Reunification of Egypt under Mentuhotep II of Thebes. Building work at Deir el-Bahri.

2004 BC   Death of Mentuhotep II.

2004–1992 BC   Reign of Mentuhotep III.

1992–1985 BC   Reign of Mentuhotep IV.

1985–1795 BC   Dynasty 12.

1985–1955 BC   Reign of Amenemhat I, founder of Dynasty 12. Capital moved to Lisht in Middle Egypt.

1965 BC   Senusret I named as coregent.

1955 BC   Assassination of Amenemhat I. Sole rule of Senusret I.

1922 BC   Amenemhat II named as coregent.

1920 BC   Death of Senusret I. Sole Rule of Amenemhat II.

1880 BC   Senusret II named as coregent.

1878 BC   Death of Amenemhat II. Sole rule of Senusret II.

1874 BC   Death of Senusret II. Accession of Senusret III.

1855 BC   Death of Senusret III. Accession of Amenemhat III.

1808 BC   Death of Amenemhat III. Accession of Amenemhat IV.

1799 BC   Death of Amenemhat IV.

1799–1795 BC   Reign of Queen Sobekneferu. End of Dynasty 12.

1795–1650 BC   Dynasties 13–14. Second Intermediate Period. Disintegration of central authority. Infiltration and conquest of the north by Hyksos.

1650–1550 BC   Rule of Hyksos. Dynasties 15–16 in the north. Dynasty 17 at Thebes.

1560 BC   Campaign of Thebes against the Hyksos begins.

1550–1069 BC   New Kingdom.

1550 BC   Sack of Avaris and expulsion of Hyksos. Reunification of Egypt under Ahmose I of Dynasty 18. Elevation of Amun as chief god. Expansion into Nubia.

1525 BC   Death of Ahmose I. Accession of Amenhotep I.

1504 BC   Death of Amenhotep I. Accession of Thutmose I.

1504–1492 BC   Reign of Thutmose I. Egyptian armies in the Levant. Founding of Deir el-Medina and Valley of the Kings.

1492 BC   Death of Thutmose I. Accession of Thutmose II.

1479 BC   Death of Thutmose II. Accession of Thutmose III. Hatshepsut as regent.

1472–1458 BC   Reign of Hatshepsut. Expedition to Punt. Building at Deir el-Bahri.

1458 BC   Death or disappearance of Hatshepsut. Battle of Megiddo.

1458–1425 BC   Thutmose III consolidates Egypt's empire in Syria-Palestine and in Nubia.

1425 BC   Death of Thutmose III. Accession of Amenhotep II. Rebellion in Syria and Nubia.

1400 BC   Death of Amenhotep II. Accession of Thutmose IV.

1390 BC   Death of Thutmose IV. Accession of Amenhotep III.

1389 BC   Marriage of Amenhotep III and Tiy.

1381 BC   Marriage of Amenhotep III and Gilikhepa of Mitanni.

1352 BC   Death of Amenhotep III. Accession of Amenhotep IV Akhenaten.

1352–1336 BC   Reign of Akhenaten. Attempt at religious change to worship of Aten. Loss of northern part of Syrian province to the Hittites.

1336–1338 BC   Reign of Smenkhkare.

1336 BC   Accession of Tutankhamun. Return to former religious practices.

1327 BC   Death of Tutankhamun. Accession of Ay.

1323 BC   Death of Ay. Accession of Horemheb.

1295 BC   Death of Horemheb. Accession of Ramesses I. Founding of Dynasty 19.

1294 BC   Death of Ramesses I. Accession of Sety I.

1279 BC   Death of Sety I. Accession of Ramesses II.

1274 BC   Battle of Kadesh. Ramesses II fails to win back lost Syrian provinces from Hittites.

1258 BC Egyptian–Hittite peace treaty.

1245 BC Egyptian–Hittite marriage alliance.

1213 BC Death of Ramesses II. Accession of Merenptah.

1209 BC War against the Libyans and Sea Peoples. First mention of Israel.

1202 BC Death of Merenptah. Civil war between Sety II and Amenmesse.

1199 BC Overthrow of Amenmesse. Rule of Sety II over a reunited Egypt.

1196 BC Death of Sety II. Accession of Siptah.

1190 BC Death of Siptah. Accession of Queen Tewosret.

1189 BC Accession of Sethnakhte. Inception of Dynasty 20.

1184 BC Death of Sethnakhte. Accession of Ramesses III.

1179 BC War against the Libyans.

1176 BC War against the Sea Peoples.

1153 BC Assassination of Ramesses III. Accession of Ramesses IV.

1126 BC Death of Ramesses VIII. Accession of Ramesses IX.

1153–1069 BC Later Dynasty 20. Loss of Egyptian empire in Syria-Palestine and Nubia.

1069–702 BC Third Intermediate Period.

1069 BC Accession of Nesbanebdjed. Founding of Dynasty 21. Political division of Egypt between north and south.

945 BC Accession of Sheshonq I. Founding of Dynasty 22.

924 BC Death of Sheshonq I. Accession of Osorkon I.

925 BC Campaign of Sheshonq I in Palestine.

850–715 BC Gradual disintegration of Egypt into various principalities. Dynasties 22–24.

728 BC   Invasion of Egypt by the Kushite king Piye.

720 BC   Death of King Piye. Accession of Shabaqo in Nubia.

719 BC   Conquest of Egypt by Shabaqo. Execution of Bakenrenef of Dynasty 24. Founding of Dynasty 25.

706 BC   Death of Shabaqo. Accession of Shebitqo.

701 BC   Battle of Eltekeh. Defeat of Egyptians by the Assyrians.

690 BC   Death of Shebitqo. Accession of Taharqo. First definite date in Egyptian history.

671 BC   First Assyrian invasion of Egypt. Temporary flight of Taharqo to Nubia.

667/666 BC   Renewed Assyrian invasion. Retreat of Taharqo to Nubia.

664 BC   Reconquest of Egypt by Tantamani. Death of Nekau I. Flight of Psamtik I to Assyria.

663 BC   Assyrian invasion of Egypt. Sack of Thebes. Installation of Psamtik I as vassal of Dynasty 26.

656 BC   Installation of Nitocris, daughter of Psamtik I, as God's wife in Thebes.

610 BC   Death of Psamtik I. Accession of Nekau II.

609 BC   Battle of Carchemish. Defeat of Nekau II by the Babylonians.

595 BC   Death of Nekau II. Accession of Psamtik II. Invasion of Nubia. Adoption of Ankhnesneferibre as heiress to God's wife of Amun.

589 BC   Death of Psamtik II. Accession of Wahibre.

586 BC   Installation of Ankhnesneferibre as God's wife of Amun.

570 BC   Overthrow of Wahibre by Ahmose II.

526 BC   Death of Ahmose II. Accession of Psamtik III.

525 BC   Persian conquest of Egypt. Dynasty 27.

486 BC   Revolt against Persian rule.

484 BC   Restoration of Persian rule. Appointment of Achaemenes as satrap.

459 BC   Rebellion of Inaros. Death of Achaemenes in battle.

454 BC   Defeat of the rebellion of Inaros. Restoration of Persian rule.

404 BC   Expulsion of Persians by Amyrtaeos of Dynasty 28.

399 BC   Overthrow of Amyrtaeos. Accession of Nefaarud I of Dynasty 29.

393 BC   Death of Nefaarud I. Accession of Hakor.

380 BC   Death of Hakor. Accession and deposition of Nefaarud II. Accession of Nakhtnebef of Dynasty 30.

373 BC   Abortive Persian invasion.

362 BC   Death of Nakhtnebef. Accession of Djedhor.

360 BC   Campaign against Persia. Overthrow of Djedhor. Acccession of Nakhthorheb.

343 BC   Second conquest of Egypt by Persia. Flight of Nakhthorheb to Nubia.

332 BC   Conquest of Egypt by Alexander the Great.

323 BC   Death of Alexander the Great. Accession of joint kings Philip III Arrhidaeus and Alexander IV. Ptolemy I becomes satrap of Egypt.

317 BC   Murder of King Philip III.

310 BC   Murder of King Alexander IV.

305 BC   Official acknowledgment of the death of King Alexander IV. Reign of Ptolemy I.

282 BC   Death of Ptolemy I. Accession of Ptolemy II.

c. 270 BC   Marriage of Ptolemy II and his sister Arsinoe I.

246 BC   Death of Ptolemy II. Accession of Ptolemy III.

222 BC   Death of Ptolemy III. Accession of Ptolemy IV.

217 BC   Marriage of Ptolemy IV and his sister Arsinoe III.

205 BC   Death of Ptolemy IV. Accession of Ptolemy V. Revolt of Harwennefer in southern Egypt.

199 BC   Thebes temporarily taken by Ptolemaic forces. Accession of rebel Ankhwennefer.

191 BC   Thebes retaken by Ptolemaic forces.

186 BC   Final suppression of rebellion in the south.

180 BC   Death of Ptolemy V. Accession of Ptolemy VI.

176 BC   Marriage of Ptolemy VI and his sister Cleopatra III.

170 BC   Joint rule of Ptolemy VI, Ptolemy VIII, and Cleopatra III.

170/169 BC   First invasion of the Seleucid king Antiochus IV.

168 BC   Second invasion of Antiochus IV. Withdrawal of Antiochus IV under Roman pressure.

168/167 BC   Revolt of Dionysius Petosarapis.

163 BC   Expulsion of Ptolemy VIII to Cyrenaica.

145 BC   Death of Ptolemy VII in battle in Syria. Accession of Ptolemy VII. Accession of Ptolemy VIII and marriage to Cleopatra III. Murder of Ptolemy VII.

c. 140 BC   Marriage of Ptolemy VIII to his niece, Cleopatra IV.

132–124 BC   Civil War between Cleopatra II and Ptolemy VIII and Cleopatra IV.

116 BC   Death of Ptolemy VIII. Accession of Ptolemy IX.

107 BC   Expulsion of Ptolemy IX to Cyprus. Accession of Ptolemy X.

89 BC   Expulsion of Ptolemy X. Restoration of Ptolemy IX.

88 BC   Death of Ptolemy X in battle. Death of Ptolemy IX. Accession of Ptolemy XI. Murder of Ptolemy XI. Accession of Ptolemy XII.

58 BC   Expulsion of Ptolemy XII. Reign of Berenice IV.

55 BC   Restoration of Ptolemy XII. Murder of Berenice IV.

51 BC   Death of Ptolemy XII. Accession of Ptolemy XIII and Cleopatra VII.

48 BC   Civil War between Ptolemy XIII and Cleopatra VII. Arrival of Caesar in Alexandria.

47 BC   Defeat and death of Ptolemy XIII. Accession of Ptolemy XIV as husband of Cleopatra VII.

44 BC   Death of Ptolemy XIV.

36 BC   Accession of Ptolemy XV Caesarion son of Cleopatra VII and Caesar as joint rulers.

30 BC   Conquest of Egypt by Rome.

69 AD   Accession of Emperor Vespasian.

130 AD   Visit of Emperor Hadrian.

312 AD   Triumph of Constantine. Official recognition of Christianity.

391–2 AD   Edicts of Emperor Theodosius against paganism.

394 AD   Last dated hieroglyphic inscription found at Philae.

395 AD   Division of the Roman Empire. Egypt becomes part of the Eastern (Byzantine) Empire.

452 AD   Last attested demotic inscription found at Philae.

c. 530 AD   Closure of the temple of Philae.

617–629 AD   Persian (Sassanian) occupation of Egypt.

641 AD   Arab invasion. Surrender of Alexandria.

642 AD   Departure of Byzantine forces. Arab occupation of Egypt.

Introduction

Ancient Egypt owed its prosperity, wealth, and power to its geographic location along the banks and in the Delta formed by the river Nile. The annual floods of the Nile brought down rich silt from the interior that enriched the fertility of the soil and made food production dependable and plentiful. The agricultural region was protected in the east, west, and south by desert areas and in the north by the Mediterranean Sea, which tended to discourage but not necessarily prevent invasions. The desert areas were also rich in minerals and stone, which could be exploited as tools and building materials.

The original inhabitants of Egypt appear to have belonged to the Hamito-Semitic group of peoples, along with the ancient Libyans and Berbers. The Egyptian language had affinities with both the ancient Hamitic and Semitic languages but was an autonomous linguistic branch. The Egyptians clearly differentiated themselves from their Semitic neighbors to the northeast, the Libyans to the west, and the Nubians to the south. They appear to have inhabited the Nile Valley from the earliest times and essentially remained a homogeneous group absorbing the intermittent flow of immigrants mainly from the northeast.

Inhabitants of the Nile Valley can be identified from the Palaeolithic Period at various sites beginning in 200,000 BC as hunter-gatherers living off the land and using flint tools. During the Neolithic Period, farming communities developed, growing emmer wheat, barley, and flax. These groups also domesticated animals and made and used pottery. Such sites have been found at Merimda Beni Salama in the Delta and in the Fayum, but the earliest phase of the Predynastic Period is known as Badarian from the site of el-Badari in Middle Egypt (5000–4000 BC). The subsequent phases of the Predynastic Period take their name from Naqada in Upper Egypt. Naqada I (4000–3500 BC) witnessed the growth of settlement sites in Upper Egypt noted for its black-topped red pottery. During the Naqada II Period (3500–3100 BC), the culture is attested as far north as the Delta at Minshat Abu Omar, although an apparently separate culture is attested at Maadi near modern Cairo.

According to late Egyptian traditions, two kingdoms emerged during the late Predynastic Period: those of Upper Egypt and Lower Egypt, which were merged to form the united kingdom of Egypt through the actions of the legendary king Menes. Modern historians have speculated that the historical king Narmer of Upper Egypt conquered Lower Egypt to unite the country, but the historical process was probably more complicated. A strong kingdom under Dynasty 0 emerged in the south, possibly based at Hierakonpolis, but those rulers were buried in mastaba tombs at Abydos. Little is known about developments in the north or even if the kingdom of Lower Egypt existed, but certainly by about 3100 BC, the country was unified under Dynasty 1.

The union of Egypt is also alleged to have led to the founding of a new capital at Memphis; certainly the tombs of such officials as Hemaka in the nearby cemetery at Saqqara testify to the early importance of Memphis, although the rulers continued to the buried at Abydos. The tombs became increasingly elaborate with niched facades, and the royal tombs were surrounded by those of sacrificed retainers. Hieroglyphic writing appeared during the late Predynastic Period, as attested in the titulary of the rulers, who were identified with the sky god Horus. The writing became more complex, appearing on labels and surviving tomb inscriptions. During Dynasty 2, it appears that there were religious conflicts between the followers of the gods Seth and Horus, which apparently were resolved by Khasekhemwy. During his reign, the first bronze vessels and royal sculptures are attested. He was the last ruler to be buried at Abydos.

Dynasty 3 marked a shift in royal policy. The rulers were now buried at Saqqara. The mastaba tomb and royal sacrifices were abandoned in favor of the newly developed step pyramid, a series of mastabas placed on top of one another using stone on a large scale. The step pyramid was allegedly conceived by the vizier Imhotep, minister of King Djoser. The complex of Djoser also includes other buildings and reliefs of the king undertaking ritual activities. The names of the rulers of Dynasty 3 are attested at the mines of the Wadi Maghara on the Sinai Peninsula. Dynasty 3 marked the first appearance of the sun god Re, who became the main god, displacing the sky god Horus.

Some scholars include Dynasty 3 in the Old Kingdom, and others begin the period with Dynasty 4.

Dynasty 4 marked the high point of royal power and control during the Old Kingdom. The forces of the first ruler, Snefru, campaigned in Nubia, and Egypt entered into commercial relations with Byblos and the Levant. Expeditions penetrated to Buhen in Nubia, where a copper-smelting operation and supporting town site have been discovered, and stone from quarries near Abu Simbel was used for royal statuary. The most visible sign of royal power was the royal tombs at Meidum, Dahshur, and later Giza, where the true stone pyramid was constructed to contain the royal burial. Each pyramid was in fact an architectural complex consisting of the royal pyramid, to which was attached a mortuary temple linked by a causeway to a valley temple on the edge of the cultivation where the royal body was received prior to its burial. Smaller pyramids of the queens adjoined the main pyramid, which was surrounded by the mastaba tombs of the princes and courtiers of the reign.

The royal court was unable to maintain the degree of economic control needed for the continual construction of stone pyramids in succeeding reigns, and only three were built. Dynasty 4 ended in some chaos, and future rulers were content to build pyramids with rubble case and only stone casing. The new rulers of Dynasty 5 enhanced the prestige of their patron deity, the sun god Re, who was elevated to the top of the pantheon and in one form absorbed the sky god Horus to appear as Re-Harakhty. New sun temples were built at Abusir, where most of the rulers chose to be buried. The earliest known written documents on papyrus, which are temple accounts, date to this period. Dynasty 6 maintained control over the entire country, but the minority and the long reign of Pepy II led to a loosening of central control. The dynasty apparently ended in confusion, and the central authority of the Old Kingdom collapsed, ushering in the First Intermediate Period.

The term *Intermediate Period* is used to designate phases when the central government was weak or nonexistent and, partly as a consequence, written documentation is also less abundant. At the end of the Old Kingdom, the country was divided into warring factions whose leaders adopted the titularies of rulers. Dynasties 7 and 8 briefly maintained themselves at Memphis but were superseded by two main contenders for power: the princes of Herakleopolis (Dynasties 9 and 10) and Thebes (Dynasty 11). Other provincial rulers, or nomarchs, increased their local power, backing one side or the other. The surviving monuments of the period demonstrate the growth of different provincial schools of art as opposed to the previous uniform school emanating from the royal court of Memphis.

Around 2040 BC, Mentuhotep II of Dynasty 11 finally overcame the forces of Herakleopolis and reunited Egypt to establish the Middle Kingdom. A new capital was established at Thebes, where the king built his funerary monument at Deir el-Bahri. Trade links were reopened with the south and the Levant. His dynasty did not endure for long and was replaced by Dynasty 12, inaugurated by the southerner Amenemhat I, probably the vizier of the last ruler of Dynasty 11.

Amenemhat I proved a vigorous and inventive ruler. He strengthened Egypt's defenses on the Sinai Peninsula by building fortifications to control the growing influx of Semitic peoples. He moved the capital to Itjtawy near the Fayum in the center of the country, and the region was further developed by his successors. Amenemhat I sought to ensure political stability by appointing his son, Senusret I, as his coregent. During his reign, the military occupation of Nubia began. His court also patronized writers who wrote favorably of the dynasty, and the literature of the Middle Kingdom became the classic reading of the Egyptian literate classes long after stories like the *Tale of Sinuhe*. This strong reign ended with the assassination of Amenemhat I in obscure circumstances, but Senusret I was able to secure the throne and continue his father's policies.

Expansion continued south into Nubia as far as Semna under Senusret I and Senusret III, and a series of fortifications were erected at strategic points to keep Nubia under control. The extent of Egyptian influence in the Levant is unclear. Trade links were maintained with coastal cities like Byblos. Egyptian couriers passed through Palestine, and the execration texts reveal an intimate knowledge of local rulers. Some texts report Egyptian military action in the Levant region. It is probable that Egypt maintained political influence in the area through diplomacy and the occasional military expedition. The period is distinguished by its fine and intricate craftsmanship, notably the production of jewelry, examples of which have been recovered from several royal tombs, including those of princesses Sithathoriunet and Nefruptah.

Dynasty 12 appears to have died out in the male line with Amenemhat IV, who was briefly succeeded by his sister, Sobeknefru, the first unequivocal female ruler. Her reign was brief, and the succeeding Dynasty 13 is considered by most Egyptologists to have begun the Second Intermediate Period. At first, the country remained stable and united, although there was a continuous succession of rulers who generally ruled for a very short period. However, the unity of Egypt began to dissolve with the creation of a contemporary Dynasty 14 at Xois. Egyptian forces withdrew from Nubia, where a strong native kingdom emerged based at Kerma. The country also faced an increasing influx of Asiatic settlers from the east, centering on the town of Avaris. Later Egyptian accounts infer a brutal invasion with much destruction. It is known that peaceful Asiatic settlement had continued throughout Dynasty 12 and Dynasty 13, but the final conquest of the north by the Asiatics or Hyksos may have been made under more violent circumstances. Certainly the Hyksos rulers of Dynasty 15 and Dynasty 16 adopted Egyptian styles of titulary and so must have had some Egyptian advisers at court. The Hyksos appeared to have controlled Lower Egypt and Middle Egypt, but Thebes remained independent under a series of rulers who also adopted royal titularies, although they may at one point have been obliged to become vassals of the Hyksos rulers in the north.

It is clear that the Thebans and Egyptians as a whole resented the rule of this foreign dynasty, and as before, the rulers of Thebes led the resistance to the Hyksos and sought to oust them from Egypt. According to a fragmentary literary tale, the revolt against their rule appears to have been initiated by Tao of Dynasty 17 against the Hyksos ruler Apepi of Dynasty 15. Tao may have died in battle, but the struggle was carried on by his successor, Kamose, who besieged the Hyksos capital at Avaris' and prevented a coalition between Hyksos and Nubian forces. He too appears to have failed, and it was left to his successor, Ahmose I, to capture Avaris around 1550 BC, expel the Hyksos forces from Egypt, and reunite Egypt under the control of his new Dynasty 18. The victorious Egyptians pursued their defeated foes into southern Palestine, and under successive monarchs, notably Thutmose III, they extended their domination of the Levant to the Euphrates River, attempting to forestall any future Asiatic resurgence. At the same time, Egyptian forces penetrated south of Elephantine (Aswan), destroying the Nubian kingdom based at Kerma and annexing much of Nubia as far south as Kurgus near the Fifth Cataract.

These further conquests brought wealth and prosperity back into Egypt. The rulers of Dynasty 18 embarked on important building projects, notably in the temple of Karnak at Thebes, whose god, Amun, was elevated to chief god of Egypt and identified with the sun god Re. The temples were also awarded large land grants and portable wealth to confirm their support of the dynasty. The royal family altered its burial customs, choosing the more secluded Valley of the Kings. The control of an empire and the southern gold mines made Egypt a superpower on the world stage. Direct contact was established with Greece, Asia Minor, and Babylon. Egyptian prestige reached its height during the reign of Amenhotep III, whose harem was filled with many foreign princesses, although his chief wife was an Egyptian commoner, Tiy.

Religious discontent surfaced during the reign of Amenhotep III's son, Akhenaten, who sought to suppress the cult of Amun in favor of his own patron deity, Aton, a form of the sun god Re. Although he tried to eliminate many of the old gods, as well as Amun, he was not a monotheist, denying neither his own divinity nor that of his father. In his new capital at Amarna, a distinctive new art style developed. Akhenaten also faced the growth of a new superpower in the Hittite empire, which annexed the Egyptian provinces of southern Syria. The failure of Akhenaten's program led to a return to the old gods and the old capital under his eventual successor, Tutankhamun, who was apparently the last of the royal line. The final rulers of Dynasty 18 sought to restore Egypt's position at home and abroad.

This new militaristic approach was favored by the rulers of Dynasty 19, who came from a military background. The attempt to restore the former empire ended in failure around 1274 BC, when Ramesses II was defeated by the Hittites; however, he held on to his inherited borders and eventually reached a peaceful accommodation with his enemy, relinquishing claims on lost territory and in due course marrying Hittite princesses. He was able to undertake major building projects at Abu Simbel and other temples and at his new capital, Pi-Ramesses. Egypt had become a cosmopolitan country no longer immune to outside influences in language and customs and even accepting foreign deities, but the era of Ramesses II marked the beginning of the end of Egypt as a prosperous superpower.

The successors of Ramesses II faced invasions from the west by the Libyans allied to the Sea Peoples, as well as a civil war leading to the establishment of Dynasty 20. Ramesses III managed to fend off a further onslaught of the Sea Peoples, who had apparently destroyed the Hittite empire, but his successors gradually became impoverished and withdrew from all Egyptian possessions in the east and in Nubia. Another civil war led to the end of the New Kingdom and the beginning of the Third Intermediate Period.

The Third Intermediate Period is marked by the fragmentation of authority within the country, notably the division between north and south. During Dynasty 21, the authority of the pharaoh situated in the north was only nominally recognized in Thebes under the control of the high priest of Amun. Sheshonq I, of Libyan extraction, attempted to restore the unity of Egypt by establishing his son as high priest, and he also sought to restore Egyptian prestige abroad by invading Palestine; however, the tendency of Dynasty 22 to install princes in key areas of Egypt led to disunity and constant civil war, with Dynasty 22 and Dynasty 23 vying for nominal authority amid other local princes, notably of Sais (Dynasty 24). Unity was only restored with the invasion and conquest of Egypt by the Nubian kings Piye and Shabaqo, who put an end to Dynasty 24 and reduced the local princes to vassals. The Nubian rule (Dynasty 25) in Egypt was brief, as a weakened Egypt faced new superpowers in the cast who cast covetous eyes on the natural wealth and historic treasures of the country. A series of Assyrian invasions devastated the country, culminating in the expulsion of Dynasty 25; the sack of Thebes; and the installation of a puppet ruler, Psamtik I of Sais, in 663 BC.

Psamtik I made use of his Assyrian master and later Greek mercenaries to eliminate all rival princes, and he won control of the south through the adoption of his daughter as God's wife of Amun at Thebes. His Saite dynasty (Dynasty 26) represented a brief revival of Egypt's prosperity and power. Artistic trends toward archaism and simplicity, which began during the Third Intermediate Period, continued. The hieratic written script gave way to the new, more abbreviated demotic, which also indicated a shift in the spoken language. The weakening of Assyria allowed Egypt to become virtually independent, and under Nekau II, the country was even able to intervene in an attempt to support Assyria, which failed, and vainly to try to restore Egyptian influence in the Levant in the face of the new threat from Babylon. Closer relations were initiated with Cyrene in North Africa, sealed through a marriage alliance by Ahmose II, and with the Greek states leading to the designation of Naukratis as a Greek entrepôt in Egypt.

Egypt, however, remained too weak to resist the onslaught of the Persian king Cambyses, who added the country to his Persian empire as a province ruled by a satrap of royal birth. The Persian conquest (Dynasty 27) was deeply resented, especially as the Persian authorities appear to have limited the funds available to the temples, many of which had suffered varying degrees damage during the invasion. There was a series of revolts aided and abetted by the Greeks, which eventually succeeded in expelling the Persians around 404 BC. The new rulers of Egypt, Dynasties 28, 29, and 30, were Delta dynasties recognized throughout Egypt whose principal aim was to prevent any new Persian incursion. The most prominent were the rulers Nakhtnebef and Nakhthorheb, who embarked on an ambitious building program on most of the temples of Egypt.

This last native dynasty was deposed by the reinvading Persians in 343 BC, but their rule was brief as Egypt fell to Alexander the Great in 332 BC. Alexander was welcomed by the Egyptians as a liberator. His sojourn in Egypt was short but significant. He visited the Siwa Oasis, where the oracle is alleged to have confirmed his divinity and made arrangements for the founding of Alexandria. Upon his death, Egypt was secured by his general, Ptolemy, who founded a new dynasty and secured Alexander's body for burial at Alexandria.

Unlike some of Alexander's successors, Ptolemy did not aspire to recreate his empire but was content to rule Egypt and its dependencies. This did not mean that he refrained from expanding Egypt's influence and control in Greece, Asia Minor, and especially Syria when possible, and the Ptolemaic dynasty became embroiled in frequent wars over Syrian territories with the Seleucid Empire, which weakened both powers. Egypt was ruled from the court at Alexandria, which was almost exclusively Greek. Native Egyptians did not fill the top administrative positions and had to learn the Greek language for advancement. Greek settlers, mostly veteran soldiers, were given land, notably in the Fayum area where agricultural land was increased by improved irrigation. Many settlers married local women, and a bilingual class arose that acted as an intermediary between the Greek rulers and the bulk of the Egyptian population. Greek settlers also benefited from tax privileges denied to the locals; however, the court patronized Egyptian temples and sponsored building works to win the loyalty of the priestly class. This did not prevent occasional rebellion on the part of the Egyptians, especially in the south where the rulers Harwennefer and Ankhwennefer maintained their independence for a time.

The Ptolemaic dynasty was severely weakened by civil war and the growth of Roman power in the Mediterranean. Ptolemy XII was forced to accede to Roman financial demands, leading to his expulsion and reinstatement by Roman force of arms. Cleopatra VII was also given power by Roman might but used her charms on Caesar and Marcus Antonius to expand Egyptian influence and restore its prestige in the Levant. Her partnership with Antonius was used by his enemies in Rome to blacken his reputation and inexorably led to a military clash with Roman forces under the future Augustus. His victory at Actium in 30 BC resulted in the conquest of Egypt and the suicides of Cleopatra and Antonius.

The Roman conquest resulted in a change of government in Egypt. Egypt was regarded as the private property of the Roman emperor, ruled in his name by the prefect, and the source of cheap grain to keep the Roman populace happy. Few emperors visited Egypt after Augustus, most notably Hadrian. Roman senators were barred from entering the country without imperial permission. The Greek population in major cities— Alexandria, Naukratis, Ptolemais, and later Antinoopolis—were allowed to enjoy favored tax status, but the mixed Greek-Egyptian population of the provincial cities lost their special status, being regarded as equivalent to the native population, although prominent local citizens enjoyed some privileges. While the emperors occasionally endowed Egyptian temples, the Roman administration tended not to actively support ancient Egyptian institutions. The Egyptian language was no longer considered valid in the courts, where only Greek and Latin were recognized. As a result, written Egyptian in the form of demotic and residual hieroglyphic writing gradually died out in ordinary usage, although it was kept fitfully alive by the priesthood until the 5th century. The temples and the priests they supported grew steadily impoverished.

The weakened pagan culture was unable to resist the spread of Christianity, which gained official recognition under Emperor Constantine. Egyptian Christianity was marked by a certain asceticism, which led individual hermits like Anthony to seek solace in isolated locations, but soon under Pachomius the religion gave rise to settled monastic communities, which helped foster Christianity. Christians were intolerant of the pagan past—both Egyptian and Greek—and made destructive attacks on ancient temples and monuments, especially following the official suppression of paganism under the Emperor Theodosius I in 391–392 AD. Only the temple of Philae remained open because of its diplomatic importance in Egyptian–Nubian relations until the time of the Emperor Justinian, when it was closed in the 530s AD. Funeral customs also changed with the abandonment of mummification and substantial grave goods.

A new form of written Egyptian emerged known as Coptic. The ancient language was written in Greek letters with the addition of seven new letters to represent specific Egyptian sounds. The spoken language had already been altered through the influx of Greek words into the vocabulary. It is thought that the Coptic alphabet may have been devised by the early Christians to translate religious texts, but it was also used for new religious compositions, biographical texts, letters, and administrative texts, notably in the new monastic communities. The development of Coptic proved to be of immense importance in the modern understanding of the ancient Egyptian language.

The adoption of Christianity and the suppression of the ancient cults did not lead to stability in Egypt. The division of the Roman Empire in 395 AD meant that Egypt was now ruled from Constantinople and became part of the Byzantine Empire. Attempts by the emperor to impose an agreed uniform Christian creed foundered on the doctrinal differences between orthodoxy as understood by Rome and the tendency toward Monophysitism in the Coptic Church. Opposition to what the patriarchs at Alexandria, including Cyril and Dioscorus, saw as unorthodox doctrines gradually estranged the Egyptian church from the imperial court, which vainly sought a compromise and then increasingly opted to impose orthodoxy by force, leading to the foundation of a Coptic Church separate from the Orthodox Church. Religious dissension weakened Byzantine rule and led sections of the population to welcome the Arab conquest of 641–642 AD.

The Arab conquest ultimately put an end to the last vestiges of the ancient Egyptian culture, in which the new rulers, like their Christian predecessors, had no interest. It was not their immediate intention to convert the entire population to Islam, as this would have drastically affected their new revenues from the poll tax on nonbelievers; however, later bouts of fanaticism and social and economic pressure led to the conversion of the bulk of the population to Islam. Islamicization led to the adoption of Arabic as the common language of the new administration, and its use also spread to the non-Muslim population so that Coptic had died out as a spoken language by the 15th century. It was preserved only in a few places in the Christian service, although even the speakers no longer knew the meaning of the words. Ancient sites, when not despoiled or destroyed, were gradually buried and forgotten. Memories of ancient Egypt survived only in the neglected works of classical authors in European monastic libraries.

Very few Europeans visited Egypt during the medieval period apart from occasional pilgrims or merchants who brought back a few objects. The growth of learning during the Renaissance led to a rediscovery of classical antiquity and interest in the country. Coptic works, including Biblical translations, were acquired for Western libraries, and the language was soon deciphered, although it was not connected with ancient Egyptian. Haphazard excavations took place at Saqqara to supply *mumiya*, ground-up mummy dust prized for its alleged medicinal properties, during the course of which minor Egyptian antiquities were uncovered. More substantial pieces were found in Rome, where they had been imported during the period of Roman control. Minor pieces continued to arrive in Europe as a result of more intrepid travelers who penetrated further into Egypt during the 18th century. The major impetus to the study of ancient Egypt came with the invasion of the country by Napoleon in 1798 as part of a plan to cut off the British from India. Napoleon took with him a team of scholars who went about the country recording and collecting monuments. The expedition ended in failure, as the French were eventually forced to surrender to a combined Turkish–British force. The monuments that had been collected for shipment to Paris, including the Rosetta Stone, were awarded to the British by treaty and ended up in the British Museum. The French scholars returned with their papers and published the multivolume *Description de l'Égypte*, which made Egyptian sites and monuments known to a wider public.

Peace in Europe in 1815 and a stable government in Egypt under Mohammed Ali allowed scholars, artists, and collectors to visit Egypt; record its monuments; and collect antiquities with the permission of the

Egyptian government. A major breakthrough was made by the decipherment of the hieroglyphic script by Jean-François Champollion using the Rosetta Stone and other bilingual monuments. His realization that the ancient Egyptian language was an earlier form of Coptic, which he already knew, greatly aided his work. His work was carried on by other scholars after his early death. The hieroglyphic, hieratic, and demotic scripts used by the ancient Egyptians can now be read, although grammatical and lexical difficulties still remain.

The major European collections of Egyptian antiquities at the British Museum in London, England, the Louvre Museum in Paris, France, and the Museo Egizio in Turin, Italy, were formed during the first part of the 19th century mainly by purchase from collectors, notably those of the British and French consuls in Egypt, Henry Salt and Bernardino Drovetti, who used such agents as Giovanni Battista Belzoni to acquire objects either directly from the locals or from excavations. The Egyptian government approved the export of most antiquities, in which it took no interest, until in 1858 the efforts of Auguste Mariette persuaded the ruler to create an Egyptian Antiquities Service to supervise and approve all excavations and exports of antiquities and a Cairo museum, which opened in 1862, to display the best discoveries that were to remain in Egypt.

Serious excavation began toward the end of the century with the creation of the French Institute of Archaeology in 1880 and the Egypt Exploration Fund (now the Egypt Exploration Society) in 1882. The method of excavation was revolutionized by the work of the British archaeologist Flinders Petrie, whose attention to detail and such small objects as pottery enabled archaeological levels to be more clearly dated. Important contributions were made during the first half of the 20th century by such American institutions as the Metropolitan Museum of Art in New York and the Museum of Fine Arts in Boston under its excavator George Reisner. Under agreements at the time, the chief finds remained in Egypt, but a portion of the discoveries were awarded to institutions that financed excavations.

The discovery of the tomb of Tutankhamun led to increased public awareness of ancient Egyptian history and archaeology. Apart from interruptions due to wars, excavation and study of ancient Egypt have continued unabated. Following the revolution of 1952, the sale and export of antiquities from Egypt were banned apart from divisions of duplicate archaeological material with foreign archaeological missions. During the 1960s, a major international rescue campaign was undertaken to excavate sites in Nubia in danger of flooding by Lake Nasser, the lake created by the Aswan High Dam. More recently, excavation by the Egyptian Antiquities Service and foreign missions have shifted from desert sites to lesser known town sites, especially in the Delta region. Continual discovery of new material necessitates constant revision of ancient Egyptian chronology and history, which still have many problems awaiting solutions. The more material that is recovered, the more we learn how little we know of ancient Egypt despite the riches of its archaeological heritage.

The Dictionary

– A –

ABDI-ASHIRTA (fl. 1350 BC). Ruler of **Amurru**. He was a vassal of the Egyptians in Syria. His career is known from the **Amarna letters**. Abdi-Ashirta embarked on a campaign of conquest against his neighbors with the help of the **Habiru**. Abdi-Ashirta argued that his acts were in Egypt's best interest and protested his loyalty to the **pharaoh**. He was later arrested by the Egyptian authorities and possibly executed. His son, **Aziru**, succeeded him.

ABRAHAM (fl. 590–620). Abbot of the monastery of St. Phiobammon at **Deir el-Bahri** and Bishop of **Armant**. Son of Sabinus and Rebecca. He founded the monastery on the ruins of **Queen Hatshepsut**'s mortuary temple to replace an earlier monastery of St. Phoibammon in the nearby western desert, which had fallen in ruins. Abraham is known primarily from the many **ostraca**, some in his own hand, and **papyri** in both Greek and **Coptic**, which were excavated by **Henri Edouard Naville** at the monastic site. Both his will written in Greek and a portrait of him have survived. *See also* ANTHONY; COPTIC CHURCH; PACHOMIUS; SHENOUTE.

ABU MINA. A major pilgrimage site and town on the edge of the western Delta southwest of **Alexandria** built over the supposed burial place of the Christian martyr **St. Menas**. It was begun in the fourth century and consisted of a series of churches and buildings, including the Great Basilica, the largest church in Egypt. Abu Mina was destroyed by Persian invaders about 619 AD but was partially rebuilt and occupied until the 11th century. It was initially cleared in 1905–1907 and more recently has been excavated by a German

1

expedition since 1961. The site is the origin of the many St. Menas **pottery** flasks that contained holy water.

ABU ROASH. Modern name for the site of the funerary complex of **Djedefre** of **Dynasty 4**, which includes the remains of his **pyramid** and associated **temples**, as well as a major cemetery of the **Early Dynastic Period** and a pyramid of **Dynasty 3**. The site has been excavated by French expeditions since 1901, notably under Fernand Bisson de la Roque in 1922–1924 and **Pierre Montet** in 1937; a Dutch expedition in 1957–1959; and a joint French–Swiss team since 1995.

ABU SIMBEL. Modern name for the site in **Nubia** where **Ramesses II** erected two **temples**. The larger temple, with four colossal statues of the king on the facade, is dedicated to **Amun-Re**, **Re-Harakhty**, **Ptah**, and Ramesses II and is aligned so the rays of the rising sun illuminate the cult statues in the interior sanctuary twice a year. The smaller temple, with statues of the king and his **queen**, **Nefertari**, with their children on the front wall, is dedicated to the goddess **Hathor**. The site was rediscovered by Swiss explorer Johann Ludwig Burckhardt in 1813, and the main temple was entered in 1817 by **Giovanni Battista Belzoni**, who removed some of the statuary, now in the **British Museum**. The temples were disassembled and moved to a higher site nearby from 1964–1968, when the area was flooded in the wake of the construction of the new Aswan High Dam. *See also* AMADA; BEIT EL-WALI; GERF HUSSEIN; KALABSHA; SOLEB.

ABUSIR. Modern name for the area between **Giza** and **Saqqara** that served as the burial place for the kings and courtiers of **Dynasty 5** and also the location of **temples** dedicated to the sun god **Re**. Four **pyramids** with their temples have been found here. The area was examined by a German expedition under Friedrich von Bissing and then under Ludwig Borchardt in 1898–1913, followed by a Swiss expedition in 1954–1957, and it has been excavated by a Czech expedition since the 1960s. *See also* NEFERIRKARE; NIUSERRE; RANEFEREF; SAHURE.

ABUSIR PAPYRI. The earliest written documents from Egypt consisting of **temple** accounts found in the temple of **Neferirkare** at **Abusir** dating to **Dynasty 5** and **Dynasty 6**. The texts are written in early **hieratic**. Similar texts were found by a Czech expedition working in the pyramid complex of **Khentkaues** and more importantly in the nearby temple of **Raneferef** during 1982–1984. *See also* PAPYRUS.

ABYDOS. Greek name for the sacred city of Abdju in **Upper Egypt** and burial place of **Osiris**, god of the dead, located south of modern Sohag. The kings of **Dynasty 0**, **Dynasty 1**, and **Dynasty 2** were buried there at the site now known as Umm el-Qaab. The local god, Kentiamentiu, became identified with Osiris, who was believed to be buried there. In the **Middle Kingdom**, with the growth in worship of Osiris, the site became a place of pilgrimage and a desirable location for burial. In the **New Kingdom**, **temples** were erected by **Sety I** and **Ramesses II**, as well as a cenotaph for Osiris, the Osireion.

The area was excavated by French archaeologists **Auguste Mariette** in the 1850s and Émile Amélineau in 1894–1998. The **Egypt Exploration Fund** worked here under **Flinders Petrie** and later other archaeologists in 1899–1904, 1909–1914, and 1925–1930, and also sponsored the copying of the temple of Sety I since 1928. Another British archaeologist, John Garstang, was active in 1907. Excavations have been carried out by an American expedition from Yale University and the University of Pennsylvania since 1967, German archaeologists in the archaic cemetery since 1977, and an American team from the University of Michigan in the **Old Kingdom** cemetery since 1995. *See also* AHA; ANEDJIB; DEN; DJER; DJET; NARMER; QAA; SEMERKHET.

ACHAEMENES (fl. c. 484–459 BC). Persian **satrap** of Egypt. Son of **Darius I**, king of **Persia**, and Atossa, daughter of Cyrus the Great. He was appointed to office in 484 BC after a rebellion in Egypt and governed until he was killed in 459 BC during another rebellion against Persian rule led by **Inaros**. *See also* ARSAMES; XERXES I.

ACHILLAS (fl. 48–49 BC). Military commander of **Ptolemy XIII**. He supported the king and his minister, **Pothinus**, in ousting **Cleopatra VII** from power. Achillas supervised the murder of **Gnaeus Pompeius** and besieged Caesar in **Alexandria**. He was murdered in 48 BC in a power struggle with the supporters of **Arsinoe IV**.

ADAIMA. Modern name for a site on the west bank of the **Nile** south of **Esna** in **Upper Egypt**. It contains the remains of a settlement and cemeteries from the **Naqada I** Period of the **Predynastic Period** to the **Early Dynastic Period**. Adaima was first excavated on behalf of the Brooklyn Museum from 1906–1908. The site was examined by a team from the **French Institute** in 1973 and since 1989 by a French expedition. *See also* GERZEH; KAFR HASSAN DAOUD; MIN-SHAT ABU OMAR; TELL EL-FARKHA; TELL IBRAHIM AWAD.

AFRICANUS, PUBLIUS CORNELIUS SCIPIO AEMILIANUS. *See* CORNELIUS SCIPIO AEMILIANUS AFRICANUS, PUBLIUS.

AFTERLIFE. The ancient Egyptians firmly believed in an afterlife, although conceptions of its nature varied. It was generally regarded as a continuation of the **agricultural** life along the **Nile**, hence servant figures, or **shabtis**, were required to avoid manual labor. It was also believed that the dead rested in suspended animation and were only revived when the sun god **Re** descended into the underworld during the hours of darkness on earth.

To enjoy an afterlife, the deceased had to have led a virtuous life according to the precepts of *maat*. He would have to pass through the various gates of the underworld, guarded by demons, to reach the court of the god of the dead **Osiris**, where he would be judged in the **weighing of the heart** ceremony. Various spells in the **Book of the Dead** were designed to ensure that this procedure was carried out successfully.

The Egyptians also believed that the body of the deceased had to be preserved as a home for the *ka*, or life spirit, and the *ba*, or free spirit, of the deceased so that he or she might continue to live after death. The technique of mummification was developed to accomplish this. The **mummy** was buried in the **tomb** after the opening of the mouth ceremony in which it was magically revived. Depending on the cost of burial, the mummy could be interred in a series of wooden decorated coffins that might be placed in a large stone coffin or **sarcophagus**. The family or priests would then make periodic food offerings to the spirit of the deceased. Statues would also be provided as a home for the spirits in case the body decayed. The Egyptians expected to enjoy the same life after death, so they provided the deceased with the appropriate grave goods. *See also* NAME; PYRAMID TEXTS; RELIGION.

A-GROUP. A term invented by **George Reisner** and used by Egyptologists to designate the inhabitants of **Nubia** in the **Predynastic Period**, **Early Dynastic Period**, and the early **Old Kingdom**. The people appear to have been herders and farmers. They are known from cemetery sites and a few Egyptian texts that describe Egyptian military activities against them. Such action may have contributed to their eventual disappearance. An alleged B-Group who succeeded them is now regarded as fictitious. *See also* C-GROUP.

AGRICULTURE. Egypt was an agricultural country in which the bulk of the population were peasant farmers involved in work on the land. The fertility of the land caused by the **Nile** floods ensured that crops were generally abundant and famines, while they did occur, were rare. The main crops were wheat and barley used to make bread and beer, the staple diet of the people. Vegetables were also produced, and vineyards are attested. Flax was planted to produce linen for clothing, and fodder was grown for livestock.

The life of the countryside was dominated by the agricultural schedule. Planting followed the Nile flood in the early summer, and the peasantry was available for government-forced labor toward the end of the growing season. Government inspectors determined the amount of tax due from the individual plots, and the collected grain was stored and used to feed government employees, as at **Deir el-Medina**. In Egypt's barter **economy**, a measure of wheat was used to value less expensive goods.

Most of the land was owned by the royal court, the **temples**, and the bureaucracy, but along with the large estates, small private plots are also attested. Most of the people were presumably landless peasants who worked on the large estates as sharecroppers or laborers, but some peasants owned their own land by inheritance or gift of the crown. Enterprising farmers owned some land, rented out more from the estates, and hired laborers, so the status of the agricultural population may be varied. *See also* DIET; TRADE.

AHA (reigned c. 3080 BC). Second king of **Dynasty 1**. Successor of **Narmer**, as confirmed by the dynastic seal. He appears to have been buried at **Abydos**, and **tombs** of officials of his reign are known at **Saqqara**. Aha is probably not to be identified as **Menes**. He was succeeded by **Djet**, who was probably his son and whose mother was **Khenethap**.

AHHIYAWA. An important power whose kingdom bordered on the Mediterranean Sea. The country and its ruler are mentioned in **Hittite** records. It is now generally believed that the term corresponds to Achaea, the country of the Mycenaean Greeks. A statue base of **Amenhotep III** mentions the names of various towns in Greece. Quantities of Mycenaean **pottery** have been found in Egypt at the end of **Dynasty 18** and in **Dynasty 19**. Egyptian objects have been found on mainland Greece, so the two countries are known to have been in contact, although not necessarily directly.

AHHOTEP (fl. 1570–1540 BC). Sister and **queen** of probably Seqenenre **Tao** of **Dynasty 17** and thus daughter of Senakhtenre and **Tetisheri**. She was the mother of **Ahmose I**, who founded **Dynasty 18**, and his sister-wife **Ahmose-Nefertari**. Ahhotep apparently acted as regent of her son on his accession and exercised great influence during his reign. A second queen, Ahhotep, is known from a burial at **Thebes** and is probably to be identified as a queen of **Kamose** or Seqenenre Tao. The gilded coffin from this burial and jewelry are now in the **Cairo Egyptian Museum**.

AHMOSE (fl. 1560–1500 BC). Military officer. Son of Baba, a soldier of King Seqenenre **Tao**, and his wife Ebana, from whose name her son is generally known as Ahmose, son of Ebana. He was the owner of a **tomb** at **Elkab**, which contains a major autobiographical inscription describing his exploits in the wars against the **Hyksos**. Ahmose was present at the siege of **Avaris** and later took part in campaigns in Palestine, Syria, and **Nubia** under **Ahmose I**, **Amenhotep I**, and **Thutmose I**. *See also* WARFARE.

AHMOSE. The name of several princes and princesses of **Dynasty 17** and early **Dynasty 18**. Their separate identities are confusing, as Ahmose seems to have been used both as a distinct name and as part of a more complex name, like Ahmose-**Meritamun**, daughter of **Ahmose I** and wife of **Amenhotep I**. The most prominent prince seems to have been **Ahmose-Sipair**.

AHMOSE (fl. 1504–1470 BC). Sister-wife of **Thutmose I** and mother of **Hatshepsut**. Her parentage is not known, but she was not a royal princess as previously believed.

AHMOSE I (reigned c. 1552–1527 BC). Throne name Nebpehtyre. Founder of **Dynasty 18**. Probably son of Seqenenre **Tao** and **Queen Ahhotep**. He succeeded **Kamose**, who may have been his brother, apparently under the regency of his grandmother, **Tetisheri**, and his mother, Ahhotep. Ahmose I continued the campaign of the rulers of **Thebes** against the **Hyksos** rulers in the north, and his army successfully took the Hyksos capital, **Avaris**, and expelled the Hyksos from Egypt, reuniting the country under his rule. His army penetrated at least into southern Palestine in pursuit of the enemy. He also began the Egyptian invasion of **Nubia**. His wife and probable sister, **Ahmose-Nefertari**, became regent for their son, **Amenhotep I**, on his death. *See also* AHMOSE-SIPAIR; WARFARE.

AHMOSE II (reigned 570–526 BC). The Greek form of his name is Amasis. Throne name Khnumibre. A military commander of **Wahibre** (Apries), whom he overthrew following a brief civil war. He sought to ally Egypt with the Greeks to face the continuing threat of **Persia**, including a marriage alliance with Laodike, a Greek lady from **Cyrene**. Ahmose II ruled effectively for 45 years and died conveniently just before the Persian invasion of 525 BC, as a result of which his son, **Psamtik III**, was deposed and later executed.

AHMOSE-NEFERTARI (fl. 1550–1500 BC). Wife and probably sister of **Ahmose I** and thus daughter of Seqenenre **Tao** and **Ahhotep**. She appears to have been the first **queen** to use the title **God's wife of Amun** and is portrayed with her husband on several monuments of the reign. Ahmose-Nefertari may have acted as regent for her son, **Amenhotep I**, and seems to have survived him. She was deified with him after his death and is worshipped with him, especially at the village of **Deir el-Medina**.

AHMOSE-SIPAIR (fl. 1520 BC). A prince of **Dynasty 18**. He was probably the eldest son of **Ahmose I**. He was venerated in the later **New Kingdom** and appears in **tomb** paintings in **Deir el-Medina** of the **Ramesside Period**. Ahmose-Sipair was worshipped together with **Ahmose-Nefertari**, who may have been his mother, and **Amenhotep I**. It has been suggested that he was the brother of Ahmose I and the father of **Thutmose I**. This appears less likely in view of his association with Ahmose-Nefertari, and it is equally probable that he died young. *See also* MERITAMUN; SITAMUN.

AITAKAMA (fl. 1350–1320 BC). Ruler of **Kadesh**. Son of Shutatarra, ruler of Kadesh. Loyal of Egypt, his father was defeated and deposed by the **Hittite** king **Suppiluliuma I**, and Aitakama was installed in Kadesh as a Hittite vassal. He joined **Aziru** of **Amurru** in attacks on Egyptian territory, yet he wrote an **Amarna letter** declaring his loyalty to Egypt. Upon the death of his Hittite overlord, he broke this allegiance but was assassinated by a son who returned to the Hittite fold.

AKHENATEN (reigned c. 1352–1336 BC). Throne name Neferkheperure waenre. Original name Amenhotep IV. Son of **Amenhotep III** and **Tiy**. It is probable that he was not the eldest son, as a Prince **Thutmose** is attested but presumably died young. It is also not clear if there was a **coregency** between his father and himself or whether he succeeded only upon his father's death. Akhenaten sought to establish the primacy of the cult of **Re**-Harakhty in the form of **Aten**, the sun's disk. Following opposition in **Thebes** from the followers of **Amun**, he established a new capital at Akhetaten, now **Amarna**, and built his royal **tomb** nearby. His opposition to the older cults gradually grew more intense, and they were eventually proscribed. His religious beliefs have been wrongly described as monotheism, as Akhenaten did not abandon those cults associated with the sun god or with kingship, namely his deified father and himself.

His reign is also noted for a revolutionary new art style, which is far freer than older Egyptian conventions and depicted the royal family and he himself in a particular manner. Some have sought to identify a medical problem in this style, but it may simply have been a new artistic convention. His wife, **Nefertiti**, assumed a prominent role in royal scenes, and it has been suggested that she even succeeded him. The circumstances that ended the reign are unknown. Akhenaten's eventual successor, **Tutankhamun**, who may have been his son, abandoned Amarna and reverted to the worship of Amun. Akhenaten's name and that of his immediate successors were later proscribed. *See also* ANKHESENAMUN; ART; AY; BAKETATEN; HOREMHEB; MEKETATEN; MERITAMUN; MERITATEN-TASHERIT; NEFERNEFRUATEN; NEFERNEFRURE; RELIGION; SETEPENRE; SITAMUN; SMENKHKARE; TALATAT.

AKHETATEN. *See* AMARNA.

AKHMIM. Modern name for the Egyptian *Khent-Min*, Greek Khemmis or Panopolis in the ninth **Upper Egyptian nome**. Little remains of the ancient city under the modern town. Akhmim is the home city of **Ay**. In 1981, colossal statues of **Ramesses II** and his daughter and **Queen Meritamun** were discovered there. Unsupervised excavations at the end of the 19th century led to the discovery of many textiles and textile fragments from the **Coptic** Period. The nearby **tombs** of the **Old Kingdom** at el-Hawawish were copied and published by an Australian expedition from Macquarie University in 1979–1992. *See also* ATHRIBIS; MIN.

AKORIS. A town site in **Middle Egypt** north of **Beni Hasan** and Ashmunein (**Hermopolis**). Probably ancient *Mer-nefer*, late *Ta-dehnet*. Modern Tihneh-el-Gebel. It is attested from the **Middle Kingdom** until the **Coptic** Period. A limestone quarry was located nearby. It has been excavated by a Japanese expedition since 1981.

ALARA (reigned c. 770 BC). Nubian ruler. The first known member of the later **Dynasty 25**. He is not known to have been active in Egypt, but his successor, **Kashta**, extended Nubian rule over the Theban area. *See also* PIYE.

ALASIA. A foreign country named in Egyptian documents during **Dynasty 18, Dynasty 19**, and **Dynasty 20**, notably in the **Amarna letters**. The country could be reached by sea, as described in the story of **Wenamun**. Alasia is generally identified with all or part of

Cyprus, although some authors situate it on the Levant coast. However, recent advances in the understanding of the geography of Aisa Minor through **Hittite** documents render this last theory increasingly untenable.

ALEXANDER II (IV of Macedon) (reigned 317–310 BC). Posthumous son of **Alexander the Great** and the Bactrian princess Roxana. He reigned jointly with his uncle, **Philip Arrhidaeus**, until the murder of the latter in 317 BC. Alexander II was imprisoned by Cassander and murdered in 310 BC, but he was still acknowledged as ruler until 305 BC, when Cassander, **Ptolemy I**, and other Macedonian generals assumed independent kingships over parts of Alexander the Great's empire.

ALEXANDER THE GREAT (356–323 BC). King of Macedon and conqueror of the Persian Empire, including Egypt. Son of King Philip of Macedon and Olympias of Epirus. Alexander succeeded to the Macedonian throne upon the assassination of his father in 336 BC and in 334 BC embarked on the conquest of **Persia**. In 332 BC, his army entered Egypt, whose **satrap** surrendered peacefully. Alexander assumed the status of an Egyptian ruler and visited the **Siwa Oasis**, where he received an oracular pronouncement, later believed to indicate that he was the son of a god. He indicated the position of a new city to be built on the coast and named **Alexandria** after himself. He left Egypt in 331 BC to continue his conquests elsewhere, arranging for the country to be divided under various officials, the chief of whom was **Cleomenes**, the chief financial officer. Alexander died in Babylon in 323 BC upon his return from India. His **mummified** body was eventually buried in a special mausoleum in Alexandria, where it remained on display until at least the 3rd century AD. *See also* ALEXANDER II; PHILIP ARRHIDAEUS; PTOLEMY I SOTER.

ALEXANDER HELIOS (b. 40 BC). Son of **Marcus Antonius** and **Cleopatra VII**. Twin of **Cleopatra Selene**. He was declared king of Armenia, Parthia, and Media in 34 BC and betrothed to Princess Iotape of Media. He was captured by **Augustus** in 30 BC and displayed in his triumph in Rome in 29 BC. His ultimate fate is unknown. *See also* PTOLEMY PHILADELPHUS.

ALEXANDER, TIBERIUS IULIUS. *See* IULIUS ALEXANDER, TIBERIUS.

ALEXANDRIA. City on the Mediterranean coast of the western Delta founded by **Alexander the Great** in 331 BC on the site of the Egyptian village of *Rakedet*, Greek Rakotis. It became the capital of Ptolemaic and Roman Egypt and included many fine buildings, notably the famed Library of Alexandria and the **Pharos**, or Lighthouse, of Alexandria, regarded as one of the seven wonders of the ancient world. Alexander's body was preserved in a special mausoleum in the city. The city was also decorated with Egyptian monuments removed from earlier sites, notably **Heliopolis**. The large cosmopolitan population included Egyptians, Greeks, and Jews.

The city later suffered damage from earthquakes and invasion and declined following the move of the capital to Cairo after the Arab conquest in 642 AD. Many parts of the city appear to have sunk beneath the harbor. Little of the ancient metropolis remains today, apart from the area adjacent to the so-called Pompey's Pillar. Excavations by successive directors of the Graeco-Roman Museum have uncovered many local burial catacombs with reliefs in a mixed Egyptian-Roman style. Since 1960, a Polish expedition has worked at the site of Kom el-Dikka uncovering a theater and baths. A French rescue expedition excavated part of the main cemetery at Gabbari from 1997–2000, prior to the construction of a new expressway. Recent surveys by teams of French divers have begun to reveal the parts of the city now underwater and recovered Egyptian sculptures and reliefs. Blocks in the sea near the fort of Qait Bey have been identified as belonging to the original lighthouse.

AMADA. Modern name for a site in Lower **Nubia** of a **temple** built by **Thutmose III** and his son, **Amenhotep II,** in honor of **Amun**-Re and **Re**-Harakhty. The area is now flooded by Lake Nasser, the lake formed by the Aswan High Dam, but the temple was removed and reerected at a higher level. *See also* ABU SIMBEL; BEIT EL-WALI; GERF HUSSEIN; KALABSHA; SOLEB.

AMARA WEST. Modern name for a site in Upper **Nubia** where a major Ramesside settlement and **temple** have been discovered. The town appears to have been founded by **Sety I**, with further construction by his son, **Ramesses II**. It was probably the major administrative center for Upper Nubia. It was excavated by the **Egypt Exploration Society** in 1938–1939 and 1947–1950.

AMARNA. The modern Arabic name el-Amarna or Tell el-Amarna denotes the site of the capital city *Akhetaten* founded by **Akhenaten** in **Middle Egypt** in his year 5 (1348 BC). Akhenaten claimed to have chosen a virgin site to become the new capital, away from the religious intolerance of **Thebes** and where he was free to pursue the worship of **Aten**. The site consists of the remains of royal palaces, villas, **temples**, private dwellings, and a workmen's village, and the boundaries were marked by a series of **stelae**. The sculptor **Thutmose**'s workshop yielded the famous bust of **Nefertiti**, now in the **Berlin Egyptian Museum**. Tombs for officials were cut in the nearby cliffs, and a royal tomb was built for the king. The scenes on the walls are not fully preserved, but one depicts the death of the Princess **Meketaten**, although the circumstances of her passing are unclear.

The city was abandoned by **Tutankhamun** and used as building material by later rulers, notably **Ramesses II**. The site was first excavated by **Flinders Petrie** in 1891–1892 and then a German expedition in 1907 and 1911–1914. The tombs were copied by an expedition of the **Egypt Exploration Fund** in 1901–1907. In 1921–1936, further excavations were carried out by the British organization, renamed the Egypt Exploration Society, and work was resumed under its auspices in 1977.

AMARNA LETTERS. A large number of clay tablets inscribed in cuneiform, the script used in Mesopotamia and western Asia, found at the site of el-**Amarna**. The letters consist of the diplomatic correspondence of the royal court at the end of **Dynasty 18** with the princes of Syria and Palestine under Egyptian control as well as other royal courts in Babylonia, **Assyria**, and Anatolia. Most of the documents date to the reign of **Akhenaten**, but some letters may belong to the time of his predecessor, **Amenhotep III**, or his successor, **Tutankhamun**. The letters reflect a state of disarray in the Egyptian empire, although the extent of the disorder may be exaggerated. *See also* ABDI-ASHIRTA; AITAKAMA; AMMISTAMRU I; AZIRU; MEGIDDO; RIB-HADDA.

AMARNA PERIOD (c. 1352–1327 BC). A term used by Egyptologists to denote the reigns of **Akhenaten** and his successors, **Smenkhkare** and **Tutankhamun.** The period is notable for innovations in art and religious belief and ended with the abandonment of **Amarna** as Egypt's capital. The rulers of the Amarna period were later suppressed from Egypt's historical record by their successors. *See also* AY; HOREMHEB; NEFERTITI; RELIGION.

AMASIS. *See* AHMOSE II.

AMENEMHAT. The name of several Egyptian princes of **Dynasty 18.** One is known solely from an inscription on a coffin that had been made for his reburial toward the end of **Dynasty 20** or early **Dynasty 21** and was rediscovered in 1918–1920 at **Deir el-Bahri.** He has been wrongly described as a son of **Amenhotep I,** but his actual parentage remains unknown. His very existence might be doubtful if the later embalmers were mistaken in their identification of the body, which was that of a one-year-old child. The eldest son of **Thutmose III,** who died before his father but was alive in his year 24 (1456 BC), was named Amenemhat but cannot be identified with this child as his titles indicate an older individual. Another Prince Amenemhat may have been a son of **Thutmose IV.**

AMENEMHAT I (reigned c. 1985–1955 BC). Throne name Sehetepibre. Son of Senusret and Nefret. He is first attested as **vizier** of **Mentuhotep IV** of **Dynasty 11** and must be identical to the founder of **Dynasty 12,** although it is not clear if he came to the throne peacefully or as a result of a coup d'état. Amenemhat I proved a strong and effective ruler, establishing a new capital at *Itjtawy,* now **Lisht** in the **Fayum.** He began the campaign of conquest of **Nubia** and also built a series of fortifications along Egypt's Sinai border known as the Walls of the Ruler. He apparently installed his son **Senusret I** as **coregent,** although this has been doubted by some Egyptologists. Amenemhat I was assassinated after 30 years of rule in an apparent palace conspiracy that was later crushed by his son. He was buried in a **pyramid** complex at **Lisht.** A **wisdom** text in his name, *The Instruction of Amenemhat I,* was composed after his death, presumably during his son's reign. *See also* INTEFYOKER; KHETY; SINUHE.

AMENEMHAT II (reigned c. 1922–1878 BC). Throne name Nubkaure. Son of **Senusret I** of **Dynasty 12** and **Nefru**. He continued Egyptian expansion in **Nubia** and sent expeditions to the Red Sea and **Punt**. An inscription gives details of campaigns in the Sinai Peninsula and possibly further north. Amenemhat II maintained contacts with **Byblos**. He was buried in a **pyramid** complex at **Dahshur**. *See also* KHENEMET-NEFER-HEDJET; SENUSRET II.

AMENEMHAT III (reigned c. 1855–1808 BC). Throne name Nimaatre. Son of **Senusret III** of **Dynasty 12**. His principal monuments are located in the **Fayum** area, which seems to have been extensively developed during his reign. He built two **pyramids**, one at **Dahshur**, where he appears to have been buried, and another at **Hawara**, where his mortuary **temple** was later known to the Greeks as the Labyrinth. *See also* AMENEMHAT IV; NEFRUPTAH; SOBEKNEFRU.

AMENEMHAT IV (reigned c. 1808–1799 BC). Throne name Maatkherure. Son of **Amenemhat III** of **Dynasty 12**. He is principally known from several monuments in the **Fayum**. Amenemhat IV appears to have died without issue and was succeeded by his sister, **Sobeknefru**. His burial place has not been securely identified.

AMENEMHAT V (reigned c. 1796–1783 BC). Throne name Sekhemkare. A minor king of **Dynasty 13**. He is only known from the **Turin Royal Canon** and a statue found at **Elephantine**.

AMENEMHAT VI (reigned c. 1788–1785 BC). Throne name Sankhibre. A minor king of **Dynasty 13**. He is attested in the **Turin Royal Canon** and on several monuments from **Heliopolis**, **Abydos**, and **Karnak**. His full name is given as Ameny Intef Amenemhat, which may imply that his father was named Intef and his grandfather Ameny, an abbreviation for Amenemhat, and was possibly **Amenemhat V**.

AMENEMHAT VII (reigned 1769–1766 BC). Throne name Sedjefakare. A minor king of **Dynasty 13**. Possibly son of Kay. He is named on the **Turin Royal Canon** and on several monuments.

AMENEMNISU (reigned c. 1043–1039 BC). Throne name Neferkare. Second ruler of **Dynasty 21** of unknown origin. He was cited in **Manetho** by his throne name, which was generally considered to be an error until an inscription with his titulary was discovered in the **tomb** of **Pasebakhaenniut I** at **Tanis**. His reign appears to have been brief. *See also* AMENEMOPE; NESBANEBDJED.

AMENEMOPE (reigned c. 993–984 BC). Throne name Usermaatre setepenamun. Epithet meryamun. Fourth ruler of **Dynasty 21** and successor of **Pasebakhaenniut I**. Little is known of his reign. His burial was discovered at **Tanis** by French excavator **Pierre Montet**.

AMENHERKHEPESHEF (fl. 1285–1255 BC). Eldest son of **Ramesses II** of **Dynasty 19** and **Nefertari**. The prince appears to have been also known as Amenherwenemef and Setiherkhepeshef. He was named crown prince by his father and is attested until year 21 of the reign, when he was involved in diplomatic correspondence with the **Hittites** along with his mother. Amenherkhepeshef died before his father. He was buried in the tomb of the sons of Ramesses II **(KV5)** in the **Valley of the Kings**. A like-named son of **Ramesses III**, who died young, was buried in the **Valley of the Queens (QV55)**. *See also* KHAEMWESE; MERENPTAH; MERYATUM; PREHERWENEMEF; SETY.

AMENHOTEP I (reigned c. 1525–1504 BC). The Greek form of his personal name is Amenophis. Throne name Djeserkare. Son of **Ahmose I** of **Dynasty 18** and **Ahmose-Nefertari**. He seems to have succeeded as a child under the regency of his mother. During his reign, the workmen's community at **Deir el-Medina** appears to have been founded, and he was the first king to be buried in a cliff **tomb** in or near the **Valley of the Kings**, but this remains to be identified. Amenhotep I apparently died without issue by his sister and **queen Meritamun** and was succeeded by **Thutmose I**. He was later worshipped as a god, along with his mother, especially at Deir el-Medina. His body was recovered in the **royal cache** at **Deir el-Bahri** in 1881.

AMENHOTEP II (reigned c. 1427–1400 BC). Throne name Akheperure. Son of **Thutmose III** of **Dynasty 18** and **Meryetre Hatshepsut**. He appears to have been named as **coregent** by his father and succeeded as sole ruler in 1425 BC. Upon his accession, he faced a revolt in his Asiatic domains, which he ruthlessly crushed, exhibiting the remains of the rebels as far south as **Nubia**. His inscriptions boast of his athletic prowess. He appears to have largely maintained the northern conquests of his father. Amenhotep II was buried in **tomb KV35** in the **Valley of the Kings**, and his body was recovered from his tomb in 1898, along with the remains of other rulers who had been buried there in a **royal cache**. His mortuary temple at **Thebes** is in ruins, but some **foundation deposits** have been recovered. It was excavated in 1896 by **Flinders Petrie** and since 1998 by an Italian expedition. He was succeeded by his son **Thutmose IV** and by the lady **Tiaa**.

AMENHOTEP III (reigned c. 1390–1352 BC). Throne name Nebmare. Son of **Thutmose IV** of **Dynasty 18** and **Mutemwia**. He may have succeeded as a child and reigned 32 years. His supremecy is known for its magnificence in construction and artworks. He maintained the Egyptian empire in Asia and was in communication with the many princes of the area, as shown in the **Amarna letters**. His chief **queen** commoner, **Tiy**, was the mother of his eventual heir, **Akhenaten**, as it appears that his eldest son, Thutmose, predeceased him. Amenhotep III married several foreign princesses from **Mitanni** and Babylon. He also had several daughters, notably **Sitamun**, whom he married. A proposed **coregency** between father and son is debatable, and most Egyptologists reject the notion. He was buried in **tomb KV22** in the **Valley of the Kings**, and his body was recovered from the **royal cache** in tomb **KV35** of **Amenhotep II**. His mortuary **temple** at Kom el-Hetan on the west bank opposite **Thebes** is largely in ruins but featured the **Colossi of Memnon** and inscriptions mentioning the **Keftyu**. It has been under excavation by a German expedition since 1998. *See also* GILUKHEPA; TADUKHEPA.

AMENHOTEP IV. *See* AKHENATEN.

AMENHOTEP, SON OF HAPU (fl. c. 1390–1360 BC). Overseer of works for **Amenhotep III**. He was born in **Athribis** and was likely responsible for the construction of many of the king's monuments, including his mortuary **temple** at **Thebes** and his **Nubian** temple at **Soleb**, where he was commemorated. He was buried at Thebes. Amenhotep, son of Hapu, acquired a reputation for wisdom and was deified after his death, being worshipped in his own mortuary temple. *See also* MEMNON, COLOSSI OF.

AMENIRDIS. The name of two princesses of **Dynasty 25** who were adopted as **God's wife of Amun**. Amenirdis I was the daughter of **Kashta** and Pebtama, and her adoption by **Shepenwepet I** was an indication of the control of **Thebes** exercised by the ruler of **Nubia**. Amenirdis II, daughter of **Taharqo**, was adopted by Shepenwepet II as her heir, but it is not certain if she succeeded, as Dynasty 25 was ousted from Thebes by **Psamtik I** of **Dynasty 26**, who sent his daughter, **Nitocris**, to become God's wife.

AMENMESSE (reigned c. 1202–1199 BC). Throne name Menmire. Of unknown parentage, he contended with **Sety II** for the throne upon the death of **Merenptah**. Amenmesse was defeated and his memory largely obliterated. He had prepared **tomb KV10** in the **Valley of the Kings** for his burial. *See also* DYNASTY 19.

AMENMOSE (fl. 1504–1499 BC). Egyptian prince of **Dynasty 18**. He was the eldest son of **Thutmose I**, possibly by the lady **Mutnefret**. He is attested in his father's reign with the title of general and in a tomb scene with his younger brother, **Wadjmose**. Both predeceased their father, and the throne eventually passed to their brother or half brother, **Thutmose II**.

AMENOPHIS. *See* AMENHOTEP.

AMENY QEMAU (reigned c. 1793–1783 BC). Throne name uncertain. An ephemeral king of **Dynasty 13**. His **pyramid tomb** was discovered at **Dahshur** in 1957 but has never been properly excavated or published. The name Qemau has been wrongly interpreted in the past with the meaning of Asiatic. He may have been the father of **Harnedjitef**, who also bore the epithet that might be read as son of Qemau. The name of Ameny Qemau might be interpreted to indicate that he was the son of a previous ruler named Ameny, who in turn might be identified with one of the obscure rulers named Amenemhat of Dynasty 13, probably **Amenemhat V**.

AMETHYST. Ancient Egyptian *hesmen*. A violet-colored quartz used in miniature vessels, amulets, and jewelry, mainly from the late **Predynastic Period** to the end of the **Middle Kingdom** and again in the **Graeco-Roman Period**. The main quarries were at **Wadi el-Hudi** during the Middle Kingdom and Wadi Abu Diyeiba during the Graeco-Roman Period, which was discovered in 1914 and surveyed by an U.S. team in 2004.

AMHEIDA. Ancient Trimithis. A town in the northwest **Dakhla Oasis**. It has been excavated by an American expedition since 2004. The site was occupied during the **Old Kingdom**, but the present remains date from the **Third Intermediate Period** to the late **Roman Period**. The town was abandoned at the end of the 4th century. The main temple, now destroyed, was dedicated to the god **Thoth**.

AMMISTAMRU I (fl. 1360–1340 BC). Ruler of **Ugarit**. He was a correspondent in the **Amarna letters**. As a vassal ruler, he wrote to declare his loyalty to Egypt. His son and succesor, Niqmaddu, challenged his allegiance and acknowledged **Hittite** king **Suppiluliuma I** as his overlord.

AMUN. Chief god of the **New Kingdom** and later. Originally a minor god at **Thebes**, he rose to prominence in **Dynasty 12**, which came from the south, and was promoted to the head of the pantheon under the Theban **Dynasty 18** through a fusion with the sun god **Re**, becoming Amen-Re, king of the gods. Amun is usually represented as a human figure with two plumed feathers but can also have the head of a hawk. He is viewed as one of the creator gods. His main **temple** was at **Karnak** in Thebes, where he formed part of the Theban **triad** with his wife, the goddess **Mut**, and his son, the moon god **Khonsu**. He was later worshipped as one of the main gods in **Nubia** at Gebel Barkal and other temples. His sacred animals were the ram and the goose. *See also* RELIGION.

AMURRU. A kingdom in Syria that was the northenmost area conquered by **Thutmose III.** In the time of **Amenhotep III** and **Akhenaten**, it was ruled by **Abdi-Ashirta** and his son, **Aziru**, who expanded their power with the help of the **Habiru**. Aziru later defected to the **Hittite** king **Suppiluliuma I** and became his vassal. A later ruler, Benteshina, returned to the Egyptian allegiance under **Ramesses II** but was deposed by the Hittites in the aftermath of the battle of **Kadesh**. He was later restored by **Hattusili III**. By the time of the Egyptian–Hittite peace treaty, Egypt finally recognized the loss of Amurru.

AMYRTAEOS (reigned 404–399 BC). Greek name for the Egyptian ruler of **Dynasty 28**, Amenirdis of **Sais**, who led a rebellion against the Persian occupation and succeeded in expelling them from the country. He apparently invaded Phoenicia to prevent a Persian counterattack. No inscriptions of his are known, but Amyrtaeos is mentioned in a **demotic** papyrus. Amyrtaeos was later overthrown by **Nefaarud** I, founder of **Dynasty 29**.

ANAT. Canaanite goddess of war. Her worship was adopted in Egypt during the **Ramesside Period**, and **Ramesses II** gave his eldest daughter, **Bintanat**, her name. The Egyptians considered Anat one of the wives of **Seth,** along with **Astarte**. *See also* QUDSHU; RELIGION; RESHEP.

ANCHMACHIS. *See* ANKHWENNEFER.

ANEDJIB (reigned c. 2935 BC). Sixth ruler of **Dynasty 1** and successor of **Den**. He was buried in a modest **tomb** at **Abydos**, and his name has been erased in some instances, indicating possible unrest at the end of his reign. *See also* SEMERKHET.

ANHUR. Egyptian god known to the Greeks as Onuris and considered a god of war. He is depicted as a bearded man wearing feathered plumes and carrying a spear. His principal place of worship was **Thinis** in the eighth **nome** of **Upper Egypt**, but he was also worshipped in combination with **Shu** at **Sebennytos**. Anhur's wife was the lioness-headed goddess **Mehit**. *See also* RELIGION.

ANIBA. Site in Lower **Nubia** in the Second **Cataract** region. Egyptian *Miam*. A fortress was constructed here during **Dynasty 12** and was reoccupied during the **New Kingdom** when it became a major administrative center for the area between the First Cataract and Second Cataract. Aniba was excavated by a German expedition in the 1930s and is now flooded by Lake Nasser, the lake of the Aswan High Dam. Some monuments from the site were salvaged before the flooding. *See also* ASKUT; BUHEN; KUMMA; MIRGISSA: SHALFAK; URONARTI.

ANKHESENAMUN (fl. 1345–1327 BC). Formerly **Ankhesenpaaten**. Third daughter of **Akhenaten** and **Nefertiti** and wife of **Tutankhamun**. She joined her husband in the abandonment of her father's religious practices and capital at **Amarna** and changed her name to remove the reference to **Aten**. Upon the death of her husband, Ankhesenamun wrote to the **Hittite** king seeking a Hittite prince as a new husband, but the choice, **Zannanza**, died mysteriously on the way to Egypt. Her subsequent fate is unknown, although it has been conjectured that she married the next king, **Ay**, as her name appears joined with his on two rings. *See also* AMARNA PERIOD; ANKHESENPAATEN-TASHERIT; BAKETATEN; MEKETATEN; MERITAMUN; MERITATEN-TASHERIT; NEFERNEFRUATEN; NEFERNEFRURE; SETEPENRE.

ANKHESENMERYRE I AND II (fl. 2305–2270 BC). Also named **Ankhesenpepy**. The name of two sister **queens** of **Pepy I** and daughters of Huy. The elder became the mother of **Nemtyemsaf** I and the younger of **Pepy II**. The **pyramid tomb** of the younger sister Ankhesenmeryre II/Ankhesenpepy II was identified at **Saqqara** in 1999.

ANKHESENPAATEN. *See* ANKHESENAMUN.

ANKHESENPAATEN-TASHERIT (fl. 1336 BC). A princess of the **Amarna Period**. She is attested on some monuments originating from **Amarna** found at **Hermopolis**. Her origin is unknown, but she may be a daughter of **Akhenaten** or **Smenkhkare**, and her mother may be Ankhesenpaaten, later **Ankhesenamun**. *See also* BAKETATEN; MEKETATEN; MERITAMUN; MERITATEN-TASHERIT; NEFERNEFRUATEN; NEFERNEFRURE; SETEPENRE.

ANKHESENPEPY I AND II. *See* ANKHESENMERYRE I AND II.

ANKHESENPEPY III. (fl. 2230 BC). A princess and **queen** of **Dynasty 6**. She was the daughter of **Nemtyemsaf** I and married her uncle, **Pepy II**. Her **tomb** at **Saqqara** was identified and excavated by a French expedition beginning in 1999.

ANKHESENPEPY IV (fl. 2220 BC). The name of a wife of **Pepy II**. Her **sarcophagus** was found in the **tomb** of **Iput**, another of his queens, at **Saqqara**. She was the mother of an ephemeral king of **Dynasty 7** or **Dynasty 8** whose throne name was Neferkare.

ANKHNESNEFERIBRE (fl. c. 590–525 BC). Daughter of **Psamtik II** of **Dynasty 26** and Takhut. She was adopted by her great-aunt **Nitocris** in 595 BC and succeeded her as **God's wife of Amun** in 586 BC. She held the post until the Persian invasion of 525 BC, after which there is no further record of her. Ankhnesneferibre is the last attested God's wife, although a later classical source implies that the office continued. Her reused **sarcophagus** was discovered at **Deir el-Medina** and is now in the **British Museum**.

ANKHWENNEFER (reigned c. 199–186 BC). The Greek form of his name is Chaonnophris, previously wrongly read as Anchmachis. Rebel ruler in the south during the reign of **Ptolemy V**. He succeeded **Harwennefer** and was able to regain **Thebes**, controlling as far north as **Asyut**. Ankhwennefer was driven from Thebes in 191 BC and finally defeated and captured in battle in 186 BC. His ultimate fate is unknown.

ANTHONY (c. 251–356 AD). Egyptian saint and hermit. He was the son of Christians from the village of Qiman, and upon their death, he gave away his worldly possessions and lived the life of an ascetic hermit near the village and later in the eastern desert. Anthony inspired other hermits to live near him for a time, forming the first ascetic community, although he himself moved to the desert to be on his own. Several of his letters survive, and his life, written by **Athanasius**, spread the idea of ascetic life in the Christian world. **Pachomius**, another ascetic, was to change the solitary existence of the hermit into that of a monastic community. *See also* ABRAHAM; COPTIC CHURCH; SHENOUTE.

ANTINOOPOLIS. Greek name of the city in **Middle Egypt** founded by **Hadrian** in 130 AD in honor of his favorite, Antinous, who had drowned in the **Nile**. Now modern Sheikh Ibada, it is located on the east bank of the Nile opposite **Hermopolis**. The inhabitants were drawn from the major Greek cities in Egypt. The site was originally an Egyptian city with a **temple** erected by **Ramesses II** and has remains dating from the **Predynastic Period**. Antinoopolis was excavated by the French archaeologist Albert Gayet from 1895–1914, by a British expedition from 1913–1914, and more recently by an Italian expedition.

ANTIOCHUS IV (reigned 175–164 BC). Ruler of the Seleucid Empire encompassing Syria, Asia Minor, Mesopotamia, and parts of Iran. Son of **Antiochus** III and Laodice of Pontus and brother of **Cleopatra I**. He succeeded to the throne upon the assassination of his brother, Seleucus IV, in association with his nephew, Antiochus, whom he adopted and later executed. Conflict with Egypt over Syria was renewed in 170–169 BC, but an invading Egyptian army was defeated. Antiochus in turn invaded Egypt, taking the border town of Pelusium and capturing **Ptolemy VI** and **Memphis**, but he failed to take **Alexandria** and withdrew in 169 BC. He invaded again in 168 BC and may have aimed to crown himself ruler of Egypt, but he was forced to withdraw under pressure from Rome. He then turned his attention eastward to Iran and died at Tabae in 164 BC. *See also* POPILLIUS LAENAS, CAIUS; WARFARE.

ANTONIUS, MARCUS (83–30 BC). Roman politician. Son of Marcus Antonius and Julia of the family of the Julii Caesares. He was an early supporter of his distant relation, **Caius Iulius Caesar**, and sought to inherit his political power after the latter's assassination in 44 BC, but he was forced to ally himself with the future **Augustus** to crush their political opponents. Antonius was given the eastern part of the empire in the division of the territory after the victory at Philippi in 42 BC and married Augustus's sister as part of their political alliance. He soon formed a political and personal connection with **Cleopatra VII** of Egypt, which estranged him from Augustus, who used this oriental entanglement to vilify Antonius in Rome. War was eventually declared against Egypt, and Antonius was defeated at the battle of Actium in 31 BC and committed suicide in 30 BC as Augustus's forces entered **Alexandria**. *See also* ALEXANDER HELIOS; CLEOPATRA SELENE; PTOLEMY PHILADELPHUS.

ANTYEMSAF. *See* NEMTYEMSAF.

ANUBIS. Egyptian god of the necropolis and embalming represented as a jackal or a jackal-headed man. He was responsible for conducting the deceased to **Osiris**, god of the dead. *See also* RELIGION.

ANUKIS. Daughter of the god **Khnum** of **Elephantine** and **Satis**. She is depicted as a human female figure wearing a feathered headdress and was principally worshipped at Elephantine and in **Nubia**. *See also* RELIGION.

APEPI (reigned c. 1585–1550 BC). The Greek form of his name is Apophis. Throne name Aawoserre. Last or penultimate **Hyksos** ruler of **Dynasty 15**. He is attested as an opponent of the rulers of **Thebes**, **Tao**, and **Kamose**. Apepi tried to fashion an alliance with the ruler of Kush against the Thebans, but this attempt apparently failed. It is not clear whether he was still reigning when his capital, **Avaris,** fell to the Theban forces under **Ahmose I**. Two other throne names, Aakenenre and Nebkhepeshre, are associated with Apepi and may refer to different monarchs or more likely to the same man who changed his throne name. He may have been briefly succeeded by Khamudy, the last of the dynasty. *See also* IANNAS; KHAYAN; SALITIS.

APEREL (fl. 1370 BC). Northern **vizier** of **Amenhotep III**. His intact **tomb** was excavated at **Saqqara** beginning in 1976, culminating in the opening of the burial chamber in 1987. His existence was hitherto unknown. Aperel's name is Semitic, but his burial was thoroughly Egyptian, so it cannot be necessarily assumed that he was of foreign origin as Semitic names were sometimes used by Egyptians. *See also* AMENEMHAT I; AY; HEMIUNU; IMHOTEP; INTEFYOKER; KAGEMNI; MERERUKA; NEFERMAAT; PASER; PTAHHOTEP; PTAHSHEPSES; RAMESSES I; REKHMIRE.

APION. Family of Egyptian landowners and officials in the **Byzantine Period**, known from documents from **Oxyrhynchus**, where they had estates. The earliest known member appears to have been Flavius Strategius I, who died before 469. His probable son was Apion I, a patrician and vice **prefect** of the East in 503–504 and later praetorian prefect in the East in 518–519, who held an honorary consulship at the end of the 5th century AD and died between 524 and 532.

Other family members included Flavius Strategius II, prefect of Egypt from 518–523, and Flavius Strategius Apion II, consul in 539 who died around 578. The family supported the orthodox imperial view in the religious controversies with the nascent **Coptic Church**. The last known member was Apion III, who died or disappeared in late 619, possibly a victim of the Persian invasion. The Apions represent one of the few Egyptian families to have exercised political influence on the imperial court.

APIS. Greek name for the sacred bull of **Memphis**. Egyptian *Hapi*. The bull was the living embodiment of the god **Ptah** and after death was identified with **Osiris**. He was recognized by distinct signs and housed in the **temple** complex. Upon his death, a new bull was sought born near the time of death of the old. The bulls were buried in the **Serapeum** at **Saqqara**. The mother of the bull was also accorded special honors, and the burial catacombs for the cows were discovered by a British expedition in the 1970s. The cult is known from **Dynasty 1**, but it became particularly important during the **Late Period**. *See also* RELIGION.

APRIES. *See* WAHIBRE.

ARCHAIC PERIOD. *See* EARLY DYNASTIC PERIOD.

ARIUS (c. 270–336 AD). Egyptian Christian priest in **Alexandria** of Libyan origin who enunciated the doctrine of Arianism indicating that Christ had only one nature—human as against the orthodox view of two natures, human and divine intermingled. He was fiercely opposed by **Athanasius**, later patriarch of Alexandria, who forced him to leave the city. Arius died in Constantinople in 336. His doctrine found little support in Egypt, although Athanasius was for a time deposed by an Arian, but it influenced several emperors and later spread to barbarian converts outside the empire.

ARMANT. Modern name for the Egyptian *Iuny*, Greek Hermonthis, capital of the fourth **nome** of **Upper Egypt** until superseded by **Thebes**. It was located on the west bank of the **Nile** opposite **Tod**. The principal deity of the site was the god **Montu**, whose **temple** is now destroyed. Archaeological remains date from the **Predynastic Period** to the **Roman Period**, when it again became the nome capital. The burials of the sacred ram **Buchis** have also been located. Armant was excavated on behalf of the **Egypt Exploration Society** in 1927–1932, and the texts in the temple have been recorded by the **French Institute** since 2002.

ARSAMES (fl. 423-404 BC). Persian **satrap** of Egypt during the reign of **Darius II** of **Persia** (423–404 BC). Member of the royal family. Part of his official correspondence written in Aramaic has been discovered. His governorship may have been ended by the revolt that brought **Amyrtaeos** to power. *See also* ACHAEMENES.

ARSAPHES. *See* HERYSHEF.

ARSINOE I (born c. 300 BC). Daughter of King Lysimachus of Thrace and Nicaea. First wife of **Ptolemy II** and mother of **Ptolemy III**. She was exiled to **Coptos** in 279 BC on a charge of conspiracy after she was supplanted in the king's affections by **Arsinoe II**.

ARSINOE II (c. 316–270 BC). Daughter of **Ptolemy I** and **Berenice I**. She married King Lysimachus of Thrace, who killed his son by his first marriage possibly by her influence. This resulted in civil strife leading to the king's death in battle in 281 BC. She then married her half brother Ptolemy, king of Macedonia, who murdered two of her sons and died in battle with the Celts in 279 BC. She returned to Egypt and entered into her third marriage around 276 BC to her full brother, **Ptolemy II**. She was highly influential at court and was deified with her husband.

ARSINOE III (c. 235–205 BC). Daughter of **Ptolemy III** and **Berenice II** and wife of her full brother **Ptolemy IV**, whom she married in 217 BC. She was estranged from her husband and apparently murdered by his courtiers shortly after his death to prevent her becoming regent. *See also* SOSIBIOS.

ARSINOE IV (c. 63–41 BC). Daughter of **Ptolemy XII** and possibly **Cleopatra VI Tryphaena**. She supported her brother, **Ptolemy XIII**, against **Cleopatra VII** and was taken to Rome by **Iulius Caesar** to appear in his triumph in 46 BC. She later took refuge in Ephesus but was executed at the order of her sister, Cleopatra VII, in 41 BC. *See also* ACHILLAS.

ART. In ancient Egypt, monumental and most private art was designed for religious rather than decorative purposes. The statue was originally developed as a substitute home for the spirit in the **afterlife**, and later statues were also placed in **temples** where the **name** of the deceased could be read, causing the deceased to live again. The block statue, which first appeared in the early **Middle Kingdom**, was particularly favored because of the amount of space available for text. Incised reliefs and wall paintings in **tombs** depicted the goods and activities the deceased wished to enjoy in the next life. Royal reliefs on temple walls showed the majesty and power of the king and the beneficence of the gods. Most statues and reliefs were in fact painted, but much of this paint has worn away.

Egyptian artists worked to a canon of proportions for the human figure. A standard style was set by the royal court, although regional variations appeared during the **First Intermediate Period**, **Second Intermediate Period**, and **Third Intermediate Period**, when central government and artistic patronage had broken down. Egyptian art was not static, as the canon of proportions varied over time. The most obvious change occurred during the **Amarna Period**, when the canon was changed and the human figure was depicted in an exaggerated style with a long, narrow neck and full hips. During the **Late Period**, artists drew inspiration from the works of the **Old Kingdom** and **Middle Kingdom**.

Very little decoration in royal and private buildings survives. The remaining fragments of tiles and frescoes show that the decorative scheme of the royal palace sought to display the might of the sovereign as a conqueror, although more intimate scenes are known from the Amarna Period. Egyptian craftsmen were adept in the production of such small, functional objects as cosmetic spoons and other toiletry objects in a highly decorative form. *See also* SPHINX; STONE; THUTMOSE.

ARTAXERXES I (reigned 465–423 BC). King of **Persia** and ruler of Egypt. Son of **Xerxes** and Amestris. He succeeded to the throne following the murder of his father and his elder brother, Darius. He faced a major revolt in Egypt beginning in 459 BC led by **Inaros**, but his forces managed to crush the resistance in 454 BC. He installed **Arsames** as **satrap**. He also signed a peace treaty with Athens in 449 BC to end the Greco-Persian wars. Following his death, the throne was briefly occupied by his sons, Xerxes II and Sogdianus, until a third son, **Darius II**, secured his rule.

ARTAXERXES II (c. 453/445–359 BC). King of **Persia**. Son of **Darius II** and Parysatis. Egypt was in revolt upon his succession, although he seems to have been recognized in **Elephantine** until 401 BC. He faced a rebellion by his younger brother, **Cyrus**, which was suppressed and unable to reconquer Egypt despite several campaigns. *See also* AMYRTAEOS.

ARTAXERXES III (reigned in Egypt 343–338 BC). King of **Persia** and ruler of Egypt. Personal name Ochus. Son of **Artaxerxes II** and Statira. He took part in a war against Egypt around 361 BC and seized power upon the death of his father in 359 BC. He spent his reign quelling rebellions and consolidating his empire. He embarked on a campaign of reconquest of Egypt in 343 BC. He had a reputation as a cruel and ruthless ruler and was murdered by his close adviser, **Bagoas**, in 338 BC, who initially placed his son, Arses—officially Artaxerxes IV—on the throne before replacing him with **Darius III**. *See also* WARFARE.

ASHAYET (fl. 2020 BC). A minor wife of **Mentuhotep II** of **Dynasty 11**. She was commemorated in a chapel and buried in a pit **tomb** at his funerary complex at **Deir el-Bahri**. The chapel was discovered during **Henri Edouard Naville**'s excavations at the site, but Ashayet's tomb was found largely intact by an American expedition from the **Metropolitan Museum of Art** in excavations from 1920–1921. Her **sarcophagus** and **mummy** are now in the **Cairo Egyptian Museum**. *See also* HENHENET; KAWIT; KEMSIT; MYT; NEFRU; SADEH; TEM.

ASKUT. Modern name for the site of a fortress in the Second **Cataract** region of **Nubia**. Egyptian *Djer Setiu*. It appears to have been constructed during the **Middle Kingdom** as part of a series of fortresses from **Buhen** to **Semna** by **Senusret III** to control the native Nubians. The fortress was abandoned during the **Second Intermediate Period** but reused during the **New Kingdom**. Askut was excavated in 1962–1964 by an expedition from the University of California at Los Angeles before the site was flooded by Lake Nasser, the lake created by the Aswan High Dam. *See also* ANIBA; BUHEN; KUMMA; MIRGISSA; SEMNA; SHALFAK; URONARTI.

ASSYRIA. A kingdom situated in northern Iraq that was renowned for its warring capabilities. Assyria benefited from the destruction of **Mitanni** and the **Hittite** Empire and expanded southward to conquer Mesopotamia and westward to Syria and Palestine, whose states were annexed or reduced to vassal status. The kingdom came into conflict with Egypt at the beginning of **Dynasty 25**, but its forces were kept at bay until the reign of Esarhaddon (681–69 BC), who invaded Egypt in 671 BC. Nubian ruler **Taharqo** of Dynasty 25 was defeated and driven south, and members of the royal family were captured, but Assyrian forces were eventually expelled.

The son and successor of Esarhaddon, Ashurbanipal (669–27 BC), renewed the campaign, took **Memphis**, and drove Taharqo south again. The local princes of the Delta submitted, notably **Nekau I** of **Sais** of **Dynasty 26**, who became the chief Assyrian vassal after the other princes were executed for disloyalty. The new ruler of Dynasty 25, **Tantamani**, invaded Egypt from **Nubia** in 664 BC, after the departure of the main Assyrian forces, and killed Nekau, whose son, **Psamtik I**, fled to Assyria for protection. In 663 BC, the Assyrians returned, defeated the Nubians, and sacked **Thebes**. During Psamtik I's long reign, the control of Assyria gradually weakened due to internal difficulties, and Egypt regained independence. When the Assyrian kingdom was destroyed in 612 BC, the remnants appealed to Egypt for help, and **Nekau II** invaded Palestine as an ally but was defeated by the Babylonians at the battle of Carchemish in 609 BC, after which Assyria disappeared as a political entity.

ASTARTE. Canaanite goddess of love and fertility. Her worship spread to Egypt during the **New Kingdom**. She was considered one of the wives of the god **Seth**, along with **Anat**. *See also* QUDSHU; RELIGION; RESHEP.

ASWAN. *See* ELEPHANTINE.

ASYUT. Arabic name for the Egyptian *Sauty*, Greek Lycopolis, capital of the 13th **nome** of **Upper Egypt**. The chief deity of the city was the god **Wepwawet**. Very little remains of the town, but the **tombs** of the nomarchs of the **First Intermediate Period** and the **Middle Kingdom** have been uncovered. Excavations were performed by a French team in 1903, an Italian expedition in 1905–1913, and British excavators in 1906–1907 and 1922. A joint German–Egyptian expedition has been working on tombs in the necropolis since 2003.

ATEN. The sun's disk and so a form of the sun god **Re**-Harakhty. Aten was worshipped as a god in his own right toward the end of **Dynasty 18** and raised to position of supreme deity by **Akhenaten** in opposition to the cult of **Amun**. In his honor, the king took a name compounded with that of the god and founded a new city at **Amarna**. The king sought to suppress the cults of other rival gods, but his new **religion** was not monotheistic since he did not proscribe cults connected with the sun god, like the **Mnevis** bull or those deifying the kingship of his father or himself. Following Akhenaten's death, the cult of Aten was abandoned and proscribed, although there are occasional references to the Aten in its old form as the sun's disk.

ATET. *See* NEFERMAAT.

ATHANASIUS (c. 296–373 AD). Egyptian Christian patriarch. He was born in **Alexandria**, where he was educated and became the secretary of Patriarch Alexander, whom he succeeded in 326. Prior to his accession, he took part in the Council of Nicaea in 325, where the orthodox creed was laid down, and thereafter he became a staunch opponent of the doctrine of **Arius**. Athanasius was exiled from 334–337 and deposed from 340–345 and 356-61 and briefly exiled in 363 and 365 by various emperors for his views. He set the example for opposition by the patriarchs of Alexandria to imperial policy when it conflicted with their religious beliefs. He died in May 373. His surviving writings include an influential life of St. **Anthony**. *See also* BENJAMIN; COPTIC CHURCH; CYRIL; CYRUS; DIOSCORUS; THEOPHILUS.

ATHRIBIS. Greek name for the Egyptian *Hutheryib*, modern Tell Atrib, capital of the 10th **nome** of **Lower Egypt**. The town is attested from at least the **Old Kingdom** but was particularly prominent in the **Late Period** and **Graeco-Roman Period**. Little remains on the site, but it was excavated by **Flinders Petrie** in 1907 and subsequently by Alan Rowe in 1939 and has been under excavation by a Polish expedition since 1957. The **tomb** of **queen** Takhut, wife of **Psamtik II** and mother of **Wahibre**, was discovered here in 1951.

A second site named Athribis is located at modern Nag ash-Shaykh Hamad in the ninth nome of **Upper Egypt** on the west bank of the **Nile** opposite **Akhmim**, ancient *Hutrepit*. The surviving remains are dated from the **Late Period** to the **Coptic Period** and include Graeco-Roman tombs and a **temple** dedicated to the local goddess **Repit** with her consort **Min**. The site has been examined by a German–Egyptian expedition since 1998.

ATUM. Primeval creator god who was believed to have arisen from chaos, or **Nun**, and then produced the deities **Shu** and **Tefnut** by spitting or masturbation. He can be depicted as a human figure or serpent. Atum worshipped at **Heliopolis**, where he was identified with the sun god **Re**. His sacred animal was the ichneumon or shrew. *See also* RELIGION.

AUGUSTUS (63 BC–14 AD). First Roman emperor. Original name Caius Octavius. Son of Caius Octavius and Atia and great-nephew of **Iulius Caesar** who adopted him in his will. He used his adoptive father's name and his own political skills following Caesar's assassination in 44 BC to become one of the rulers of the Roman world, alongside Marcus Aemilius Lepidus and **Marcus Antonius**. Augusttus eventually forced Lepidus's resignation and clashed with Antonius and his ally **Cleopatra VII**, whom he defeated and drove to suicide in 30 BC. He then annexed Egypt as the personal property of the emperor, forbidding any senator to go there without imperial permission and putting Egypt under the control of a **prefect**. His rule restricted the rights of the native Egyptians and refused to recognize the use of the Egyptian language in official documentation. Augustus was considered **pharaoh** by the Egyptians, and his name appears in **cartouches** with the prenomen autocrator, the Greek equivalent of imperator, his official Roman designation.

AVARIS. Modern Tell el-Daba. Capital city of the **Hyksos Dynasty 15** situated in the Delta. Very little is known of its history. It was founded in **Dynasty 12** and settled by immigrants from Syria-Palestine and later served as the Hyksos stronghold. Avaris was attacked by **Kamose** and later captured by **Ahmose I** of **Dynasty 18**, after which it fell into ruins. Excavations on the site have been carried out by an Austrian expedition since 1966 and have revealed palace structures and wall frescoes in the Minoan style.

AVIDIUS CASSIUS, CAIUS (c. 130–175 AD). Roman general. He was born in Egypt c. 130 AD as son of Caius Avidius Heliodorus, **prefect** of Egypt. He served the Roman emperor Marcus Aurelius and took part in the Parthian War from 162–166. He became consul in 166 AD and was then named governor of Syria. On a rumor of the death of the emperor, he was proclaimed his successor in 175 AD and controlled Egypt and the East, but his revolt collapsed, and he was killed when the news of the emperor's death proved false.

AY (reigned c. 1327–1323 BC). Throne name Kheperkheprure. High official during the reign of **Akhenaten** and **Tutankhamun** with the title **God's father** and **vizier**. It has been speculated that he was the brother of **Tiy** and the father of **Nefertiti**, but nothing definite is known about his family apart from the fact that his wife, also **Tiy**, was the nurse of Nefertiti. Ay succeeded Tutankhamun, probably against the wishes of **Queen Ankhesenamun**, and conducted the burial rites for the late monarch, as depicted in Tutankhamun's **tomb**. His reign was brief and he was buried in tomb **KV23** in the **Valley of the Kings**, which was discovered in 1816, but his **mummy** has not been preserved or identified. His memory was later suppressed in **Dynasty 19**. *See also* HOREMHEB; NAKHTMIN.

AYN SOKHA. Modern name for a site on the Gulf of Suez south of the city of Suez. There are remains of **copper**-smelting facilities from the **Old Kingdom** to the **Middle Kingdom**. The area has been under excavation by a French expedition since 2001.

AZIRU (fl. 1350–1320 BC). Ruler of **Amurru**. Son of **Abdi-Ashirta**. He continued his father's policy of conquest and took over the local Egyptian capital, killing the Egyptian commissioner. He still protested his loyalty to **Akhenaten** in the **Amarna letters**. Aziru was summoned to Egypt to explain his actions but was allowed to return to Amurru to face a **Hittite** advance. He renounced his Egyptian allegiance and became a vassal of the Hittite king **Suppiluliuma I**. *See also* BENTESHINA.

– **B** –

BACCHIAS. A town in the northeastern **Fayum** from the **Graeco-Roman Period**. Modern Tell Umm et-Atl. It flourished from the 3rd century BC until the 4th century AD. The main **temple** was dedicated to the local god Soknobkonneus. It was excavated by British archaeologists briefly in 1896, and excavation work has been carried out by an Italian expedition since 1993. Remains of houses and **papyri** have been discovered. *See also* DEIR EL-NAQLUN; GUROB; HARAGEH; HAWARA; KARANIS; KOM KHELWA; KOM TALIT; LAHUN; LISHT; MEDINET MADI; SOKNOPAIOU NESOS; TEBTUNIS.

BADARI, EL-. Modern name for a site in **Upper Egypt** dated to the **Predynastic Period**. The black-topped red **pottery** found here gave the name Badarian to a phase of predynastic culture.

BAGOAS (fl. 360–336 BC). Persian eunuch. He was a close adviser of **Artaxerxes III** and led his army in the reconquest of Egypt in 343 BC. He quarreled with his Greek mercenaries and was recalled to **Persia**. Bagoas murdered Artaxerxes III in 338 BC, as well as his son and successor, Arses, in 336 BC but was then executed by **Darius III**, whom he had placed on the throne. *See also* NAKHTHORHEB.

BAHARIYA OASIS. Ancient Egyptia *Djesdjes* or *Wehat mehyt*, meaning northern oasis. An oasis in the Western Desert west of **Luxor**. Archaeological remains have been discovered from the **Middle Kingdom** to the **Byzantine Period**, including **tombs** of local governors from **Dynasty 19** and **Dynasty 26**. There are also **temples** dedicated to Hercules and **Alexander the Great**. A major cemetery of the **Graeco-Roman Period** was discovered by Egyptian archaeologists in 1996. The late Roman fortress site at Qaret el-Tub has been excavated by a French team beginning in 2001 and the settlement site from Dynasty 26 at Qasr Allam since 2002. *See also* DAKHLA OASIS; FARFARA OASIS; KHARGA OASIS; SIWA OASIS.

BAKENKHONS (fl. 1300–1220). High priest of Amun at Thebes. He came from a priestly family, being the son of Roma, second prophet of **Amun**, and **Amenemope**. His lengthy biography is inscribed on a block statue, now in the Munich Museum. During his youth, he served in the stable of **Sety I** and then succesively held the offices of fourth, third, and second prophets of Amun during the reign of **Ramesses II** until being promoted to the post of high priest, first prophet of Amun. He supervised the king's building of the **temple** of **Karnak**. He was succeeded by Roma-Roy, probably a close relation. A second high priest of Amun, Bakenkhons held office during the reigns of **Sethnakhte** and **Ramesses III**. A stela of his dated to year 4 of Sethnakhte was discovered in 2007 during clearance of the alley of ram-headed **sphinxes** between the temples of Karnak and **Luxor**. *See also* PASER; WENNEFER.

BAKENRENEF (reigned c. 725–719 BC). The Greek form of his name is Bocchoris. Throne name Wahkare. Ruler of **Dynasty 24**. He succeeded his father, **Tefnakhte**, as prince of **Sais** and claimant to the throne of Egypt. The extent of his rule is unclear, but he was opposed and finally defeated by **Shabaqo** of **Dynasty 25**. Later sources indicate that Bakenrenef was executed by the new ruler. *See also* THIRD INTERMEDIATE PERIOD.

BAKETATEN (fl. c. 1350 BC). Royal princess known only from a relief at **Amarna**, where she is depicted with her mother, **Queen Tiy**. It is presumed that she was an otherwise unattested daughter of **Amenhotep III**, but it is possible that she was in fact a granddaughter of Tiy and daughter of **Akhenaten**. *See also* AMARNA PERIOD; SITAMUN; THUTMOSE.

BALAMUN. *See* TELL EL-BALAMUN.

BALAT. Modern name for a site near Ayn Asil in the **Dakhla Oasis**. Ancient *Dmi-iw*. It flourished during the **Old Kingdom** and was the center of the oasis and seat of the local governor. The site was discovered by Egyptian archaeologist Ahmad Fakhry, who excavated the area from 1968–1972. Excavations were continued by a French expedition beginning in 1977. Since 1985, the group has uncovered the palace of the governor built during **Dynasty 6**, where two caches of clay tablets inscribed in hieratic and seal impressions have been found. The nearby **tombs** of the governors of the oasis, Ima-Pepy I, Ima-Pepy II, **Khentikha** and Medu-nefer, who served under **Pepy I** and **Pepy II**, have also been cleared and published.

BALBILLA, JULIA (fl. 130 AD). Daughter of Caius Iulius Antiochus Epiphanes and Claudia Capitolina and granddaughter of King Antiochus IV of Commagene and Tiberius Claudius Balbillus, **prefect** of Egypt. She accompanied Emperor **Hadrian** and his wife, **Vibia Sabina**, to Egypt in 130 AD and took part in their visit to the **Colossi of Memnon**. Balbilla recorded the event in a poem inscribed on one of the statues, which still survives.

BALLANA. Modern name for a site in **Nubia** on the west bank of the **Nile** south of **Qasr Ibrim** where, together with the site of Qustul on the east bank, many graves have been excavated from different phases of Nubian culture. Some 180 **tombs**, dating from the 4th through 7th centuries AD, were discovered, of which 40 contained material of such richness that they might be called royal, including jewelry, crowns, weapons, horse fittings, and vessels. These items are now housed in the **Cairo Egyptian Museum**. The site has given its name to the Ballana culture, or X-group culture, which can be identified from graves elsewhere in Nubia. Ballana was excavated by the Egyptian Antiquities Service in 1931–1934 and more recently by an Egyptian expedition in 1958–1959 and the University of Chicago in the 1960s in advance of flooding caused by the Aswan High Dam.

BASTET. Cat goddess of **Bubastis** represented as a cat-headed or lioness-headed human figure, often with a sistrum rattle or kittens. The worship of her cult became popular during the **Late Period**, from which time cemeteries of cats killed as votive offerings to her have been discovered. *See also* RELIGION; SAKHMET.

BAUEFRE (fl. 2570 BC). A royal prince of **Dynasty 4**. Son of **Khufu**. He is named in the literary tale on the **Westcar Papyrus**, and his name appears in a **cartouche** in a later inscription in the **Wadi Hammamat**. He is otherwise unknown. *See also* DJEDEFRE; HARDJEDEF; KAWAB; KHAFRE.

BAWIT. Modern name for a monastic site of Apa Apollo in **Upper Egypt** on the west bank of the **Nile** between **Asyut** and Ashmunein (**Hermopolis**), which flourished from the late 3rd century AD until at least the end of the 12th century. It was apparently founded by the monk Apa Apollo. Excavations by French archaeologists from 1901–1904 and in 1913 uncovered part of the site and found architectural elements and stone and wooden sculpture, as well as important paintings. Further excavations have been conducted by an Egyptian expedition in 1976 and from 1984–1985 and a French team since 2002.

BAY (fl. 1196 BC). Ruler of the throne at the end of **Dynasty 19**. He claims to have arranged the succession of **Siptah** after the death of **Sety II**. Egyptian inscriptions give him the title of chancellor, but a text from **Ugarit** calls him commander of the king's guard. He had a **tomb (KV13)** in the **Valley of the Kings**. Bay has been identified as a Syrian by modern Egyptologists due to a later ambiguous reference, but there is no firm evidence of his background. He is now known to have been executed in year 5 of Siptah (1189 BC) by order of the king. Since the king was a minor, it is obvious that a rival faction at court, possibly head by **Queen** Dowager **Tewosret**, arranged for his demise. Tewosret succeeded to the throne the next year after the death of the king, so she was the ultimate beneficiary of Bay's execution. He was presumably never buried in his valley tomb. *See also* SETHNAKHTE.

BEIT EL-WALI. Modern name for the site of a **temple** of **Ramesses II** in **Nubia**, built early in his reign and depicting his wars. The area is now flooded by the lake of the Aswan High Dam, but the temple has been moved to a site near Aswan. *See also* ABU SIMBEL; AMADA; GERF HUSSEIN; KALABSHA; SOLEB.

BELZONI, GIOVANNI BATTISTA (1778–1823). Italian adventurer and excavator. He was born in Padua on 5 November 1778 and later joined a circus troupe in London. He went to Egypt in 1815 to seek work as a technical adviser but was unsuccessful. Belzoni was employed by **Henry Salt**, the British consul general, to move a head of **Ramesses II** from the **Ramesseum** to England for placement in the **British Museum** and thereafter to acquire antiquities for Salt's collections, which were later sold to the British Museum and the **Louvre Museum**. He supervised excavations at **Giza**, **Thebes**, and **Abu Simbel** and acquired material from locals. He quarreled with Salt over the terms of his employment, and in 1819, he returned to London with some antiquities and watercolors of **tomb** scenes. While there he put on a successful exhibition and wrote his memoirs. Belzoni died at Gwato in Benin, West Africa, on 3 December 1823, during an expedition seeking the source of the Niger River. *See also* DROVETTI, BERNARDINO MICHELE MARIA.

BENI HASAN. Modern name for the site in **Middle Egypt** containing the rock **tombs** of the nomarchs of the 16th **nome** of **Upper Egypt** and other officials dating to **Dynasty 11** and **Dynasty 12**. One tomb is notable for the depiction of Asiatics who had traveled to Egypt. The site also contains a **New Kingdom** rock chapel dedicated by **Hatshepsut** and **Thutmose III**. The tombs were copied by an expedition from the **Egypt Exploration Fund** in 1890–1891. *See also* KHNUMHOTEP I; KHNUMHOTEP II.

BENJAMIN (c. 590–661 AD). Coptic patriarch of **Alexandria**. He was born at Barshut in the western Delta and in 620 joined a monastic community at Canopus. He later served as assistant to the patriarch Andronicus of the **Coptic Church**, succeeding him in 622. In 631, he opposed **Cyrus**, the newly appointed orthodox patriarch and **prefect** of Egypt who tried to end the religious divisions in Egypt by force. Benjamin fled into hiding, and the resultant instability undoubtedly aided the Arabic conquest of Egypt in 642. He was later restored to office, but the division of the Christians into Coptic and orthodox communities with separate patriarchs remained permanent. He remained on amicable terms with the new Islamic rulers. He died on 3 January 661. *See also* ATHANASIUS; CYRIL; CYRUS; DIOSCORUS; THEOPHILUS.

BENTESHINA (fl. 1290–1235 BC). King of **Amurru**. Son of Tuppi-Teshub, king of Amurru, and great-grandson of **Aziru**, son of **Abdi-Ashirta**. Originally a **Hittite** vassal, he defected to Egypt probably under **Sety I**. Benteshina was deposed by **Muwattili II**, the Hittite king, in the aftermath of the battle of **Kadesh** when the Hittites regained control of Amurru. He was restored to the throne by **Urhi-Teshub** or **Hattusili III**, whose daughter he married.

BERENICE I (c. 340–278/7 BC). Daughter of Magas and Antigone and wife of a Macedonian named Philip by whom she had several children. She came to Egypt with Eurydice, second wife of **Ptolemy I**, and soon became the mistress and then wife of the king. Berenice I was the mother of his successor, **Ptolemy II**, and his sister-wife, **Arsinoe II**.

BERENICE II (c. 273–221 BC). Daughter of King Magas of **Cyrene** and Apama. She was engaged to **Ptolemy III**, but her mother attempted to marry her to a Macedonian prince against whom she led a revolt ending in his execution. She married the Egyptian king in 246 BC. Berenice II was the mother of **Ptolemy IV**, who apparently had her killed shortly after his accession.

BERENICE III. *See* CLEOPATRA BERENICE III.

BERENICE IV (c. 78–55 BC). Eldest daughter of **Ptolemy XII** and **Cleopatra VI Tryphaena**. When her father was expelled in 58 BC, she was named joint ruler apparently with her mother. In 56 BC, Berenice IV first married Seleucus, a Syrian prince whom she murdered shortly after the marriage. She then wed Archelaus of Cappadocia, who was killed in 55 BC trying to defeat the Roman forces supporting his father-in-law. Upon his restoration, Ptolemy XII executed his daughter.

BERENIKE. Ptolemaic port on the Red Sea on a parallel with Aswan and connected by a **trade** route to **Edfu**. It was founded by **Ptolemy II** around 275 BC and named after his mother, **Berenice I**. It was the main port for trade with Arabia and India during the **Ptolemaic Period** when important imports included elephants for the Ptolemaic army, but it declined during the **Roman Period** when **Myos Hormos**, located further north, became more prominent. Berenike appears to have been refurbished during the 4th century AD and flourished until the 6th century AD. The town was excavated by an American expedition from 1994–2001.

BERLIN EGYPTIAN MUSEUM. Founded by the King of Prussia on 1 July 1828 following the acquisition of the collections of Heinrich von Minutoli and Giuseppe Passalacqua, who became the first director, and the collection of **Bernardino Drovetti** in 1836. The collection was increased during the expedition to Egypt in 1842–1845 by **Richard Lepsius**, who became the second director of the institution in 1865. A new museum for Egyptain antiquities was opened in 1850. The collection was enriched by the gift of **Amarna** sculpture, notably the head of **Queen Nefertiti** by a merchant who had financed the German excavations at Amarna. The museum was badly damaged during World War II, and the collections were later divided between East Berlin and West Berlin. The management of the Egyptian collection has now been unified, and plans are under way to rebuild the museum at its old site. *See also* BOSTON MUSEUM OF FINE ARTS; BRITISH MUSEUM; CAIRO EGYPTIAN MUSEUM; LOUVRE MUSEUM; METROPOLITAN MUSEUM OF ART; TURIN EGYPTIAN MUSEUM.

BIBI UMM FAWAKHIR. A **gold** mining site in the Eastern Desert northeast of the **Wadi Hammamat** between **Coptos** and Quseir (**Myos Hormos**). It flourished in the 5th and 6th centuries AD, but there is earlier evidence of **New Kingdom** and Ptolemaic activity. Bibi Umm Fawakhir was excavated by an expedition from the University of Chicago from 1992–2001.

BINTANAT (fl. c. 1280–1210 BC). Eldest daughter of **Ramesses II** and **Isitnofret**. She married her father and was influential during the latter part of his reign and into that of her full brother, **Merenptah**. Bintanat had her own tomb (**QV71**) in the **Valley of the Queens**, where she is depicted with a daughter whose royal parentage is not explicitly stated. *See also* HENTTAWY; HENUTMIRE; MAATHORNEFERURE; MERITAMUN; NEBTTAWY; NEFERTARI.

BOOK OF THE DEAD. The name given to a type of **papyrus** often buried with the dead from the **New Kingdom** onward. The papyrus contained a number of magical spells that would enable the deceased to successfully reach the next world. The most important spell concerned the ritual of the **weighing of the heart** against the feather of *maat* to determine the deceased's worthiness to enter the **afterlife**, and the spell was supposed to fix the balance in the deceased's favor. Some books of the dead were decorated with elaborate vignettes and scenes depicting funerals and rituals. Some were obviously produced as special commissions, but there were stock examples available for purchase in which the name of the deceased could be filled in blank spaces or in some cases not filled in at all. *See also* RELIGION.

BOSTON MUSEUM OF FINE ARTS. Founded in 1872, the museum immediately acquired its first Egyptian objects from the collection of C. Granville Way, who had purchased them from the estate of Robert Hay, an early traveler in Egypt. Further acquisitions were made from the collection of John Lowell of Boston, another early traveler, and from donations from the **Egypt Exploration Fund**. In 1909, a new museum building was inaugurated. Following the appointment of **George Reisner** as curator of Egyptian antiquities in 1910, the museum received substantial numbers of objects from his archaeological work at **Giza**, **Naga el-Deir**, **Deir el-Bersha**, and various **Nubian**

sites. *See also* BERLIN EGYPTIAN MUSEUM; BRITISH MU-
SEUM; CAIRO EGYPTIAN MUSEUM; LOUVRE MUSEUM;
METROPOLITAN MUSEUM OF ART; TURIN EGYPTIAN
MUSEUM.

BREASTED, JAMES HENRY (1865–1935). American Egyptologist.
He was born in Rockford, Illinois, on 27 August 1865. He studied at
Yale University and later in Berlin. Breasted obtained a post at the
University of Chicago in 1895, where later in 1905 he became professor of egyptology. With funds from John D. Rockefeller, he
founded the Oriental Institute at the University of Chicago, which became the leading research and teaching center for Near Eastern studies in the United States. He also directed expeditions in Egypt and
published translations of Egyptian historical texts. He died in New
York on 2 December 1935.

BRITISH MUSEUM. Founded in 1753 as a national museum of Great
Britain to house collections bequeathed to the nation. It was funded
by a lottery that allowed the purchase of property in London, now on
Great Russell Street. The original building was demolished and rebuilt during the first half of the 19th century. Small Egyptian items
were initially part of the collection, but major Egyptian antiquities
were acquired in 1802 with the surrender of objects, including the
Rosetta Stone, collected by the French invaders of Egypt who were
defeated by a combined British and Turkish force. Egyptian holdings
then expanded with the purchase of individual collections, including
those of **Henry Salt** in 1823, Joseph Sams in 1834, and Giovanni
Anastasi in 1839, as well as items acquired at auction or by donation.
The collection was further enhanced by the efforts of the keeper of
Egyptian antiquities, E. A. Wallis Budge (1857–1934). Since 1882,
the museum has received a share of the objects excavated by the
Egypt Exploration Fund/Egypt Exploration Society. Since 1980,
the British Museum has conducted its own excavations at **Hermopo-
lis** and **Tell el-Balamun**. It houses one of the finest collections of
Egyptian antiquities outside the **Cairo Egyptian Museum**. *See also*
BERLIN EGYPTIAN MUSEUM; BOSTON MUSEUM OF FINE
ARTS; LOUVRE MUSEUM; METROPOLITAN MUSEUM OF
ART; TURIN EGYPTIAN MUSEUM.

BRONZE. An alloy of **copper** and tin. It is attested infrequently in Egypt before the **Middle Kingdom**, although some vessels from the tomb of **Khasekhemwy** of **Dynasty 2** of the **Early Dynastic Period** are known from **Abydos**. Bronze gradually superceded the use of copper in the **New Kingdom**. It became the standard material for weapons, pins, vessels, and especially votive statues during the **Late Period**. See also GOLD; IRON; SILVER.

BRUCE, JAMES (1730–1794). British traveler. He was born in Kinnaird, Scotland, on 14 December 1730. He traveled extensively in Africa, visiting Egypt in 1768, where he toured the **Valley of the Kings** at **Thebes**. He entered the **tomb** of **Ramesses III (KV3)**, which was thereafter known as Bruce's tomb, and made drawings. Bruce later spent several years in Ethiopia, returning to Europe in 1773. His publication of his travels in 1790 contained the first engraving of a scene from a royal tomb. He died in Kinnaird on 27 April 1794.

BUBASTIS. Greek name for the Egyptian city of *Per-Bastet*, capital of the 18th **nome** of **Lower Egypt**, now Tell Basta. The principal deity worshipped in Bubastis was the cat-headed or lioness-headed goddess **Bastet**. Remains have been found from the **Old Kingdom**, but the town was most prominent in **Dynasty 22**, which is said to have originated there. It was excavated by a British expedition from the **Egypt Exploration Fund** from 1887–1889 and by Egyptian Egyptologists, notably Labib Habachi in 1939 and from 1943–1944, Shafik Farid from 1961–1967, Ahmad el-Sawi from 1967–1971, and more recently Muhammad Bakr since 1978 and a joint expedition of Zagazig University and Potsdam University since 1996.

BUCHIS. Sacred ram of the city of **Armant**. The Bucheum or catacombs of the rams were excavated from 1926–1932 by a British expedition sponsored by the **Egypt Exploration Society** and date from **Dynasty 30** to the **Roman Period**. See also RELIGION.

BUDGE, SIR ERNEST ALFRED THOMPSON WALLIS (1857–1934). British orientalist. He was born in Bodmin, England, on 27 July 1857 of illegitimate birth. While working in London as a youth, he was attracted to the displays of the ancient Egyptian and

Assyrian world in the **British Museum**. His enthusiasm was noted by the then keeper of Oriental antiquities Samuel Birch, who raised enough money to send him to study the topic at the University of Cambridge. He joined the staff of the museum in 1883 and through intrigue managed to oust Keeper Renouf, Birch's successor, and obtain his position in 1892. Budge proved an active collector of objects for the museum, establishing links with agents and dealers in antiquities in Egypt and Mesopotamia. He grudgingly accepted excavated material from the **Egypt Exploration Fund** and other sources and was opposed to **Flinders Petrie**'s ideas about the importance of archaeology. He wrote extensively and often hastily on Egyptian, **Coptic**, Assyrological, and Ethiopian topics and was well known as a popularizer of the subjects. Although completely outdated, his books are still being reprinted. Budge retired in 1924 and died in London on 23 November 1934.

BUHEN. Site in **Nubia** at the Second **Cataract**. The Egyptians had penetrated this far south during the **Old Kingdom**, where remains of **copper**-smelting production have been found. A major fort was constructed in the **Middle Kingdom** as part of the Egyptian garrison. The site and its vicinity were excavated by a British expedition from the **Egypt Exploration Society** from 1960–1965 before the area was flooded by Nasser Lake, the lake formed behind the Aswan High Dam. *See also* ANIBA; ASKUT; KUMMA; MIRGISSA; SEMNA; SHALFAK; URONARTI.

BUTO. Greek name for the Egyptian twin cities of *Pe* and *Dep*, also known as *Per-Wadjet*, modern Tell el-Farain. Ancient capital city of **Lower Egypt** whose principal deity was the cobra goddess **Wadjet**. Some remains can be traced from the **Predynastic Period** until Roman occupation. The site was briefly examined by **Flinders Petrie** in 1886 and excavated by Charles Currelly in 1904 and Veronica Seton-Williams for the **Egypt Exploration Society** from 1964–1968 but has since been examined more extensively by an Egyptian expedition and a German expedition since 1985.

BYBLOS. Major town and seaport on the eastern Mediterranean coast in modern Lebanon, ancient *Gubla*. It was the principal port through which timber and other goods were exported to Egypt from the **Early Dynastic Period** onward. Relations are attested in the **Old Kingdom**, **Middle Kingdom**, and **New Kingdoms**. The city became part of the Egyptian empire as a result of the campaigns of **Thutmose III**. Toward the end of **Dynasty 18**, Byblos was menaced by the aggressive intentions of the kings of **Amurru**, who had become **Hittite** vassals. This was reported in detail by King **Rib-Hadda** in the **Amarna letters**. The city escaped destruction by the **Sea Peoples** and is mentioned in the tale of **Wenamun** at the end of **Dynasty 20** when Egyptian influence there was negligible due to the weakness of the Egyptian state. *See also* YANTIN.

BYZANTINE PERIOD (395–642 AD). The period during which Egypt was ruled from Constantinople by the eastern Roman emperor. The era is marked by increasing religious differences between the orthodox court and the Monophysite church in Egypt, which became increasingly nationalistic, eventually breaking away to form the separate **Coptic Church**. The period ended with the Arabic conquest of Egypt in 642 AD. *See also* RELIGION.

– C –

CAESAR. *See* IULIUS CAESAR, CAIUS.

CAIRO EGYPTIAN MUSEUM. Established in 1862 by the Egyptian ruler Said at the request of **Auguste Mariette**, the head of the Antiquities Service, and opened at Bulaq in October 1863. It houses and preserves the largest and finest number of Egyptian antiquities in the world. The museum was filled with objects from Mariette's excavations and subsequent work by Egyptian and foreign archaeologists. It supervised the division of antiquities agreed upon with foreign excavators and kept all important pieces in Egypt. In 1891, the museum was moved to Giza, and in 1902 it was again relocated to its present site in Cairo. A large selection of objects acquired in the 19th century and the early 20th century were published in a series of catalogs by international scholars. Masterpieces in the collection include the **Narmer** Palette, the statues of **Khafre** and **Menkaure** from **Giza**, royal jewelry from **Dahshur**, the **Tutankhamun** treasures, and the finds from the royal **tombs** at **Tanis**. A new museum is slated for construction in Giza. *See also* BERLIN EGYPTIAN MUSEUM; BOSTON MUSEUM OF FINE ARTS; BRITISH MUSEUM; LOUVRE MUSEUM; METROPOLITAN MUSEUM OF ART; TURIN EGYPTIAN MUSEUM.

CAMBYSES (reigned 525–522 BC). Persian ruler, son of **Cyrus**, king of **Persia** and Mesopotamia. He carried out a successful invasion of Egypt in 525 BC, overthrowing **Dynasty 26**. The invasion caused some damage, although the extent of cannot be determined. Cambyses adopted a few Egyptian royal customs, including taking the throne name Mesutire, chosen by **Udjahorresnet**. He canceled many of the privileges of Egyptian **temples** and so became unpopular with the Egyptian priesthood. Later stories of his cruelty, including the murder of the **Apis** bull, cannot be substantiated and may be exaggerated. He was briefly succeeded by his supposed brother, Bardiya, and then his cousin, **Darius I**.

CANOPIC JARS. Modern term for the four jars in which the soft internal tissues of the deceased were stored after the mummification of the body. Canopic chests in which packages of these organs—the liver, lungs, stomach, and intestines—were placed are known from the early **Old Kingdom**, but actual jars with ovoid lids appeared slightly later. By the **Middle Kingdom**, the set of jars dedicated to the four **sons of Horus** had evolved. The jars were all originally human-headed, but by the **New Kingdom** they bore separate heads—human, baboon, jackal, and hawk. From **Dynasty 21** onward, the internal organs were wrapped in packages and placed in the body, but the funerary equipment continued to include dummy canopic jars. The use of actual jars was revived in **Dynasty 26**. The term canopic derives from confusion with Canopus, a deity depicted as a human-headed jar during the **Graeco-Roman Period**. *See also* AFTERLIFE; MUMMY.

CARACALLA (188–217 AD). Roman emperor. He was born on 4 April 188, the eldest son of **Septimius Severus** and Julia Domna. His original name appears to have been Lucius Septimius Bassianus, but he was renamed Marcus Aurelius Antoninus after his father's accession. Caracalla was his nickname. Caracalla was named coemperor with his father on 28 January 198 and succeeded his father in 211 with his younger brother Geta, whose murder he ordered in late 211. Geta's image has been erased from a relief in the **temple** of **Esna**. In the same year, he issued a proclamation granting Roman citizenship to all inhabitants of the empire to raise taxes. Caracalla conducted several military campaigns, notably an eastern war beginning in 215. He visited Egypt from December 215 to March/April 216 and massacred part of the population of **Alexandria**, whom he regarded as disrespectful. Caracalla was assassinated on the road between Edessa and Carrhae in Syria on 8 April 217.

CARTER, HOWARD (1874–1939). British excavator. He was born in London on 9 May 1874, the son of an artist who trained him in the trade. He was sent to Egypt in 1891 as an artist draughtsman at **Beni Hasan** by the **Egypt Exploration Fund** and later worked as an assistant to **Flinders Petrie** at **Amarna** and **Deir el-Bahri**. Carter was appointed chief inspector for **Upper Egypt** in 1899 and transferred to **Lower Egypt** in 1904 but left the Antiquities Service in 1905 after a disagreement. He was employed by the Earl of Carnarvon beginning in 1909 as an archaeologist in the Theban area, especially in the **Valley of the Kings**, where he made significant discoveries before finding the intact **tomb** of **Tutankhamun** in 1922. Carter took 10 years to clear the tomb, but he lacked the academic background to undertake a definitive archaeological report on his work. His detailed notes are preserved in the Griffith Institute in Oxford, United Kingdom, and have been used to prepare a series of reports on groups of materials from the tomb. He died in London on 2 March 1939. *See also* MARIETTE, (FRANÇOIS) AUGUSTE FERDINAND; MONTET, (JEAN) PIERRE MARIE; NAVILLE, (HENRI) EDOUARD; REISNER, GEORGE ANDREW; WINLOCK, HERBERT EUSTIS.

CARTOUCHE. The modern French name used by Egyptologists to denote the ring that encircles the prenomen and nomen in the royal **titulary**, ancient Egyptian *shenu*. The identification of the cartouche as the marker of the royal name aided the decipherment of **hieroglyphic** writing.

CATARACT. The modern name for the rocky stone areas in the bed of the **Nile** that render navigation impossible. The First Cataract is situated just south of **Elephantine**, modern Aswan, and marks the original border between Egypt and **Nubia**. There are six numbered cataracts in the course of the Nile in Sudan before it divides into the White Nile and Blue Nile near Khartoum.

C-GROUP. The term invented by **George Reisner** and used by Egyptologists to designate the inhabitants of Lower **Nubia** during the late **Old Kingdom** to the **Middle Kingdom**. They may have been connected to the **A-Group** but were more likely a new more warlike people who moved north as the Egyptians abandoned Nubia during the **First Intermediate Period**. Their kingdoms are mentioned in texts of **Dynasty 6**. The northern regions were conquered by the Egyptians during the Middle Kingdom, while the southern part of Nubia evolved into the kingdom of **Kerma** or Kush, which reoccupied the north during the **Second Intermediate Period** and was finally conquered at the beginning of **Dynasty 18**.

CHAMPOLLION, JEAN-FRANÇOIS (1790–1832). French scholar. He was born in Figeac on 23 December 1790. He very early conceived the desire to decipher the ancient Egyptian **hieroglyphic** script and prepared himself by studying oriental languages, including **Coptic**. He eventually obtained an academic post in Grenoble, France, which gave him time to devote to his studies. Champollion first regarded the script as symbolic; however, Englishman **Thomas Young** demonstrated that the names of the Ptolemaic rulers were written alphabetically. Champollion later disingenuously claimed that he was unaware of Young's research, but he adopted this approach and soon, with the help of such bilingual inscriptions as the **Rosetta Stone**, surpassed Young's work. Champollion established that the hieroglyphic script was both alphabetic and pictographic and was able to read ancient Egyptian for the first time and realize that it was an older form of Coptic.

He achieved widespread recognition for his work and in 1826 was appointed first curator of Egyptian antiquities at the **Louvre Museum**. From 1828–1829 he visited Egypt. Champollion was appointed professor of Egyptian history and archaeology at the Collège de France in Paris in 1831. He died in Paris on 4 March 1832. Although respected as a scholar, he was regarded by his contemporaries as an arrogant and difficult man.

CHEOPS. *See* KHUFU.

CHEPHREN. *See* KHAFRE.

CHRONOLOGY. The ancient Egyptian calendar consisted of a year of 360 days divided into the three seasons *akhet* (flood), *peret* (sowing) and *shemu* (harvest), plus five extra days at the end of the year. Each season was comprised of four months of 30 days and was in turn divided into three weeks of 10 days of 24 hours split between night and day. Because the calendar did not include the extra one-quarter day of the earth's rotation, the civil calendar gradually diverged from the solar year so that the months moved, and the two only harmonized briefly every 1,460 years. The solar year was measured from the annual rising of the star Sirius, which becomes visible around July of each year in the modern calendar.

A third calendar used for administrative purposes was the regnal year initially based on the biennial cattle count during the **Old Kingdom** and from the **Middle Kingdom** onward the king's actual years, although his first year was foreshortened, so the beginning of his second might coincide with the beginning of the civil year. This practice was abandoned during the **New Kingdom** when the full regnal year was dated from the king's accession, but calculation of the regnal year reverted to the old system during the **Late Period**. Thus three different dating systems—solar, civil, and regnal—were used during the New Kingdom.

The conversion of Egyptian dates to the modern Julian calendar is not exact. Dating from the **Late Period** is fixed by synchronisms with Assyrian, Persian, Greek, and Roman dating systems. It is known that the solar and civil calendars coincided in 139 AD, thus the previous coincidence would have occurred 1,460 years earlier—the period being known as a Sothic cycle—but the use of astronomical references to the rising of the star Sirius are too unclear to be of use. The most effective method for determining chronology is through use of the detailed **king lists** known from such documents as the **Palermo Stone** or **Turin Royal Canon** or authors following **Manetho** supplemented by synchronisms with Mesopotamian or **Hittite** kings and astronomical dating when available. For earlier periods, radiocarbon dating has proved most useful. The chronology of ancient Egypt is under constant revision as new discoveries are made.

CLEOMENES (fl. c. 350–322 BC). Born in **Naukratis**, he was appointed the chief financial administrator of Egypt by **Alexander the Great** and soon became the leading power in the country. Cleomenes undertook the building of **Alexandria**. He was executed by **Ptolemy I** following his appointment as **satrap** in 322 BC.

CLEOPATRA I (c. 215–176 BC). Wife of **Ptolemy V** and daughter of Antiochus III, ruler of the Seleucid Empire, and Laodice of Pontus. She was engaged to Ptolemy V in 196 BC and married him in 194–193 BC as part of a peace settlement between Egypt and the Seleucid Empire. She had three children, including **Cleopatra II**, **Ptolemy VI**, and **Ptolemy VIII.** Upon the death of her husband in 180 BC, she acted as regent until her own death between April and July 176 BC.

CLEOPATRA II (c. 185–116 BC). Daughter of **Ptolemy V** and **Cleopatra I** and wife of **Ptolemy VI** and **Ptolemy VIII**. She was married to her brother, Ptolemy VI, in April 176 BC and declared joint ruler of Egypt in 170 BC in the face of the threat of invasion by the Seleucid king **Antiochus IV**. When her husband was captured by the enemy, she and her younger brother, Ptolemy VIII, held out in **Alexandria**. Antiochus IV was forced to abandon Egypt under Roman pressure, and the joint rule of the three siblings was restored. In 164 BC, civil war broke out between the brothers, and Ptolemy VIII was expelled to **Cyrene**. Cleopatra II bore four children to Ptolemy VI, including **Ptolemy Eupator**, **Ptolemy VII**, **Cleopatra Thea**, and **Cleopatra III**. Her husband was killed in 145 BC, and she briefly acted as regent for her son, Ptolemy VII, until power was seized by her brother, Ptolemy VIII, who married her and murdered her son.

Cleopatra bore her new husband one son, **Ptolemy Memphites**, but he soon preferred her daughter Cleopatra III. Civil war broke out between the spouses in 132 BC during which Ptolemy VIII murdered his son, Memphites, before regaining control in 130 BC. Peace was eventually restored between the spouses in 124 BC, when Cleopatra II was recognized as senior **queen**. She is last recorded in 116 BC having survived her second husband.

CLEOPATRA III (c. 158–101 BC). Daughter of **Ptolemy VI** and **Cleopatra II**. She became the second consort of her uncle, **Ptolemy VIII**, around 141 BC, which eventually led to a civil war between her mother, Cleopatra II, who was the first consort, and her husband. Peace was eventually restored in 124 BC. Cleopatra bore her husband five children, including **Ptolemy IX**, **Ptolemy X**, **Cleopatra IV**, **Cleopatra VI Tryphaena**, and **Cleopatra V Selene**. Upon Ptolemy VIII's death in 116 BC, she was given the choice of which son would rule with her. She preferred her younger son, Ptolemy X, but was forced by public pressure to accept her elder son, Ptolemy IX, who was eventually ousted in favor of his younger brother in 107 BC. This led to civil war between the rival kings in **Cyprus** and Syria. Cleopatra III died in 101 BC, allegedly murdered by her ungrateful son, Ptolemy X.

CLEOPATRA IV (d. 113 BC). Daughter of **Ptolemy VIII** and **Cleopatra III**. Consort of her brother, **Ptolemy IX**, who was forced to divorce her by their mother around 116 BC. Cleopatra IV fled to **Cyprus** and then Syria, where she married the Seleucid king Antiochus IX Cyzicenus. She was in Antioch in 113 BC when it fell to his rival, Antiochus VIII Grypus, whose wife, her sister **Cleopatra VI Tryphaena**, ordered her execution.

CLEOPATRA V SELENE (c. 140/35–69 BC). Daughter of **Ptolemy VIII** and **Cleopatra III**. Around 116 BC, she married her brother, **Ptolemy IX**, after he was forced by his mother to divorce his first wife and their sister, **Cleopatra IV**. She remained in Egypt when her husband was expelled in 107 BC, and in 103 BC she married her cousin, Antiochus VIII Grypus, ruler of Syria, son of her aunt **Cleopatra Thea**, and former husband of her sister, **Cleopatra VI Tryphaena**. Antiochus VIII Grypus was killed in 96 BC. Cleopatra Selene then married two further rulers of Syria, Antiochus IX Cyzicenus (d. 95 BC), cousin of her husband but also his maternal half brother through Cleopatra Thea and former husband of her other sister, Cleopatra IV, and finally her stepson, Antiochus X Eusebes (killed around 89 BC). She apparently had two sons by her first husband, whose fate is uncertain, and two sons by her last husband, who aspired to rule in Syria. Cleopatra Selene was captured during an invasion of Syria by Tigranes, king of Armenia, and executed in Seleucia-on-the-Tigris in 69 BC. Because the former Cleopatra V Tryphaena and Cleopatra VI Tryphaena are now regarded as identical, Cleopatra Selene is cited in more recent scholarship as Cleopatra V Selene.

CLEOPATRA VI TRYPHAENA (d. 57 BC). Wife of **Ptolemy XII**. Her origin is unknown, but she was presumably his sister or half sister and so daughter of **Ptolemy IX**. She evidently remained in the country when her husband was expelled in 58 BC and ruled jointly with her daughter, **Berenice IV**. Earlier scholars had supposed that the coruler was a sister of Berenice IV and counted Cleopatra V Tryphaena as the mother and Cleopatra VI Tryphaena as the daughter, but these two are now regarded as one and the same; the designation Cleopatra V has now been assigned to **Cleopatra V Selene**.

CLEOPATRA VII PHILOPATOR (c. 69–30 BC). Egyptian **queen**. Daughter of **Ptolemy XII** and possibly **Cleopatra VI Tryphaena**. She succeeded her father alongside her younger brother and consort, **Ptolemy XIII**, with whom she soon fell out. Their civil war was interrupted by the arrival in Egypt of **Iulius Caesar** who soon sided with Cleopatra and defeated her brother's forces in 47 BC during a battle in which he was killed. Cleopatra VII Philopator was installed as ruler of Egypt with her younger brother, **Ptolemy XIV**, as consort, but she had become Caesar's mistress and claimed him as the father of her son, Ptolemy Caesarion. She was in Rome in 44 BC when Caesar was assassinated and hurriedly returned to Egypt. Her brother soon died and was replaced as ruling **pharaoh** by her son as **Ptolemy XV**.

Cleopatra VII Philopator formed an alliance with **Marcus Antonius**, who was in charge of the eastern Roman Empire, and bore him three children. She used her intimacy with Antonius to aggrandize Egypt to the detriment of other eastern states. Their relationship gave

Antonius's rival, **Augustus**, the opportunity to vilify him in Rome and declare war on Egypt as a threat to Rome. Egyptian forces were defeated at the battle of Actium in 31 BC and, after the fall of **Alexandria** in 30 BC, Cleopatra VII Philopator committed suicide rather than be taken captive to Rome. *See also* ALEXANDER HELIOS; ARSINOE IV; BERENICE IV; CLEOPATRA SELENE; PTOLEMY PHILADELPHUS.

CLEOPATRA BERENICE III (d. 80 BC). Daughter of **Ptolemy IX** and **Cleopatra IV**. She became the official consort of her uncle, **Ptolemy X**, after he took over the throne from her father, and following the former's deposition in 88 BC of her father Ptolemy IX. She became sole ruler of Egypt upon his death in 80 BC but was forced by the Romans to accept her first cousin and stepson, **Ptolemy XI Alexander II**, as her consort. He murdered her within days of their marriage in June 80 BC and was promptly killed himself.

CLEOPATRA SELENE (fl. c. 40 BC–11/7 AD). Daughter of **Marcus Antonius** and **Cleopatra VII**. She was born in 40 BC with her twin brother, **Alexander Helios**. She was captured by **Augustus** in 30 BC and displayed in his triumph in Rome in 29 BC. She was brought up by Octavia, the sister of Augustus and Roman wife of Antonius, and married to King Juba II of Mauretania (modern Morocco) around 20 BC. Cleopatra Selene may have acted as regent for her husband during his absences from the kingdom, and she appears on his coinage. She had at least one son, King Ptolemy of Mauretania, who was executed by Caligula in 40 AD and is the last known descendant of the Ptolemaic dynasty.

CLEOPATRA THEA (c. 165–121/0 BC). Daughter of **Ptolemy VI** and **Cleopatra II**. She was married in 150 BC to the Syrian pretender Alexander I Balas, who was installed as Seleucid ruler with the aid of his father-in-law, but the allies soon fell out. Cleopatra Thea was given to his rival, Demetrius II. Balas was defeated in battle by Ptolemy VI in 145 BC, after which he was killed and Ptolemy died of wounds. Demetrius II was captured in battle with the Parthians in 139 BC, and Cleopatra Thea married his brother, Antiochus VII Sidetes, who was himself killed in battle with the Parthians in 129

BC. Demetrius II was restored but proved unpopular and was killed at Tyre in 126/125 BC. His widow ruled alone or in association with her sons by Demetrius II, Seleucus V (allegedly killed by her), and Antiochus VIII Grypus. She was apparently poisoned by her son in 121/120 BC after her attempt to murder him had failed. Her other son, Antiochus IX Cyzicenus, by Antiochus VII, became a rival to his half brother, Antiochus VIII Grypus. Both brothers married Ptolemaic princesses, the former **Cleopatra IV** and **Cleopatra Selene**, and the latter **Cleopatra Tryphaena** and his brother's widow, Cleopatra Selene.

CLEOPATRA TRYPHAENA (d. 112 BC). Daughter of **Ptolemy VIII** and **Cleopatra III**. She married her first cousin, Seleucid king Antiochus VIII Grypus, son of Demetrius II and **Cleopatra Thea**, but he faced a rival in his half brother, Antiochus IX Cyzicenus, who was married to **Cleopatra IV**, sister of Cleopatra Tryphaena. When Cleopatra IV was captured in 113 BC, she was executed at her sister's behest. Cleopatra Tryphaena was then herself killed when she fell into the hands of Antiochus IX in 112 BC.

COLOSSI OF MEMNON. *See* MEMNON, COLOSSI OF.

COMINIUS LEUGAS, CAIUS (fl. 18 AD). Roman explorer and discoverer of the mines at **Mons Porphyrites**. He built a sanctuary there in honor of the gods Pan (Egyptian **Min**) and **Sarapis**, in which he erected a black porphyry stela in 18 AD, indicating that he must have discovered the site that year or slightly earlier.

CONTENDINGS OF HORUS AND SETH, THE. A mythological story found in a single manuscript from the **Ramesside Period** written in the Late Egyptian form of the Egyptian **language**. Fragments of an earlier version of the text written in Middle Egyptian of the **Middle Kingdom** have been found at **Lahun**. The story relates the contest of **Horus**, son of **Osiris**, and Isis and his uncle **Seth** for the throne of Egypt in which Horus eventually triumphs. The text is notable for its depiction of the gods as foolish, quarrelsome, and incompetent.

COPPER. A metal used extensively by the Egyptians for tools, weapons, and vessels. Its use is attested in beads from the early **Predynastic Period**. Such rare copper statues as those of **Pepy I** and his son, **Nemtyemsaf** I, survive. Copper was found in the Eastern Desert, where copper-smelting activity has been uncovered at **Ayn Sokha**, Sinai at **Wadi Maghara**, **Nubia** near **Buhen**, and elsewhere. The metal was also mined at times by the Egyptians at **Timna** in the Negev Desert. It was often hardened by the use of arsenic. It was superceded by **bronze** from the **Middle Kingdom**. *See also* GOLD; IRON; SILVER.

COPTIC. The final phase of the Egyptian **language** and writing in which Greek script, with the addition of six new letters, was used to write ancient Egyptian. It is believed that the script was developed by Christians to spread their faith to the Egyptian populace. The script was used to translate Christian religious works, including the Bible, but also ordinary correspondence, business and legal texts, and funerary and other inscriptions in stone. Following the Arabic conquest in 642 AD, Coptic was gradually superseded by Arabic and fell out of use by the 16th century, with the exception of certain religious phrases no longer understood by the priests or general population. European scholars learned the language from exported Biblical and other religious manuscripts but were unaware that it was ancient Egyptian until the decipherment of the **hieroglyphic** script. Knowledge of Coptic greatly aided in the decoding and understanding of ancient Egyptian. *See also* CHAMPOLLION, JEAN-FRANÇOIS.

COPTIC CHURCH. Egyptian Christianity developed during the 1st century AD under the patriarch of **Alexandria**. The **Coptic** script was used to translate the Holy Scriptures and religious works. Strains soon appeared between the orthodox formula for the nature of Christ, which was two natures—human and divine intermingled—as set down by the councils of Nicaea in 334 and Chalcedon in 454, and the belief in Egypt of one divine nature known as Monophysitism.

After failing to find a compromise, the Byzantine emperors, with the support of the Roman popes, sought to impose orthodoxy in Egypt, leading to a schism when a Coptic patriarch of Alexandria was elected in opposition to the orthodox one. Most Egyptians supported the Coptic church, and their loyalty to the emperor was weakened, facilitating the Arab conquest. This in turn led to the eventual decline of the native church, since large parts of the population eventually converted to Islam, and the Coptic **language** was replaced by Arabic. The Coptic church is more vigorous at present than it was for several centuries. *See also* BENJAMIN; RELIGION.

COPTIC MUSEUM. This museum was founded in 1902 through the efforts of Marcus Simaika Pasha and established in its current position in Old Cairo in 1908. It was taken over by the Egyptian Antiquities Service in 1931 and enlarged in 1947. The collection contains more than 14,000 objects from the **Coptic** Period, including stone sculptures, frescoes, icons, textiles, ivory objects, wood, metal, ceramic, and such important manuscripts as the **Nag Hammadi Codices**.

COPTOS. Greek name for a site in northern **Upper Egypt**, modern Qift. Ancient Egytian *Gebtu*, capital of the fifth Upper Egyptian **nome**. The chief deity of the town was the fertility god **Min**, who was also regarded as the god of the Eastern Desert. The town was an important center for expeditions into the desert to the stone quarries or to the Red Sea coast to connect to trade routes to **Punt** and other key locations. The **temple** that survives there dates to the **Ptolemaic Period** with Roman additions, but earlier remains have been found that date back to the **Early Dynastic Period**. The site was partly excavated by **Flinders Petrie** from 1893–1894 and a French expedition from 1910–1911. Further excavations took place from 1987–1992 by an American expedition from the University of Michigan, and a French team has been working the area since 2002. *See also* BERENIKE; MYOS HORMOS; WADI HAMMAMAT.

COREGENCY. A system of dual rule that was devised to ensure the automatic transfer of power to the junior ruler upon the death of the elder. It seems to have first been employed by **Amenemhat I**, who made his son, **Senusret I**, a joint ruler, although in this case the succession was disputed. Two types of coregency are known whereby the junior partner has a full royal **titulary** and regnal dates or simply the titulary and no separate year dates until his succession as sole ruler. Coregencies have complicated the determination of the exact **chronology** of rulers as they are not always attested clearly or taken account of in the surviving **king lists**. Some coregencies proposed by some modern Egyptologists like that between **Amenhotep III** and **Akhenaten** are disputed.

CORNELIUS GALLUS, CAIUS (c. 70–26 BC). Roman poet and official. First **prefect** of Egypt from 30–26 BC. He took part in the Egyptian campaign of **Augustus** and was put in charge of the newly conquered province of Egypt. He suppressed a revolt in **Thebes**. His inscriptions praising his own deeds annoyed the emperor, and he was recalled and forced to commit suicide in 26 BC. *See also* PETRONIUS, PUBLIUS.

CORNELIUS SCIPIO AEMILIANUS AFRICANUS, PUBLIUS (d. 129 BC). Roman general. He was born 185/184 BC, son of Lucius Aemilus Paulus, conqueror of Macedonia, and Papiria and was adopted by Publius Cornelius Scipio, a son of the conqueror of Hannibal. He was consul in 147 BC and led the campaign that destroyed Carthage in 146 BC. He visited **Alexandria** in 140/139 BC as part of a Roman delegation to the East and met with **Ptolemy VIII**. The Romans were taken aback by the extravagance of the Ptolemaic court and the demeanor of the king, whom they persuaded to walk through the city with them to the surprise of his subjects.

CRETE. *See* KEFTYU.

CYPRUS. *See* ALASIA.

CYRENE. An area of eastern Libya colonized by Greek settlers c. 630 BC. An independent dynasty emerged but later recognized the suzerainty of **Cambyses** and subsequently **Alexander the Great**. First ruled by **Ptolemy I**, Cyrene became sovereign again, but the country was annexed to Egypt through the marriage of **Berenice II** to **Ptolemy III**. It briefly became independent once again under **Ptolemy VIII** before his accession and under **Ptolemy Apion**, the illegitimate son of Ptolemy VIII, who died childless in 96 BC and left his kingdom to Rome.

CYRIL (c. 378–444 AD). Patriarch of **Alexandria**. He was the son of the sister of the patriarch **Theophilus** and was born in Theodosiu c. 378 and educated at the monastery of Deir Anba Macarius in the Nitrian Valley. He became a priest in Alexandria and succeeded his uncle as patriarch in 412. Cyril was a vigorous opponent of Neoplatonism and Nestorianism and took a leading part in the Council of Ephesus in 431, when the teachings of Nestorius were condemned as heresy. He died in Alexandria on 27 June 444 and was succeeded by **Dioscorus**. *See also* ATHANASIUS; BENJAMIN; COPTIC CHURCH; CYRUS.

CYRUS (d. 642 AD). Byzantine official. Bishop of Phasis in the Caucasus until 631, when he was named by Emperor **Heraclius** as **prefect** of Egypt and patriarch of **Alexandria** in opposition to the **Coptic Church** and its patriarch, **Benjamin**. He was entrusted with putting an end to dissension by enforcing orthodoxy in Egypt, and he attempted to carry out this policy with ruthless persecution of the Copts, though he was unsuccessful. Cyrus faced the Arabic invasion in 641 and was forced to agree by a treaty on 8 November 641 to surrender Alexandria and Egypt to the invaders and withdraw imperial forces the following year. He died in Alexandria on 21 March 642 before the end of Byzantine rule in the city. *See also* ATHANASIUS; BYZANTINE PERIOD; CYRIL; DIOSCORUS; THEOPHILUS.

– D –

DAHSHUR. Modern name for the area south of **Saqqara** where several royal **tombs** from **Dynasty 4**, **Dynasty 12**, and **Dynasty 13** are located. Two **pyramids**, the Bent and the Red, are assigned to **Snefru** and were the first built as true pyramids from the start. The pyramids of **Amenemhat II, Senusret III**, and **Amenemhat III** are also located here, as well as the tombs of **queens** and princesses from which much fine jewelry has been excavated. The tomb of King **Hor** of Dynasty 13 has also been discovered. The area was excavated by the French from 1894–1895; the Egyptians under Ahmad Fakhry from 1951–1955; and the German Archaeological Institute, later taken over by the **Metropolitan Museum of Art** beginning in 1980, a Japanese expedition since 1996, and a German expedition from Berlin since 1997.

DAKHLA OASIS. An oasis in the Western Desert west of **Luxor**. Excavations have uncovered remains possibly from the **Early Dynastic Period** and from the **Old Kingdom** to the **Byzantine Period**. The site was visited by **Herbert Winlock** in 1908 and again examined by Egyptian archaeologist Ahmed Fakhry from 1968–1972. A settlement and **tombs** from **Dynasty 6** have been excavated at **Balat** by a French expedition since 1977, while a joint Canadian–Australian expedition has conducted a survey and excavations in the oasis since 1978 and found a Roman and Byzantine town site and associated **temples** at **Ismant el-Kharb**, which has yielded documentary and literary texts on **papyrus** and wooden tablets. The site of the main temple at Mut el-Kharb, the later capital of the oasis, has been under investigation since 2001, and remains have been found from the **New Kingdom** to the **Graeco-Roman Period**. An American expedition is now working at the site of **Amheida**. *See also* BAHARIYA OASIS; FARFARA OASIS; KHARGA OASIS; SIWA OASIS.

DARIUS I (reigned 522–486 BC). King of **Persia** and ruler of Egypt. Throne name in Egypt Setutre. Son of Hystaspes and Rhodogune. He supposedly came from a junior line of the royal family. He accompanied **Cambyses** on his conquest of Egypt. Darius I seized the throne in September 522 after the ephemeral reign of Bardiya, alleged brother of Cambyses, whom Darius denounced as an imposter. His forces spent the early years of his rule resisting revolts in the empire, including Egypt, which he may have visited c. 518 BC and perhaps on a second occasion. He ordered the codification of Egyptian law and the completion of a canal between the **Nile** and Red Sea begun by **Nekau II**. Darius I is best known for his military campaign in Greece, which resulted in the defeat of the Persians at the battle of Marathon in 490 BC. There appears to have been further unrest in Egypt at the end of his reign. He died in October 486 and was succeeded by his son, **Xerxes I**, born to his chief wife Atossa, daughter of **Cyrus** and sister of Cambyses.

DARIUS II (reigned 423–404 BC). Personal name Ochus. King of **Persia** and ruler of Egypt. Illegitimate son of **Artaxerxes I**. He succeeded to the throne after the ephemeral reigns of his brothers Xerxes II and Sogdianus. He then married his half sister, Parysatis. Darius II faced a major revolt in Egypt toward the end of his reign led by **Amyrtaeos**.

DARIUS III (reigned in Egypt 336–332 BC). King of **Persia** and ruler of Egypt. Original name Codomanus. Son of Arsames, an alleged grandson of **Darius II**, and Sisygambis. He distinguished himself in battle during the reign of **Artaxerxes III**. He was put on the throne by **Bagoas** after the murder of Arses and then executed the ambitious minister. Darius III faced the invasion of **Alexander the Great**, who defeated his forces at Granicus in 334 BC and Issus in 333 BC, when he was present. He lost Egypt in 332 BC when his **satrap**, Mazaces, surrendered without a struggle. After a further defeat at Gaugamela in 331 BC, he fled to eastern Iran, where he was murdered in 330 BC by rebellious nobles.

DEIR EL-BAHRI. Modern name for a site on the cliffs of the western bank of the **Nile** opposite **Thebes**. It was apparently first used to construct the **tomb** and mortuary **temple** of **Mentuhotep II** of **Dynasty 11** and the tombs of his successors, as well as the chief officials of the court. During **Dynasty 18** it was chosen as the site of the mortuary temple of **Queen Hatshepsut**, the building of which was supervised by her official, **Senenmut**. The temple is well preserved and is famous for its reliefs of the expedition to **Punt** and the transportation of an **obelisk**. Next to Deir el-Bahri a mortuary temple was constructed by **Thutmose III**, but this shrine has been largely destroyed by an earthquake, leaving only a pillared hall with **Hathor** capitals and a chapel. The site became a **Coptic** monastery during the Christian period but was later abandoned.

Deir el-Bahri was first excavated by **Auguste Mariette** in 1850, 1862, and 1866. Major excavations were undertaken in the Hatshepsut temple from 1893–1896 and the Mentuhotep II temple from 1903–1907 by a British expedition of the **Egypt Exploration Fund**. Further work in the area was carried out by **Herbert Winlock** of the **Metropolitan Museum of Art** from 1911–1931. The Mentuhotep II temple was reexamined by a German expedition from 1965–1972, and the Hatshepsut temple has been the subject of excavation and restoration work by a Polish team since 1961, during which time the Thutmose III temple was also discovered.

DEIR EL-BALLAS. Modern name for a site in **Upper Egypt** north of **Thebes** where the remains of a major royal palace and town have been discovered. The area appears to have been occupied at the end of **Dynasty 17** and the beginning of **Dynasty 18**. It was partially excavated by **George Reisner** from 1900–1902, and work has more recently been carried out by an expedition from the **Boston Museum of Fine Arts** since 1980.

DEIR EL-BERSHA. Modern name for a site in **Middle Egypt** on the east bank of the **Nile** near **Hermopolis**. The most important features of the area are the rock-cut **tombs** of the governors of the 15th **nome** of **Upper Egypt** from **Dynasty 12**, notably the tomb of Djehutihotep, which features a scene of the transport of a colossal seated statue from the quarry at **Hatnub**. The tombs were excavated and copied by expeditions of the **Egypt Exploration Fund** from 1891–1892, the Egyptian Antiquities Service in 1897 and from 1900–1902, and the **Boston Museum of Fine Arts** in 1915 and 1990. The area has been investigated by a Belgian expedition since 2002.

DEIR EL-GABRAWI. Modern name for a site in **Middle Egypt** on the east bank of the **Nile** north of **Asyut** where the governors of the 12th **nome** of **Upper Egypt** were buried in rock-cut **tombs** during **Dynasty 6**. Some of the scenes in one tomb served as a model for similar scenes in a tomb at **Thebes** dated to the **Saite Period**. The tombs were copied by Norman de Garis Davies in 1900 and in 2004 by an Australian expedition.

DEIR EL-MEDINA. Modern name for the site of the workmen's village on the west bank of the Nile opposite **Thebes** near the **Valley of the Kings**. The village was founded either by **Amenhotep I**, who was worshipped there as a god, or his successor, **Thutmose I**, whose name appears on bricks at the site. The workmen were organized to construct the royal **tombs** in the Valley of the Kings, but little material has survived from **Dynasty 18** apart from several tombs of such workmen as the foreman **Kha**, whose tomb was found intact, and some **stelae**. The village may have been abandoned during the reign of **Akhenaten** but was certainly in operation under **Tutankhamun** and reorganized during the reign of **Horemheb**.

Much material survives from the **Ramesside Period**, including stelae, **papyri**, **ostraca**, and tombs that give a detailed picture of community life. Deir el-Medina was under the direct control of the southern **vizier** but was effectively governed by the two foremen of each side of the workforce, which was divided into two sections, and the **scribe** or scribes. Local disputes were settled in the village court made up of the chief men of the village, but criminal cases were sent to the vizier. The workmen were supplied with payments of wheat and beer and other commodities, and surviving daybooks show that the work period was not overly onerous and there was generous time off. In their spare time the workmen prepared material for their own tombs and accepted commissions for tomb equipment from outside the community. The village possessed a series of small chapels in which such gods and goddesses as **Amun** and **Meretseger** were worshipped by the workmen themselves in the roles of priests. The village was abandoned at the end of **Dynasty 20** when royal burials ceased and conditions deteriorated due to Libyan raids. Some workmen remained at **Medinet Habu** and took part in the preparation of the **royal caches** during **Dynasty 21**.

The site was discovered in the early 19th century, and objects were acquired by several museum collections, notably the **British Museum**, **Louvre Museum**, and **Turin Egyptian Museum**. Deir el-Medina was excavated by an Italian expedition from Turin from 1905–1906 and in 1909, a German expedition in 1913, and since 1917 has been excavated and published by the **French Institute** in Cairo. *See also* HESUNEBEF; KENHERKHEPESHEF; KHA; PANEB; RAMOSE; SENNEDJEM.

DEIR EL-NAQLUN. A **Coptic** monastic site in the **Fayum** consisting of a monastery and hermitages with a church dedicated to the archangel Gabriel. Since 1986, Deir el-Naqlun has been excavated by a Polish expedition and, apart from architectural remains, it has yielded much documentary evidence. *See also* BACCHIAS; GUROB; HARAGEH; HAWARA; KARANIS; KOM KHELWA; KOM TALIT; LAHUN; LISHT; MEDINET MADI; SOKNOPAIOU NESOS; TEBTUNIS.

DELTA. *See* LOWER EGYPT.

DEMOTIC. Term derived from the Greek for the cursive Egyptian script, which was derived from and then superseded **hieratic** from the **Saite Period**. It was used primarily on **papyri** and **ostraca** but also occasionally on carved stone, notably the **Rosetta Stone**. Use of the script declined following the Roman conquest as it was no longer recognized in the courts and solely used by priests. The last known text has been found in the temple of **Philae** dated to 452 AD. *See also* HIEROGLYPHIC.

DEN (reigned c. 2985 BC). Fifth king of **Dynasty 1**. Successor and probably son of **Djet** and **Queen Merneith**, who may have acted as regent for her son. His **tomb** has been excavated at **Abydos**, and among the finds were ivory labels that showed the king in various poses, including smiting Asiatics. *See also* ANEDJIB.

DENDERA. Modern name for the Egyptian city of *Iunet*, later known as Tentyris in Greek, capital of the sixth **nome** of **Upper Egypt**. The site is known from the **Early Dynastic Period**, and there are **tombs** from the **First Intermediate Period,** when the regional rulers were semi-independent. Its main feature is the magnificent Graeco-Roman **temple** dedicated to the goddess **Hathor**, from which came the famous Dendera zodiac now in the **Louvre Museum**. The site was excavated by **Flinders Petrie** from 1897–1898 and the University of Pennsylvania from 1915–1918. The temple inscriptions are being published by a French expedition. *See also* EDFU; ESNA; KOM OMBO.

DENDUR. Site in Lower **Nubia** of a small **temple** built during the reign of **Augustus** to two deified brothers. The site has now been flooded by Lake Nasser, the lake behind the Aswan High Dam, but the temple was removed in 1963 and presented to the **Metropolitan Museum of Art**.

DERR. Site in Lower **Nubia** of a small **temple** built by **Ramesses II**. The site has now been flooded by Lake Nasser, the lake behind the Aswan High Dam, but the temple was removed to higher ground in 1964.

DIET. The main food items in ancient Egypt were bread and beer. Depending on wealth, the diet could be supplemented by fish from the **Nile**; such fowl as ducks and geese, either domestic or killed in the wild; and meat in the form of cattle, sheep, or goats. Chickens were not introduced until the **New Kingdom**. The evidence indicating the existence of pigs is inconsistent since they are clearly attested during the **Predynastic Period** at **Kahun** during the **Middle Kingdom** and at **Amarna** during the **New Kingdom**, and they are depicted in some **tombs**, but religious texts imply that the eating of pig meat was taboo. Their use becomes more evident during the **Graeco-Roman Period**. Such vegetables as onions, garlic, radishes, beans, lentils, and lettuce were available, as were some fruit trees, including as date, fig, pomegranate, and persea. Vineyards produced wine for the upper classes. A sweetener was provided by bee honey. *See also* AGRICULTURE.

DIOCLETIAN (reigned 284–305 AD). Roman emperor. Original name Diocles. Full name Gaius Aurelius Valerius Diocletianus. Born in Dalmatia on 22 December 243/245, he joined the army and rose to the rank of commander of the Royal Bodyguard. Upon the mysterious death of the Emperor Numerian, he was proclaimed emperor on 20 November 284. In a series of campaigns, Diocletian reunited the empire under his rule. In 298, he crushed the revolt of **Lucius Domitius Domitianus** in **Alexandria**. Diocletian reorganized the empire and instituted the system of two emperors with a Caesar to assist each. He also undertook the systematic persecution of Christians in an attempt to restore old Roman values. Diocletian abdicated on 1 May 305 and retired to Salonae, where he saw the empire relapse into civil war among his successors. He died in Salonae on 3 December 316 or possibly 311. *See also* GALERIUS VALERIUS MAXIMIANUS, CAIUS.

DIONYSIUS PETOSARAPIS (fl. 168 BC). A rebel against the rule of King **Ptolemy VI**. He led a revolt in **Alexandria** c. 168/167 BC but fled to the countryside to continue resistance after it was crushed. His subsequent fate is unknown.

DIOSCORUS (d. 454 or 458 AD). Patriarch of **Alexandria**. He was possibly born in Alexandria and became archdeacon to the patriarch **Cyril**, with whom he attended the council of Ephesus in 431 and whom he succeeded in 444. Dioscorus soon came into conflict with the pope in Rome when he headed the Second Council of Ephesus in 449 over the issue of Monophysitism. Here his opponent, the patriarch of Constantinople. Flavian, was deposed and died soon after as a result of ill treatment by Egyptian monks in the entourage of Dioscorus. The orthodox view was reaffirmed at the Council of Chalcedon in 451, and Dioscorus was deposed and exiled to Gangra in Paphlagonia. The decisions of the Council of Chalcedon and the deposition of the Alexandrian patriarch increased the tension between the **Coptic** population of Egypt, who supported their patriarch and the imperial power in Constantinople, which led to continued dissension in Egypt. *See also* ATHANASIUS; BENJAMIN; COPTIC CHURCH; CYRIL; CYRUS; THEOPHILUS.

DIOSCORUS (c. 520–585 AD). Egyptian landholder, lawyer, and poet. He was the son of Apollos, village headman of Aphrodito in **Middle Egypt**, modern Kom Ishgaw, and later founder and monk of the monastery of Apa Apollos. He received a good classical education, probably at **Alexandria**, and pursued a legal career during which he visited Constantinople. Many of his papers, which include both documentary and literary texts of his own composition written in Greek and **Coptic**, were discovered from 1901–1907 and are now divided among several museum collections.

DIVINE BIRTH. According to the official theology, each ruler of ancient Egypt was a son of the chief god of the period who impregnated the **queen** mother. This belief was reflected in the **Westcar Papyrus**, where the first three rulers of **Dynasty 5** are described as the sons of **Re**. During the **New Kingdom**, the mother of **Hatshepsut** is depicted being embraced by the god **Amun** in reliefs at **Deir el-Bahri**, and the mother of **Amenhotep III** is shown in a similar position in the **temple** of **Luxor**. *See also* RELIGION.

DJEDEFRE (reigned c. 2566–2558 BC). Variant Redjedef. Eldest son and successor of **Khufu** of **Dynasty 4**. He is apparently mentioned in the destroyed section of the **Westcar Papyrus**. Djedefre's reign is obscure, and he is mainly known from his funerary **pyramid** at **Abu Roash**. He was succeeded by his brother, **Khafre**.

DJEDHOR (reigned 361–362 BC). The Greek form of his name is given as Tachos or Teos. Throne name Irmaatenre. Epithet setepenanhur. Second ruler of **Dynasty 30**. Son of **Nakhtnebef.** Upon his accession, he embarked on a military campaign against **Persia** in Asia financed by a heavy levy on **temples** to pay his expenses, including Greek mercenaries. Djedhor left his brother, Tjaihapimu, as regent in Egypt, but the latter's son, **Nakhthorheb**, revolted against his uncle and won over the army, whereupon Djedhor fled to Persia.

DJEDKARE (reigned c. 2414–2375 BC). Personal name Isesi. Penultimate ruler of **Dynasty 5**. His **pyramid** at **Saqqara** was discovered in 1880, but the owner remained unidentified until an Egyptian expedition in 1945. Further work was carried out in the 1950s and 1980s, and a French expedition began work on the site in 2000. The pyramid complex has not yet been fully published. *See also* MENKAUHOR; UNAS.

DJEHUTY (fl. 1460 BC). A leading general of **Thutmose III** who took part in his wars in the Levant. He is the hero of the tale *The Taking of Joppa*, in which his soldiers took this seaport by hiding in large jars, thus secretly gaining access to the fortress.

DJER (reigned c. 3050 BC). Third king of **Dynasty 1**. Successor and probable son of **Aha**. His mother was **Khenethap**. His **tomb** has been excavated at **Abydos**, and among the finds was an arm with fine jewelry of the period. His tomb was later identified as the tomb of **Osiris**. *See also* DJET.

DJET (reigned c. 3000 BC). Fourth king of **Dynasty 1**. Successor of **Djer**. His **tomb** has been excavated at **Abydos**, and among the finds was a finely carved **stela** with the royal name written as a serpent, now in the **Louvre Museum**. His son and successor, **Den**, may have been a child upon his accession, as Djer's wife, **Merneith**, appears to have acted as regent.

DJOSER (reigned c. 2686–2667 BC). Horus name Netjerihet. Probably the first king of **Dynasty 3**. He is famed for his **tomb**, the first step **pyramid** and the first building constructed in stone, supposedly designed by his **vizier Imhotep**. Nothing is known about his reign. *See also* SANAKHTE.

DODEKASCHOENUS. The border area between Aswan and the kingdom of **Meroe** from **Philae** to Maharraqa. This stretch of the **Nile** river was under the control of Egypt during most of the **Ptolemaic Period**, except from around about 207–160s BC, when it was occupied by Meroe. Under **Ptolemy VI**, Egyptian control briefly extended to the Second **Cataract**. Dodekaschoenus was awarded to Roman Egypt under the peace treaty negotiated by **Publius Petronius** in 21 BC. The income tax here supported the priesthood at Philae. The area was abandoned by Rome during the reign of **Diocletian**.

DOMITIANUS, LUCIUS DOMITIUS. A rival emperor to **Diocletian**. He is known only from **papyri** but appears to have a led a revolt from August to December 297 centered in **Alexandria**. Literary sources record a revolt by a certain Aurelius Achilles in Alexandria at this time, who may have been Domitianus's supporter and successor. The revolt was crushed by early 298, and both men must have perished as a result.

DROVETTI, BERNARDINO MICHELE MARIA (1776–1852). French soldier and diplomat of Italian extraction. He was born in Barbania, Piedmont, Italy, on 4 January 1776. When Italy came under French control under Napoleon, he joined the French army, and he was later promoted to French vice consul in **Alexandria** in 1802, although he did not arrive there until 1803. He became vice consul general in Egypt in 1806 and then consul general in 1811. Drovetti was dismissed in 1814 after the fall of Napoleon, but he remained in Egypt as a private businessman until being reappointed as consul from 1821–1829. He became an avid collector of Egyptian antiquities and financed agents to collect or dig for objects mostly at **Saqqara** and **Thebes**. Drovetti has been harshly depicted by **Giovanni Battista Belzoni**, who saw his men as rivals. His first collection was sold in 1824 and became the foundation for the **Turin Egyptian Museum**, and his second went to the **Louvre Museum** in 1827, while his third was acquired by the **Berlin Egyptian Museum** in 1836. He died in Turin, Italy, on 9 March 1852.

DUAMUTEF. *See* SONS OF HORUS.

DUATENTOPET (fl. 1150 BC). Queen of **Ramesses IV** of **Dynasty 20.** She was buried in **QV**73 in the **Valley of the Queens**.

DUDIMOSE (reigned c. 1674 BC). Throne name Djedneferre. One of the last rulers of **Dynasty 13**. He is generally identified with the ruler Tutimaios, mentioned by the historian Josephus probably following **Manetho**, during whose reign the **Hyksos** seized power in Egypt. However, it has recently been suggested that the passage in Josephus does not contain a royal name and Dudimose should be assigned to **Dynasty 16**. *See also* SECOND INTERMEDIATE PERIOD.

DYNASTIES. The Egyptian writer **Manetho** divided Egyptian rulers into numbered dynasties or families. His original manuscript apparently contained 30 dynasties, and later copyists seemingly added **Dynasty 31**, the later **Persian** kings, but the Macedonian and Ptolemaic kings and Roman emperors were never part of the numbered sequence. This concept of dynastic tabulation has been followed by modern Egyptologists. The concept appears already in use during the **Ramesside Period** in the **Turin Royal Canon**.

DYNASTY 0 (c. 3500–3100 BC). The designation given by Egyptologists to those kings of **Upper Egypt** before the official union of Egypt. They are attested mostly by their **tombs** at **Abydos**. It is not clear how much of **Lower Egypt** they controlled. The system of **hieroglyphic** writing had not developed sufficiently for their names to be clearly read, so they are known by their royal symbols, for example, King **Scorpion**.

DYNASTY 1 (c. 3100–2890 BC). First dynasty of the Archaic or **Early Dynastic Period**. Stated by **Manetho** to comprise eight kings of **Thinis**, the dynasty was founded by the legendary **Menes**, the first king of united Egypt. All can be identified from later **king lists**. The royal seal of Dynasty 1, recently discovered at **Abydos**, confirms the order of the first five kings beginning with **Narmer**, who may be identified with Menes. The kings were buried at **Abydos** and their high officials at **Saqqara**.

DYNASTY 2 (c. 2890–2686 BC). Stated by **Manetho** to comprise nine kings of **Thinis**. The names given by Manetho and earlier **king lists** are difficult to reconcile with those on contemporary inscriptions. The rulers were buried either at **Saqqara** or in the royal cemetery at **Abydos**.

DYNASTY 3 (c. 2686–2613 BC). Stated by **Manetho** to comprise nine kings of **Memphis**. Very little is known about this dynasty, the most famous ruler being **Djoser**, for whose burial the step **pyramid** was allegedly designed by **Imhotep**. These rulers were buried at **Saqqara**. This dynasty is usually considered to mark the beginning of the **Old Kingdom**.

DYNASTY 4 (c. 2613–2494 BC). Sometimes considered the first dynasty of the **Old Kingdom**. Stated by **Manetho** to consist of eight kings of **Memphis** belonging to a different line. Most of these rulers can be identified from contemporary monuments and later **king lists**, although the number varies. The rulers include **Snefru**, who built two **pyramids** at **Dahshur**, and **Khufu**, **Khafre**, and **Menkaure**, the builders of the three pyramids at **Giza**.

DYNASTY 5 (c. 2494–2345 BC). Stated by **Manetho** to consist of eight kings from **Elephantine**, although he names nine. All nine are easily identifiable on monuments and later **king lists**. They were buried in **pyramids** at **Abusir** and **Saqqara**, notably **Unas**, whose pyramid was the first to be inscribed.

DYNASTY 6 (c. 2345–2181 BC). Stated by **Manetho** to comprise six kings of **Memphis**. The first five, notably **Pepy II**, are all identifiable from contemporary monuments and later **king lists**. They were buried in **pyramids** at **Saqqara**. The last, **Nitocris**, is known from the **Turin Royal Canon** and later legend.

DYNASTY 7 (c. 2181 BC). Stated by **Manetho** to consist of 70 kings of **Memphis** who reigned for 70 days. No rulers have been identified, and the entire dynasty may be nonexistent.

DYNASTY 8 (c. 2181–2125 BC). Stated by **Manetho** to comprise 27 kings of **Memphis** who reigned for 146 years. This dynasty, or the preceding if it existed, marks the beginning of the **First Intermediate Period**. A number of rulers are known from **king lists**.

DYNASTY 9 (c. 2160–2130 BC). Stated by **Manetho** to consist of 19 kings of **Herakleopolis** who reigned for 146 years. *See also* DYNASTY 10.

DYNASTY 10 (c. 2130–2040 BC). Stated by **Manetho** to consist of 19 kings of **Herakleopolis** who reigned for 185 years. The numbers and figures for **Dynasty 9** and Dynasty 10 are dubious. The **Turin Royal Canon** seems to list 18 rulers for both dynasties, but they are ignored on other **king lists**. Contemporary monuments mention kings with the name of **Khety**, and **Merykare** is known from literature. Dynasty 10 was contemporary in part with **Dynasty 11** and was overthrown by **Mentuhotep II**.

DYNASTY 11 (c. 2125–1985 BC). Stated by **Manetho** to consist of 16 kings of **Thebes** who reigned for 43 years. Only seven kings are known, although the first king, **Mentuhotep I**, never reigned but was honored with the royal title by his descendants. The family may have originally been governors of Thebes, but independence was probably declared by **Intef I**, who adopted the royal title. **Mentuhotep II** reunited Egypt and inaugurated the **Middle Kingdom**. The later kings were buried at **Deir el-Bahri**.

DYNASTY 12 (c. 1985–1795 BC). Stated by **Manetho** to comprise seven kings of **Thebes**. There were in fact eight, as the founder, **Amenemhat I**, was erroneously mentioned by Manetho under **Dynasty 11**. Much detail on this dynasty is preserved in the **Turin Royal Canon** and on many contemporary monuments. The dynasty moved its capital to Itjtawy, modern **Lisht**, and the kings were buried in **pyramids** in the **Fayum** area and **Dahshur**.

DYNASTY 13 (c. 1795–1650 BC). Stated by **Manetho** to consist of 60 kings of **Thebes** who reigned for 453 years. With this dynasty began the **Second Intermediate Period**. Manetho's numbers and total of years are clearly inaccurate, but the **Turin Royal Canon** reveals a long list of kings, many with short reigns. Many rulers can be identified from contemporary monuments.

DYNASTY 14 (c. 1750–1650 BC). Stated by **Manetho** to comprise 76 kings of **Xois** who reigned for 184 years. Nothing is known of this dynasty, which was probably contemporary with **Dynasty 13** in part. Some of the minor **Hyksos** kings have recently been assigned to this dynasty rather than **Dynasty 16**. Manetho's figures are again suspect.

DYNASTY 15 (c. 1650–1550 BC). The dynasty of the **Hyksos**. Stated by **Manetho** to comprise six kings, although the figures for this dynasty vary in different versions from 250 to 284 years. The **Turin Royal Canon** gives a more accurate assessment of 108 years. Few monuments survive, but most kings can be identified from **scarabs** or other references, notably **Khayan** and **Apepi**.

DYNASTY 16 (c. 1650–1580 BC). The surviving sources of **Manetho** are confused regarding this dynasty. Versions range from 32 **Hyksos** rulers reigning for 518 years to five kings of **Thebes** reigning for 190 years. Some Egyptologists assign minor Hyksos chieftains, probably contemporary with **Dynasty 15**, to this dynasty, but more recently it has been suggested that some of the Theban rulers previously listed in **Dynasty 17** should be listed here.

DYNASTY 17 (c. 1580–1550 BC). The versions of **Manetho** are confused, sometimes identifying this dynasty with **Dynasty 15** or naming 43 kings of **Thebes**. Egyptologists place here some of the rulers of Thebes before the reunification of Egypt under **Dynasty 18**, many of which are known from the **Turin Royal Canon** or contemporary monuments.

DYNASTY 18 (c. 1550–1295 BC). The first dynasty of the **New Kingdom** starting with **Ahmose I**, who drove out the **Hyksos** and reunified Egypt. **Manetho** names 14 or 16 kings of **Thebes**, but his names are not all identifiable with evidence from contemporary monuments, which yield detailed information on 14 rulers.

DYNASTY 19 (c. 1295–1186 BC). The famous Ramesside dynasty founded by **Ramesses I**. The sources for **Manetho** name five kings of **Thebes** reigning for 194 to 209 years, but Ramesses I is usually misplaced in **Dynasty 18**. Contemporary monuments yield eight rulers.

DYNASTY 20 (c. 1186–1069 BC). Manetho names 12 kings of **Thebes** reigning for 135 years. Contemporary monuments name 10 kings from the founder, **Sethnakhte**, to **Ramesses XI**. With the exception of the first ruler, all kings bore the dynastic name Ramesses. The rulers were all buried in the **Valley of the Kings**, except the last, whose tomb was unfinished.

DYNASTY 21 (c. 1069–945 BC). Stated by **Manetho** to consist of seven kings of **Tanis** reigning for 130 years. Most can be identified from contemporary sources. The dynasty was founded by **Nesbanebdjed** (Smendes), ruler of Tanis, but he apparently only ruled the north of the country, while the south was virtually independent under the **high priest of Amun** at **Thebes**. Some royal burials have been discovered at Tanis.

DYNASTY 22 (c. 945–715 BC). The Libyan dynasty founded by **Sheshonq I**. Stated by **Manetho** to consist of nine kings of **Bubastis** reigning for 120 years. Nine kings with the names of **Sheshonq**, **Osorkon**, and **Takelot** can be identified from contemporary monuments, but the situation is confused, as **Dynasty 23** was in part contemporary with Dynasty 22, and other local rulers also assumed pharaonic **titularies**. The royal burials have been discovered at **Tanis**.

DYNASTY 23 (c. 818–715 BC). Manetho's excerptors name three kings of **Tanis** reigning for 44 years or four kings reigning for 89 years. This dynasty was wholly contemporary with **Dynasty 22** and appears to have consisted of local rulers of Libyan origin, possibly offshoots of the previous dynasty, who became independent. The first ruler, **Pedubast I**, and the second, **Osorkon III**, are easily identifiable from contemporary monuments. It is not clear exactly where their capital city was located, but they were recognized in **Thebes**.

DYNASTY 24 (c. 727–715 BC). Stated by the copyists of **Manetho** to comprise one king of **Sais**, Bocchoris, who reigned for six or 44 years. The former figure is probably more accurate. That king, whose Egyptian name was **Bakenrenef**, is known from contemporary sources, but Egyptologists also include his predecessor, **Tefnakhte**, in this dynasty.

DYNASTY 25 (c. 747–656 BC). **Manetho** names three Nubian rulers, **Shabaqo**, **Shebitqo**, and **Taharqo**, who reigned for 40 or 44 years. Contemporary monuments confirm these three kings, as well as two previous rulers, **Kashta** and **Piye**, and a final one, **Tantamani**, whose rule was recognized in parts of Egypt.

DYNASTY 26 (664–525 BC). **Manetho** names nine rulers of **Sais** reigning for 150 to 167 years, of whom the first three appear to have been only local rulers of Sais. The first authenticated member of the dynasty was **Nekau I** (d. 664 BC), and his son, **Psamtik I**, was the first to rule a reunited Egypt. The later kings are well attested on contemporary monuments and documents. Dynasty 26 was overthrown by the invasion of King **Cambyses** of **Persia** in 525 BC.

DYNASTY 27 (525–404 BC). The kings of **Persia** who ruled in Egypt from **Cambyses** to **Darius II**. **Manetho** lists eight kings reigning for 120 or 124 years and four months, but the names vary slightly in his copyists. The kings are known from some monuments in Egypt and Persian and classical sources.

DYNASTY 28 (404–399 BC). Stated by **Manetho** to consist of **Amyrtaeos** of **Sais**, who reigned for six years. The king is known from contemporary classical sources. He was evidently deposed by the founder of the succeeding dynasty.

DYNASTY 29 (399–380 BC). **Manetho** lists four kings of **Mendes** who reigned for 21 years and four months but actually gives five names. Some of the kings, like **Nefaarud** and **Hakor**, are known from contemporary documentation.

DYNASTY 30 (380–343 BC). Stated by **Manetho** to consist of three kings from **Sebennytos** who reigned for 20 or 38 years. The names of these rulers, **Nakhtnebef**, **Djedhor**, and **Nakhthorheb**, all appear on contemporary monuments and in classical sources. The last ruler of the dynasty was forced to flee to **Nubia** by the second Persian invasion in 343 BC.

DYNASTY 31 (343–332 BC). This dynasty was apparently added to **Manetho** and refers to the kings of **Persia** who ruled Egypt following the conquest by **Artaxerxes III** until the arrival of **Alexander the Great**.

– E –

EARLY DYNASTIC PERIOD (c. 3100–2686 BC). The term used by Egyptologists for the period of **Dynasty 1** and **Dynasty 2**; some also include **Dynasty 3**. The term *Archaic Period* is also used for this era. This period witnessed the development of the unitary Egyptian state; the growth of royal power as shown in the **tombs** at **Abydos**; and most importantly, the development of writing in the form of **hieroglyphs**.

ECONOMY. The Egyptian economy was primarily based on **agriculture** as the fertility of the soil engendered by the **Nile** flood allowed a crop surplus to fulfill the population's basic food needs. The excess crops could be collected, stored, and recirculated. Egypt's natural resources provided for most mineral needs, in particular control of the **gold** mines of **Nubia**.

Egypt never developed a monetary economy, but a sophisticated barter system was used. Goods were valued in measures of wheat if of low worth, or weights of **copper**, **silver** or gold for more highly valued objects. These items would be paid for with goods of a similar value and not usually with the materials used in the valuation.

Major imports were normally received as part of state diplomatic relations. These included wood from Lebanon, tin, **lapis lazuli**, and other luxury goods accepted as tribute when Egypt was strong or reciprocated with such Egyptian products as gold. There is little evidence of a strong merchant class in Egypt, and foreign **trade**, not on the diplomatic level, appears to have been carried out by foreigners based in their own quarters in **Memphis** or later in such special areas as **Naukratis**. *See also* TRAVEL.

EDFU. Modern name for a site on the west bank of the **Nile** in the second **nome** of **Upper Egypt**, halfway between **Thebes** and **Elephantine** (Aswan), ancient Egyptian *Djeba*, Greek Apollonopolis Magna, where a major **temple** dedicated to the god **Horus**, which was rebuilt during the **Ptolemaic Period** from 237 BC to 57 BC, is located. The inscriptions include a long text, which may be the text of a ritual play. Remains of the earlier temple have been uncovered in the foundations. The Edfu **triad** consists of Horus, his wife **Hathor**, and **Isis**. Tombs from the **Old Kingdom** to the **Byzantine Period** are located there, along with a Coptic monastery. Excavations have been performed by **Auguste Mariette** around 1860, a French expedition from 1914–1933, and a Franco–Polish team from 1937–1939. The temple inscriptions are being published by a French team. The main town site, largely buried under the modern town, has been examined by an international expedition beginning in 2000, and a German expedition has been surveying the locality since 1994. The sacred site of *Behdet* was located nearby. *See also* DENDERA; ESNA; KOM OMBO.

EDUCATION. The bulk of the Egyptian population consisted of agricultural laborers, while not more than 10 percent or less were literate. There is little evidence of formal schools but some did exist, possibly attached to **temples** or run in a semiprivate capacity by trained **scribes**. One such institution is mentioned in the *Tale of Truth and Falsehood* attended by the illegitimate son of the hero presumably because his mother is a wealthy woman. Many would have simply been educated by their father or a close relation. People from nonscribal backgrounds would have found it difficult to gain an education unless their father had come into wealth, usually by war booty. It is probable that even many of the educated Egyptian people living in the later periods could only read **hieratic** and not **hieroglyphic**. With the growth of **demotic**, the ability to read was probably confined to a smaller population of scribes and, when not recognized by the Roman authorities for legal purposes, it was eventually confined to the priests, so the advent of Christianity caused the forms of ancient Egyptian writing to be lost. *See also* WISDOM LITERATURE.

EDWARDS, AMELIA ANN BLANFORD (1831–1892). British author, traveler, and patroness. She was born in London on 7 June 1831, the daughter of an army officer. She edited and published popular books and articles and visited Egypt and Syria from 1873–1874 and wrote the best seller *A Thousand Miles up the Nile* in 1877. She became concerned with the destruction of Egyptian monuments and founded the **Egypt Exploration Fund** in 1882 to encourage the accurate study, conservation, and excavation of Egyptian antiquities. She was the funds secretary and worked tirelessly on its behalf, lecturing both in England and the United States to raise money. She was an active supporter of **Flinders Petrie** and left money in her will to found the professorship at University College London for him. She died at Westbury-on-Trym, England, on 15 April 1892.

EGYPT. Modern name derived from the Greek *Aigyptos* for the country comprising the **Nile** Delta and the Nile Valley up to **Elephantine** (Aswan) and the adjacent deserts. The Greek name may be derived from the name *Hikuptah*, which was sometimes used for ancient **Memphis**. The ancient Egyptians called their country *Kemet*, the Black Land, referring to the fertile soil left by the Nile inundation.

EGYPT EXPLORATION FUND (AKA EGYPT EXPLORATION SOCIETY). This organization was founded in London in 1882 to sponsor excavations in Egypt, largely through the efforts of novelist **Amelia Edwards**. The name was changed from Egypt Exploration Fund to Egypt Exploration Society in 1919. It has been responsible for archaeological work at many sites in Egypt, notably at **Tanis** and **Bubastis** in the Delta, **Abydos**, **Amarna**, **Deir el-Bahri**, **Memphis**, **Saqqara**, and **Buhen** and **Qasr Ibrim** in **Nubia**. Among the archaeologists employed by the society have been **Flinders Petrie** and **Howard Carter**. The society has also encouraged the copying of **tomb** and **temple** reliefs and inscriptions, and from 1895–1907 it sponsored the work of Bernard Grenfell and Arthur Hunt in collecting Graeco-Roman **papyri**, notably at **Oxyrhynchus**, which are still in the course of publication. In the past, the society received from the Egyptian authorities a division of the antiquities found during its excavations, which were then distributed to various museums throughout the world.

EGYPT EXPLORATION SOCIETY. *See* EGYPT EXPLORATION FUND.

EGYPTIAN ANTIQUITIES SERVICE. *See* SUPREME COUNCIL FOR ANTIQUITIES.

ELEPHANTINE. Greek name for the Egyptian *Abu*, modern Aswan, capital of the first **nome** of **Upper Egypt**. The site located on an island in the **Nile** marked the southern limit of the border of Egypt proper and was the main entrepôt for goods imported from the south, notably ivory, from which its name in Egyptian and Greek derives. Remains have been found from the **Predynastic Period (Naqada** III) to the **Roman Period**. The principal deity worshipped at the main **temple** was the ram-headed god **Khnum**, together with the goddesses **Satis** and **Anukis**. There was a smaller temple devoted to Satis erected by **Thutmose III** and **Hatshepsut**. The important shrine of the deified **Heqaib** is also located here. Rock **tombs** from the **Old Kingdom** to the **New Kingdom** are located on the west bank of the Nile at Qubbet el-Hawa. The Nilometer records the levels of the flood and dates from the Roman Period. Interesting records of a Jewish colony during the Persian Period have been discovered here. Elephantine was excavated by German archaeologists from 1906–1907, by a French team from 1907–1909, by Egyptian archaeologists in 1932 and from 1946–1947, and by a Swiss archaeologist from 1953–1954, and it has been systematically excavated by a German-Swiss expedition since 1969. The nearby tombs were examined by a second German expedition from 1960–1973. *See also* NUBIA.

ELEPHANTINE PAPYRI. Hieratic, Demotic, and Greek **papyri** have been discovered during the excavations at **Elephantine**, but the term generally refers to the archives of Aramaic papyri found at this site at the end of the 19th century. These disclose a hitherto unknown Jewish colony resident there as part of the Persian garrison during the Persian Period. The texts indicate tensions between the local population and the Jewish residents and also point to the construction of a Jewish temple. Most of the texts are now preserved in the **Berlin Egyptian Museum,** the Brooklyn Museum, and the **Cairo Egyptian Museum**.

ELKAB. Arabic name for a site in **Upper Egypt** south of **Thebes**, ancient Egyptian *Nekheb*, Greek Eileithyiapolis, on the east side of the **Nile**, opposite **Hierakonpolis** in the third **nome** of Upper Egypt, of which became the capital during the **New Kingdom**. The principal deity of the city was the goddess **Nekhbet**, tutelary goddess of

Upper Egypt. Remains date from the **Prehistoric Period** to the **Graeco-Roman Period** from 7000 BC to the 4th century AD. The remains include the foundations of the **temple** of Nekhbet, whose standing remains were destroyed in 1828; the foundations of the smaller temple of **Thoth**; **mastabas** from the **Early Dynastic Period**; **Old Kingdom** rock **tombs**; and tombs from **Dynasty 18** and **Dynasty 19**. Those of **Ahmose,** son of Ebana, and Ahmose Pennekhbet contain biographical texts concerning the war against the **Hyksos** and the early rulers of Dynasty 18. Elkab was excavated by British archaeologists from 1892–1904 and has been worked by a Belgian expedition since 1937 and more recently also by a team from the **British Museum.**

ESNA. Modern name for a site in southern **Upper Egypt** on the west bank of the **Nile**, ancient Egyptian *Iunet*, Greek Latopolis. The surviving **temple** dedicated to **Khnum** dates to the **Ptolemaic Period** and **Roman Period** and includes a relief of **Septimius Severus** with his family, in which the image of his younger son, Geta, has been erased by the order of his older brother, **Caracalla**, who murdered him. Esna was excavated by the British archaeologist John Garstang from 1905–1906 and since 1951 has been excavated and the temple inscriptions copied by a French expedition. *See also* DENDERA; EDFU; KOM OMBO.

EXECRATION TEXTS. These texts are found during the **Middle Kingdom** inscribed on figures and pots that were ritually broken. They contain curses against the enemies of the king, both internal and external. The ceremony of breaking their names may have been thought to render these enemies powerless. The texts range from the general to the specific, giving names of individuals and foreign princes in Palestine and **Nubia** otherwise unknown. The texts give the earliest citation of the city of Jerusalem.

EXODUS. A book of the Hebrew Bible that describes the captivity of the Israelites in Egypt and their delivery by Moses from the oppression of the **pharaoh**. Much has been written to try to identify the route of the Exodus out of Egypt and the pharaoh concerned. The pharaoh of the oppression has usually been identified as **Ramesses II**

or his son. **Merenptah**; however, the story, as described in Exodus, is in some respects legendary. Most Egyptologists do not accept the complete tale as historical fact. Some doubt its entire historicity, while others are willing to subscribe to a minor flight of slaves but not the full dramatic account. It has been recently argued that the Exodus is to some extent a rewriting of the expulsion of the **Hyksos** from a Canaanite or Israelite point of view. *See also* JOSEPH.

– F –

FAIENCE. Egyptian *Thnt*. Material used for the production of amulets, inlays, jewelry, **shabtis**, votive offerings, vases, and bowls. It consists of a core of crushed quartz covered in a glaze composed of soda, lime, and silica, usually but not exclusively blue. The technique was in use from **Predynastic Period** to the Arabic Period. *See also* GLASS.

FARAS. Modern Arabic name for a site in **Nubia**, Greek name Pachoras, south of **Abu Simbel** in modern Sudan. The earliest remains appear to date to the Meroitic Period, as blocks of **Thutmose III** found here are now known to have been reused from **Buhen**. The most extensive period of occupation dates to the **Coptic** Period and includes several churches and a cathedral with frescoes. The site was briefly excavated in 1905 by an expedition from the University of Pennsylvania, from 1910–1913 by Francis L. Griffith for the University of Oxford, from 1960–1962 by the Sudan Antiquities Service, and from 1961–1964 by a Polish expedition that discovered the cathedral and much inscriptional evidence. The area was flooded in 1964 by Lake Nasser, the lake formed by the waters of the Aswan High Dam. The frescoes were rescued and divided between the National Museums in Khartoum and Warsaw.

FARFARA OASIS. Ancient Egyptian *Ta-ihu*. An oasis in the Western Desert between the **Dakhla Oasis** and the **Bahariya Oasis**. It is possibly mentioned in the famous stela of **Kamose**. It is cited in later records, but little excavation has taken place there and no pharaonic remains have been uncovered. An Italian expedition has been examining

Palaeolithic and Neolithic remains in the oasis. *See also* KHARGA OASIS; SIWA OASIS.

FAYUM. A fertile depression south of **Memphis** where a large lake was located during the Pharaonic Period. The area was developed during the course of **Dynasty 12**, whose capital at **Lisht** was close to the Fayum. Several of the rulers were buried either in the Fayum at **Hawara** or nearby at **Lahun**. The principal god of the region was the crocodile god **Sobek**.

The area was further extensively settled during the **Ptolemaic Period** due to major drainage works carried out to release new land for retired Greek soldiers of the royal army. The area was quite prosperous at the time, as well as during the **Roman Period**, and the remains of many settlements exist from which many objects, notably literary and nonliterary **papyri** and **mummy portraits**, have been recovered. *See also* BACCHIAS; DEIR EL-NAQLUN; GUROB; HARAGEH; HAWARA; KARANIS; KOM KHELWA; KOM TALIT; LAHUN; LISHT; MEDINET MADI; SOKNOPAIOU NESOS; TEBTUNIS.

FAYUM PORTRAITS. *See* MUMMY PORTRAITS.

FIRST INTERMEDIATE PERIOD (c. 2181–2055 BC). The term used by Egyptologists to denote the period from the end of **Dynasty 6** to the reunification of Egypt under **Dynasty 11**. The era is marked by the collapse of royal power and the growth of the authority of the local rulers or nomarchs of the **nomes**. Local autonomy also led to distinct provincial art styles. Following the disappearance of the ruling line in **Memphis**, the governors of **Herakleopolis** (**Dynasty 9** and **Dynasty 10**) and **Thebes** (Dynasty 11) vied for supreme authority, and the period came to an end with the victory of **Mentuhotep II** of **Thebes**, who reunited the country under his rule. *See also* MIDDLE KINGDOM; OLD KINGDOM.

FOUNDATION DEPOSITS. A series of ritual objects buried at the corners and important axis points of **temples** and **tombs**, sometimes in brick-lined pits. The deposits often consist of inscribed plaques of **faience**, stone, and precious metals, as well as food offerings, model tools, vessels, and other religious symbols, also often in faience or other materials. They are a useful dating material for construction. They were used consistently from the **Old Kingdom** to the **Graeco-Roman Period** and also in the Meroitic Empire.

FRENCH INSTITUTE. Originally Ecole française and from 1898 Institut français d'archéologie orientale. It was founded in 1880 by the French government as a research center in Cairo to undertake the study of ancient and Islamic Egypt and carry out archaeological excavations. It has had its headquarters at the Munira Palace since 1907. Several directors later became the heads of the Egyptian Antiquities Service. At first it organized epigraphic work, copying texts notably in **Graeco-Roman Period temples** at **Edfu** and later **Dendera** and **Esna**. Beginning in 1898, archaeological excavations have been undertaken at various sites in Egypt, particularly **Deir el-Medina**, **Karnak**, **Medamud**, and more recently at the **Dakhla Oasis** and **Kharga Oasis**. The findings of its projects have been published by its own press.

– G –

GALERIUS VALERIUS MAXIMIANUS, CAIUS (d. 311). Roman Emperor. He was born at Serdica in the Balkans. He was named Caesar by **Diocletian** on 1 March 293 and crushed a revolt in Egypt in the same year. He became Augustus, one of the two senior emperors, in 305. He died in May 311.

GALLUS, CAIUS CORNELIUS. See CORNELIUS GALLUS, CAIUS.

GEB. Egyptian god of the earth. Son of **Shu** and **Tefnut**, husband of the sky goddess **Nut**, and father of **Osiris**, **Isis**, **Seth**, and **Nephthys**. According to legend, Geb and Nut were separated in the act of sexual union, and he can be depicted lying flat as the earth with the overvaulting Nut as the sky. See also RELIGION.

GEBEL EL-HARIDI. The site of a limestone quarry and rock-cut **tombs** in **Upper Egypt** near Sohag. The remains date from the **Old**

Kingdom to the **Coptic** Period. It was investigated by a British expedition from 1991–1993 and in 1998.

GEBEL EL-SILSILA. Ancient *Khenu*. A sandstone quarry on the banks of the **Nile** between **Thebes** and **Elephantine** (Aswan) that was used from the **New Kingdom** onward. There are remains of rock-cut shrines, notably one of **Horemheb**.

GEBEL EL-ZEIT. Modern name for a site in the Eastern Desert on the Red Sea coast north of modern Hurghada where the lead mines exploited by the ancient Egyptians from the **Middle Kingdom** to the **New Kingdom** were located. The site was discovered in 1982 and excavated from 1982–1986 by a French expedition. Apart from the mines, the site included small sanctuaries erected by the miners, notably to the deities **Hathor**, **Horus**, and **Min**, as well as graffiti. The lead was used for the production of eye makeup known by the Arabic word *kohl*.

GEBELEIN. Greek Pathyris. Modern name for a site in the third **nome** of **Upper Egypt** where remains from the **Old Kingdom** to the **Roman Period** have been uncovered, including an important early **papyrus**. The patron goddess was **Hathor** linked to **Anubis**. The site was excavated by an Italian expedition from 1910–1814, from 1919–1920, and again in 1930, 1935, and 1937.

GERF HUSSEIN. Former location of a sandstone **temple** in **Nubia** built by the **viceroy of Kush**, Setau, in honor of **Ptah** and the deified **Ramesses II**. The inscriptions on the temple were copied and certain parts cut out before the site was flooded by Lake Nasser, the lake caused by the Aswan High Dam in the 1960s. *See also* ABU SIMBEL; AMADA; BEIT EL-WALI; KALABSHA; SOLEB.

GERMANICUS (15 BC–19 AD). Roman prince. Son of Nero Claudius Drusus and Antonia, daughter of **Marcus Antonius**. He was likely born in Rome on 24 May 15 BC. His original name was probably Nero Claudius Germanicus, but he was known as Germanicus Julius Caesar following his adoption by Emperor Tiberius in 4 AD. He was destined to succeed to imperial power and held several high appointments, including governor of Germany and Syria. In 19 AD, he traveled to Egypt despite the ban on senatorial visits and was well received in **Alexandria**. He died in Antioch upon his return on 10 October 19 AD.

GERZEH. The modern name for a cemetery site northwest of **Meidum**. It was excavated by a British expedition in 1911. The cemetery comprised graves of the **Predynastic Period** with a few graves from the **Early Dynastic Period** and the **New Kingdom**. Flinders Petrie adopted the term *Gerzean* to describe the culture, but it is recognized as a form of **Naqada** II culture from the south. *See also* ADAIMA; KAFR HASSAN DAOUD; MINSHAT ABU OMAR; TELL EL-FARKHA; TELL IBRAHIM AWAD.

GILUKHEPA (fl. 1381 BC). A princess of **Mitanni** and daughter of Shuttarna II, who married **Amenhotep III** when he was 10 years old. Her fate is unknown, although she is mentioned when arrangements were made for the marriage of her niece, **Tadukhepa**, to the king. *See also* TIY.

GIZA. Modern name for the area near modern Cairo that was the main burial site for the rulers of **Dynasty 4**. The site is dominated by the three **pyramid** complexes of **Khufu** and Khufu's son, **Khafre**, and grandson, **Menkaure**. The **Sphinx** appears to have been constructed under Khafre but was renovated by the later king, **Thutmose IV**. The pyramids are surrounded by the **tombs** of the wives, children, and officials of the monarchs.

The most important early excavations here were carried out by the Italian Giovanni Battista Caviglia in 1817 and the British John Perring and Howard Vyse from 1837–1838. In more modern times, the site has been excavated by several expeditions, the most notable led by **Auguste Mariette** in 1853; **Flinders Petrie** from 1880–1881; the **Boston Museum of Fine Arts** under **George Reisner** from 1902–1939, whose discoveries included the tomb of **Hetepheres**, which was examined from 1924–1927; the Italian Ernesto Schiaparelli in 1903; the Austrian Hermann Junker from 1912–1929; the American Clarence Fisher for the University of Pennsylvania in 1915; and Egyptian archaeologists Selim Hassan from 1929–1939,

Abdel-Moneim Abu Bakr for the University of Cairo from 1949–1976, an Egyptian team that excavated one of the boat graves beside the pyramid of Khufu in 1954; and more recently Zahi Hawass and Mark Lehner in 1978, 1980, and since 1989. The University of Cairo resumed work in the area in 2000.

GLASS. A material produced in Egypt beginning in the **New Kingdom**. The earliest dated vessel is belongs to the reign of **Thutmose III**, and he may have imported glassmakers from Syria after his conquests. Glass was used for the production of inlays, amulets, and cosmetic vessels. *See also* FAIENCE.

GNOSTICISM. A religious doctrine that combined elements of Christianity and Platonist Greek philosophy. These beliefs were later deemed heretical by the orthodox Christian church, and gnostic texts were proscribed. The discovery of gnostic texts in Egypt written in **Coptic**, notably at **Nag Hammadi**, have enabled gnostic beliefs to be better understood. *See also* MANICHEISM; RELIGION.

GOD'S FATHER. Title used beginning in the **Middle Kingdom** for the father of a ruler who was not himself a king. During late **Dynasty 18**, it may have designated a king's father-in-law, although the exact reason that it was used by future king **Ay** is unclear. It is not to be confused with the minor priestly title of god's father used for priests of a certain god.

GOD'S WIFE OF AMUN. Title first attested for **queens** and some princesses during **Dynasty 18**. The office was eventually bestowed on unmarried princesses, who were regarded as brides of the god **Amun** rather than the king. The first known princess to hold the office under these conditions was **Isis**, daughter of **Ramesses VI of Dynasty 20**. The importance of the office gradually eclipsed the status of that of **high priest of Amun** by **Dynasty 25**, and the latter office fell into disuse in **Dynasty 26**, the title being absorbed by the God's wife. The office was used by both Dynasty 25 and Dynasty 26 to exert control over **Thebes** by having their princesses installed, although true power rested with the steward of the God's wife. The last attested God's wife was **Ankhnesneferibre**, daughter of **Psamtik II**, who was in office at the time of the Persian invasion in 525 BC. Classical sources during the **Ptolemaic Period** imply that the office may have continued or been revived on a more modest scale. The tombs of the God's wives were built in the precinct of the **temple** of **Medinet Habu**.

GOLD. A precious metal highly valued from antiquity. Egyptian *Nbw*. It was mainly used for jewelry, personal adornment, and royal funerary equipment. The trade of gold appears to have been a royal monopoly. The metal was found in the Eastern Desert in such locations as **Wadi Hammamat** and **Nubia** so much so that Egypt was regarded as a prime source of the metal by foreign countries. According to Egyptian myth, the flesh of the gods was made of gold. *See also* BRONZE; COPPER; IRON; SILVER.

GRAECO-ROMAN PERIOD (332 BC–642 AD). A term used by Egyptologists for the entire span of rule by the Greeks and later the Romans in Egypt. It is usually divided into the **Ptolemaic Period**, **Roman Period**, and **Byzantine Period**.

GRAFFITI. Singular graffito. Short inscriptions carved or painted on **temple** walls, **tomb** walls, cliff faces, or prominent boulders that usually give the name of the author and sometimes the date and reason for his presence. Lengthier texts can occur. Graffiti can also be pictorial, notably during the **Prehistoric Period** when they are known as rock art. The texts are useful for dating purposes and are attested throughout Egyptian history to the Arabic Period and unfortunately in modern times when they can disfigure the monuments.

GRIFFITH, FRANCIS LLEWELLYN (1862–1934). British Egyptologist. He was born in Brighton, England, on 27 May 1862. He studied at Oxford and excavated in Egypt with **Flinders Petrie** and **Henri Edouard Naville**. He became reader in 1901 and then in 1924 professor of Egyptology at Oxford. He was one of the leading scholars of Egyptian texts and deciphered the script of ancient **Meroe**. He died in Oxford on 14 March 1934. According to his will, he founded the Griffith Institute in Oxford, a major research center for Egyptology.

GUROB. Modern name for a site in the **Fayum** west of the **Nile**. Ancient Egyptian *Merwer*. A palace complex and associated town and cemetery were located here during **Dynasty 18**, **Dynasty 19**, and **Dynasty 20**. The finds included imported Mycenaean **pottery**. It is believed that the famous sycamore head of **Queen Tiy**, now in the **Berlin Egyptian Museum**, came from this vicinity. Other cemeteries date from the late **Predynastic Period** to the **First Intermediate Period** and the **Ptolemaic Period**. The area was excavated by **Flinders Petrie** from 1888–1890 and again by his team from 1903–1904 and in 1920. It was briefly surveyed in 1978 and 1983 and since 2005 has been investigated by a team from the University of Liverpool. *See also* BACCHIAS; DEIR EL-NAQLUN; HARAGEH; HAWARA; KARANIS; KOM KHELWA; KOM TALIT; LAHUN; LISHT; MEDINET MADI; SOKNOPAIOU NESOS; TEBTUNIS.

– H –

HABIRU. A term found in cuneiform documents to signify nomads, renegades, or mercenaries. They are mentioned in the **Amarna letters** as allies of **Abdi-Ashirta**, king of **Amurru**. The term is obviously the ancestor of the word Hebrews but does not necessarily designate the same people in all its references.

HADRIAN (76–138 AD). Roman emperor. Original name Publius Aelius Hadrianus. He was born in Baetica in 76, son of Publius Aelius Hadrianus and Domitia Paulina, and was great-nephew of the Emperor Trajan, who adopted him on his deathbed in 117. Hadrian was noted for his policy of favoring Greek culture and his constant travels throughout the empire. He visited Egypt in 130 along with his wife, Vibia **Sabina**, and his favorite, Antinous, who drowned in the Nile. Hadrian founded the city of **Antinoopolis** in his honor. His visit to the **Colossi of Memnon** is recorded in **graffiti**.

HAKOR (reigned 393–380 BC). The Greek form of his name is Achoris. Throne name Khnummaatre setepenkhnum. Second ruler of **Dynasty 29** and successor of **Nefaarud** I. He allied with Greek states and rebels in Cyprus against Persian rule.

HAPUSENEB (fl. 1470 BC). High priest of Amun. He was a strong supporter of **Queen Hatshepsut** and supervised the construction work for her **tomb** in the **Valley of the Kings**, and at **Karnak**, he supervised the removal of two **obelisks** from **Elephantine** for the **temple**. His own badly damaged tomb (nunber 67) at **Thebes** has a scene depicting the Egyptian expedition to **Punt** during Hatshepsut's reign.

HAPY. Fertility god who was a personification of the annual **Nile** flood. He is depicted as a fat, effeminate man with large breasts and marsh plants on his head. A different god Hapy with a baboon head was one of the **Sons of Horus**. *See also* RELIGION.

HARAGEH. A cemetery site near **Lahun** at the entrance to the **Fayum** dating from the **Predynastic Period** to the **Coptic** Period. It was excavated by a British expedition from 1912–1914. *See also* BACCHIAS; DEIR EL-NAQLUN; GUROB; HAWARA; KARANIS; KOM KHELWA; KOM TALIT; LAHUN; LISHT; MEDINET MADI; SOKNOPAIOU NESOS; TEBTUNIS.

HARDJEDEF (fl. 2570 BC). Son of Khufu of Dynasty 4. During later times, he was regarded as the author of a text of **wisdom literature**, and he was named among the princes in the literary tale of the **Westcar Papyrus**. An isolated later text in the **Wadi Hammamat** writes his name in a royal **cartouche**. In later legend, he was credited with the discovery of the text of the **Book of the Dead**. *See also* BAUEFRE; DJEDEFRE; KAWAB; KHAFRE.

HAREM CONSPIRACY PAPYRI. An archive of papyri that date to the reign of **Ramesses IV** detailing the investigation of a conspiracy against his predecessor, **Ramesses III**. It appears that the king was assassinated in an attempt by a lady of the harem and certain officials to put her son, Pentaweret, on the throne. The conspiracy was thwarted by the king's appointed heir. The judgements of the special court are recorded. Many of the culprits were sentenced to death or suicide.

HARKHUF (fl. 2280 BC). Egyptian official during the reigns of **Nemtyemsaf** I and **Pepy II** of **Dynasty 6** who held the post of governor of **Upper Egypt**, possibly as successor to **Weni**. He was buried at

Elephantine, and his **tomb** contains a major autobiographical inscription. He undertook four expeditions to **Nubia** during which he acquired exotic goods for the royal court, including a pygmy or dwarf for which he was personally congratulated by the king.

HARMACHIS. *See* HARWENNEFER.

HARNEDJITEF (reigned c. 1770 BC). Throne name Hetepibre. Ruler at the beginning of **Dynasty 13**. Possibly son of a previous ruler, **Ameny Qemau**, whose name appears in his **cartouche** and has been wrongly interpreted as meaning "the Asiatic." A statue of Harnedjitef has been found in the Delta near **Avaris**. A mace with his throne name has been found in the Syrian city of Ebla, indicating that trade and political links with the Levant were still active in this period. *See also* SECOND INTERMEDIATE PERIOD.

HARRIS PAPYRUS. Also known as Great Harris Papyrus or Papyrus Harris I. It was acquired by collector Anthony Charles Harris (1790–1869) from illicit excavations at **Thebes** in 1855, possibly at **Deir el-Medina**. It is an account written during the reign of **Ramesses IV** of the state of Egypt and its **temples** during the reign of his father, **Ramesses III**, which the new king inherited. A historical summary describes in general terms the rise of **Dynasty 20** under his grandfather, **Sethnakhte**. The papyrus is now housed in the **British Museum**.

HARSAPHES. *See* HERYSHEF.

HARSIESE (reigned c. 870–860 BC). Throne name Hedjkheperre setepenamun. Son of the **high priest of Amun** Sheshonq, who may have succeeded as **Sheshonq II** and Nestanebtashru. Grandson of **Osorkon I** of **Dynasty 22** and great-grandson of **Pasebakhaenniut II** of **Dynasty 21**. He succeeded as high priest of Amun and then adopted the royal **titulary** during the reign of his cousin, **Osorkon II**. Upon Harsiese's death, Osorkon II installed his own son, **Nimlot**, as high priest to reassert central control of **Thebes**. *See also* KAROMAMA; MAATKARE.

HARWENNEFER (reigned c. 205–199 BC). The Greek form of his name is Haronnophris and was previously wrongly read as Harmachis. Rebel king during the reign of **Ptolemy V**. His rebellion was centered in the south, and he controlled the area from south of **Thebes** to north of **Abydos**, while the Ptolemaic government remained in control of **Elephantine** and the north. Thebes was retaken in 199 BC, when Harwennefer was succeeded in unknown circumstances by **Ankhwennefer**.

HATHOR. Egyptian goddess of sexual love and music. She was originally the mother of the sky god **Horus** and so mother of the king who was identified with Horus. She was later regarded as the daughter of **Re** and wife of Horus. She is depicted as a cow or human figure with the ears of a cow or wearing a crown with the horns of a cow. Her principal place of worship was **Dendera**, but she also had connections with such desert and foreign areas as **Serabit el-Khadim**, where she was worshipped as the lady of turquoise. She is also associated as a protective deity with the necropolis area of **Thebes**. *See also* RELIGION.

HATNUB. Site in the Eastern Desert used as a quarry for Egyptian alabaster from the **Early Dynastic Period** to the **Roman Period**. *See also* AKORIS; GEBEL EL-HARIDI; GEBEL EL-SILSILA; MONS CLAUDIANUS; MONS PORPHYRITES; SERABIT EL-KHADIM; WADI EL-HUDI; WADI MAGHARA; WADI HAMMAMAT.

HATSHEPSUT (reigned c. 1472–1458 BC). Throne name Makare. **Queen**-regnant of Egypt. She was the daughter of **Thutmose I** and Queen **Ahmose** and married her half brother, **Thutmose II**, by whom she had at least one daughter, **Nefrure**. Hatshepsut became regent for her stepson, **Thutmose III**, but she soon ascended the throne in her own right, although the date for this act is disputed. She claimed that she had been designated as heir to the throne by her father. Hatshepsut built her mortuary **temple** at **Deir el-Bahri** with scenes showing the great events of her reign, including an expedition to **Punt** and the erection of an **obelisk**. The work was supervised by her chief architect, **Senenmut**, whose relations with the queen have been the subject of much speculation.

Her reign ended after 21 years, presumably upon her death, and her stepson became sole ruler. Hatshepsut initially built her **tomb** as king's wife in the **Wadi Gabbanat al-Qurud**. Her **sarcophagus** from this tomb is now housed in the **Cairo Egyptian Museum**. She appears to have been buried with her father in a joint tomb (**KV20**) built later in the **Valley of the Kings**. Thutmose III later attempted to expunge all mention of his aunt, although he appears to have been on relatively good terms with her during her reign. Her **mummy** was identified in 2007 as one of two women found in **KV60**. *See also* NE-FRUBITY; WOMEN.

HATTUSILI III (fl. 1300–1237 BC). King of the **Hittites**. Youngest son of Mursili II and Gassuliyawiya. He served with his brother, **Muwattalli II**, and was granted an important viceroyalty in the northern part of the kingdom. He was with the Hittite forces in Syria at the time of the battle of **Kadesh** in which he may have fought. He fell out with his brother's successor, his nephew, **Urhi-Teshub**, and deposed him c. 1295 BC. He faced hostility from Egypt but negotiated a famous peace treaty in 1258 BC. His daughter, **Maathorneferure**, later married **Ramesses II** c. 1245 BC. Correspondence between the two monarchs has been found at the Hittite capital Hattusha. *See also* PUDUHEPA.

HAWARA. Modern name for the area in the **Fayum** where the **pyramid** complex of **Amenemhat III** of **Dynasty 12** was built. The remains of the mortuary **temple** were later identified by the Greeks as the Labyrinth. The area was excavated by **Flinders Petrie** from 1888–1889 and in 1911, when in a cemetery close to the complex he discovered pits from the **Roman Period** that contained many burials with finely painted **mummy portraits**. In 1955–1956, an Egyptian expedition uncovered the intact burial of Princess **Nefruptah**, daughter of the king. *See also* BACCHIAS; DEIR EL-NAQLUN; GUROB; HARAGEH; KARANIS; KOM KHELWA; KOM TALIT; LAHUN; LISHT; MEDINET MADI; SOKNOPAIOU NESOS; TEBTUNIS.

HEIRESS CONCEPT. A theory invented by Egyptologists whereby the right to the throne passed through a **woman** and thus necessitated brother–sister marriages by the ruler. The theory was based on the inscriptions of **Queen Hatshepsut** and the number of brother–sister marriages during early **Dynasty 18**. This concept has now been proven false, as succession passed through the male line. Many rulers chose not to marry their sisters, preferring commoners.

HEKANAKHTE (fl. 1950 BC). Landholder and priest at **Thebes** during the reign of **Senusret I**. He is known from his letters, which were discovered in 1921–1922 at **Deir el-Bahri**. These letters were written to his household while he was away in the north and give details about the practice of Egyptian **agriculture** and personal relations within his family.

HELIOPOLIS. Greek name for the Egyptian city of *Iunu*, capital of the 13th **Lower Egyptian nome** in the suburbs of present-day Cairo. Its main **temple** was dedicated to the creator god **Atum**, who was identified with the sun god **Re**, elevated to the chief god in Egypt beginning during **Dynasty 5**. Very little remains of the original city and temple apart from an **obelisk** of **Senusret I**. Many of the monuments appear to have been transported to decorate **Alexandria** during the **Ptolemaic Period** and **Roman Period**. Excavations were carried out by an Italian expedition in 1903, **Flinders Petrie** from 1911–1912, the University of Cairo from 1976–1981, and Egyptian inspectors since 1988.

HELWAN. Modern name for a site south of Cairo where a major cemetery of the **Early Dynastic Period** was excavated from 1942–1954 by Egyptian archaeologist Zaki Saad. Objects from **Dynasty 1** and **Dynasty 2**, including **pottery**, stone vessels, palettes, and jewelry, were recovered. An Australian expedition began work there again in 1997.

HEMAKA (fl. 2950 BC). High official of King **Den** of **Dynasty 1**. His large **tomb** (number 3035), excavated at **Saqqara**, has been ascribed to the king but is now generally accepted as that of his chancellor. It was discovered by Cecil Firth, a British archaeologist working for the Egyptian Antiquities Service in 1931, and was cleared by his successor, Walter B. Emery, in 1936.

HEMIUNU (fl. 2600-2560 BC). Egyptian prince of the **Old Kingdom**. Probably identified with a like-named son of **Nefermaat**. He served as **vizier** under **Khufu**. He was buried in a **mastaba tomb** at **Giza**. It is speculated that he may have been in charge of the construction of the Great **Pyramid**. A statue from his tomb is now housed in the Pelizaeus Museum in Hildesheim, Germany. *See also* AMENEMHAT I; APEREL; AY; IMHOTEP; INTEFYOKER; KAGEMNI; MERERUKA; PASER; PTAHHOTEP; PTAHSHEPSES; RAMESSES I; REKHMIRE.

HENHENET (fl. 2020 BC). A minor wife of **Mentuhotep II** of **Dynasty 11**. She was commemorated in a chapel and buried in a pit **tomb** at his funerary complex at **Deir el-Bahri** discovered during **Henri Edouard Naville**'s excavations at the site. Her **sarcophagus** is now housed in the **Metropolitan Museum of Art**. *See also* ASHAYET; KAWIT; KEMSIT; MYT; NEFRU; SADEH; TEM.

HENTTAWY (fl. 1270–1240 BC). A princess of **Dynasty 19**. Seventh daughter of **Ramesses II**. She was buried in **tomb QV73** in the **Valley of the Queens**. *See also* BINTANAT; HENUTMIRE; MAATHORNEFERURE; MERITAMUN; NEBETTAWY; NEFERTARI.

HENTTAWY. The name of several ladies related to the family of the **high priests of Amun** and the royal family during **Dynasty 21**. The most important seems to have been the wife of **Pinudjem** I and daughter of **Queen Tentamun**. The inscriptions concerning these women are not always precise, so their exact relationships are still uncertain.

HENUTMIRE (fl. 1275 BC). Royal princess and **queen** of **Dynasty 19**. She is probably a daughter of **Sety** I and appears on a statue with his wife, **Tuy**. She later married her brother, **Ramesses II**. She was buried in **QV75** in the **Valley of the Queens**. *See also* BINTANAT;

HENTTAWY; ISITNOFRET; MAATHORNEFERURE; MERITA-
MUN; NEBETTAWY; NEFERTARI.

HEQAIB (fl. 2240 BC). Military official and probable governor of **Elephantine** at the end of the **Old Kingdom**. His full name was
Pepinakht, also known as Heqaib, and he was buried at Qubbet el-
Hawa **(tomb** number 35) on the west bank of the **Nile** opposite the island of Elephantine. He appears to have played a leading role in Egyptian military activity in **Nubia** and was deified after his death. A shrine
was built in his honor by Sarenput I, governor of Elephantine, at the beginning of **Dynasty 12**. It was excavated in 1932 and 1946 by Egyptian archaeologists and yielded a large number of statues, **stelae**, and offering tables of kings and officials of **Dynasty 12** and **Dynasty 13**. The
shrine was abandoned during the **Second Intermediate Period**.

HERACLIUS (c. 575–641 AD). Byzantine emperor. Son of Heraclius,
the governor of Africa, of Armenian origin, and Epiphania. His father
organized a revolt against the usurper Phocas in 610, sending a
nephew, Nicetas, to secure Egypt while the younger Heraclius sailed
to Constantinople, where he was crowned emperor on 7 October 610.
The new emperor tried without success to reconcile the religious differences within the empire between the orthodox and Monophysite
beliefs. He had to fight and expel the Persians, who occupied Egypt
and other eastern provinces between 617 and 629, only to lose them
to the Arabs from 641–642. He died in Constantinople on 11 February 641. *See also* BENJAMIN; CYRUS.

HERAKLEOPOLIS. Greek name, more properly Herakleopolis
Magna, for the Egyptian site of *Nen-nesu*, modern Ihnasya el-
Medina in **Middle Egypt**. It became the capital of Egypt under **Dynasty 9** and **Dynasty 10**, until the overthrow of the last ruler by the
prince of **Thebes**. Its main **temple** was dedicated to the local god
Heryshef and enlarged by **Ramesses II**. The city was an important
military garrison during **Dynasty 22**, and a branch of the royal family was established there. Excavations were carried out by British archaeologists from 1890–1891 and 1903–1904 and more recently by
a Spanish expedition from 1966–1969, from 1976–1979, and since
1984, which has uncovered **tombs** of the royal family of Dynasty 22.

HERIHOR (fl. 1075 BC). High priest of Amun and military general of unknown but possibly Libyan origin at the end of **Dynasty 20**. It is not certain if he preceded or followed **Piankh** in office. He adopted the style of king at **Thebes**, using his title as high priest as his throne name, and was virtually an independent ruler in the south. His rule may not have ended peacefully, as his figure on one **stela** is defaced. He may have been the first of a line of independent Theban high priests.

HERMOPOLIS. Greek name, more properly Hermopolis Magna, for the ancient Egyptian *Khmunu*, modern el-Ashmunein, capital of the 15th **nome** of **Upper Egypt**. The site is virtually destroyed, but there are remains from the **Middle Kingdom** to the **Roman Period**. It has been excavated by expeditions from Italy in 1903, Germany from 1929–1939, the University of Alexandria during the late 1940s, various Egyptian inspectors, and more recently a **British Museum** expedition from 1980–1990. Many of the blocks from **Amarna** were reused in construction work here by **Ramesses II**. *See also* AKHENATEN; TALATAT.

HERODOTUS (c. 484–420 BC). Greek author from Halicarnassus. He visited Egypt during the course of his travels, and his *The Histories* (c. 440 BC) contains valuable information about Egyptian history and customs. Much of this information would have been supplied by Egyptian priests and is uneven in content. *See also* MANETHO.

HERYSHEF. Chief god of **Herakleopolis** whose Greek name was Arsaphes and who was identified with the Greek god Herakles. He is depicted as a ram-headed human figure. *See also* RELIGION.

HESIRE (fl. 2650 BC). A high official of **Dynasty 3**. His **tomb** at **Saqqara** yielded delicately carved wooden panels depicting the owner and his titles. The tomb was first discovered by **Auguste Mariette** and later recleared from 1911–1912.

HESUNEBEF (fl. 1210–1175 BC). Workman in the **Deir el-Medina** community during **Dynasty 19** and **Dynasty 20**. He is first attested as a **slave** boy of the foreman **Neferhotep**, who freed him and arranged a post for him as a workman. Neferhotep also obtained a bride for him from a community family. Hesunebef remained in the workforce after his patron's death, but the new foreman, **Paneb**, Neferhotep's adopted son, was later accused of adulterous relations with his wife and sexual misconduct with his daughter, who was then passed on to Paneb's son. The truth of this accusation is unclear, but Hesunebef and his wife divorced. During the reign of **Ramesses III**, Hesunebef rose to the post of deputy foreman. He remained loyal to the memory of his patron, naming his son after him and erecting a **stela** in his honor. *See also* KENHERKHEPESHEF; KHA; RAMOSE; SENNEDJEM.

HETEPHERES. The name of several princesses and **queens** of **Dynasty 4**. The most important was Hetepheres I, the wife of **Snefru** and mother of **Khufu**. Her intact burial missing a body was recovered at **Giza** by **George Reisner** during an expedition from 1925–1927. Hetepheres II was the daughter of Khufu, wife of her brother **Kawab**, and mother of **Meresankh** III.

HIBA, EL-. Modern name for the Egyptian *Teudjoi* and Greek Ankyronpolis. This location was an important military garrison during **Dynasty 21** and **Dynasty 22**. The cemetery of the **Roman Period** was excavated by British explorers in 1903, and **papyri** and **mummy portraits** were found. It was investigated by an American expedition in 1980 and again by a team from the University of California, Berkeley, beginning in 2001.

HIERAKONPOLIS. Greek name for the Egyptian city of *Nekhen*, modern Kom el-Ahmar on the west bank of the **Nile** opposite **Elkab**. The city was a major settlement during the **Predynastic Period** and **Early Dynastic Period** and probably the capital of the kings of **Upper Egypt** before the unification of the country. Important remains and objects from this period were discovered in Hierakonpolis during a British expedition from 1897–1899, including the famous **Narmer** Palette and the **Scorpion** Macehead. The main deity of the city was the falcon god **Horus**. The site continued to be occupied through the **Roman Period** and **Coptic** Period. Further excavation took place during an expedition by the University of Liverpool from

1905–1906, the Brooklyn Museum from 1907–1908, a British expedition in 1927, and the **Metropolitan Museum of Art** from 1934–1935. Work was resumed by an American expedition from 1967–1969 and since 1978.

HIERATIC. Modern term derived from the Greek word for the abbreviated form of writing the **hieroglyphic** script, which developed during the **Early Dynastic Period** and was used primarily on **papyri** and **ostraca** for correspondence and religious and literary texts. The earliest complete texts are the **Abusir Papyri** of **Dynasty 5**. The script fell out of use during the **Saite Period**, when it was largely replaced by **demotic**, but it persisted in use in religious texts until the **Roman Period**.

HIEROGLYPHIC. Modern term derived from the Greek word used to describe the standard form of Egyptian writing to express the Egyptian **language**. The earliest forms appear at the end of the **Predynastic Period** and the **Early Dynastic Period**, but the script does not become fully intelligible until the **Old Kingdom**. The writing consists of two types of signs: phonograms that represent single consonants or consonantal clusters (biliterals or triliterals) and ideograms that indicate the sense of the word, usually written at the end of the word to reinforce the meaning. The basic consonantal alphabet consists of 24 signs; vowels were not written. Hieroglyphic writing was soon replaced by **hieratic** for ordinary usage, and the hieroglyphic script was reserved for monumental work in stone or paint and for religious texts. The script was deciphered in modern times by **Jean-François Champollion**, building on the work of **Thomas Young**, with the help of bilingual texts such as the **Rosetta Stone**. The subsequent realization that **Coptic** was a later form of the same language immeasurably aided the understanding of ancient Egyptian texts. *See also* DEMOTIC.

HIGH PRIEST OF AMUN. The chief religious office in the **temple** of **Amun** at **Karnak** in **Thebes**. The office grew in importance and wealth with the elevation of Amun to the position of chief god of Egypt during **Dynasty 18** and the extensive endowments bestowed upon the temple by various rulers. The appointment of the high priest appears to have been carefully controlled by the ruler to avoid any conflict of power, and incumbents were often chosen not from the Theban clergy but from priesthoods in other cities or from court officials. The reforms of **Akhenaten** appeared in part designed to limit the influence of the priesthood of Amun.

During **Dynasty 20**, the office became more influential and hereditary in one family, resulting in a civil war in Thebes under **Ramesses XI**, whose generals, **Herihor** and **Piankh**, suppressed the high priest **Amenhotep** but took over his office and power. During **Dynasty 21**, the south was virtually independent under the family of high priests descended from Piankh. Under **Dynasty 22**, an attempt was made to control Thebes through the appointment of royal princes as high priests, but conflict soon arose, especially over the appointment of the high priest **Osorkon**. During **Dynasty 25**, the office was still held by royal descendants of the dynasty, but it appears to have been suppressed during **Dynasty 26**, when the titles were assumed by the **God's wife of Amun**. The office is again attested during the **Ptolemaic Period**, when it appears to have been primarily religious and shorn of political power. *See also* BAKENKHONS; IUPUT; NEBWENNEF; PASER; WENNEFER.

HIGH PRIEST OF PTAH. Chief religious office in the **temple** of **Ptah** at **Memphis**. The lack of documentation limits knowledge of the influence and power of this office. As administrator of the main temple of the second capital of Egypt, the high priest had great resources under his control, but any political power would have been limited by the proximity of the court, which resided in the north during the **New Kingdom**. There is no evidence of conflict, as is recorded in the case of the **high priest of Amun**. The officeholders included Prince **Khaemwese**, son of **Ramesses II**, and several princes during **Dynasty 22**, but also local priests allegedly of one family. An inscription listing many of the officeholders and the rulers they served is an important chronological tool in studying Egyptian history. The office took on new importance during the **Ptolemaic Period**, when the high priest served as the chief Egyptian religious official at the royal court, and many funerary inscriptions of the family survive. The office may have been suppressed by the Roman government, as only one high priest is attested after the conquest.

HITTITES. An Indo-European-speaking people who established a kingdom in central Anatolia, modern Turkey, which in the second millennium BC gradually built up an empire that included much of Anatolia and Syria. The Hittites helped destroy the kingdom of **Mitanni** and sought to inherit their overlordship in Syria, leading them into conflict with Egypt during the reign of **Akhenaten**. The Hittite king **Suppiluliuma I** managed to detach the Egyptian vassal kingdom of **Amurru** from Egyptian control. Upon the death of **Tutankhamun**, his widow, **Ankhesenamun**, sought a Hittite husband, but this plan proved abortive.

Sety I and Ramesses II sought to restore Egyptian control in Syria, but the Egyptians were driven back at the battle of **Kadesh** in 1274 BC. A peace treaty was eventually signed between the two powers in 1258 BC, whereby the border between the two empires in Syria was recognized with the loss of Amurru to the Hittites. Around 1245 BC, a marriage was arranged by Ramesses II with the daughter of the Hittite king, who was known in Egypt as **Maathorneferure**, and he later appears to have married a second daughter. Relations between the two powers remained friendly until the destruction of the Hittite kingdom around 1195 BC, probably as a result of the movement of the **Sea Peoples** perhaps aided by local tribesmen. *See also* HATTUSILI III; MUWATTALLI II; PUDUHEPA; URHI-TESHUB.

HOR (reigned c. 1760 BC). Throne name Awibre. Ruler of **Dynasty 13**. He was buried at **Dahshur**, where statues of the king have been recovered from his **tomb**, which was discovered in 1894. The nearby tomb shaft of the royal lady Nubheteptikhered may well be one of his female relations. *See also* SECOND INTERMEDIATE PERIOD.

HOREMHEB (reigned c. 1323–1295 BC). Throne name Djeserkheperure. Of unknown parentage from Henes. Possibly to be identified with Paatonemheb attested during the reign of **Akhenaten**, he was a military commander during the reign of **Tutankhamun**. He was married to **Mutnodjmet**, possibly a sister of **Nefertiti**. Horemheb conducted campaigns in **Nubia** and Palestine to restore Egyptian power and alongside **Ay** conducted affairs in the minority of Tutankhamun and helped organize the return to orthodoxy after the **Amarna Period**. His **tomb** at **Saqqara**, built when he was a commoner, was first seen in the 19th century and was rediscovered and excavated by an expedition of the **Egypt Exploration Society** from 1975–1980.

Horemheb succeeded to the throne upon the death of Ay and continued the policy of rebuilding Egypt at home and abroad and suppressed the names of his immediate predecessors since **Amenhotep III**. He died childless and appears to have arranged the succession of his **vizier**, **Ramesses I**, founder of **Dynasty 19**. He was buried in tomb **KV57** in the **Valley of the Kings**, but his **mummy** has not been recovered or identified. *See also* DYNASTY 18.

HORUS. Egyptian god. Horus was originally a sky god identified with the ruler during the **Early Dynastic Period** who bore a Horus name in a **serekh** as part of the royal **titulary**. In later legend, Horus became the son of **Osiris** and **Isis** and the legitimate ruler of Egypt upon his father's death. In his former aspect, he was worshipped as Haroeris or Horus the elder and in the latter as Harpocrates or Horus the child, often depicted as a youth with a sidelock protected by his mother. Horus was also identified with the sun god **Re** and was worshipped as Re-Harakhty. His sacred animal was the hawk, and his particular places of worship were at **Hierakonpolis** and **Edfu**. The *udjat*-cyc of Horus was considered a potent amulet. *See also* RELIGION.

HOTEPSEKHEMWY (reigned c. 2880 BC). First ruler of **Dynasty 2**. The reasons for his accession and the start of a new dynasty are unknown. His **tomb** appears to have been at **Saqqara**. *See also* RANEB.

HRERE (fl. 1075 BC). Wife of a **high priest of Amun** and mother of **Nodjmet** and an unnamed king. She may be the wife of **Piankh**, who wrote to her in his absence to carry out administrative duties in **Thebes**, but it has also been suggested that she may have been the wife of the high priest **Amenhotep**. It is not altogether clear whether there were one or two Hreres. *See also* HERIHOR.

HU. A site in **Upper Egypt** near **Nag Hammadi**. Graeco-Roman Diospolis Parva. Capital of the seventh **nome** of Upper Egypt. Remains have been found from the **Predynastic Period** to the **Graeco-Roman Period**. The main **temple** was dedicated to the goddess

Hathor. The site was excavated by **Flinders Petrie** from 1898–1899 and by an American expedition from 1989–1991.

HUNI (reigned c. 2638–2615 BC). Last ruler of **Dynasty 3**. He is often said to have been buried in the **pyramid** at **Meidum**, but this may well have been built for **Snefru** or completed by him. There is no basis for the contention that Snefru was his son since Snefru's mother does not have a queenly title. No reason is known for the change in dynasty.

HYKSOS. The Greek form of the Egyptian *Heka Khasut*, "ruler of foreign lands." This title was used by the Egyptians for the various Asiatic chieftains in Palestine and Syria. The later derivation of "shepherd kings" is erroneous. The Egyptians were always wary of Asiatic encroachment, and during **Dynasty 12 Amenemhat I** built a wall to exclude unwanted Asiatics. Nevertheless, some immigration was permitted as an Asiatic settlement grew up around **Avaris**, and Asiatic travelers are depicted at **Beni Hasan**. During the **Second Intermediate Period**, large numbers of Asiatics settled in Egypt and eventually took over most of the country, founding the Hyksos **Dynasty 15** and adopting many of the attributes of Egyptian rulers. **Thebes** apparently became a vassal state but ultimately rebelled and succeeded in capturing the Hyksos capital at Avaris and driving them from Egypt. *See also* APEPI; IANNAS; KHAYAN; SALITIS.

HYPATIA (d. 415 AD). Pagan martyr. Daughter of the mathematician Theon of **Alexandria**. She was educated in mathematics, astronomy, and philosophy and taught Neoplatonist philosophy in Alexandria. As a pagan, she was opposed by Christians in the city and was killed by a mob incited by fanatical monks. It is not clear if the murder had the approval of the patriarch **Cyril**.

– I –

IAH. Moon god of Egypt. He was popular at the beginning of **Dynasty 18** when such royal names as **Ahmose** and **Ahhotep** were composed from his name. He was later identified with **Khonsu**. *See also* RELIGION.

IANNAS (reigned c. 1590 BC). Greek name given by the Hebrew historian Josephus, who derived it from **Manetho** for one of the **Hyksos** kings of **Dynasty 15**. A **stela** fragment recently discovered at **Avaris** bears the **cartouches** of **Khayan** and names his eldest son, Ianassi, presumably to be identified with the future king. Nothing is known of his actual reign. *See also* APEPI; SALITIS.

IARET (fl. 1400 BC). Sister-**queen** of **Thutmose IV** and daughter of **Amenhotep II**. She appears on several monuments from her husband's reign. *See also* MUTEMWIA; NEFERTIRY.

IBI (reigned c. 2140 BC). Throne name Kakare. A minor ruler of **Dynasty 8**. Nothing is known of his reign, but he was buried in a **pyramid** at **Saqqara**, which was excavated in the 1930s. *See also* FIRST INTERMEDIATE PERIOD.

IMHOTEP (fl. 2660 BC). **Vizier** of **Djoser** of **Dynasty 3**. He is credited with devising the construction of the step **pyramid**, the first stone structure in Egypt. He had a reputation for wisdom and was deified after his death and worshipped as a minor deity. He is usually depicted as a seated **scribe** with an open **papyrus** on his lap. He was identified by the Greeks with Aesculapius, god of medicine. *See also* AMENEMHAT I; APEREL; AY; HEMIUNU; INTEFYOKER; KAGEMNI; MERERUKA; NEFERMAAT; PASER; PTAHHOTEP; PTAHSHEPSES; RAMESSES I; REKHMIRE.

IMSETY. *See* SONS OF HORUS.

INAROS (fl. 459–454 BC). Greek form of the Egyptian name Irethorru. Son of **Psamtik**, a local Egyptian dynast. Egyptian rebel against the rule of **Persia**. Allied with forces from Athens, he took **Memphis** and defeated and killed the **satrap Achaemenes** in 459 BC, but his army was later crushed by superior Persian troops. He was captured and taken to Persia, where he was executed. His son, Amyrtaeos, was said to have been reinstated in his father's possessions and may have been an ancestor of the later king **Amyrtaeos**. An inscription from **Kharga Oasis** mentions his rule.

INENI (fl. 1510–1470 BC). A high official at the beginning of **Dynasty 18**, serving in the reigns of **Amenhotep I, Thutmose I, Thutmose II**, and **Thutmose III** with the title of overseer of the granary of **Amun**. Son of the judge Ineni and the lady Sit-Djehuty. He was in charge of building works at **Karnak** for the first two rulers and supervised the construction of the royal **tomb** of Thutmose I in the **Valley of the Kings**. He was buried in a tomb (number 81) at **Thebes**, which contains a detailed biographical inscription.

INTEF (fl. 2150 BC). Governor of **Thebes** during the **First Intermediate Period**. Son of the lady Ikuy. He was worshipped as the ancestor of the later rulers of **Dynasty 11** and so was probably the father or ancestor of **Mentuhotep I**.

INTEF I (reigned c. 2125–2112 BC). First declared ruler of **Dynasty 11**. **Horus** name Sehertawy. Son of **Mentuhotep I**. At first governor of **Thebes**, he appears to have revolted against **Herakleopolis** and adopted the title of king, although he did not adopt the full royal **titulary**. He was buried in a rock-cut **tomb** on the west bank at Thebes.

INTEF II (reigned c. 2112–2063 BC). Successor to **Intef I** of **Dynasty 11**. **Horus** name Wahankh. Son of the lady **Nefru** and possibly **Mentuhotep I**, so likely the brother of his predecessor. He consolidated Theban control of **Upper Egypt**, capturing **Thinis**. He was buried in a rock-cut **tomb** on the west bank at **Thebes** where a funerary **stela** mentioning his pet dogs was set up. The stela is mentioned in a tomb robbery **papyrus** of **Dynasty 20**, and part of it was recovered by **Auguste Mariette** in excavations in 1860.

INTEF III (reigned c. 2063–2055 BC). Successor and presumably son of **Intef II** of **Dynasty 11** and the lady **Nefru**. **Horus** name Nakhtnebtepnefer. Little is known of his brief reign except that a famine occurred in the region of **Abydos**. He too was buried in a rock-cut **tomb** at **Thebes**. He married the lady Iah, by whom he had his son and successor, **Mentuhotep II**, who conquered the rest of Egypt and ended the **First Intermediate Period**.

INTEF IV (reigned c. 1740 BC). Throne name Sehetepkare. A minor king of **Dynasty 13.** A statue of his has been discovered in the **Fayum.**

INTEF V (reigned c. 1571–1566 BC). A king of **Dynasty 17.** Prenomen Nubkheperre. His position in the dynasty is unclear. He has hitherto been regarded as one of the earlier rulers, but in more recent research, it has been suggested that he may be a son of **Sobekemsaf** I and brother and successor of **Intef VI.** He is known from a large number of inscriptions at **Abydos, Coptos,** and **Thebes.** He was buried on the west bank at Thebes, and his **tomb** was mentioned in the **Tomb Robbery Papyri** as still intact. His coffin is now housed in the **British Museum.** His tomb was rediscovered and excavated by a German expedition from 2001–2002.

INTEF VI (reigned c. 1566 BC). Throne name Sekhemrewepmaat. A king of **Dynasty 17.** He has generally been regarded as a successor of **Intef V,** but more recently it has been suggested that he may be a son of **Sobekemsaf** I and brother and predecessor of Intef V. He was buried on the west bank at **Thebes,** and his **tomb** is mentioned in the **Tomb Robbery Papyri** as still intact. The **pyramidion** of his tomb in now housed in the **British Museum,** while his coffin is preserved in the **Louvre Museum.**

INTEF VII (reigned c. 1566 BC). A king of **Dynasty 17.** Prenomen Sekhemreherhermaat. His coffin is now housed in the **Louvre Museum.** He was possibly a **coregent** of **Intef VI.**

INTEFYOKER (fl. 1945–1950 BC). Vizier of **Amenemhat I** and **Senusret I** of **Dynasty 12.** He is attested in office toward the end of the reign of Amenemhat I and was presumably one of the most powerful officials of the period. He was buried in a **tomb** near the **pyramid** of Amenemhat I at **Lisht;** however, his family is cursed in the **execration texts,** so it is speculated that they eventually fell from power. *See also* APEREL; AY; HEMIUNU; IMHOTEP; KAGEMNI; MERERUKA; NEFERMAAT; PASER; PTAHHOTEP; PTAHSHEPSES; RAMESSES I; REKHMIRE.

IPUT. The name of two **queens** of **Dynasty 6**. Iput I appears to have been the wife of **Teti** and mother of **Pepy I** and was buried in a subsidiary **pyramid** next to that of Teti. Iput II was the wife of **Pepy II** and was buried in a subsidiary pyramid next to her husband's.

IPUWER. The ostensible author of a text of **wisdom literature** composed during the late **Middle Kingdom** that describes Egypt in a state of chaos. While this has been taken as a reference to a historical event, it is now regarded as simply a literary device.

IRETHORRU. *See* INAROS.

IRON. A metal rarely used in Egypt until the **Saite Period** that later became widespread during the **Roman Period**. Isolated examples are known from the **Old Kingdom** onward, but the most notable examples are an iron dagger, iron chisel heads, and amulets from the **tomb** of **Tutankhamun** of **Dynasty 18**. *See also* BRONZE; COPPER; GOLD; SILVER.

ISIS. Greek name of the major female deity of Egypt, Egyptian *Ast*. Daughter of **Geb** and **Nut** and consort of her brother, **Osiris**, mythological ruler of Egypt. Following the murder of her husband by their brother **Seth**, she assiduously collected the remains of Osiris and, according to one version, was impregnated by him after death, if not before. She fought tirelessly for the rights of her son, **Horus**, to succeed to Egypt in opposition to Seth. This contest is reflected in the bawdy tale *The Contendings of Horus and Seth*. The worship of Isis became particularly strong during the **Graeco-Roman Period**, when Osiris was displaced as her husband by the composite god **Sarapis**. Her cult spread throughout the Roman Empire, being particularly attractive to **women**. It was suppressed at the advent of Christianity. *See also* RELIGION.

ISIS (fl. 1485 BC). The name of a junior wife of **Thutmose II** who was the mother of his successor, **Thutmose III**. She is only attested during the reign of her son as the king's mother. Princess Isis is probably her granddaughter. *See also* HATSHEPSUT.

ISITNOFRET (fl. 1300–1245 BC). Junior wife and **queen** of **Ramesses II**. He married her at the same time as **Nefertari**, and she bore his eldest daughter, **Bintanat**, as well as three sons, his second, **Ramesses**, his fourth, **Khaemwese**, and his 13th, **Merenptah**. She appears to have succeeded Nefertari as chief queen but died before her husband and was replaced by Bintanat. The name was also borne by princesses of **Dynasty 19** and a later queen, wife of **Merenptah**, who may have been his niece, daughter of **Khaemwese**. *See also* HENUTMIRE; HENTTAWY; MAATHORNEFERURE; MERITA-MUN; NEBETTAWY.

ISMANT AL-KHARB. Ancient Kellis. A Roman town in the **Dakhla Oasis** that flourished from the 1st to the 4th centuries AD. The main **temple** of the site was dedicated to the local god Tutu. The area has been excavated by a joint Canadian and Australian team since 1986. Apart from the temple, houses have been uncovered that contained documents in Greek and **Coptic**, including many associated with the Manichean sect opposed to orthodox Christianity. *See also* MANICHEISM.

ISRAELITES. The people of the Old Testament Bible who founded the state of Israel in the former Egyptian province of Canaan. They are later known as the Hebrews (**Habiru**). Their origins are obscure, but modern archaeologists believe that they were the original inhabitants of the hill country in Canaan joined perhaps by other elements. According to Isrealite legend, they immigrated to Egypt and then escaped in the **Exodus**. They conquered most of Canaan apart from the coastal fringe held by the **Philistines**. This must have occurred after the withdrawal of the Egyptians in late **Dynasty 20**. The only reference to the Israelites in an Egyptian text is the inscription of **Merenptah** of **Dynasty 19**, where they are mentioned as a defeated tribe not yet a state.

The extant and importance of the state of Israel is much debated by many scholars regarding the Biblical account as unsupportable by archaeological discoveries. The area was eventually divided into two states, Judah in the north and Israel in the south. The former was conqured by the Assryrians. According to the Bible, the forces of **Nekau**

II defeated those of Josiah, king of Israel, when he invaded the area in support of **Assyria**. The state of Israel was later annexed by the Babylonians. *See also* JOSEPH.

ISTEMKHEB. The name of several princesses and members of the family of the **high priests of Amun** during **Dynasty 21**. The most important appears to have been a wife of the high priest **Pinudjem** I and a daughter of **Pasebakhaenniut I**, who married the high priest **Menkheperre**.

IULIUS ALEXANDER, TIBERIUS (c. 10–75 AD). Roman official. He was born in **Alexandria**, son of Alexander Lysimachus, head of the Jewish community. Alexander served as governor of Judaea (c. 46–48) and as **prefect** of Egypt, in which capacity he helped engineer the accession of **Vespasian**. He served on the staff of **Titus** during the siege of Jerusalem.

IULIUS CAESAR, CAIUS (100–44 BC). Roman dictator. Son of Caius Iulius Caesar and Aurelia. He had a successful political career culminating in the consulship of 59 BC. Caesar obtained an appointment as governor of Roman Gaul (then only covering modern Provence) and exhibited exceptional military skill in conquering the whole of Gaul (modern France and part of Belgium). Attacked by political opponents at home, he invaded Italy in 49 BC and was proclaimed dictator. Caesar defeated his rival, **Gnaeus Pompeius**, at Pharsalus and followed the latter's flight to Egypt, where he discovered that Pompeius had been murdered and Egypt was engulfed in civil war between **Ptolemy XIII** and his sister, **Cleopatra VII**. He sided with Cleopatra, who became his mistress, and following the defeat and death of Ptolemy, he installed her as ruler of Egypt alongside her younger brother, **Ptolemy XIV**. She claimed that Caesar was the father of her son, **Ptolemy XV**, known as Caesarion. Cleopatra was in Rome when Caesar was assassinated in 44 BC. *See also* ANTONIUS, MARCUS.

IUPUT. The name of two kings and a royal prince of **Dynasty 22** and **Dynasty 23**. Iuput (fl. 944–924), son of **Sheshonq I**, was installed as **high priest of Amun** to control **Thebes** on behalf of his father. Iuput I (reigned c. 805–783 BC) is attested as ruler in association with **Pe-**

dubast I of **Dynasty 23**, but nothing is known of him. Iuput II (reigned c. 731–720 BC) had the throne name Usimaatre setepenamun and the epithet meryamun sibast. He is attested as ruler of **Leontopolis** in the **stela** of **Piye**.

– J –

JOSEPH. Biblical hero, son of Jacob and Rachel, who was sold into **slavery** in Egypt and rose to the position of king's chief minister or **vizier**. He later welcomed his father and family to settle in Egypt. The story exhibits knowledge of Egyptian customs, but it is debatable whether Joseph represents a historical figure. The background of the story may refer to the period when the **Hyksos** had gained power in Egypt. *See also* EXODUS; ISRAELITES.

JUBILEE. This *heb-sed* festival or jubilee was usually performed in a king's 30th year and presumably consisted of rituals to rejuvenate him to continue his rule. It is possible that during prehistoric times the king may have been killed if he failed the ritual. Subsequent jubilees were performed at frequent intervals after year 30 until the death of the monarch.

JUSTINIAN (482–565 AD). Byzantine emperor. He was born as Petrus Sabbatius, son of Sabbatius in Tauresium 482. He was adopted by his maternal uncle, Emperor Justin I, and made coemperor in 527, succeeding to sole rule later in the year. He sought to expand the empire regaining Italy, North Africa, and parts of Spain. He also undetook the codification of the laws of the empire. He was a staunch adherent to the orthodox faith and unsympathetic to the **Coptic church**. He encouraged orthodox missionaries in **Nubia** and closed the **temple** of **Philae**, ending paganism in Egypt. He died in Constantinople on 14 November 565. *See also* THEODORA.

– K –

KADESH. An important city-state, now located in Syria; modern Tell Nebi Mend. The city became part of the Egyptian empire during

Dynasty 18. Its prince rebelled against **Thutmose III** but was forced to submit after the battle of **Megiddo**. The city later fell under **Hittite** control during the reign of **Suppiluliuma I**. It may have been briefly regained by **Sety I**. Around 1274 BC, **Ramesses II** sought to regain the lost Egyptian territory, but his forces were ambushed outside Kadesh by the Hittite army. Although his army was severely mauled, the Egyptian king managed to hold the Hittites back from his camp and avoid capture. The battle itself ended in stalemate, but the campaign was lost, and the Egyptians were forced to retreat.

Upon his return to Egypt, Ramesses II had an account of the battle written and inscribed on **temple** walls to glorify his personal bravery despite the unfortunate outcome of the campaign. The Hittites more succinctly recorded an Egyptian defeat, and the northern part of the Egyptian empire in Syria, notably **Amurru**, remained in Hittite hands. *See also* WARFARE.

KAFR HASSAN DAOUD. Modern name for a cemetery site on the eastern edge of the Delta of **Lower Egypt** in the **Wadi Tumilat**. The area was surveyed in 1983, and remains were identified from the **Predynastic Period** to the **Graeco-Roman Period**. Kafr Hassan Daoud was excavated by an Egyptian expedition from 1988–1995 and since 1995 by a British-Egyptian expedition, which has uncovered more than 1,000 graves from the Predynastic Period (**Naqada** II) to the **Early Dynastic Period**. These burial places contain **pottery** and stone vessels, and the names of the kings **Narmer** and **Qaa** have been identified. *See also* ADAIMA; GERZEH; MINSHAT ABU OMAR; TELL EL-FARKHA; TELL IBRAHIM AWAD.

KAGEMNI (fl. 2613 BC). Legendary **vizier** of **Huni** of **Dynasty 3** and **Snefru** of **Dynasty 4**. He was the recipient of a text of **wisdom literature** that has only survived in fragments and was undoubtedly composed at a later date. A historical vizier of this name is known from the reign of **Teti** of **Dynasty 6** and may have served as a model for the literary text. His **tomb** was discovered in 1893 and more fully excavated during the 1920s. *See also* AMENEMHAT I; APEREL; AY; HEMIUNU; IMHOTEP; INTEFYOKER; MERERUKA; NEFERMAAT; PASER; PTAHHOTEP; PTAHSHEPSES; RAMESSES I; REKHMIRE.

KAHUN. *See* LAHUN.

KALABSHA. Modern name for the site in **Nubia** 50 kilometres south of **Elephantine** (Aswan) on the west bank of the **Nile**; Greek Talmis. There stood a **temple** rebuilt under **Augustus** dedicated to the Nubian god Mandulis. The area was flooded by Lake Nasser, the lake formed by the Aswan High Dam, but the temple was moved to a safer location from 1961–1963. During the course of this work, a gateway of the **Graeco-Roman Period** was discovered, which is now housed in the **Berlin Egyptian Museum**. *See also* ABU SIMBEL; AMADA; BEIT EL-WALI; GERF HUSSEIN; SOLEB.

KAMOSE (reigned c. 1555–1552 BC). Throne name Wadjkheperre. Last ruler of **Dynasty 17** and prince of **Thebes**. He succeeded Seqenenre **Tao**, who may have been his father, and continued the war against the **Hyksos**. Kamose campaigned up to the walls of the Hyksos capital **Avaris** and also in **Nubia**. A **stela** giving details of his campaign was found at **Karnak**. His fate is unknown, but he was followed by **Ahmose I**, possibly his brother, who expelled the Hyksos from Egypt. *See also* AHHOTEP.

KARANIS. Modern Kom Aushim. A town during the **Graeco-Roman Period** in the Arsinoite **nome** of the **Fayum**. It flourished from the **Ptolemaic Period** until the 5th century AD. It was excavated by an expedition from the University of Michigan from 1924–1935 and found in an excellent state of preservation. Approximately 5,000 inscribed documents were recovered that illustrate life in Karanis, mainly in the 2nd and 3rd centuries AD. *See also* BACCHIAS; DEIR EL-NAQLUN; GUROB; HARAGEH; HAWARA; KOM KHELWA; KOM TALIT; LAHUN; LISHT; MEDINET MADI; SOKNOPAIOU NESOS; TEBTUNIS.

KARNAK. The main **temple** of the god **Amun** at **Thebes** known in Egyptian as *Iput-sut*. The temple was known during the **Middle Kingdom** and was enlarged and embellished by successive rulers of the **New Kingdom**. Its great wealth led to an increase of political power for the **high priest of Amun**, under whom Thebes became virtually independent during the **Third Intermediate Period**. The temple was sacked by the **Assyrians** in 663 BC, and although it was restored during the **Ptolemaic Period**, it never regained prominence. The site has been extensively excavated beginning in the 20th century and is currently being restored by the Centre Franco-Égyptien. More recent expeditions include the work of the Brooklyn Museum at the subsidiary temple of **Mut** since 1976.

KAROMAMA. Variants Karoma, Kamama. The name of several **queens** and princesses of **Dynasty 22** and **Dynasty 23**, the first of which was the wife of **Sheshonq I** and mother of his heir, **Osorkon I**. A second was the wife of **Osorkon II**. Another queen, Karomama, was the daughter of **Osorkon II**'s Prince **Nimlot**, wife of **Takelot II**, and mother of the **high priest of Amun Osorkon**. The mother of **Osorkon III** was also named Kamama, probably a form of the name. A **bronze** statue, inlaid with **gold**, **silver**, and electrum, of the God's Wife **Karomama** is now housed in the **Louvre Museum**.

KASHTA (fl. c. 750 BC). Nubian ruler. He appears to have gained control over the **Theban** region at the end of **Dynasty 23** and installed his daughter, **Amenirdis**, as the adopted daughter and heiress of the **God's wife of Amun**. *See also* ALARA.

KAWAB (fl. 2580 BC). Son of **Khufu** of **Dynasty 4** and possibly **Meritetes**. He was apparently Khufu's eldest son and destined successor, but he died before his father and was buried in a **mastaba** near Khufu's **pyramid** at **Giza**. His widow, **Hetepheres** II, then married his brother, **Khafre**.

KAWIT (fl. 2020 BC). A minor wife of **Mentuhotep II** of **Dynasty 11**. She was commemorated in a chapel and buried in a pit **tomb** at Mentuhotep's funerary complex at **Deir el-Bahri** discovered during **Henri Edouard Naville**'s excavations at the site. Her **sarcophagus** is now housed in the **Cairo Egyptian Museum**. *See also* ASHAYET; HENHENET; KEMSIT; MYT; NEFRU; SADEH; TEM.

KEFTYU. A foreign people named in Egyptian accounts mostly during **Dynasty 18** and depicted in certain **tomb** paintings with local produce. These depictions leave little doubt that they are Minoans from Crete, and the existence of Minoans in Egypt is confirmed by the discovery of Minoan **pottery** at Egyptian sites from the **Middle Kingdom**. Egyptian stone vessels found in Crete indicate a trading relationship beginning in the **Early Dynastic Period**. An inscription from the reign of **Amenhotep III** names several cities of the Keftyu, notably Knossos, but it is unclear whether the reference is contemporary or based on earlier records. Recent discoveries of Minoan frescoes at **Avaris** confirm the presence of Minoan traders or artists in Egypt beginning in the late **Second Intermediate Period** or early Dynasty 18. *See also* TRADE.

KEMSIT (fl. 2020 BC). A minor wife of **Mentuhotep II** of **Dynasty 11**. She was commemorated in a chapel and buried in a pit **tomb** at Mentuhotep's funerary complex at **Deir el-Bahri** discovered during **Henri Edouard Naville**'s excavations at the site. Fragments of her chapel and **sarcophagus** are now housed in the **British Museum**. *See also* ASHAYET; HENHENET; KAWIT; MYT; NEFRU; SADEH; TEM.

KENHERKHEPESHEF (fl. 1270–1200 BC). Chief **scribe** of the **Deir el-Medina** community from the middle of the reign of **Ramesses II** until **Sety II**. Son of Panakht and Sentnefer. He appears to have been adopted by the scribe **Ramose** and succeeded him in his office. He is known as a collector of historical and religious manuscripts, including an account of the Battle of **Kadesh** written in his own hand and a dream book giving interpretations of dreams. His interest in previous rulers is attested by a brief **king list**, also in his own hand. His **tomb** has not been discovered, and he appears to have died childless. He was survived upon his death by his widow, Naunakhte, who must have been several decades younger than him as she remarried the workman Khaemnun and had eight children. She survived until the reign of **Ramesses V** when her will was written. She apparently inherited the papers of her first husband, which were passed on to her sons by the second marriage. They added to the archive, notably with the literary text *The Contendings of Horus and Seth*. The archive was uncovered in the 1920s and is preserved in several museums. *See also* HESUNEBEF; KHA; PANEB; RAMOSE; SENNEDJEM.

KERMA. Site of a major city in **Nubia** near the Third **Cataract** and apparent capital of the Nubian kingdom, Kush, founded by a population related to the **C-group** people from the **Old Kingdom**, which was especially prominent during the **Second Intermediate Period** when an alliance was attempted with the **Hyksos** against the rulers of **Thebes** of **Dynasty 17**. The kingdom of Kush was regarded as a major threat by the Egyptians and was destroyed in a series of campaigns at the beginning of **Dynasty 18**, after which the area was incorporated as a province of Egypt. The site is dominated by two large brick constructions known as the Upper Deffufa and the Lower Deffufa of uncertain usage. The area was excavated by **George Reisner** from 1913–1916 for the **Boston Museum of Fine Arts** and more recently by a Swiss expedition under Charles Bonnet.

KHA (fl. 1390 BC). Foreman in the community of **Deir el-Medina** during **Dynasty 18**, probably during the reign of **Thutmose IV** and **Amenhotep III**. He is known from his undecorated **tomb** that was discovered with its contents still intact by an Italian expedition in 1906. The **mummies** of Kha and his wife, Meret, together with the coffins and other objects from the tomb, are now preserved in the **Turin Egyptian Museum**.

KHABA (reigned c. 2648–2640 BC). **Horus** name of an obscure king of **Dynasty 3**. He apparently was the builder of the unfinished **pyramid** located at **Zawiyet el-Aryan**.

KHABABASH (reigned c. 338–337 BC). Egyptian ruler who is attested on several documents, including an inscription on the **sarcophagus** of an **Apis** bull of his second year. He appears to have held office during the later Persian Period as a rebel against their rule, but his origin and exact date are not known.

KHAEMWESE (fl. c. 1285–1230 BC). Fourth son of **Ramesses II** by **Isitnofret**. He was appointed to the priesthood of **Ptah** and eventually reached the position of **high priest of Ptah** at **Memphis** and briefly served as crown prince before predeceasing his father. He may have been buried in the **Serapeum**. Khaemwese undertook restoration works of older monuments, including the **pyramids** at

Abusir and **Saqqara**. In later **literature**, he is portrayed as a learned but not necessarily wise magician. A like-named son of **Ramesses III**, who died young, is known from his **tomb** (**QV44**) in the **Valley of the Queens**. *See also* AMENHERKHEPESHEF; MERENPTAH; MERYATUM; PREHERWENEMEF; SETY.

KHAFRE (reigned c. 2558–2532 BC). His name might be read as Rakhaef and was known in Greek as Chephren. Son of **Khufu** of **Dynasty 4**. He succeeded his brother, **Djedefre**. For his burial, he moved back to the site at **Giza** and erected the second **pyramid** at that site close to that of his father. His valley **temple** was excavated in 1860 and yielded much fine sculpture. It is believed that his architects fashioned the **Sphinx** after his likeness from a rocky outcrop near his pyramid. *See also* HARDJEDEF; MENKAURE.

KHAKHEPERRESENEB. The ostensible author of a text of **wisdom literature** composed during the **Middle Kingdom** that consists of a series of complaints about the state of Egypt.

KHAMERERNEBTY. The name of two **queens**, mother and daughter, of **Dynasty 4**. It is generally thought that the elder married **Khafre** and that their daughter then became the wife of **Menkaure**, but formal proof is lacking, although it seems likely that the elder was the mother of Menkaure. The younger was buried in a **tomb** at **Giza** in the cemetery near the **pyramid** of Khafre originally designed for her mother.

KHARGA OASIS. Possibly Ancient Egyptian *Wehat resyt*, meaning southern oasis. An oasis in the Western Desert west of **Luxor**. Prehistoric remains have been discovered there, but evidence from the Pharaonic Period is lacking. The surviving archaeological sites date from the **Graeco-Roman Period** and **Byzantine Period**, apart from the **temple** at Hibis, which was begun during the Persian Period. The area was excavated by an expedition from the **Metropolitan Museum of Art** from 1907–1909, 1927–1928, and 1930–1931. These were followed by French expeditions, notably beginning in 1976 at the site of Dush, a Roman settlement abandoned during the 5th century AD; since 1993 at Ayn Manawir, which dates from the **Late**

Period to the **Graeco-Roman Period**; and since 1998 at El-Deir. *See also* BAHARIYA OASIS; DAKHLA OASIS; FARFARA OASIS; SIWA OASIS.

KHASEKHEMWY (reigned c. 2710 BC). Final ruler of **Dynasty 2**. Probably identical with a King Khasekhem attested on contemporary monuments. He appears to have ended the religious conflict between the supporters of **Horus** and **Seth** by adopting both gods as part of the **serekh** of the royal **titulary**. His statues found at **Hierakonpolis** represent the king as victorious over northern enemies in **Lower Egypt**. He built an elaborate **tomb** at **Abydos** and a massive palace structure that may have served as a mortuary **temple**.

KHAYAN (reigned c. 1600 BC). Throne name Sewoserenre. **Hyksos** ruler of **Dynasty 15**. Monuments of his have been found in Crete and Baghdad, but it is uncertain when they were removed from Egypt. The discovery of Cretan frescoes at his capital, **Avaris**, strengthens the idea of direct relations between Crete and Egypt at the time. A **stela** names his eldest son and presumed successor, **Iannas**. *See also* APEPI; SALITIS.

KHENDJER (reigned c. 1750 BC). Throne name Userkare. A ruler of **Dynasty 13**. He is known principally for his **pyramid tomb**, which was built at **Saqqara** and excavated by Gustave Jécquier from 1929–1931. *See also* SECOND INTERMEDIATE PERIOD.

KHENEMET-NEFER-HEDJET. The name of a princess and two **queens** of **Dynasty 12**. The princess was a daughter of **Amenemhat II**, but her fate is unknown, although she might be identical with Queen Khenemet-nefer-hedjet the elder. Queen Khenemet-nefer-hedjet the elder was the chief wife of **Senusret II** and mother of **Senusret III**, while Khenemet-nefer-hedjet the younger was the wife of Senusret III. The parentage of either queen is uncertain. The name was later used as a royal title for the queen.

KHENETHAP (fl. 3080). Queen of Egypt. Wife of **Aha** of **Dynasty 1** and mother of **Djer**. She may be the earliest attested queen in Egypt, but the position of **Neithhotep** is uncertain.

KHENTIKHA (fl. 2225 BC). Governor of **Dakhla Oasis** under **Pepy II** of **Dynasty 6**. Son of Ima-Pepy II, a previous governor. His **tomb** is the most impressive in the series of official tombs. He is also credited with the building of the governor's palace at **Balat**.

KHENTKAUES. The name of two **queen** mothers of **Dynasty 5**. Khentkaues I was buried at **Giza**, where her **tomb** was excavated in 1932, while the tomb of Khentkaues II was excavated at **Abusir** from 1978–1981. The theory that Khentkaues I was a princess of **Dynasty 4** who linked the two dynasties has been abandoned since she is nowhere styled the daughter of a king. She was the mother or wife of **Userkaf** or **Sahure**, while Khentkaues II was the wife of **Neferirkare** and mother of **Raneferef** and **Niuserre**. It seems that both may have been mothers of two kings and played important political roles, possibly as regents for a minor king or during a disputed succession. *See also* ABUSIR PAPYRI.

KHEPRI. An Egyptian deity in the form of a **scarab**-headed figure. He was an aspect of the sun god at dawn and often identified with the god **Atum** and so associated with resurrection. *See also* ATEN; RE; RELIGION.

KHETY. The name of several kings of **Dynasty 9** and **Dynasty 10** based in **Herakleopolis**. Their reigns are obscure, and little documentation survives from the period.

KHETY (fl. 1960 BC). Author and sage who lived during **Dynasty 12**. He was the author of *The Satire on Trades*, a popular composition extolling the profession of the **scribe** and denigrating others. He may also have composed *The Instructions of King Amenemhat I*, which was assigned to the king.

KHNUM. The ram-headed creator god of **Elephantine**. He was believed to fashion the souls of the living on his potter's wheel and so was also a patron of potters. He was associated with the goddesses **Anukis** and **Satis**. *See also* RELIGION.

KHNUMHOTEP I (fl. 1985–1945 BC). Nomarch of the 16th **Upper Egyptian nome** and governor of the Eastern Desert. He was a contemporary of **Amenemhat I** of **Dynasty 12**, who confirmed him in office, and **Senusret I**. He took part in military expeditions to **Nubia** and against the Asiatics. His **tomb** with biographical texts is located at **Beni Hasan** in **Middle Egypt**.

KHNUMHOTEP II (fl. 1910–1874 BC). Nomarch of the 16th **Upper Egyptian nome** and governor of the Eastern Desert. Son of Nehri and Baqet, daughter of **Khnumhotep I**. He was a contemporary of **Amenemhat II** and **Senusret II**. He maintained the family's power in **Middle Egypt**. His **tomb**, which depicts a famous scene of the arrival of Asiatic nomads, with biographical texts is located at **Beni Hasan**.

KHONSU. Moon god. His principal place of worship was **Thebes**, where he was regarded as a son of **Amun** and his consort, **Mut**. He is attested from the **Old Kingdom** but gained greater prominence during the **New Kingdom** with the growth of the cult of Amun. He had a separate **temple** within the **Karnak** complex. He is depicted as a human or hawk-headed deity with a lunar crescent. His cult continued during the **Graeco-Roman Period**, and at **Kom Ombo** he was worshipped as a son of **Sobek** and **Hathor**. *See also* IAH; RELIGION.

KHUFU (reigned c. 2592–2566 BC). The Greek form of his name is Cheops. Second king of **Dynasty 4**, son of **Snefru** and **Hetepheres I**. The Great **Pyramid** at **Giza** was built during his reign as his **tomb**, surrounded by the **mastaba** tombs of his family and officials, including his vizier, **Hemiunu**. Little is known about his reign, but he was remembered in later times as a harsh ruler. According to the **Turin Royal Canon**, he reigned for 23 years, but an inscription, apparently of his year 27, has recently been discovered. *See also* BAUEFRE; DJEDEFRE; HARDJEDEF; KAWAB; KHAFRE; MERITETES.

KING LISTS. Lists of kings and their reign lengths seem to have been kept in early dynastic times for religious and chronological use. No complete list has survived, but the **Turin Royal Canon** written during the **Ramesside Period** is the most complete record with many exact reign lengths. Other offering lists to deceased kings appear in **tombs** and **temples**. One difficulty with these lists lies in the fact that some rulers reigned contemporaneously as **coregents** or rivals, which is rarely indicated. *See also* CHRONOLOGY; MANETHO.

KIYA (fl. 1340 BC). Secondary wife of **Akhenaten**, of unknown origin. There has been much speculation about her background and possible children, but nothing is known about her except her name, which is found erased on many monuments. *See also* NEFERTITI.

KOM ABU BILLO. Modern name for a site in the third **nome** of **Lower Egypt** on the western edge of the Delta; Greek Terenuthis, possibly ancient Egyptian *Perhathornebetmefkat*. The principal deity of the town may have originally been **Hathor** and later the snake goddess **Renenutet**. The necropolis dates from the **Old Kingdom** but has yielded many **stelae** from the **Roman Period** that depict the deceased in Greek costume either standing with arms raised or reclining on a couch often associated with such Egyptian gods as **Anubis** or **Horus**, sometimes with texts in Greek. The area was first excavated on behalf of the **Egypt Exploration Fund** from 1887–1888 when remains of a Ptolemaic **temple** were discovered. Further excavations were carried out by the University of Michigan in 1935 and the Egyptian Antiquities Service from 1970–1971.

KOM AL-KHILGAN. Modern name for a site in the northeastern Delta of **Lower Egypt** near **Tell el-Farkha** and **Minshat Abu Omar**. The remains date from the **Predynastic Period** to the **Second Intermediate Period**. It has been excavated since 2002 by a joint French–Egyptian team.

KOM EL-AHMAR SAWARIS. Possibly ancient *Hut-nesut*, capital of the 18th **nome** of **Upper Egypt**. The site near modern Sharuna dates from the **Old Kingdom** to the **Coptic** Period and features Old Kingdom **tombs**, notably one of Pepiankh of **Dynasty 6** and the remains of a Ptolemaic **temple** from the **Graeco-Roman Period**. It was excavated by a Polish team in 1907, Egyptian archaeologists in 1976 and 1980, and a German expedition from 1984–1989.

KOM EL-HISN. The modern name for a site in the western Delta south of **Naukratis**, ancient *Imu*. Remains have been found from the **Old Kingdom** to the **Roman Period**. The main **temple** was dedicated to the dual goddess **Sakhmet-Hathor**. It became the capital of the third **nome** of **Lower Egypt** during the **New Kingdom**. Kom el-Hisn was first surveyed in 1885 and again in 1980, and excavations were carried out by an Egyptian expedition from 1943–1946, an American team in 1984 and 1986, and an Egyptian expedition from the University of Alexandria, Damanhur branch beginning in 2001.

KOM FIRIN. Modern name for a settlement site in the western Delta of **Lower Egypt** whose surviving remains date from the **New Kingdom** to the **Late Period**. At least one **temple** with inscriptions of **Ramesses II** have been identified. The site was excavated by the Egyptian Antiquities Service in 1911 and from 1949–1951 and has been the subject of a survey and excavations by a British team since 2002.

KOM KHELWA. Modern name for a site in the northwest **Fayum** near **Medinet Madi**. It is the site of a **Middle Kingdom** cemetery that includes the **tomb** of **Wadjet**, governor of the Fayum during **Dynasty 12**. It was surveyed by an Italian expedition in 1981 and excavations commenced in 1991. *See also* BACCHIAS; DEIR EL-NAQLUN; GUROB; HARAGEH; HAWARA; KARANIS; KOM TALIT; LAHUN; LISHT; MEDINET MADI; SOKNOPAIOU NESOS; TEBTUNIS.

KOM OMBO. The modern name for a site on the east bank of the **Nile** in the first **nome** of southern **Upper Egypt**, ancient Egyptian *Nebit*, Greek Ombos. The principal surviving monument consists of a **temple** from the **Ptolemaic Period** dedicated to the gods **Sobek** and **Horus** in the form of Haroeris and their respective wives and sons. The temple was cleared by the Egyptian Antiquities Service in 1893 and is being published by a French expedition. The nearby town has not been excavated. *See also* DENDERA; EDFU; ESNA.

KOM TALIT. Ancient Talit, a Graeco-Roman site in the **Fayum**, now largely destroyed. It once featured a temple to **Taweret**. The area was surveyed by a Britsh expedition in 1995. *See also* BACCHIAS; DEIR EL-NAQLUN; GUROB; HARAGEH; HAWARA; KARANIS; KOM KHELWA; LAHUN; LISHT; MEDINET MADI; SOKNOPAIOU NESOS; TEBTUNIS.

KOPTOS. *See* COPTOS.

KUMMA. Modern name for a site in lower **Nubia** in the Second **Cataract** region where a fortress was erected during **Dynasty 12**, probably by **Senusret III**, as part of the Egyptian garrison. Egyptian *Itnw Pedjut*. The area has now been flooded by Lake Nasser, the lake of the Aswan High Dam. *See also* ANIBA; ASKUT; BUHEN; MIRGISSA; SEMNA; SHALFAK; URONARTI.

KV. An abbreviation used by Egyptologists to denote the **Valley of the Kings** on the west bank of the Nile opposite **Thebes**. Sometimes the further abbreviation of WV is used to denote the west valley of the burial ground. The numbering of the **tombs** was begun by **John Gardner Wilkinson**. Some pit tombs and tentative constructions have not been numbered. Most of the tombs had been plundered in antiquity, although the royal tomb of **Tutankhamun** and several pri vate tombs have been found intact. The royal tombs of **Dynasty 18** were decorated by painted plaster, but from **Horemheb** onward the tombs were carved in raised relief and then painted. *See also* DEIR EL-MEDINA.

KV1. The **tomb** of **Ramesses VII** of **Dynasty 20** in the **Valley of the Kings**. It has stood open since antiquity and was noted by traveler **Richard Pococke** during his visit to the valley in 1738. The tomb was cleared by Edwin Brock during the 1980s and 1990s. The king's **mummy** remains unidentified.

KV2. The **tomb** of **Ramesses IV** of **Dynasty 20** in the **Valley of the Kings**. It has stood open since antiquity and was noted by traveler **Richard Pococke** during his visit to the valley in 1738. A sketch plan of the tomb has survived on a **papyrus** in **Turin Egyptian Museum** and on an **ostracon**. The **mummy** of the king was found in the **royal cache** in **KV35** in 1898.

KV3. An unfinished **tomb** in the **Valley of the Kings** dated by a **cartouche** to the time of **Ramesses III**. It was seen by James Burton in the early 19th century and cleared by Harry Burton in 1912. It is not certain if it was originally intended for the king and then abandoned or was for one of his children.

KV4. The **tomb** of **Ramesses XI** of **Dynasty 20** in the **Valley of the Kings**. It has stood open since antiquity and was cleared by an American expedition in 1979, when **foundation deposits** were discovered. It was the last royal tomb built in the valley and was never used by the king, who was buried in the north.

KV5. The **tomb** of the children of **Ramesses II** of **Dynasty 19** in the **Valley of the Kings**. It may have been seen by the traveler **Richard Pococke** during his visit to the valley in 1738 but was first firmly recorded by James Burton in 1825, although not cleared. American archaeologist Kent Weeks began clearance in 1987 and found evidence of the burial of the sons of Ramesses II, including inscriptions of **Ameherkhepeshef, Ramesses, Sety,** and **Meryatum**. The design of the tomb is unique, with more than 150 rooms, including chapels for the various sons. It is undoubtedly the tomb of the royal children mentioned on a **papyrus** now in the **Turin Egyptian Museum.**

KV6. The **tomb** of **Ramesses IX** of **Dynasty 20** in the **Valley of the Kings**. It has stood open since antiquity. It was examined by British consul **Henry Salt**, and a number of objects were recovered, which are now housed in the **British Musuem**. It was further cleared by Georges Daressy in 1888. A plan of the tomb can be found on an **ostracon** in the **Cairo Egyptian Museum**. The king's **mummy** was discovered in the **royal cache** at **Deir el-Bahri**.

KV7. The **tomb** of **Ramesses II** of **Dynasty 19** in the **Valley of the Kings**. It has stood open since antiquity but has been badly damaged by flooding. It has not been throughly excavated until recently, but it was investigated by a French expedition beginning in 1991. The king's **mummy** was found in the **royal cache** at **Deir el-Bahri** in 1881.

KV8. The **tomb** of **Merenptah** of **Dynasty 19** in the **Valley of the Kings**. It has been stood open since antiquity. It was seen by traveler **Richard Pococke** during his visit to the valley in 1738. It was cleared by **Howard Carter** in 1903 and Edwin Brock from 1987–1988 and 1994–1995. A French expedition has been working in the tomb since 2002. The king's **mummy** was discovered in **KV35** in 1898. One of the king's stone **sarcophagi** was reused for the burial of King **Pasebakhaenniut I** at **Tanis**.

KV9. The **tomb** of **Ramesses VI** of **Dynasty 20** in the **Valley of the Kings**. It was known as the tomb of Memnon and has stood open since antiquity. It was seen by traveler **Richard Pococke** during his visit to the valley in 1738. It was cleared by James Burton in the 1820s and Georges Daressy in 1888 and later examined by Edwin Brock beginning in 1985. The first chambers are inscribed for **Ramesses V**, and it is probable that the tomb was originally intended for him and usurped by his successor. It is unlikely that a double burial was intended. The **mummies** of both kings were found in the **royal cache** in **KV35**. The head of a **sarcophagus** lid found there is now housed in the **British Museum**.

KV10. The **tomb** of **Amenmesse** of **Dynasty 20** in the **Valley of the Kings**. It has stood open since antiquity. It was noted by traveler **Richard Pococke** during his visit to the valley in 1738. It was cleared by Edward Ayrton in 1907 and has been investigated by American archaeologist Otto Schaden since 1993. The tomb has yielded objects mentioning **Queen Takhat**, who may be Amenmesse's mother. The king's **mummy** has not been recovered.

KV11. The **tomb** of **Ramesses III** of **Dynasty 20** in the **Valley of the Kings**. It has stood open since antiquity. The tomb was originally intended for **Sethnakhte** but was abandoned when it broke into **KV10**. The builders for Ramesses III realigned the axis of the tomb to complete it for the king. It was seen by traveler **James Bruce** in 1768, and he later printed an engraving of the scene of the harper, the first scene from the royal tombs to be published. Since then it has also been known as Bruce's tomb. The tomb was entered by **Giovanni**

Battista Belzoni in 1816, when he removed the **sarcophagus**. Its lid is now in the Fitzwilliam Museum in Cambridge, and the lower part is in the **Louvre Museum**. The king's **mummy** was found in the **royal cache** at **Deir el-Bahri** in 1881.

KV12. An undecorated multichamber **tomb** in the **Valley of the Kings**. It may have been seen by traveler **Richard Pococke** during his visit to the valley in 1738 and was cleared by James Burton during the 1820s. The site was also examined by Harold Jones from 1908–1909, **Howard Carter** from 1920–1921, and Otto Schaden from 1993–1994.

KV13. The **tomb** of the chancellor **Bay**, an official of **Siptah** of **Dynasty 19,** in the **Valley of the Kings**. It has stood open since antiquity. Following Bay's execution, the tomb was vandalized, and his name was excised so that only his title remains. It appears to have been reused for two princes of **Dynasty 20**. The tomb was cleared by a German expedition from 1988–1994.

KV14. The **tomb** of **Sethnakhte** of **Dynasty 20** in the **Valley of the Kings**. It was originally built for **Queen Tewosret** and possibly her husband, **Sety II**, but taken over by Sethnakhte. It has stood open since antiquity. There is a record of work on the queen's tomb in year 2, probably by her husband. It was seen by traveler **Richard Pococke** during his visit to the valley in 1738. The tomb was cleared by a German expedition from 1983–1987. The king's **mummy** was found in the **royal cache** at **Deir el-Bahri** in 1881.

KV15. The **tomb** of **Sety II** of **Dynasty 19** in the **Valley of the Kings**. It has stood open since antiquity. It was seen by traveler **Richard Pococke** during his visit to the valley in 1738. The tomb is unfinished. It is not certain if it was his original tomb or whether he was moved here after **KV14** was taken over by **Sethnakhte**. It was examined by **Howard Carter** from 1903–1904. The king's **mummy** was found in the **royal cache** in **KV35** in 1898. A plan of the tomb on an **ostracon** is now housed in the **Cairo Egyptian Museum**.

KV16. The **tomb** of **Ramesses I** of **Dynasty 19** in the **Valley of the Kings**. It was discovered in October 1817 by **Giovanni Battista Bel-**

zoni. Some surviving wooden objects from the tomb are now housed in the **British Museum**. The king's **mummy** has not been securely identified, but an alleged mummy, which was formerly in the Niagara Falls Museum in Canada and the William C. Carlos Museum in Atlanta, was returned to the **Cairo Egyptian Museum** in 2003.

KV17. The **tomb** of **Sety I** of **Dynasty 19** in the **Valley of the Kings**. It was discovered by **Giovanni Battista Belzoni** in October 1817. It is one of the best preserved tombs in the valley with most of the painted scenes intact. Belzoni's rather garbled copies created a sensation when exhibited in London. The tomb has been damaged, with some scenes lost since its discovery. The alabaster **sarcophagus** was removed by Belzoni and now is in Sir John Soane's Museum in London. The king's **mummy** was discovered in the **royal cache** at **Deir el-Bahri** in 1881.

KV18. The **tomb** of **Ramesses X** of **Dynasty 20** in the **Valley of the Kings**. It has stood open since antiquity. It was recorded by traveler **Richard Pococke** during his visit to the valley in 1738 and James Burton in 1825. **Howard Carter** found **foundation deposits** in 1902. A full clearance of the tomb commenced in 1998 by a Swiss expedition. The king's **mummy** has not been located.

KV19. The **tomb** of Prince Ramesses-**Mentuherkhepeshef**, son of **Ramesses IX** of **Dynasty 20** in the **Valley of the Kings**. It was discovered by **Giovanni Battista Belzoni** in 1817 and cleared by Edward Ayrton from 1905–1906.

KV20. An undecorated **tomb** in the **Valley of the Kings** sometimes attributed to **Thutmose I** of **Dynasty 18**, in which case it was his original tomb built by **Ineni**, but it is more likely that of his daughter, **Hatshepsut**. If the latter, Hatshepsut likely intended it as a double burial with her father, as funerary equipment of both were found there. The tomb descent is very steep, and at 100 yards, is the longest in the Valley of the Kings. Hatshepsut's **sarcophagus** is now housed in the **Cairo Egyptian Museum**, while that of her father is preserved in the **Boston Museum of Fine Arts**. The tomb was opened in 1799 and recorded by **Giovanni Battista Belzoni** in 1817 but not entirely cleared until 1903–1904 by **Howard Carter**. It was reexamined again in 1980. *See also* KV38.

KV21. A small, undecorated **tomb** in the **Valley of the Kings**. It was discovered by **Giovanni Battista Belzoni** in October 1817 and reexamined by a team from Pacific Lutheran University from 1989–1990. It consists of a single chamber with a small side storage room. It was robbed in antiquity. Two female **mummies** were found there. It possibly dates to **Dynasty 18**.

KV22. The **tomb** of **Amenhotep III** of **Dynasty 18** in the west valley of the **Valley of the Kings**. It was first noted by members of a French expedition in 1799, and it was cleared by **Howard Carter** in 1915 and has been reexamined by a Japanese expedition since 1989. The tomb may well have been begun by **Thutmose IV**, whose **foundation deposits** were found. The king's **mummy** was found in the **royal cache** in **KV35** in 1898. It has been speculated that his wife, **Tiy**, was also buried in the tomb, as frgaments of her **sarcophagus** were discovered.

KV23. The **tomb** of **Ay** of **Dynasty 18** in the west valley of the **Valley of the Kings**. It was discovered by **Giovanni Battista Belzoni** in 1816 and reexamined by Otto Schaden in 1972. It has been suggested that it was originally destined for **Tutankhamun** but was taken over by Ay, who buried his predecessor in a lesser tomb. The king's **mummy** has not been identified.

KV24. A small, one-chamber **tomb** in the west valley of the **Valley of the Kings**. It was noted by **John Gardner Wilkinson** and excavated by Otto Schaden from 1991–1992, when evidence of later burials was found. The tomb probably dates to **Dynasty 18**.

KV25. An unfinished **tomb** in the west valley of the **Valley of the Kings**. It consists of only two corridors. It was discovered by **Giovanni Battista Belzoni** in 1817 and cleared by Otto Schaden in 1972. It dates to the end of **Dynasty 18**. It has been speculated that it may be the original Theban tomb of **Akhenaten** before his move to **Amarna**.

KV26. An undecorated, single-chamber **tomb** in the **Valley of the Kings**. It was noted by James Burton in the 1820s and Victor Loret in 1898 but has never been fully cleared.

KV27. A small, undecorated, multichamber **tomb** in the **Valley of the Kings**. It was noted by **John Gardner Wilkinson** and examined by a team from Pacific Lutheran University in 1990. It likely dates to **Dynasty 18**.

KV28. An undecorated, single-chamber **tomb** in the **Valley of the Kings**. It was noted by **John Gardner Wilkinson** and cleared by an American expedition from the Pacific Lutheran University in 1990. It likely dates to **Dynasty 18**.

KV29. A small, undecorated **tomb** in the **Valley of the Kings**. It was noted by James Burton and **John Gardner Wilkinson** but has not since been examined.

KV30. A small, undecorated, multichamber **tomb** in the **Valley of the Kings**. It was discovered by **Giovanni Battista Belzoni** in 1817. It likely dates to **Dynasty 18**.

KV31. A small **tomb** or pit in the **Valley of the Kings**. It was discovered in 1817 by the Earl of Belmore under the direction of **Giovanni Battista Belzoni**. Its present location is unknown.

KV32. A small, undecorated, single-chamber **tomb** in the **Valley of the Kings**. It was discovered by Victor Loret in 1898 and reexcavated by a Swiss team beginning in 2001 and identified from fragments of a canopic chest as made for **Queen Tiaa**, mother of **Thutmose IV**. It dates to **Dynasty 18**.

KV33. A small, undecorated, two-chamber **tomb** the **Valley of the Kings**. It was discovered by Victor Loret in 1898 but never cleared.

KV34. The **tomb** of **Thutmose III** of **Dynasty 18** in the **Valley of the Kings**. It was discovered by Victor Loret in 1898 and contains such architectural innovations as a well to deter floodwater and tomb robbers. It uniquely mentions the king's mother and his wives. The king's **mummy** was found in the **royal cache** at **Deir el-Bahri**.

KV35. The **tomb** of **Amenhotep II** of **Dynasty 18** in the **Valley of the Kings**. It was discovered by Victor Loret in 1898. This tomb was used as a **royal cache** for some mummies of **pharaohs**, so it was presumably sealed during **Dynasty 21**. The king's **mummy** is the only royal one, aside from **Tutankhamun**, found in its original tomb.

KV36. The **tomb** of the royal fanbearer Maiherperi of **Dynasty 18** in the **Valley of the Kings**. It was discovered largely intact by Victor Loret in 1899 and consists of a single, undecorated chamber with a small annex. It was robbed in antiquity, but only a few precious items have been removed. Most of the funerary equipment and the **mummy**, although damaged, remained. The occupant is otherwise unknown but must have been a favored courtier.

KV37. A small, undecorated, single-chamber **tomb** in the **Valley of the Kings**. It was discovered by Victor Loret in 1899. It likely dates to **Dynasty 18**.

KV38. The **tomb** of **Thutmose I** of **Dynasty 18** in the **Valley of the Kings**. It was discovered by Victor Loret in 1899. It is not clear if the tomb was the king's original burial place constructed by **Ineni** from which his body was transferred to **KV20** and then back again or a reburial when his body was removed from KV20. His **mummy** has not been securely identified.

KV39. An undecorated royal **tomb** in the **Valley of the Kings**. It was discovered by Victor Loret in 1899 and reexamined by John Rose from 1989–1994. It has been speculated that it may be the lost tomb of **Amenhotep I**.

KV40. A small **tomb** in the **Valley of the Kings**. It was discovered by Victor Loret in 1899, but no details have been published. It likely dates to **Dynasty 18**.

KV41. A small **tomb** in the **Valley of the Kings**. It was discovered by Victor Loret in 1899, but no details have been published. It likely dates to **Dynasty 18**.

KV42. An undecorated, multichambered **tomb** with such royal attributes as a **cartouche**-shaped burial chamber in the **Valley of the Kings**. It may have ben discovered by Victor Loret at the end of the 19th century, but it was cleared under the supervision of **Howard Carter** in 1900. Remains from private burials of **Dynasty 18** were found but were probably intrusive. In 1921, Carter discovered **foundation deposits** of **Queen Meryetre Hatshepsut**, wife of **Thutmose III** and mother of **Amenhotep II**, so the tomb was likely intended for her.

KV43. The **tomb** of **Thutmose IV** of **Dynasty 18** in the **Valley of the Kings**. It was discovered by **Howard Carter** in 1903. Although robbed, a number of pieces of funerary equipment were recovered, including **shabtis** and **foundation deposits**. The king's **mummy** was found in the **royal cache** in **KV35**.

KV44. An undecorated, single-chamber **tomb** in the **Valley of the Kings**. It was discovered by **Howard Carter** in 1901. It contained several private coffins and **mummies**. It was examined again by a team from Pacific Lutheran University from 1990–1991. It likely dates to **Dynasty 18**.

KV45. An undecorated, single-chamber **tomb** in the **Valley of the Kings**. It was discovered by **Howard Carter** in 1902. It contained **canopic jar** fragments of Userhat of **Dynasty 18**, who may have been the original occupant, as well as later material. It was examined again by a team from Pacific Lutheran University from 1990–1991.

KV46. The intact **tomb** of **Yuya**, father of **Queen Tiy** and father-in-law of **Amenhotep III**, and his wife, Tuya, in the **Valley of the Kings**. It was discovered by James Quibell in 1905. The contents, which include the **mummies** of the couple, are now housed in the **Cairo Egyptian Museum**.

KV47. The **tomb** of **Siptah** of **Dynasty 19** in the **Valley of the Kings**. It was discovered by Edward Ayrton in 1905 and cleared inside by Harry Burton in 1912 and outside by **Howard Carter** in 1922. The tomb and its environs have been under investigation by a Swiss expedition since 1998. The king's **mummy** was found in the **royal cache** in **KV35** in 1898.

KV48. A single, undecorated, single-chamber **tomb** in the **Valley of the Kings**. It was discovered by Edward Ayrton in 1906. The tomb had been robbed, but a **mummy** and some funerary equipment were recovered, naming the **vizier** Amenemopet under **Amenhotep II** of **Dynasty 18**, the presumed original owner.

KV49. A small corridor **tomb** in the **Valley of the Kings**. It was discovered by Edward Ayrton in 1906. It likely dates to **Dynasty 18** and may later have been used as a storeroom.

KV50. An undecorated, single-chamber **tomb** in the **Valley of the Kings**. It was discovered by Edward Ayrton in 1906. It contained a **mummified** monkey and dog.

KV51. An undecorated, single-chamber **tomb** in the **Valley of the Kings**. It was discovered by Edward Ayrton in 1906. It contained **mummified** animals.

KV52. An undecorated, single-chamber **tomb** in the **Valley of the Kings**. It was discovered by Edward Ayrton in 1906. It contained a **mummified** monkey.

KV53. An undecorated, single-chamber **tomb** in the **Valley of the Kings**. It was discovered by Edward Ayrton in 1906.

KV54. A small pit **tomb** in the **Valley of the Kings**. It was discovered in 1907 and contained embalming materials from the burial of **Tutankhamun**. It was relocated and examined by a Swiss expedition from 1998–1999.

KV55. One of the most controversial **tombs** in the **Valley of the Kings**. It was discovered by Edward Ayrton in 1907. It had remained largely intact and contained a skeleton in a wooden coffin and other funerary equipment, some inscribed with the name of **Queen Tiy**. The names on the coffin had been erased. The body has been scientifically examined and proved to be that of a young male. It has been tentatively identified as that of **Smenkhkare**, but some believe that it is the body of **Akhenaten**, although the age does not fit. The tomb was evidently a reburial brought from **Amarna**. The material is now in the **Cairo Egyptian Museum.** The tomb was recleared by Lyla Pinch Brock from 1993–1996.

KV56. An undecorated single-chamber **tomb** in the **Valley of the Kings** known as the Gold Tomb. It was discovered by Edward Ayrton in January 1906. **Gold** and **silver** jewelry was recovered bearing the names **Sety II** and **Queen Tewosret**. It has been speculated that this was material from the queen's tomb or perhaps that the tomb belonged to a child of the royal couple.

KV57. The **tomb** of **Horemheb** in the **Valley of the Kings**. It was discovered by Edward Ayrton in February 1906. It is one of the finest tombs in the valley, with most of the painting preserved, apart from scenes in sketch outline. It is the first tomb with painted raised relief instead of the painted plaster walls of earlier **Dynasty 18** tombs. The king's **mummy** has not been recovered. A British expedition is currently reexcavating material in the tomb.

KV58. A small, undecorated **tomb** in the **Valley of the Kings**. It was discovered by Harold Jones in 1909. The finds consisted of an alabsater **shabti**, sheets of **gold** foil, alabaster knobs, and **faience** box handles, which may have come from the tomb of **Ay**.

KV59. A small, undecorated pit **tomb** in the **Valley of the Kings**.

KV60. A small, undecorated **tomb** in the **Valley of the Kings**. It was discovered by **Howard Carter** in 1903. It contained some **mummified** geese and meat offerings and two female mummies. One mummy was in a coffin inscibed with the name of the great royal nurse In-Sitre. The tomb was reopened by Edward Ayrton in 1906, and the coffin and mummy were likely then removed to the **Cairo Egyptian Museum**. The other mummy remained in the tomb, which was opened again in 1989–1990, when it was cleared by a team from Pacific Lutheran University. It was long suggested that one of the female mummies might be that of **Queen Hatshepsut**, and it was confirmed that the mummy in the coffin was indeed hers in 2007 by matching a broken tooth in a box with her name to a similar broken tooth on the mummy.

KV61. A small, undecorated pit **tomb** in the **Valley of the Kings**. It was discovered by Harold Jones in 1910. It appears to have been abandoned unused.

KV62. The **tomb** of **Tutankhamun** in the **Valley of the Kings**. It was discovered intact by **Howard Carter** in 1922. It consists of three rooms on one level: an antechamber leading to the main burial chamber and a storage annex off the antechamber. Only the burial chamber was decorated with painted reliefs. These works of art depict the funeral of the king carried out by his successor, **Ay**. It appears that the tomb was hastily built upon the unexpected death of the king. The rich contents have been removed to the **Cairo Egyptian Museum**, but the inner coffin and the king's **mummy** remain in the tomb.

KV63. The most recently discovered **tomb** in the **Valley of the Kings**. It was discovered by an American expedition in February 2006. It consists of one small, undecorated chamber off the main shaft. Seven coffins, filled mainly with funerary material and 28 storage jars, were found inside. The tomb is dated to the end of **Dynasty 18** by necropolis sealings.

– L –

LAENAS, CAIUS POPILLIUS. *See* POPILLIUS LAENAS, CAIUS.

LAHUN. Modern name for a site near the **Fayum**, also known as Illahun, where the **pyramid** complex of **Senusret II** of **Dynasty 12** was built. At Kahun, a nearby site, the village for the workmen who constructed the pyramid was laid out and later used by the community of priests that served the royal cult. The area was excavated from

1889–1890 by **Flinders Petrie**, who discovered much material of daily life at Kahun, including **papyri**, and in the pyramid, he found jewelry belonging to Princess **Sithathoriunet**. *See also* BACCHIAS; DEIR EL-NAQLUN; GUROB; HARAGEH; HAWARA; KARA-NIS; KOM KHELWA; KOM TALIT; LISHT; MEDINET MADI; SOKNOPAIOU NESOS; TEBTUNIS.

LANGUAGE. The ancient Egyptian language belongs to the Afro-Asiatic group of languages and has affinities with both North African and Semitic languages and possibly devolved before these two groups separated. The language did not remain unchanged but rather went through five linguistic stages. Old Egyptian was used during the **Old Kingdom** and expressed in written form by **hieroglyphic** and **hieratic** writing. The next phase, Middle Egyptian, was first used during the **Middle Kingdom** and later regarded as the classical form of the language by subsequent generations. Late Egyptian was in use during the **New Kingdom** but was replaced by **demotic** during the **Late Period**, which used new grammatical and written forms until it also died out as a written language during the **Roman Period**. **Coptic** was introduced during the Christian period. Regional variations only become apparent during the Coptic period but must have existed in earlier times. During its long history, the Egyptian language borrowed many words from Semitic languages during the New Kingdom and later from Greek languages.

LAPIS LAZULI. A blue gemstone thought to originate in Afghanistan during ancient times. It has been used for jewelry and vessels in Egypt since the **Predynastic Period** (**Naqada** I) and must have reached Egypt via **trade** routes. The gem was highly prized and during the **New Kingdom** was imitated by blue **glass**.

LATE PERIOD (664–332 BC). A term used by Egyptologists for the period from the beginning of **Dynasty 26** until the conquest of Egypt by **Alexander the Great**. Some scholars also include **Dynasty 25**. During this time, the royal court was located in the Delta at **Sais** and other cities. Egyptian rulers attempted to maintain the independence of the country against outside aggression from **Persia** but were ultimately unsuccessful.

LEONTOPOLIS. Greek name for the Egyptian *Ta-remu*, modern Tell el-Muqdam in the Delta 50 miles north of Cairo. Capital of the 11th **nome** of **Lower Egypt**. The principal deity was the lion god **Mahes**. The remains date from the **Middle Kingdom** to the **Graeco-Roman Period**. Little is left of the city now. It was examined by **Auguste Mariette** in 1889 and excavated by **Henri Edouard Naville** in 1892. In 1915, the burial of a **Queen** Kama, possibly a shortened form of **Karomama**, of the **Third Intermediate Period** was discovered at the site. The city was investigated by an American expedition from 1992–1998.

LEPSIUS, (KARL) RICHARD (1810–1884). German Egyptologist. He was born in Naumburg, Germany, on 23 December 1810. He studied Egyptology in Paris and Germany. From 1842–1845, Lepsius was sent to Egypt with a Prussian expedition that collected antiquities for the **Berlin Egyptian Museum**, but he and his colleagues also took copious notes on and made drawings of standing monuments, which were later published in 12 volumes. In 1846, he was appointed professor at Berlin University and in 1855 vice director of the Berlin Museum, succeeding as director in 1865. Lepsius continued **Jean-François Champollion's** research into ancient Egyptian grammar and helped perfect the understanding of the ancient **language**. He died in Berlin, Germany, on 10 July 1884.

LIGHTHOUSE. *See* PHAROS.

LISHT. Modern name for the city of *Itjtawy*, capital of **Dynasty 12** located in the **Fayum**. The town itself is unexcavated, but the **pyramids** of **Amenemhat I** and his son, **Senusret I**, and their officials are located nearby. The site was excavated by the French from 1894–1995 and the **Metropolitan Museum of Art** from 1906–1934 and 1984–1989. *See also* BACCHIAS; DEIR EL-NAQLUN; GUROB; HARAGEH; HAWARA; INTEFYOKER; KARANIS; KOM KHELWA; KOM TALIT; LAHUN; MEDINET MADI; SOKNOPAIOU NESOS; TEBTUNIS.

LITERATURE. A great variety of types of literature has survived from ancient Egypt from all periods. These include the didactic **wisdom**

literature; poetry, including love poems from the **New Kingdom**; hymns; and a large number of stories and folktales, some purely entertaining but with a moral point and others mythological in content. Royal inscriptions and religious texts could be written in a poetical vein. *See also* DJEHUTY; SHIPWRECKED SAILOR; SINUHE; *TALE OF THE DOOMED PRINCE, THE; TALE OF THE ELOQUENT PEASANT, THE; TALE OF THE TWO BROTHERS, THE; TALE OF TRUTH AND FALSEHOOD, THE*; WENAMUN; WESTCAR PAPYRUS.

LOUVRE MUSEUM. Following the French Revolution, the Louvre Palace in Paris, France, was turned into a museum but contained only few Egyptian objects. In 1824, the French government acquired the Durand collection of 1,225 small Egyptian antiquities, and in 1826, through the efforts of **Jean-François Champollion**, the second collection of **Henry Salt**, the British consul general in Egypt, comprising 4,000 pieces, was purchased. A separate Egyptian section was established in the Louvre in 1826, with Champollion as its curator. The collection was enriched by further purchases, notably the **Bernardino Drovetti** collection in 1827, and objects acquired by Champollion during his tour of Egypt from 1828–1829.

Further antiquities were received from the excavations of **Auguste Mariette** at the **Serapeum** and the work of the **French Institute**, which undertook excavations throughout Egypt. Among its chief pieces are a **stela** from King **Djet's tomb** dating to **Dynasty 1** from **Abydos**, the Seated **Scribe** from the **Old Kingdom**, and the **bronze** statue inlaid with **gold**, **silver**, and electrum of Princess **Karomama** of **Dynasty 22**. *See also* BERLIN EGYPTIAN MUSEUM; BOSTON MUSEUM OF FINE ARTS; BRITISH MUSEUM; CAIRO EGYPTIAN MUSEUM; METROPOLITAN MUSEUM OF ART; TURIN EGYPTIAN MUSEUM.

LOWER EGYPT. Ancient Egyptian *Tamehu*. The area of Egypt comprising the **Nile** Delta from the Mediterranean Sea north to **Memphis**. It appears to have evolved into a separate kingdom, possibly with its capital at **Buto**, during the **Predynastic Period** and was united, forcibly or not, with **Upper Egypt** to form a single country described in Egyptian texts as the Two Lands. The symbol of Lower Egypt was the sedge plant, which formed part of the royal title with the bee of Upper Egypt. The tutelary goddess **Wadjet** was represented as a serpent, or **uraeus**, on the royal brow. The royal crown of Lower Egypt, known as the red crown, consisted of a flat top with a vertical section at the back. *See also* MIDDLE EGYPT.

LUXOR. Modern name for the town on the site of ancient **Thebes**. The name is used by Egyptologists to refer to the **temple** in Luxor, known to the Egyptians as *Iput-rsyt*, as distinct from the temple of **Karnak**, or *Iput-sut*, now on the outskirts of the town. The Luxor temple was built by **Amenhotep III** and apparently dedicated to the *ka*, the soul of the king. Reliefs feature the **divine birth** of the king. The temple was later enlarged by **Tutankhamun** and **Ramesses II**. A procession of ram-headed **sphinxes** connected the temple to that of Karnak. During the main religious festival, the sacred image of the god **Amun** would proceed from Karnak to Luxor on a barque carried by priests. During the 4th century AD, part of the temple was converted into a church and later a mosque. A Muslim religious festival celebrating a local saint incorporates some features of the ancient Egyptian ritual. A major cache of **New Kingdom** statues was recovered here in 1989.

– M –

MAADI. Modern name for a suburb south of Cairo where excavations by Cairo University from 1930–1953 uncovered a settlement and cemeteries dating to the late **Predynastic Period**. The remains included huts and storage pits for grain and **pottery**, both local and imported, from Palestine. The local culture is different from that of **Upper Egypt** of the **Naqada** Period, which is believed to be in part contemporary and was thought to represent a separate culture of **Lower Egypt**, although excavations at **Minshat Abu Omar** and elsewhere in the Delta reveal Naqada culture there. A German expedition investigated the site from 1999–2002.

MAAT. The Egyptian concept of righteous order, often translated as truth and symbolized by a feather or a goddess with a feather on her head. The king was obliged to maintain *maat* on earth through just rule and the maintenance of the constant religious rituals in the **tem-**

ples, which placated the gods. Individuals were supposed to follow *maat* in their daily lives to ensure passage to the next life and, according to religious belief, their heart would be weighed against the feather of *maat* to determine their worthiness to enter the **afterlife**, although **Books of the Dead** were used to avoid any possible problems if there was doubt about the worthiness of the individual. *See also* RELIGION.

MAATHORNEFERURE (fl. 1245 BC). Egyptian name of the **Hittite** princess, daughter of **Hattusili III** and **Puduhepa**, who married **Ramesses II** in his year 34, c. 1245 BC. The marriage is recorded on several monuments, and this **queen** is known from **scarabs** and other textual evidence. She appears to have been a resident for a time at the royal palace at **Gurob**. *See also* BINTANAT; HENTTAWY; HENUTMIRE; ISITNOFRET; MERITAMUN; NEBETTAWY; NEFERTARI.

MAATKARE (fl. 1030 BC). Daughter of the **high priest of Amun Pinudjem** I and **Henttawy** II. She was appointed **God's wife of Amun**. Her body was recovered from the **royal cache** at **Deir el-Bahri** in 1881. Her virgin status was disputed, as a small body, believed to be her child, was found in her coffin, but x-ray analysis later revealed this to be her pet monkey. A later Maatkare, daughter of **Pasebakhaenniut II** of **Dynasty 21**, was the wife of **Osorkon I** of **Dynasty 22**.

MAHES. Greek Mihos. A lion god said to be the son of **Bastet** or **Sakhmet**. He was regarded as a god of war and protector of sacred environs. He was primarily worshipped in **Lower Egypt** at **Leontopolis** and had a chapel at **Bubastis**. His cult became more widespread during the **Graeco-Roman Period**. *See also* RELIGION.

MALKATA. Modern name for an area on the west bank of the **Nile** opposite **Thebes** known as *Aten Tjehen*. Here the remains of a palace of **Amenhotep III** have been found, as well as a pleasure lake at nearby Birket Habu. The site was discovered in 1888 and excavated by the American R. Tytus from 1901–1903, the **Metropolitan Museum of Art** from 1910–1920, and an American expedition from Pennsylvania from 1971–1974. It has been more recently examined by a Japanese expedition from Waseda University from 1972–1980 and 1985–1988.

MANETHO (fl. 270 BC). Egyptian priest and author during the reign of **Ptolemy II**. He came from **Sebennytos** and appears to have held the post of high priest at **Heliopolis**. He wrote *Aegyptiaca*, a history of Egypt penned in Greek based on **temple** records. The complete text is now lost, but part of it is known from garbled excerpts in the works of other authors. His **king list** and division of **dynasties** were instrumental in establishing Egyptian **chronology** but must be carefully evaluated. The names and reign lengths are often distorted and must be checked against contemporary sources. It is now known that this division of dynasties was based on earlier documents, like the **Turin Royal Canon**. Manetho was also involved in the establishment of the cult of **Sarapis** in Egypt. *See also* DYNASTY 1–DYNASTY 30.

MANHATA. A wife of **Thutmose III**. She was buried with her cowives, Manuwai and Maruta, in a **tomb** in **Wadi Gabbanat al-Qurud**. Their names have also been transliterated as **Menhet**, Menwi, and Merti. The tomb was discovered almost intact by illicit diggers in 1916, and the bulk of the objects were sold to the **Metropolitan Museum of Art** from 1918 onward. The names indicate that the ladies were of Caananite or Syrian extraction and were probably acquired as a result of the king's levantine conquests.

MANICHEISM. A religious doctrine developed from gnosticism that was preached throughout the Mediterranean world by the Bablylon-born Mani and his disciples from the 3rd century AD. It is a dualistic **religion** of good and evil, light and dark in which good is identified with Jesus Christ and heaven and evil with Satan and earth. It was proscribed during the Roman Empire both before and after the triumph of orthodox Christianity. It was prevalent in Egypt, and Manichean texts have been discovered at **Medinet Madi** and the **Dakhla Oasis**.

MANUWAI. *See* MANHATA.

MARIETTE, (FRANÇOIS) AUGUSTE FERDINAND (1821–1881).
French excavator. He was born in Boulogne-sur-Mer, France, on 11
February 1821, and he first became a teacher. His interest in Egypt
was aroused by papers of a relative who had visited the country, and
he taught himself both the Egyptian and **Coptic languages.** In 1850,
he was sent to Egypt to purchase Coptic manuscripts but used the
money to discover and excavate the **Serapeum** at **Saqqara.**

In 1858, he was appointed head of the newly founded Egyptian
Antiquities Service (now the **Supreme Council for Antiquities**) and
organized archaeological excavations at all major sites in Egypt, notably **Abydos, Thebes, Dendera, Saqqara, Giza,** and various sites
in the Delta region. In 1863, he opened the first **Cairo Egyptian Museum.** Mariette tried to put an end to illicit excavation and restricted
foreign excavators. The bulk of his discoveries went to the Cairo
Egyptian Museum, which henceforth had first choice of excavated
material in Egypt. He died in Cairo on 18 January 1881, and he was
later reburied in front of the new Cairo Museum. *See also* CARTER,
HOWARD; MONTET, (JEAN) PIERRE MARIE; NAVILLE,
(HENRI) EDOUARD; PETRIE, WILLIAM MATTHEW FLINDERS;
REISNER, GEORGE ANDREW; WINLOCK, HERBERT EUSTIS.

MARINA EL-ALAMEIN. Modern name for an ancient site on the
Mediterranean coast near modern el-Alamein where Egyptian and
Polish excavations since 1986 have uncovered a town from the
Graeco-Roman Period with nearby **tombs.** The tombs consist of
burial chambers off a central altar and a room for the funeral and subsequent feasts in honor of the dead. **Mummy portraits** have been recovered with some of the burials, indicating that this practice was
also carried on in northern Egypt; this had not been hitherto attested
due to the wetter climate here.

MARRIAGE. Although marriage undoubtedly existed in ancient
Egypt, there is no evidence of any marriage ceremonies, and it may
be that a couple merely declared their intention and lived together. It
is probable that there was a family celebration of some sort, but no
legal or religious notification was necessary. Marriage contracts from
the **Late Period** have survived that specify the terms of relationships.
Most Egyptian men appear to have had monogamous marriages with

one wife at a time, and certainly this state of affairs was the ideal in **wisdom literature**. Because of the high mortality rate, it is likely that some men and women had additional partners, although evidence for remarriage is not always clearly indicated. Divorce was freely available but was limited by economic and social pressures. A divorced wife or widow was entitled to one-third of the matrimonial property unless guilty of adultery, in which case her financial claims were diminished.

Polygamy, although permitted, is rarely attested, except for the king. Total fidelity on the part of men was not realistically expected, but most men appear to have preferred to consort with prostitutes, concubines, or **slave** girls rather than take a second wife, as this procedure was expensive and might lead to legal disputes. In one known case of a childless couple, the husband fathered children by a slave girl, and the offspring were then adopted by the wife.

Aside from the royal family, ancient Egyptians did not marry their sisters. Early Egyptologists were confused by the fact that wives are often referred to as a sister as a term of endearment. The king as a god could marry his sister, although this was not obligatory, and only a few cases of full brother–sister marriage are recorded during the Pharaonic Period, possibly **Mentuhotep II** and his sister, **Nefru**; Seqenenre **Tao** and **Ahhotep**; and **Ahmose I** and **Ahmose-Nefertari**. Others married half sisters, or the identity of the mother of the **queen** is uncertain. The practice was revived by some of the Ptolemaic kings, beginning with **Ptolemy II**. Only during the **Graeco-Roman Period** are brother–sister marriages attested for commoners, and this development seems to have arisen as a means to control family property. *See also* SEX.

MARUTA. *See* MANHATA.

MASAHARTA (fl. 1044–1036 BC). High priest of Amun at **Thebes** during **Dynasty 21**. Son of **Pinudjem** I. He succeeded his father as high priest apparently when the latter adopted royal titles but may have predeceased him. He was eventually succeeded by his brother, **Menkheperre**. His body was recovered from the **royal cache**.

MASTABA. Arabic term used by Egyptologists to describe freestanding **tombs** from the late **Predynastic Period** onward. The superstructure of these tombs is rectangular in shape and composed of mudbrick or stone. Within the core of the superstructure are various storerooms or chapels, sometimes filled in to present a seemingly solid appearance. A shaft within the body of the tomb leads to the underground burial chamber. *See also* PYRAMID.

MAXIMIANUS, CAIUS GALERIUS VALERIUS. *See* GALERIUS VALERIUS MAXIMIANUS, CAIUS.

MEDAMUD. Modern name for a site in **Upper Egypt** just northeast of **Luxor**. Ancient Egyptian *Madu*. The main deity of the site was the god **Montu**, whose **temple** is attested during the **Middle Kingdom**, although the surviving remains date to the **Graeco-Roman Period**. A cult of a sacred bull similar to the **Mnevis** is known from here. The site was excavated by French archaeologists from 1929–1940.

MEDINET HABU. Modern name for the site of the mortuary **temple** of **Ramesses III** on the west bank of the **Nile** at **Thebes**. The temple is well preserved and contains a major inscription detailing the king's war against the **Sea Peoples**. The workmen from **Deir el-Medina** sought refuge here at the end of **Dynasty 20**. The site also contains a temple of **Thutmose III** and the burial chapels of the **God's wives of Amun**.

MEDINET MADI. Modern name of a town site in the **Fayum**. Ancient Egyptian *Dja*, named Narmuthis during the **Graeco-Roman Period**. The earliest remains date to the **Middle Kingdom** when a **temple** to the goddess **Renenutet** is attested. Later evidence dates from the 4th century AD to the early Arabic Period, when the main temple was dedicated to **Isis**-Termouthis. The late Roman fort Castrum Narmoutheos was identified in 2006. The site was excavated by a French expedition in 1900; a German expedition from 1909–1910; and an Italian expedition from 1934–1939 and since 1966, recovering much documentary evidence in the form of **ostraca** and **papyri** pertaining to the Manichean religious sect. *See also* BACCHIAS; DEIR EL-NAQLUN; GUROB; HARAGEH; HAWARA; KARANIS; KOM KHELWA; SOKNOPAIOU NESOS; TEBTUNIS.

MEGIDDO. A city-state in Syria-Palestine that became a vassal of Egypt after the campaigns of **Thutmose I**. In 1458 BC, it became the center of a revolt against Egypt headed by the prince of **Kadesh**. The city was attacked and beseiged by **Thutmose III** in a surprise assault and forced to surrender. The captured princes were obliged to renew their allegiance to Egypt. The city and its ruler, Biridiya, appear in the **Amarna letters**. The city remained under Egyptian control until the middle of **Dynasty 20**, when the last attested Egyptain ruler there is **Ramesses VI**. *See also* WARFARE.

MEHIT. A lioness-headed goddess of the desert regions and wife of **Anhur** of the eighth **Upper Egyptian nome**.

MEHY (fl. 1290 BC). An Egyptian army officer depicted by the side of **Sety I** in his war reliefs at **Karnak**. His figure was later erased by **Ramesses II**. Early Egyptologists mistakenly assumed that the erased reliefs originally depicted an older son of Sety I suppressed by Ramesses II, but the correct name and titles of Mehy have now been deciphered. However, his exact position in the court and subsequent career remains unknown.

MEIDUM. Modern name for ancient Egyptian *Mertem*, where the earliest known true **pyramid** is located, although it was not originally designed as such. It was built as a step pyramid, but the steps were later filled in, although most of the filling has now collapsed. The pyramid has been attributed to **Huni** or his successor, **Snefru**. It is surrounded by the **tombs** of royal officials, including that of Prince **Rahotep**, which contained finely painted statues of him and his wife, Nefret, now housed in the **Cairo Egyptian Museum**, and Prince **Nefermaat**, who served as **vizier**. The site was examined by **Auguste Mariette** from 1871–1872, **Flinders Petrie** from 1890–1891 and 1909–1911, Alan Rowe from 1929–1932, an Egyptian expedition and later a Polish–Egyptian expedition that conserved the tombs from 1985–1988, and a Spanish expedition since 1996.

MEIR. Modern name for a site in **Middle Egypt** south of **Amarna**, ancient Egyptian *Qis*, capital of the 14th **nome** of **Upper Egypt** whose patron goddess was **Hathor**. The most important features of the area are the rock-cut **tombs** of the nomarchs from **Dynasties 6–12**. The reliefs were copied by an expedition sponsored by the **Egypt Exploration Society** from 1912–1914, in 1921, and from 1949–1950. Another nearby burial site was located at Quseir el-Amarna recorded by an Australian expedition in 1989.

MEKETATEN (fl. 1340 BC). Second daughter of **Akhenaten** and **Nefertiti**. She appears on many monuments with her sisters during the early part of her father's reign. The deathbed scene of this princess is vividly depicted in the royal **tomb** at **Amarna**. This scene might be interpreted to suggest that she died during childbirth, but this is not certain. *See also* ANKHESENAMUN; ANKHESENPAATEN-TASHERIT; BAKETATEN; MERITAMUN; MERITATEN-TASHERIT; NEFERNEFRUATEN; NEFERNEFRURE; SETEPENRE.

MEKETRE (fl. 2000 BC). Chancellor at the end of **Dynasty 11** and possibly the beginning of **Dynasty 12**. He was buried at **Deir el-Bahri**, and his **tomb** was excavated by an expedition from the **Metropolitan Museum of Art** in 1921. Among the objects discovered were fine models of activities of daily life, which are a feature of tombs of the **Middle Kingdom**.

MEMNON, COLOSSI OF. The two colossal statues of **Amenhotep III** that stood before his mortuary **temple** on the west bank of the **Nile** at **Thebes**. The statues were named by the Greeks after the legendary Ethiopian king Memnon, who fought in the Trojan War. One was believed to sing, probably the action of wind through cracks, and became a favorite tourist attraction during the **Roman Period**, being visited notably by **Hadrian** and his wife. The statue was repaired by order of **Septimius Severus**, and it sang no more. The temple behind the statues was heavily plundered by **Merenptah**, who used many blocks and statues for the construction of his own mortuary temple.

MEMPHIS. Greek name for the capital of the first **nome** of **Lower Egypt** located at modern Mit Rahina. The city is said to have been founded by **Menes**. It then served as the capital of a united Egypt and was first called *Inebu-hedj*, meaning "White Wall." It was later known by the name *Men-nefer*, derived from the **pyramid** of **Pepy I**, from which the Greek form of its name developed. Memphis remained the first or second capital of Egypt throughout most of dynastic history. Its principal monument was the **temple** to its local god, **Ptah**, which is now in ruins but was largely rebuilt by **Ramesses II**. The remains of smaller temples and palaces, mainly from the **Ramesside Period**, have also been uncovered.

The site has not been systematically excavated and so is less well known than the southern capital at **Thebes**. Investigations were carried out by Jospeh Hekekyan in 1852. Excavations were carried out by **Auguste Mariette**; **Flinder**s **Petrie** from 1909–1913; the University of Pennsylvania from 1915–1919, 1921–1923, and 1955–1956; Egyptian archaeologists notably in 1931 and 1942 when **tombs** of the Ramesside Period and **Dynasty 22** were uncovered; and the **Egypt Exploration Society** since 1981. The kings and courtiers who resided here were buried at the nearby desert sites of **Abusir**, **Dahshur**, **Giza**, **Meidum**, and **Saqqara**.

MENAS, ST. Legendary Christian martyr and popular saint of **Coptic** Egypt. He was supposedly a Roman soldier of Egyptian parentage serving in Phrygia. As a committed Christian, he was martyred during the persecutions of the Emperor **Diocletian**. His body was brought to Egypt by his military comrades and buried in the Delta at the site now known as **Abu Mina**.

MENDES. Greek name for the Egyptian *Per-Banebdjet*, now Tell el-Ruba, capital of the 16th **nome** of **Lower Egypt**. Capital of **Dynasty 29**. The principal deity of the site was the sacred ram Banebdjet. Remains include **tombs** from the **Old Kingdom** and later eras and the cemetery of the sacred rams. The site has been excavated by a number of American Egyptologists since 1964. The nearby site of Tell el-Timai, Greek Thmuis, marked the area of residence during the **Graeco-Roman Period**.

MENES. Legendary first king of Egypt who founded **Dynasty 1** and founder of the city of **Memphis**. There are no certain contemporary references to a king of this name, but he appears on Ramesside **king lists** 2,000 years later. He may be identified with **Narmer**, although some scholars have suggested that he may be **Aha**.

MENHET. *See* MANHATA.

MENKAUHOR (reigned c. 2421–2414 BC). Ruler of **Dynasty 5.** Successor of **Niuserre.** Very little is known about his reign, and although the name of his **pyramid** has been discovered, the actual structure has yet to be located at either **Saqqara** or **Abusir.** *See also* DJEDKARE.

MENKAURE (reigned c. 2532–2503 BC). The Greek form of his name is Mycerinus. Ruler of **Dynasty 4.** Son and successor of **Khafre** and probably **Queen Khamerernebty I.** He built the third **pyramid** complex at **Giza** next to that of his father and his grandfather, **Khufu.** His pyramid was opened in 1837, and his **sarcophagus** was shipped to London but was lost at sea. The associated **temples** and chapels were excavated by **George Reisner** for the **Boston Museum of Fine Arts** from 1906–1910 and in 1923 and yielded fine pieces of sculpture depicting the king with various goddesses.

MENKHEPERRE (fl. 1060–986 BC). High priest of Amun at **Thebes** during **Dynasty 21.** Son of **Pinudjem I.** He eventually succeeded his brother, **Masaharta,** at Thebes in year 25 of **Nesbanebdjed** (c. 1035 BC) after some political dissension resulting in the banishment of his rivals. Menkheperre held office for approximately 50 years, after which he was followed by his sons, Nesbanebdjed and Pinudjem II. *See also* THIRD INTERMEDIATE PERIOD.

MENNA (fl. 1395 BC). Owner of the well-preserved **tomb** 69 in the necropolis of **Thebes,** probably dating to the reign of **Thutmose IV.** He held the title of **scribe** of the fields of the king. The scenes in his tomb include those of the harvest and fishing and fowling.

MENTUEMHAT (fl. 700–650 BC). Fourth prophet of **Amun** and mayor of **Thebes.** Son of Nesptah, who had similar titles, and **Istemkheb.** He was the virtual ruler of Thebes and **Upper Egypt** at the end of **Dynasty 25** and is named in Assyrian accounts as prince of Thebes. Mentuemhat skilfully kept his position during and after the Assyrian conquest but submitted in 656 BC to **Psamtik I,** who recognized his position. He was succeeded by his son, Nesptah, but Psamtik I eventually managed to remove the family from power. His large **tomb** is located on the western bank of the **Nile** and has not been fully excavated.

MENTUHERKHEPESHEF. The name of several princes of **Dynasty 19** and **Dynasty 20**. The name was first used for the fifth son of **Ramesses II** (fl. 1270 BC). A like-named son of **Ramesses IX** was buried in **tomb KV19** in the **Valley of the Kings**, first rediscovered in 1817.

MENTUHOTEP I (fl. 2125 BC). Ancestor of **Dynasty 11**. He apparently never actually ruled but was probably a governor of **Thebes** and was awarded a posthumous royal **Horus** name as the father of **Intef I**. *See also* FIRST INTERMEDIATE PERIOD.

MENTUHOTEP II (reigned c. 2055–2004 BC). Throne name Nebhepetre. Son of **Intef III** and **Iah**, ruler of **Thebes** of **Dynasty 11**. He reestablished the unity of Egypt c. 2040 BC by defeating the ruler of **Herakleopolis** during **Dynasty 10**, thus ending the **First Intermediate Period** and inaugurating the **Middle Kingdom**. He established Thebes for the first time as capital of Egypt. Mentuhotep II appears to have undertaken campaigns in **Nubia**, in Sinai, and against the Libyans to safeguard and possibly expand Egypt's borders. He built his **tomb** and mortuary **temple** at **Deir el-Bahri**. He married his sister, **Nefru**, and the lady **Tem**, mother of his successor, **Mentuhotep III**.

MENTUHOTEP III (reigned c. 2004–1992 BC). Throne name Sankhkare. Son and successor of **Mentuhotep II** and **Tem**. He also built a funerary complex at **Deir el-Bahri**, but it has not survived. This site was examined by George Schweinfurth in 1904 and **Flinders Petrie** in 1909 and excavated by a Hungarian expedition from 1995–1998.

MENTUHOTEP IV (reigned c. 1992–1985 BC). Throne name Nebtawyre. Successor and probable son of **Mentuhotep III** and Imi. He is not listed in any of the surviving **king lists** but is known from contemporary documents, including inscriptions of mining expeditions to the **Wadi el-Hudi** and the **Wadi Hammamat**. The latter records a visit by his **vizier**, **Amenemhat**, who is generally believed to be the future **Amenemhat I** who may well have overthrown his master.

MENTUHOTEP V–VII. Ephemeral kings of **Dynasty 13** and **Dynasty 17**. Meryankhre Mentuhotep V is known from two statues, Sewadjre Mentuhotep VI from a fragmentary inscription, and Sankhenre Mentuhotep VII from some inscriptions and the **Turin Royal Canon.** *See also* SECOND INTERMEDIATE PERIOD.

MENWI. *See* MANHATA.

MERENPTAH (reigned c. 1212–1202 BC). Throne name Baenre. Thirteenth son of **Ramesses II** by **Isitnofret.** He apparently survived all his older brothers or those eligible for the throne and became virtual **coregent** of his father toward the end of his father's reign. After his succession, he faced invasions from the Libyans and **Sea Peoples** that were successfully repulsed. Diplomatic correspondence with the king of **Ugarit** was discovered in 1994. He was buried in **tomb KV8** in the **Valley of the Kings,** and his **mummy** was found in the **royal cache** in the tomb of **Amenhotep II.** The remains of his mortuary **temple** on the west bank of the **Nile** opposite **Thebes** were excavated by **Flinders Petrie** in 1896 and a Swiss expedition since 1971. His temple was built with material removed from the nearby mortuary temple of **Amenhotep III.** *See also* AMENHERKHEPESHEF; KHAEMWESE; MERYATUM; PREHERWENEMEF; SETY.

MERENRE. *See* NEMTYEMSAF.

MERERUKA (fl. 2340 BC). Vizier of **Teti** of **Dynasty 6** and successor of **Kagemni.** Son of the lady Nedjetempet. He married a royal princess, Watetkhekher, alias **Sesheseshet.** His **tomb** is located near the **pyramid** of Teti at **Saqqara,** and it is one of the largest in the cemetery. There are many fine reliefs of daily life and a massive statue of the deceased in the main hall. The tomb was discovered in 1893 but was only fully copied by an expedition from the University of Chicago from 1930–1936. Mereruka's mother's tomb has recently been discovered next to his. *See also* AMENEMHAT I; APEREL; AY; HEMIUNU; IMHOTEP; INTEFYOKER; KAGEMNI;

NEFERMAAT; PASER; PTAHHOTEP; PTAHSHEPSES; RAMESSES I; REKHMIRE.

MERESANKH. The name of several princesses and **queens** of **Dynasty 4**. Meresankh I was the mother of **Snefru**. Meresankh II was the daughter of **Khufu**, and Meresankh III was the daughter of Khufu's son, **Kawab**; both were wives of **Khafre** and were buried at **Giza**.

MERETSEGER. Snake goddess of **Thebes**. She was worshipped primarily by the royal workmen at **Deir el-Medina**, no doubt to avoid the dangers of snakebites. She was sometimes represented as a woman with a snake's head. Meretseger was identified with el-Qorn, the highest mountain peak on the west bank of the **Nile** opposite Thebes. *See also* RELIGION.

MERIMDA BENI SALAMA. Modern name of an archaeological site in the Delta northwest of Cairo where a prehistoric town settlement was located. The later phases include mudbrick houses apparently built in a town plan. The culture is contemporary with that of **el-Badari** and **Naqada** I but exhibits differences that were originally thought to indicate separate cultural development for **Lower Egypt**. The site was excavated by a German expedition from 1928–1939 and 1977–1983. Recent discoveries at **Minshat Abu Omar** indicate that Naqada culture was also present in the north.

MERITAMUN (fl. 1540–1500 BC). Egyptian princess and **queen**. Sister and wife of **Amenhotep I** of **Dynasty 18** and thus likely daughter of **Ahmose I** and **Ahmose-Nefertari**. She appears to have had no issue. She was buried in **tomb** number 358 at **Deir el-Bahri**, which was discovered in the 1920s. A body identified as hers in the **royal cache** is thought to be a misattribution. *See also* AHMOSE-SIPAIR; SITAMUN.

MERITAMUN (fl. 1450 BC). Egyptian princess of **Dynasty 18**. Likely daughter of **Thutmose III**. She is attested in the chapel at **Deir el-Bahri** and several other monuments and is not to be confused with Meritamun of 1540–1500 BC.

MERITAMUN (fl. 1352–1338 BC). Original name Meritaten. Eldest daughter of **Akhenaten** and **Nefertiti**. She appears as **queen** toward the end of **Dynasty 18**, and it has been suggested that she was the wife of **Smenkhkare** or was possibly Smenkhkare herself. Her ultimate fate is unknown. A Princess **Meritaten-tasherit** attested on monuments from **Amarna** may be her daughter. *See also* AMARNA PERIOD; ANKHESENAMUN; ANKHESENPAATEN-TASHERIT; BAKETATEN; MEKETATEN; MERITATEN-TASHERIT; NEFER-NEFRUATEN; NEFERNEFRURE; SETEPENRE.

MERITAMUN (fl. 1279–1240 BC). A princess of **Dynasty 19**. She was the fourth daughter of **Ramesses II** by **Nefertari**. She became one of her father's **queens**, and a colossal statue of her was discovered at **Akhmim** in 1981. She was buried in **tomb QV68** in the **Valley of the Queens**. *See also* BINTANAT; HENTTAWY; HENUTMIRE; ISITNOFRET; MAATHORNEFERURE; MERITAMUN; NEBETTAWY.

MERITATEN. *See* MERITAMUN (fl. 1352–1338 BC).

MERITATEN-TASHERIT (fl. 1336 BC). A princess of the **Amarna Period**. She is attested on some monuments originating from **Amarna** found at **Hermopolis**. Her origin is unknown, but she may be a daughter of **Akhenaten** or **Smenkhkare**, and her mother may be Meritaten/**Meritamun**. *See also* ANKHESENAMUN; ANKHESENPAATEN-TASHERIT; BAKETATEN; MEKETATEN; NEFERNEFRUATEN; NEFERNEFRURE; SETEPENRE.

MERITETES (fl. 2580 BC). A **queen** of **Khufu** of **Dynasty 4**. She is known from a now lost inscription and is believed to have been buried in one of the unnnamed queen's **pyramids** near her husband's pyramid at **Giza**. She may have been the mother of **Kawab**. Two princesses of Dynasty 4 also bore this name. A later Queen Meritetes was the wife of **Pepy I** of **Dynasty 6**.

MERNEITH (fl. 2985 BC). A **Queen** of **Dynasty 1**. Wife of **Djet** and mother of **Den**, who appears on the royal seals of her son. She apparently acted as regent or coruler with her son, the first **woman** attested in this position. *See also* EARLY DYNASTIC PERIOD.

MEROE. Capital of the Kushite kingdom in **Nubia** from the **Late Period** until the **Roman Period**. Following the expulsion of **Dynasty 25** from Egypt, their successors reigned first at **Napata** and then further south at Meroe. The rulers were buried in **pyramids** near the city. Hostilities with the Egyptian authorities occasionally occurred, the most notable being during the reign of **Augustus**. Little is known about the internal workings of the kingdom, as Meroitic script has yet to be deciphered. The city-site has been excavated by the British John Garstang from 1909–1914, a Canadian expedition from 1965–1977 and 1983–1984, a joint German–Sudanese expedition in 1992, and a joint Canadian–Sudanese expedition since 1999. The pyramid site has been explored by **George Reisner** from 1920–1923 and more recently by a German expedition.

MERSA GAWASIS. Modern name for the site of an ancient Egyptian port on the Red Sea north of Quseir al-Khadim (**Myos Hormos**). Ancient *Saww*. It lies at the entrance to the Wadi Gawasis and is accessed via the Eastern Desert to the **Nile** Valley. The port flourished from the end of the **Old Kingdom** to the early **New Kingdom**, but the period of its greatest activity appears to be during the **Middle Kingdom**. It was used by expeditions to **Punt**. Inscriptions have been recovered naming **Senusret I**; Senusret's **vizier, Intefyoker**; and **Amenemhat III**. The site was discovered and examined by an Egyptian team from 1976–1977 and has been under excavation by a joint American–Italian expedition since 2001.

MERTI. *See* MANHATA.

MERYATUM (fl. 1270–1230 BC). Sixteenth son of **Ramesses II** by **Nefertari**. He was appointed to the post of high priest of **Re** at **Heliopolis** c. 1254 BC. He was buried in **KV5** in the **Valley of the Kings**. *See also* AMENHERKHEPESHEF; KHAEMWESE; MERENPTAH; PREHERWENEMEF; SETY.

MERYETRE HATSHEPSUT (fl. 1445–1420 BC). Queen of **Thutmose III** and possibly daughter of the lady Huy. She is depicted in Thutmose's **tomb** in the **Valley of the Kings** and named on other monuments. She was his wife at the end of his reign, as her son,

Amenhotep II, who succeeded to the throne, was a young man upon his accession. *See also* NEBTU; NEFRURE; SITIAH.

MERYKARE (reigned c. 2050 BC). Throne name of a ruler of **Dynasty 9** or **10** who ruled from **Herakleopolis** during the **First Intermediate Period**. He is known as the recipient of advice in a text of **wisdom literature** where the name of the author is missing but was presumably a King **Khety**. The personal name and fate of King Merykare are unknown.

METROPOLITAN MUSEUM OF ART. One of the major collections of Egyptian antiquities located in New York City. The Egyptian galleries were first opened in 1911. The collection was assembled from such purchases as the antiquities of the Earl of Carnarvon; donations from the **Egypt Exploration Fund**; and most importantly archaeological work in Egypt carried out by director **Herbert Winlock**, mainly at **Deir el-Bahri**, **Thebes**, and **Lisht**. Major pieces include the statue of **Sahure** of **Dynasty 5**, the jewelry of Princess **Sithathoriunet**, a wooden statue of **Senusret I**, and the jewelry of the minor wives of **Thutmose III**. Following the **Nubian Rescue Campaign**, the museum was presented with the **temple** of Dandur by the Egyptian government. *See also* BERLIN EGYPTIAN MUSEUM; BOSTON MUSEUM OF FINE ARTS; BRITISH MUSEUM; CAIRO EGYPTIAN MUSEUM; LOUVRE MUSEUM; TURIN EGYPTIAN MUSEUM.

MIDDLE EGYPT. A geographical term used by modern Egyptologists to refer to the area from **Lisht** to **Asyut** in the **Nile** Valley. During ancient times, it was considered to be the northern part of **Upper Egypt**. *See also* LOWER EGYPT.

MIDDLE KINGDOM (c. 2040–1795 BC). The term used by Egyptologists for the period from the reunion of Egypt by **Mentuhotep II** of **Dynasty 11**, which terminated the **First Intermediate Period**, until the end of **Dynasty 12**, although some academics continue the period until the middle or end of **Dynasty 13**. The Middle Kingdom witnessed Egyptian expansion into **Nubia** and increased influence in the Middle East, the establishment of a new capital at **Lisht** under

Dynasty 12, increased **agricultural** development in the **Fayum** region, and the development of Egyptian classical literature. Political instability and pressure from Asiatic neighbors brought about its collapse and the beginning of the **Second Intermediate Period**. *See also* NEW KINGDOM; OLD KINGDOM.

MIN. Egyptian god of fertility represented as a standing mummiform man with an erect phallus and feathered plumes. His right arm is usually raised with a flail at hand. He was the chief god of **Coptos** and **Akhmim**. Min was also regarded as a protector of desert areas and was often identified with **Amun** as a creator god. During the **Roman Period**, he was identified with the god Pan. Near Akhmin, his wife, was considered to be the goddess **Repit**. *See also* ATHRIBIS; RELIGION.

MINSHAT ABU OMAR. Modern name for a site of a cemetery in the northeastern Delta of **Lower Egypt**. The graves date from the late **Predynastic Period** to the **Early Dynastic Period**, and **pottery** found there shows strong affinities with the **Naqada** culture of **Upper Egypt** but also includes imports from Palestine. Minshat Abu Omar was excavated by a German expedition from 1978–1991. *See also* ADAIMA; GERZEH; KAFR HASSAN DAOUD; TELL EL-FARKHA; TELL IBRAHIM AWAD.

MIRGISSA. Modern name for a site in lower **Nubia** near the end of the Second **Cataract**. Ancient Egyptian *Iken*. The area was the location of a **Dynasty 12** fort that served as a major **trading** center and entrepôt. The site was excavated by a French expedition before the region was flooded by Lake Nasser, the lake formed by the waters of the Aswan High Dam. *See also* ANIBA; ASKUT; BUHEN; KUMMA; SEMNA; SHALFAK; URONARTI.

MITANNI. A major Asiatic kingdom formed in the middle of the second millennium covering northern Iraq, southern Turkey, and eastern Syria. Its rulers exercised sway over many of the local princes of Syria and Palestine. The invading Egyptian armies from **Thutmose I** onward clashed with Mitanni, known to the Egyptians as Naharin, and restricted its influence. Peace seems to have been arranged between the powers by the reign of **Thutmose IV**, who married a Mitannian princess, as did his son **Amenhotep III**, who had two Mitannian wives, **Tadukhepa** and **Gilukhepa**. The Mitannian kingdom was reduced to vassal status by the **Hittites** and finally destroyed by the Assyrians toward the end of the second millennium. *See also* WARFARE.

MNEVIS. Greek name for the sacred bull of **Heliopolis**, regarded as the living embodiment of the sun god **Re**. He ranked next in importance to the **Apis** bull of **Memphis**. Some burials have been discovered at Heliopolis, but information on the succession of Mnevis bulls is less documented than that of the Apis. *See also* BUCHIS; RELIGION.

MOALLA, EL-. A site in **Upper Egypt** near **Thebes** where painted rock-cut **tombs** of the **First Intermediate Period** have been discovered. The most interesting of these tombs is that of Ankhtifi, who described the civil **wars** at that time. It was copied by Jacques Vandier, a French archaeologist, beginning in 1935 and was published in 1950. It has since been the subject of reexamination by an expedition from the University of Liverpool since 2001.

MONS CLAUDIANUS. Roman name for the site of the Roman granodiorite quarry and associated settlement in the Eastern Desert 500 kilometers south of Cairo in the mountains bordering the Red Sea. The area was in use from the time of Trajan (98–117 AD). The surviving remains include a fortress with administrative buildings, animal lines, and a **temple** of **Sarapis**. The site was excavated by a joint British–French expedition from 1987–1993, which recovered among other objects 9,000 **ostraca**. *See also* HATNUB; MONS PORPHYRITES; SERABIT EL-KHADIM; WADI EL-HUDI; WADI HAMMAMAT; WADI MAGHARA.

MONS PORPHYRITES. Roman name for the site of the Roman porphyry quarry and associated settlement in the mountains of the Eastern Desert 30 kilometers from the Red Sea coast. The site was discovered around 18 AD by **Caius Cominius Leugas** and was worked throughout the **Roman Period**. Archaeological investigations of the area were conducted by a British expedition from 1994–1998. *See also* HATNUB; MONS CLAUDIANUS; SERABIT EL-KHADIM; WADI EL-HUDI; WADI HAMMAMAT; WADI MAGHARA.

MONTET, (JEAN) PIERRE MARIE (1885–1966). French Egyptologist. He was born at Villefranche-sur-Saone, France, on 27 June 1885, and studied at the University of Lyons and the **French Institute** in Cairo. He excavated at Byblos in Lebanon from 1921–1924; in Egypt at **Abu Roash** in 1937; and at the important site of **Tanis** from 1929–1940, 1945–1951, and 1954–1956. His most important finds were the royal **tombs** of **Dynasty 21** and **Dynasty 22** at Tanis from 1939–1940. Montet later became professor at the University of Strasbourg. He died in Paris on 18 June 1966. *See also* CARTER, HOWARD; MARIETTE, (FRANÇOIS) AUGUSTE FERDINAND; NAVILLE, (HENRI) EDOUARD; PETRIE, WILLIAM MATTHEW FLINDERS; REISNER, GEORGE ANDREW; TAKELOT I; WINLOCK, HERBERT EUSTIS.

MONTU. Hawk-headed god of **war** whose major place of worship was at **Thebes** and nearby **Armant** and **Tod**. Prominent during **Dynasty 11**, he was eclipsed by the popularity of **Amun**. *See also* RELIGION.

MOSES. *See* EXODUS.

MUDBRICK. The basic material used for construction in ancient Egypt. **Nile** clay mixed with sand and straw was poured into molds and dried to form bricks used in the building of most domestic buildings and palaces. Straw was used in the bricks found at **Amarna**. Mudbricks were also used in the lower courses of **temple** construction. They were placed on a bed of clean sand and topped by the **stone** structure. As mudbrick buildings decay over time, only the bottom courses are generally preserved. The Egyptian word for brick was *tob*, which then passed into Arabic and Spanish to produce the modern word adobe.

MUMMY. Modern word derived from the Arabic *mumiya* to describe the embalmed bodies of the ancient Egyptians. The earliest preserved bodies from the late **Predynastic Period**, c. 3200 BC, are not mummies strictly speaking since they have been preserved by natural means in the dry Egyptian sand without any human intervention. Possibly inspired by these examples, the Egyptians came to believe that it was necessary to maintain the body of the deceased as home for the soul. Mummification efforts were undertaken beginning in the **Old Kingdom**. The first results were not very successful. The bodies were wrapped in linen, presumably after the removal of the internal organs, and then covered with mud to model human features. Only a few of these mummies have been discovered intact, notably one in the **tomb** of **Nefer** during **Dynasty 5**.

By the **New Kingdom**, the method of embalming had been perfected, and it reached its most advanced state during **Dynasty 21**. The internal organs were removed and placed in **canopic jars** or returned to the body in packages, apart from the heart, which was left in the body. The brain was extracted via the nose and discarded. The body was then dried out with dry natron, a natural salt; packed and anointed with resins and aromatics; and then wrapped in bandages, beneath and between which various amulets were often placed.

The method of mummification declined in succeeding periods, although the outer covering of bandages became more elaborate and during the **Roman Period** included painted **mummy portraits**. Mummification was abandoned during the **Coptic** Period as a pagan rite. During the medieval period, bodies were ground to a powder, known in Arabic as *mumiya*, which was considered beneficial for health. This practice led to a minor industry of excavating and disposing of mummies, which incidentally also resulted in some early archaeological discoveries. The present term *mummy* derives from the Arabic name of the powder. *See also* AFTERLIFE.

MUMMY PORTRAITS. Painted wooden panels with a head and shoulders portrait of the deceased attached to the head of the **mummy** popular during the **Roman Period**. The portrait was painted in tempera or wax encaustic. Painting in wax is mentioned by ancient authors, but the mummy portraits from **Hawara** are the only surviving examples of this technique, which has not been successfully replicated in modern times. The portraits are often called **Fayum** portraits, as the majority of them have been found in the Fayum, but examples have also been excavated throughout the country from

Marina el-Alamein in the north to **Aswan** in the south. *See also* HIBA, EL-.

MURSILI III. *See* URHI-TESHUB.

MUSIC. No textual information has survived on ancient Egyptian music, but original instruments have been recovered, and musical instruments are depicted on **tomb** reliefs. Music was used as a background for songs and hymns and for dancing in a religious context or at private banquet functions. The musical instruments of the period included the flute, depicted in the **Old Kingdom**; the double clarinet of the **Old Kingdom**, which was replaced in the **New Kingdom** by the double oboe; harps of various types; lyres and lutes introduced from the Levant in the New Kingdom; drums; and tambourines. Hand clapping and clappers were also used for rhythm. The trumpet was used in militray contexts and the **sistrum** in religious ceremonies.

MUT. Egyptian goddess. Consort of **Amun**. She is usually depicted as a female figure with a vulture headdress surmounted by the double crown of Egypt, but she is also portrayed with the head of a lioness. Her sacred animal was a lion, and her principal place of worship was her **temple** at **Karnak** linked to the main temple of Amun. The temple was adorned by many statues of the goddess **Sakhmet**, who was thus linked to Mut. *See also* RELIGION.

MUTEMWIA (fl. 1350 BC). Queen-mother of **Amenhotep III** and wife of **Thutmose IV**. She is not attested until the reign of her son and must have been a minor wife of his father. There is no evidence identifying her with the **Mitannian** princess who was also wife to Thutmose IV. In the **temple** of **Luxor**, she is depicted in the embrace of the god **Amun**, who according to tradition was the father of each Egyptian ruler.

MUTNEFRET (fl. 1500 BC). Wife of **Thutmose I** and mother of **Thutmose II**. Her origin is unknown, but she is generally described by Egyptologists as a minor or secondary wife. There is no evidence for this assertion, as she may have been the wife of Thutmose I before his accession to the throne, at which time he may have wed his sister, **Queen Ahmose**. Mutnefret may have been the mother of the king's other sons, **Amenmose** and **Wadjmose**. A Princess Mutnefret was probably her granddaughter or great-granddaughter.

MUTNODJMET (fl. 1310 BC). Queen of **Horemheb**. She appears in the reign of **Akhenaten**, apparently as the sister of his queen, **Nefertiti**, but her parentage is unknown. It is not clear when she married Horemheb, who appears to have had an earlier wife. She apparently died childless before her husband and is possibly buried in his **tomb** at **Saqqara**.

MUTNODJMET (fl. 1039–991 BC). Queen of **Pasebakhaenniut I**. She is mentioned in texts in his **tomb** at **Tanis**. She bears the titles of king's daughter and king's sister, so she may the daughter of **Pinudjem** I, who had a daughter of this name.

MUWATTALLI II (c. 1310–1272 BC). King of the **Hittites**. Son of Mursili II and Gassuliyawiya. He faced a renewed attempt by Egypt to regain its lost territories in Syria resulting in the battle of **Kadesh** with **Ramesses II**. The Hittite victory there assured that these areas remained in Hittite possession. He also led campaigns against his northern and western neighbors. *See also* URHI-TESHUB; WARFARE.

MYCENAE. *See* AHHIYAWA.

MYCERINUS. *See* MENKAURE.

MYOS HORMOS. Modern Quseir al-Khadim. A seaport on the Red Sea built during the **Ptolemaic Period** but that was more prominent during the **Roman Period** until the 3rd century AD. It was the major port for **trade** with Arabia and India and was connected to **Coptos** via the **Wadi Hammamat**. **Hadrian** later built a road to connect it with **Antinoopolis**. The historian Stabo visited the port with the prefect Aelius Gallus. The town was excavated by an American expedition in 1978, 1980, and 1982 and a British team from 1999–2003, when it was securely identified. The remains of an ancient Egyptian port on the Red Sea have been identified nearby at **Mersa Gawasis**.

MYT (fl. 2020 BC). Also Tamyt. An intended minor wife or daughter of **Mentuhotep II** of **Dynasty 11**. She was commemorated in a chapel at the funerary complex at **Deir el-Bahri** discovered during **Henri Edouard Naville**'s excavations at the site. Her largely intact **tomb** was discovered nearby by an American expedition from the **Metropolitan Museum of Art** from 1920–1921, and her **sarcophagus** is now housed in the museum. Her **mummy** indicates that she was a young child. *See also* ASHAYET; HENHENET; KAWIT; KEMSIT; NEFRU; SADEH; TEM.

– N –

NAG HAMMADI CODICES. Thirteen codices written in **Coptic** during the 4th century AD discovered by a peasant in 1945 near the modern city of Nag Hammadi in **Upper Egypt**. After being sold separately, they have all been reunited in the **Coptic Museum** in Cairo and fully published. The texts are religious tractates pertaining to the dualistic gnostic sect that combined features of Christianity and paganism and was proscribed following the triumph of Christianity. *See also* GNOSTICISM; MANICHEISM.

NAG EL-MASHAYIKH. Modern name for a site in **Upper Egypt** close to **Nag el-Deir**. Ancient Egyptian *Behdet-iabett* but later called Lepidotonpolis by the Greeks. A possible **tomb** from the **Old Kingdom** and two tombs from the **Ramesside Period** are located in the nearby cliffs. There are remains of a **New Kingdom temple** dedicated to the goddess **Mehit**.

NAGA EL-DEIR. Modern name for a site in northern **Upper Egypt** on the east bank of the **Nile** south of Sohag. It likely served as a cemetery for the city of **Thinis**, capital of the eighth Upper Egyptian **nome**. The remains date from the **Predynastic Period** to the **Middle Kingdom**. The site was excavated by **George Reisner** from 1901–1904, in 1912, and from 1923–1924, and the examination yielded much inscribed material in the form of **stelae** and the **Reisner Papyri**.

NAKHT (fl. 1395 BC). Owner of **tomb** 52 in the necropolis of **Thebes**, probably dating to the reign of **Thutmose IV**. He held the title of astronomer. The tomb is decorated with scenes of a blind harper and agricultural activities.

NAKHTHORHEB (reigned 360–343 BC). The Greek form of his name is Nectanebos, usually rendered as Nectanebo II. Throne name Senedjemibre setepenanhur. Epithet meryhathor. Last ruler of **Dynasty 30**. Son of Tjaihepimu, who was the brother of King **Djedhor**. Nakhthorheb accompanied his uncle, Djedhor, on a campaign in Syria and there rebelled with the assistance of his father, who had been left as regent in Egypt. Nakhthorheb was joined by the Greek mercenaries in the army, and his uncle fled to **Persia**. He continued the policies of his grandfather, **Nakhtnebef**, in supporting Egyptian temples.

Nakhthorheb faced continued attempts by Persia to reconquer Egypt, and his armies were eventually defeated in 343 BC, and he was forced to flee to the south, disappearing from history. The **sarcophagus**, which he prepared for his burial, was reused and is now housed in the **British Museum**. Later legend views him as a wise magician who escaped to Macedon and through an affair with Queen Olympias fathered **Alexander the Great**, who drove the Persians from Egypt. The legend is chronologically impossible but reflects the Egyptian tendency to try to give an Egyptian background to their foreign conquerors. *See also* WARFARE.

NAKHTMIN (fl. 1327 BC). An Egyptian army officer under **Tutankhamun**. He dedicated some **shabtis** to the king's **tomb** and so must have been of some importance. It has been speculated that he was related to **Ay** and rival to **Horemheb** for the throne. His ultimate fate is unknown.

NAKHTNEBEF (reigned 380–362 BC). The Greek form of his name is Nectanebes, usually rendered as Nectanebo I. Throne name Kheperkare. Founder of **Dynasty 30**. Son of Djedhor, a military officer from **Sebennytos**. He overthrew **Nefaarud** II of **Dynasty 29**. He managed to defeat a Persian invasion of Egypt in 373 BC and embarked on a major program of refurbishing Egypt's **temples**. *See also* DJEDHOR; NAKHTHORHEB; WARFARE.

NAME. Ancient Egyptian *rn*. Much importance was attached in ancient Egypt to preserving the name of an individual throughout eternity as this imparted immortality to the deceased. Statues and **stelae** were erected especially in **tombs** and **temples** for this purpose. One of the standard prayers of an ancient Egyptian was that someone "cause his name to live."

NAOS. Greek name for the sacred shrine of a **temple**. The naos usually consisted of a hollowed-out stone or wooden container fitted with wooden doors into which the image of the deity was placed. Such monuments are depicted on statues and survive from some temples. Model naoi are also known to exist in **bronze** and wood.

NAPATA. First capital of the later kingdom of Kush in **Nubia**. The site is 30 kilometers south of the Second **Cataract** and appears to have been initially occupied during the **New Kingdom**. Following the Egyptian withdrawal, a Nubian kingdom centered on Napata developed and under **Kashta** and **Piye**, and finally **Shabaqo** conquered Egypt as **Dynasty 25** or the Napatan Dynasty. The area includes the royal cemeteries at el-Kurru and Nuri and the holy mountain of Gebel Barkal with its **temple** to **Amun**. The capital of the kingdom was eventually transferred to the site of **Meroe**.

NAQADA. Modern name for ancient *Nubt*, Greek Ombos. A site in **Upper Egypt** north of **Thebes** where important remains from the late **Predynastic Period** were excavated by **Flinders Petrie** in 1895. The name is now used to denote the final phase of predynastic culture, divided into the periods Naqada I (c. 3900–3600 BC); Naqada II (c. 3600–3200 BC), which is best attested by its painted designs on **pottery**; and Naqada III (c. 3200–3100 BC), when the elements of kingship (**Dynasty 0**) and writing are first discernible. *See also* ADAIMA; GERZEH; KAFR HASSAN DAOUD; MINSHAT ABU OMAR; TELL EL-FARKHA; TELL IBRAHIM AWAD.

NARMER (reigned c. 3100 BC). First king of **Dynasty 1**, as named in the royal seal of the dynasty. He may be identified with the legendary King **Menes**. He is known from a palette and macehead found at **Hierakonpolis**, which record his military victories. He was buried at **Abydos**, where his **tomb** has recently been reexcavated by a German expedition. *See also* AHA.

NAUKRATIS. Greek name for a site in the fifth **nome** of **Lower Egypt** that became a settlement for Greek merchants during **Dynasty 26**, probably founded by **Psamtik I** rather than **Ahmose II**, as stated in **Herodotus**, and that flourished into the **Roman Period**. It was excavated by **Flinders Petrie** in 1885; other British archaeologists in 1886, 1899, and 1903; and an American expedition from 1977–1978 and 1980–1983.

NAVILLE, (HENRI) EDOUARD (1844–1926). Swiss Egyptologist and archaeologist. He was born in Geneva, Switzerland, on 14 June 1844. He studied Egyptology at several universities and visited Egypt in 1865 for the first time. He first worked on texts but was chosen as a field archaeologist by the **Egypt Exploration Fund** in 1882. He excavated at many sites in the **Lower Egypt**, notably **Tell el-Maskhuta**, **Bubastis**, and also at **Herakleopolis** and **Abydos**. He also cleared the **temple** of **Hatshepsut** at **Deir el-Bahri** near **Thebes**. He clashed with **Flinders Petrie** over archaeological methods, as he was mainly interested in inscribed material and monumental architecture and often ignored small finds. He died in Malagny near Geneva on 17 October 1926. *See also* CARTER, HOWARD; MARIETTE, (FRANÇOIS) AUGUSTE FERDINAND; MONTET, (JEAN) PIERRE MARIE; REISNER, GEORGE ANDREW; WINLOCK, HERBERT EUSTIS.

NEBETTAWY (fl. 1270–1240 BC). Princess of **Dynasty 19**. She was the fifth daughter of **Ramesses II**. She was given the title of **queen**, but it is not known if this means that she actually married her father. She was buried in **QV60** in the **Valley of the Queens**. *See also* BINTANAT; HENTTAWY; HENUTMIRE; ISITNOFRET; MAATHORNEFERURE; MERITAMUN; NEFERTARI.

NEBTU (fl. 1450 BC). A wife of **Thutmose III**. She is depicted in his **tomb** in the **Valley of the Kings**. It is not certain if she was a contemporary of his other wives or if she followed **Sitiah** and preceded **Meryetre Hatshepsut**. *See also* NEFRURE.

NEBWENNEF (fl. 1279 BC). High priest of Amun at **Thebes**. Formerly high priest of **Anhur** and of **Hathor** at **Dendera**. He was appointed to the post in Thebes during the first year of **Ramesses II** and records this in a long inscription in his **tomb** (number 157) in the Theban necropolis on the west bank of the **Nile**. *See also* BAKENKHONS; PASER; WENNEFER.

NECHO. *See* NEKAU I; NEKAU II.

NECTANEBO I. *See* NAKHTNEBEF.

NECTANEBO II. *See* NAKHTHORHEB.

NEFAARUD. The Greek form of the name is Nepherites. The name of two kings of **Dynasty 29** from **Mendes**. Nefaarud I, throne name Baenre merynetjeru, reigned from 399–93 BC. He overthrew **Amyrtaeos**, but little is known of his reign. Nefaarud II, who reigned in 380 BC, was in turn ousted by **Nakhtnebef** (Nectanebo I), founder of **Dynasty 30**.

NEFER (fl. 2400 BC). The owner of a **tomb** built at **Saqqara** south of the causeway of the **pyramid** of **Unas** that was discovered by Egyptian archaeologists in 1966. Son of the overseer of singers Kahay and Meretites, who were also buried here. Nefer inherited his father's rank and built the tomb for the family during **Dynasty 5**. The tomb contains fine painted reliefs and is remarkable for the survival of a male **mummy** in a fine state of preservation.

NEFEREFRE. *See* RANEFEREF.

NEFERHOTEP I (reigned c. 1740–1730 BC). Throne name Khasekhemre. Son of the **God's father** Haankhef and the lady Kemi. The circumstances of his accession to power as ruler 22 during **Dy-**

nasty 13 are unclear. He was one of the more important rulers of the period, and he recorded his family origins on **graffiti** near **Elephantine**. He was acknowledged as sovereign by **Yantin**, ruler of **Byblos**. He was succeeded by his brothers, **Sihathor** and **Sobekhotep IV**. *See also* SECOND INTERMEDIATE PERIOD.

NEFERIRKARE (reigned c. 2475–2455 BC). Personal name Kakai. Third ruler of **Dynasty 5**. According to the later **Westcar Papyrus**, he was a brother of his predecessors, **Userkaf** and **Sahure**, but this is doubtful. It has recently been suggested that he was the son of Sahure. He built his **pyramid** complex at **Abusir**, which was excavated by the German Ludwig Borchardt in 1900 and from 1903–1907. He is the first ruler to use two **cartouches** with his prenomen and nomen in the royal **titulary**. *See also* RANEFEREF.

NEFERMAAT (fl. 2620–2580). Egyptian prince during the **Old Kingdom**. He was either a son of **Huni** of **Dynasty 3** or **Snefru** of **Dynasty 4**. He served as **vizier**, probably under Snefru or **Khufu**. He and his wife, Atet, were buried in a **mastaba tomb** at **Meidum**. Many of the wall paintings from the tomb have been preserved, including a famous scene of geese from the chapel of Atet now housed in the **Cairo Egyptian Museum**. He was possibly succeeded in office by his probable son, **Hemiunu**. *See also* AMENEMHAT I; APEREL; AY; IMHOTEP; INTEFYOKER; KAGEMNI; MERERUKA; PASER; PTAHHOTEP; PTAHSHEPSES; RAMESSES I; REKHMIRE.

NEFERNEFRUATEN (fl. 1336 BC). Fourth daughter of **Akhenaten** and **Nefertiti**. She is named in **tomb** reliefs from **Amarna**. She may be one of two princesses who appear on a painted fresco now housed in the Ashmolean Museum of Art and Archaeology in Oxford, United Kingdom. Her fate is unknown. *See also* ANKHESENAMUN; ANKHESENPAATEN-TASHERIT; BAKETATEN; MEKETATEN; MERITAMUN; MERITATEN-TASHERIT; NEFERNEFRURE; SETEPENRE.

NEFERNEFRURE (fl. 1336 BC). Fifth daughter of **Akhenaten** and **Nefertiti**. She is named in **tomb** reliefs from **Amarna** and on a box from the tomb of **Tutankhamun**. She may be one of two princesses who appear on a painted fresco now housed in the Ashmolean Museum of Art and Archaeology in Oxford, United Kingdom. Her fate is unknown. *See also* ANKHESENAMUN; ANKHESENPAATEN-TASHERIT; BAKETATEN; MEKETATEN; MERITAMUN; MERITATEN-TASHERIT; NEFERNEFRUATEN; SETEPENRE.

NEFERTARI (fl. c. 1300–1255 BC). Favorite wife of **Ramesses II** of unknown origin. She is represented in his **temples** at **Abu Simbel** and has her own magnificent **tomb (QV66)** in the **Valley of the Queens**. She had six children, including sons **Amenherkhepeshef**, **Preherwenemef**, Meryre, and **Meryatum**, and daughters **Meritamun** and **Henttawy**. She carried out diplomatic correspondence with **Queen Puduhepa** of the **Hittites**. *See also* BINTANAT; HENUTMIRE; ISITNOFRET; MAATHORNEFERURE; MERITAMUN; NEBETTAWY.

NEFERTI. The fictional author of a literary text set during the reign of **Snefru** in which he prophesies civil war and confusion in Egypt, which will be ended by the succession of **Amenemhat I** of **Dynasty 12**. The text was doubtlessly written during the reign of the latter as a justification of his accession to the throne.

NEFERTIRY (fl. 1395 BC). A wife of King **Thutmose IV**. She appears on several of his monuments. *See also* IARET; MUTEMWIA.

NEFERTITI (fl. 1370–1336 BC). Chief wife of **Akhenaten** of unknown origin. She is represented as an equal of her husband on reliefs and in a style not previously used for **queens**. She is best known for the famous bust found at **Amarna** now housed in the **Berlin Egyptian Museum**. She was apparently the mother of six daughters, including Meritaten (later **Meritamun**), **Meketaten**, Ankhesenpaaten (later **Ankhesenamun**, wife of **Tutankhamun**), **Nefernefruaten**, **Nefernefrure**, and **Setepenre**. Her ultimate fate is unknown, but it has been suggested that she briefly acted as ruler or regent upon her husband's death. *See also* AY; SMENKHKARE; TIY.

NEFERTUM. Egyptian god of vegetation. Son of **Ptah** and **Sakhmet** and part of the **triad** of **Memphis**. He is represented as a human figure with a beard and a floral headdress of a lotus. *See also* RE.

NEFRU. The name of several **queens** of **Dynasty 11** and **Dynasty 12**. The mothers of **Intef II** and **Intef III** of Dynasty 11 were both named Nefru, as was the daughter of Intef III and **Iah**, who married her brother, **Mentuhotep II**. The **tomb** of the last was discovered at her husband's funerary complex at **Deir el-Bahri**. During Dynasty 12, Nefru, daughter of **Amenemhat I**, married her brother, **Senusret I**, and was the mother of his successor, **Amenemhat II**. She is mentioned at the royal court in the story of **Sinuhe**.

NEFRUBITY (fl. 1480 BC). Daughter of King **Thutmose I** and **Queen Ahmose** and sister of Queen **Hatshepsut**. She is named in the **temple** reliefs at **Deir el-Bahri** but is otherwise unknown.

NEFRUPTAH (fl. 1810 BC). The name of at least two royal princesses of **Dynasty 12**. The more notable was the daughter of **Amenemhat III**, whose intact **tomb** was discovered in 1955 at **Hawara** near the **pyramid** of her father. Her body had been dissolved by water seepage, but jewelry and funerary material were recovered. A **sarcophagus** inscribed for her was also found in her father's burial chamber, but it was either not used or used only temporarily. Her importance is witnessed by the fact that her name is written in a **cartouche**.

NEFRURE (fl. 1480–1459 BC). Only daughter of **Thutmose II** and **Queen Hatshepsut**. She was given a prominent role at court by her mother and was placed in the care of **Senenmut**. She was possibly destined to marry her half brother, **Thutmose III**. It is not certain if she survived her mother or if this marriage took place, but she undoubtedly died fairly young and without issue. *See also* MERYETRE HATSHEPSUT; NEBTU; SITIAH.

NEHESY (reigned c. 1700 BC). Throne name Aasehre. Ruler of **Dynasty 14** during the **Second Intermediate Period**. He is known from several monuments discovered in the eastern Delta region, notably from **Tanis**, **Bubastis**, **Leontopolis**, **Avaris**, and **Tell Hebua**. His capital was probably at **Xois** or Avaris, and his rule undoubtedly extended over part of the Delta region.

NEITH. Primeval Egyptian goddess worshipped primarily at **Sais**. She is represented as a woman with the red crown of **Lower Egypt**. Her symbol was a shield with crossed arrows representing an ancient connection with war. She was one of the tutelary goddesses protecting **canopic jars**. *See also* RELIGION.

NEITH (fl. 2275 BC). Egyptian princess and **queen**. Daughter of **Pepy I**. She married her brother, **Pepy II**, and was buried in a subsidiary **pyramid** next to his at **Saqqara**.

NEITHHOTEP (fl. 3080 BC). A **queen** of **Dynasty 1**. Her position remains uncertain, as she appears to be connected with kings **Aha** and **Djer**. It may even be possible that there were two ladies of this name.

NEKAU I (d. 664 BC). The Greek form of his name is Necho. Throne name **Menkheperre**. Originally prince of **Sais**, he was installed as puppet ruler of Egypt by the Assyrians and was killed by **Tantamani** during his reconquest of Egypt. He was the ancestor of **Dynasty 26**. *See also* PSAMTIK I.

NEKAU II (reigned 610–595 BC). Throne name Wehemibre. Son of **Psamtik I**. He attempted to stop the growth of Babylonian power by supporting the remnants of the defeated Assyrian army. Nekau defeated the army of King Josiah of Israel, killing the king when the **Israelites** attempted to block his forces, but he himself was defeated by the Babylonians at the battle of Carchemish in 609 BC. He was forced to retreat but prevented a Babylonian invasion of Egypt. He attempted to build a canal between the **Nile** and Red Sea, which was later finished by **Darius I**. *See also* PSAMTIK II; WARFARE.

NEKHBET. Egyptian goddess of *Nekheb*, modern **Elkab**, represented as a vulture. She was the tutelary deity of **Upper Egypt** and as such appears in the *nebty* or two ladies name of the royal **titulary** and on the royal crown with the **uraeus** of **Wadjet**. *See also* RELIGION.

NEMTYEMSAF. The name of two kings of **Dynasty 6** who both had brief reigns. The name was wrongly read Antyemsaf by earlier Egyptologists. Nemtyemsaf I (reigned c. 2287–2278 BC), throne name Merenre, was the elder son of **Pepy I**. He died young and was buried at **Saqqara**. His **pyramid** was opened in 1880, and its complex was excavated by a French team from 1971–1973 and in 1980.

Nemtyemsaf II (reigned c. 2184–2183 BC) was the son of **Pepy II** and nephew of his namesake. If a later story reported by **Herodotus** is correct, he was assassinated after a brief reign and succeeded by his sister-**queen**, **Nitocris**.

NEPHERITES. *See* NEFAARUD.

NEPHTHYS. Egyptian goddess. Daughter of **Geb** and **Nut** and sister of **Isis**, **Osiris**, and **Seth**, whom she married. She was the chief mourner for Osiris, along with Isis. Nephthys was one of the tutelary goddesses protecting coffins and **canopic jars**. *See also* RELIGION.

NESBANEBDJED (reigned c. 1069–1043 BC). The Greek form of his name is Smendes. Throne name Hedjkheperre. Founder of **Dynasty 21**. Mayor of **Tanis** at the end of **Dynasty 20**, he succeeded to the throne after **Ramesses XI** in obscure circumstances. His control of southern Egypt appears to have been minimal. He and his wife, **Tentamun**, are mentioned in the story of **Wenamun**.

NESKHONS. The wife of **Pinudjem** II, **high priest of Amun** at **Thebes**. Possibly a daughter of the high priest **Nesbanebdjed** and so niece of her husband. She was buried in the **royal cache** at Thebes. She bore the title of **viceroy of Kush**, which must have been purely nominal and was used for the last time by her. *See also* DYNASTY 21.

NEW KINGDOM (c. 1550–1069 BC). The term used by Egyptologists to describe the period from **Dynasty 18** to **Dynasty 20** when Egypt was at the height of its power and prosperity and ruled an empire covering **Nubia** and Palestine-Syria. The era began with the expulsion of the **Hyksos** from Egypt and the reunion of the country under **Ahmose I** and ended with the **Second Intermediate Period**. There followed the expansion into Nubia and the Levant, culminating in the campaigns of **Thutmose III**. The increased wealth generated by these conquests led to major building campaigns, notably at **Karnak** and later under **Ramesses II** at **Pi-Ramesses**, **Abu Simbel**, and other sites. The god of **Thebes**, **Amun**, was elevated to the head of the divine pantheon. Increasing political and economic instability and aggressive external threats led to the gradual abandonment of the empire by the end of **Dynasty 20** and the division of the country, heralding the **Third Intermediate Period**. *See also* MIDDLE KINGDOM; OLD KINGDOM; WARFARE.

NILE. Modern word derived from Greek for the main waterway of ancient Egypt known simply then as the *itrw* (river), since there was no other river. It was the main artery for irrigation and transportation in Egypt. The Nile flooded annually from July to September fed by the rains in Ethiopia, and it brought fertile topsoil down to Egyptian farmlands and washed out harmful salts. As a result, Egypt was guaranteed hefty crop harvests unless the Nile was exceptionally low or high and thus presented the most stable area for settlement in the Middle East. The Nile also served as the main means of communication throughout the Nile Valley up to **Elephantine** (Aswan), where a series of **cataracts** or rapids impeded river traffic and so marked the historical border of Egypt. *See also* AGRICULTURE; CHRONOLOGY.

NIMLOT. The name of several princes of **Dynasty 22**. The earliest was the brother of King **Osorkon** the Elder and father of **Sheshonq I**. Both Sheshonq I and **Osorkon II** had sons named Nimlot who were placed in control of the town of **Hierakonpolis**. During the invasion of **Piye**, King Nimlot of **Hermopolis** was one of his chief opponents. *See also* KAROMAMA.

NITOCRIS (reigned c. 2183–81 BC). The Greek form of the name of a legendary **queen**. She is alleged by **Herodotus** to have succeeded her assassinated brother and husband and to have executed his murderers before committing suicide. If the legend is correct, she might have been the wife of **Nemtyemsaf** II. The Egyptian name Neithikert, from whom the Greek Nitocris may be derived, appears as the last ruler of **Dynasty 6** in the **Turin Royal Canon**, but nothing historical is known of the ruler, who may well have been a man. *See also* FIRST INTERMEDIATE PERIOD.

NITOCRIS (fl. 665–586 BC). Daughter of **Psamtik I** and Mehitenweskhet, daughter of the priest Harsiese. She was appointed in 656 BC as eventual heiress to the title of **God's wife of Amun** and was thereby ensured the recognition of her father as **pharaoh** by the authorities in **Thebes** headed by **Mentuemhat**. She later adopted her great-niece, **Ankhnesneferibre**, in 595 BC, and she died on 16 December 586 BC. A second Nitocris, daughter of **Ahmose II**, was destined to be the successor of Ankhnesneferibre, but her fate is unknown after the Persian conquest of Egypt.

NIUSERRE (reigned c. 2445–2421 BC). Personal name Ini. Ruler of **Dynasty 5**. Son of **Neferirkare** and probably **Khentkaues** II. He was the eventual successor of the short-lived **Raneferef**, possibly after some confusion. He built a sun **temple** at Abu Ghurab near **Abusir**, which was excavated by a German expedition at the end of the 19th century, and a **pyramid** and mortuary complex at Abusir excavated by Ludwig Borchardt from 1902–1904, from which many fine reliefs were recovered. The **Palermo Stone** indicates that he sent expeditions to Sinai and **Punt**. *See also* MENKAUHOR.

NODJMET (fl. c. 1075 BC). Wife of the **high priest of Amun** and titular king **Herihor**. A surviving letter indicates that she served in an administrative capacity in **Thebes** while the high priest **Piankh** was absent in **Nubia**. It has been suggested that she might have married Piankh as well, but his wife may have been **Hrere**.

NOMARCH. *See* NOME.

NOME. Greek name for the 42 provincial divisions of Egypt known as *sepat* to the Egyptians. There were traditionally 22 **Upper Egyptian** nomes and 20 **Lower Egyptian** nomes, each with its own standard and symbols. The governors of the nomes, known as nomarchs in Greek, tended to increase their power at times of weakness of the central government, notably during the **First Intermediate Period**, but their powers were curbed during **Dynasty 12**, and the offices may well have been suppressed under **Senusret III**.

NUBIA. Modern name for the area of the **Nile** Valley and its adjacent region south of **Elephantine**. It became important to Egypt as a source of minerals and served as an intermediary between Egypt and sub-Saharan Africa for luxury **trade** goods. Egyptian expeditions penetrated the area beginning in the late **Predynastic Period** during raiding forays, and in the **Old Kingdom**, **copper** was mined and smelted at **Buhen**, although it is unclear whether the Egyptian presence was permanent.

During the **Middle Kingdom**, a determined attempt was made to subjugate the area, and extensive fortresses were built along the Nile with the new border fixed at **Semna**. The collapse of the **Second Intermediate Period** led to an Egyptian withdrawal and the growth of a native kingdom based in **Kerma** in the area now known in Egyptian sources as Kush. The **Hyksos** sought an alliance with Kush against the rulers of **Thebes**, but both were destroyed by **Dynasty 18**, which renewed the Egyptian conquest of the south, conquering Nubia down to **Napata** by the reign of **Thutmose III** and putting the new province under the rule of the **viceroy of Kush**.

Some native chieftains were allowed to remain under strict control, but their families were sent to the Egyptian court to be Egyptianized. Nubia was exploited principally for its **gold** reserves, which greatly enhanced Egyptian prestige and power. Numerous **temples** were built, and Egyptian **religion**, especially worship of the god **Amun**, took a strong hold on the population. Egyptian administration collapsed into civil war and confusion at the end of **Dynasty 20**.

A new native kingdom was formed based at **Napata** and eventually under **Piye**, and **Shabaqo** conquered Egypt itself to found **Dynasty 25**. The Nubians were driven out of Egypt by **Assyria**, but the dynasty persisted in Nubia and later moved its capital to **Meroe**. Tension remained between the Meroitic kingdom and the Ptolemaic and Roman rulers of Egypt over control of the area just south of Elephantine, and Nubian rulers were assiduous in their worship at the temple of **Philae**, even after Egypt was Christianized.

The Meroitic kingdom fell apart during the 4th century AD, partly under pressure from such invading desert tribes as the Nobatae, which gave the area its modern name. Three local kingdoms developed and adopted Christianity in the 6th century but were eventually overwhelmed by Muslim forces and disappeared during the 15th century. The successive constructions of dams at Aswan and the subsequent flooding have led to major archaeological campaigns in Lower

Nubia from 1898–1902, 1907–1912, 1929–1934, and 1960–1965 so that, although the region is now flooded, its archaeological record is better attested than many areas of Egypt proper. *See also* A-GROUP; C-GROUP; NUBIAN RESCUE CAMPAIGN.

NUBIAN RESCUE CAMPAIGN. The construction of the new Aswan High Dam, which commenced in 1960, resulted in the creation of Lake Nasser, a massive lake flooding much of Lower Nubia from the First **Cataract** at Aswan to almost the Third Cataract. Under the auspices of the United Nations Educational, Scientific, and Cultural Organization, following an appeal by the Egyptian and Sudanese governments in 1959, an intensive archaeological campaign was organized by the international community from 1960–1965, involving 27 nations. Nineteen **temples** or monuments were removed from threatened sites, notably the temples at **Abu Simbel**, **Dendur**, and **Philae**, and also parts of the temples of **Gerf Hussein** and **Semna**.

NUN. God of the primeval waters of chaos from which emerged a mound on which the god **Atum** appeared. *See also* RELIGION.

NUT. Egyptian goddess of the sky and wife of **Geb**, the god of earth. Mother of **Osiris**, **Isis**, **Seth**, and **Nephthys**. She is represented as a naked woman often in an arched position over her husband and is depicted on the inside of coffins as a protector of the dead. *See also* RELIGION.

NYMAATHAP (fl. 2667 BC). Queen of **Dynasty 3**. Either mother or wife of **Djoser**. She has been seen as a link between **Dynasty 2** and Dynasty 3, but no firm evidence has been found of her exact position in either dynasty.

NYNETJER (reigned c. 2810 BC). Third ruler of **Dynasty 2** and successor to **Raneb**. Part of his reign is recorded on the **Palermo Stone**, which mentions military campaigns and the **Apis** bull. He appears to have been buried at **Saqqara**. His **tomb** has been examined by a German expedition since 2004. *See also* PERIBSEN.

– O –

OBELISK. Modern word for an Egyptian monolithic stone monument consisting of a thin shaft with a top is shaped as a **pyramidion**. Ancient Egyptian *tekhen*. Small obelisks are known, but most are tall and were located in **temples**. The development of the monument was linked to the introduction of the cult of the sun god **Re**, whose rising rays would strike the top of the obelisk, often sheeted in **gold**. The first obelisks seem to have been constructed at **Heliopolis** and the sun temples of **Dynasty 5**, but their use in temples in the **New Kingdom** and later periods was widespread. Two obelisks were placed in front of the main **pylon** of the major temples. Scenes from the temple of **Hatshepsut** at **Deir el-Bahri** depict the transport of an obelisk from the quarries at Aswan to **Thebes**, while a broken monument remains in the quarry. Many obelisks were carried off by Roman conquerors to decorate Rome, while others were removed in modern times to major European and North American cities.

OLD KINGDOM (c. 2686–2181 BC). A term used by Egyptologists to refer to the stable period beginning in either **Dynasty 3** or **Dynasty 4** to the end of **Dynasty 6**, which followed the **Early Dynastic Period**. It appeared that Egypt at the time had a highly organized autocratic government that could mobilize its resources and manpower in massive construction efforts, like the building of the **pyramids**. The period ended with the collapse of central authority possibly due to famine or increasingly powerful regional governors or nomarchs ushering in the **First Intermediate Period**. *See also* MIDDLE KINGDOM; NEW KINGDOM.

ONURIS. *See* ANHUR.

OSIRIS. The Greek form for the Egyptian god of the dead *Wsir*, lord of the underworld. Son of **Geb** and **Nut** and husband of **Isis**. According to legend, he was originally a king of Egypt but was murdered and dismembered by his brother, **Seth**. His widow, Isis, recovered and buried his remains. He was also a god of vegetation and renewal. The dead king, and later any deceased individual, was identified with Osiris, but the individual also had to be judged by Osiris before entering the next life. Osiris is depicted as a mummiform figure with a feathered crown holding a crook and flail. He was early amalgamated with the god Khentyamnetyu of **Abydos**, which became the principal place of his worship and where his **tomb** was said to be located. *See also* RELIGION.

OSORKON (fl. 850–785 BC). The name of a **high priest of Amun**, son of **Takelot II** and **Queen Karomama**. He was installed in office by his father but faced opposition from the Thebans and was involved in a series of campaigns to claim his position. He recorded his biography on a long inscription on the **temple** wall at **Karnak**. It has been suggested that he is to be identified with a later King **Osorkon III**, who also had the title of high priest and is known mainly from monuments in **Thebes** and **Middle Egypt**. If this is true, Osorkon must have lived to an old age.

OSORKON (reigned c. 984–978 BC). Throne name Aakheperre setepenre. A king of **Dynasty 21**, now known to Egyptologists as Osorkon the Elder. Son of the Libyan chief Sheshonq and Mehtenweskhet. He briefly gained the throne from the Tanite king **Amenemope**, but it then passed to **Siamun**, apparently of another family. His nephew, **Sheshonq I**, reestablished the Libyans to the throne, founding **Dynasty 22**. The true form of his name was only established after the later kings Osorkon had been numbered, so he does not appear in that sequence.

OSORKON I (reigned c. 924–889 BC). Throne name Sekhemkheperre setepenre. Epithet meryamun. Son of **Sheshonq I** of **Dynasty 22** and **Queen Karomama**. He established a major fortress at Per-Sekhemkheperre. He is attested in close relations with the port of **Byblos** on the eastern Mediterranean coast. He married **Maatkare**, daughter of **Pasebakhaenniut II**, by whom he was the father of Sheshonq, whom he installed as **high priest of Amun** in succession to his brother, **Iuput**. This son wrote his name in a royal **cartouche** and may be identified with the ephemeral king **Sheshonq II**. *See also* TAKELOT I.

OSORKON II (reigned c. 874–850 BC). Throne name Usimaatre setepenamun. Epithet meryamun sibast. Son of **Takelot I** of **Dynasty 22**

and Kapes. He continued the dynastic policy of putting sons in key positions, installing **Sheshonq** as **high priest of Ptah** in **Memphis** and **Nimlot** as high priest of **Heryshef** in **Herakleopolis** and later **high priest of Amun** in **Karnak**. He erected a festival hall in **Bubastis** to celebrate his **jubilee**. He was buried at **Tanis**, and his intact **tomb** was rediscovered in 1939. *See also* TAKELOT II.

OSORKON III (reigned c. 777–749 BC). Throne name Usimaatre setepenamun. Epithet siese. Ruler of **Dynasty 23**. Son of **Queen Karomama**. He is attested mainly by monuments in **Thebes** and **Middle Egypt**. He installed his son, **Takelot III**, as **high priest of Amun** in **Karnak** and his daughter, **Shepenwepet** I, as **God's wife of Amun**. He was recognized as ruler in Thebes and Middle Egypt. *See also* OSORKON; RUDAMUN.

OSORKON IV (reigned c. 730–715 BC). Throne name possibly Aakheperre setepenamun. He was probably the last ruler of **Dynasty 22** and ruled only in the areas of **Tanis** and **Bubastis**. He is named on the **stela** of **Piye** and attested in Assyrian sources in 716 BC. He may be the ruler who appears in the Bible as So, king of Egypt. He was followed by the Nubian rulers of **Dynasty 25**.

OSTRACON. Plural ostraca. Greek name used by Egyptologists to designate flakes of limestone or **pottery** with ink inscriptions in **hieroglyphic**, **hieratic**, **demotic**, and later Greek that are often found at many sites in Egypt. Some texts may be trial pieces or school exercises, but many are complete documents that may contain literary texts or such nonliterary material as legal texts, tax documents, or letters. These often provide valuable contributions to the study of Egyptian **literature** and daily life, notably the thousands of ostraca found at **Deir el-Medina**.

OXYRHYNCHUS. Greek name of a town in **Middle Egypt**, ancient *Per-medjed*, capital of the 19th **Upper Egyptian nome** and modern el-Bahnasa. Little is known of the site during the Pharaonic Period as it is attested only from the **New Kingdom** onward. The principal deity worshipped there was **Seth**, along with the sacred oxyrhynchus fish. Remains date from the **Graeco-Roman Period** into the Muslim

Period. The site was excavated from 1896–1907 by a British expedi-ton, when thousands of **papyri** from that time were recovered. These finds included both known and lost literary texts and a large volume of documentary material. Further excavations at the site were carried out by an Italian team from 1910–1914, **Flinders Petrie** in 1922, and another Italian expedition from 1927–1934. The area has been exca-vated more recently by a Kuwaiti-financed expedition from 1985–1987, which concentrated on Islamic remains; an Egyptian dig in 1993, and a Spanish–Egyptian expedition from 1992–2002.

– P –

PACHOMIUS (292–346 AD). Egyptian Christian monk and saint. He was born in **Upper Egypt** and later served in the Roman army in Egypt. Upon leaving the army, he settled at the village of Shenest in **Middle Egypt** and converted to Christianity, becoming an ascetic hermit at Tabennese. He was joined by other disciples, whom he or-ganized into the first monastic community with a common rule. This gradually expanded during his lifetime to nine monasteries and two convents. He transformed the previously ascetic solitary style of liv-ing into that of a monastic existence, an idea that soon spread throughout the Christian world. *See also* ABRAHAM; ANTHONY; COPTIC CHURCH; SHENOUTE.

PALERMO STONE. A fragment of diorite that was inscribed with the annals of the kings of Egypt from the **Predynastic Period** to **Dy-nasty 5**, now housed in the Palermo Museum in Italy. While the early section is vague, later reigns are listed year by year with mention of the one important event of the year. Other fragments of the stone or similar stones have been located; however, all remain too broken to give a detailed account of the period. *See also* CHRONOLOGY.

PANEB (fl. 1235–1190 BC). Foreman of the community of **Deir el-Medina** at the end of **Dynasty 19**. Son of the workman Nefersenut and Iuy. He was adopted by the childless foreman Neferhotep. He ap-pears in the workforce at the end of the reign of **Ramesses II**, when he is attested with his wife, Wab. Upon the death of Neferhotep, who was apparently killed in the civil war between **Sety II** and **Amenmesse**, he succeeded to his adopted father's office. At the end of Dynasty 19 or possibly early **Dynasty 20**, he was accused by Amennakhte, brother of Neferhotep, of various crimes, including bribing the **vizier** to obtain the office of foreman; stealing from the royal **tombs;** and oppressive behavior toward his fellow workmen, notably adultery with some of their wives. He disappears abruptly from the records, and a later reference implies that he was punished for his misdeeds. *See also* HESUNEBEF; KENHERKHEPESHEF; KHA; RAMOSE; SENNEDJEM.

PAPYRUS. Plural papyri. An aquatic plant found in the swamps of ancient Egypt but is now extinct in that country. The name derives from Greek and probably ancient Egyptian. The pith of the plant was cut into strips and joined using its natural adhesive properties to form sheets that were never more than 50 centimeters high. The sheets could be glued together to form rolls or cut down to form smaller writing surfaces. Papyrus became the standard medium of written communication in ancient Egypt, and many examples of literary, religious, and documentary uses survive. The earliest uninscribed example dates to **Dynasty 1**. Papyrus was later used outside of Egypt throughout the ancient world before the invention of paper. *See also* LITERATURE; WISDOM LITERATURE.

PARENNEFER. *See* WENNEFER.

PASEBAKHAENNIUT I (reigned c. 1039–991 BC). The Greek form of his name is Psusennes. Throne name Akheperre setepenre. He ruled in the north while **Thebes** was under the control of the **high priests of Amun**. He was buried in **Tanis**, and his **tomb** was discovered intact by a French expedition headed by **Pierre Montet** in 1939. *See also* MUTNODJMET; THIRD INTERMEDIATE PERIOD.

PASEBAKHAENNIUT II (reigned 959–945 BC). Throne name Titkheperure setepenre. Epithets hor and meryamun. Last ruler of **Dynasty 21**. He is generally believed to be identical to the likenamed **high priest of Amun**, son of **Pinudjem** II. Little is known about his reign. His daughter, **Maatkare**, married **Osorkon I**, second ruler of **Dynasty 22**. *See also* THIRD INTERMEDIATE PERIOD.

PASER (fl. 1300–1255 BC). Southern **vizier** of **Sety I** and **Ramesses II**. Son of the **high priest of Amun** Nebnejteru and Meritre. He began his career as chamberlain and later chief chamberlain to Sety I, who promoted him to vizier. Paser continued in office under Ramesses until at least year 21, when he was in correspondence with the **Hittite** court at the time of the peace treaty with Egypt. He was in direct charge of the community at **Deir el-Medina**, where he appears to have been highly respected. Paser is known from a large number of monuments, including his **tomb** (number 106) at **Thebes**. He was later rewarded with the post of high priest of Amun. *See also* AMENEMHAT I; APEREL; AY; BAKENKHONS: HEMIUNU; IMHOTEP; INTEFYOKER; KAGEMNI; MERERUKA; NEB-WENNEF; NEFERMAAT; PTAHHOTEP; PTAHSHEPSES; RAMESSES I; REKHMIRE; WENNEFER.

PASER (fl. 1116 BC). Mayor of **Thebes** under **Ramesses IX**. According to the **Tomb Robbery Papyri**, he first alerted authorities to the pillaging of the royal **tombs** in the **Valley of the Kings**. He was initially rebuffed, but he eventually forced an inquiry that identified the thefts and culprits. His investigation was hindered by Paweraa, mayor of Western Thebes, who managed to keep his office in spite of the robberies.

PASHERMUT (reigned c. 393 BC). The Greek form of his name is Psammuthis. Throne name Userre setepenptah. Obscure ruler of **Dynasty 29** and probable successor to **Nefaarud** I and rival to **Hakor**. He is attested in inscriptions from **Thebes** and **Memphis**.

PEDUBAST I (reigned c. 818–793 BC). Throne name Usermaatre setepenenamun. Epithet meryamun. Founder of **Dynasty 23**. He appears to have assumed the royal **titulary** during the reign of **Sheshonq III** of **Dynasty 22** and founded a parallel line of rulers recognized in **Thebes**. Little is known about his reign or that of his contemporary, **Iuput I**. His effective successor was **Osorkon III**. *See also* THIRD INTERMEDIATE PERIOD.

PEDUBAST II. Throne name Sehetepibre. Minor kinglet who flourished at the end of the **Third Intermediate Period**. He may well be the king of **Tanis**, who is mentioned in an Assyrian inscription from 671 BC.

PEFTJAUAWYBAST (reigned c. 730 BC). Throne name Neferkare. He is attested as ruler of **Herakleopolis** at the end of the **Third Intermediate Period** when the country was divided into various local kinglets with full royal **titularies**. He married a daughter of **Rudamun** of **Dynasty 23**.

PELUSIUM. Ancient *Sjn* or *P3y-ir-Imn*. Modern Tell Farama. Major town on Egypt's eastern border in the 14th **Upper Egyptian nome**. It is attested from the **Old Kingdom** to the Arabic Period. Pelusium was the first destination of invaders across the Sinai desert, and its fall inevitably left the country open to such invaders as **Alexander the Great**. The town has not been fully investigated apart from rescue excavations by international teams in the 1990s. A Polish expedition has been working in the area of the newly discovered theater since 2003.

PEPY I (reigned c. 2321–2287 BC). Throne name Meryre. Son of **Teti** of **Dynasty 6** and **Queen Iput** I. He had a lengthy reign and is attested at various sites, notably at **Hierakonpolis**, where a life-size **copper** statue of the king and a smaller figure, possibly of his son **Nemtyemsaf** I, were discovered. There is a mysterious reference in the inscription of **Weni** to a disgraced **queen** who was replaced by two sisters, both renamed **Ankhesenmeryre**, otherwise Ankhesenpepy I and II. His other wives included Nubwenet, Inenek-Inti, and **Meritetes**, whose **tombs** next to the **pyramid** of the king were identified in 1990, 1992, and 1995. Another **queen**, Nedjeftet, was named in texts found in the tomb of Inenek-Inti, while Mehaa was named in the tomb of her son, Prince Hornetjerikhet, excavated in 1996. The king was buried in a pyramid at **Saqqara**, whose discovery in 1880 revealed the first examples of **pyramid texts** and has been the subject of excavation by a French team since 1966. He was succeeded by his son, **Nemtyemsaf** I.

PEPY II (reigned c. 2278–2184 BC). Throne name Neferkare. Son of **Pepy I** and **Ankhesenmeryre II**. He succeeded his half brother, **Nemtyemsaf** I. As he was still a child, his mother and her brother apparently ruled on his behalf. Very little information has survived about his reign, except its length. Both the **Turin Royal Canon** and **Manetho** imply that he reigned for more than 90 years, but this date has recently been disputed, as only about 64 years are attested. The dynasty ended in confusion shortly after his death, so his longevity and increasing loss of power may have contributed to its downfall. The king was buried in a **pyramid** at **Saqqara** surrounded by the subsidiary pyramids of his **queens, Iput** II; **Neith,** who was his sister or half sister; Udjebten; and **Ankhesenpepy IV,** who was buried in the **tomb** of Iput. Another queen was **Ankhesenpepy III,** whose tomb was discovered in the funerary complex of Pepy I. He was succeeded by his son, **Nemtyemsaf** II.

PERIBSEN (reigned c. 2760 BC). Ruler of **Dynasty 2** and successor to **Nynetjer**. There appears to have been a religious conflict during his reign between the followers of the gods **Horus** and **Seth**. Peribsen changed the standard inscription of the royal **titulary,** writing his name in a **serekh** not as a Horus name but as one preceded by that of Seth.

PERSIA. Ancient kingdom situated in modern Iran. The Persian king, Cyrus the Great, overthrew the Babylonian kingdom and annexed most of western Asia, creating the largest empire then known. His son, **Cambyses,** conquered Egypt in 525 BC and added it to the empire. Persian rule in Egypt was unpopular, and the Persians were later accused of neglecting Egyptian **religion** and withdrawing **temple** privileges. The Persian governor or **satrap** was usually a member of the royal family. The Persians were expelled by **Amyrtaeos** in 404 BC. In 343 BC, the Persian king Artaxerxes III reconquered Egypt, driving out the last native ruler, **Nakhthorheb. Alexander the Great** put an end to Persian rule in 332 BC and was welcomed as a liberator by the Egyptians. *See also* ACHAEMENES; ARSAMES; ARTAXERXES I; ARTAXERXES II; ARTAXERXES III; BAGOAS; DARIUS I; DARIUS II; XERXES I.

PETOSIRIS (fl. 330 BC). High priest of **Thoth** at **Hermopolis**. Son of the high priest of Thoth, Sishu, and Ankhefenkhons. He succeeded his elder brother as high priest and probably held office at the end of the Persian Period and the beginning of Greek rule. He was the owner of a magnificent **tomb** at **Tuna el-Gebel** discovered in 1919. In the biographical inscriptions there, he claims to have restored the neglected **temples** of his city. *See also* GRAECO-ROMAN PERIOD.

PETRIE, WILLIAM MATTHEW FLINDERS (1853–1942). British archaeologist. He was born in Charlton, England, on 3 June 1853. He was educated at home, his interest in archaeology being encouraged by his father. Petrie was first sent to Egypt to survey the **pyramid** of **Khufu** from 1880–1882. He later excavated for the **Egypt Exploration Fund** from 1884–1986 and again from 1896–1905, but disagreements led to his founding of the Egyptian Research Account and later the British School of Archaeology in Egypt to finance his independent excavations by donations from subscribers. Petrie carried out work in many sites in Egypt, notably **Tanis**, **Abydos**, **Hawara**, **Lahun**, **Amarna**, and **Thebes**. He was the first archaeologist to stress the importance of such small, uninscribed objects as amulets and **pottery**, which could be used to date the consecutive archaeological levels of a site, and he strongly criticized those like his rival **Edouard Naville**, who sought only monumental, inscribed antiquities. He believed in prompt publication but then often omitted much detailed evidence. He also laid down the basic framework for the study of **Predynastic** and **Early Dynastic** Egypt through the through study of pottery. Petrie's rather austere lifestyle in the field owed much to his desire to expend his resources on the excavations. He was appointed as the first professor of Egyptology at University College London in 1892, retiring in 1933. During the 1920s, he turned his attention to excavation in Palestine. He died in Jerusalem on 28 July 1942. His personal collection of antiquities, notebooks, and papers is preserved in the Petrie Museum of Egyptian Archaeology at University College in London. *See also* CARTER, HOWARD; MARIETTE, (FRANÇOIS) AUGUSTE FERDINAND; MONTET, (JEAN) PIERRE MARIE; REISNER, GEORGE ANDREW; WINLOCK, HERBERT EUSTIS.

PETRONIUS, PUBLIUS (fl. 25–21 BC). Roman **prefect** of Egypt c. 25–21 BC. He led Roman forces in two campaigns against **Meroe** after Meroitic forces raided Aswan and the **temple** of **Philae** and carried off booty, including statues of the emperor. A **bronze** head of

Augustus was discovered buried in Meroe in 1910 and is now housed in the **British Museum**. Roman forces marched to **Qasr Ibrim**, which they garrisoned, and sacked the Nubian city of **Napata** from 24–25 BC and in 22 BC. The war ended around 21 BC with a treaty that fixed the Egyptian border at Maharraqa south of Aswan and so awarded the **Dodekaschoenus** to Rome. *See also* CORNELIUS GALLUS, CAIUS.

PHARAOH. Modern word derived from Hebrew to designate the ruler of Egypt. The ancient Egyptian term *peraa*, or great house, was used at first to refer to the royal court as a whole and was not originally a synonym for king, ancient Egyptian *nesu*, but it was used with this meaning from the **New Kingdom** onward. Its first known use as a title was during the reign of **Sheshonq I**.

PHAROS. The famous Lighthouse of Alexandria and one of the seven wonders of the ancient world. Its construction was apparently initiated under Ptolemy I but was completed during the reign of **Ptolemy II**. Monumental statues of the latter king and his wife, **Arsinoe**, were placed before the entrance. The building was dedicated to the god Zeus. The lighthouse was destroyed by a series of earthquakes, notably in the 14th century AD, and left in ruins. The fort of Qait Bey was built on the site, probably reusing some of the original building materials. Blocks and the possible remains of the royal statues have been found in the sea nearby.

PHILAE. Greek name for an island in the **Nile** south of **Elephantine** where a **temple** to **Isis** and associated buildings were constructed dating from the **Late Period** to the **Roman Period**. Temples were also erected to deities from **Nubia**, and the site became a place of pilgrimage for Nubians and Egyptians. The last known **hieroglyphic** inscription (394 AD) and the last **demotic** inscription (452 AD) are recorded here. Following the advent of Christianity in Egypt, the temples remained open to accommodate the worshippers from the empire of **Meroe** until the time of Justinian, who closed them. From 1972–1979, the buildings on the site were dismantled and reconstructed on a neighboring island to rescue them from Lake Nasser, the new lake formed by the construction of the Aswan High Dam.

PHILIP ARRHIDAEUS (reigned 323–317 BC). Son of Philip II of Macedon and Larinna and half brother of **Alexander the Great**. Although mentally incompetent, he was proclaimed his brother's successor and ruled jointly with his nephew, **Alexander II** (IV), until he was murdered at the order of his stepmother, Olympias. He never visited Egypt, but his name is recorded on work in the **temples** of **Karnak**, **Hermopolis**, and **Sebennytos**.

PHILISTINES. A people named the Peleset who formed part of the coalition known as the **Sea Peoples** who invaded Egypt during the reign of **Ramesses III** of **Dynasty 20**. Ramesses III claims that they were defeated and that he allowed them to settle in southern Canaan. They had likely already occupied the area, and he won a nominal pledge of allegiance from them that lapsed when the Egyptians withdrew from Canaan in late Dynasty 20. The Philistine cities were in constant conflict with their new neighbors, the **Israelites**, as indicated in the Bible. They were subsequently absorbed in the Babylonian, Persian, and later empires. Recent excavations in Ashdod and other Philistine sites have shown new light on the Philistine material culture, but their origins remain obscure. They gave their name to the larger area now known as Palestine.

PIANKH (fl. c. 1094–1064 BC). High priest of Amun and military general at the end of **Dynasty 20**. He led his army against the **viceroy of Kush**, Panehsi, whose forces had overrun **Thebes**, advancing into **Nubia**, although it is not clear if he gained an outright victory. Letters written by him while on campaign have survived. It is not clear if he followed or preceded **Herihor**, but he was an ancestor of such independent high priests as **Pinudjem** I, who flourished under **Dynasty 21**. *See also* HRERE; NODJMET.

PIANKHY. *See* PIYE.

PIMAY (reigned c. 773–767 BC). Throne name Usimmatre setepenere or setepenamun. Epithet meryamun. An obscure monarch of **Dynasty 22**. Probably son of **Sheshonq III** or **Sheshonq IV**. He was the father of **Sheshonq V**. *See also* THIRD INTERMEDIATE PERIOD.

PINUDJEM. The name of two **high priests of Amun** who flourished during **Dynasty 21**. Pinudjem I (fl. 1064–26 BC) was the son of **Piankh**, and he succeeded as high priest and governor of **Upper Egypt** during the reign of **Nesbanebdjed**. He was an effective ruler of the south and later took royal titles with the throne name Khaheperre setepenamun. He was succeeded by his two sons, **Masaharta** and **Menkheperre,** and his two grandsons, Nesbanebdjed and Pinudjem II, who maintained Theban independence. The **marriage** links between the Theban family and the royal family of Dynasty 21 in **Tanis** are not always clear. His great-grandson, **Pasebakhaenniut II,** eventually became ruler of the entire country.

PI-RAMESSES. The northern capital city of **Ramesses II** built on the Delta at modern Qantir near the site of the **Hyksos** capital **Avaris**. Building seems to have begun under **Sety I**, but Ramesses II enlarged the city and gave it his name. Several poems in praise of the city survive. Pi-Ramesses seems to have been abandoned after **Dynasty 20**, and many of its monuments were used to decorate the cities of **Tanis** and **Bubastis**. It is currently being excavated by a German expedition that has uncovered the royal stables and other palace buildings.

PIYE (reigned c. 747–720 BC). Throne names Usimaatre and Sneferre. Ruler of **Nubia** formerly known as Piankhy. Successor of **Kashta**. He is known principally from a **stela** detailing his military campaign against Egypt around 728 BC. He appears to have inherited control over parts of southern Egypt, and he temporarily extended Nubian control throughout the country by defeating local princes, notably **Tefnakhte**, prince of **Sais**, although control was largely lost upon his return to Nubia. He was buried in el-Kurru near **Napata** and was succeeded by his brother, **Shabaqo**, who conquered Egypt and founded **Dynasty 25**. *See also* SHEPENWEPET.

POCOCKE, RICHARD (1704–1763). British traveler. He was born in Southampton, Great Britain, in 1704 and educated at Oxford. He visited Egypt from 1737–1738, journeying as far up the **Nile** as **Philae**. He visited the **Valley of the Kings** and left the first map of the area. He then traveled in Palestine and the East before returning to Egypt in late 1738 and 1739 to visit Sinai. Upon his return to Great Britain, he published an account of his travels. He later became bishop of Ossory and then Meath. He died in Charleville, Ireland, on 25 September 1765.

POMPEIUS, GNAEUS (106–48 BC). Roman general. He was the son of Gnaeus Pompeius Strabo, a leading general. He took part in the Roman civil wars of the 80s BC, serving in Sicily, Italy, and Africa, and he later led Roman armies in Spain from 77–71 BC and Asia and Syria from 66–62 BC. He was consul in 70 BC and later in 52 BC. He formed a political allaince with **Iulius Caesar**, whose daughter he married, known as the First Triumvirate. He backed the restoration of **Ptolemy XII** but failed to arrange it in person. He fell out with Caesar and led the senatorial focres against him. Upon his defeat, he fled to Egypt, where he supposed the government of **Ptolemy XIII** would support him, as he had been a friend of the king's father. Instead the king's advisors regarded him as a political embarassment and possible threat, and he was killed as he landed on Egyptian soil.

POPILLIUS LAENAS, CAIUS (fl. 200–158 BC). Roman senator. He was consul in 172 and 158 BC. He served in the Roman army in Greece from 170–169 BC and visited Egypt in 168 BC, when he forced King **Antiochus IV** to halt his invasion.

POSTUMUS, CAIUS RABIRIUS. *See* RABIRIUS POSTUMUS, CAIUS.

POTHINUS (fl. 49–48 BC). Chief minister of **Ptolemy XIII**. Together with **Achillas**, he deposed **Cleopatra VII**, igniting civil war in Egypt. He also advised the murder of **Gnaeus Pompeius**. He opposed the intervention of **Iulius Caesar** and was executed by him in 48 BC.

POTTERY. The use of pottery for storage vessels and eating utensils began during prehistoric times and continued throughout Egyptian history. Pottery is found in sites in the eastern Sahara and Sudan dating back to 9000–8000 BC. It appears in Egypt in the seventh millennium from sites in the **Fayum** and **Merimda Beni Salama**. Handmade painted pottery became common during the **Predynastic Period** with such distinctive designs as the Badarian and **Naqada** sequences. From these pieces, **Flinders Petrie** divised a scheme of sequence dating pottery, which is especially useful for working with objects from nonhistoric periods of time. These early periods are distinguished by their handmade pottery. The use of the potter's wheel appears to have originated in **Dynasty 4** or **Dynasty 5**. Scenes of pottery production appear on **Old Kingdom tomb** reliefs. The pottery of the historic periods is decorated in a simpler manner, is more utiliarian, and has not been the subject of detailed studies until recently. Scholars can now differentiate the types of clay used, for example silt or marl clays, and they are beginning to identify the exact locations of manufacture. Kilns used in the production of pottery have been discovered in excavations, like those found at predynastic **Hierakonpolis**. Imports of foreign pottery from Syria-Palestine, Crete, and Greece can prove useful dating tools as well. *See also* BADARI, EL-; TELL EL-YAHUDIYA.

PREDYNASTIC PERIOD (c. 5000–3100 BC). The period in Egyptian history from the development of permanent settlements until the creation of the united Egyptian state with **Dynasty I**. The period is subdivided into the cultures named from the sites of **el-Badari** and **Naqada**.

PREFECT. The title of the governor of Egypt during the **Roman Period**. The official was directly appointed by the Roman emperor from the equestrian order, namely the nonsenatorial official class. As Egypt supplied most of Rome's grain, it was essential that the prefect not be a threat to the emperor or a potential rival. Senators were barred from entering Egypt without the emperor's express approval. During the later Roman Empire, Egypt was divided into several provinces, but the senior official based in **Alexandria** retained the title of prefect. *See also* APION; CORNELIUS GALLUS, CAIUS; PETRONIUS, PUBLIUS; IULIUS ALEXANDER, TIBERIUS.

PREHERWENEMEF (fl. c. 1280–1260 BC). Fourth son of **Ramesses II** but the king's third son by his **queen**, **Nefertari**. He appears in inscriptions from the beginning of Ramesses II's reign. His fate is not known, but he presumably died before his father and was buried in the **tomb** of the king's sons (**KV5**) in the **Valley of the Kings**. A like-named son of **Ramesses III** is known from his tomb (**QV**42) in the **Valley of the Queens**. *See also* AMENHERKHEPESHEF; KHAEMWESE; MERENPTAH; MERYATUM; SETY.

PSAMMETICHUS. *See* PSAMTIK I.

PSAMMUTHIS. *See* PASHERMUT.

PSAMTIK I (reigned 664–610 BC). The Greek form of his name is Psammetichus. Throne name Wahibre. Son of **Nekau I** of **Sais**. Upon his father's death in battle against **Tantamani** in 664 BC, he fled to Assyria and was restored as puppet ruler by Assyrian forces in 663 BC, founding **Dynasty 26**. He skillfully reunited Egypt under his rule with the help of Greek mercenaries and by installing his daughter, **Nitocris**, as **God's wife of Amun** in **Thebes**. He gradually disentangled himself from Assyrian control and restored Egyptian independence. *See also* MENTUEMHAT.

PSAMTIK II (reigned 595–589 BC). Throne name Neferibre. Son and successor of **Nekau II**. He sought to restore Egyptian prestige by a campaign into **Nubia** recorded by **graffiti** of his soldiers at **Abu Simbel** and also intrigued in Palestine. He arranged the adoption of his daughter, **Ankhnesneferibre**, as **God's wife of Amun**. He died on 10 February 589 BC. *See also* WAHIBRE.

PSAMTIK III (reigned 526–525 BC). Throne name Ankhkaenre. Son of **Ahmose II** and Tantheta, daughter of the priest of **Ptah** Padineith. Shortly after his accession, he faced an invasion by **Cambyses**, king of **Persia**, who conquered Egypt and took him prisoner. He and his son were later executed for plotting against the new ruler.

PTAH. Chief god of **Memphis** depicted as a mummiform man with a cap and beard holding a sceptre. His principal epithet was Lord of *Maat*, or Truth. He was associated with crafts. Ptah was worshipped throughout the country as one of the main deities. The priests of Memphis credited him with the first act of creation. His consort was the goddess **Sakhmet**, and with their son, **Nefertum**, they formed the Memphite **triad**. The **temple** of Ptah at Memphis is now in a ruined state with little remaining of its ancient splendor, which may have rivaled that of **Karnak**. *See also* RELIGION.

PTAH-SOKAR-OSIRIS. *See* SOKAR.

PTAHHOTEP (fl. 2400 BC). **Vizier** of **Djedkare** Isesi of **Dynasty 5**. He is the alleged author of a text of **wisdom literature** known from later copies from the **Middle Kingdom** and **New Kingdom**. *See also* AMENEMHAT I; APEREL; AY; HEMIUNU; IMHOTEP; INTE-FYOKER; KAGEMNI; MERERUKA; NEFERMAAT; PASER; PTAHSHEPSES; RAMESSES I; REKHMIRE.

PTAHSHEPSES (fl. 2440 BC). **Vizier** who held office under **Niuserre**, whose daughter Khamerernebty, he married. He had a magnificent **tomb** built at **Abusir**, which has been excavated by a Czech expedition since the 1970s. *See also* AMENEMHAT I; APEREL; AY; HEMIUNU; IMHOTEP; INTEFYOKER; KAGEMNI; MERERUKA; NEFERMAAT; PASER; PTAHHOTEP; RAMESSES I; REKHMIRE.

PTOLEMAIC PERIOD (323–30 BC). The term used by Egyptologists for the period during which Egypt was ruled by the Macedonian general **Ptolemy I** and his descendants. The beginning of the period varies, as Ptolemy was in charge from 323 BC, but he did not openly assume independent rule until 305 BC. Many **temples** from **Upper Egypt** erected or refurbished by the Ptolemies survive; however, the government was continued from **Alexandria** by the Greek ruling class, and Egyptian culture, although respected, remained secondary to the interests of the rulers. *See also* PTOLEMY II–PTOLEMY XV.

PTOLEMY (d. 58 BC). King of Cyprus. Illegitimate son of **Ptolemy IX** by an unknown mistress. When his brother became **Ptolemy XII** of Egypt in 80 BC, he was given Cyprus to rule. His kingdom was unilaterally annexed by Rome in 58 BC. He was offered the position of high priest at Paphos but commited suicide. The failure of his brother, Ptolemy XII, to support him led to a rebellion in Egypt that temporarily ousted him from the throne.

PTOLEMY I SOTER (c. 367–282 BC). Son of Lagus and Arsinoe. Macedonian nobleman and military commander under **Alexander the Great**. In 323 BC, upon the death of Alexander the Great, he secured the governorship of Egypt, which he virtually ruled as an independent state after disposing of **Cleomenes**. He expanded his control to Cyprus and parts of Syria, Greece, and Asia Minor. He assumed the title of king in 305 BC. Unlike other would-be successors of Alexander the Great, he had no pretensions to try to control the entire empire. Ptolemy I had several wives, including the Persian Artacama, daughter of Artabazus, whom he presumably abandoned; the Macedonian Eurydice, daughter of the regent Antipater; and finally **Berenice I**, leading to court intrigues over his succession until he made his son **Ptolemy II**, by his last wife, **coregent**. He apparently died during the first half of 282 BC. *See also* ALEXANDER II; PHILIP ARRHIDAEUS.

PTOLEMY II PHILADELPHUS (308–246 BC). Son of **Ptolemy I** and **Berenice I**. He was named **coregent** with his father in 285 BC and succeeded to sole rule in 282 BC. His reign was prosperous, allowing the king to undertake major building works, including the **Pharos**, or Lighthouse, of **Alexandria**; Library of Alexandria; and Museum of Alexandria. He scandalized Greek public opinion by divorcing his wife, **Arsinoe I**, and marrying his full sister, **Arsinoe II**. He died in January 246 BC and was succeeded by his son, **Ptolemy III**.

PTOLEMY III EUERGETES (c. 284–222 BC). Son of **Ptolemy II** and his first wife, **Arsinoe I**. He succeeded to the throne in 246 BC and continued to expand Egypt's control in Syria and Asia Minor. He also acquired **Cyrene** through marriage with its heiress **Berenice II**. He died between October and December 222 BC and was succeeded by his son, **Ptolemy IV**.

PTOLEMY IV PHILOPATOR (c. 244–205 BC). Son of **Ptolemy III** and **Berenice II**. He married his sister, **Arsinoe III**. He pursued an aggressive policy in Asia in an attempt to gain control of Palestine-Syria but faced a major revolt in the south where native rulers **Harwennefer** and **Ankhwennefer** were proclaimed. His chief minister was **Sosibios**, who arranged a series of murders of members of the royal family to strengthen his hold on power. The king appears to have died in late 205 BC, but his death was initially concealed by his court. He was succeeded by his son, **Ptolemy V**.

PTOLEMY V EPIPHANES (210–180 BC). Son of **Ptolemy IV** and **Arsinoe III**. He was born on 9 October 210 and was at first under the regency of various courtiers, notably **Sosibios**. He faced difficulties throughout his reign with revolts in Egypt that were eventually suppressed and clashes over Ptolemaic possessions in Syria and Palestine that were lost in 200 BC. He married a Seleucid princess, **Cleopatra I**. He died in September/October 180 BC and was succeeded by his son, **Ptolemy VI**.

PTOLEMY VI PHILOMETER (c. 186–145 BC). Son of **Ptolemy V** and **Cleopatra I**. He succeeded in 180 BC at a young age under the regency of his mother and later courtiers. When Egypt was threatened by **Antiochus IV**, the royal family was united through his **marriage** to his sister, **Cleopatra II**, in 176 BC and their joint rule together with his brother, **Ptolemy VIII**, beginning in 170 BC. He was briefly captured and then released by Antiochus IV during the latter's invasion in 169 BC, and his rule was restored by a Roman ultimatum to the Syrian king to withdraw from Egypt in 168 BC after a second invasion. His reign was undermined by war with his brother, who was expelled to **Cyrene** in 163 BC. Ptolemy VI attempted to regain Egyptian possessions in Syria in 145 BC but died of wounds sustained in a battle near Antioch in which his forces were victorious. His elder son, **Ptolemy Eupator**, died during his lifetime, so he was initially succeeded by his younger son, **Ptolemy VII**.

PTOLEMY VII NEOS PHILOPATOR (c. 162–145 BC). Son of **Ptolemy VI** and **Cleopatra II**. He was made joint ruler with his father but was killed in 145 BC when his uncle, **Ptolemy VIII**, returned to Egypt and seized the throne.

PTOLEMY VIII EUERGETES II (c. 182–116 BC). Nicknamed Physcon, or potbelly. Younger son of **Ptolemy V** and **Cleopatra I**. He was made joint ruler with his brother, **Ptolemy VI**, in 170 BC and expelled him from the country in 164 but was himself forced to retire to **Cyrene** in 163 BC. Upon his brother's death in 145 BC, Ptolemy VIII returned to Egypt and seized the throne, murdering his nephew, **Ptolemy VII**. He first married in 145 BC his sister, **Cleopatra II**, by whom he had one son, **Ptolemy Memphites**, whom he eventually put to death. Around 140 BC, he married his niece, Cleopatra II's daughter, **Cleopatra III**, thus precipitating a civil war with his sister in 132 BC. He was initially driven out of Egypt but regained control in 130 BC. The civil war was finally resolved in 124 BC by the recognition of Cleopatra II's position as senior **queen**. Ptolemy VIII died on 28 June 116 BC, leaving Egypt to Cleopatra III and whichever of her two sons, **Ptolemy IX** or **Ptolemy X**, she chose to rule with her.

PTOLEMY IX SOTER II (142–80 BC). Nicknamed Lathyros or chickpea. Elder son of **Ptolemy VIII** and **Cleopatra III**. He was possibly born on 18 February 142 BC. King of Cyprus under his father, he succeeded him despite the wishes of his mother, who preferred his younger brother, the future **Ptolemy X**. He was forced to divorce his sister-wife **Cleopatra IV** in favor of a younger sister, **Cleopatra V Selene**. He was expelled from Egypt in 107 BC by his mother and brother but was able to return in 88 BC and reigned with his daughter, **Cleopatra Berenice III**, until his death in March 80 BC.

PTOLEMY X ALEXANDER I (c. 140–88 BC). Younger son of **Ptolemy VIII** and **Cleopatra III**. He was his mother's choice as ruler in 116 BC but was forced to acknowledge his elder brother, **Ptolemy IX**. Later king of Cyprus, he ousted his elder brother in 107 BC and reigned in Egypt with his niece, **Cleopatra Berenice III,** as consort until they were expelled by a popular revolt in 89 BC. He returned with Syrian forces but was again expelled to Lycia. He was killed in a battle at sea in March 88 BC as he attempted to flee to Cyprus.

PTOLEMY XI ALEXANDER II (c. 105–80 BC). Son of **Ptolemy X** and an unknown wife. He was living in exile until he was chosen as the consort of his cousin, **Cleopatra Berenice III**, upon the death of her father, **Ptolemy IX**. He murdered his wife shortly afterward and was in turn killed by the **Alexandrian** mob in June 80 BC. He was succeeded by his cousin, **Ptolemy XII**.

PTOLEMY XII THEOS PHILOPATOR PHILADELPHUS NEOS DIONYSIUS (d. 51 BC). Illegitimate son of **Ptolemy IX** by an unknown mistress. He was chosen as ruler upon the murder of **Ptolemy XI** and soon gained the nickname Auletes, or flute player. He was expelled in 58 BC, following his failure to support his brother, Ptolemy, king of Cyprus. He was replaced by his daughter, **Berenice IV**, but he was restored in 55 BC by Roman troops and executed his daughter. He appointed the Roman **Rabirius Postumus**, who loaned him the money to pay for his restoration, as his finance minister. His wife was **Cleopatra VI Tryphaena** and may have been his sister, but it is not known if she was the mother of all of his children, notably **Cleopatra VII**. *See also* ARSINOE IV; PTOLEMY XIII, PTOLEMY XIV PHILOPATOR.

PTOLEMY XIII (c. 61–47 BC). Elder son of **Ptolemy XII** and possibly **Cleopatra VI Tryphaena**. He succeeded jointly with his sister and wife, **Cleopatra VII**, but he soon fell out with her, and civil war broke out between the siblings. The situation was changed by the arrival of **Iulius Caesar**, who soon supported Cleopatra. The king was defeated in battle against Roman forces and apparently drowned in the **Nile** during the action in January 47 BC. *See also* ACHILLAS; ARSINOE IV; POTHINUS.

PTOLEMY XIV PHILOPATOR (c. 59–44 BC). Younger son of **Ptolemy XII** and possibly **Cleopatra VI Tryphaena**. He replaced his older brother as consort of **Cleopatra VII**, but his position was purely nominal, and he was probably murdered by her.

PTOLEMY XV PHILOPATOR PHILOMETER (47–30 BC). Son of **Cleopatra VII**, who named **Iulius Caesar** as the father. The boy was nicknamed Caesarion. He was made joint ruler of Egypt with his mother in 44 BC upon the death of his uncle, **Ptolemy XIV**. He was executed while trying to escape from Roman forces following the conquest of Egypt in 30 BC.

PTOLEMY APION (d. 96 BC). Son of **Ptolemy VIII** by his concubine, Irene. His father made him ruler of **Cyrene** in 145 BC, where he ruled until his childless death in 96 BC. He left his kingdom to Rome.

PTOLEMY EUPATOR (c. 163–152 BC). Elder son of **Ptolemy VI** and **Cleopatra II**. He was named **coregent** with his father but died young.

PTOLEMY MEMPHITES (c. 144–131 BC). Son of **Ptolemy VIII** and **Cleopatra II**. Heir to the throne, he was executed by his father in 131 BC after his mother had revolted in an attempt to overthrow her husband.

PTOLEMY PHILADELPHUS (b. 36 BC). Younger son of **Marcus Antonius** and **Cleopatra VII**. He was assigned Syria and the eastern part of the Roman Empire by his father in 34 BC. He was taken prisoner by **Augustus** in 30 BC, but his ultimate fate is unknown. *See also* ALEXANDER HELIOS; CLEOPATRA SELENE.

PUDUHEPA (fl. 1285–1220 BC). Queen of the **Hittites**. Daughter of Pentipsharri, priest of Ishtar at Lawazantiya. She married the future **Hattusili III** and supported his usurpation of the throne. She played an important role in his government, especially in foreign policy. She arranged **marriage** alliances with foreign monarchs, including the marriage of her daughter, **Maathorneferure**, with **Ramesses II**. Her correspondence with the Egyptian king and his wife, **Nefertari**, has been recovered at the Hittite capital.

PUNT. A country located along the Red Sea coast, probably in Somalia, to which Egyptian expeditions were periodically sent from the time of the **Old Kingdom** to the **New Kingdom** to obtain such exotic products as incense. An expedition sent by **Queen Hatshepsut** is recorded in detail on reliefs on her funerary **temple** at **Deir el-Bahri**. The expedition reached the Red Sea via the **Wadi Hammamat** and sailed from a port located at **Mersa Gawasis**.

PYLON. Greek name for the massive stone gateway in front of Egyptian **temples** and also within several of the larger temples. The pylon was decorated with scenes of the king triumphant over his enemies and had emplacements for massive flagstaffs. **Obelisks** and large royal sculptures were often placed in front of the pylon.

PYRAMID. Greek name for the four-sided, triangular-shaped monument that marked the burial of kings from the **Old Kingdom** to the **Middle Kingdom**. Rulers from **Dynasty 1** and **Dynasty 2** were buried in mudbrick **mastaba tombs**, but during **Dynasty 3** a new architectural form in stone was evolved ascribed according to legend to the **vizier Imhotep** for his master, **Djoser**. The stone step **pyramid** at **Saqqara** consisted of a series of six mastabas placed on top of each other covering the burial chamber beneath. The tomb complex also included a mortuary **temple** and other ritual buildings.

This type of complex was used during the course of the dynasty, but at the beginning of **Dynasty 4**, the true pyramid with its **pyramidion** capstone was created for **Snefru** at **Meidum** and later **Dahshur**. The pyramids of **Khufu**, **Khafre**, and **Menkaure** at **Giza** represent the high point of pyramid construction. Each of these pyramids had a mortuary temple associated with it, as well as a valley **temple** reached by water and connected to the main pyramid by a dry causeway. The tombs of the **queens** in small pyramids and favored courtiers in mastabas surrounded the king's tomb.

Later pyramids were built on a less lavish scale with rubble cores and only one course of stone masonry on the outside, but they were highly decorated with reliefs in the temples and causeway walls and **pyramid texts** inscribed inside the burial chamber. Pyramid construction continued into the **Middle Kingdom**, although the pyramids of **Dynasty 12** in the **Fayum** area often had a **mudbrick** core. At the beginning of **Dynasty 18**, pyramids were abandoned by rulers in favor of secluded tombs in the **Valley of the Kings**, but the royal mortuary temples remained, now located near the **Nile**, and some are of considerable size. Small mudbrick pyramids with a stone pyramidion were used to mark burials of private individuals. The use of small pyramids for royal burials with associated chapels was revived by **Dynasty 25** at cemeteries near **Napata** and **Meroe**.

PYRAMID TEXTS. Religious texts inscribed on the walls of the royal **pyramid** to enable the king to pass safely to the next life. The earliest texts are inscribed in the pyramid of **Unas**, last ruler of **Dynasty 5**, and were discovered in 1881. The texts were first discovered in 1880 in the pyramid of **Pepy I** of **Dynasty 6**. *See also* AFTERLIFE.

PYRAMIDION. The capstone of a **pyramid**. After the use of pyramids for royal burials was discontinued, **mudbrick** pyramids were placed on top of private **tombs**, as at **Thebes** surmounted by a stone pyramidion often inscribed with a prayer to and decorated with a figure of the sun god **Re**-Harakhty.

– Q –

QAA (reigned c. 2915 BC). Eighth and final ruler of **Dynasty 1** and successor to **Semerkhet**. Like his predecessors, he was buried in **Abydos**, where his **tomb** has recently been reexcavated by a German expedition. A fine **stela** of the king is now housed in the **Louvre Museum**. *See also* DYNASTY 2.

QADESH. *See* KADESH.

QANTIR. *See* PI-RAMESSES.

QASR IBRIM. Modern name for a site in **Nubia** situated on the east bank of the **Nile** 116 kilometers north of Wadi Halfa. Greek name Primis. The site consists of a Roman fortress but includes isolated blocks and **stelae** from the **New Kingdom** and a **temple** from **Dynasty 25**, as well as later Meroitic occupation and a Christian cathedral. The town later housed a Turkish garrison. The construction of the Aswan High Dam in the 1960s has led to flooding of part of the site, which is now an island, by Lake Nasser. The site and its vicinity have been excavated by the **Egypt Exploration Society** since 1961. Much documentary material from the **Coptic** Period and Turkish Period has been discovered, along with interesting material from the Napatan Period, Meroitic Period, and **Roman Period** occupation. Nearby chapels were dedicated by the **viceroys of Kush** of **Dynasty 18** and **Dynasty 19**, and a rock-cut stela of **Sety I** was removed before the area was covered by the new lake.

QAU EL-KEBIR. Modern name for a site in the 10th **Upper Egyptian nome**. Ancient *Djuqa*, Graeco-Roman Antaeopolis. The settlement site is destroyed but once had the remains of a Graeco-Roman **temple**. The cemeteries date from the **Old Kingdom** to the **Graeco-Roman Period**. The most important items at the site are the **tombs** of the nomarchs of the **First Intermediate Period** and the early **Middle Kingdom**. The site was excavated by an Italian expedition from 1905–1906, a German expedition from 1913–1914, and **Flinders Petrie**'s team from 1923–1925. Another cemetery for the elite of the area in the **Old Kingdom** was located at nearby El-Hammumiya, which was also examined by the Petrie expedition and later recorded by an Australian team from 1989–1990.

QEBEHSENUEF. *See* SONS OF HORUS.

QEMAU. *See* AMENY QEMAU.

QENHERKHEPESHEF. *See* KENHERKHEPESHEF.

QUDSHU. Canaanite fertility goddess whose worship became popular in Egypt during **Dynasty 18** and **Dynasty 19**. She is represented as a full-frontal nude woman and is often depicted with the Syrian war god **Reshep**. *See also* ANAT; ASTARTE; RELIGION.

QUEEN. The wife of the king. The most common term for the position was *hmt nswt*, or "king's wife," and from the **Second Intermediate Period** onward, the term *hmt nswt wrt*, or "king's great wife," was used to denote the chief queen. Other terms were used, particularly during the **Old Kingdom**. It appears that there was normally only one chief queen at a time, although **Ramesses II** may have bestowed this title more frequently. The king appears to have had a relatively free choice of wives, although many **women** were picked for political reasons. The king was not obliged to marry his sister, and the **heiress concept** has been shown to be false. Kings may have married their sisters to enhance their divine status, as the gods married their sisters. Similarly, **Amenhotep III** and Ramesses II appear to have granted the title of queen to some of their daughters, although it remains unclear whether such marriages were honorific. The son of the chief queen may have been favored in the royal **succession**, but the known succession of sons of minor queens and concubines indicates that this was not necessarily always the case. The king's mother, if a minor wife, was then raised to the status of chief queen.

QUSTUL. *See* BALLANA.

QV. The abbreviation used by Egyptologist to denote a burial in the **Valley of the Queens**.

– R –

RABIRIUS POSTUMUS, CAIUS (fl. 80–43 BC). Roman banker. Son of Caius Curtius and Rabiria. He was adopted by his mother's brother. He lent money to **Ptolemy XII** and later financed the king's restoration to the throne in 55 BC to recover his debts. To obtain repayment of his loan, he was made finance minister of Egypt from 55–54 BC. He became a supporter of **Iulius Caesar** and was made a senator. He possibly returned to Egypt as a member of Caesar's entourage. He later supported **Augustus**.

RAHOTEP (fl. 2600 BC). A prince of **Dynasty 4**, probably a son of **Huni** or **Snefru**. He held the post of high priest of **Re** at **Heliopolis**. His intact **tomb** was discovered at **Meidum** in 1871, and it is famous for the painted statues of the owner and his wife, Nefret, now housed in the **Cairo Egyptian Museum**. It is noteworthy that the moustache on his statue in the style of **Old Kingdom** males still survives, whereas this feature, which is usually painted on, has faded on other sculptures of the time.

RAMESSES (fl. 1279–1229). Second son of **Ramesses II** and eldest son of **Queen Isitnofret**. He appears in inscriptions during the early part of his father's reign. He held the position of general and was crown prince from approximately 1254–1229 BC, but he died before his father. He was buried in **KV5** in the **Valley of the Kings**. *See also* BINTANAT; KHAEMWESE; MERENPTAH.

The Step Pyramid of Djoser at Saqqara. Dynasty 3. *Photo: M. L. Bierbrier.*

The Sphinx and the Great Pyramid of Khufu at Giza. Dynasty 4. *Photo: M. L. Bierbrier.*

The tomb of Nefer at Saqqara. Dynasty 5. *Photo: M. L. Bierbrier.*

The tomb of Ti at Saqqara, Dynasty 5. *Photo: M. L. Bierbrier.*

The tomb of Ankhtifi at el-Moalla. First Intermediate Period. *Photo: M. L. Bierbrier.*

A relief of Tuthmose III at Deir el-Bahri. Dynasty 18. *Photo: M. L. Bierbrier.*

The tomb of Ramose at Thebes. Dynasty 18. *Photo: M. L. Bierbrier.*

The tombs of Tutankhamun and Ramesses VI in the Valley of the Kings, Thebes. Dynasties 18–20. *Photo: M. L. Bierbrier.*

An unfinished pillar in the tomb of Sety I in the Valley of the Kings. Dynasty 19. *Photo: M. L. Bierbrier.*

The Workman's Village at Deir el-Medina. Dynasties 18–20. *Photo: L. Collins.*

A hieroglyphic inscription from the tomb of Ramesses VI in the Valley of the Kings. *Photo: M. L. Bierbrier.*

A relief of Cleopatra VII and her son Ptolemy XV Caesarion on the Temple of Dendera. *Photo: M. L. Bierbrier.*

The Necropolis of Tuna el-Gebel. Graeco-Roman Period. *Photo: M. L. Bierbrier.*

The lighthouse at Taposiris Magna. Graeco-Roman Period. *Photo: M. L. Bierbrier.*

A view of the Cataract at Aswan before the flooding by the High Dam Project. *Photo: M. L. Bierbrier.*

A view of the site of Qasr Ibrim in Nubia after the flooding by the High Dam Project. *Photo: M. L. Bierbrier.*

RAMESSES I (reigned c. 1295–1294 BC). Throne name Menpehtyre. Son of a military officer named Sety. First ruler of **Dynasty 19**. He was **vizier** to the apparently childless **Horemheb** and succeeded to the throne upon the latter's death. His reign was short, but he left a son, **Sety I**, to reestablish Egyptian prestige at home and abroad. He was buried in **tomb KV16** in the **Valley of the Kings**, but his **mummy** has not been recovered or identified. He is commemorated in the mortuary **temple** of his son at Qurna.

RAMESSES II (reigned c. 1279–1212 BC). Throne name Usermaatre setepenre. Epithet meryamun. Son of **Sety I** and **Tuy**, daughter of the lieutenant of the chariotry, Raia. As an apparently only son, he was named crown prince at an early age by his father and provided with the accoutrements of kingship, including a royal harem. Upon his accession, Ramesses II sought to restore Egyptian control in Syria but was defeated by the **Hittites** at the battle of **Kadesh** in year 5 (c. 1274 BC). In year 21 (c. 1258 BC), he signed a formal treaty with the Hittites ending the conflict. In year 34 (c. 1245 BC), he married **Maathorneferure**, the daughter of the Hittite king, to cement the alliance. He apparently later married a second daughter.

Ramesses II emphasized Egyptian power through many construction projects, notably his new capital at **Pi-Ramesses** and many Nubian **temples**, including at **Abu Simbel**. His wives included **Nefertari**, for whom he had a splendid **tomb** built in the **Valley of the Queens** at **Thebes**, and **Isitnofret**. Ramesses II also married three of his daughters, the eldest Princess **Bintanat**, **Meritamun**, and **Nebettawy**. He had around 100 children, including his eldest son, **Amenherkhepeshef**, by Nefertari, and **Khaemwese** and his eventual heir, **Merenptah**, both by Isitnofret. Ramesses II reigned for 66 years and two months and is remembered in legend as a great conqueror. His tomb (**KV7**) in the **Valley of the Kings** has suffered severe damage and awaits a proper publication. An extensive tomb, which he had built for his many sons, has recently been uncovered in **KV5**. His **mummy** survived in the **royal cache** at **Deir el-Bahri** and was recovered in 1881. His mortuary temple, known as the **Ramessum**, is well preserved. *See also* HENTTAWY; MEHY; MERYATUM; PREHERWENEMEF; RAMESSES; SETY.

RAMESSES III (reigned c. 1186–1153 BC). Throne name Usermaatre meryamun. Epithet heka iunu. Son of **Sethnakhte** and Tiyemerenese of **Dynasty 20**. His reign was distinguished by his successful campaign against the **Sea Peoples**, whose invasion of Egypt he crushed. He was able to maintain most of Egypt's Asian empire. His principal surviving monuments are his mortuary **temple** at **Medinet Habu** and his **tomb (KV11)** in the **Valley of the Kings**. Ramesses III was apparently assassinated during a conspiracy against his appointed heir, **Ramesses IV**, who successfully countered the plot and punished the conspirators as recounted in the **Harem Conspiracy Papyri**. His **mummy** was recovered from the **royal cache** at **Deir el-Bahri** in 1881. *See also* KV3; PREHERWENEMEF; SETHHERKHEPESHEF.

RAMESSES IV (reigned c. 1153–1147 BC). Throne name Usermaatre, later Hekamaatre. Son and successor of **Ramesses III**. He may be identical with a Prince Ramesses, son of Ramesses III, whose **tomb (KV53)** was prepared in the **Valley of the Queens** but obviously abandoned upon his accession. He successfully overcame the conspirators who assassinated his father and had them tried and punished. The Harris **Papyrus** recording the benefactions of his father was compiled during his reign. Ramesses IV appeared to have intended to undertake massive construction works in the Theban area, but he died when the work was barely begun. He doubled the number of the workmen at **Deir el-Medina** so his tomb **KV2** in the **Valley of the Kings** would be completed. His body was recovered from the **royal cache** in the tomb of **Amenhotep II** in 1898. *See also* DUATENTOPET.

RAMESSES V (reigned c. 1147–1143 BC). Throne name Usermaatre sekheperenre. Personal name Amenherkhepeshef. Epithet meryamun. Successor and possibly son of **Ramesses IV**. The principal document of his brief reign is the extensive **Wilbour Papyrus** outlining the possessions of the **temple** of **Amun** at **Thebes** throughout Egypt. He prepared **tomb KV9** in the **Valley of the Kings** for his burial, but it was taken over by his successor, **Ramesses VI**, so it is not certain if he was buried here. His body was recovered from the **royal cache** in the tomb of **Amenhotep II** in 1898.

RAMESSES VI (reigned c. 1143–1136 BC). Throne name Nebmaatre meryamun. Personal name Amenherkhepeshef. Epithet netjer heka iunu. Successor of **Ramesses V** and possible son of **Ramesses III**. He installed his daughter, Princess **Isis**, as **God's wife of Amun**, apparently the first known virgin princess to hold the post. He was buried in **tomb KV9** in the **Valley of the Kings**, which he had taken over from his predecessor. His body was recovered from the **royal cache** in the tomb of **Amenhotep II** in 1898.

RAMESSES VII (reigned c. 1136–1129 BC). Throne name Usermaatre meryamun setepenre. Personal name Itamun. Epithet netjer heka iunu. Successor and possibly son of **Ramesses VI**. He was buried in **tomb KV1** in the **Valley of the Kings**, but his **mummy** has not been identified.

RAMESSES VIII (reigned c. 1129–1126 BC). Throne name Usermaatre akhenamun. Personal name Sethherkhepeshef. Epithet meryamun. Successor of **Ramesses VII** and possibly son of **Ramesses III**. His reign was brief, and no **tomb** has been identified for him.

RAMESSES IX (reigned c. 1126–1108 BC). Throne name Neferkare setepenre. Personal name **Khaemwese**. Epithet mereramun. A member of the royal family of **Dynasty 20** whose exact origin is uncertain. Successor to **Ramesses VIII**. A large volume of documentation survives from his reign concerning the affairs of **Deir el-Medina** and the Theban area, notably the **Tomb Robbery Papyri**, which illustrates the gradual breakdown in law and order and the growing independence of the Theban area under its high priest. He was buried in **tomb KV6** in the **Valley of the Kings**, and his body was recovered from the **royal cache** at **Deir el-Bahri** in 1881.

RAMESSES X (reigned c. 1108–1099). Throne name Khepermaatre setepenre. Successor and possibly son of **Ramesses IX**. The length of his reign is uncertain. He was buried in **tomb KV18** in the **Valley of the Kings**, but his **mummy** has not been identified.

RAMESSES XI (reigned c. 1099–1069 BC). Throne name Menmaatre setepenptah. Personal name **Khaemwese**. Epithet mereramun netjer heka iunu. Successor and possibly son of **Ramesses X**. His reign marked the end of **Dynasty 20**. Contemporary documents refer to civil war and **tomb** robberies in **Thebes**, which became increasingly independent under the **high priest of Amun**. The king's tomb (**KV4**) in the **Valley of the Kings** was left unfinished. It is presumed that he spent most of his time in the north, but the circumstances of his death and the change of the dynasty are unknown. His body has not been recovered. *See also* HERIHOR; PIANKH.

RAMESSEUM. Modern name for the site of the mortuary **temple** of **Ramesses II** on the west bank of the Nile opposite **Thebes** near **Deir el-Bahri**. Originally named *Hnm-W3st*. The temple is noted for its fallen colossal statue of the king, which inspired the poetic work of Percy Bysshe Shelley. The inscriptions also detail the royal children and the king's wars. The site was excavated by British archaeologist John Quibell in 1896. A Franco–Egyptian team has been in charge of the publication and excavation of the temple since the 1970s.

RAMESSIDE PERIOD (c. 1295–1069 BC). A term used to describe the rule of **Dynasty 19** and **Dynasty 20**, when the most common royal name was Ramesses. The period marked the time of Egypt's imperial power, with an empire encompassing **Nubia** and Syria-Palestine. It was also a period when Egypt was open to foreign influence, especially from Syria in **language** and **religion**. *See also* RAMESSES I–RAMESSES XI.

RAMOSE (fl. 1300–1240 BC). Chief **scribe** of the **Deir el-Medina** community. Son of Amenemheb and Kakaia. He previously served at the mortuary **temple** of **Thutmose IV** and was appointed to Deir el-Medina in year 5 of **Ramesses II**. He was still in office in year 38. He appears to have been one of the wealthiest members of the community and had three **tombs** (numbers 7, 212, and 250) built for himself and his dependants. He and his wife, **Mutemwia**, were childless and adopted **Kenherkhepeshef**, who succeeded to Ramose's office. *See also* HESUNEBEF; KHA; PANEB; SENNEDJEM.

RANEB (reigned c. 2850 BC). Second ruler of **Dynasty 2** and successor to **Hotepsekhemwy**. Little is known about his reign. **Manetho**

credits him with the introduction of the animal cults at **Mendes, Heliopolis**, and **Memphis**, although the **Apis** bull cult is attested earlier in **Dynasty 1**. His **tomb** appears to be located at **Saqqara**. *See also* NYNETJER.

RANEFEREF (reigned c. 2448–2445 BC). Variant transcription of the name also transcribed as Neferefre. Personal name Isi. Fourth ruler of **Dynasty 5**. Son of **Neferirkare** and probably **Khentkaues** II. His reign was short, and his funerary complex at **Abusir** was left unfinished. It was examined and excavated by a Czech expedition from 1978–2002. Several fine pieces of sculpture were recovered, as well as more **Abusir papyri**. *See also* NIUSERRE; SHEPSEKARE.

RE. The ancient Egyptian sun god whose main place of worship was at **Heliopolis**. The sun god became the principal god of Egypt beginning in **Dynasty 4**, displacing the sky god **Horus**, with whom Re is often combined in the form of the god Re-Harakhty. He was usually combined with other gods who were placed at the head of the pantheon, notably **Sobek** and **Amun**. During late **Dynasty 18**, the worship of Re in the form of the sun's disk, or **Aten**, was promoted by **Akhenaten** but failed to displace Amun. Re is usually depicted as a human figure with a feathered headdress but can be represented with a hawk head. *See also* RELIGION.

RE-HARAKHTY. *See* RE.

REISNER, GEORGE ANDREW (1867–1942). American excavator. He was born in Indianapolis, Indiana, on 5 November 1867. A Harvard graduate, he then studied Egyptology at Berlin. He became director of archaeological work in Egypt, the Hearst Expedition, for the University of California, financed by the Hearst family, from 1899–1905 and then directed the Nubian Archaeological Survey for the Egyptian Antiquities Service from 1907–1909. He was appointed curator of the Egyptian Department of the **Boston Museum of Fine Arts** in 1910, and until his death he conducted excavations at various sites in Egypt, including **Zawiyet el-Aryan**; several sites in **Nubia**; and especially **Giza**, where he discovered the **tomb** of **Queen Hetepheres**, and **Nag el-Deir**, where he found the **Reisner Papyri**.

Reisner kept meticulous and detailed notes of his work, but this inevitably delayed publication, so many of his excavations were published posthumously by his assistant, Dows Dunham. He died in Giza, Egypt, on 6 June 1942. *See also* CARTER, HOWARD; MARIETTE, (FRANÇOIS) AUGUSTE FERDINAND; MONTET, (JEAN) PIERRE MARIE; NAVILLE, (HENRI) EDOUARD; PETRIE, WILLIAM MATTHEW FLINDERS; WINLOCK, HERBERT EUSTIS.

REISNER PAPYRI. Four papyrus rolls discovered in a **tomb** at **Nag el-Deir** by **George Reisner** in 1904. These date to the **Middle Kingdom** and the reign of **Amenemhat I** or **Senusret I** and describe administrative projects.

REKHMIRE (fl. 1425 BC). Vizier toward the end of the reign of **Thutmose III** and the beginning of that of **Amenhotep II**. Son of Neferweben and Bata. He came from a prominent official family, as his grandfather, Ahmose, and his uncle, Woser, had both held the post of vizier. He was buried at **Thebes** (Theban **tomb** number 100), and his tomb contains a major inscription that details the duties of the vizier as well as scenes of foreign peoples bringing tribute to the Egyptian court. *See also* AMENEMHAT I; AY; HEMIUNU; IMHOTEP; INTEFYOKER; KAGEMNI; MERERUKA; NEFERMAAT; PASER; PTAHHOTEP; PTAHSHEPSES; RAMESSES I.

RELIGION. For most of Egyptian history no attempt was made to develop a coherent religious theology for the entire country. Egypt consisted of many cities, each of which had a god or goddess to whom the inhabitants were particularly attached, along with the deity's family represented in a local **triad** and often an animal or animals sacred to the local divinity. For example, **Meretseger**, the snake goddess of **Thebes**, represented a purely regional deity; however, some gods and goddesses, for example, **Ptah** of **Memphis**; **Thoth** of **Hermopolis**; or **Osiris**, the god of the dead, were worshipped on a national level throughout the country. The patronage of the king elevated others to the status of supreme deity, like the sky god **Horus**, the sun god **Re** of **Heliopolis**, the formerly obscure god **Amun** of Thebes, the Ptolemaic deity **Sarapis**, and the goddess **Isis** during the **Roman Period**.

More influential deities might absorb a local god or combine to form a composite god, like Re-Harakhty or Amun-Re. Various local **temples** as at Heliopolis or Hermopolis conceived different myths of creation in which their god naturally played the crucial role. The only attempt to impose a more uniform worship—that of the **Aten** disk—by **Akhenaten** ended in failure.

In most cities, the gods were worshipped in major temples built or enlarged through the favor of the king and staffed with priests appointed by him. It was their duty to carry out the rituals to maintain *maat* and appease the gods. The bulk of the priests inherited their rank and were trained in their calling by temple schools and their relations, but the king could and did assign the top posts to royal favorites who could have been from priestly families but also from the royal family, the bureaucracy, or the military. He could also shift priests from one temple to another. Worship was not confined to the temples.

Unlike the state temples from which the local population would have been largely barred, common folk would have access to small local shrines and chapels, sometimes in their own homes, as reflected in the religious practice at **Deir el-Medina**. **Stelae** and statues of the deceased with prayers giving their **name** were erected in the shrines, **tombs**, and temples to keep the individual's memory alive. The ancient religion was eventually replaced by Christianity and evolved into the distinctive **Coptic Church**. *See also* AFTERLIFE; ANAT; ANHUR; ANUBIS; ANUKIS; APIS; ASTARTE; BASTET; BUCHIS; GEB; HAPY; HATHOR; HERYSHEF; HORUS; IAH; KHEPRI; KHNUM; KHONSU; MAHES; MEHIT; MERETSEGER; MIN; MNEVIS; MONTU; MUT; NEFERTUM; NEITH; NEKHBET; NEPHTHYS; NUN; NUT; QUDSHU; RENENUTET; REPIT; RESHEP; SAKHMET; SATIS; SETH; SHAI; SHU; SOKAR; SONS OF HORUS; SOPDU; SOTHIS; TATENEN; TAWERET; TEFNUT; WADJET; WEPWAWET.

RENENUTET. Egyptian goddess of fertility. She was also regarded as a protector of the king and depicted as a cobra. She was worshipped in the **Fayum**, notably at the site of **Medinet Madi**. She was known as Termouthis during the **Graeco-Roman Period** and identified with **Isis**. *See also* RELIGION.

REPIT. Greek Triphis. A goddess whose principal place of worship was at the southern **Athribis** in **Upper Egypt**. She is attested from the **Early Dynastic Period** to the **Graeco-Roman Period**. She is associated with the god **Min** and **Sokar-Osiris**. *See also* RELIGION.

RESHEP. Canaanite war god worshipped in Egypt during the **New Kingdom**. He is usually depicted as a bearded man carrying military weapons. He is found associated with the Canaanite fertility goddess **Qudshu** and the Egyptian fertility god **Min** at **Deir el-Medina**. *See also* ANAT; ASTARTE.

RIB-HADDA (fl. 1350–1330 BC). Ruler of **Byblos**. He was a frequent correspondent in the **Amarna letters**. He complained bitterly about the encroachments of **Abdi-Ashirta** and **Aziru**, kings of **Amurru** to his north, and demanded Egyptian assistance. He was eventually driven from Byblos and sought refuge in Beirut. His ultimate fate is unclear.

RISHI COFFIN. This term is used to denote a type of anthropoid coffin used during the late **Second Intermediate Period** and early **Dynasty 18**. The body of the coffin was decorated in a feather pattern that was probably meant to evoke the goddess **Nut** to envelop the deceased in her protective embrace. *See also* SARCOPHAGUS.

ROAD SYSTEM. Although the most convenient method of travel was through navigation on the river **Nile**, marked desert tracks did exist along the Nile and **Delta** in the Eastern Desert and between the oases in the Western Desert. These were often bordered by pebbling and marked by cairns to give guidance to travelers. These roads could be traversed on foot or on donkeys. Water reserves seem to have been arranged at intervals on the route to the oases. The study of these roadways has only recently been undertaken and has resulted in the discovery of new **graffiti** from all periods.

ROMAN PERIOD (30 BC–395 AD). The term used by Egyptologists to designate the period when Egypt was under the direct rule of Roman emperors in Rome whose representative, the **prefect** of Egypt, was the effective governor of the country. Egypt was regarded as the private property of the Roman ruler, and Roman citizens were not allowed to enter the country without imperial permission. Privileges were granted to Greek residents, but these were strictly defined and more limited than during the **Ptolemaic Period**. Construction work on Egyptian **temples** was undertaken, but there was no official recognition of the use of the Egyptian **language**, especially in legal contexts. After the court was moved to Constantinople, Egypt was ruled as part of the Eastern Empire during the **Byzantine Period**.

ROSETTA STONE. A bilingual decree of 196 BC built into the fort at Rosetta discovered by the French during reconstruction work in 1797. The same decree is written in the **hieroglyphic, demotic**, and Greek scripts. The importance of these texts for the decipherment of the Egyptian scripts was immediately realized, and copies were sent to Paris, where the stone was to be shipped. Following the surrender of French forces in 1801, however, the Rosetta Stone was given, with Turkish approval, to the British by the Treaty of Alexandria and assigned to the **British Museum** in 1802. Decipherment of the hieroglyphic writing proved difficult and centered on the royal names in **cartouches**. The major breakthrough was made by **Jean-François Champollion** in 1822, when he recognized the alphabetic and ideogrammatic nature of the hieroglyphic text. The Rosetta Stone has become the symbol of the key that unlocks mysteries. *See also* YOUNG, THOMAS.

ROYAL CACHES. During **Dynasty 21**, the royal **mummies** in the **Valley of the Kings** whose **tombs** had been plundered were gathered together and reburied in two separate locations, one group in a cliff tomb near **Deir el-Bahri** and a second in the tomb of **Amenhotep II**. The first group was discovered by local residents in the 1870s, who sold some of the equipment, leading to the discovery of the tomb in 1881. The second group was recovered in 1898 from **KV35**. The mummies include most rulers of **Dynasty 18, Dynasty 19**, and **Dynasty 20**, as well as some **queens**, princes, and princesses of Dynasty 18 and members of the family of the **high priest of Amun** of **Dynasty 21**. Most are identified by inscriptions, but it is not absolutely clear that all the identifications made by the priests of Dynasty 21 are correct. Modern attempts to distinguish relationships and ages through bone structure or DNA have so far proved inconclusive. The cliff tomb at Deir el-Bahri was reexamined by a German–Russian expedition from 1998–2003.

RUDAMUN (reigned c. 734–731 BC). Throne name Usimaatre setepenamun. Epithet meryamun. Younger son of **Osorkon III** of **Dynasty 23** and successor of his brother, **Takelot III**. He is attested from a few monuments in **Thebes**. His daughter married **Peftjauawybast**, ruler of **Herakleopolis**. *See also* THIRD INTERMEDIATE PERIOD.

– S –

SABINA, VIBIA (d. 136/7). Empress of Rome. Wife of **Hadrian** and daughter of Lucius Vibius Sabinus and Matidia, niece of the previous ruler Trajan. She accompanied her husband on his many travels and visited Egypt in 130 AD when she went with her husband to view the **Colossi of Memnon**. The visit is recorded by her attendant, **Julia Balbilla**.

SADEH (fl. 2020 BC). A minor wife of **Mentuhotep II** of **Dynasty 11**. She was commemorated in a chapel and buried in a pit **tomb** at his funerary complex at **Deir el-Bahri** discovered during **Henri Edouard Naville**'s excavations at the site. *See also* ASHAYET; HENHENET; KAWIT; KEMSIT; MYT; NEFRU; TEM.

SAFT EL-HENNA. Modern name for the site of *Pr-Spdw*, located southeast of **Bubastis** in the eastern Delta of **Lower Egypt** at the beginning of the **Wadi Tumilat**. The remains date from the **Late Period** to the **Graeco-Roman Period**. It was excavated by **Henri Edouard Naville** from 1884–1885, and its cemetery was examined by **Flinders Petrie** in 1906. During the 1980s, it was surveyed by a team from the University of Liverpool, and it has been under excavation by an Italian expedition since 1988.

SAHURE (reigned c. 2487–2475 BC). Second ruler of **Dynasty 5**. According to the later **Westcar Papyrus**, he was a brother of his predecessor, **Userkaf**, but he was more likely his son. He continued the policy of sun worship, constructing his own sun **temple** and a **pyramid** and temple complex at **Abusir**. The reliefs from the temple depict a **trade** expedition, probably to Lebanon. The area was excavated by the German Ludwig Borchardt from 1907–1908. Sahure's only known **queen** was Meretnebty. *See also* NEFERIRKARE.

SAIS. Greek name for the Egyptian town *Sau*, modern Sa el-Hagar, on the east bank of the Rosetta branch of the **Nile**. Capital of the fifth **nome** of **Lower Egypt**. The chief deity of the town was the goddess **Neith**. The town gained prominence during the **Third Intermediate Period**, when it was ruled by local princes, one of whom, **Nekau I**, was installed by the Assyrians as ruler of Egypt and founded **Dynasty 26**. The city became the capital of Egypt at the time, but very little remains of the site today. Sais has never been properly excavated by archaeologists. In 1997, the **Egypt Exploration Society** began a survey of the area and found remains from the **Prehistoric Period** to the **Roman Period** with some notable gaps in the time sequence.

SAITE PERIOD (664–525 BC). A term used to describe the rule of **Dynasty 26** from **Sais**. It marked the last dynastic period of Egypt's greatness with political reunification of the country, revival in art that had begun during **Dynasty 25** combining styles from the **Old Kingdom** and **Middle Kingdom** in deliberate archaisms, and Egyptian intervention in **Nubia** and Palestine.

SAKHMET. Egyptian goddess. Daughter of the sun god **Re** and wife of the god **Ptah** of **Memphis**. She is usually depicted as a lioness-headed human figure. She was regarded as fierce and bloodthirsty and a destroyer of the king's enemies, but she also had a healing aspect. In **Thebes** she was identified with the goddess **Mut**, and her statues were erected in the **temple** of Mut in the city. *See also* RELIGION.

SALITIS. Greek name given by the Hebrew historian Josephus, who derived it from **Manetho** for the first **Hyksos** ruler of **Dynasty 15**. The Austrian expedition at **Avaris** recently discovered a fragmentary inscription with part of a royal **titulary** of King Seker-Hor, who may well be identifiable with the first Hyksos ruler. *See also* APEPI; IAN-NAS; KHAYAN.

SALT, HENRY (1780–1827). British artist and diplomat. He was born in Lichfield, England, on 14 June 1780 and trained as an artist. He accompanied George Annesley, viscount valentia, as his secretary on a tour of the East, including Egypt, Ethiopia, and India from 1802–1806. He was sent on a mission to Ethiopia from 1809–1811. In 1815, he was appointed British consul general in Egypt, arriving there in 1816. Salt showed great interest in Egyptian antiquities and employed **Giovanni Battista Belzoni** and other agents to form a collection while the French consul, **Bernardino Drovetti**, was doing likewise. Salt also helped direct excavations at **Giza** and **Thebes**. He sold his first collection to the **British Museum** in 1823 after some haggling, apart from the **sarcophagus** of **Sety I**, which went to Sir John Soane's Museum in London. His second collection went to the **Louvre Museum** in 1826, and his third was sold at auction in 1835. He died at Desuke near **Alexandria** on 30 October 1827.

SANAKHTE (reigned c. 2640–2638 BC). Horus name of a king of **Dynasty 3** whose personal name is uncertain, possibly Nebka. He is known from a relief from Sinai, but his order in the dynasty is unclear. He is generally stated to be the first king, but it is probable that he was a later successor rather than a predecessor of **Djoser**.

SAQQARA. Modern name for the main necropolis of ancient **Memphis** in use from **Dynasty 1** to the **Roman Period**. The area contains the **tombs** of the high officials of the **Early Dynastic Period**; the step **pyramids** of **Dynasty 3**, notably the pyramid complex of **Djoser**; the tomb of **Shepseskaf** of **Dynasty 4**; three pyramids of **Dynasty 5**, including that of **Unas** with the first inscribed **pyramid texts**; the pyramids of **Dynasty 6**; many private tombs from all periods; and the **Serapeum**, the burial place of the **Apis** bull. The area has been under continuous excavation since the late 19th century, and recent discoveries by Egyptian, British, and French excavators include the late **Dynasty 18** and **Ramesside Period** cemeteries, notably the tombs of **Horemheb** as a commoner and the **vizier Aperel**.

SARAPIS. Egyptian god prominent during the **Graeco-Roman Period**. The name seems to have been derived from **Osiris Apis**, the deceased form of the Apis bull worshipped at **Memphis**. The deity was adopted by **Ptolemy I** and depicted with Greek features as a bearded man similar to the Greek god Zeus but with attributes derived from other Greek gods, like Dionysius and Aesculapius. Sarapis was promoted to the head of the Egyptian pantheon and considered the husband of **Isis**. He was regarded as a god of fertility and healing.

SARCOPHAGUS. The term used by Egyptologists to denote the stone coffins used in the burials of members of the royal family and high officials that contained the wooden coffin or coffins in which the **mummy** of the deceased rested. These first appeared during the **Old Kingdom** and were rectangular in shape, being plain or decorated on the outside with a palace facade or **serekh** motif. In some cases, the name and titles of the deceased were inscribed on the inside or outside. More lengthy inscribed prayers and decorations were in evidence from the **Middle Kingdom**. During the **New Kingdom**, anthropoid sarcophagi came into use with texts on the inside and outside. The sky goddess **Nut** was often depicted on the inside, especially in sarcophagi from the **Late Period** and **Graeco-Roman Period**. The term *sarcophagus* has also been loosely used to refer to wooden or cartonnage coffins, but it is now generally restricted to those made of stone. *See also* RISHI COFFIN; TOMB.

SATIRE ON TRADES, THE. A literary work composed by **Khety** during the **Middle Kingdom**. It purports to be his advice as a father to his son on the choice of profession. It points out the drawbacks to all professions, except that of **scribe**, of which it extols its virtues. *See also* LITERATURE.

SATIS. Consort of the god **Khnum** of **Elephantine**. She is depicted as a human female figure with a white crown with horns. She was principally worshipped at Elephantine and in **Nubia**. *See also* ANUKIS; RELIGION.

SATRAP. The Persian term for governor of a province. The Persian satraps of Egypt were generally members of the royal family or nobility. The last Persian satrap surrendered to **Alexander the Great**, upon whose death the Macedonian general, **Ptolemy**, became the last satrap, as he eventually took the title of king. *See also* ACHAEMENES; ARSAMES.

SCARAB. Modern name for the dung beetle that was regarded as sacred by the ancient Egyptians as, according to one perception, the sun was pushed through the sky by a celestial beetle. The ancient Egyptian name for the beetle was *kheper*. The scarab was a popular form of amulet usually made of steatite and then glazed and pierced vertically to fit on necklaces or rings. The underside could carry a prayer or **name** when used as a seal. The larger heart scarab was unpierced and made of hard stone, like schist. It was placed over the heart of the **mummy**, as the underside carried a spell to enable the heart to act favorably toward the deceased during the **weighing of the heart** ceremony. Winged and smaller scarabs all made of **faience** were also placed amid the wrappings of the mummy. *See also* KHEPRI.

SCORPION (reigned c. 3200 BC). A major king of **Dynasty 0** whose name is uncertain but was written as a scorpion hieroglyph. He reigned in **Upper Egypt** but is attested from an inscription in **Nubia**. His principal monument is a decorated macehead found at **Hierakonpolis**. He was buried at **Abydos**, and his **tomb** has recently been excavated by a German expedition.

SCRIBE. Ancient Egyptian *Sesh*. The title designates a literate man as well as a profession. The scribe was the essential backbone of the Egyptian administration and was essential for the the country to run smoothly. The range of tasks of a scribe varied from humble village scribes to key members of the elite. While general **education** was limited, scribal schools were believed to be attached to the **temples** and the court, although many scribes would have learned their skill from their fathers or relatives. It was rare but not impossible for a member of the nonscribal classes to join their ranks. Many high officials style themselves scribe to indicate their literacy, although presumably they left the writing of administrative documents to their underlings. The scribes tended to regard themselves as superior to the bulk of the population, as reflected in the *The Satire on Trades*.

SEA PEOPLES. A term used by the Egyptians for a group of allied foreign peoples who threatened Egypt from the middle of **Dynasty 19** until the beginning of **Dynasty 20**. They first appeared as an entity in year 5 of **Merenptah** when, allied with the Libyans, they invaded Egypt but were driven back and defeated. The Sea Peoples are described as Ekwesh, Lukka, Shekelesh, and Sherden, some of whom had been noted separately in Egyptian texts from late **Dynasty 18**.

The Sea Peoples returned in year 8 of **Ramesses III** after, according to the Egyptians, destroying the **Hittite** empire and several Syrian centers, including **Ugarit**. Their coalition was now described as Denen, Peleset, Shekelesh, Sherden, Tjekker, Teresh, and Weshwesh. Ramesses III claimed to have defeated and pushed them back from Egypt. The intention of the Sea Peoples was to settle in newly occupied lands, as they were accompanied by their families and possessions. Ramesses III stated that he agreed to the defeated forces settling along the Levantine coast in what was then the Egyptian empire, although he may have been obliged to do so since they could not be expelled. The Tjekker are later recorded there during late Dynasty 20, and the Peleset, later known as the **Philistines**, also settled on the coast. The origin of the Sea Peoples in unclear, but they may have originated in Asia Minor or the northern Aegean. Some groups may have migrated elsewhere, from Sherden to Sardinia, but this is speculative. *See also* WARFARE.

SEBENNYTOS. Greek name for the ancient Egyptian town of *Tjebnetjer*, capital of the 12th **nome** of **Lower Egypt**. Modern Samanud on the west bank of the Damietta branch of the **Nile**. The main **temple** was dedicated to the god Onuris (**Anhur**)-**Shu** and his wife, **Mehit**. Although some objects from the **Old Kingdom** to **New Kingdom** have been found in the vicinity, no remains have been found on-site earlier than **Dynasty 30**, whose royal family is stated to have come from Sebennytos, but the area has not yet been thoroughly excavated. The town remained prominent during the **Graeco-Roman Period**, its most famous citizen being the historian **Manetho**. It was surveyed by a British expedition from 1998–1999.

SECOND INTERMEDIATE PERIOD (c. 1795–1550 BC). The term used by Egyptologists to designate the period between the end of

Dynasty 12 or, according to some, the middle of **Dynasty 13** until the accession of **Dynasty 18**. During this period, the kingship was weak and divided, and Egypt was occupied by the **Hyksos** until they were driven out by the princes of **Thebes**.

SEDMENT. The modern name for a cemetery site northwest of **Herakleopolis** consisting of cliff **tombs** and desert burials. The tombs date from the **Early Dynastic Period** to the **Graeco-Roman Period**, including important official tombs from **Dynasty 19**. The site was excavated by **Flinders Petrie** from 1920–1921.

SEKER-HOR. *See* SALITIS.

SEKHEMKHET (reigned c. 2667–2648 BC). **Horus** name of a king of **Dynasty 3** and probable successor to **Djoser**. His personal name is uncertain, possibly Djoser Teti. His unfinished **pyramid** at **Saqqara** was excavated between 1951 and 1954 by Zakaria Goneim, an Egyptian archaeologist, but Sekhemkhet's closed **sarcophagus** was found empty. His successor is uncertain. *See also* HUNI.

SEMERKHET (reigned c. 2915 BC). Seventh ruler of **Dynasty 1** and successor of **Anedjib**. He was buried in an elaborate **tomb** at **Abydos**, but little is known of his reign, which may have been a time of unrest.

SEMNA. Modern name for a site in **Nubia** near the Second **Cataract** of the **Nile** where a fortress, **temple**, and settlement were erected during **Dynasty 12** on the west bank, probably begun under **Senusret I** and completed under **Senusret III**, after who it was named *Sekhem-Khakaure*. Nearby was a second fort, now known as Semna South, ancient Egyptian *Dair Seti*. Semna marked the limit of Egyptian control during the **Middle Kingdom**. The site was excavated by **George Reisner** from 1924–1928 and again during the 1960s. The area is now flooded by Lake Nasser, the lake formed by the Aswan High Dam, but part of the temple was removed to safety. *See also* ANIBA; ASKUT; BUHEN; KUMMA; MIRGISSA; SHALFAK; URONARTI.

SENAKHTENRE. *See* TAO.

SENENMUT (fl. 1479–1455 BC). High official during the reign of **Queen Hatshepsut**. Son of **Ramose** and Hatnefer of apparently humble origin. He held the office of chief steward and tutor of Princess **Nefrure**. He was in charge of the queen's building works, notably at **Deir el-Bahri**. Numerous statues of him survive, most badly damaged, although it is not certain when the damage occurred. There has been much speculation about his relationship with the queen. He may have fallen into disgrace before the end of the reign. No family of his is known. His major **tomb** at Deir el-Bahri was never completed and is defaced. *See also* THUTMOSE III.

SENNEDJEM (fl. 1280 BC). Workman in the community of royal **tomb** builders at **Deir el-Medina**. Son of Khabekhnet and Tahenen. He served in the workforce probably during the reign of **Sety I** and the early part of that of **Ramesses II** during **Dynasty 19**. His **tomb** (number 1) was discovered intact in 1886, including several **mummies** of his immediate family along with their burial equipment. Most of the material is now housed in the **Cairo Egyptian Museum**, but some has been dispersed to other institutions. The painted plaster scenes in his tomb are well preserved and remarkable for their vividness. *See also* HESUNEBEF; KENHERKHEPESHEF; KHA; PANEB; RAMOSE.

SENNEFER (fl. 1400 BC). Mayor of **Thebes** under **Amenhotep II**. He was the owner of the well-preserved Theban **tomb** (number 96), which includes scenes of his family and is noted for its grapevine decoration.

SENUSRET I (reigned c. 1965–1920 BC). Throne name Kheperkare. Son of **Amenemhat I**, founder of **Dynasty 12**. He was named **coregent** with his father c. 1965 BC to secure the new dynasty and succeeded to sole rule following his father's assassination about 1955 BC. The circumstances are mentioned in the tale of **Sinuhe**, but the motive for the assassination and the means by which the conspiracy was crushed remain unclear. Senusret I maintained the policy of expansion in **Nubia**. His reign appears to have fostered literary composition, as evidenced by the production of the story of *Sinuhe, the Prophecy of Neferti*, and the **wisdom** text *The Instruction of Amenemhat*

I. An important example of his construction work at **Karnak** has survived in the form of a kiosk with intricately carved **hieroglyphs**. He also erected a pair of **obelisks** in the **temple** at **Heliopolis**, of which one survives. He was buried in a **pyramid** complex at **Lisht**, which was excavated by the **Metropolitan Museum of Art** from 1908–1934 and 1984–1989. His principal wife was his sister, **Nefru**, and he was succeeded by his son, **Amenemhat II**.

SENUSRET II (reigned c. 1880–1874 BC). Throne name Khakheperre. Son of **Amenemhat II**. He continued the expansionist policy of **Dynasty 12** with **trade** relations recorded with Palestine. He was buried at **Lahun** in the **Fayum**. His principal wife was **Queen Khenemet-nefer-hedjet**, and he was succeeded by his son, **Senusret III**.

SENUSRET III (reigned c. 1874–1855 BC). Throne name Khakaure. Son of **Senusret II** and **Khenemet-nefer-hedjet**. He undertook military expeditions in **Nubia**, where he strengthened Egyptian fortresses and attacked the town of Shechem in Palestine. He is credited with eliminating the provincial nomarchs who are last attested in his reign. Senusret III was buried in a **pyramid** at **Dahshur**, which was recently excavated by the **Metropolitan Museum of Art**. His military activities were later confused with those of **Ramesses II** to form the deeds of conquest of a mythical King Sesostris. His principal wife was **Khenemet-nefer-hedjet** the younger. *See also* WARFARE.

SEPTIMIUS SEVERUS (145–211 AD). Roman emperor. Full name Lucius Septimius Severus, son of Publius Septimius Geta and Fulvia Pia. He was born in Leptis Magna, Libya, around 145 AD. He had a successful military and senatorial career, finally occupying the post of governor of Pannonia. Severus was proclaimed emperor in 193 AD and eventually defeated his rivals in the eastern and western parts of the Roman Empire. He visited Egypt from 199–201 AD, granting **Alexandria** and other major cities municipal councils and ordering new building work in Alexandria and the restoration of one of the **Colossi of Memnon**, which was alleged to sing but did so no more after this work. The imperial family is depicted on a relief from the **temple** of **Esna**, although the image of the younger son was later erased. He also admited Egyptians into the Roman senate, although the first Egyptian senator was not appointed until 212 AD. Severus died in York on 4 February 211 AD and was succeeded by his son, **Caracalla**.

SERABIT EL-KHADIM. Site in the Sinai used as a quarry for turquoise beginning in the **Middle Kingdom**, largely replacing **Wadi Maghara**, and also the location of a **temple** dedicated to **Hathor**, lady of turquoise, where many texts dedicated by the leaders of mining expeditions have been found. The site was first excavated by Major Charles Macdonald in the 1860s, **Flinders Petrie** from 1904–1905, and a French expedition from 1993–1996. *See also* HATNUB; MONS CLAUDIANUS; MONS PORPHYRITES; WADI EL-HUDI; WADI HAMMAMAT; WADI MAGHARA.

SERAPEUM. Greek name for the catacombs of the sacred **Apis** bull at **Saqqara**. The underground vault contained separate chambers for each burial in a massive **sarcophagus**, and on the walls were attached **stelae** of the workmen involved in the burials. The Serapeum was discovered by **Auguste Mariette** in 1851, but the continuous sequence of burials has only been traced from the **Third Intermediate Period** to the **Ptolemaic Period**, although a few isolated earlier burials have been located. Prince **Khaemwese**, son of **Ramesses II**, may have been buried here. *See also* MEMPHIS.

SERAPIS. *See* SARAPIS.

SEREKH. The stylized palace facade used beginning in **Dynasty 0** to enclose the **Horus** name of the king in the royal **titulary**.

SESEBI. Modern name for a settlement in Upper **Nubia** founded at the end of **Dynasty 18**. The **temple** was dedicated to the Theban **triad**. The area was excavated by a British expedition from 1936–1938 but has not been properly published.

SESHESESHET. The name of two royal ladies of **Dynasty 6**. The first was the mother of **Teti**, founder of the dynasty, whose husband is unknown. She apparently was alive at her son's accession and was given the title of **queen** mother. Her granddaughter, Sesheseshet, the daughter of Teti, was the wife of the **vizier Mereruka**.

SETEPENRE (fl. 1336 BC). Sixth daughter of **Akhenaten** and **Nefertiti**. She is named in **tomb** reliefs from **Amarna**. She may be one of two princesses who appear on a painted fresco now in the Ashmolean Museum of Art and Archaeology in Oxford, United Kingdom. Her fate is unknown. *See also* ANKHESENAMUN; ANKHESEN-PAATEN-TASHERIT; BAKETATEN; MEKETATEN; MERITA-MUN; MERITATEN-TASHERIT; NEFERNEFRUATEN; NEFER-NEFRURE.

SETH. Egyptian god of thunder and the desert. Son of **Geb** and **Nut**. Brother of **Osiris**, **Isis**, and **Nephthys**. According to Egyptian legend, he murdered his brother, Osiris, in order to claim the crown of Egypt but was thwarted by Isis and her son, **Horus**. He was therefore regarded as an evil god and abominated in most parts of Egypt, although he was still worshipped in areas of the Delta. He was identified with the Syrian god Baal and hence associated with the **Hyksos**. In another myth, he appears as a protector of the sun god **Re**. *See also* RELIGION.

SETHHERKHEPESHEF. The name of several royal princes in **Dynasty 19** and **Dynasty 20**. The first known was a son of **Ramesses II**, but it appears that this name was merely an alternate name of Prince **Amenherkhepeshef**. The **tomb** (number 43) of Sethherkhepeshef (fl. c. 1185 BC), son of **Ramesses III**, is located in the **Valley of the Queens**, and it appears from his depiction that he died as a child. A second Prince Sethherkhepeshef succeeded as **Ramesses VIII** and may well have been a younger son of Ramesses III of the same name.

SETHNAKHTE (reigned c. 1189–1184 BC). Throne name Userkhaure. Founder of **Dynasty 20** of unknown origin. He overthrew the rule of **Tewosret** and claimed to have restored the land from the chaos that **Bay** had left when he fled the country. A recently discovered **stela** in **Luxor** is dated to his year 4, indicating that he reigned at least three full years. He was succeeded by his son, **Ramesses III**. He was buried in **tomb KV14** in the **Valley of the Kings**, which he had taken over from Tewosret. His body may have been found in the **royal cache** in the tomb of **Amenhotep II** in 1898.

SETY (fl. 1279–1230 BC). Ninth son of **Ramesses II**. He appears in inscriptions during the early part of his father's reign. He was buried in **tomb KV5** in the **Valley of the Kings**, where some of his **canopic** equipment was discovered. *See also* AMENHERKHEPESHEF; KHAEMWESE; MERENPTAH; MERYATUM; PREHERWENEMEF; SETY.

SETY I (reigned c. 1294–1279 BC). Throne name Menmare. Son of **Ramesses I** and Sitre. Second ruler of **Dynasty 19**. He pursued a vigorous policy of reestablishing Egyptian control in Palestine and Syria. At home he undertook important construction works, notably the **temple** at **Abydos** with a detailed **king list** and his finely painted **tomb (KV17)** in the **Valley of the Kings** discovered in 1817. He established his son, **Ramesses II**, as his **coregent**. His **mummy** was recovered in the **royal cache** at **Deir el-Bahri** in 1881. His mortuary temple at Qurna on the west bank of the **Nile** opposite **Thebes** is well preserved and has been recently excavated, recorded, and restored by a German expedition from 1970–1984 and after flood damage from 1995–2000.

SETY II (reigned c. 1202–1196 BC). Throne name Userkheprure. Son of **Merenptah** of **Dynasty 19**. His claim to the throne was challenged by **Amenmesse**, and he only established himself after a civil war that weakened the dynasty. After a short reign, Sety II was followed by his son, **Siptah**, although power remained in the hands of his widow, **Tewosret**, and **Bay**. He was buried in **tomb KV15** in the **Valley of the Kings**, and his body was recovered from the **royal cache** in the tomb of **Amenhotep II** in 1898.

SEVERUS, SEPTIMUS. *See* SEPTIMIUS SEVERUS.

SEX. Unlike some Semitic peoples of the Near East, the ancient Egyptians had a rather relaxed view of sex and sexuality. While **wisdom literature** advised moderation in sexual life and also in drinking, sex was regarded as a natural and enjoyable part of the human condition. Men were certainly not expected to be monogamous in **marriage**, although discretion for the sake of the family in regard to other relationships was preferable. **Women** were expected to be faithful if married, but if not, divorce was available for the husband if he wished, and adultery was not normally treated as a major offense in ordinary life despite the fact that in literature faithless wives always suffer misfortune. Independent women could behave as they chose, as in the *Tale of Truth and Falsehood*. The repeated allegations of "rape" at **Deir el-Medina** imply that sexual relationships between individuals, whether married or unmarried, were not uncommon.

Homosexuality is also mentioned in some texts, and it is clear that sexual relationships between men were regarded as abnormal but not of any great concern of the state or other individuals. It was the passive partner, who played the part of a woman, who was viewed with greater contempt. The Egyptians believed that sexual practices were the concern of the individuals themselves and were of no interest to the community unless sexual jealousy happened to arouse tensions that required the interference of the authorities.

SHABAQO (reigned c. 720–706 BC). Throne name Neferkare. Son of **Kashta** and successor of **Piye**. **Nubian** ruler who conquered Egypt around 720 BC, executing **Bakenrenef** of **Dynasty 24** and establishing **Dynasty 25**. He maintained good relations with **Assyria**, whose empire had spread to the Egyptian border. He was buried in a **pyramid tomb** at el-Kurru in **Nubia**. He was succeeded by **Shebitqo**, whose relationship to him is uncertain.

SHABTI. The earliest royal burials of **Dynasty 1** and **Dynasty 2** were surrounded by the graves of royal retainers who had been sacrificed to accompany their master as servants in the next life. This practice was eventually abandoned, and models of servants appear in **tombs** in the **Old Kingdom** and **Middle Kingdom**. The deceased was expected to perform some manual activities in the **afterlife**, so from the late Middle Kingdom to the **Ptolemaic Period** burials included *shabtis*, or servant figures, with inscriptions naming the deceased and obliging the figure to carry out any work demanded of him or her.

Elaborate burials had 365 *shabtis*, 1 for each day of the year plus overseer *shabtis* for every 10 worker figures. The figures would be placed in *shabti* boxes in the tomb.

SHAI. Egyptian god of fate. He is represented as a human figure. *See also* RELIGION.

SHALFAK. Modern name for the site of a fortress in the Second **Cataract** region of the **Nile** in **Nubia** probably built by **Senusret III**. Ancient Egyptian *Waf Khasut*. *See also* ANIBA; ASKUT; BUHEN; KUMMA; MIRGISSA; SEMNA; URONARTI.

SHANHUR. Modern name for a site in **Upper Egypt** south of **Coptos** where a **temple** to **Isis** built during the **Roman Period** is located. It has been investigated by a Belgian expedition since 1992.

SHARUNA. *See* KOM EL-AHMAR SAWARIS.

SHEBITQO (reigned c. 706–690 BC). Throne name Djedkaure. Successor of **Shabaqo** of **Dynasty 25**. He faced mounting pressure from the expanding Assyrian empire and supported a rebellion of the Palestinian states against Assyrian domination. Egyptian forces under the command of **Taharqo** were defeated at Eltekeh in 701 BC, and **Assyria** remained a constant threat. He was buried at el-Kurru in **Nubia**. *See also* WARFARE.

SHENOUTE (d. c. 466 AD). **Coptic** abbot of the White Monastery near modern Sohag. He was born in the village of Shenalolet near **Akhmim** and entered the White Monastery in 371, where he served as a monk and later succeeded his uncle, Pjol, the founder of the monastery, as head of the community. His rule was quite strict and harsher than that of **Pachomius**, and Shenoute introduced a written profession of obedience. He was a staunch opponent of paganism and encouraged the destruction of pagan monuments. In 431, he took part in the Council of Ephesus with the patriarch **Cyril**. Many of his literary compositions, all on religious subjects, have survived, and he is regarded as the most original author of the Coptic Period. *See also* ABRAHAM; ANTHONY; COPTIC CHURCH.

SHEPENWEPET. The name of two princesses who succeeded as **God's wife of Amun**. Shepenwepet I, daughter of **Osorkon III** of **Dynasty 23**, and Karoatjet held office until the advent of the Nubian **Dynasty 25**, when she was obliged to adopt **Amenirdis** I, daughter of **Kashta**, as her heir. Shepenwepet II, daughter of **Piye**, succeeded Amenirdis I and adopted Amenirdis II, daughter of **Taharqo**, but in 656 BC she was obliged to adopt **Nitocris**, daughter of **Psamtik I** of **Dynasty 26**, who had ousted her family from power.

SHEPSEKARE (reigned c. 2455–2448 BC). Obscure monarch of **Dynasty 5**. He appears to have been either the predecessor or the successor of **Raneferef**, but no details are known about his reign.

SHEPSESKAF (reigned c. 2503–2498 BC). Ruler of **Dynasty 4**. Successor and possibly son of **Menkaure**. The waning power of the monarch is demonstrated by his failure to build a **pyramid**. He was buried in a large **mastaba tomb** near **Saqqara**.

SHESHI. Throne name Maaibre. Ruler of the **Second Intermediate Period** attested on many **scarabs**. He is generally considered to be a member of the **Hyksos Dynasty 15** but may well belong to **Dynasty 14**.

SHESHONQ I (reigned c. 945–924 BC). Throne name Hedjkheperre setepenre. Epithet meryamun. Founder of **Dynasty 22B**. Son of the Libyan chieftain **Nimlot** and his wife, Tentsepeh, and nephew of King **Osorkon** the Elder. He succeeded to the throne despite opposition in **Thebes** and reestablished Egyptian prestige with a campaign in Palestine, being mentioned in the Bible as Shishak. A statue of him has been discovered at **Byblos**. Sheshonq I described his campaign on a victory relief carved in the **temple** of **Karnak**. He placed his sons in strategic positions, such as that of **high priest of Amun**, to strengthen his rule. *See also* WARFARE.

SHESHONQ II (reigned c. 890 BC). Throne name Heqakheperre setepenre. Epithet meryamun. Ephemeral monarch of **Dynasty 22** who is known from his burial at **Tanis** in the **tomb** of **Pasebakhaenniut I**.

He is usually identified with Prince Sheshonq, son of **Osorkon I**, and **Maatkare**, daughter of **Pasebakhaenniut II** of **Dynasty 21**, but he appears never to have reigned alone, only as **coregent** with his father.

SHESHONQ III (reigned c. 825–785 BC). Throne name Usermaatre setepenre or setepenamun. Epithet meryamun si-bast netjer heka iunu. Successor of **Takelot II** of **Dynasty 22**. It appears that during his reign the unity of Egypt was broken and a rival line of rulers was established as **Dynasty 23**, beginning with **Pedubast I**. Sheshonq III carried out building works at **Tanis** with material brought from **Pi-Ramesses**. His intact **tomb** at Tanis was discovered in 1939. A King Usimaatre meryamun Sheshonq is known to have lived during this time in **Thebes**, and his name may be a variant of Sheshonq's title or a separate king now to be known as Sheshonq VI. Sheshonq III may have been succeeded by **Sheshonq IV**.

SHESHONQ IV (reigned c. 785–773 BC). Throne name Hedjkheperre setepenre or setepenamun. Epithet meryamun si-bast netjer heka iunu. An obscure ruler whose existence has only recently been acknowledged. It is likely that he was a successor to **Sheshonq III**.

SHESHONQ V (reigned c. 767–730 BC). Throne name Akheperre setepenre. Epithet meryamun si-bast netjer heka waset. Son and successor of **Pimay**. His control appears to have been restricted to the Delta area. He celebrated his **jubilee** and carried out building works at **Tanis** but is otherwise little known. *See also* OSORKON IV.

SHIPWRECKED SAILOR. A literary tale from the **Middle Kingdom** known from one manuscript. It describes the adventures of a sailor shipwrecked on a mysterious island where he meets a magical serpent. *See also* LITERATURE.

SHU. Egyptian god of the air and sunlight. According to the creation myth from **Heliopolis**, he was created by **Atum**, and by his union with **Tefnut**, goddess of moisture, he produced **Geb** and **Nut**. He is depicted in human form as a kneeling man with upraised arms and a sun disk on his head or as a lion. *See also* RELIGION.

SIAMUN (reigned c. 978–950 BC). Throne name Netjerkheperre. Penultimate king of **Dynasty 21**. Successor of **Osorkon** the Elder but of unknown origin. Little is known about his reign. He may have undertaken a campaign against Gezer in Palestine, but his identification with the unnamed ruler who took the city mentioned in the Bible is speculative. *See also* SHESHONQ I.

SICARD, CLAUDE (1677–1726). French priest. He was born in Aubagne, France, on 4 May 1677. He went to the Levant as a missionary and settled in Cairo in 1712. He made numerous exploratory journeys throughout the country and became the first known European to visit **Upper Egypt**, including the **Valley of the Kings** and Aswan in 1721 in the company of another priest, Pietro Lorenzo Pincia. His surviving papers were not completely published until 1982, and Pincia's account only appeared in 1998. He died in Cairo on 12 April 1726.

SIHATHOR (fl. 1730 BC). A possible minor ruler of **Dynasty 13**. Son of the God's father Haankhef and probably the lady Kemi. According to the **Turin Royal Canon**, he succeeded his brother, **Neferhotep I**, but his reign was brief, and he was followed by his brother, **Sobekhotep IV**. However, contemporary monuments only describe him as a royal prince, and he may have predeceased his elder brother and never reigned. The attribution of the throne name Menwadjre is dubious. *See also* SECOND INTERMEDIATE PERIOD.

SILVER. A precious metal not widely available in Egypt in its purest form, thus it had to be imported. It is attested beginning in the **Old Kingdom** in the royal burial of **Queen Hetepheres** of **Dynasty 4** and in the **Middle Kingdom** in the **Tod** treasure. It was used in the funerary equipment of the royal burials at **Tanis** of **Dynasty 21** and **Dynasty 22**. According to Egyptian myth, the bones of the gods were made of silver. *See also* BRONZE; COPPER; GOLD; IRON.

SINUHE. Hero of a **Middle Kingdom** story set during the reign of **Senusret I**. Sinuhe flees the country upon hearing of the assassination of the king's father, **Amenemhat I**, and the story outlines his adventures in the Palestine region. In old age, he longs to return to

Egypt and is pardoned and welcomed back by the king. The story reflects the strong attachment of Egyptians to their homeland. It is already attested at the end of the Middle Kingdom and was extremely popular during the **New Kingdom**, from which time many copies survive. *See also* LITERATURE.

SIPTAH (reigned c. 1196–1190 BC). Throne name Akhenre. Probably son of **Sety II** of **Dynasty 19**. He was proclaimed king with the help of **Bay** when he was still a child, but he died after a short reign. His **mummy** reveals that he suffered from a clubfoot. Nothing is known of the internal politics of his reign, but it has recently been revealed that Bay was executed in 1189 BC, presumably after a power struggle at court. The king died the next year. He was succeeded by his probable stepmother, **Tewosret**. He was buried in **tomb KV47** in the **Valley of the Kings**, discovered in 1905, and his body was recovered from the **royal cache** in the tomb of **Amenhotep II** in 1898. His mortuary **temple** at **Thebes** has not been preserved, but **foundation deposits** have been recovered. The site was excavated by **Flinders Petrie** in 1896.

SISTRUM. A **musical** instrument usually made of **bronze** consisting of a vertical handle with an open curved frame above. Bronze rods are attached across the frame, and small bronze roundels are threaded on the rods that produce sound when shaken. The instrument is depicted being shaken by priestesses at religious ceremonies.

SITAMUN (fl. 1525 BC). Egyptian princess. Probably daughter of **Ahmose I** and **Ahmose-Nefertari**. She is attested in the reign of her father with the title **God's Wife** and appears to have survived into the reign of her brother **Amenhotep I**. *See also* AHMOSE-SIPAIR; MERITAMUN.

SITAMUN (fl. 1355 BC). Egyptian princess. Daughter of **Amenhotep III** and **Tiy**. An item of furniture inscribed with her name was found in the **tomb** of **Yuya**, Tiy's father. She was given the title of **queen** on inscriptions from her father's reign and so probably married him, but her subsequent fate is not known. *See also* AKHENATEN; BAKETATEN.

SITHATHORIUNET (fl. 1875 BC). A princess of **Dynasty 12**. Probable daughter of **Senusret II**. Her **tomb** was discovered near her father's **pyramid** at **Lahun** and contained a large of collection of jewelry now housed in the **Cairo Egyptian Museum** and the **Metropolitan Museum of Art**.

SITIAH (fl. 1460 BC). Wife of **Thutmose III** and daughter of the royal nurse Ipu. She is depicted in Thutmose III's **tomb (KV34)** in the **Valley of the Kings** and presumably succeeded **Nefrure** as a royal wife. *See also* MERYETRE HATSHEPSUT; NEBTU.

SITRE (fl. 1290 BC). Queen of **Ramesses I** of **Dynasty 19** and mother of **Sety I**. Her origin is unknown. She was buried in **QV38** in the **Valley of the Queens**.

SIWA OASIS. An oasis in the northern part of the Western Desert just east of the present Libyan border. There is no direct evidence for Egyptian control until **Dynasty 26**, when the famous **temple** to **Amun** was built, although this does not preclude earlier Egyptian influence. The oracle of the temple became well known in the classical world. **Cambyses** was alleged to have tried and failed to conquer the oasis. The oracle was consulted by **Alexander the Great** and was believed to have confirmed his divine origin. There are a number of **tombs** probably from the **Late Period** and the **Graeco-Roman Period**, notably the **tomb** of **Siamun**, who is depicted in Greek fashion. A German expedition has been working there since 1993. *See also* BAHARIYA OASIS; DAKHLA OASIS; FARFARA OASIS; KHARGA OASIS.

SLAVERY. Slavery played a minor role in ancient Egypt, contrary to modern expectations. There was no large-scale exploitation of slavery. Most slaves were acquired as booty in war or to a lesser extent from the sale of criminals or debtors. Most slaves were used in a domestic context as local servants, although they may have been employed in certain industrial concerns, for example as slave **women** used for the preparation of textiles. Slaves seem to have been on the whole well treated and absorbed into the community in due course. There is the example of **Hesunebef**, who was freed by his patron and found a position, and references to slaves who inherited the property of their master or mistress. The Biblical **Israelites** in Egypt were not technically slaves but were subject to indentured labor, as were all Egyptian subjects. The position of slaves undoubtedly worsened during the **Graeco-Roman Period**, when classical views on slavery prevailed.

SMATAWYTEFNAKHT (fl. 340–330 BC). A chief priest of **Sakhmet** from **Herakleopolis**. Son of the priest of **Amun-Re**, Djedsmatawyefankh, and Ankhet. He left a long biographical **stela** discovered in 1765 in Pompeii, Italy, and now housed in the Naples National Archaeological Museum in Italy, in which he mentions his presence in the battle between the Persians and the Greeks, presumably referring to the campaign of **Alexander the Great**.

SMENKHKARE (reigned c. 1338–1336 BC). Throne name Ankhkheperure. Mysterious and ephemeral ruler at the end of **Dynasty 18** who was **coregent** and successor of **Akhenaten**. It has been suggested that this ruler was in fact Akhenaten's widow, **Nefertiti**, or daughter, **Meritamun**, or a man who reigned with one of these **women**, but his existence remains obscure. It has also been suggested that his presumed body found in **tomb KV55** in the **Valley of the Kings** was in fact that of Akhenaten, although the age of the skeleton renders this theory dubious. *See also* AY; HOREMHEB; TUTANKHAMUN.

SNEFRU (reigned c. 2615–2592 BC). First king of **Dynasty 4** of unknown origin. His mother, **Meresankh** I, bore the title of **queen** mother but not queen, so his father is unlikely to have been **Huni**, last ruler of the previous dynasty. He built possibly three **pyramids**, two at **Dahshur** and possibly one at **Meidum**. Snefru undertook campaigns in **Nubia** and had **trade** relations with Lebanon. He was remembered in the later **literature** as a wise and just monarch. He was succeeded by **Khufu**, his son by his chief queen, **Hetepheres**. *See also* NEFERMAAT; RAHOTEP.

SOBEK. Crocodile god often depicted as a crocodile-headed human figure. His principal places of worship were the **Fayum** and **Kom**

Ombo. He was especially popular during the late **Middle Kingdom** and early **Second Intermediate Period**, when he is often equated with **Re** as the god Sobek-Re.

SOBEKEMSAF. The name of two kings of **Dynasty 17**. The more important was Sobekemsaf II, throne name Sekhemre Shedtawy, of whom several monuments survive, including a colossal statue now housed in the **British Museum**. He was buried on the western bank of the **Nile** at **Thebes**, and his **tomb** is recorded as being violated in **Dynasty 20**. *See also* SECOND INTERMEDIATE PERIOD.

SOBEKHOTEP. The name of several kings of **Dynasty 13**, the numbering of whom is not absolutely certain. The most successful appears to have been **Sobekhotep III** and **Sobekhotep IV**.

SOBEKHOTEP III (reigned c. 1740 BC). Throne name Sekhemresewadjtawy. Son of the God's father Mentuhotep and the lady Iuhetibu. He is attested on monuments in **Middle Egypt** and **Upper Egypt** and on **graffiti** near the First **Cataract**. A **papyrus** from his reign documents the presence of Asiatic servants in Egypt.

SOBEKHOTEP IV (reigned c. 1730–1722 BC). Throne name Khaneferre. He was a younger son of the God's father Haankhef and the lady Kemi and succeeded his brothers, **Neferhotep I** and **Sihathor**. He is attested on **graffiti** in the region of **Elephantine** and the **Wadi Hammamat** and on monuments in **Karnak** and Palestine.

SOBEKNAKHT (fl. 1560 BC). Governor of **Elkab** and possibly **Hierakonpolis** during **Dynasty 17**. He is known principally from his **tomb**, which was partially published in 1896. A vessel inscribed with his name has been found in a tomb at **Kerma**. A recent reexamination of his burial site discovered an inscription that recounts a raid by invaders from Kush in the vicinity of Elkab and thus explains the presence of the vessel in the Kushite capital as loot.

SOBEKNEFRU (reigned c. 1799–1795 BC). Throne name Sobekkare. Last ruler of **Dynasty 12**. Daughter of **Amenemhat III** and possibly wife of her brother, **Amenemhat IV**. She succeeded to the throne presumably for lack of male heirs, but her reign was brief, and she was followed by the unstable **Dynasty 13** beginning the **Second Intermediate Period**.

SOCIETY. Ancient Egyptian society consisted of two classes divided by the ability to read and write. The bulk of the population were illiterate peasants engaged in **agriculture** with a relatively small number of craftsmen who either lived alongside the rural communities or, like workers in **faience**, **glass**, or jewelery, were attached to wealthy private or government establishments. The literate population of not more than 5 percent comprised the royal court and the bureaucracy covering civil, priestly, and military. Although it was an Egyptian ideal for a son to follow in his father's office, the major appointments were the prerogative of the king and the **vizier**, or high officials, for more minor offices, so posts often did not follow a hereditary line, although the sons of a literate official could find other positions. Thus it is inaccurate to speak of a member of Egyptian nobility. Rather there existed a hereditary bureaucratic class.

It would have been difficult to rise from one class to another. Presumably an enterprising farmer who managed to build up a small estate, like **Hekanakhte**, might become literate or have his children educated so they could join the official class. Similarly the army might prove the vehicle for the acquisition of land and wealth for someone from a peasant background, but such cases appear to be rare. *See also* MARRIAGE; SEX; SCRIBE; SLAVERY.

SOKAR. Protective god of the necropolis of **Memphis**. He is usually depicted as a hawk-headed human. As a funerary god, he was often identified with **Osiris**, but he was also seen as a craftsman and maker of unguents and so identified with **Ptah**. The composite god Ptah-Sokar-Osiris is attested during the **Middle Kingdom** but becomes more prominent during the **Late Period**, when statues dedicated to him become a standard part of funerary equipment. *See also* RELIGION; REPIT.

SOKNOPAIOU NESOS. Also known as Dime. A town site in the northeastern **Fayum**. It flourished during the **Graeco-Roman Period** and was abandoned in the middle of the 3d century AD. The ruins of the houses, **temples**, and cemeteries are extant. The main temple is dedicated to the crocodile god Soknopaius. Numbers of **papyri** have been found here. It was briefly excavated by a British expedition from 1900–1901, a German expedition from 1908–1909, and an American team from the University of Michigan from 1931–1932. Since 2001 it has been investigated by an Italian expedition from the University of Bologna and the University of Lecce. *See also* BACCHIAS; DEIR EL-NAQLUN; GUROB; HARAGEH; HAWARA; KARANIS; KOM KHELWA; KOM TALIT; LAHUN; LISHT; MEDINET MADI; TEBTUNIS.

SOLEB. Modern name for a site in Upper **Nubia** where a major **temple** was erected by **Amenhotep III** dedicated to Amen-Re and the deified king himself as Nebmaatre, lord of Nubia. The site also includes the remains of a town and cemeteries. The area was excavated by an Italian-French expedition from 1957–1977. *See also* ABU SIMBEL; AMADA; BEIT EL-WALI; GERF HUSSEIN; KALABSHA.

SONS OF HORUS. The four deities who were associated with the protection of the internal organs removed during the embalming procedure and placed in **canopic jars** or packages. They were originally represented as human figures, but by the **New Kingdom**, three of them had acquired animal heads. Imsety, in human form, protected the liver; **Hapy**, with a baboon head, guarded the lungs; Duamutef, with a jackal head, safeguarded the stomach; and Qebehsenuef, with a hawk head, watched over the intestines. The gods appear as heads on canopic jars and on amulets placed on the **mummy**. *See also* RELIGION.

SOPDU. Falcon god worshipped in the eastern Delta of **Lower Egypt**, especially at **Saft el-Henna**. He is attested beginning in the **Early Dynastic Period**. He is associated with Sinai and the lands fàrther east as lord of the East. *See also* RELIGION.

SOSIBIOS (fl. 240–204 BC). Chief minister of **Ptolemy IV**. He came from **Alexandria**. He arranged the murder of the king's uncle, brother, and mother upon his accession. Later, upon the king's death, he murdered the **queen**, who was to be regent for her son, **Ptolemy V**, and took over power together with the late king's mistress, Agathoclea, and her brother, Agathocles. Sosibios died in 204 BC. His associates were overthrown and killed in 203 BC, but his son, Sosibios was briefly guardian for the king. *See also* ARSINOE III; BERENICE II.

SOTHIC CYCLE. *See* CHRONOLOGY.

SOTHIS. Greek name for the Egyptian astral goddess *Sopdet*, the personification of the dog-star Sirius, whose time of best visibility marked the beginning of the **Nile** flood. The goddess is represented as a human female figure with a star on her headdress. *See also* RELIGION.

SPHINX. Greek name for the human-headed lion depicted in Egyptian art, especially large sculpture. The most famous example is the Great Sphinx at **Giza**, which was carved from a rocky knoll in the form of King **Khafre**. This sphinx was later identified with a form of the sun god Harmakhis. In particular, it was venerated and restored by **Thutmose IV**, who attributed his unexpected succession to its divine intercession. Monumental sphinxes were produced during **Dynasty 12**, although they were wrongly assigned to the **Hyksos** by early Egyptologists. The Great Sphinx was first cleared by Giovanni Battista Caviglia in 1817 and subsequently by **Auguste Mariette** in 1853, Gaston Maspero in 1889, and Eugene Baraize from 1923–1936. It has recently been restored.

ST. MENAS. *See* MENAS, ST.

STELA. Plural stelae. Greek word used by Egyptologists for a freestanding inscribed stone, often but not necessarily round-topped. A stela can vary in size from several inches to several feet. Most record prayers with dedications to gods on behalf of an individual, often naming members of his family, and they can run to several registers with both inscribed scenes and texts. Historical stelae record the deeds of kings. Some inscriptions on **temple** walls or cliffs have a surround in imitation of the freestanding stelae.

STONE. Egypt is rich in a variety of stones used for both construction and **art**. Stone was first used for construction in **Early Dynastic tombs** at **Saqqara** and **Abydos**. The first fully stone building was the step **pyramid** of **Djoser** allegedly designed by **Imhotep** and built of limestone. Different types of limestone were used in the later pyramids and their associated **temples**. The finest limestone from the Tura quarries faced the pyramidal structure. Basalt was used for paving stones in the buildings. Granite was also used in the construction of the pyramids. Temples in the north were usually made of limestone, while many in the south were built of sandstone. Limestone could be melted down to make lime during the **Roman Period**, and as a result, very few temples made of this material survive; however, most domestic buildings and palaces were made of mudbrick rather than stone, so few survive.

From the **Predynastic Period** onward, stone was also used to produce vessels, statues and jewelry. The various types included alabaster, anhydrite, basalt, breccia, gneiss, granodiorite, greywacke, jasper, serpentine, and later porphyry. **Amethyst**, carnelian, and turquoise were favored for jewelry. Only **lapis lazuli** appears to have been imported. Many of the quarries used by the Egyptians have been identified and studied. The most notable is the granite quarry at Aswan (**Elephantine**), but there were alabster and basalt quarries in the **Fayum**. Other quarries have been located in the Eastern Desert at **Serabit el-Khadim** and **Wadi Maghara** for turquoise and in the Western Desert at Gebel el-Asr, northwest of **Abu Simbel**, for gneiss, which was rediscovered in 1997. *See also* AKORIS; GEBEL El-HARIDI; GEBEL EL-SILSILA; HATNUB; MONS CLAUDI-ANUS; MONS PORPHYRITES; WADI EL-HUDI; WADI HAM-MAMAT.

SUCCESSION. The mechanics of the succession to the throne are never indicated in Egyptian sources. It is generally assumed that the eldest son of the king by his **queen** was the likely successor, but a more ambitious and politically competent son by a minor wife might have proven succesful. This lack of a clear law of succession appears to have led to various harem conspiracies, of which only a few are known. During **Dynasty 12**, the post of **coregent** was established whereby the designated successor was crowned as joint king during his father's lifetime, but even this procedure did not prevent an unsuccessful attempt to dispose of both **Amenemhat I** and his coregent, **Senusret I**, in favor of a rival candidate. During **Dynasty 19**, the post of crown prince, or *iry pct*, was created, but this too seems to have lapsed during **Dynasty 20**. It is a curious fact that royal princes are rarely attested during the reigns of their fathers except during the later period of Egyptian history. *See also* HAREM CONSPIRACY PAPYRI.

SUPPILULIUMA I (fl. 1370–1322 BC). King of the **Hittites**. Son of King Tudhaliya III. He seized the throne after a succession dispute and embarked on an aggressive military campaign of expansion defeating **Tushratta**, king of **Mitanni**, and severely weakening his kingdom. He expanded into Syria occupying Egyptian territory, including **Kadesh**, and detaching the kings of **Amurru** and **Ugarit** from alliance with Egypt. He is a correspondent in the **Amarna letters**. An attempt to marry his son, Zannanza, to the **queen** of Egypt failed and led to increased **warfare**. He died of the plague c. 1322 BC.

SUPREME COUNCIL FOR ANTIQUITIES. The organization in charge of excavation and preservation of all archaeological sites in Egypt and all museums, including the **Cairo Egyptian Museum**. It was founded by **Auguste Mariette** in 1858 as the Egyptian Antiquities Service (Service des Antiquités). It was traditionally run by the French with a few foreign (British and German) curators and inspectors. During the 20th century, the number of locally trained Egyptians gradually increased, and the organization was completely Egyptianized after the revolution of 1952. It is the body that grants foreign expeditions the right to excavate designated sites in Egypt. Formerly foreign excavators were allowed to remove a certain amount of duplicate objects for museums outside Egypt, but this practice has now been suspended, and all finds are kept in Egypt.

– T –

TACHOS. *See* DJEDHOR.

TADUKHEPA (fl. 1350 BC). A princess from **Mitanni**. Daughter of King **Tushratta**, who was married to **Amenhotep III** toward the end of his reign and possibly married his successor, **Akhenaten**. She has sometimes been identified with the lady **Kiya**, but there is no evidence for this. *See also* GILUKHEPA.

TAHARQO (reigned 690–664 BC). Throne name Khunefertemre. Son of **Piye** and Abar. He was summoned from **Nubia** after the accession of his relation, **Shebitqo**, and he commanded his army in Palestine in 701 BC against the Assyrians. He succeeded Shebitqo and undertook extensive building works, especially at **Karnak**, where he installed his daughter, **Amenirdis** II, as prospective **God's wife of Amun**. He defeated an initial Assyrian invasion but was driven out of Egypt by another invasion in 671 BC, in which his family was captured. He retired to Nubia, where he died in 664 BC and was buried in the royal cemetery at Nuri near **Napata**. *See also* TANTAMANI; WARFARE.

TAKELOT I (reigned c. 889–874 BC). Throne name Hedjkheperre. Son of **Osorkon I** and Tashedkhons. His reign is obscure. He has recently been identified as the king of this name buried at **Tanis** in the **tomb** of his son, **Osorkon II**, whose body was uncovered in 1939 by the French excavator **Pierre Montet**.

TAKELOT II (reigned c. 850–825 BC). Throne name Hedjkheperre setepenre. Epithet meryamun siese. Successor and probable son of **Osorkon II**. His reign is badly attested, but his attempt to install his son, **Osorkon**, as **high priest of Amun** in **Karnak** led to prolonged civil strife. *See also* KAROMAMA.

TAKELOT III (reigned c. 754–734 BC). Throne name Usermaatre setepenamun. Epithet meryamun siese. Son of **Osorkon III** of **Dynasty 23** and Tentsai. He held the title of **high priest of Amun** before his accession. He is attested on monuments from **Thebes**. *See also* RUDAMUN.

TAKHAT (fl. 1270 BC). A royal princess and possible **queen**. She was the fourteenth daughter of **Ramesses II**. A later Queen Takhat is shown in possible association with either **Sety II** or **Amenmesse**. It has been assumed that she may be the same woman as the princess and the mother of Amenmesse and perhaps even the wife of Sethos II, although these conjectures are debatable.

TALATAT. Arabic name employed by Egyptologists for the small **stone** blocks decorated with relief used to build **temples** by **Akhenaten** during the **Amarna Period**. Following the destruction of Akhenaten's temples, the blocks were reused as filling in temple contruction in **Karnak, Hermopolis, Antinoopolis**, and other sites and so have been preserved. A talatat block from Hermopolis is the only evidence that **Tutankhamun** was the son of a king.

TALE OF THE DOOMED PRINCE, THE. A story found in a single manuscript from the **Ramesside Period** written in the Late Egyptian form of the Egyptian **language**. The hero is an Egyptian prince doomed from birth to die at the hand of a dog, snake, or crocodile. The tale follows his adventures in Syria, marriage to a local princess, and escape from two of his fates. Unfortunately, the manuscript is lost at the end, but it is probable that he escapes his doom and returns to reign in Egypt. The story has some affinities to modern fairy tales, notably a princess in a tower. *See also* LITERATURE.

TALE OF THE ELOQUENT PEASANT, THE. A literary tale from the **Middle Kingdom** that describes the pleadings of the peasant Khunanup for justice at the hands of the Egyptian bureaucracy. His complaints were so eloquently worded that his case was prolonged by officials so they could hear his words until its eventual successful conclusion. *See also* LITERATURE.

TALE OF THE TWO BROTHERS, THE. A semimythological story found in a single manuscript from the **Ramesside Period** written in the Late Egyptian form of the Egyptian **language**. The hero, Bata, is the handsome younger brother of a farmer, Anubis, whose wife attempts to seduce him and when rebuffed accuses him of rape. After proving his innocence to his brother by castrating himself, his brother kills Bata's wife, and Bata goes off to Syria where the gods provide him with a wife. She too proves faithless and deserts him for the king of Egypt. Bata eventually becomes king of Egypt, punishes his wife, and dies, leaving the throne to his brother. The tale paints a rather bleak picture of **women**'s motives. *See also* LITERATURE.

TALE OF TRUTH AND FALSEHOOD, THE. A story found in a single manuscript from the **Ramesside Period** written in the Late

Egyptian form of the Egyptian **language**. The hero, Truth, is falsely accused of theft by his jealous brother, Falsehood. Truth is found guilty by a tribunal of the gods and blinded. Falsehood's attempt to then kill his brother is frustrated, and Truth is vindicated and avenged by his illegitimate son. The story is notable for its admission that the gods are fallible and the depiction of the independent lifestyle of the mother of Truth's son. *See also* LITERATURE.

TANIS. Greek name for ancient Egyptian *Djane*, modern San el-Hagara, a city in the northeastern part of the Delta in the 19th Egyptian **nome** of Lower Egypt. It came into prominence during **Dynasty 21** as the residence of the royal family founded by **Nesbanebdjed**, mayor of Tanis. The town was decorated with monuments moved from other sites, like **Pi-Ramesses**. The town was excavated by **Auguste Mariette** in the 1860s and **Flinders Petrie** in 1884. A French expedition worked the site from 1929–1940, 1945–1951, and 1954–1956 under **Pierre Montet**; worked the area from 1965–1985 under Jean Yoyotte; and has worked the site since 1985 under Philippe Brissaud. In 1939, inside the **temple** complex dedicated to **Amun**, Montet found the **tombs** of the some of the rulers of Dynasty 21 and **Dynasty 22**.

TANTAMANI (reigned 664–656 BC). Throne name Bakare. Last ruler of **Dynasty 25** in Egypt. He succeeded **Taharqo** and embarked on a reconquest of Egypt, defeating the ruler **Nekau I**, who was installed by the Assyrians. In 663 BC, the Assyrian army returned and defeated him, marching as far south as **Thebes**, which was sacked, and appointing **Psamtik I** as ruler. Tantamani retreated to **Nubia** but was recognized as ruler in southern Egypt until 657 BC. He died in 656 BC and was buried at el-Kurru. *See also* MENTUEMHAT; WARFARE.

TAO (reigned c. 1555 BC). Throne name Seqenenre. Penultimate ruler of **Dynasty 17** and prince of **Thebes**. Son of **Queen Tetisheri** and possibly Senakhtenre. Likely a vassal of the **Hyksos**, he later led Theban forces against them in the north. A literary tale implies conflict between him and the Hyksos ruler **Apepi**. His **mummy** was recovered in the **royal cache** and shows that he died violently. He is often referred to as Tao II since his predecessor, whose throne name was Senakhtenre, may have had the same personal name, although this is not certain. *See also* AHHOTEP; AHMOSE; AHMOSE-NEFERTARI; KAMOSE.

TAPOSIRIS MAGNA. A city west of **Alexandria** between the Mediterranean Sea and Lake Mareotis attested from the **Ptolemaic Period** to the early Christian Period. Its principal ruins consist of a tower believed to be modeled after the **Pharos**, or Lighthouse, of Alexandria and a **temple** dedicated to **Isis** erected by **Ptolemy II** and used as a fortress during the **Roman Period** and later as a monastery. The site was excavated from 1905–1907, 1937–1940, and 1946–1948 through the auspices of the Museum of Alexandria and since 1998 by a Hungarian expedition.

TARKHAN. The site of a major cemetery dating from the **Predynastic Period** to the **Roman Period** south of Cairo on the west bank of the **Nile** near Kafr Ammar in the 21st **nome** of **Upper Egypt**. The bulk of the 2,000 **tombs** date to the foundation of the Egyptian state around 3000 BC. It was excavated by **Flinders Petrie** from 1911–1913.

TATENEN. Primeval god of the fertility of the enriched soil left by the **Nile** flood. He was later identified with the god **Ptah** of **Memphis**. He is represented as a human figure with plumes and is often painted green. *See also* RELIGION.

TAWERET. Egyptian goddess. Protector of **women** during childbirth. She is represented as a pregnant hippopotamus with female breasts and a crocodile tail. Her appearance was supposed to frighten off demons that might harm the pregnant woman or her child. *See also* RELIGION.

TEBTUNIS. A town of the **Ptolemaic Period** and **Roman Period** in the southwest **Fayum**. Ancient *T3-nbt-tn*, modern Umm el-Baragat/Breigat. It flourished from the 4th century BC to the early Arabic Period. The principal god of the town was Soknebtunis, a form of **Sobek**. It was excavated from 1899–1900 by British papyrologists on behalf of American heiress Mrs. Phoebe Hearst. Among the objects recovered were **papyri** and **mummy portraits**, all now housed in the Robert H. Lowie Museum of Anthropology at the University of California, Berkeley. It was later examined by Italian archaeologists from 1929–1935 and has been excavated by a joint Franco–Italian expedition since 1988. *See also* BACCHIAS; DEIR EL-NAQLUN; GUROB; HARAGEH; HAWARA; KARANIS; KOM KHELWA; KOM TALIT; LAHUN; LISHT; MEDINET MADI; SOKNOPAIOU NESOS.

TEFNAKHTE (reigned c. 733–725 BC). Throne name Shepsesre. Prince of **Sais**. He is named as the main opponent of the Nubian ruler **Piye** during his invasion of Egypt, although he is not named there as a king. Despite his submission, it appears that Tefnakhte still assumed royal status and was succeeded by his son, **Bakenrenef**, of **Dynasty 24**.

TEFNUT. Egyptian goddess of moisture. Created by **Atum**, she produced **Geb** and **Nut** from a union with **Shu**, the god of air. She can be depicted as a lioness or a lioness-headed human figure. *See also* RELIGION.

TELL DAFANA. Modern name for a site on the eastern edge of the Delta of **Lower Egypt**. The remains date from **Dynasty 26** to the **Graeco-Roman Period**. It is likely to be identified with the ancient Daphnae mentioned by **Herodotus** as a garrison town founded during the **Saite Period** to guard the frontier routes from the Sinai. Tell Dafna was excavated by **Flinders Petrie** in 1886.

TELL EL-BALAMUN. Modern name for the site of the northernmost city of Egypt situated near the Mediterranean coast of the northeastern part of the Delta. Egyptian *Behdet*, later *Paiuenamun*. Greek Diospolis Parva. The city is attested from the **Old Kingdom** until the **Roman Period** and was the capital of the 17th **nome** of **Lower Egypt** created during the **New Kingdom**, although little now remains. The principal gods worshipped here were **Horus**, lord of Behdet, and later **Amun**, to whom the main **temple** was dedicated during the New Kingdom. The site was briefly examined by **Howard**

Carter in 1913 and an Egyptian expedition from 1977–1978. Since 1991, Tell el-Balamun has been excavated by an expedition from the **British Museum**, which has traced the outlines of the main temple and subsidiary temples built during the **Saite Period** until **Dynasty 30** and has discovered burials of the **Third Intermediate Period** within the temple walls.

TELL EL-BORG. A fortress site in the north Sinai east of **Tell Hebua**. It dates to the **New Kingdom** and contains a **temple** and **tombs**. It was surveyed during the 1990s and excavated by an American expedition beginning in 2000.

TELL EL-FARKHA. Modern name for a town site in the eastern Delta southeast of **Mendes**. The site contains buildings and graves that date from the **Predynastic Period** to the early **Old Kingdom**. It appears to have been founded during the **Naqada** II period. It has yielded **pottery**, seal impressions from the **Early Dynastic Period**, and in 2006 predynastic ivory figurines and decayed wooden statues covered in **gold** foil with inlaid **lapis lazuli** eyes from the Early Dynastic Period. Tell el-Farkha was discovered by an Italian expedition in 1987, which worked there until 1990, and since 1998 the site has been excavated by a Polish team. *See also* ADAIMA; GERZEH; KAFR HASSAN DAOUD; MINSHAT ABU OMAR; TELL IBRAHIM AWAD.

TELL EL-HERR. Modern name for the site of a fortress at the edge of the easten Delta in the 14th **nome** of **Lower Egypt**. It guarded the entry route into Egypt from the east. The remains, which include a cemetery, date from the 5th century BC to the 5th century AD, thus from the **Late Period** to the **Graeco-Roman Period**. Tell el-Herr has been under excavation by a French expedition since 1985.

TELL EL-MASKHUTA. Modern name for a site excavated by the **Egypt Exploration Fund** in 1883 in the eastern Delta in the middle of the **Wadi Tumilat** just west of Ismailia. Remains dating from the **Second Intermediate Period** and the **Saite Period** to the **Roman Period** have been found at the site. The city has been identified in the past with ancient Egyptian *Pr-Itm*, or Pithom, capital of the eighth nome of **Lower Egypt**, but this identification is no longer accepted, as **Tell er-Rataba** is the more likely site. It was excavated by an expedition from the University of Toronto from 1978–1985.

TELL EL-YAHUDIYA. Modern name for a site in the Delta where remains dating from the **Middle Kingdom** to the **Graeco-Roman Period** have been excavated. The site has given its name to a form of black **pottery** juglet decorated with incised designs painted in white that have been found throughout the Levant, although their exact place of manufacture is still unclear. Tell el-Yahudiya was excavated by the **Egypt Exploration Fund** in 1887 and **Flinders Petrie** in 1906.

TELL ER-RATABA. Modern name for site on the eastern edge of the Delta in the **Wadi Tumilat**. Objects found here date from the **First Intermediate Period** to **Dynasty 23**. There are the remains of a **temple** of **Ramesses II** dedicated to the god **Atum**. The site is now identified with ancient Egyptian *Pr-Itm*, or Pithom, capital of the eighth nome of **Lower Egypt**. Tell er-Rataba was excavated by **Henri Edouard Naville** in 1894 and **Flinders Petrie** from 1905–1906.

TELL HEBUA. Modern name for a fortified settlement site on the eastern edge of the Delta of **Lower Egypt** north of Ismailia. It dates from the **Middle Kingdom** to the **New Kingdom**. Inscriptions found there name the **Hyksos** king **Nehesy**. The area was excavated by an Egyptian expedition from 1981–1991, and the cemetery area of the New Kingdom has been examined by an Austrian team since 1995.

TELL IBRAHIM AWAD. Modern name for a site in the eastern Delta of **Lower Egypt** north of **Minshat Abu Omar** and southeast of **Tanis**. The remains date from the **Naqada** II Period of the late **Predynastic Period** to the **Middle Kingdom**. The finds include **pottery** and votive ivories. It has been excavated by a Dutch expedition since 1988. *See also* ADAIMA; GERZEH; KAFR HASSAN DAOUD; TELL EL-FARKHA.

TEM (fl. 2020 BC). A minor wife of **Mentuhotep II** of **Dynasty 11**. She was buried in a pit **tomb** at his funerary complex at **Deir el-**

Bahri, which was discovered in 1883. She was the mother of **Mentuhotep III**. *See also* ASHAYET; HENHENET; KAWIT; KEMSIT; MYT; NEFRU; SADEH; TEM.

TEMPLE. The site of worship for a deity or a series of deities located in each Egyptian center. During the **New Kingdom** and later, a major temple consisted of a **pylon** in front of an open courtyard followed by a hypostyle or columned hall and then a series of rooms leading to the **naos**, or sacred shrine, in which the image of the deity was contained. The general public was admitted only to the first courtyard, and only the priests and officials were granted access to the rest of the building. It was believed that for stability to be maintained, the sacred rituals had to be carried out daily. These ceremonies consisted of waking the deity in his or her shrine, clothing the image, and offering food regularly. The image might be carried into the courtyard or out of the temple on festive days on a sacred boat or barque. The temple also contained royal and private statuary, as the king and officials would hope that their **names** might be read by the priests, thus they would become immortal. Religious worship was not confined to the main temples but also took place more directly between supplicant and deity at various small local shrines. Mortuary temples for deceased rulers were initially associated with the burial site but during the New Kingdom were located some distance away. *See also* PYRAMID; RELIGION.

TENTAMUN (fl. 1085 BC). Wife of **Nesbanebdjed**, mayor of **Tanis** and later first ruler of **Dynasty 21**. She is mentioned along with her husband in the tale of **Wenamun**. There is no reason to doubt her identification with **Queen** Tentamun, daughter of the official Nebseny, thus she did not have a royal pedigree since it has been previously suggested that she might be a daughter of **Ramesses XI**. Her daughter, **Henttawy**, apparently married the **high priest of Amun Pinudjem** I.

TEOS. *See* DJEDHOR.

TETI (reigned c. 2345–321 BC). Founder of **Dynasty 6** and son of **Queen** Mother **Sesheseshet**. His origin is unknown, and it is not clear how he came to power. He had a long and apparently successful reign. He was buried in a **pyramid tomb** at **Saqqara**, which was opened in 1882. Nearby were the tombs of his queens, **Iput** I, Khuit, and Khentet, whose complete name is lost. The area surrounding his pyramid was excavated by the Egyptian Antiquities Service under Victor Loret in 1893 and from 1897–1899, James Quibell from 1905–1907, and Cecil Firth from 1920–1922. It was also examined during the 1950s and 1960s by a French team, and the Egyptian archaeologist Zahi Hawass has been working there since 1993. *See also* PEPY I.

TETISHERI (fl. c. 1570–540 BC). Possibly wife of Senakhtenre, the ruler of **Thebes** during **Dynasty 17**, and daughter of Tjenna and **Nefru**. She was the mother of **Tao** and grandmother of **Ahmose I** and **Ahmose-Nefertari**. She possibly acted as regent for her grandson and played a prominent role in his reign. A funerary **temple** in her honor was founded in **Abydos**.

TEWOSRET (reigned c. 1190–189 BC). Throne name Sitre. Wife of **Sety II** and stepmother of his successor, **Siptah**. She remained a powerful figure at court and may have benefited from the execution of the king's protector, **Bay**. Upon the death of the king, she took the throne and counted her regnal years from the death of her husband. She was apparently overthrown by **Sethnakhte**. She prepared **tomb KV14** in the **Valley of the Kings** for her burial, but it was taken over by Sethnakhte. Her **mummy** has not been securely identified. Her mortuary **temple** at **Thebes**, excavated by **Flinders Petrie** in 1896, has not been preserved apart from some **foundation deposits**. In 2006, an American expedition began a reinvestigation of the site.

THEBES. Greek name for the Egyptian city of *Waset* in the fourth **nome** of **Upper Egypt**. Also known as Diospolis Magna. The early history of the city is obscure, but during the **First Intermediate Period**, its rulers took the royal title. It became the capital of Egypt when **Mentuhotep I** reunited Egypt under **Dynasty 11**. While the rulers of **Dynasty 12** were southerners, they moved the capital to Itjtawy in the north, although Thebes remained the most important city in the south. It regained its prominent position at the end of the **Second Intermediate Period** when the princes of Thebes led the fight against the **Hyksos** rulers in the north and reunited Egypt under **Dynasty 18**. Its god, **Amun**, was elevated to the position of chief god of Egypt, and his **temple** at **Karnak** was enlarged and richly endowed. A second major temple was built at **Luxor** within the city. The royal **tombs** from Dynasty 18 to **Dynasty 20** were constructed on the west bank of the **Nile** opposite the city in the **Valley of the Kings**. The **queens**, princesses, and some princes were buried in the **Valley of the Queens**, while the tombs of the officials were located in the nearby cliffs. Also on the west bank near the edge of cultivation such mortuary temples of the kings as **Deir el-Bahri**, the **Ramesseum**, and **Medinet Habu** were constructed.

During **Dynasty 19**, the king began to reside more frequently in the north, but the city remained the main religious capital and southern administrative center. It was often known simply as *niwt*, the city. Beginning at the end of Dynasty 20, Thebes and the southern region became increasingly independent of central rule under the **high priests of Amun**. The city was sacked during the Assyrian invasion of 666 BC and never recovered its prominence. It remained a bastion of Egyptian nationalism during the **Ptolemaic Period** and was held by various rebel kings. Following the Roman conquest, Thebes became a tourist center. After the adoption of Christianity, its temples were converted into churches or desecrated and abandoned, and it reverted to a minor provincial town after the Arabic conquest. The temples and tombs have been cleared and excavated during modern times, but few remains of the living quarters of the ancient city have been located.

THEODORA (d. 548). Byzantine empress from 527–548. Wife of **Justinian**. She was the daughter of Acacius, an animal keeper at the circus in Constantinople. After a disreputable youth, she married Justinian, then heir to the throne. She was a strong support to her husband, especially during the riots of 532, which nearly cost him the throne. Theodora was a Monophysite and opposed her husband's orthodox line. She thus supported the **Coptic Church** and the rival Monophysite missionary work in **Nubia**. She died in Constantinople on 28 June 548.

THEOPHILUS (345–412 AD). Patriarch of **Alexandria**. He was born in **Memphis** in 345 and became the secretary of the patriarch **Athanasius**. He then became archdeacon of Alexandria and succeeded as patriarch in 385. He was a vigorous opponent of paganism and was involved in the destruction of the **Serapeum** in Alexandria, over which he built a church. He played an active role in church politics and was partly responsible for the deposition of the patriarch of Constantinople, John Chrysostom. He died in Alexandria on 15 October 412. *See also* BENJAMIN; COPTIC CHURCH; CYRIL; CYRUS; DIOSCORUS.

THINIS. Greek name for a city in northern **Upper Egypt**, possibly in or near modern Girga. Ancient Egyptian *Tjeny*, capital of the eighth Upper Egyptian **nome**. The major god worshipped at the site was **Anhur**, later identified with the god **Shu**. The city is named by **Manetho** as the native town of the kings of **Dynasty 1** and **Dynasty 2**, and the population may have been buried in the nearby cemetery of **Naga el-Deir**. Thinis is mentioned in texts of the **First Intermediate Period**, when it was fought over by rivals **Dynasty 10** and **Dynasty 11** until its final capture by **Mentuhotep II**. It is also mentioned in Egyptian texts during the **Middle Kingdom** and **New Kingdom**, and in the **Third Intermediate Period** it became the seat of the **vizier** of Upper Egypt. During the **Ptolemaic Period**, the capital of the **nome** was moved elsewhere. The site has never been securely identified.

THIRD INTERMEDIATE PERIOD (c. 1069–716 BC). The term used by some Egyptologists for the period between the end of **Dynasty 20** and the beginning of **Dynasty 26**, although some end it with the inception of **Dynasty 25**. During this time, Egypt was again divided, with the south virtually independent for much of the time. Later local rulers sprang up in various cities, and **Dynasty 22**, **Dynasty 23**, and **Dynasty 24** vied for recognition. *See also* NEW KINGDOM; LATE PERIOD.

THOTH. Greek name for the Egyptian god *Djehuty*. He is depicted in the form of an ibis-headed human with a moon's disk on his head. His principal seat of worship was **Hermopolis**, and the ibis and baboon were sacred to him. He was worshipped throughout Egypt as the god of scribal arts who wrote the judgement of **Osiris** at the **weighing of the heart**. *See also* RELIGION; SCRIBE.

THUTEMHAT (reigned c. 720 BC). Throne name Neferkheperre Kha-khau. Minor kinglet at the end of the **Third Intermediate Period**. He is attested as a ruler in **Hermopolis**, but it is not certain whether he was a predecessor or successor of King **Nimlot** of Hermopolis attested on the **stela** of **Piye**.

THUTMOSE (fl. 1375 BC). Royal prince. Eldest son of King **Amenhotep III** and presumably **Queen Tiy**. He held a senior position in the priesthood of **Ptah** at **Memphis**. Objects bearing his name have been found in the burial of the **Apis** bull in the **Serapeum** at **Saqqara**. He presumably died young since his father's successor to the throne was his brother, **Akhenaten**. *See also* BAKETATEN; SITAMUN.

THUTMOSE (fl. 1330 BC). The name of a sculptor at **Amarna** whose house has been excavated and in which important royal sculptures, notably busts of **Queen Nefertiti**, have been found. He is one of the few Egyptian artists whose works can be identified.

THUTMOSE I (reigned c. 1504–1492 BC). Throne name Akheperre. Son of the lady Seniseneb by an unknown father. He succeeded the childless **Amenhotep I** and must have been related to the ruling family. Thutmose I continued Egyptian expansion south in **Nubia** and in Asia penetrating as far as the Euphrates River and defeating the army of **Mitanni**. He married his sister, **Ahmose**, possibly after his accession, and had two daughters, notably **Hatshepsut**, but his successor, **Thutmose II**, was the son of another wife, **Mutnefret**. At least two other older sons, possibly by Mutnefret, **Amenmose** and **Wadjmose**, predeceased their father. Thutmose I appears to have been the first ruler to be buried in the **Valley of the Kings** and is the first attested ruler at the village of **Deir el-Medina** where the **tomb** builders were located. The construction of his tomb is described in a text by his official, **Ineni**, and may have been tomb **KV20**, although his final burial might have been in tomb **KV38** discovered in 1899, to which he may have been moved later by his grandson, **Thutmose III**. His **mummy** has not been recovered.

THUTMOSE II (reigned c. 1492–1479 BC). Throne name Aakheperenre. Son of **Thutmose I** and **Mutnefret**. He may have been fairly young upon his accession, and he married his half sister, **Hatshepsut**. The length of his reign is uncertain. His forces put down a revolt in **Nubia** early in the reign. He left one daughter, **Nefrure**, by Hatshepsut, and a son and successor, **Thutmose III**, by a minor wife or concubine, **Isis**. His **tomb** has not been identified, but his **mummy** was recovered from the **royal cache** in 1881.

THUTMOSE III (reigned c. 1479–1425 BC). Throne name Menkheperre. Son of **Thutmose II** and **Isis**. He succeeded his father as a young child under the regency of his stepmother, **Hatshepsut**, who soon took the royal title. He remained in relative obscurity until year 21, when Hatshepsut presumably died, and he appeared at the head of his army invading Palestine-Syria. Thutmose III defeated the local princes at the battle of Megiddo and firmly established Egyptian rule in the area with a series of campaigns that led to the defeat of **Mitanni**. Later in his reign, he ordered the removal of all inscriptions concerning his stepmother. He was regarded in later times as one of the most effective rulers, and **scarabs** with his throne name were produced centuries after his death. It is not clear if he married his half sister, **Nefrure**, but he had at least three other principal wives, Satiah, **Nebtu**, and **Meryetre Hatshepsut**, not of royal birth, who was the mother of his successor, **Amenhotep II**, as his eldest son, **Amenemhat**, had predeceased him. Thutmose III was buried in the **Valley of the Kings (KV34)**, which was discovered in 1898, and his body was recovered from the **royal cache** in 1881. He has been erroneously described as being very short, but this is due to damage to the lower part of his **mummy**. His mortuary temple, *Djeser-akhet* at **Deir el-Bahri**, next to that of Hatshepsut, has been largely destroyed by an earthquake and was rediscovered by a Polish expedition in 1982. *See also* WARFARE.

THUTMOSE IV (reigned c. 1400–1390 BC). Throne name Menkheperure. Son of **Amenhotep II** and **Tiaa**. He was apparently a younger son and not destined to rule, but in his dream **stela**, he recounts that after hunting in the desert, he rested at the foot of the **Sphinx** and in a dream was promised the throne if he would undertake clearance and restoration of the monument, which he did upon his accession. Little is known of his reign, but he concluded peace with **Mitanni** and is the first ruler attested with a Mitannian princess, the daughter of Artatama I, as a wife. His principal wives were **Nefertari** and the Princess **Iaret**, who was either his sister or daughter. Thutmose IV was succeeded by **Amenhotep III**, his son by a minor wife, **Mutemwia**, whose origin is not known. He was buried in **KV43** in the **Valley of the Kings**, which was discovered in 1903, and his **mummy** was recovered from the **royal cache** in the **tomb** of **Amenhotep II** in 1898. The remains of his mortuary **temple** on the west bank of the **Nile** opposite **Thebes** were excavated by **Flinders Petrie** in 1896.

TI (fl. 2450 BC). High official during **Dynasty 5**. He held the post of overseer of the **pyramids** of **Neferirkare** and **Niuserre** and the sun **temples** of **Sahure**, Neferirkare, **Raneferef**, and Niuserre. His **mastaba tomb** at **Saqqara** contains some of the finest carved scenes of daily life from the period. It was discovered by **Auguste Mariette** in 1860.

TIAA (fl. 1430–1380 BC). A wife of **Amenhotep II** and mother of **Thutmose IV**. She was buried in **KV32** in the **Valley of the Kings**. Objects from her **tomb** equipment found their way into the nearby tomb of **Siptah**, so it was mistakenly assumed that he had a mother of this name. The name was used by several princesses during the **New Kingdom**.

TIMNA. A site in the Wadi Arabah that lies between the Red Sea and the Dead Sea alongside the south Negev desert. The area is rich in **copper** ore and has been mined since Chalcolithic times. The site was excavated from 1964–1970, 1974–1976, and 1978–1983 by a team from the Institute of Archaeology at Tel Aviv University. They discovered copper mining and smelting made by Egyptian expeditions during the **New Kingdom** during **Dynasty 19** and **Dynasty 20**. The archaeologists found the remains of a small **temple** dedicated to the goddess **Hathor** with votive offerings from **Sety I** to **Ramesses V**. The site also seems to have been worked under **Dynasty 22**. It may be the site Atika, which is mentioned in the **Harris Papyrus** from the reign of **Ramesses IV**.

TITULARY, ROYAL. The full style of the royal titulary consisted of five names and is attested in complete form beginning in the **Middle Kingdom**. During **Dynasty 1**, only two names were used: the **Horus** name, which identified the king with the sky god **Horus**, and the *nebty* name, which associated the king with the goddesses **Nekhbet** and **Wadjet**, the "two ladies," mistresses of **Upper Egypt** and **Lower Egypt**. The Horus name was generally used on its own as the royal name during **Dynasty 1**, **Dynasty 2**, and **Dynasty 3**, so it is difficult to match these with personal names from other sources. The personal name, or nomen, becomes more prominent beginning in **Dynasty 4**, when it appears in a **cartouche** from the reign of **Snefru**, but it is clearly distinguished beginning in **Dynasty 5**, when there also appears the prenomen or throne name adopted upon accession and compounded with the name of the sun god **Re**. The Golden Horus name gradually evolved from a title and was also adopted upon accession. The Horus name was written in a **serekh**, a recessed palace facade, while the prenomen and nomen were written in the cartouche ring. From **Dynasty 19** onward, epithets were adopted to be added to the prenomen and nomen.

TITUS (39–81 AD). Roman emperor. Original name Titus Flavius Vespasianus. He was born in Rome on 30 December 39, son of Titus Flavius Vespasianus, the future Emperor **Vespasian**, and Flavia Domitilla. Titus headed one of the legions that his father took on his campaign against the Jewish Revolt in 67. When his father was proclaimed emperor in 69, he then took over command of the expedition against Jerusalem. Titus captured Jerusalem in August 70 and returned to Rome via Egypt, where he was present at **Memphis** for the installation of an **Apis** bull. He became his father's staunchest supporter in Rome and succeeded him in 79. He proved an effective and popular emperor but died after a short rule at Aquae Cutilae on 13 September 81.

TIY (fl. 1400–1340 BC). Chief wife of **Amenhotep III** and daughter of **Yuya** and Tuya. She was already married in year 2 of the reign and is depicted prominently on many monuments. She was the mother of **Akhenaten** and probably his elder brother, the crown prince **Thutmose**, who predeceased his father, as well as several daughters, notably **Sitamun**, who married her father; Henuttaneb; **Isis**; and Nebetah. Tiy survived into the reign of her son and is depicted at **Amarna** with a Princess **Baketaten**, who may have been a daughter or granddaughter. Her original burial place is uncertain, and some of her funerary equipment was apparently reused in **tomb KV55** in the **Valley of the Kings**. A previously unidentified female **mummy** in the **royal cache** has recently been suggested to be that of the **queen**.

TIY (fl. 1370–1323 BC). Wife of **Ay**. She first appears during the **Amarna Period**, when she is described as the nurse of **Nefertiti**. It has been conjectured that Ay was the father of Nefertiti, in which case Tiy would be her stepmother. She is later depicted as Ay's queen after he ascended the throne, which makes it unlikely that he married **Ankhesenamun**. *See also* AKHENATEN.

TOD. Modern name for ancient Egyptian *Djerty*, a site in **Upper Egypt** just south of **Thebes** where there are remains of the **temple** of **Montu** from the **Middle Kingdom** to the **Roman Period**. The site was excavated by French archaeologists from 1934–1936. During the last year of the excavation, the Tod treasure consisting of **silver** vessels, bars of precious material, and cylinder seals dating to the reign of **Amenemhat II** and probably of foreign origin was discovered. The temple site has been the subject of recording by the **French Institute** again since 1999.

TOMB. The Egyptians were at first buried in simple pit tombs in the desert sand with such grave goods as **pottery** and slate palettes. This remained the normal state of burial for the bulk of the population throughout Egypt's history, although the type of grave goods varied. However, the king and wealthier members of society demanded more elaborate burials, so the **mastaba** tomb was developed during the late **Predynastic Period**. This burial place initially consisted of a rectangular mudbrick superstructure over the tomb shaft in which were a number of chambers for storage of grave goods and for use as a chapel. Beginning in **Dynasty 3**, the king began to use a **pyramid** burial built in **stone**, and his courtiers later followed his example using stone or stone-lined mastabas that enabled the production of carved reliefs of religious scenes and more particularly scenes of daily life. Some earlier private tombs, like those at **Meidum**, were decorated with painted wall reliefs, but these have rarely survived.

While the use of freestanding tombs continued throughout history in such locations as **Saqqara** in **Upper Egypt**, it was more common for the elite to be buried in rock-cut tombs in the cliffs that lined the **Nile** Valley. The scenes in the tombs could be painted on a mud plaster base or more elaborately carved into the rock. The bulk of these tombs survive from the **New Kingdom** at **Thebes**, but earlier examples are known throughout the country in the **Middle Kingdom** tombs at **Beni Hasan** and elsewhere. The royal family adopted this method to hide their tombs in the **Valley of the Kings** and **Valley of the Queens** during **Dynasty 18**, **Dynasty 19**, and **Dynasty 20**. During later periods of Egyptian history, when the country was not so properous, many tombs were reused, and the royal family and priests were buried in tombs built within **temple** precincts for greater protection, like those at **Tanis**. During the **Graeco-Roman Period**, large communal cemeteries with mausolea containing individual family vaults were built at **Alexandria** and are only just being investigated. *See also* AFTERLIFE; KV–KV 63.

TOMB ROBBERY PAPYRI. A series of **papyri** dating from the reigns of **Ramesses IX** and **Ramesses XI** consisting of the official reports into claims that the royal **tombs** in the **Valley of the Kings** and elsewhere on the west bank of the **Nile** had been violated and robbed. After some dispute, the claims were investigated, and the culprits were severely punished. *See also* PASER.

TRADE. Egypt was largely self-sufficient in **agriculture** and raw materials; nevertheless, trade developed in the Levant beginning in the **Predynastic Period** for such luxury imports as wine, olive oil, **lapis lazuli**, and later for such necessities as **copper** and cedar wood. External trade was regarded as a royal monopoly and was controlled by the court. It was largely in the hands of foreign traders who were officially stated to be bringing tribute to the king and then rewarded for doing so. Royal expeditions were occasionally sent to the south and the Levant, presumably to seize goods when able or trade for them if required, and by sea to the Levant in the search for cedar and other woods. **Temples** used agents for internal trade, and local markets flourished, but a thriving merchant class never developed. Foreign traders settled in Egypt during the **New Kingdom** in **Memphis** and **Pi-Ramesse** and later during the **Saite Period** when Greeks were assigned the town of **Naukratis**.

TRAVEL. The ancient Egyptians did not as a rule travel extensively, but the king and officials needed to traverse the country, and farmers needed to visit local markets. Then, as now, most people either walked or rode donkeys for local visits. An important official was often carried in a palanquin for short distances. For longer journeys, the most convenient way to move from place to place was by boat on the **Nile** and its canals. During the flood season, this was the most practical way to travel. The use of the desert **road system** for internal travel and journeys to the oases and mines is only now being studied and fully appreciated.

The Egyptians were not very keen on foreign travel, as they regarded Egypt as the height of civilization. Their armies and **trade** expeditions marched on foot with officers later in chariots and supplies on pack mules, but maritime sailing expeditions are recorded to the Syrian ports mainly for purposes of trade. The *Tale of Sinuhe* and the *Tale of Wenamun* illustrate the distaste felt by Egyptians for traveling abroad. *See also* WARFARE.

TRIAD. A term used by Egyptologists to refer to the standard divine family of each city, which usually consisted of the chief god of the city, his wife, and his son. For example, the triad from **Thebes** consisted of the god **Amun**, his wife, **Mut**; and his son, **Khonsu**. That of **Memphis** comprised the god **Ptah**; his wife, **Sakhmet**; and his son, **Nefertum**. A triad could also have consisted of a god or goddess and two consorts. *See also* RELIGION.

TUNA EL-GEBEL. Arabic name for the necropolis of **Hermopolis** in the desert near the city. A boundary **stela** of **Akhenaten** marks it as the edge of his city at **Amarna**. The site is primarily known for its decorated **tombs** from the **Persian Period** to the **Roman Period**, notably that of **Petosiris** discovered in 1920, and underground galleries for the burials of ibis **mummies** sacred to the god **Thoth**. The site was excavated by the Egyptian Antiquities Service from 1919–1920 and 1931–1952, a German expedition beginning in 1983, and a joint German–Egyptian expedition since 1989.

TURA. Modern name for the site south of Cairo of the principal limestone quarry used by the ancient Egyptians for fine stone, notably for the outside blocks for the **pyramids** at **Giza**. The quarries are still in use. *See also* HATNUB.

TURIN EGYPTIAN MUSEUM. The Museo Egizio, or Egyptian Museum, in Turin, Italy, was founded in 1824 with the purchase of the collection of the French consul general in Egypt, **Bernardino Drovetti**. The collection included 100 statues, particularly an extremely fine representation of **Ramesses II**, along with other Egyptian objects, many from **Deir el-Medina**, notably **papyri** and the important **Turin Royal Canon**. The collection was further enlarged by the director of the museum from 1894–1927, Ernesto Schiaparelli, who conducted excavations in the **Valley of the Queens**, Deir el-Medina, where he found the intact **tomb** of **Kha**; **Giza**; **Heliopolis**; Qau el-Kebir; and **Gebelein**. The museum took part in the **Nubian Rescue Campaign** and was rewarded with the gift of the temple of Ellesiya. *See also* BERLIN EGYPTIAN MUSEUM; BOSTON MUSEUM OF FINE ARTS; BRITISH MUSEUM; CAIRO EGYPTIAN MUSEUM; LOUVRE MUSEUM; METROPOLITAN MUSEUM OF ART.

TURIN ROYAL CANON. The only **king list** to survive on **papyrus**, although the text is now damaged and incomplete. It was written during the **Ramesside Period**. When complete, it was extremely detailed, listing almost every king with the years of his reign, all divided into **dynasties**. A similar text was used by the later historian **Manetho**.

TUSHRATTA (fl. 1342–27 BC). King of **Mitanni**. Son of Shuttarna II of Mitanni. He succeeded to the throne after a **succession** crisis in which his brother was killed. His aunt was married to **Thutmose IV**; his sister, **Gilukhepa**, to **Amenhotep III**; and his daughter, **Tadukhepa**, to Amenhotep III and then **Akhenaten**. He was one of the correspondents in the **Amarna letters**. His kingdom was weakened by **Hittite** aggression under **Suppiluliuma I** and dynastic disputes that resulted in his assassination. His kingdom was then reduced to vassalage by the Hittites. *See also* WARFARE.

TUTANKHAMUN (reigned c. 1336–1327 BC). Throne name Nebkheperre, formerly Tutankhaten. Son of a king, probably **Akhenaten**. Still a child, he succeeded Akhenaten after the ephemeral rule of **Smenkhkare**, presumably under the tutelage of **Ay** and **Horemheb**. His reign is marked by the return to orthodoxy and the worship of **Amun** and the move of the capital back to **Thebes** from **Amarna**. He married his probable half sister, Ankhesenpaaten, who later changed her name to **Ankhesenamun**, but he had no surviving children. He was the last ruler of the family of **Dynasty 18** and was succeeded by Ay, who buried him in **tomb KV62** in the **Valley of the Kings**. His memory was suppressed under **Dynasty 19**. The discovery of his intact tomb by **Howard Carter** in 1922 has ensured his fame, although as he died young, he took no independent actions during his reign.

TUY (fl. 1300–1275 BC). Egyptian **queen**. She was the wife of **Sety I** and mother of **Ramesses II**. She came from a minor military family, being the daughter of the lieutenant of the chariotry Raia. She was buried in **QV80** in the **Valley of the Queens**.

TYTI. A **queen** of **Dynasty 20**. She was the daughter, wife, and mother of kings, but her exact position in the royal family is not certain. She may have been the daughter of **Ramesses IX**, wife of **Ramesses X**, and mother of **Ramesses XI**. She was buried in **QV57** in the **Valley of the Queens**.

– U –

UDJAHORRESNET (fl. 530–520 BC). Egyptian officer from **Sais**. Commander of the navy under **Ahmose II** and **Psamtik III**. He became chief physician to **Cambyses** of **Persia** following his conquest of Egypt in 525 BC, and he claimed to choose the royal **titulary** of Cambyses. He left a long autobiographical inscription on a statue now housed in the Vatican Museum in Rome. He used his influence to benefit Sais and its **temple**. His **tomb** has recently been discovered at **Abusir**.

UGARIT. A major town and seaport on the eastern Mediterranean coast in modern Syria, modern Ras Shamra. Relations with Egypt are attested beginning in the **Middle Kingdom**, and the city became part of the Egyptian empire during the **New Kingdom** until it switched its allegiance to the **Hittites** at the end of **Dynasty 18**. It was destroyed by the **Sea Peoples** around year 8 of **Ramesses III**. Excavations by a French expedition began in 1928 and have yielded much material, including inscribed tablets. *See also* AMMISTAMRU I.

UNAS (reigned c. 2375–2345 BC). Final ruler of **Dynasty 5** and successor of **Djedkare**. His name has also been transcribed as Wenis. He is principally known for his **pyramid tomb** at **Saqqara**, opened in 1881, which is the earliest pyramid to be inscribed on the inside walls with the religious texts now known as **pyramid texts**. The causeway to his mortuary **temple** was also decorated with fine reliefs. His pyramid complex has been the subject of excavations from 1899–1901, in 1903, and during the 1930s and 1940s. It has been examined more recently from 1971–1981 and 1986–1990 by succesive teams from the Egyptian Antiquities Service.

UPPER EGYPT. Ancient Egyptian *Shemau*. The area of Egypt comprising the **Nile** Valley from **Memphis** north to **Elephantine** during ancient times. The area seems to have evolved into a separate kingdom with its capital at **Hierakonpolis** during the late **Predynastic Period** and was united with **Lower Egypt** by **Narmer**, probably by conquest. It was one of the two lands ruled by the Egyptian monarch. In the royal **titulary**, the symbol of Upper Egypt was a bee, and its crown was the tall white crown. The term is sometimes used by modern Egyptologists with a more restrictive meaning, covering the area from **Asyut** south, the northern part being termed *Middle Egypt*.

URAEUS. Name for the cobra, representing the goddess **Wadjet**, which appears on the brow of the headdress of the monarch and so signifies royalty and kingship. During **Dynasty 25**, the Nubian rulers of Egypt wore a double uraeus. *See also* NEKHBET.

URHI-TESHUB (fl. 1292–1255 BC). King of the **Hittites** under the throne name Mursili III. Son of **Muwattalli II** by a secondary wife. He succeeded his father but faced hostility from his powerful uncle, **Hattusili II**, who eventually deposed him after a short reign c. 1267 BC. He was banished to Syria and later Cyprus but fled to Egypt and was granted asylum by **Ramesses II**. His presence was undoubtedly used by the Egyptians in the negotiations over the Egyptian–Hittite peace treaty in 1258 BC. Despite Hittite protests, he was not handed over but rather allowed to depart to Palestine, where he may have obtained some territory to rule. His ultimate fate is unknown.

URONARTI. Modern name for a site in Lower **Nubia** in the Second **Cataract** region of the **Nile** where a fortress was constructed on an island under **Senusret III** as part of the Egyptian garrison. Egyptian *Khesef Iunu*. It was abandoned during the **Second Intermediate Period**. The site has now been flooded by Lake Nasser, the lake created by the Aswan High Dam. *See also* ANIBA; ASKUT; BUHEN; KUMMA; MIRGISSA; SEMNA; SHALFAK.

USERKAF (reigned c. 2494–2487 BC). First ruler of **Dynasty 5**. According to a later legend in the **Westcar Papyrus**, he was the eldest of triplet sons of Rededet, a priestess of **Re**. The story is fictitious but emphasizes the attachment of the new dynasty to the cult of Re. The king built a sun **temple** at Abu Ghurab near **Abusir**, which was excavated by a Swiss expedition during the 1950s, but he was buried in a **pyramid** at **Saqqara**, which was opened in 1881. His pyramid complex was excavated by various archaeologists from 1889 onward and more recently by a French team from 1966–1973, in 1979, from 1987–1988, and from 1993–1997.

USERKARE (reigned c. 2321 BC). An obscure king of **Dynasty 6**. He appears to have been the direct successor of **Teti**, possibly his son by

Khentet, whose full name is lost), but he was quickly followed by **Pepy I**, who may have been his brother. It is possible that he was eliminated by his more ambitious brother.

USHABTI. *See* SHABTI.

– V –

VALLEY OF THE KINGS. Known in Arabic as Biban el-Moluk. A secluded desert area in the cliffs on the west bank of the Nile opposite **Thebes** consisting of two valleys chosen as the burial place for the kings of **Dynasty 18**, **Dynasty 19**, and **Dynasty 20**. There are 62 **tombs** there, mainly in the eastern valley. It is probable that the first ruler buried here was **Thutmose I**, and with the subsequent burials of the later monarchs, it became standard practice to inter royalty at the location. Apart from kings, there are tombs of some princes and favored courtiers. The tombs were constructed by a crew of royal workmen based at **Deir el-Medina**. The walls of the tombs were decorated with religious texts and contain very little in the way of historical information. The last tomb built was that of **Ramesses XI**, but it appears never to have been completed. Future rulers were buried in the north where they lived.

Most of the tombs were plundered at the end of Dynasty 20 and beginning of **Dynasty 21**. Some remained open during the **Graeco-Roman Period** and later periods, while others were rediscovered and excavated during the 19th and early 20th century, notably the tomb of **Tutankhamun**, the only royal tomb to be recovered intact. Most tombs still await full publication. The valley was first visited during modern times by the priests **Claude Sicard** and Pietro Pincia on 2 January 1721. The first plan was drawn by explorer **Richard Pococke** in 1738. Recent work has focused on the unexplored tomb of **Ramesses II** and that of his sons and a newly discovered tomb **KV63**. Following the desecration of the royal tombs, the **mummies** of many of the rulers were gathered in two secret **royal caches** from which they were recovered during the 20th century.

VALLEY OF THE QUEENS. An area on the west bank of the Nile opposite **Thebes** where the **tombs** of the **queens** and some princes of

Dynasty 18, **Dynasty 19**, and **Dynasty 20** were constructed. The most notable is the tomb of **Nefertari**, wife of **Ramesses II**. The area was explored by an Italian expedition under Ernesto Schiaparelli from 1903–1905, and since 1970, it has been extensively examined by a French team who began excavations in 1984. *See also* QV.

VESPASIAN (9–79 AD). Roman emperor. Full name Titus Flavius Vespasianus. Son of Titus Flavius Sabinus and Vespasia Polla. He was born at Falacrina near Rieti, Italy, on 17 November 9,. He pursued a senatorial career, taking part in the conquest of Britain in 43 and governing Africa. He was put in command of the army sent to crush the Jewish revolt in 67. On 1 July 69, he was proclaimed emperor by the **prefect** of Egypt, Tiberius Julius **Alexander** and his forces and was supported by the Eastern and Balkan armies. He moved to **Alexandria** to cut wheat exports to Italy and is recorded as visiting the **temple** of **Sarapis** there. His forces took Rome in December 69, and he reached Italy in 70. Vespasian proved an effective ruler. He died at Aquae Clutiae near Rieti on 23 or 24 June 79.

VICEROY OF KUSH. Governor of Egyptian **Nubia** during the **New Kingdom** whose title was literally King's son of Kush, although no royal princes ever held this office. The title was established in early **Dynasty 18** and continued until the end of **Dynasty 20** when Viceroy Panehsi became embroiled in the civil war in the Theban region at first by royal command but was eventually driven back to Nubia by **Piankh**. Egyptian control of Nubia seems to have lapsed at his death, but the title was used purely symbolically by descendants of Piankh.

VIZIER. Modern name based on the Arabic *wazir* for the chief administrative official of the Egyptian kingdom. Ancient Egyptian *tjaty*. The office appears to be attested since the **Early Dynastic Period**. It was the chief administrative office in the country, and the vizier was responsible for law and order. Beginning in the **New Kingdom**, the post was divided into two positions—one vizier for **Lower Egypt** and one for **Upper Egypt**. The post was the most powerful next to that of the ruler, and an ambitious vizier was often a threat to the king, as in the case of **Amenemhat I**.

– W –

WADI EL-HUDI. Site in the Eastern Desert used as a quarry for **amethyst** beginning in the **Middle Kingdom** during **Dynasty 11**, **Dynasty 12**, and **Dynasty 13**. The site was rediscovered in 1923, first surveyed in 1939, and explored by the Egyptian archaeologist Ahmed Fakhry from 1944–1945 and in 1949, when he copied surviving inscriptions. It was again surveyed by A. I. Sadek in 1975, a British team in 1993, and a German expedition in 1993. *See also* AKORIS; GEBEL EL-HARIDI; GEBEL EL-SILSILA; HATNUB; MONS CLAUDIANUS; MONS PORPHYRITES; SERABIT EL-KHADIM; STONE; WADI HAMMAMAT; WADI MAGHARA.

WADI ES-SEBUA. A site in Lower **Nubia** that contained **temples** of **Amenhotep III** and **Ramesses II**. This area has been flooded by Lake Nasser, the lake of the Aswan High Dam, but the main temple was removed and reerected elsewhere. *See also* GERF HUSSEIN.

WADI GABBANAT AL-QURUD. A desert wadi on the west bank of the Nile opposite **Thebes** in which a number of **tombs** of **Dynasty 18 queens** are located, including **Manhata** and other foreign wives of **Thutmose III**, and **Hatshepsut**'s first tomb and possibly that of her mother, **Ahmose**, and daughter, **Nefrure**. The site also yielded burials of baboons from the **Ptolemaic Period**.

WADI HAMMAMAT. Site in the Eastern Desert used as a quarry for siltstone (greywacke) beginning in the **Old Kingdom**. **Gold** mines were also located here. There are many inscriptions recording expeditions, notably those of **Mentuhotep III** and **Mentuhotep IV** of **Dynasty 11**. The desert wadi was the major access route to the Red Sea coast and its ports at **Mersa Gawasis** during ancient Egyptian times, **Berenike** and **Myos Hormos** during the **Graeco-Roman Period**, and the land of **Punt** and later India. The Roman bases along the desert route, like Krokodilo, were excavated by a French expedition from 1994–1997. *See also* AKORIS; GEBEL EL-HARIDI; GEBEL EL-SILSILA; HATNUB; MONS CLAUDIANUS; MONS PORPHYRITES; SERABIT EL-KHADIM; WADI EL-HUDI; WADI MAGHARA.

WADI MAGHARA. Site in the southwest of the Sinai Peninsula used as a quarry for turquoise and **copper** beginning in **Dynasty 3** until the **Middle Kingdom**. The area is noted for important royal inscriptions of the **Old Kingdom**. *See also* AKORIS; GEBEL EL-HARIDI; GEBEL EL-SILSILA; HATNUB; MONS CLAUDIANUS; MONS PORPHYRITES; SERABIT EL-KHADIM; WADI EL-HUDI; WADI HAMMAMAT.

WADI NATRUN. Coptic Scetis. A valley in the Western Desert southwest of the Delta of **Lower Egypt**. It became a place of settlement for monks during the **Coptic** Period to the middle of the 4th century. The monks initially formed individual cells grouped around four churches rather than creating a tight monastic settlement as envisioned by **Pachomius**, but later unrest and bedouin raids encouraged the growth of fortified monasteries. One of the earliest was Deir al-Baramus, whose original site was discovered by a Dutch expedition in 1994. Several monasteries still exist.

WADI SHATT ER-RIGAL. A wadi or desert gully in **Upper Egypt** near Aswan (**Elephantine**). Carved in the cliffs are predynastic rock drawings and an important relief from **Dynasty 11** that names **Mentuhotep II** and his parents, **Intef III** and **Iah**.

WADI TUMILAT. A desert valley formed by a dry river bed that runs from the Eastern Delta in **Lower Egypt** to Ismailia. The area appears to have been uninhabited except during the **Second Intermediate Period** and the **Late Period** to the **Graeco-Roman Period**. The archaeological site of **Tell er-Rataba** is located at the Delta edge of the wadi and that of **Tell el-Maskhuta** in the middle. The area was probably known as *Tjeku* during the **New Kingdom** and was closely guarded as one of the desert routes into Egypt.

WADJET. Egyptian goddess of **Buto**, usually represented as a cobra. She was the tutelary goddess of **Lower Egypt** and as such appears as part of the *nebty*, or "two ladies," name in the royal **titulary** and as the **uraeus** on the royal crown. During the **Late Period**, she is often represented as a lioness-headed goddess. *See also* NEKHBET; RELIGION.

WADJMOSE (fl. 1504–1490 BC). Egyptian prince of **Dynasty 18**. He was the son of **Thutmose I** probably by the lady **Mutnefret**. He is attested during the reign of his father and may have become heir to the throne after the death of his elder brother, **Amenmose**. Wadjmose predeceased his father, and a mortuary **temple** was built in his honor near the **Ramesseum**, in which he and Mutnefret were commemorated. *See also* THUTMOSE II.

WAHIBRE (reigned 589–570 BC). The Greek form of his name is Apries. Throne name Haaibre. Son of **Psamtik II** and Takhut. He embarked on a military expedition against **Cyrene**, which ended in failure. His troops mutinied and proclaimed **Ahmose II** as ruler. His forces were defeated, and he apparently perished then or after his capture. *See also* WARFARE.

WARFARE. Warfare appeared to have been endemic in the Nile Valley during the **Predynastic Period** until the unification of Egypt under **Narmer**, who is depicted with his captives. Military expeditions are known to have taken place into **Nubia**, notably under **Snefru**. The collapse of the **Old Kingdom** was followed by civil wars during the **First Intermediate Period** until the reunification of Egypt under **Mentuhtep II** of **Dynasty 11**. The bodies of soldiers slain during the conflict have been found buried at **Thebes**. During **Dynasty 12**, the Egyptian army conquered Nubia and built a string of fortresses to control the area. Little is known of the organization of the army during this time. The basic weapons were axes, maces, daggers, small swords, spears, and bows and arrows.

The fall of the **Middle Kingdom** and the invasion of the **Hyksos** brought about the introduction of the chariot during the **Second Intermediate Period**, while the long sword is first attested during the **New Kingdom**. Under **Dynasty 18**, a more professional standing army emerged that campaigned successfully in Nubia and in the Levant under **Ahmose**, **Thutmose II**, and notably **Thutmose III** at the battle of **Megiddo**. *The Satire on Trade*s gives a dim view of the life of a soldier. The rise of the **Hittites** led to reversals that **Ramesses II** of **Dynasty 19** failed to stem at the battle of **Kadesh**. During the **Third Intermediate Period**, there were bouts of civil war followed by the conquest by **Assyria**. The rise of **Dynasty 26** brought some

Egyptian victories in the Levant under **Nekau II** and in Nubia under **Psamtik II**, but Egypt was defeated by the Babylonians and later conquered by **Persia**. During the **Ptolemaic Period**, there were several attempts to annex Syria, but the state was weakened by civil wars and finally annexed by Rome. Roman rule was generally peaceful, but as it weakened, Egypt was invaded by the forces of **Septimia Zenobia** of Palmyra; later the Sassanian Persians; and finally the Arabs, who overran Egypt in 642 AD.

WEGAF (reigned c. 1795–1792 BC). Throne name Khutawyre. He is generally regarded as the first ruler of **Dynasty 13**, although his position in the dynasty has recently been questioned. He appears to have been of common origin, but the circumstances of his accession are obscure. His reign was brief. *See also* SECOND INTERMEDIATE PERIOD.

WEIGHING OF THE HEART. The main feature of the judgement of the dead when the heart of the deceased, regarded by Egyptians as the seat of intelligence, was weighed on a balance against the feather of *maat*, representing truth and righteousness. A virtuous heart would balance and admit the deceased to the **afterlife**, while a heavy heart would indicate an evildoer whose heart would then be devoured by a monster and hence denied an afterlife. The **Book of the Dead** was designed to fix the balance with magic spells to enable the deceased to enter the afterlife without difficulty. A heart **scarab** was often placed over the heart of the deceased with the same intention. *See also* RELIGION.

WENAMUN. Hero of a literary tale set at the end of **Dynasty 20**. The *Tale of Wenamun* outlines his adventures on a trip to Lebanon seeking wood for religious constructions at **Thebes**. The story reflects the loss of Egyptian influence in the Near East and the political divisions in Egypt. It survives in only one incomplete copy. *See also* LITERATURE; SINUHE.

WENI (fl. 2325–2275 BC). Royal official during the reigns of **Teti**, **Pepy I**, and **Nemtyemsaf** I of **Dynasty 6**, who rose to the position of governor of **Upper Egypt**. He is known from his autobiographical inscription found at **Abydos** now housed in the **Cairo Egyptian Museum**. During his career, he managed quarrying expeditions to **Tura** and **Hatnub**, commanded a military expedition against Asiatic raiders, and was part of a royal inquiry into the conduct of a **queen** of Pepy I.

WENNEFER (fl. 1320 BC). Also known as Parennefer. **High priest of Amun** at the **temple** of **Karnak** at **Thebes**. Son of Minhotep and Maia. He served at the end of **Dynasty 18** probably in the reigns of **Tutankhamun** and **Horemheb**. He was initially wrongly dated to the reign of **Ramesses II**, but the excavation of his **tomb** on the west bank of the **Nile** at Thebes by a German expedition from 1990–1993 revealed his true chronology. His son, Amenemone, served in the army and was later chief of works in the **Ramesseum** for Ramesses II. *See also* BAKENKHONS; NEBWENNEF; PASER.

WEPWAWET. Egyptian god in the form of a canine, originally a jackal but later identified by the Greeks as a wolf. Chief god of **Asyut**. His name "opener of the ways" associated him with royal conquests and as a protector and guide of the deceased through the underworld. *See also* RELIGION.

WESTCAR PAPYRUS. A **papyrus** that contains a literary tale set during the reign of **Khufu** of **Dynasty 4** but predicts the eventual triumph of **Dynasty 5**. The beginning and end of the text are missing. The king is entertained by tales of the feats of magicians, each told by one of his sons. The final magician foretells the end of the dynasty with Khufu's grandson and the advent of **Dynasty 5**. The papyrus is named after its earliest known owner and is now housed in the **Berlin Egyptian Museum**. *See also* LITERATURE.

WILBOUR PAPYRUS. A **papyrus** is named after the Egyptologist Charles Wilbour, who acquired it in Egypt and whose heirs bequeathed it to the Brooklyn Museum. It outlines in great detail the possessions of the **temple** of **Amun** throughout Egypt in **Dynasty 20** and the tenants in place and is important in understanding Egyptian land tenure and onomastics during the late **New Kingdom**. *See also* RAMESSES V.

WILKINSON, SIR JOHN GARDNER (1797–1875). British Egyptologist. He was born in Little Missenden, Buckinghamshire, England, on 5 October 1797. Educated at Harrow and Oxford, he was persuaded to devote his studies to Egyptology, and from 1821–1833 he studied hieroglyphs and recording inscriptions in Egypt. He initiated the numbering of the **tombs** in the **Valley of the Kings**. Wilkinson can be regarded as the founder of Egyptology in Great Britain, and he wrote several books, including his best seller *The Manners and Customs of the Ancient Egyptians* (1837). He died in Llandovery, Wales, on 29 October 1875. *See also* CHAMPOLLION, JEAN-FRANÇOIS; LEPSIUS, (KARL) RICHARD.

WINLOCK, HERBERT EUSTIS (1884–1950). American archaeologist. He was born in Washington, D.C., on 1 February 1884. He was educated at the University of Michigan and Harvard University and went on to work for the **Metropolitan Museum of Art**, where he became curator and later director from 1932–1939. He excavated extensively in Egypt at **Lisht**, **Kharga Oasis**, **Malkata**, and particularly at **Deir el-Bahri** from 1906–1931.

Winlock was regarded as one of the most distinguished archaeologists in Egypt of his generation. He died in Venice, Florida, on 26 January 1950. *See also* CARTER, HOWARD; MARIETTE, (FRANÇOIS) AUGUSTE FERDINAND; MONTET, (JEAN) PIERRE MARIE; NAVILLE, (HENRI) EDOUARD; PETRIE, WILLIAM MATTHEW FLINDERS; REISNER, GEORGE ANDREW.

WISDOM LITERATURE. A genre of Egyptian **literature** that consists of precepts by sages or kings to guide the reader in a virtuous life, known as *sebayet*, or lamentations on the failure of mankind to do so. Surviving examples date from most periods of Egyptian history. The earliest texts are alleged to have been composed during the **Old Kingdom** by Prince **Hardjedef**, which have not survived intact, and the **viziers Kagemni** and **Ptahhotep**. *See also* KHAKHEPER-RESENEB; MERYKARE.

WOMEN. Women in Egypt had the most secure position of females anywhere in the ancient world. During the Pharaonic Period, women were recognized as having equal legal rights as men and therefore had the right to own, inherit, and manage property and appear in court in their own capacity and not with a male guardian. The wife had a valued position in any household and was normally in a monogamous **marriage**, although sexual fidelity on the part of the husband was not expected. Women found it difficult to exercise their legal rights unless they were backed by male protection, so their legal rights were often more theoretical than practical. During the **Graeco-Roman Period**, these rights were restricted in accordance with classical practice.

The principal role of a woman of all classes was to be a wife and manage her household, so she was invariably known by the title *nebet per*, mistress of the house. She had to bear and rear children and feed and clothe her husband and offspring, thus a large part of their time was taken up with food preparation, including the grinding of wheat into flour, and textile manufacture. Wealthy women had servants, but even royal wives and princesses were involved in the weaving process. There is little evidence supporting the use of peasant women in **agriculture** apart from the winnowing process and in the harvesting of flax. Women were normally barred from administrative and political offices and so wielded their influence from behind the scenes, although there were powerful **queens**, like **Tiy** and **Nefertiti**, and queen mothers, like **Merneith** and **Ankhesenmeryre**. The few queens regnant in Egyptain history, for example, **Nitocris**, **Sobeknefru**, and **Tewosret**, were ephemeral stopgaps and marked the end of their **dynasties**. The only exception was **Hatshepsut**, who usurped the throne and reigned for a lengthy period. Only during the **Ptolemaic Period** did Egyptian queens wield real power, notably **Cleopatra VII**. *See also* MARRIAGE; SEX.

– X –

XERXES I (reigned 486–465 BC). King of **Persia** and ruler of Egypt. Son of **Darius I** and Amestris, daughter of **Cyrus**. He is best known for his attempted invasion of Greece resulting in defeats at the battles of Salamis (480 BC) and Mycale (479 BC). Thereafter, the Greek states encouraged unrest in Egypt. He was assassinated in a court intrigue in 465 BC and succeeded by his son, **Artaxerxes I**. *See also* WARFARE.

XOIS. Greek name for the capital of the sixth **nome** of **Lower Egypt**. Ancient Egyptian *Khasuu*, modern Sakha. Little is known about the site, which was briefly excavated by **Howard Carter** in 1912. It is alleged by **Manetho** to have been the seat of **Dynasty 14** during the **Second Intermediate Period**.

– Y –

YANTIN (fl. 1735 BC). Ruler of **Byblos**. Son of Yakin. He is attested on a relief dated to **Neferhotep I**. He uses an Egyptian title implying Egypt's sovereignty over Byblos. He may be identified with Yantin-ammu, ruler of Byblos, and his father with Yakin-ilu, a contemporary of an earlier Egyptian ruler, Sehetepibre.

YAQUB-HER (reigned c. 1600 BC). Throne name Meruserre. Ruler during the **Second Intermediate Period** attested on **scarabs**. He is probably one of the **Hyksos** chieftains, but it is unclear whether he belongs to **Dynasty 15** or is simply a minor ruler of **Dynasty 14**. His name is similar to the Biblical patriarch Jacob whose sojourn in Egypt might derive from an account of this king.

YOUNG, THOMAS (1773–1829). British scholar. He was born at Milverton, Somerset, England, on 13 June 1773. He studied medicine at the University of London and the University of Edinburgh and undertook further studies at the University of Göttingen and University of Cambridge. He was extremely precocious and gained a reputation as a polymath interested in both science and linguistics. He attempted to decipher the **hieroglyphic language** and was the first to recognize that it was in fact partly alphabetic. He identified several of the letters from the **cartouches** in the **Rosetta Stone**. He later abandoned his studies, but they were continued by **Jean-François Champollion**, who made the major breakthrough in the decipherment; however, Champollion never acknowledged his debt to Young, claiming inaccurately that he was unaware of his work. Young died in London on 10 May 1829.

YUYA (fl. 1390–1360 BC). High official. Father of **Tiy** and father-in-law of **Amenhotep III**. He and his wife, Tuya, were given the honor of a **tomb** in the **Valley of the Kings**, which was discovered intact in 1905. Their **mummies** and funerary equipment are now in the **Cairo Egyptian Museum**.

– Z –

ZANNANZA (fl. 1327). Son of **Suppiluliuma I**, king of the **Hittites**. He was sent to Egypt as the prospective husband of the widowed **queen**, who was probably **Ankhesenamun**, widow of **Tutankhamun**, after she had appealed for help. He died mysteriously on the way, and his father blamed the new Egyptian ruler **Ay** for his death.

ZAWIYET EL-ARYAN. Modern name for a site south of **Giza** where two unfinished **pyramids** are located. The older structure probably belongs to **Khaba** of **Dynasty 3** and the other to **Dynasty 4**. There are also graves dating to the **Early Dynastic Period**, **New Kingdom**, and **Roman Period**. The site was excavated by the Egyptian Antiquities Service in 1903 and the **Boston Museum of Fine Arts** from 1910–1911.

ZAWIYET SULTAN. Also known as Zawiyet al-Mayetin and Zawiyet el-Amwat. Modern names for a site in **Middle Egypt** south of modern Minya on the east bank of the **Nile**. It has remains from the **Predynastic Period** to the **Graeco-Roman Period**, but its main features are a ruined step **pyramid** of **Dynasty 3** and **Old Kingdom** and **New Kingdom tombs**. The site was investigated by a German expedition in 1976, 1977 and 1985, and by a joint Egyptian–British team beginning in 2000.

ZAWIYET UMM EL-RAKAN. The site of a Ramesside fortress built by **Ramesses II** on the Libyan border near Mersa Matruh as a defensive measure against Libyan incursions. It contains a small **temple** to **Ptah** and **Sakhmet**, chapels to the deified king, and storage magazines. It was discovered and partially excavated by the British archaeologist Alan Rowe in 1946. It has been under excavation by a team of archaeologists from the University of Liverpool since 1994.

ZENOBIA, SEPTIMIA (fl. 240–272 AD). Queen of Palmyra. She was the wife of Septimius Odenathus, king of Palmyra in Syria, and she took over as regent for her son, Vaballathus, upon her husband's assassination in 268 AD. Her forces conquered Egypt in 270 and expanded throughout the Levant. She proclaimed her son as a rival emperor to Aurelian in Rome, but his forces recaptured Egypt in 272 and later seized Palmyra. Zenobia was taken captive to Rome. *See also* WARFARE.

ZENON (fl. 260–240 BC). Son of Agreophon of Kaunos in Caria, Asia Minor. Secretary and later manager of the gift-estate of Apollonius c. 256–248 BC and finance minister of **Ptolemy II**, located at Philadelphia in the **Fayum**. He is known from his volumious correspondence of more than 1,000 **papyri**, which give valuable insight into the administration of Egypt during the early **Ptolemaic Period**.

Appendix A: Dynastic List

Note: All dates before 690 BC are approximate. Some dynasties or kings were contemporary with each other. Revisions of Egyptian chronology are ongoing and will often differ in other publications. An asterisk indicates that the full name is unknown.

PREHISTORIC PERIOD TO C. 5000 BC

PREDYNASTIC PERIOD	**C. 5000–3100 BC**
EARLY DYNASTIC PERIOD	**C. 3100–2686 BC**

First Dynasty	**c. 3100–2890 BC**
Narmer	c. 3100 BC
Aha	c. 3080 BC
Djer	c. 3050 BC
Djet	c. 3000 BC
Den	c. 2985 BC
Anedjib	c. 2935 BC
Semerkhet	c. 2925 BC
Qaa	c. 2915 BC

Second Dynasty	**c. 2890–2686 BC**
Hotepsekhkemwy	c. 2890 BC
Raneb	c. 2850 BC
Nynetjer	c. 2810 BC
Peribsen	c. 2760 BC
Khasekhem (Khasekhemwy)	c. 2710 BC

OLD KINGDOM

C. 2686–2181 BC

Third Dynasty

c. 2686–2617 BC

Netjerkhet Djoser	2686–2667 BC
Sekhemkhet	2667–2648 BC
Khaba	2648–2640 BC
Sanakhte Nebka	2640–2638 BC
Huni	2638–2615 BC

Fourth Dynasty

c. 2615–2494 BC

Snefru	2615–2592 BC
Khufu (Cheops)	2592–2566 BC
Radjedef	2566–2558 BC
Khafre (Chephren)	2558–2532 BC
Menkaure (Mycerinus)	2532–2503 BC
Shepseskaf	2503–2498 BC

Fifth Dynasty

c. 2494–2345 BC

Userkaf	2494–2487 BC
Sahure	2487–2475 BC
Neferirkare Kakai	2475–2455 BC
Shepseskare	2455–2448 BC
Raneferef Isi	2448–2445 BC
Niuserre	2445–2421 BC
Menkauhor	2421–2414 BC
Djedkare Isesi	2414–2375 BC
Unas	2375–2345 BC

Sixth Dynasty

c. 2345–2181 BC

Teti	2345–2323 BC
Userkare	2323–2321 BC
Meryre Pepy I	2321–2287 BC
Merenre Nemtyemsaf I	2287–2278 BC
Neferkare Pepy II	2278–2184 BC

| Merenre Nemtyemsaf II | 2184–2183 BC |
| Nitocris | 2183–2181 BC |

FIRST INTERMEDIATE PERIOD C. 2181–2000 BC

Seventh/Eighth Dynasties c. 2181–2125 B

Ninth/Tenth Dynasties c. 2160–2130 BC,
  c. 2130–2040 BC

Meryibre Khety	
Wahkare Khety	
Merykare	c. 2050 BC

Eleventh Dynasty c. 2125–1985 BC

Rulers of Thebes

Mentuhotep I	c. 2125 BC
Sehertawy Intef I	2125–2112 BC
Wahankh Intef II	2112–2063 BC
Nakhtnebtepnefer Intef III	2063–2055 BC

MIDDLE KINGDOM C. 2040–1795 BC

Kings of Egypt

Nebhepetre Mentuhotep II	2055–2004 BC
Sankhkare Mentuhotep III	2004–1992 BC
Nebtawyre Mentuhotep IV	1992–1985 BC

Twelfth Dynasty c. 1985–1795

Sehetepibre Amenemhat	1985–1955 BC
Kheperkare Senusret I	1965–1920 BC
Nubkaure Amenemhat II	1922–1878 BC
Khakheperre Senusret II	1880–1874 BC
Khakaure Senusret III	1874–1855 BC

Nymaatre Amenemhat III	1855–1808 BC
Maakherure Amenemhat IV	1808–1799 BC
Sobekkare Sobeknefru	1799–1795 BC

SECOND INTERMEDIATE PERIOD   C. 1795–1550 BC

Thirteenth Dynasty   c. 1795–1650 BC

Khutawyre Wegaf
Sekhemkare Amenemhat V
    Senebef
Sehetepibre
Iufni
Seankhibre Amenemhat VI
Semenkare Nebnun
Hetepibre Harnedjitef
Sewadjkare
Nedejemibre
Khaankhre Sobekhotep I
Renseneb
Awibre Hor
Sedjefakare Amenemhat VII
Sekhemre-khutawy Sobekhotep II
Userkare Khendjer
Semenkhkare Imiermesha
Sehetepkare Intef IV
Seth
Sekhemre-sewadjtawy
    Sobekhotep III
Khasekhemre Neferhotep I
Sihathor
Khaneferre Sobekhotep IV
Khahetepre Sobekhotep V
Wahibre Iaib
Merneferre Ay
Merhetepre Sobekhotep VI
Seankhenre-sewadjtu

Mersekhemre Ined
Sewadjkare Hori
Merkare Sobekhotep VII
Djednefere Dudimose

Fourteenth Dynasty   c. 1750–1650 BC

Aasehre Nehesy

Fifteenth Dynasty (Hyksos)   c. 1650–1550 B

Salitis (Seker-her)
Meruserre Yaqub-her
Seuserenre Khayan
Iannas
Aauserre Apepi
Khamudy

Sixteenth Dynasty   c. 1650–1580 BC

Rulers of Thebes

Sekhemresementawy Djehuty
Sekhemrewosertawy
   Sobekhotep VIII
Seakhemre-seankhtawy
   Neferhotep III Iykhernefret
Seankhenre Mentuhotep
Sewadjenre Nebirirau I
Seuserenre Bebiankh

Seventeenth Dynasty   c. 1580–1550 BC

Rulers of Thebes

Sekhemre-wahkaw Rahotep
Sekhemre-shedtawy Sobekemsaf I
Nubkheperre Intef V
Sekhemre-wepmaat Intef VI

Sekhemre-herhermaat Intef VII
Sekhemre-wadjkhaw
   Sobekemsaf II
Senakhtenre
Seqenenre Taa
Wadjkheperre Kamose

NEW KINGDOM   C. 1550–1069 BC

Eighteenth Dynasty   c. 1550–1295 BC

Nebpehtyre Ahmose I	1550–1525 BC
Djeserkare Amenhotep I	1525–1504 BC
Aakheperkare Thutmose I	1504–1492 BC
Aakheperenre Thutmose II	1492–1479 BC
Maatkare Hatshepsut	1472–1458 BC
Menkheperre Thutmose III	1479–1425 BC
Aakheperure Amenhotep II	1425–1400 BC
Menkheperure Thutmose IV	1400–1390 BC
Nebmaatre Amenhotep III	1390–1352 BC
Neferkheperure waenre Amenhote p IV (Akhenaten)	1352–1336 BC
Neferneferuaten Smenkhkare	1338–1336 BC
Nebkheperure Tutankhamun	1336–1327 BC
Kheperkheperure Ay	1327–1323 BC
Djeserkheperure Horemheb	1323–1295 BC

Nineteenth Dynasty   c. 1295–1186 BC

Menpehtyre Ramesses I	1295–1294 BC
Menmaatre Sety I merenptah	1294–1279 BC
Usermaatre setepenre Ramesses II meryamun	1279–1212 BC
Baenre meryamun Merenptah hotephermaat	1212–1202 BC
Menmire setepenre Amenmesse heka waset	1202–1199 BC

Userkheperure setepenre/
   meryamun Sety II merenptah   1202–1196 BC
Sekhaenre meryamun Ramesses
   Siptah, later Akhenre setepenre
   Siptah merenptah   1196–1190 BC
Sitre meritamun Tewosret
   setepenmut   1190–1189

Twentieth Dynasty   c. 1189–1069 BC

Userkhaure setepenre meryamun
   Sethnakhte mereramun   1189–1184 BC
Usermaatre meryamun Ramesses
   III heka iunu   1184–1153 BC
Usermaatre setepenamun, later
   Hekamaatre setepenamun
   Ramesses IV heka maat
   meryamun   1153–1147 BC
Usermaatre sekheperenre
   Ramesses V Amenherkhepeshef
   meryamun   1147–1143 BC
Nebmaatre meryamun Ramesses
   VI Amenherkhepeshef nejter
   heka iunu   1143–1136 BC
Usermaatre setepenre meryamun
   Ramesses VII Itamun netjer
   heka iunu   1136–1129 BC
Usermaatre akhenamun Ramesses
   VIII Sethherkhepeshef
   meryamun   1129–1126 BC
Neferkare setepenre Ramesses IX
   Khaemwaset meryamun   1126–1108 BC
Khepermaatre setepenre Ramesses
   X Amenherkhepeshef meryamun 1108–1099 BC
Menmaatre setepenptah Ramesses
   XI Khaemwaset mereramun
   netjer heka iunu   1099–1069 BC

THIRD INTERMEDIATE PERIOD C. 1069–656 BC

Twenty-First Dynasty	c. 1069–945 BC
Hedjkheperre setepenre Nesbanebded (Smendes) meryamun	1069–1043 BC
Neferkare heka waset Amenemnisu meryamun	1043–1039 BC
Aakheperre setepenamun Pasebakhaenniut (Psusennes) I meryamun	1039–991 BC
Usermaatre setepenamun Amenemope meryamun	993–984 BC
Aakheperre setepenre Osorkon	984–978 BC
Netjerkheperre setepenamun Siamun meryamun	978–959 BC
Titkheperure setepenre Hor-Pasebakhaenniut (Psusennes) II meryamun	959–945 BC

Twenty-Second Dynasty	c. 945–715 BC
Hedjkheperre setepenre Sheshonq I meryamun	945–924 BC
Sekhemkheperre setepenre Osorkon I meryamun	924–889 BC
Hekakhepere setepenre Sheshonq II meryamun	890 BC
Hedjkheperre setepenre Takelot I meryamun	889–874 BC
Usermaatre setepenamun Osorkon II sibast meryamun	874–850 BC
Hedjkheperre setepenamun Harsiese meryamun	
Hedjkheperre setepenre Takelot II siese meryamun	850–825 BC
Usermaatre setepenre/setepenamun Sheshonq III si-bast meryamun netjer heka iunu	825–785 BC

Hedjkeheperre setepenre Sheshonq IV si-bast meryamun netjer heka iunu	785–773 BC
Usermaatre setepenamun Pimay meryamun	773–767 BC
Aakheperre setepenre Sheshonq V meryamun si-bast netjer heka waset	767–730 BC
Aakhepere setepenamun Osorkon IV meryamun	730–715 BC

Twenty-Third Dynasty   c. 818–715 BC

Usermaatre setepenamun Pedibast I si-bast meryamun	818–793 BC
Iuput I meryamun	805–783 BC
Usermaatre setepenamun Osorkon III si-ese meryamun	777–749 BC
Usermaatre setepenamun Takelot III si-ese meryamun	754–734 BC
Usermaatre setepenamun Rudamun meryamun	734–731 BC
Usermaatre setepenamun Iuput II si-bast meryamun	731–720 BC

Twenty-Fourth Dynasty   c. 733–719 BC

Shepsesre Tefnakht	733–725 BC
Wahkare Bakenrenef (Bocchoris)	725-719 BC

Twenty-Fifth Dynasty (Nubian or Kushite)   c. 747–656 BC

Menkheperre/Usermaatre/ Seneferre Piye (Piankhi)	747–720 BC
Neferkare Shabaqo	720–702 BC
Djedkaure Shebitqu	706–690 BC
Khunefertemre Taharqa	690–664 BC
Bakare Tanutamani	664–656 BC

Ruler of Sais

Menkheperre Nekau I	672–664 BC

LATE PERIOD

664–332 BC

Twenty-Sixth Dynasty (Saite)

664–525 BC

Wahibre Psamtek I	664–610 BC
Wehemibre Nekau II	610–595 BC
Neferibre Psamtek II	595–589 BC
Haaibre Wahibre (Apries)	589–570 BC
Khnemibre Ahmose II (Amasis) si-neith	570–526 BC
Ankhkaenre Psamtek III	526–525 BC

Twenty-Seventh Dynasty (Persian Kings)

525–401 BC

Mesutire Cambyses	525–522 BC
Bardiya	522 BC
Setutre Darius I	522–486 BC
Xerxes I	486–465 BC
Artaxerxes I	465–423 BC
Xerxes II	423–424 BC
Sogdianus	424 BC
Darius II	424–405 BC
Artaxerxes II	405–401 BC

Twenty-Eighth Dynasty

404–399 BC

Amyrtaeos (Amenirdis)	404–399 BC

Twenty-Ninth Dynasty

399–380 BC

Baenre merynetjeru Nefaarud (Nepherites) I	399–393 BC
Userre setepeenptah Pasherenmut (Psamuthis)	393 BC

Khnemmaatre setepenkhnum/
   setepenanhur Hakor (Achoris)   393–380 BC
Nefaarud II   380 BC

Thirtieth Dynasty   380–343 BC

Kheperkare Nakhtnebef
   (Nectanebo I)   380–362 BC
Irmaatenre Djedhor (Teos)
   setepenanhur   362–360 BC
Snedjemibre setepenanhur/
   setepenhathor Nakhthorheb
   (Nectanebo II) meryanhur
   sibastt/sihathor   360–343 BC

PERSIAN KINGS   343–332 BC

Artaxerxes III Ochus   343–338 BC
Arses (Artaxerxes IV)   338–336 BC
Darius III   336–332 BC

MACEDONIAN KINGS   332–305 BC

Alexander the Great   332–323 BC
Philip Arrhidaeus   323–317 BC
Alexander IV   317–305 BC

THE PTOLEMIES   305–30 BC

Ptolemy I Soter I   305–282 BC
Ptolemy II Philadelphus   285–246 BC
Ptolemy III Euergetes I   246–222 BC
Ptolemy IV Philopator   222–205 BC
Ptolemy V Epiphanes   205–180 BC
Ptolemy VI Philometer   180–145 BC
Ptolemy VII Neos Philopator   145 BC

Ptolemy VIII Euergetes II	170–163, 145–116 BC
Ptolemy IX Soter II (Lathyros)	116–107 BC
Ptolemy X Alexander I	107–88 BC
Ptolemy IX Soter II (restored)	88–80 BC
Ptolemy XI Alexander II	80 BC
Ptolemy XII Neos Dionysos (Auletes)	80–58, 55–51 BC
Berenice Cleopatra III	58–55 BC
Ptolemy XIII	51–47 BC
Cleopatra VII Philopator	51–30 BC
Ptolemy XIV	47–44 BC
Ptolemy XV (Caesarion)	44–30 BC

ROMAN EMPERORS 30 BC–395 AD

Augustus	30 BC–14 AD
Tiberius	14–37 AD
Gaius (Caligula)	37–41 AD
Claudius	41–54 AD
Nero	54–68 AD
Galba	68–69 AD
Otho	69 AD
Vespasian	69–79 AD
Titus	79–81 AD
Domitian	81–96 AD
Nerva	96–98 AD
Trajan	98–117 AD
Hadrian	117–138 AD
Antoninus Pius	138–161 AD
Marcus Aurelius	161–180 AD
Lucius Verus	161–169 AD
Commodus	180–192 AD
Septimius Severus	193–211 AD
Caracalla	198–217 AD
Geta	209–212 AD
Macrinus	217–218 AD
Diadumenianus	218 AD

Severus Alexander	222–235 AD
Gordian III	238–244 AD
Philip	244–249 AD
Decius	249–251 AD
Gallus and Volusianus	251–253 AD
Valerian	253–260 AD
Gallienus	253–268 AD
Macrianus and Quietus	260–261 AD
Aurelian	270–275 AD
Probus	276–282 AD
Carus	282–283 AD
Numerian	283–284 AD
Diocletian	284–305 AD
Galerius	293–311 AD
Constantine I	306–337 AD
Constantius	337–361 AD
Julian	361–363 AD
Jovian	363–364 AD
Valens	364–378 AD
Theodosius I the Great	379–395 AD

BYZANTINE EMPERORS	**395–642 AD**
Arcadius	395–408 AD
Theodosius II	408–450 AD
Marcian	450–457 AD
Leo I	457–474 AD
Zeno	474–491 AD
Anastasius I	491–518 AD
Justin I	518–527
Justinian I	527–565 AD
Justin II	565–578 AD
Tiberius	578–582 AD
Maurice	582–602 AD
Phocas	602–610 AD
Heraclius	610–642 AD

SATRAPS OF EGYPT

The list is incomplete, and all dates of office are approximate.

Aryandes	522–490s BC, executed
Pherendates	492–486/485, killed by rebels
Achaemenes, son of Darius I	484–459 BC, killed by rebels
Arsames	424–404 BC
Pherendates	c. 343BC
Sabaces	333 BC, killed at the battle of Issus
Mazaces	323–332 BC, surrendered to Alexander the Great

PREFECTS OF EGYPT

The list is incomplete, and all dates of office are approximate.

Caius Cornelius Gallus	30–26 BC
Lucius Aelius Gallus	26–24 BC
Publius Petronius	24–22 BC
Publius Rubirius Barbarus	15–12 BC
Caius Turranius	7–4 BC
Publius Octavius	2/1 BC–3 AD
Publius Ostorius Scapula	9–10 AD
Caius Iulius Aquila	10–11 AD
*Pedo	11–13 AD
Marcus Magius Maximus	11–14 AD
Caius Galerius	15–31 AD
*Hiberus (acting)	31–32 AD
Aulus Avillius Flaccus	32–Oct 38 AD
Caius Vitrasius Pollio	38–41 AD
Lucius Aemilius Rectus	41–42 AD
Marcus Heius	42–45 AD
Caius Iulius Postumus	45–47 AD
Gnaeus Vergilius Capito	47–52 AD
Lucius Lusius Geta	54 AD
Tiberius Claudius Balbillus	55–59 AD
Lucius Iulius Vestinus	60–62 AD
Caius Caecina Tuscus	63–64 AD

Tiberius Iulius Alexander	66–70 AD
Lucius Peducaeus Colon	70–72 AD
Tiberius Iulius Lupus	72–73 AD
*Valerius Paulinus	73 AD
Caius Aeternius Fronto	78–79 AD
Caius Tettius Africanus Cassianus Priscus	80/81–82 AD
Lucius Laberius Maximus	83 AD
Lucius Iulius Ursus	83/84 AD
Caius Septimius Vegetus	85–88/89 AD
Marcus Jetties Rufus	88/89–91/92 AD
Titus Petronius Secundus	91/92–93 AD
Marcus Iunius Rufus	94–98 AD
Caius Pompeius Planta	98–100 AD
Caius Minicius Italus	101/103 AD
Caius Vibius Maximus	103–7 AD
Servius Sulpicius Similis	107–112 AD
Marcus Rutilius Rufus	113–117 AD
Quintus Rammius Martialis	117–119 AD
Titus Haterius Nepos	120–124 AD
Titus Flavius Titianus	126–133 AD
Marcus Petronius Mamertinus	133–137 AD
Caius Avidius Heliodorus	137–142 AD
Caius Valerius Eudaemon	142–143 AD
Lucius Valerius Proculus	144–147 AD
Marcus Petronius Honoratus	147–148 AD
Lucius Munatius Felix	150–154 AD
Marcus Sempronius Liberalis	154–159 AD
Titus Furius Victorinus	159–160 AD
Lucius Volusius Maecianus	160–161 AD
Marcus Annius Syriacus	161–164 AD
Titus Flavius Titianius	164–167 AD
Quintus Baienus Blassianus	167–168 AD
Marcus Bassaeus Rufus	168–169 AD
Caius Calvisius Statianus	170–175 AD
Caius Caecilius Salvianus (acting)	176 AD
Titus Pactumeius Magnus	176–179 AD
Titus Aius Sanctus	179–180 AD

Titus Flavius Piso
Decimus Veturius Marcinus   181–183 AD
*Vernasius Facundus
Titus Longaeus Rufus   185 AD
*Pomponius Faustinianus   186–187 AD
Marcus Aurelius Verianus   188 AD
Marcus Aurelius Papirius Dionysus
*Tineius Demetrius   189–190 AD
*Claudius Lucilianus   190 AD
*Larcius Memor   191–192 AD
Lucius Mantennius Sabinus   193–194 AD
Marcus Ulpius Primianus   195–196 AD
Quintus Aemilius Saturninus   197–199/200 AD
Quintus Maecius Laetus   200–203 AD
*Claudius Iulianus   203–205/206 AD
Tiberius Claudius Subatianus
    Aquila   206–211 AD
Lucius Baebius Aurelius Iuncinus   212/213 AD
Marcus Aurelius Septimius
    Heraclitus   214–215 AD
*Aurelius Antinous (acting)   216 AD
Lucius Valerius Datus   216–217 AD
*Iulius Basilianus   218 AD
*Callistianus (acting)   218/219 AD
*Geminus Chrestus   219–220/221 AD
Lucius Domitius Honoratus   222 AD
Marcus Aedinius Iulianus   222–223 AD
*alerius   223 AD
Marcus Aurelius Epagathus   223–224 AD
Tiberius Claudius Herennianus
    (acting)   224–225 AD
*Claudius Claudianus   225–229 AD
*Claudius Masculinus   229–230 AD
*Mevius Honoratianus   232–237 AD
*Corellius Galba   237 AD
Lucius Lucretius Annianus   239 AD
*Aurelius Basileus   242–245 AD
Caius Valerius Firmus   245–247 AD

*Aurelius Appius Sabinus	249–250 AD
*Faltonius Restitutianus	252 AD
*Lissenius Proculus	252–253 AD
Lucius Titinius Clodianus otherwise Consultius (acting)	252–253 AD
*Septimius	253 AD
Titus Magnius Felix Crescentillianus	253–256 AD
*Ulpius Pasion	257–258 AD
*Claudius Theodorus	258 AD
Lucius Mussius Aemilianus otherwise Aegippius (acting)	259–261 AD
*Aurelius Theodotus	262–263 AD
Caius Claudius Firmus	264 AD
*Iuvenius Genialis	267 AD
*Tenagino Probus	270 AD
Iulius Marcellinus (acting)	270 AD
Palmyrene control	270–272 AD
Statilius Ammianus	270/271–272/273
Caius Claudius Firmus	273–274 AD
*Sallustius Hadrianius	279–280 AD
*Celerinus	283 AD
*Pomponius Ianuarius	283–284 AD
Marcus Aurelius Diogenes	284/286 AD
*Aurelius Mercurius	285 AD
*Bellicius Peregrinus	286 AD
Caius Valerius Pompeianus	287–290 AD
*Titius Honoratus	290–292 AD
*Rupilius Felix	292/293 AD
c. 295 AD the Thebaid with Middle Egypt was split off and made into a separate province	
*Aristius Optatus	297 AD
*Aurelius Achilleus	297–298 AD (in rebellion)
*Aurelius Rusticianus (acting)	298 AD
Aelius Publius	298–299 AD
c. 314 Egypt was divided into several provinces which were	

reunited under the prefect c.
324/325 apart from the Thebaid

Clodius Culcianus	303–306 AD
Sossianus Hierocles	307 AD
Valerius Victorinus	308 AD
Aelius Hyginus	308–309 AD
Titinnius Clodianus	c. 310 AD
Aurelius Ammonius	312 AD
Iulius Iulianus	314 AD
Aurelius Apion	
Tiberius Flavius Laetus	326 AD
Septimius Zenius	328–329 AD
Flavius Magnilianus	330 AD
Florentius	331 AD
Flavius Hyginus	331–332 AD
Paternus	333–335 AD
Flavius Philaorius	335–337 AD
Flavius Antonius Theodorus	338 AD
Flavius Philagrinus	338–340 AD
Longinus	341–343 AD
Palladius	344 AD
Nestorius	345–352 AD
Sebastianus	353–354 AD
Maximus	355–356 AD
Cataphronius	356–357 AD
Parnassius	357–359 AD
Italicianus	359 AD
Faustinus	359–361 AD
Hermogenes	361 AD
Gerontius	361–362 AD
Ecdicius Olympus	362–363 AD
Hierius	364 AD
Maximus	364 AD
Flavianus	364–365 AD
Proclianus	366–367 AD
Flavius Eutolmius Tatianus	367–370 AD
Olympius Palladius	370–371 AD
Aelius Palladius	371–374 AD

Iulianus	380 AD
Palaldius	382 AD
Hypatius	383 AD
Optatus	384 AD
Florentius	384–386 AD
Paulinus	386 AD
Eusebius	387 AD
Flavius Ulpius Erythrius	388 AD
Alexander	388–390 AD
Evagrius	391 AD
Hypatius	392 AD
Potamius	392 AD
Damonicus	
Theodorus	
Gennadius Torquatus	396 AD
Remigius	396 AD
Archelaus	397 AD
Pentadius	403/404 AD
Euthalius	403/404 AD
Orestes	415 AD
Theodorus	420/430 AD
Callistus	c. 422 AD
Aelianus	
Cleopater	435 AD
Charmosynus	c. 443 AD
Theodorus	451 AD
Florus	453 AD
Nicolaus	457 AD
Flavius Alexander	468–469 AD
Boethius	475/476 AD
Anthemius	477 AD
Theoctistus	470/480 AD
Theognostus	482 AD
Pergamius	482 AD
Entrecitus	482/490 AD
Theodorus	487 AD
Arsenius	487 AD
Theodosius	516 AD

Flavius Strategius	518–523 AD
Zeno	527/848 AD
Dioscorus	535 AD
Rhodon	538 AD
Licinius	
Victor	
Cyrus	631–640, 641–642 AD

PATRIARCHS OF ALEXANDRIA

The names and dates of the first eleven patriarchs are traditional. Some of the later dates of office can vary according to authorities.

Mark	43–68 AD
Anianus	68–85 AD
Ablilius	85–98 AD
Cerdon	98–109 AD
Primus	109–122 AD
Justus	122–130 AD
Eumenius	130–142 AD
Marcianus	143–152 AD
Celadion	157–167 AD
Agrippinus	167–180 AD
Julianus	180–189 AD
Demetrius I	189–231 AD
Heraclas	231–247 AD
Dionysius	242–264 AD
Maximus	264–282 AD
Theonas	282–300 AD
Peter I	300–311 AD, martyr
Achillas	311–312 AD
Alexander I	312–328 AD
Athanasius I	328–373 AD
Peter II	373 AD
Lucius	373–378 AD, not recognized by the Orthodox and Coptic Church
Peter II	restored 378–385 AD

Timothy I	380–385 AD
Theophilus	385–412 AD
Cyril I	412–444 AD
Dioscorus I	44–451 AD, deposed
Proterius	451–457 AD, not recognized by the Coptic Church
Timothy II	457–460 AD, deposed
Timothy III	60–475 AD, deposed, not recognized by the Coptic Church
Timothy II	restored 474–477 AD
Timothy III	restored 477–482 AD, not recognized by the Coptic Church
John (I)	482 AD, not recognized by the Coptic Church
Peter III	elected 477 AD, not recognized by the Orthodox Church, officially recognized 482-489 AD
Athansius II	489–496 AD
John I	496–505 AD
John II	505–516 AD
Dioscorus II	516–517 AD
Timothy IV (III in Coptic Church)	517–535 AD
Theodosius I	535–537, deposed, still recognized by the Coptic Church until his death in 566 AD
Paul	537–540 AD, not recognized by the Coptic Church
Zoilus	540–541 AD, not recognized by the Coptic Church
Appollinarius	541–570 AD, not recognized by the Coptic Church
John III	570–580 AD, not recognized by the Coptic Church
Eulogius	580–608 AD, not recognized by the Coptic Church

Theodore	608–609 AD, not recognized by the Coptic Church
John IV	609–619, not recognized by the Coptic Church, fled the Persian invasion
Cyrus	631–642 AD, not recognized by the Coptic Church Orthodox succession thereafter

Coptic Patriarchs

Peter IV	575–578 AD
Damian	578–604 AD
Anastasius	604–619 AD
Andronicus	619–622 AD
Benjamin I	622–661 AD
Coptic succession thereafter	

ARABIC CONQUEST	**642 AD**

Appendix B: Museums with Egyptian Collections

Note: An asterisk indicates large or important collections.

ARGENTINA

Buenos Aires

Programa de Estudios de
 Egiptologia
Florida, 165
Entrada San Martin, Piso 5°, Of.
 542
1333 Buenos Aires

AUSTRALIA

Adelaide

South Australian Museum
North Terrace
Adelaide
South Australia 5000

Melbourne

Museum of Victoria
328 Swanson Street
Melbourne, Victoria 3000

Sydney

Australian Museum
6-8 College Street
Sydney, NSW 2000

Nicholson Museum of
 Antiquities*
University of Sydney
Sydney, NSW 2006

AUSTRIA

Vienna

Kunsthistorisches Museum*
Ägyptisch-Orientalische
 Sammlung
Burgring 5
A-1010 Wien

BELGIUM

Antwerp

Museum Vleeshuis
Vleeshouwersstraat, 38
2000 Antwerp

Brussels

Musées Royaux d'Art et
d'Histoire*
Collection Égyptienne
Parc du Cinquantenaire, 10
B-1000 Bruxelles

Liège

Musée Curtius
13 quai de Maastricht
4000 Liège

Mariemont

Musée Royal de Mariemont
Section Égypte et Proche-Orient
100 Chaussée de Mariemont
B-7140 Morlanwelz-Mariemont

Namur

Bibliothèque Universitaire
Moretus Plantin
Rue Grandgagnage 19
B-5000 Namur

BRAZIL

Rio de Janeiro

Museu Nacional
Quinta da Boa Vista
20942 Rio de Janeiro

CANADA

Montreal

Montreal Museum of Fine Arts
1379 Sherbrooke Street West
Montreal, Quebec H3G 1K3

Redpath Museum
McGill University
859 Sherbrooke Street West
Montreal, Quebec H3A 2K6

Toronto

Royal Ontario Museum*
Department of Near Eastern and
Asian Civilizations
100 Queen's Park
Toronto, Ontario M5S 2C6

CROATIA

Zagreb

Arheoloski Muzej
41000 Zagreb
Zrinjski trg 19

CUBA

Havana

Museo Nacional de Bellas Artes
Animas entre Zulueta y
Monserrate
CP 10200 Havana

CZECH REPUBLIC

Prague

Náprstkovo Muzeum
Betlémské námestí 1
CZ-11000 Praha 1

Univerzita Karlova
Cesky egyptologicky ústav
Celetná 20
CZ-11000 Praha 1

DENMARK

Copenhagen

Carsten Niebuhr Institute
University of Copenhagen
Snorresgade 17-19
DK-2300 Copenhagen S

The National Museum of
Denmark*
Department of Classical and Near
Eastern Antiquities
Ny Vestergade, 10
DK-1220 Copenhagen

Ny Carlsberg Glyptotek*
Egyptian Collection
Dantes Plads
DK-1556 Copenhagen

Thorvaldsens Museum
Porthusgade, 2
1213 Copenhagen

EGYPT

Alexandria

Greco-Roman Museum
Al Mathaf Street
Alexandria

Aswan

Aswan Museum
Elephantine Island
Aswan

Nubia Museum
Aswan

Cairo

Coptic Museum*
Masr Ateeka
Old Cairo
Cairo

The Egyptian Museum*
Midan el-Tahrir
Cairo

Luxor

Luxor Museum*

Mummification Museum

Mallawi

Mallawi Museum
Mallawi

FRANCE

Aix-en-Provence

Musée Granet
Place Saint-Jean-de-Malte
13100 Aix-en-Provence

Aix-les-Bains

Musée Archéologique
Place Maurice-Mollard
73100 Aix-les-Bains

Amiens

Musée de Picardie
48 rue de la République
80000 Amiens

Angers

Musée Pincé
32 bis rue Lenepveu
49100 Angers

Annecy

Musée-Château
Place du Château
74000 Annecy

Autun

Musée Rolin
5 rue des Bancs
71400 Autun

Avignon

Musée Calvet
Fine Arts Section
65 rue Joseph Vernet
84000 Avignon

Bordeaux

Musée d'Aquitaine
20 cours Pasteur
33000 Bordeaux

Cannes

Musée-château de la Castre
Le Suquet
06400 Cannes

Chalon-sur-Saône

Musée Vivant Denon
Place de l'Hôtel de Ville
7100 Chalon-sur-Saône

Chambéry

Musées d'Art et d'Histoire
Chambéry

Figeac

Musée Champollion
4 rue Champollion
46100 Figeac

Grenoble

Musée de Beaux-Arts
Place de Verdun
38000 Grenoble

Lille

Institut de Papyrologie et
    d'Égyptologie
URA 1275 CNRS
Université Charles-de-Gaulle,
    Lille III
59653 Villeneuve d'Ascq Cedex

Limoges

Musée Municipal
Place de la Cathédrale
87000 Limoges

Lyon

Musée des Beaux-Arts
20 place des Terreaux
69001 Lyon

Marseilles

Musée d'Archéologie
    Mediterranéenne*
Collection Egyptienne
2 Rue de la Charité
13002 Marseille

Meudon

Musée Rodin
Meudon

Nantes

Musée Dobrée
18 rue Voltaire
Nantes

Orléans

Musée Historique et
    Archéologique de l'Orléanais
Hôtel Cabu
Square Abbé Desnoyers
45000 Orléans

Paris

Bibliothèque Nationale
Département des Monnaies,
    Médailles et Antiques
58 rue Richelieu
75002 Paris Cedex 02

Musée de Cluny
6 Place Paul Pinlevé
75005 Paris

Musée du Louvre*
Département des Antiquités
    égyptiennes
Palais du Louvre
75058 Paris Cedex 01

Musée Jacquemart André
158 Bld Hausman
75008 Paris

Roanne

Musée Joseph Déchelette
22 rue Anatole France
42300 Roanne

Rouen

Musée des Antiquités de la Seine-
  Maritime
198 rue Beauvoisine
76000 Rouen

Saint-Germain-en-Laye

Chateau de Saint-Germain
Saint-Germain-en-Laye

Sèvres

Musée National de Céramique
Place de la Manufacture
92310 Sèvres

Strasbourg

Université de Strasbourg
Institut d'Égyptologie
Palais Universitaire
67000 Strasbourg

Toulouse

Musée Georges-Labit
43 rue des Martyrs de la
  Libération
31000 Toulouse

Varzy

Musée Auguste Grasset
Varzy

GERMANY

Berlin

Ägyptisches Museum und
  Papyrussammlung*
Staatliche Museen zu Berlin,
  Preussischer Kulturbesitz
Bodestrasse, 1-3
D-10178 Berlin

Museumsinsel (Berlin Mitte)
Schlossstrasse, 70
D-14059 Berlin
  (Charlottenburg)

Bremen

Übersee-Museum Bremen
Bahnhofsplatz, 13
D-28195 Bremen

Darmstadt

Hessisches Landesmuseum
  Darmstadt
Friedensplatz, 1
D-64283 Darmstadt

Dresden

Staatliche Kunstsammlungen
Dresden
Georg-Treu-Platz, 1
Albertinum
O-8012 Dresden

Essen

Museum Folkwang
Goethestrasse, 41
D-4300 Essen 1

Frankfurt-am-Main

Städtische Galerie
Liebieghaus
Museum Alter Plastik
Schaumainkal, 71
D-60596 Frankfurt-am-Main

Gotha

Schlossmuseum
Schloss Friedenstein
Ägyptische Sammlung
D-99867 Gotha

Hamburg

Hamburgisches Museum für
Völkerkunde
Binderstrasse, 14
D-2000 Hamburg 13

Museum für Kunst und Gewerbe
Hamburg
Steintorplatz, 1
D-2000 Hamburg 1

Hannover

Kestner-Museum
Trammplatz, 3
D-30159 Hannover

Heidelberg

Sammlung des Ägyptologischen
Instituts der Universität
Heidelberg
Marstallhof, 4
D-69117 Heidelberg

Hildesheim

Pelizaeus-Museum*
Am Steine, 1-2
D-31134 Hildesheim

Karlsruhe

Badisches Landesmuseum
Schlossplatz, 1
D-7500 Karlsruhe

Leipzig

Ägyptisches Museum der
Universität Leipzig
Schillerstrasse, 6
D-04109 Leipzig

Munich

Staatliche Sammlung Ägyptischer
Kunst*
Hofgartenstrasse
D-80333 München

Tübingen

Ägyptologisches Institut der
Universität Tübingen
Schloss Hohentübingen
D-72070 Tübingen

Würzburg

Martin von Wagner Museum der
Universität
Bayerisches-Julius-Maximilians-
Universität
Sanderring, 2
D-97070 Würzburg

GREECE

Athens

National Archaeological Museum
1 Tositsa Street
82 Athens 147

HUNGARY

Budapest

Szépmüvészeti Múzeum
Egyiptomi Osztály
Dózsa György út 41
H-1396 Budapest 62

IRELAND

Dublin

National Museum of Ireland
Kildare Street
Dublin 2

ISRAEL

Haifa

The Reuben and Edith Hecht
Museum
University of Haifa
Mount Carmel
Haifa 31905

Jerusalem

Bible Lands Museum
Granot, 25
Jerusalem 93706

Israel Museum
Department of Egyptian Art
Hakiriya
Jerusalem 91710

ITALY

Asti

Museo Archeologico e
Paleontologico
Corso Alfieri, 2
14100 Asti

Bergamo

Civico Museo Archeologico
Piazza Cittadella, 9
24100 Bergamo

Bologna

Museo Civico Archeologico*
Via dell'Archiginnasio, 2
I-40124 Bologna

Como

Museo Civico Archeologico "P
Giovio"
Piazza Medaglie d'Oro, 1
22100 Como

Cortona

Museo dell'Accademia Etrusca
Piazza Signorelli
52044 Cortona

Florence

Museo Archeologico*
Via della Colonna, 38
I-50121 Florence

Mantua

Museo di Palazzo Ducale
Piazza Sordello
46100 Mantua

Milan

Civiche Raccolte Archeologiche e
Numismatiche
Castella Sforzesco
20121 Milano

Naples

Museo Archeologico Nazionale
Via Museo, 18
80135 Naples

Palermo

Museo Regionale Archeologico
Piazza Olivella
90133 Palermo

Parma

Museo Archeologico Nazionale
Via della Pilotta, 4
43100 Parma

Pisa

Collezioni Egittologiche di
Ateneo
Via S. Frediano, 12
I-56126 Pisa

Rome

Museo Barracco
Corso Vittorio Emanuele, 168
00186 Rome

Museo Capitolino
Piazza del Campidoglio, 1471
00186 Rome

Museo Nazionale Romano
Piazza dei Cinquecento, 79
00185 Rome

Rovigo

Museo dell'Accademia dei
  Concordi
Piazza V. Emanuele II, 14
45100 Rovigo

Trieste

Civico Museo di Storia ed
  Arte
Via Cattedrale, 15
34121 Trieste

Turin

Museo Egizio
Via Accademia delle
  Scienze, 6
I-10123 Torino

Venice

Museo Archeologico
  Nazionale
Piazzetta San Marco, 17
30124 Venice

JAPAN

Kyoto

Heian Museum of Ancient
  History
3rd Archaeological Section
8-1 Takeda Nanasegawa
  Fushimu-ku
Kyoto 612

Tokyo

Ancient Orient Museum
1-4 Higashi Ukebukuro 3 chome
Toshima-ku
Tokyo 170

Tokyo National Museum
13-9 Ueno Park
Taitoku
Tokyo 110

LITHUANIA

Kaunas

M. K. Ciurlionis National
  Museum of Art
Vlado Putvinskio 55
LT-3000 Kaunas

MEXICO

Mexico City

Museo Nacional de Antropología
Paseo de la Reforma y Gandhi
México 5

NETHERLANDS

Amsterdam

Allard Pierson Museum
Oude Turfmarkt, 127
1012 GC Amsterdam

The Hague

Museum Meermanno-
   Westreenianum
Prinsessegracht, 30
2514 AP The Hague

Leiden

Rijksmuseum van Oudheden*
Egyptische afdeling
Rapenburg, 28
2301 EC Leiden

Otterlo

Rijksmuseum Kröller-Müller
Nationale Park de Hoge Veluwe
Houtkampweg, 6
6731 AW Otterlo

NORWAY

Oslo

Etnografisk Museum
Frederiksgate, 2
N-0164 Oslo

POLAND

Kraków

Archaeological Museum
Department of Mediterranean
   Archaeology and the Ancient
   Cultures of America
3 Senacka Str.
31-002 Kraków

Czartoryski Museum
   (Foundation) at the National
   Museum Kraków
ul. Pijarska 8 (The Town Arsenal)
31-015 Kraków

Jagiellonian University
Department of Mediterranean
   Archaeology
ul. Golebia 11
31-007 Kraków

Poznan

Museum Archeologiczne
Palac Górków
Dzial Archeologii Powszechnej
(Department of Extra-European
   Archaeology)
ul. Wodna 27
61-781 Poznan

Warsaw

Muzeum Narodowe*
Gallery of Ancient Art
Al. Jerozolimskie, 3
00-495 Warszawa

PORTUGAL

Lisbon

Fundação Calouste Gulbenkian
Av. Berna 45
1093 Lisbon

Museu Nacional de Arqueologia
Colecção de Antiguidades
Egípcias
Praça do Império
P-1400 Lisboa

RUSSIA

Moscow

State Pushkin Museum of Fine
Arts*
Oriental Department
Volchonka, 12
121019 Moscow

St. Petersburg

Hermitage Museum*
Oriental Department
Dvortsovaya Naberezhnaya, 34
191186 St Petersburg

SPAIN

Barcelona

Museu Egipci de Barcelona
Fundació Arquelògica Clos
Rambla de Catalunya, 57-59
E-08007 Barcelona

Madrid

Museo Arqueológico Nacional
Departamento de Antigüedafes
Egipcias y del Próximo Oriente
Serrano, 13
E-28001 Madrid

Santa Cruz de Tenerife

Museo Municipal de Belles Artes
Calle José Murphy 12
Plaza del Principe
38002 Santa Cruz de Tenerife

Seville

Universidad Hispalense
San Fernando s/n
Glorieta de San Diego
41004 Seville

SUDAN

Khartoum

National Museum*
El Neel Avenue
P. O. Box 178
Khartoum

SWEDEN

Stockholm

Medelhavsmuseet*
Egyptiska Samlingen
Fredsgatan, 2
S-11484 Stockholm

Uppsala

Institute of Egyptology
Victoriamuseet för egyptiska
    fornsaker
Gustavianum
S-75220 Uppsala

SWITZERLAND

Basel

Ägyptologisches Seminar der
    Universität
Schönbeinstrasse, 20
4056 Basel

Antikenmuseum Basel und
    Sammlung Ludwig
St Albangraben, 5
CH-4051 Basel

Museum für Völkerkunde
POB 1048
Augustinergasse, 2
4051 Basel

Bern

Bernisches Historisches Museum
Helvetiaplatz, 5
3005 Bern

Burgdorf

Museum für Völkerkunde
Kirchbühl, 11
3400 Burgdorf

Fribourg

Institut Biblique de l'Université
Miséricorde
1700 Fribourg

Geneva

Bibliotheca Bodmeriana
Fondation Martin Bodmer
Route de Guignard, 19-21
1223 Cology

Musée d'Art et d'Histoire*
Rue Charles-Galland, 2
CH-1211 Geneva 3

Lausanne

Musée Cantonal d'Archéologie et
    d'Histoire
Palais de Rumine
Place de la Riponne, 6
1005 Lausanne

Lenzburg

Historisches Museum Aargau
Kantonale Sammlungen
Schloss Lenzburg
5600 Lenzburg

Neuchâtel

Musée d'Ethnographie
Rue Saint-Nicholas, 4
2006 Neuchâtel

Riggisberg

Abegg-Stiftung
Werner Abeggstrasse, 67
3132 Riggisberg

St. Gallen

Sammlung für Völkerkunde
Museumstrasse, 50
9000 St. Gallen

Yverdon-les-Bains

Musée du Château
Le Château
1400 Yverdon

Zurich

Archäologische Sammlung der
Universitât Zürich
Rämistrasse, 73
8006 Zürich

UKRAINE

Odessa

Odessa Archaeological Museum
Vul. Lastochkina, 4
Odessa

UNITED KINGDOM

Aberdeen

Aberdeen University
Anthropological Museum*
Marischal College
Aberdeen AB9 1AS

Aylesbury

Buckinghamshire County
Museum
Church Street
Aylesbury HP20 2QP

Banbury

Banbury Museum
8 Horsefair
Banbury
Oxon

Batley

Bagshaw Museum
Wilton Park Batley
W Yorkshire WF17 0AS

Bedford

Bedford Museum
Castle Lane
Bedford MK40 3XD

Belfast

Ulster Museum
Botanic Gardens
Belfast
N Ireland BT9 5AB

Bexley

Bexley Museum
Hall Place
Bourne Road
Bexley
Kent DA5 1PQ

Birkenhead

Williamson Art Gallery and
    Museum
Slatey Road
Birkenhead
Wirral L43 4UE

Birmingham

Birmingham City Museums and
    Art Gallery
Department of Antiquities
Chamberlain Square
Birmingham B3 3DH

Blackburn

Blackburn Museum and Art
    Gallery
Museum Street
Blackburn
Lancs BB1 7AJ

Bolton

Bolton Museum and Art Gallery*
Le Mans Crescent
Bolton
Lancs BL1 1SE

Bournemouth

Bournemouth Natural Science
    Society
39 Christchurch Road
Bournemouth
Dorset BH1 3NS

Russell-Cotes Art Gallery and
    Museum
Russell-Cotes Road
East Cliff
Bournemouth
Dorset BH1 3AA

Brighton

The Royal Pavilion
Art Gallery and Museum
Brighton BN1 1UE

Bristol

City of Bristol Museum and Art
    Gallery*
Queen's Road
Bristol BS8 1RL

Bromley

Bromley Museum
The Priory
Church Hill
Bromley
Orpington
Kent BR6 0H4

Burnley

Towneley Hall
Art Gallery and Museums
Burnley BB11 3RQ

Cambridge

Fitzwilliam Museum*
Department of Antiquities
Trumpington Street
Cambridge CB2 1RB

University Museum of
   Archaeology and Anthropology
Downing Street
Cambridge CB2 3DZ

Canterbury

Royal Museum and Art Gallery
High Street
Canterbury CT1 2JE

Carlisle

Carlisle Museums and Art
   Gallery
Tullie House
Castle Street
Carlisle CA3 8TP

Carmarthen

Carmarthen Museum
Carmarthen
Dyfed

Chelmsford

Chelmsford Museums Service
Civic Centre
Chelmsford
Essex CM1 1JE

Cheltenham

Cheltenham Art Gallery and
   Museum
Clarence Street
Cheltenham
Glos GL50 3JT

Chiddingstone

Denys Eyre Bower Collection*
Chiddingstone Castle
Chiddingstone
nr Edenbridge
Kent TN8 7AD

Colchester

Colchester and Essex
   Museums
The Museum Resource
   Centre
14 Ryegate Road
Colchester
Essex CO1 1YG

Darlington

Borough of Darlington
   Museum
Tubwell Road
Darlington
co Durham DL1 1PD

Derby

Derby Museum and Art Gallery
The Strand
Derby DE1 1BS

Dundee

Dundee Art Galleries and
   Museums
Albert Square
Dundee DD1 1DA

Durham

Oriental Museum*
University of Durham
Elvet Hill
Durham DH1 3TH

Edinburgh

National Museums of Scotland*
Department of History and
    Applied Art
Royal Museum of Scotland
Chambers Street
Edinburgh EH1 1JF

Exeter

Royal Albert Memorial Museum
Queen Street
Exeter EX4 3RX

Glasgow

Art Gallery and Museum
Kelvingrove
Glasgow G3 8AG

Burrell Collection
2060 Pollockshaws Road
Glasgow G43 1AT

Hunterian Museum and Art
    Gallery
Egyptian Department
University of Glasgow
University Avenue
Glasgow G12 8QQ

Godalming

The Museum
Charterhouse
Godalming
Surrey GU7 2DX

Grantham

Grantham Museum
St Peter's Hill
Grantham
Lincolnshire NG31 6PY

Greenock

McLean Museum and Art
    Gallery
9 Union Street
Greenock PA16 8JH

Halifax

Bankfield Museum
Boothtown Road
Halifax
W Yorkshire HX3 6HG

Harrogate

Harrogate Museum and Art
    Gallery Service
Royal Pump Room
    Museum
Crown Place
Harrogate HG2 0LZ

Harrow

Old Speech Room Gallery
Harrow School
5 High Street
Harrow on the Hill
Middlesex HA1 3HP

Hartlepool

Gray Art Gallery and Museum
Hartlepool Museum Service
Clarence Road
Hartlepool
Cleveland TS24

Haslemere

Haslemere Educational
   Museum
78 High Street
Haslemere
Surrey GU27 2LA

Hawick

Roxburgh District Museums
   Collection
Hawick Museum
Wilton Lodge Park
Hawick
Roxburghshire TD9 7JL

Hereford

Hereford City Museums
Broad Street
Hereford HR4 9AU

Highclere

Highclere Castle
Highclere
nr Newbury
Berkshire RG15 9RN

Ipswich

Ipswich Museum
High Street
Ipswich
Suffolk IP1 3QH

Kendal

Kendal Museum
Station Road
Kendal
Cumbria LA9 6BT

King's Lynn

King's Lynn Museums
Market Street
King's Lynn
Norfolk PE30 1NL

Kingston Lacy

Kingston Lacy House*
Wimborne
Dorset BH21 4EA

Leicester

Leicester Museums and Record
   Service
96 New Walk
Leicester LE1 6TD

Letchworth

Letchworth Museum and Art
  Gallery
Broadway
Letchworth
Hertfordshire SG6 3PF

Lincoln

City and County Museum
Greyfriars
Broadgate
Lincoln

Liverpool

Liverpool Museum*
William Brown Street
Liverpool L3 8EN

School of Archaeology, Classics,
  and Oriental Studies
University of Liverpool
P.O. Box 147
Liverpool L69 3BX

London

British Museum*
Department of Egyptian
  Antiquities
Great Russell Street
London WC1B 3DG

Cuming Museum
155/157 Walworth Road
London SE17 1RS

Freud Museum
Maresfield Gardens
London NW3 5SX

Horniman Museum
London Road
Forest Hill
London SE23 3PQ

Museum of London
London Wall
London EC2Y 5HN

Petrie Museum of Egyptian
  Archaeology*
University College London
Gower Street
London WC1E 6BT

Soane Museum
Lincoln's Inn Fields
London WC2A 3BP

Victoria and Albert Museum
South Kensington
London SW7 2RL

Macclesfield

West Park Museum
Prestbury Road
Macclesfield

Macclesfield Museums
The Heritage Centre
Roe Street
Macclesfield
Cheshire SK11 6UT

Maidstone

Maidstone Museum and Art
   Gallery
St. Faith's Street
Maidstone
Kent ME14 1LH

Manchester

Manchester Museum*
University of Manchester
Oxford Road
Manchester M13 9PL

Newbury

Newbury District Museum
The Wharf
Newbury
Berkshire RG14 5AS

Newcastle upon Tyne

Hancock Museum
University of Newcastle upon
   Tyne
Barras Bridge
Newcastle upon Tyne NE2
   4PT

Northampton

Central Museum and Art
   Gallery
Guildhall Road
Northampton NN1 1DP

Norwich

Castle Museum
Archaeology Department
Norfolk Museums Service
Norwich NR1 3JU

Sainsbury Centre for Visual
   Arts
University of East Anglia
University Plain
Norwich NR4 7TJ

Nottingham

Castle Museum
Brewhouse Yard Museum
Castle Boulevard
Nottingham NG7 1FB

Oxford

Ashmolean Museum*
Department of Antiquities
University of Oxford
Beaumont Street
Oxford OX1 2PH

Pitt Rivers Museum
South Parks Road
Oxford OX1 3PP

Plymouth

City Museum and Art Gallery
Drake Circus
Plymouth PL4 8AJ

Reading

Ure Museum of Greek
 Archaeology
Department of Classics
Faculty of Letters
The University
Whiteknights
Reading RG6 2AA

Rochester

Guildhall Museum
High Street
Rochester
Kent ME1 1PY

Saffron Walden

Saffron Walden Museum
Museum Street
Saffron Walden
Essex CB10 1JL

St. Albans

Verulamium Museum
St. Michaels
St. Albans
Herts AL3 4SW

St. Helens

St. Helens Museum and Art
 Gallery
College Street
St. Helens
Merseyside WA10 1TW

Salford

Salford Museums and Art
 Galleries
Peel Park
The Crescent
Salford M5 4WU

Scarborough

Rotunda Museum
Vernon Road
Scarborough
N Yorkshire YO11 2PW

Sheffield

Sheffield City Museum
Weston Park
Sheffield S10 2TP

Southend on Sea

Southend Museum Service
Central Museum
Victoria Avenue
Southend on Sea
Essex SS2 6EW

Southport

Botanic Gardens Museum
Goodison Egyptology
 Collection
Churchtown
Southport PR9 7NB

Stoke on Trent

City Museum and Art Gallery
Hanley
Stoke on Trent ST1 3DW

Swansea

The Wellcome Museum of
    Egyptian and Graeco-Roman
    Antiquities
University of Wales Swansea
Singleton Park
Swansea SA2 8PP

Swindon

Thamesdown Museums
    Service
Bath Road
Swindon
Wiltshire SN5 8AQ

Torquay

Torquay Museum
529 Babbacombe Road
Torquay
S Devon TO1 1HG

Tunbridge Wells

Tunbridge Wells Museum and Art
    Gallery
Civic Centre
Mount Pleasant
Royal Tunbridge Wells
Kent TN1 1NS

Walsall

Walsall Museum and Art
    Gallery
Garman Ryan Collection
Lichfield Street
Walsall
W Midlands WS1 1TR

Warrington

Warrington Museum and Art
    Gallery
Bold Street
Warrington WA1 1JG

Warwick

Warwickshire Museum
Market Hall
Market Place
Warwick CV34 4SA

Welshpool

Powysland Museum
Salop Road
Welshpool
Powys SY21 7EG

West Malling

Kent County Museum
    Service
Kent County Council
West Malling Air Station
West Malling
Kent ME19 6QE

Windsor

Myers Museum
Eton College
Windsor
Berks SL4 6DB

Wisbech

Wisbech and Fenland Museum
Museum Square
Wisbech
Cambridgeshire PE13 1ES

UNITED STATES

Ann Arbor, Michigan

Kelsey Museum of Ancient and
    Medieval Archaeology
University of Michigan
434 South State Street
Ann Arbor, MI 48104

Atlanta, Georgia

The William C. Carlos Museum
Emory University
571 South Kilgo Street
Atlanta, GA 30322

Baltimore, Maryland

The Johns Hopkins University
Department of Near Eastern
    Studies
Charles and 34th Street
Baltimore, MD 21218

Walters Art Gallery*
600 North Charles Street
Baltimore, MD 21201-5185

Berkeley, California

The Phoebe Apperson Hearst
    Museum of Anthropology and
    Archaeology
103 Kroeber Hall
University of California
Berkeley, CA 94720-3712

Boston, Massachusetts

Museum of Fine Arts*
Department of Ancient Egyptian,
    Nubian and Near Eastern Art
465 Huntington Avenue
Boston, MA 02115

Cambridge, Massachusetts

Fogg Art Museum
Harvard University
Cambridge, MA 02138

Semitic Museum
Harvard University
Cambridge, MA 02138

Chicago, Illinois

Field Museum of Natural
    History
Roosevelt Road at Lake Shore
    Drive
Chicago, IL 60605

The Oriental Institute Museum*
University of Chicago
1155 East 58th Street
Chicago, IL 60637-1569

Cincinnati, Ohio

Art Museum
Eden Park
Cincinnati, OH 45202

Cleveland, Ohio

Museum of Art*
Department of Ancient Art
11150 East Boulevard
Cleveland, OH 44106-1797

Dallas, Texas

Dallas Museum of Art
1717 North Harwood
Dallas, TX 75201

Denver, Colorado

Art Museum
100 West 14th Avenue
Parkway
Denver, CO 80204

Detroit, Michigan

Detroit Institute of Arts*
Department of Ancient Art
5200 Woodward Avenue
Detroit, MI 48202-4008

Kansas City, Missouri

The Nelson-Atkins Museum of
Art
4525 Oak Street
Kansas City, MO 64111

Los Angeles, California

County Museum of Art
Ancient and Islamic Art
5905 Wilshire Boulevard
Los Angeles, CA 90036

Memphis, Tennessee

Memphis State University
Institute of Egyptian Art and
Archaeology
3750 Norriswood
Memphis, TN 38152

Minneapolis, Minnesota

Institute of Arts Museum
2400 Third Avenue South
Minneapolis, MN 55404

New Haven, Connecticut

Peabody Museum
Yale University
New Haven, CT 06520

New York, New York

Brooklyn Museum*
Department of Egyptian,
Classical, and Ancient Middle
Eastern Art

200 Eastern Parkway
Brooklyn, NY 11238-6052

Metropolitan Museum of Art*
Department of Egyptian Art
1000 Fifth Avenue
New York, NY 10028-0198

Newark, New Jersey

Newark Museum
The Classical Collection
49 Washington Street
Newark, NJ 07101-0540

Philadelphia, Pennsylvania

University of Pennsylvania
    Museum of Archaeology and
    Anthropology*
Egyptian Section
33rd and Spruce Streets
Philadelphia, PA 19104

Pittsburgh, Pennsylvania

The Carnegie Museum of Natural
    History
4400 Forbes Avenue
Pittsburgh, PA 15213

Princeton, New Jersey

University Art Museum
Princeton, NJ 08544

Providence, Rhode Island

Museum of Art
Rhode Island School of Design
Department of Antiquities
224 Benefit Street
Providence, RI 02903

Raleigh, North Carolina

North Carolina Museum of Art
2110 Blue Ridge Boulevard
Raleigh, NC 27607

Richmond, Virginia

Virginia Museum of Fine Arts
Department of Ancient Art
2800 Grove Avenue
Richmond, VA 23221

San Antonio, Texas

San Antonio Museum of Art
200 West Jones
San Antonio, TX 78215

San Bernardino, California

Robert V. Fullerton Art Museum
California State Museum
San Bernardino, CA 92407-2397

San Jose, California

Rosicrucian Egyptian Museum
Rosicrucian Park
1342 Naglee Avenue
San Jose, CA 95191

Seattle, Washington

Seattle Art Museum
Volunteer Park
1400 East Prospect
Seattle, WA 98112

St. Louis, Missouri

Art Museum
Forest Park
St. Louis, MO 63110

Toledo, Ohio

Toledo Museum of Art
2445 Monroe Street at
Scottswood Avenue
Toledo, OH 43697

Washington, D.C.

Freer Gallery of Art
Jefferson Drive at 12th Street,
SW
Washington, DC 20560

National Museum of Natural
History
Smithsonian Institution
Washington, DC 20560

Worcester, Massachusetts

Art Museum
55 Salisbury Street
Worcester, MA 01609

URUGUAY

Montevideo

Museo de Historia del Arte
Ejido, 1326
11100 Montevideo

Museo Egipcio de la Societal
Uruguaya de Egiptología
4 de Julio, 3068
11600 Montevideo

Museo Nacional de Historia
Natural
Buenos Aires, 652
11000 Montevideo

VATICAN CITY

Museo Gregoriano Egizio*
Vatican Museums and Galleries
00120 Vatican City

Bibliography

CONTENTS

INTRODUCTION

This bibliography is not intended to be an exhaustive and complete reference tool to the vast literature on ancient Egypt. Details on many older books can be found in the more complete bibliographies of Ibrahim Hilmy, Ida A. Pratt, and Christine Beinlich-Seeber cited in this section. With few exceptions, only monographs have been cited to limit the bibliography to a reasonable size. Modern works, especially on archaeological excavations, have been preferred to older accounts. There has been bias in favor of books published in English, but German and French works have been noted where appropriate.

GENERAL WORKS

Aldred, Cyril. *The Egyptians.* 3rd ed. Revised by Aidan Dodson. London: Thames & Hudson, 1998.

Assmann, Jan. *The Mind of Egypt: History and Meaning in the Time of the Pharaohs*, trans. Andrew Jenkins. Cambridge, Mass.: Harvard University Press, 2002.

Baines, John, and Jaromir Malek. *Atlas of Ancient Egypt.* Oxford, U.K.: Phaidon, 1980.

Brewer, Douglas J., and Emily Teeter. *Egypt and the Egyptians.* 2nd ed. Cambridge, U.K.: Cambridge University Press, 2006.

Donadoni, Sergio, ed. *The Egyptians.* Chicago: University of Chicago Press, 1997.

Harris, John R., ed. *The Legacy of Egypt.* 2nd ed. Oxford, U.K.: Clarendon Press, 1971.

Hayes, William C. *The Scepter of Egypt.* Vol. 1. New York: Harper & Brothers, 1953.

——. *The Scepter of Egypt.* Vol. 2. Cambridge, Mass.: Harvard University Press, 1959.

Helck, Wolfgang, and Eberhard Otto. *Lexikon der Ägyptologie.* 7 vols. Wiesbaden, Germany: Otto Harrassowitz, 1972–1992.

Hornung, Erik, Rolf Krauss, and David A. Warburton. *Ancient Egyptian Chronology.* Leiden, Netherlands: Brill, 2006.

Kees, Hermann. *Ancient Egypt: A Cultural Topography.* London: Faber & Faber, 1961.

Lustig, Judith, ed. *Anthropology and Egyptology: A Developing Dialogue.* Sheffield, G.B.: Sheffield Academic Press, 1997.

Malek, Jaromir, ed. *Egypt: Ancient Culture, Modern Land.* Norman: University of Oklahoma Press, 1993.

Morkot, Robert. *The Egyptians: An Introduction*. London: Routledge, 2005.
Posener, Georges. *A Dictionary of Egyptian Civilisation*. London: Methuen, 1962.
Sasson, Jack M., ed. *Civilizations of the Ancient Near East*. 4 vols. New York: Scribner's, 1995.
Shaw, Ian, and Paul Nicholson. *British Museum Dictionary of Ancient Egypt*. New ed. London: British Museum Press, 2002.
Spencer, A. Jeffrey. *The British Museum Book of Ancient Egypt*. Rev. ed. London: British Museum Press, 2007.
Wilkinson, Toby. *The Egyptian World*. London: Routledge, 2007.
———. *The Thames and Hudson Dictionary of Ancient Egypt*. London: Thames & Hudson, 2005.

HISTORY

General

Beckerath, Jürgen von. *Handbuch der Ägyptischen Königsnamen*. Münchner Ägyptologische Studien 20. Munich, Germany: Deutscher Kunstverlag, 1984.
The Cambridge Ancient History. 14 vols. 2nd and 3rd eds. Cambridge, U.K.: Cambridge University Press, 1981–2005.
Clayton, Peter. *Chronicle of the Pharaohs*. London: Thames & Hudson, 1994, 2006.
Davies, W. Vivian, and Louise Schofield, eds. *Egypt, the Aegean, and the Levant: Interconnections in the Second Millennium BC*. London: British Museum Press, 1995.
Dodson. Aidan, and Dyan Hilton. *The Complete Royal Families of Ancient Egypt*. London: Thames & Hudson, 2004.
Gardiner, Alan H. *Egypt of the Pharaohs*. Oxford, U.K.: Oxford University Press, 1961.
Grimal, Nicolas. *A History of Ancient Egypt*. Oxford, U.K.: Blackwell: 1992.
Helck, Wolfgang. *Die altägyptischen Gaue*. Beihefte zum Tübinger Atlas des Vorderen Orients B 5. Wiesbaden, Germany: Dr. Ludwig Reichert Verlag, 1974.
Hornung, Erik. *History of Ancient Egypt: An Introduction*. Ithaca, N.Y.: Cornell University Press, 1999.
Hornung, Erik, Rolf Krauss, and David Warburton. *Ancient Egyptian Chronology*. Leiden, Netherlands: Brill, 2006.
James, T. G. Henry. *A Short History of Ancient Egypt*. Cairo: Librairie du Liban, 1995.

Kemp, Barry J. *Ancient Egypt: Anatomy of a Civilization.* 2nd ed. London: Routledge, 2006.

O'Connor, David, and David P. Silverman, eds. *Ancient Egyptian Kingship.* Leiden, Netherlands: Brill, 1995.

Redford, Donald B. *The Oxford Encyclopedia of Ancient Egypt.* 3 vols. Oxford, U.K.: Oxford University Press, 2001.

Rice, Michael. *Egypt's Making.* 2nd ed. London: Routledge, 2003.

Shaw, Ian, ed. *The Oxford History of Ancient Egypt.* Oxford, U.K.: Oxford University Press, 2000.

Trigger, B. G., B. J. Kemp, D. O'Connor, and A. B. Lloyd. *Ancient Egypt: A Social History.* Cambridge, U.K.: Cambridge University Press, 1983.

Tydesley, Joyce. *Chronicle of the Queens of Egypt.* London: Thames & Hudson, 2006.

Vandersleyen, Claude. *L'Égypte et la vallée du Nil. Tome 2. De la fin de l'Ancien Empire à la fin du Nouvel Empire.* Paris: Presses Universitaires de France, 1995.

Vercoutter, Jean. *L'Égypte et la vallée du Nil. Tome 1. Des origines à la fin de l'Ancien Empire.* Paris: Presses Universitaires de France, 1992.

Prehistoric and Predynastic Period

Adams, Barbara. *Predynastic Egypt.* Aylesbury, G.B.: Shire Publications, 1988.

Adams, Barbara, and Krzysztof Cialowicz. *Protodynastic Egypt.* Aylesbury, G.B.: Shire Publications, 1997.

Bard, Kathryn A. *From Farmers to Pharaohs.* Sheffield, G.B.: Sheffield Academic Press, 1994.

Baumgartel, Elise. *The Cultures of Prehistoric Egypt.* London: Oxford University Press, 1947.

Cialowícz, Krzystof M. *La Naissance d'un royaume. L'Égypte dès la période prédynastique à la fin de la 1er Dynastie.* Cracow, Poland: Uniwersytet Jagiellonski, Instytut Archeologii, 2001.

Hayes, William C. *Most Ancient Egypt.* Chicago: University of Chicago Press, 1965.

Hendricks, Stan, R. Friedman, Krzystof M. Cialowícz, and M. Chlodnicki, eds. *Egypt at Its Origins: Studies in Memory of Barbara Adams.* Louvain, Belgium: Peeters, 2004.

Hoffman, Michael A. *Egypt before the Pharaohs: The Prehistoric Foundations of Ancient Egypt.* London: Routledge and Kegan Paul, 1980.

Midant-Reynes, Béatrix. *The Prehistory of Egypt.* Oxford, U.K.: Blackwell, 2000.

Wengrow. David. *The Archaeology of Early Egypt.* Cambridge, U.K.: Cambridge University Press, 2006.

Wilkinson, Toby. *Genesis of the Pharaohs.* London: Thames & Hudson, 2003.

Early Dynastic Period and Old Kingdom

Aldred, Cyril. *Egypt to the End of the Old Kingdom.* London: Thames & Hudson, 1965.

Andreu, Guillemette. *Egypt in the Age of the Pyramids,* trans. David Lorton. Ithaca, N.Y.: Cornell University Press, 1997.

Baud, Michel. *Djéser et la IIIe Dynastie.* Paris: Pygmalion, 2002.

———. *Famille royale et pouvoir sous l'Ancien Empire égyptien.* Cairo: Institut français d'archéologie orientale, 2005.

Emery, Walter B. *Archaic Egypt.* London: Penguin Books, 1961.

Hart, George. *Pharaohs and Pyramids.* London: Herbert Press, 1991.

Helck, Wolfgang. *Untersuchungen zur Thinitenzeit.* Wiesbaden, Germany: Harrassowitz, 1987.

Jánosi, Peter. *Die Gräberwelt der Pyramidenzeit.* Maniz am Rhein, Germany: Philipp von Zabern, 2006.

Kahl, Jochem, Nicole Kloth, and Ursula Zimmermann. *Die Inschriften der 3. Dynastie.* Wiesbaden, Germany: Harrassowitz, 1995.

Kanawati, Naguib. *Conspiracies in the Egyptian Palace: Unis to Pepy I.* London: Routledge, 2002.

Malek, Jaroslav, and Werner Forman. *In the Shadow of the Pyramids: Egypt during the Old Kingdom.* London: Orbis, 1986.

Roth, Silke. *Die Königsmütter des Alten Ägypten von der Frühzeit bis zum Ende der 12. Dynastie.* Wiesbaden, Germany: Harrassowitz, 2001.

Spencer, A. Jeffrey. *Aspects of Early Egypt.* London: British Museum Press, 1996.

———. *Early Egypt.* London: British Museum Press, 1993.

Strudwick, Nigel. *The Administration of Egypt in the Old Kingdom.* London: Kegan Paul International, 1985.

———. *Texts from the Pyramid Age.* Leiden, Netherlands: Brill, 2005.

First Intermediate Period, Middle Kingdom, and Second Intermediate Period

Bietak, Manfred. *Pharaonen und Fremde: Dynastien im Dunkel.* Vienna, Austria: Museen der Stadt Wien, 1994.

Booth, Charlotte. *The Hyksos Period in Egypt*. London: Shire Publications, 2005.

Bourriau, Janine. *Pharaohs and Mortals: Egyptian Art in the Middle Kingdom*. Cambridge, U.K.: Fitzwilliam Museum, 1988.

Favry, Nathalie. *Le nomarque sous le règne de Sésostris Ier*. Paris: Presses de l'Université Paris-Sorbonne, 2004.

Fay, Biri. *The Louvre Sphinx and Royal Sculpture from the Reign of Amenemhat II*. Mainz am Rhein, Germany: Philipp von Zabern, 1996.

Gomaà, Farouk. *Die Besiedlung Ägyptens während des Mittleren Reiches*. 2 vols. Beihefte zum Tübinger Atlas des Vorderen Orients B 66. Wiesbaden, Germany: Dr. Ludwig Reichert Verlag, 1986.

Grajetzki, Wolfram. *The Middle Kingdom of Ancient Egypt*. London: Duckworth, 2006.

Matzker, Ingo. *Die letzten Könige der 12. Dynastie*. Frankfurt, Germany: Peter Lang, 1986.

Obsomer, Claude. *Sesostris Ier: Étude chronologique et historique du règne*. Paris: Connaissance de l'Égypte ancienne, 1995.

Quirke, Stephen. *The Administration of Egypt in the Late Middle Kingdom: The Hieratic Documents*. New Malden, G.B.: SIA Publishing, 1990.

——. *Middle Kingdom Studies*. New Malden, G.B.: SIA Publishing, 1991.

——. *Titles and Bureaux of Egypt, 1850–1700 BC*. London: Golden House Publications, 2004.

Ryholt, Kim. *The Second Intermediate Period in Egypt, c. 1800–1550 B.C*. The Carsten Niebuhr Institute of Ancient Near Eastern Studies Publications 20. Copenhagen, Denmark: Museum Tusculanum Press, 1997.

Tallet, Pierre. *Sésostris III et la Fin de la XIIe Dynastie*. Paris: Pygmalion, 2005.

Van Seters, John. *The Hyksos: A New Investigation*. New Haven, Conn.: Yale University Press, 1966.

New Kingdom: Dynasty 18

Bryan, Betsy. *The Reign of Thutmose IV*. Baltimore: Johns Hopkins University Press, 1991.

Cline, Eric, and David O'Connor, eds. *Thutmose III*. Ann Arbor: University of Michigan Press, 2005.

Cummings, Barbara, and Benedict Davies. *Egyptian Historical Records of the Later Eighteenth Dynasty*. 5 vols. Warminster, G.B.: Aris &d Phillips, 1982–1994.

Della Monica, Madeleine. *Thoutmosis III: Le plus grand des Pharaons*. Paris: Le Léopard d'Or, 1991.

Der Manuelian, Peter. *Studies in the Reign of Amenophis II.* Hildesheimer Ägyptologische Beiträge 26. Hildesheim, Germany: Gerstenberg, 1987.

Dorman, Peter. *The Monuments of Senenmut.* London: Kegan Paul International, 1988.

Gitton, Michel. *Les divines épouses de la 18e dynastie.* Besançon, France: Annales Littéraires de l'Université de Besançon, 1984.

———. *L'épouse du dieu Ahmes Néfertary.* Besançon, France: Annales Littéraires de l'Université de Besançon, 1975.

Hayes, William C. *Royal Sarcophagi of the XVIII Dynasty.* Princeton, N.J.: Princeton University, 1935.

Klug, Andrea. *Königliche Stelen aud der Zeit von Ahmose bis Amenophis III.* Turnhout, Belgium: Brepols, 2002.

Kozloff, Arielle P., and Betsy M. Bryan. *Egypt's Dazzling Sun: Amenhotep III and His World.* Cleveland, Ohio: Cleveland Museum of Art, 1992.

Maruéjol, Florence. *Thoutmosis III et la Corégence avec Hatchepsout.* Paris: Pygmalion, 2007.

O'Connor, David, and Eric Cline, eds. *Amenhotep III: Perspectives on His Reign.* Ann Arbor: University of Michigan Press, 1998.

Polz, Daniel. *Der Beginn der Neuen Reiches. Zur Vorgeschichte einer Zeitenwende.* Berlin and New York: Walter de Gruyter, 2007.

Redford, Donald B. *History and Chronology of the Eighteenth Dynasty of Egypt: Seven Studies.* Toronto: University of Toronto Press, 1967.

———. *The Wars in Syria and Palestine of Thutmose III.* Leiden, Netherlands: Brill, 2003.

Roehrig, Catherine H., ed. *Hatshepsut from Queen to Pharaoh.* New York: Metropolitan Museum of Art, 2006.

Schmitz, Franz-Jürgen. *Amenophis I.* Hildesheimer Ägyptologische Beiträge 6. Hildesheim, Germany: Gerstenberg, 1978.

Tyldesley, Joyce. *Hatchepsut: The Female Monarch.* London: Viking, 1996.

Vandersleyen, Claude. *Les guerres d'Amosis.* Brussels, Belgium: Fondation Égyptologique Reine Élisabeth, 1971.

The Amarna Period

Aldred, Cyril. *Akhenaten and Nefertiti.* London: Thames & Hudson, 1973.

———. *Akhenaten, King of Egypt.* London: Thames & Hudson, 1988.

Cohen, Raymond, and Raymond Westbrook, eds. *Amarna Diplomacy.* Baltimore: Johns Hopkins University Press, 2000.

Freed, Rita E., Yvonne J. Markowitz, and Sue H. D'Auria. *Pharaohs of the Sun: Akhenaten, Nefertiti, Tutankhamen.* London: Thames & Hudson, 1999.

Giles, Frederick J. *The Amarna Age: Egypt.* The Australian Centre of Egyptology. Warminster, G. B.: Aris & Phillips, 2001.

Hornung, Erik. *Akhenaten and the Religion of Light,* trans. David Lorton. Ithaca, N.Y.: Cornell University Press, 1999.

Krauss, Rolf. *Das Ende der Amarnazeit.* Hildesheimer Ägyptologische Beiträge 7. Hildesheim, Germany: Gerstenberg, 1978.

Martin, Geoffrey T. M. *A Bibliography of the Amarna Period and Its Aftermath: The Reigns of Akhenaten, Smenkhkare, Tutankhamun, and Ay (c. 1350–1321 BC).* London: Kegan Paul International, 1991.

Montserrat, Dominic. *Akhenaten: History, Fantasy, and Ancient Egypt.* London: Routledge, 2000.

Moran, William L. *The Amarna Letters.* Baltimore: Johns Hopkins University Press, 1992.

Redford, Donald B. *Akhenaten, the Heretic King.* Princeton, N.J.: Princeton University Press, 1984.

Silverman, David, Josef Wegner, and Jennifer H. Wegner. *Akhenaten Tutankhamun: Revolution and Restoration.* Philadelphia: University of Pennsylvania Museum of Archaeology and Anthropology, 2006.

Thomas, Angela. *Akenaten's Egypt.* Aylesbury, G.B.: Shire Publications, 1988.

Tyldesley, Joyce. *Nefertiti: Egypt's Sun Queen.* London: Viking, 1998.

Tutankhamun

Allen, Susan, and James Allen. *Tutankhamun's Tomb: The Thrill of Discovery.* New York: Metropolitan Museum of Art, 2006.

Beinlich, Horst, and Mohamed Saleh. *Corpus der Hieroglyphischen Inschriften aus dem Grab des Tutanchamun.* Oxford, U.K.: Griffith Institute, 1989.

Carter, Howard, and Arthur C. Mace. *The Tomb of Tutankhamen.* 3 vols. London: Cassell & Co., 1923.

Cerny, Jaroslav. *Hieratic Inscriptions from the Tomb of Tutankhamun.* Tutankhamun Tomb Series 2. Oxford, U.K.: Griffith Institute, 1965.

Desroches-Noblecourt, Christiane. *Life and Death of a Pharaoh: Tutankhamen.* London: The Connoisseur and Michael Joseph, 1963.

Eaton-Krauss, Marianne. *The Sarcophagus in the Tomb of Tutankhamun.* Oxford, U.K.: Griffith Institute, 1993.

Eaton-Krauss, Marianne, and Erhart Graefe. *The Small Golden Shrine from the Tomb of Tutankhamun.* Oxford, U.K.: Griffith Institute, 1985.

Edwards, I. Eiddon S. *Treasures of Tutankhamun.* London: Trustees of the British Museum, 1972.

———. *Tutankhamun: His Tomb and Its Treasures.* London: Victor Gollancz, 1979.

Hawass, Zaki. *King Tutankhamun: The Treasures of the Tomb*. London, Thames & Hudson, 2007.

James, T. G. Henry. *Great Pharaohs*. Vercelli, Italy: White Star Publications, 2004.

———. *Tutankhamun: Eternal Splendour of the Boy Pharaoh*. London: Tauris Parke, 2000.

Jones, Dilwyn. *Model Boats from the Tomb of Tutankhamun*. Tutankhamun's Tomb Series 9. Oxford, U.K.: Griffith Institute, 1990.

el-Khouli, Ali, Rostislav Holthoer, Colin Hope, and Olaf Kaper. *Stone Vessels, Pottery, and Sealings from the Tomb of Tutankhamun*. Oxfor, U.K.: Griffith Institute, 1993.

Leek, F. Filce. *The Human Remains from the Tomb of Tutankhamun*. Tutankhamun's Tomb Series 5. Oxford, U.K.: Griffith Institute, 1972.

Littauer, Miriam A., and J. H. Crouwel. *Chariots and Related Equipment from the Tomb of Tutankhamun*. Tutankhamun's Tomb Series 8. Oxford, U.K.: Griffith Institute, 1985.

el-Mallakh, Kamal, and Arnold C. Brackman. *The Gold of Tutankhamen*. New York: Newsweek Books, 1978.

Manniche, Lise. *Musical Instruments from the Tomb of Tutankhamun*. Tutankhamun's Tomb Series 6. Oxford, U.K.: Griffith Institute, 1976.

McLeod, Wallace. *Composite Bows from the Tomb of Tutankhamun*. Tutankhamun's Tomb Series 3. Oxford, U.K.: Griffith Institute, 1970.

———. *Self Bows and Other Archery Tackle from the Tomb of Tutankhamun*. Tutankhamun's Tomb Series 4. Oxford, U.K.: Griffith Institute, 1982.

Murray, Helen, and Mary Nuttall. *A Handlist of Howard Carter's Catalogue of Objects in Tutankhamun's Tomb*. Tutankhamun's Tomb Series 1. Oxford, U.K.: Griffith Institute, 1963.

Reeves, C. Nicholas. *The Complete Tutankhamun: The King, the Tomb, the Royal Treasure*. London: Thames & Hudson, 1990.

Tait, W. John. *Game-Boxes and Accessories from the Tomb of Tutankhamun*. Tutankhamun's Tomb Series 7. Oxford, U.K.: Griffith Institute, 1986.

Welsh, Frances. *Tutankhamun's Egypt*. 2nd ed. Aylesbury, G.B.: Shire Publications, 2007.

New Kingdom: Dynasties 19–20

Brand, Peter J. *The Monuments of Seti I. Epigraphic, Historical and Art Historical Analysis*. Leiden, Netherlands: Brill, 2000.

Davies, Benedict G. *Egyptian Historical Inscriptions of the Nineteenth Dynasty*. Jonsered, Sweden: Paul Åströms, 1997.

Desroches-Noblecourt, Christiane. *Ramses II: An Illustrated Biography*. Paris: Flammarion, 2007.

Fisher, Marjorie M. *The Sons of Ramesses II*. Wiesbaden, Germany: Harrassowitz, 2001.

Gomaà, Farouk. *Chaemwese, Sohn Ramses' II und Hohenpriester von Memphis*. Wiesbaden, Germany: Otto Harrassowitz, 1973.

James, T. G. Henry. *Ramesses II*. Vercelli, Italy: White Star Publications, 2002.

Kitchen, Kenneth A. *Pharaoh Triumphant: The Life and Times of Ramesses II, King of Egypt*. Warminster, G.B.: Aris & Phillips, 1982.

———. *Ramesside Inscriptions*. 8 vols. Oxford, U.K.: Blackwell, 1968–1990.

———. *Ramesside Inscriptions Translated and Annotated: Notes and Comments*. Vol. 1. Oxford, U.K.: Blackwell, 1993.

———. *Ramesside Inscriptions Translated and Annotated: Translations*. Vols 1–4. Oxford, U.K.: Blackwell, 1993–2003.

Klengel, Horst. *Hattuschili und Ramses: Hethiter und Ägypter-ihr langer Weg zum Frieden*. Mainz am Rhein, Germany: Philipp von Zabern, 2002.

Manassa, Colleen. *The Great Karnak Inscription of Merenptah: Grand Strategy in the 13th Century BC*. New Haven, Conn.: Yale University Press, 2003.

Murnane, William J. *The Road to Kadesh*. 2nd ed. Chicago: Oriental Institute of the University of Chicago, 1995.

Peden, Alexander. *Egyptian Historical Inscriptions of the Twentieth Dynasty*. Jonsered, Sweden: Paul Åströms, 1994.

———. *The Reign of Ramesses IV*. Warminster, G.B.: Aris & Phillips, 1994.

Redford, Susan. *The Harem Conspiracy: The Murder of Ramesses III*. Dekalb: Northern Illinois University Press, 2002.

Sourouzian, Hourig. *Les monuments du roi Merenptah*. Deutsches Archäologisches Institut. Abteilung Kairo. Sonderscrift 22. Mainz am Rhein, Germany: Philipp von Zabern, 1989.

Tyldesley, Joyce. *Ramesses II*. London, Viking, 2000.

Vernus, Pascal. *Affairs and Scandals in Ancient Egypt*. Ithaca, N.Y., and London: Cornell University Press, 2003.

Third Intermediate and Late Periods

Der Manulian, Peter. *Living in the Past: Studies in Archaism of the Egyptian Twenty-Sixth Dynasty*. London: Kegan Paul International, 1994.

Gomaà, Farouk. *Die libyschen Fürstentümer des Delta vom Tod Osorkons II. Bis zur Wiedervereinigung Ägyptens durch Psametik I*. Beihefte zum Tübinger Atlas des Vorderen Orient B6. Wiesbaden, Germany: Dr. Ludwig Reichert Verlag, 1974.

Gosselin, Luc. *Les Divines Épouses d'Amon dans l'Égypte de la XIXe à la XXIe Dynastie*. Paris: Cybele, 2007.

Jansen-Winkeln, Karl. *Ägyptische Biographien der 22. und 23. Dynastie.* Wiesbaden, Germany: Otto Harrassowitz, 1985.

———. *Inschriften der Spätzeit I: Die 21. Dynastie.* Wiesbaden: Otto Harrassowitz, 2006.

Kienitz, Friedrich K. *Die politische Geschichte Ägyptens vom 7. bis zum 4. Jahrhundert vor der Zeitwende.* Berlin: Akademie Verlag, 1953.

Kitchen, Kenneth A. *The Third Intermediate Period in Egypt.* 4th ed. Warminster, G.B.: Aris & Phillips, 2007.

Leahy, Anthony. *Libya and Egypt c. 1300–750 BC.* London: SOAS, Centre of Near and Middle Eastern Studies and the Society for Libyan Studies, 1990.

Morkot, Robert G. *The Black Pharaohs.* London: Rubicon Press, 2000.

Perdu, Olivier. *Recueil des inscriptions royales saïtes I: Psammétique Ier.* Paris: Cybele, 2002.

Posener, Georges. *La première domination Perse en Égypte.* Cairo: Institut français d'archéologie orientale, 1936.

Rössler-Köhler, Ursula. *Individuelle Haltungen zum Ägyptischen Königtum der Spätzeit.* Wiesbaden, Germany: Otto Harrassowitz, 1991.

Vittmann, Günther. *Priester und Beamte im Theben der Spätzeit.* Vienna, Austria: Institut für Afrikanistik und Ägyptologie der Universität Wien, 1978.

Ptolemaic and Roman Periods

Adams, Colin. *Land Transport in Roman Egypt: A Study of Economics and Administration in a Roman Province.* Oxford, U.K.: Oxford University Press, 2007.

Ashton, Sally-Anne. *The Last Queens of Egypt.* London: Pearson, 2003.

Bagnall, Roger S. *Egypt in the Byzantine World, 300–700.* Cambridge, U.K.: Cambridge University Press, 2007.

———. *Egypt in Late Antiquity.* Princeton, N.J.: Princeton University Press, 1993.

———. *Hellenistic and Roman Egypt: Sources and Approaches.* Aldershot, Hampshire: Ashgate, 2006.

———. *Reading Papyri, Writing Ancient History.* London: Routledge, 1995.

Bagnall, Roger S., and Dominic W. Rathbone. *Egypt from Alexander to the Copts.* London: British Museum Press, 2004.

Bagnall, Roger S., and Raffaella Cribiore. *Women's Letters from Ancient Egypt, 300 BC–AD 800.* Ann Arbor: University of Michigan Press, 2006.

Bianchi, Robert, ed. *Cleopatra's Egypt: Age of the Ptolemies.* Brooklyn, N.Y.: Brooklyn Museum, 1989.

Bingen, Jean. *Hellenistic Egypt: Monarchy, Society, Economy, Culture.* Edinburgh, U.K.: Edinburgh University Press, 2007.

Bowman, Alan K. *Egypt after the Pharaohs, 332 BC–AD 642: From Alexander to the Arab Conquest*. London: British Museum Publications, 1986.

Burstein, Stanley. *The Reign of Cleopatra*. Westport, Conn.: Greenwood Press, 2004.

Capponi, Livia. *Augustan Egypt: The Creation of a Roman Province*. London and New York, Routledge, 2005.

Ellis, Simon. *Graeco-Roman Egypt*. Aylesbury, G.B.: Shire Publications, 1992.

Hölbl, Günther. *Altägypen im Römischen Reich*. 2 vols. Mainz am Rhein, Germany, Philipp von Zabern, 2000–2004.

———. *A History of the Ptolemaic Empire*. London and New York: Routledge, 2001.

Jones, Prudence J. *Cleopatra: A Sourcebook*. Norman: University of Oklahoma Press, 2006.

Parsons, Peter. *City of the Sharp-Nosed Fish: Greek Lives in Roman Egypt*. London: Weidenfeld & Nicolson, 2007.

Stanwick, Paul Edmund. *Portraits of the Ptolemies: Greek Kings as Egyptian Pharaohs*. Austin: University of Texas Press, 2002.

Thompson, Dorothy J. *Memphis under the Ptolemies*. Princeton, N.J.: Princeton University Press, 1988.

Veïsse, Anne-Emmanuelle. *Les Révoltes égyptiennes*. Louvain, Belgium: Peeters, 2004.

Walker, Susan, and Sally-Anne Ashton. *Cleopatra Reassessed*. London: British Museum Press, 2004.

Whitehorne, John. *Cleopatras*. London: Routledge, 1994.

Coptic Period

Atiya, Aziz A. *The Coptic Encyclopedia*. 8 vols. New York: Macmillan, 1991.

Badawy, Alexander. *Coptic Art and Archaeology: The Art of the Christian Egyptians from the Late Antique to the Middle Ages*. Cambridge, Mass.: MIT Press, 1978.

David, Stephen J, and Gawdat Gabra. *The Popes of Egypt. Vol I: The Early Coptic Papacy*. Cairo: American University in Cairo Press, 2004.

Frend, William H. C. *The Rise of the Monophysite Movement*. Cambridge, U.K.: Cambridge University Press, 1972.

Friedman, Florence D. *Beyond the Pharaohs*. Providence: Museum of Art, Rhode Island School of Design, 1989.

Gould, Graham. *The Desert Fathers on Monastic Community*. Oxford, U.K.: Clarendon Press, 1993.

Grossmann, Peter. *Christliche Architectur in Ägypten*. Leiden, Netherlands: Brill, 2002.

Kamil, Jill. *Christianity in the Land of the Pharaohs*. London and New York: Routledge, 2002.

MacCoull, Leslie. *Dioscorus of Aphrodito*. Berkeley: University of California Press, 1988.

Rousseau, Philip. *Pachomius*. Berkeley: University of California Press, 1985.

Rubenson, Samuel. *The Letters of St. Anthony*. Minneapolis, Minn.: Fortress Press, 1995.

Russell, Norman. *Cyril of Alexandria*. London: Routledge, 2000.

———. *Theophilus of Alexandria*. London: Routledge, 2007.

Timm, Stefan. *Ägypten: Das Christentum bis zur Araberzeit (bis zum 7. Jahrhundert)*. Wiesbaden, Germany: Dr. Ludwig Reichert Verlag, 1983.

———. *Das christlich-koptische Ägypten in arabischer Zeit*. 6 vols. Wiesbaden, Germany: Dr. Ludwig Reichert Verlag, 1984–1992.

Török, László. *After the Pharaohs: Treasures of Coptic Art from Egyptian Collections*. Budapest, Hungary: Museum of Fine Arts, Budapest, 2005.

The Bible and Egypt

Freedman, David Noel, ed. *The Anchor Bible Dictionary*. 6 vols. New York: Doubleday, 1992.

Frerichs, Ernest S., and Leonard H. Lesko, eds. *Exodus: The Egyptian Evidence*. Winona Lake, Ind.: Eisenbrauns, 1998.

Hoffmeier, James. *Israel in Egypt: The Evidence for the Authority of the Exodus Tradition*. Oxford, U.K.: Oxford University Press, 1997.

Kurth, Amélie. *The Ancient Near East, c. 3000–330 BC*. 2 vols. London: Routledge, 1995.

Mitchell, Terence C. *The Bible in the British Museum*. London: British Museum Publications, 1988.

Pritchard, James B. *The Ancient Near East in Pictures Relating to the Old Testament*. 3rd ed. Princeton, N.J.: Princeton University Press, 1974.

———. *Ancient Near Eastern Texts Relating to the Old Testament*. 2nd ed. Princeton, N.J.: Princeton University Press, 1955.

Rainey, Anson F. *Egypt, Israel, Sinai*. Tel Aviv, Israel: Tel Aviv University, 1987.

Redford, Donald B. *Egypt, Canaan, and Israel in Ancient Times*. Princeton, N.J.: Princeton University Press, 1992.

Tubb, Jonathan, and Rupert L. Chapman. *Archaeology and the Bible*. London: British Museum Publications, 1990.

NUBIA

Adams, William Y. *Nubia, Corridor to Africa*. London: Allen Lane, 1977.

Bonnet, Charles, and Dominique Valbelle. *The Nubian Pharaohs: Black Kings in the Nile*. Cairo: American University in Cairo Press, 2006.

Brooklyn Museum. *Africa in Antiquity: The Arts of Ancient Nubia and the Sudan*. 2 vols. Brooklyn, N.Y.: Brooklyn Museum, 1978.

Edwards, David N. *The Nubian Past: An Archaeology of the Sudan*. London: Routledge, 2004.

Eide, Tormod, Thomas Hägg, Richard Holton Pierce, and László Török. *Fontes Historiae Nubiorum*. 4 vols. Bergen, Norway: IKRR/Deptartment of Greek, Latin, and Egyptology, 1994–2000.

Säve-Söderbergh, Torgny. *Temples and Tombs of Ancient Nubia: The International Rescue Campaign at Abu Simbel, Philae, and Other Sites*. London: Thames & Hudson, 1987.

Taylor, John H. *Egypt and Nubia*. London: British Museum Press, 1991.

Trigger, Bruce C. *Nubia under the Pharaohs*. London: Thames & Hudson, 1976.

Welsby, Derek. *The Kingdom of Kush: The Napatan and Meroitic Empires*. London: British Museum Press, 1996.

——. *The Medieval Kingdoms of Nubia*. London: British Museum Press, 2002.

ARCHAEOLOGY: GENERAL

Assman, Jan, Gunter Burkhard, and W. V. Davies, eds. *Problems and Priorities in Egyptian Archaeology*. London: Kegan Paul International, 1987.

Bard, Kathryn A., ed. *Encyclopedia of the Archaeology of Ancient Egypt*. London and New York: Routledge, 1999.

——. *An Introduction to the Archaeology of Ancient Egypt*. Oxford, U.K.: Blackwell, 2007.

Brink, Edwin C. M. van den. *The Archaeology of the Nile Delta: Problems and Priorities*. Amsterdam: Netherlands Foundation for Archaeological Research in Egypt, 1988.

Butzer, Karl W. *Early Hydraulic Civilization in Egypt: A Study in Cultural Ecology*. Chicago: University of Chicago Press, 1976.

James, T. G. Henry, ed. *Excavating in Egypt: The Egypt Exploration Society, 1882–1982*. London: British Museum Publications, 1982.

Nims, Charles F. *Thebes of the Pharaohs*. London: Elek Books, 1965.

Vandier, Jacques. *Manuel d'archéologie égyptienne*. 6 vols. Paris: Éditions A. et J. Picard, 1952–1978.

ARCHAEOLOGY: EXCAVATIONS AND SURVEYS

Abu Mina

Grossman, Peter. *Abu Mina*. Cairo: Fotiadis and Co., 1986.
———. *Abu Mina I: Die Gruftkirche und die Gruft*. Deutsches Archäologisches Institut. Abteilung Kairo. Archäologische Veröffentlichungen 44. Mainz am Rhein, Germany: Philipp von Zabern, 1989.
———. *Abu Mina II: Das Baptisterium*. Deutsches Archäologisches Institut. Abteilung Kairo. Archäologische Veröffentlichungen 54. Mainz am Rhein, Germany: Philipp von Zabern, 2004.

Abu Roash

Bisson de la Roque, Fernand. *Rapport sur les fouilles d'Abu-Roasch*. 3 vols. Cairo: Institut français d'archéologie orientale, 1924–1925.
Swelim, Nabil. *The Brick Pyramid at Abu Rawash Number "I" by Lepsius: A Preliminary Study*. Alexandria, Va.: Archaeological Society of Alexandria, 1987.

Abu Simbel

el-Achirie, Hassan, and Jean Jacquet. *Le Grand Temple d'Abou Simbel. Vol. I.1. Architecture*. Cairo: Centre d'Etudes et de Documentation sur l'Ancienne Égypte, 1984.
Cerny, Jaroslav, and A. Ahmad. *Abou-Simbel: Chapelle de Rê-Herakhty*. Cairo: Centre de Documentation Égyptologique, 1963.
Desroches-Noblecourt, Christiane, and Charles Kuentz. *Le petit temple d'Abou Simbel*. Cairo: Centre d'Etudes et de Documentation sur l'Ancienne Égypte, 1968.
Desroches-Noblecourt, Christiane, Sergio Donadoni, and Gamal Mokhtar. *Le Grand Temple d'Abou Simbel. Vol. II. La Bataille de Qadesh*. Cairo: Centre d'Etudes et de Documentation sur l'Ancienne Égypte, 1971.
Donadoni, Sergio, and Hassan el-Achirie. *Le grand temple d'Abou Simbel*. Vol. 3. Cairo: Centre d'Etudes et de Documentation sur l'Ancienne Égypte, 1975.
el-Enany, Khaled. *Le Petit Temple d'Abou Simbel. Paléographie*. Cairo: Institut français d'archéologie orientale, 2007.

MacQuitty, William. *Abu Simbel*. London: Putnam, 1965.

Zecchi, Marco. *Abu Simbel, Aswan, and the Nubian Temples*. Vercelli, Italy: White Star Publications, 2004.

Abusir

Bares, Ladislav. *Abusir IV: The Shaft Tomb of Udjahorresnet at Abusir*. Prague, Czech Republic: Karolinum Press, 1999.

Bárta, Miroslav. *Abusir V: The Cemeteries at Abusir South I*. Prague, Czech Republic: Czech Institute of Egyptology, Charles University, 2001.

Bárta, Miroslav, and Jaromír Krejcí. *Abusir and Saqqara in the Year 2000*. Prague: Academy of Sciences of the Czech Republic, Oriental Institute, 2000.

Benesovska, Hanna, and Petra Vlckova, eds. *Abusir: Secrets of the Desert and the Pyramids*. Prague, Czech Republic: Czech Institute of Egyptology, Charles University, 2006.

Borchardt, Ludwig. *Das Grabdenkmal des Königs Nefer-ir-ke-re*. Leipzig, Germany: J. C. Hinrichs, 1909.

———. *Das Grabdenkmal des Königs Ne-user-re*. Leipzig, Germany: J. C. Hinrichs, 1907.

———. *Das Grabdenkmal des Königs Sa-hu-re*. Leipzig, Germany: J. C. Hinrichs, 1910–1913.

Charvát, Peter. *The Mastaba of Ptahshepses: The Pottery*. Prague, Czech Republic: Czech Institute of Egyptology, Charles University, 1981.

Krejci, Jaromir. *Abusir XI: The Architecture of the Mastaba of Ptahshepses*. Prague, Czech Republic: Czech Institute of Egyptology, Charles University, 2006.

Landgráfová, Renata. *Abusir XIV: Faience Inlays from the Funerary Temple of King Raneferef: Raneferef's Substitute Decoration Programme*. Prague, Czech Republic: Czech Institute of Egyptology, Charles University, 2006.

Navratilova, Hana. *The Visitors' Graffiti of Dynasties XVIII and XIX in Abusir and Northern Saqqara*. Prague, Czech Republic: Czech Institute of Egyptology, Charles University, 2007.

Posener-Kriéger, Paule. *Les archives du Temple funéraire de Néferirkare-Kakai (Les papyrus d'Abousir)*. Cairo: Institut français d'archéologie orientale, 1976.

Posener-Kriéger, Paule, Miroslav Verner, and Hana Vymazalovà. *Abusir X: The Pyramid Complex of Raneferef. The Papyrus Archive*. Prague: Czech Institute of Egyptology, Charles University, 2006.

Smoláriková, Kveta. *Abusir VII: Greek Imports in Egypt*. Prague, Czech Republic: Czech Institute of Egyptology, Charles University, 2002.

Strouhal, Eugen, and Ladislav Bares. *Secondary Cemetery in the Mastaba of Ptahshepses at Abusir*. Prague, Czech Republic: Czech Institute of Egyptology, Charles University, 1993.

Vachala, Bretislav. *Abusir VIII: Die Relieffragmente aus der Mastaba des Ptahschepses in Abusir*. Prague, Czech Republic: Czech Institute of Egyptology, Charles University, 2004.

Verner, Miroslav. *Abusir: The Realm of Osiris*. Cairo: University of Cairo Press, 2002.

———. *Abusir I: The Mastaba of Ptahshepses Reliefs*. Prague, Czech Republic: Czech Institute of Egyptology, Charles University, 1977.

———. *Abusir II: Baugraffiti der Ptahschepses Mastaba*. Prague, Czech Republic: Czech Institute of Egyptology, Charles University, 1992.

———. *Abusir III: The Pyramid Complex of Khentkaus*. Prague, Czech Republic: Czech Institute of Egyptology, Charles University, 1995.

Verner, Miroslav, and Vivienne G. Callender. *Abusir VI: Djedkare's Family Cemetery*. Prague, Czech Republic: Czech Institute of Egyptology, Charles University, 2002.

Verner, Miroslav, Barta Miroslav, and Hana Benesovska. *Abusir IX: The Pyramid Complex of Raneferef*. Prague, Czech Republic: Czech Institute of Egyptology, Charles University, 2006.

Vlckovà, Petra, Petra Vickov, and Jaromer Leichmann. *Abusir XV: The Stone Vessels from the Mortuary Complex of Raneferef at Abusir*. Prague, Czech Republic: Czech Institute of Egyptology, Charles University, 2006.

Abydos

Abdalla, Aly. *Graeco-Roman Funerary Stelae from Upper Egypt*. Liverpool, U.K.: Liverpool University Press, 1992.

Amelineau, Émile. *Les nouvelles fouilles d'Abydos*. 4 vols. Paris: Ernest Leroux, 1899–1905.

———. *Le tombeau d'Osiris*. Paris: Ernest Leroux, 1899.

Ayrton, Edward R., C. T. Currelly, and A. E. P. Weigall, eds. *Abydos Part III*. London: Egypt Exploration Fund, 1904.

Calverley, Amice M. *The Temple of King Sethos I at Abydos*. 4 vols. London and Chicago: Egypt Exploration Society and University of Chicago Press, 1933–1958.

Dreyer, Gunter. *Umm El-Qaab I. Das präadynastische Köningsgrab U-j und seinefrühen Schriftzeugnisse*. Deutsches Archäologisches Institut Abteilung Kairo. Archäologische Veröffentlichungen 86. Mainz am Rhein, Germany: Philipp von Zabern, 1998.

Frankfort, Henri. *The Cenotaph of Seti I at Abydos*. London: Egypt Exploration Society, 1930.

Hartung, Ulrich. *Umm El-Qaab II. Importkeramik aus den Friedhof U in Abydos (Umm el-Qaab) und die Beziehungen Ägyptens zu Vorderasien im 4. Tausend v. Ch.* Deutsches Archäologisches Institut Abteilung Kairo. Archäologische Veröffentlichungen 92. Mainz am Rhein, Germany: Philipp von Zabern, 2001.

Mariette, Auguste. *Abydos: Description des fouilles exécutées sur l'emplacement de cette ville*. 2 vols. Paris: A. Franck, 1869–1880.

——. *Catalogue général des monuments d'Abydos découverts pendant les fouilles de cette ville*. Paris: Imprimerie nationale, 1880.

Murray, Margaret. *The Osireion at Abydos*. London: Egyptian Research Account, A. Franck, 1904.

Naville, Édouard, and Thomas E. Peet. *The Cemeteries of Abydos*. 3 vols. London: Egypt Exploration Fund, 1913–1914.

Petrie, W. M. Flinders. *Abydos*. 2 vols. London: Egypt Exploration Fund, 1902–1903.

——. *The Royal Tombs of the Earliest Dynasties*. 2 vols. London: Egypt Exploration Fund, 1900–1901.

Simpson, William Kelly. *Inscribed Material from the Pennsylvania-Yale Excavations at Abydos*. New Haven, Conn., and Philadelphia, Pa.: Peabody Museum of Natural History of Yale University and University of Pennsylvania Museum of Archaeology and Anthropology, 1995.

——. *The Terrace of the Great God at Abydos: The Offering Chapels of Dynasties 12 and 13*. New Haven, Conn., and Philadelphia, Pa.: Peabody Museum of Natural History of Yale University and University of Pennsylvania Museum of Archaeology and Anthropology, 1974.

Wegner, Josef. *The Mortuary Temple of Senwosret III at Abydos*. New Haven, Conn., and Philadelphia, Pa.: Peabody Museum of Natural History of Yale University and University of Pennsylvania Museum of Archaeology and Anthropology, 2007.

Adaima

Crubézy, Eric, Thierry Janin, and Béatrix Midant-Reynes. *Adaima II. La nécropole prédynastique*. Institut français d'archéologie orientale, 2002.

Midant-Reynes, Béatrix, and Nathalie Buchez. *Adaima I. Économie et Habitat*. Cairo: Institut français d'archéologie orientale, 2002.

Akhmim

Egberts, Arno, B. P. Muchs, and J. Van Der Vliet, eds. *Perspectives on Panopolis: An Egyptian Town from Alexander the Great to the Arab Conquest.* Leiden, Netherlands: Brill, 2002.

Hope, Colin, and Anne McFarlane. *Akhmim in the Old Kingdom. Part 2.* Sydney: Australian Centre for Egyptology, Macquarie University, 2006.

Kanawati, Naguib. *A Mountain Speaks: The First Australian Excavation in Egypt.* Sydney: Australian Centre for Egyptology, Macquarie University, 1988.

———. *The Rock Tombs of el-Hawawish: The Cemetery of Akhmim.* 10 vols. Sydney: Australian Centre for Egyptology, Macquarie University, 1980–1992.

Kuhlman, Klaus. *Materialien zur Archäologie und Geschichte des Raumes von Achmim.* Mainz am Rhein, Germany: Philipp von Zabern, 1983.

McNally, Sheila, and Ivancica D. Schrunk. *Excavations in Akhmim, Egypt: Continuity and Change in City Life from Late Antiquity to the Present.* BAR International Series 590. Oxford, U.K.: BAR, 1993.

Ockinga, Boyo G. *A Tomb from the Reign of Tutankhamun at Akhmim.* Warminster, G.B.: Aris & Phillips, 1998.

Akoris

Kawanishi, Hiroyuki, and Y. Suto. *Akoris: Report of the Excavations at Akoris in Middle Egypt, 1981–1992.* Kyoto: Palaeological Association of Japan, Inc., 1995.

Alexandria

Borkowski, Zbigniew. *Alexandrie II: Inscriptions des factions à Alexandrie.* Warsaw, Poland: PWN-Éditions scientifiques de Pologne, 1981.

Empereur, Jean-Yves. *Alexandria Rediscovered.* London: British Museum Press, 1998.

———. *Alexandrina 1–2.* Cairo: Institut français d'archéologie orientale, 1998–2001.

Empereur, Jean-Yves, and Marie-Dominique Nenna. *Necropolis 1–2.* Cairo: Institut français d'archéologie orientale, 2001–2003.

Goddio, Franck. *Topography and Excavation of Heracleion-Thonis and East Canopus (1996–2006). Underwater Archaeology in the Canopic Region in Egypt.* Oxford, U.K.: Oxford Centre for Maritime Archaeology, 2007.

Goddio, Franck, and André Bernard. *Sunken Egypt.* London, Periplus, 2004.

Goddio, Franck, and Manfred Clauss. *Sunken Treasures.* Munich, Germany: Prestel, 2006.

Goddio, Franck, Andre Bernand, Etienne Bernand, Ibrahim Darwish, Zsolt Kiss, and Jean Yoyotte. *Alexandria: The Submerged Royal Quarters.* London: Periplus, 1998.

Grimm, Günter. *Alexandria: Die eiste Königsstadt der hellenistischen Welt.* Mainz am Rhein, Germany: Philipp von Zabern, 1998.

Kiss, Zsolt. *Alexandrie V: Les ampoules de Saint Ménas découvertes à Kôm el-Dikka (1961–1981).* Warsaw, Poland: PWN-Éditions scientifiques de Pologne, 1988.

———. *Alexandrie IV: Sculptures des fouilles polonaises à Kôm el-Dikka (1960–1982).* Warsaw, Poland: PWN-Éditions scientifiques de Pologne, 1988.

Kiss, Zsolt, Grzegorz Majcherek, and Henryk Meyza. *Alexandrie VII: Fouilles polonaises à Kôm el-Dikka (1986–1987).* Warsaw, Poland: ZAS PAN, 2000.

Kolataj, Wojciech. *Alexandrie VI: Imperial Baths at Kom-el-Dikka.* Warsaw, Poland: Zaklad Archeologii Srodziemnomorskiej Polskiej Akademii Nauk, 1992.

Kolataj, Wojciech, Grzegorz Majcherek, and Ewa Parandowska. *Villa of the Birds: The Excavation and Preservation of the Kom el-Dikka Mosaics.* Cairo: American University in Cairo Press, 2007.

La Riche, William. *Alexandria: The Sunken City.* London: Weidenfeld & Nicholson, 1996.

Nenna, Marie-Dominique, and Mervate Seif-el-din. *La vaisselle en faience de l'époque gréco-romaine.* Cairo: Institut français d'archéologie orientale, 2000.

Rodziewicz, Mieczyslaw. *Alexandrie I: La céramique romaine tardive d'Alexandrie.* Warsaw, Poland: PWN-Éditions scientifiques de Pologne, 1976.

———. *Alexandrie III: Les habitations romaines tardives d'Alexandrie à la lumière des fouilles polonaises à Kôm el-Dikka.* Warsaw, Poland: PWN-Editions scientifiques de Pologne, 1984.

Steen, Gareth L., ed. *Alexandria: the Site and the History.* New York: New York University Press, 1993.

Tkaczow, Barbara. *Topography of Ancient Alexandria (An Archaeological Map).* Travaux du Centre d'Archéologie Méditerranéenne de l'Académie Polonaise des Sciences No. 32. Warsaw, Poland: Zaklad Archeologii Srodziemnomorskiej Polskiej Akademii Nauk, 1993.

Venit, Marjorie S. *Monumental Tombs of Ancient Alexandria: The Theater of the Dead*. Cambridge, U.K.: Cambridge University Press, 2002.

Amada

el-Achiery, Hassan, Paul Barguet, and Michel Dewachter. *Le Temple d'Amada*. 5 vols. Cairo: Centre d'Etudes et de Documentation sur l'Ancienne Égypte, 1967.
Gauthier, Henri. *Le Temple d'Amada*. Cairo: Institut français d'archéologie orientale, 1913–1926.

Amara West

Spencer, Patricia A. *Amara West I: The Architectural Report*. London: Egypt Exploration Society, 1997.
———. *Amara West II: The Cemetery and the Pottery Corpus*. London: Egypt Exploration Society, 2002.

Amarna

Borchardt, Ludwig, and Herbert Ricke. *Die Wohnhäuser in Tell el-Amarna*. Berlin, Germany: Gebr. Mann, 1980.
Davies, Norman de Garis. *The Rock Tombs of El Amarna*. 6 vols. London: Egypt Exploration Fund, 1903–1908.
Faiers, Jane. *Late Roman Pottery at Amarna and Related Studies*. London: Egypt Exploration Society, 2005.
Kemp, Barry J., ed. *Amarna Reports*. 6 vols. London: Egypt Exploration Society, 1984–1995.
Kemp, Barry. J., and Fran Weatherhead. *The Main Chapel at the Amarna Workmen's Village and Its Wall Paintings*. London: Egypt Exploration Society, 2007.
Kemp, Barry J., and Gillian Vogelsang-Eastwood. *The Ancient Textile Industry at Amarna*. London: Egypt Exploration Society, 2001.
Kemp, Barry J., and Salvatore Garfi. *A Survey of the Ancient City of el-Amarna*. London: Egypt Exploration Society, 1993.
el-Khouly, Aly, and Geoffrey T. Martin. *Excavations in the Royal Necropolis at El-'Amarna*. Supplément aux Annales du Service des Antiquités de l'Égypte No. 33. Cairo: Service des Antiquités de l'Égypte, 1987.
Kuckertz, Josephine. *Gefässverschlüsse aus Tell el-Amarna: Grabungen der Deutschen Orient-Gesellschaft 1911 bis 1914: Sozio-ökonomische Aspekte einer Fundgattung des Neuen Reiches*. Saarbrücken, Germany: Saarbrüker Druuckerei und Verlag, 2003.

Martin, Geoffrey T. *The Royal Tomb at el-Amarna*. 2 vols. London: Egypt Exploration Society, 1974–1989.

Murnane, William J., and Charles C. Van Siclen. *The Boundary Stelae of Akhenaten*. London: Kegan Paul International, 1993.

Nicholson, Paul. *Brilliant Things for Akhenaten: The Production of Glass, Vitreous Materials, and Pottery at Amarna Site 045.1*. London: Egypt Exploration Society, 2007.

Peet, Thomas E., and C. L. Woolleyl. *The City of Akhenaten*. 3 vols. London: Egypt Exploration Society, 1923–1951.

Petrie, W. M. Flinders. *Tell el-Amarna*. London: Methuen & Co., 1894.

Rose, Pamela J. *The Eighteenth Dynasty Pottery Corpus from Amarna*. London: Egypt Exploration Society, 2007.

Smith, Wendy. *Archaeobotanical Investigations of Agriculture at Late Antique Kom el-Nana (Tell el-Amarna)*. London: Egypt Exploration Society, 2003.

Stevens, Anna. *Private Religion at Amarna: The Material Evidence*. Oxford, U.K.: BAR, 2006.

Weatherhead, Fran. *Amarna Palace Paintings*. London: Egypt Exploration Society, 2007.

Aniba

Heykal, Faiza, and Abdul Moneim Abou-Bakr. *Tombeau de Pennout à Aniba*. Cairo: Centre de Documentation Égyptologique, 1963.

Steindorff, Georg. *Aniba*. 2 vols. Glückstadt, Germany: Service des Antiquités de l'Égypte, 1935–1937.

Antinoopolis

Calament, Florence. *La Révélation d'Antinoé par Albert Gayet*. Histoire, Archéologie, Muséographie. Cairo: Institut français d'archéologie orientale, 2005.

Hunt, Arthur S., and John Johnson. *Two Theocritus Papyri*. London: Egypt Exploration Society, 1930.

Roberts, Colin H., John Barnes, and Henrik Zilliacus. *The Antinoopolis Papyri I–III*. London: Egypt Exploration Society, 1950–1967.

Armant

Mond, Robert, and Oliver H. Myers. *The Bucheum*. 3 vols. London: Egypt Exploration Society, 1934.

———. *Cemeteries of Armant I*. London: Egypt Exploration Society, 1937.

———. *Temples of Armant: A Preliminary Survey*. London: Egypt Exploration Society, 1940.

Thiers, Christophe, and Youri Volokhine. *Ermant I: Les cryptes du temple ptolémaïque*. Cairo: Institut français d'archéologie orientale, 2005.

Askut

Smith, Stuart T. *Askut in Nubia*. London: Kegan Paul International, 1995.

Athribis (Lower Egypt)

Mysliwiec, Karol, and Zofia Sztetyllo. *Tell Atrib 1985–1995 I*. Warsaw, Poland: Editions Neriton, 2000.

Vernus, Pascal. *Athribis*. Cairo: Institut français d'archéologie orientale, 1978.

Athribis (Upper Egypt)

Kanawati, Naguib. *The Tombs of El-Hagarsa I–III*. Sydney: Australian Centre for Egyptology, 1993–1995.

Petrie, W. M. Flinders. *Athribis*. London: British School of Archaeology in Egypt, 1908.

Avaris

Bader, Bettina. *Tell el-Dab'a XIII: Typologie und Chronologie der Mergel C-Ton Keramik. Materialen zum Binnenhandel des Mittleren Reiches und der zweiten Zwischenzeit*. Vienna, Austria: Östereichische Akademie der Wissenschaften, 2001.

Bietak, Manfred. *Avaris, Capital of the Hyksos: Recent Excavations*. London: British Museum Press, 1996.

———. *Avaris and Piramesse*. 2nd ed. Oxford, U.K.: Oxford University Press, 1986.

———. *Tell el-Dab'a II: Der Fundort im Rahmen einer archäologisch-geographischen Untersuchung über das ägyptische Ostdelta*. Vienna, Austria: Österreichische Akademie der Wissenschaften, 1975.

Bietak, Manfred. *Tell el-Dab'a V: Ein Friedhofsbezirk der Mittleren Bronzezeit mit Totentempel und Siedlungsschichten*. Vienna, Austria: Österreichische Akademie der Wissenschaften, 1991.

Boessneck, Joachim. *Tell el-Dab'a III: Die Tierknochenfunde 1966–1969*. Vienna, Austria: Österreichische Akademie der Wissenschaften, 1976.

Boessneck, Joachim, and Angela von den Driesch. *Tell el-Dab'a VII: Tiere und historische Umwelt im Norost-Delta im Jahrtausend anhand der Knochenfunde der Ausgrabungen 1975–1986*. Vienna, Austria: Österreichische Akademie der Wissenschaften, 1991.

Czerny, Ernst. *Tell el-Dab'a IX: Eine Plansiedlung des frühen Mittleren Reiches*. Vienna, Austria: Östereichische Akademie der Wissenschaften, 1999.

Fuscaldo, Perla. *Tell el-Dab'a X: The Palace District of Avaris. The Pottery of the Hyksos Period and the New Kingdom (Areas H/III and H/VI), Part I: Locus 66*. Vienna, Austria: Östereichische Akademie der Wissenschaften, 2000.

Habachi, Labib. *Tell el-Dab'a I: Tell el-Dab'a and Qantir. The Site and Its Connection with Avaris and Piramesse*. Vienna, Austria: Östereichische Akademie der Wissenschaften, 2001.

Hein, Irmgard, and Peter Jánosi. *Tell el-Dab'a XI: Area A/V, siedlungsrelikte der späten Hyksoszeit*. Vienna, Austria: Östereichische Akademie der Wissenschaften, 2001.

Philip, Graham. *Tell el-Dab'a XV: Metalwork and Metalworking Evidence of the Late Middle Kingdom and the Second Intermediate Period*. Vienna, Austria: Östereichische Akademie der Wissenschaften, 2006.

Winkler, Eike-Meinrad, and Harald Wilfling. *Tell el-Dab'a VI: Anthropologische Untersuchungen an der Skelettresten der Kampagnen 1966–1969, 1975–1980, 1985*. Vienna, Austria: Östereichische Akademie der Wissenschaften, 1991.

Bacchias

Bitelli, Gabriele, ed. *The Bologna and Lecce Universities Joint Archaeological Mission in Egypt: Ten Years of Excavations at Bakchias (1993–2002)*. Naples, Italy: Centro di Studi Papirologici dell'a Università degli Studi di Lecce, 2003.

Davoli, Paola. *Oggetti in Angilla dall'area Templare di Bakchias (El-Fayyum, Egitto)*. Pisa, Italy: Giardini Editore, 2005.

Pernigotti, Sergio. *Gli dèi di Bakchias e altri Studi sul Fayyum di età tolemaica e romana*. Imola, Italy: Editrice La Mandragora, 2000.

Pernigotti, Sergio, and Mario Copasso. *Bakchias*. Naples, Italy: Procaccini, 1994.

Pernigotti, Sergio, Mario Copasso, and Paola Davoli. *Bakchias I–IX. Rapporto Preliminare della Campagna di Scavo 1993–2001*. Pisa and Imola, Italy: Giardini Editori and Editrice La Mandragora, 1994–2003.

Badari, el-

Brunton, Guy, Alan Gardiner, and Flinders Petrie. *Qau and Badari*. 3 vols. London: British School of Archaeology in Egypt, 1927–1930.
Brunton, Guy, and Gertrude Caton-Thompson. *The Badarian Civilisation and Prehistoric Remains near Badari*. London: British School of Archaeology in Egypt, 1928.

Bahariya Oasis

Fakhry, Ahmed. *Bahria Oasis*. 2 vols. Cairo: Government Press, 1942–1950.
———. *The Oases of Egypt II: Bahriyah and Farafra Oases*. Cairo: American University in Cairo Press, 1974.
Giddy, Lisa. *Egyptian Oases*. Warminster, G.B.: Aris & Phillips, 1987.
Hawass, Zahi. *Valley of the Golden Mummies*. London: Virgin Publishing, 2000.

Ballana and Qustul

Emery, Walter B., and Laurence P. Kirwan. *The Royal Tombs of Ballana and Qustul*. Cairo: Service des Antiquités de l'Égypte, 1938.
Farid, Shafik. *Excavations at Ballana 1958–1959*. Cairo: Antiquities Department of Egypt, 1963.
Williams, Bruce B. *Excavations between Abu Simbel and the Sudan Frontier*. Oriental Institute Nubia Expedition. 9 vols. Chicago: Oriental Institute of the University of Chicago, 1986–1991.

Bawit

Boud'hours, Anne. *Ostraca Grecs et Coptes des Fouilles de Jean Maspero à Baouit*. Cairo: Institut français d'archéologie orientale, 2004.
Clédat, Jean. *Le monastère et la nécropole de Baouit*. Cairo: Institut français d'archéologie orientale, 1999.

Beni Hasan

Newberry, Percy E., George W. Fraser, and M. Naville. *Beni Hasan*. 4 vols. London: 1893–1900.
Shedid, Abdel Ghaffar. *Die Felsgräber von Beni Hassan in Mittelägypten*. Zaberns Bildbände zur Archäologie 16. Mainz am Rhein, Germany: Philipp von Zabern, 1994.

Berenike

Bagnall, Roger S., Christina Helms, and Arthur Verhoogt. *Documents from Berenike I–II*. Brussels, Belgium: Fondation Égyptologique Reine Élisabeth, 2000–2005.

Cappers, René. *Roman Food Prints at Berenike*. Leiden, Netherlands: Research School CNWS, 2006.

Leguilloux, Martine. *Les objets en cuir de Didymoi. Praesidium de la route caravanière Coptos-Bérénice*. Cairo: Institut français d'archéologie orientale, 2006.

Sidebotham, Steven, and Willeke Z. Wendrich. Wendrich. *Berenike 1994*. Leiden, Netherlands: Research School CNWS, 1995.

———. *Berenike 1995*. Leiden, Netherlands: Research School CNWS, 1996.

———. *Berenike 1996*. Leiden, Netherlands: Research School CNWS, 1998.

———. *Berenike 1997*. Leiden, Netherlands: Research School CNWS, 1999.

———. *Berenike 1998*. Leiden, Netherlands: Research School CNWS, 2000.

Wendrich, Willeke Z., and Steven E. Sidebotham. *Berenike 1999–2000*. Leiden, Netherlands: Research School CNWS, 2006.

Bubastis

Bakr, Mohamed I. *Tell Basta I: Tombs and Burial Customs at Bubastis. The Area of the So-Called Western Cemetery*. Cairo: Egyptian Antiquities Organization, 1992.

Habachi, Labib. *Tell Basta*. Supplément aux Anales du Service des Antiquités de l'Égypte No. 22. Cairo: Service des Antiquités de l'Égypte, 1957.

Naville, Édouard. *Bubastis (1887–1889)*. London: Egypt Exploration Fund, 1891.

el-Sawi, Ahmad. *Excavations at Tell Basta*. Prague, Czech Republic: Charles University, 1979.

Spencer, Neal. *A Naos of Nekhthorheb from Bubastis: Religious Iconography and Temple Building in the 30th Dynasty*. London: British Museum Press, 2006.

Tietze, Christian, and Mohamed Abd El Maksoud. *Tell Basta. Ein Führer über das Grabungsgelände*. Potsdam, Germany: Universitätsverlag, 2004.

Buhen

Caminos, Ricardo. *The New-Kingdom Temples of Buhen.* 2 vols. London: Egypt Exploration Society, 1974.

Emery, Walter B., Henry S. Smith, B. J. Kemp, Geoffrey T. Martin, and D. B. O'Connor. *The Fortress of Buhen.* 2 vols. London: Egypt Exploration Society, 1976–1979.

Buto

Köhler, E. Christiana. *Tell el-Faraîn: Buto III. Die Keramik von der späten Naqada-Kultur bis zum frülen Alten Reich.* Deutsches Archäologisches Institut. Abteilung Kairo. Archäologische Veröffentlichungen 94. Mainz am Rhein, Germany: Philipp von Zabern, 1998.

Von der Way, Thomas. *Tell el-Faraîn: Buto I. Ergebnisse zum fruhen Kontext Kampagnen der Jahre 1983–1989.* Deutsches Archäologisches Institut. Abteilung Kairo. Archäologische Veröffentlichungen 83. Mainz am Rhein, Germany: Philipp von Zabern, 1997.

Coptos

Herbert, Sharon C., and Andrea M. Berlin. *Excavations at Coptos (Qift) in Upper Egypt, 1987–1992.* Portsmouth, Rhode Island: Kelsey Museum, 2003.

Petrie, W. M. Flinders. *Koptos.* London: Bernard Quaritch Ltd., 1896.

Reinach, Adolphe J. *Rapport sur les fouilles de Koptos.* Paris: Ernest Leroux, 1910.

Traunecker, Claude. *Coptos. Hommes et Dieux sur le parvis de Geb.* Louvain, Belgium: Peeters, 1992.

Dahshur

Arnolf, Dieter. *The Pyramid Complex of Senwosret III at Dahshur: Architectural Studies.* New York: Metropolitan Museum of Art, 2002.

———. *Der Pyramidenbezirk des Königs Amenemhet III in Dahschur.* Deutsches Archäologisches Institut. Abteilung Kairo. Archäologische Veröffentlichungen 53. Mainz am Rhein, Germany: Philipp von Zabern, 1987.

Fakhry, Ahmed. *The Monuments of Sneferu at Dahshur.* 2 vols. Cairo: Government Printing Office, 1959–1961.

Morgan, Jacques de. *Fouilles à Dahchour.* 2 vols. Vienna: A. Holzhausen, 1895–1903.

Dakhla Oasis

Bowen, Gillian E., and Colin A. Hope. *The Oasis Papers III*. Oxford, U.K.: Oxbow Books, 2004.

Castel, Georges, and Laure Pantalacci. *Balat VII: Les cimitières est et ouest du masataba de Khentika*. Cairo: Institut français d'archéologie orientale, 2005.

Castel, Georges, Laure Pantalacci, and Nadine Cherpion. *Balat V: Le mastaba de Khentika*. Cairo: Institut français d'archéologie orientale, 2001.

Churcher, Charles S., and Anthony J. Mills. *Reports from the Survey of the Dakhleh Oasis, 1977–87*. Oxford, U.K.: Oxbow Books, 1999.

Fakhry, Ahmed. *Denkmäler der Oase Dachla*. Deutsches Archäologisches Institut. Abteilung Kairo. Archäologische Veröffentlichungen 28. Mainz am Rhein, Germany: Philipp von Zabern, 1982.

Gardner, Iain. *Kellis Literary Texts I–II*. Oxford, U.K.: Oxbow Books, 1997–2007.

Gardner, Iain, Anthony Alcock, and Wolf-Peter Funk. *Coptic Documentary Texts from Kellis I*. Oxford, U.K.: Oxbow Books, 1997.

Giddy, Lisa. *The Egyptian Oases*. Warminster, G.B.: Aris & Phillips, 1987.

Hope, Colin A., and Antony J. Mills. *Dakhleh Oasis Project: Preliminary Reports on the 1992–1993 and 1993–1994 Field Seasons*. Oxford, U.K.: Oxbow Books, 1999.

Hope, Colin A., and Gillian E. Bowen. *Dakhleh Oasis Project: Preliminary Reports on the 1994–1995 to 1998–1999 Field Seasons*. Oxford, U.K.: Oxbow Books, 2002.

Marlow, C. A., and Anthony J. Mills. *The Oasis Papers I*. Oxford, U.K.: Oxbow Books, 2001.

Midant-Reynes, Béatrix. *Le silex de 'Ayn-Aysil Oasis de Dakhla-Balat*. Cairo: Institut français d'archéologie orientale, 1998.

Minault-Gout, Anne. *Balat II: Le mastaba d'Ima-pépi*. Cairo: Institut français d'archéologie orientale, 1992.

Schijns, Wolf, Olaf Kaper, and Joris Kila. *Vernacular Mudbrick Architecture in the Dakhleh Oasis, Egypt*. Oxford, U.K.: Oxbow Books, 2003.

Soukiassian, Georges, Michel Wuttmann, and Laure Pantalacci. *Balat VI: Le palais des gouverneurs de l'époque de Pépy II: Les sanctuaires de ka et leurs dépendences*. Cairo: Institut français d'archéologie orientale, 2002.

Soukiassian, Georges, Michel Wuttmann, Laure Pantalacci, Pascale Ballet, and Maurice Picon. *Balat III: Les ateliers de potiers d'Ayn Asil*. Cairo: Institut français d'archéologie orientale, 1990.

Vallogia, Michel P. *Balat I: Le mastaba de Medou-Nefer*. Cairo: Institut français d'archéologie orientale, 1986.

———. *Balat IV: Le monument funéraire d'Ima-Pepy/Ima-Meryrê*. Cairo: Institut français d'archéologie orientale, 1998.

Willeitner, Joachim. *Die ägyptischen Oasen*. Mainz am Rhein, Germany: Philipp von Zabern, 2003.

Winlock, Herbert E., ed. *Dakhleh Oasis*. New York: Metropolitan Museum of Art, 1936.

Wiseman, Marcia F. *The Oasis Papers II*. Oxford, U.K.: Oxbow Books, 2004.

Worp, Klaas A. *Greek Ostraca from Kellis*. Oxford, U.K.: Oxbow Books, 2004.

———. *Greek Papyri from Kellis I*. Oxford, U.K.: Oxbow Books, 1995.

———. *The Kellis Isocrates Codex*. Oxford, U.K.: Oxbow Books, 1997.

Deir el-Bahri

Arnold, Dieter. *Der Tempel des Königs Mentuhotep von Deir el-Bahari I: Architectur und Deuting*. Deutsches Archäologisches Institut. Abteilung Kairo. Archäologische Veröffentlichungen 8. Mainz am Rhein, Germany: Philipp von Zabern, 1974.

———. *Der Tempel des Königs Mentuhotep von Deir el-Bahari II: Die Wandreliefs des Sanktuares*. Deutsches Archäologisches Institut. Abteilung Kairo. Archäologische Veröffentlichungen 11. Mainz am Rhein, Germany: Philipp von Zabern, 1974.

———. *Der Tempel des Königs Mentuhotep von Deir el-Bahari III: Die Königlichen Beigaben*. Deutsches Archäologisches Institut. Abteilung Kairo. Archäologische Veröffentlichungen 23. Mainz am Rhein, Germany: Philipp von Zabern, 1981.

———. *The Temple of Mentuhotep at Deir el-Bahari*. Publications of the Metropolitan Museum of Art Egyptian Expedition 21. New York: Metropolitan Museum of Art, 1979.

Godlewski, Wlodzomierz. *Deir el-Bahari V: Le monastère de St. Phoibammon*. Warsaw, Poland: PWN-Éditions scientifiques de Pologne, 1986.

Hayes, William C. *Ostraca and Name Stones from the Tomb of Sen-Mut (No. 71) at Thebes*. New York: Metropolitan Museum of Art, 1942.

Karkowski, Janusz. *Deir el-Bahari VI: The Temple of Hatshepsut. The Solar Complex*. Warsaw, Poland: ZAS-PAN, 2002.

Laskowska-Kusztal, Ewa. *Deir el-Bahari III: Le sanctuaire ptolémaique de Deir el-Bahari*. Warsaw, Poland: PWN-Éditions scientifiques de Pologne, 1984.

Latjar, Adam. *Deir el-Bahari in the Hellenistic and Roman Periods: A Study of an Egyptian Temple Based on Greek Sources*. Warsaw, Poland: Institute of Archaeology, Warsaw University, 2006.

Lipinska, Jadwiga. *Deir el-Bahari II: The Temple of Tuthmosis III. Architecture*. Warsaw, Poland: PWN-Éditions scientifiques de Pologne, 1977.

——. *Deir el-Bahari IV: The Temple of Tuthmosis IV. Statuary and Votive Monuments.* Warsaw, Poland: PWN-Éditions scientifiques de Pologne, 1984.

Marciniak, Marek. *Deir el-Bahari I: Les inscriptions hiératiques du temple de Thoutmosis III.* Warsaw, Poland: PWN-Éditions scientifiques de Pologne, 1974.

Maspero, Gaston. *La trouvaille de Deir-el-bahari.* Cairo: F. Mourés and Cie, 1881.

Naville, Édouard. *The Temple of Deir el-Bahari.* 7 vols. London: Egypt Exploration Fund, 1894–1908.

Winlock, Herbert E. *Excavations at Deir el-Bahari, 1911–1931.* New York: Macmillan, 1942.

——. *Models of Daily Life in Ancient Egypt from the Tomb of Meket-re' at Thebes.* Cambridge, Mass.: Metropolitan Museum of Art, 1955.

——. *The Slain Soldiers of Neb-hepet-rec Mentu-hotpe.* New York: Metropolitan Museum of Art, 1945.

Deir el-Ballas

Lacovara, Peter. *Deir el-Ballas: Preliminary Report on the Deir el-Ballas Expedition, 1980–1986.* Winona Lake, Ind.: Eisenbrauns, 1990.

——. *The New Kingdom Royal City.* London: Kegan Paul, 1997.

Deir el-Bersha

Brovarski, Edward. *Bersheh Reports I,* ed. D. P. Silverman. Boston: Museum of Fine Arts, 1992.

Newberry, Percy E., and Francis L. Griffiths. *El-Bersheh.* 2 vols. London: Egypt Exploration Fund, 1892.

Willems, Harco. *Dayr al-Barsha I: The Rock Tombs of Djehutinakht (No. 17K74/1), Khnumnakht (No. 17K74/2), and Iha (No. 17K74/3).* Louvain, Belgium: Peeters, 2007.

Deir el-Gebrawi

Davies, Norman de Garis. *The Rock Tombs of Deir el-Gebrâwi.* London: Egypt Exploration Fund, 1902.

Kanawati, Naguib. *Deir el-Gebrawi I: The Northern Cliff.* Australian Centre for Egyptology. Oxford, U.K.: Aris & Phillips, 2005.

——. *Deir el-Gebrawi II: The Southern Cliff.* London: Australian Centre for Egyptology, 2006.

Deir el-Medina

Andreu, Guillemette. *Deir el-Médineh et la Valleé des Rois*. Paris: Editions Khéops, 2003.

Bierbrier, Morris. *The Tomb-Builders of the Pharaohs*. New ed. Cairo: American University in Cairo Press, 1989.

Bruyère, Bernard. *Mert Seger à Deir el-Médineh*. 2 vols. Cairo: Institut français d'archéologie orientale, 1929–1930.

———. *Rapport sur les fouilles de Deir el Médineh*. 17 vols. Cairo: Institut français d'archéologie orientale, 1924–1953.

———. *La tombe no 1 de Sen-nedjem à Deir el-Médineh*. Cairo: Institut français d'archéologie orientale, 1959.

———. *Tombes à décors monochromes*. Cairo: Institut français d'archéologie orientale, 1952.

Bruyère, Bernard, and Charles Kuentz. *Tombes thébaines: La nécropole de Deir el-Médineh. La Tombe de Nakht-Min et la tombe d'Ari-Nefer*. Cairo: Institut français d'archéologie orientale, 1926.

Cerny, Jaroslav. *Catalogue des ostraca hiératiques non littéraires de Deir el-Médineh*. 6 vols. Cairo: Institut français d'archéologie orientale, 1935–1970.

———. *Graffiti hiéroglyphiques et hiératiques de la nécropole thébaine (nos 1060–1405)*. Cairo: Institut français d'archéologie orientale, 1956.

———. *Papyrus hiératiques de Deir el-Médineh*. 2 vols. Cairo: Institut français d'archéologie orientale, 1978–1986.

Cherpion, Nadine. *Deux tombes de la XVIIIe dynastie à Deir el-Medina*. Cairo: Institut français d'archéologie orientale, 1999.

Davies, Benedict G. *Who's Who at Deir el-Medina*. Leiden: Nederlands Instituut voor het Nabije Oosten, 1999.

Demarée, Rob. J., and Arno Egberts. *Deir el-Medina in the Third Millennium AD*. Leiden: Nederlands Instituut voor het Nabije Oosten, 2000.

Donker van Heel, Koen, and Ben Haring. *Writing in a Workmen's Village*. Leiden: Nederlands Instituut voor het Nabije Oosten, 2003.

Du Bourget, Pierre. *Le temple de Deir al-Médîna*. Cairo: Institut français d'archéologie orientale, 2002.

Gasse, Annie. *Catalogue des ostraca figurés de Deir el-Médineh*. Cairo: Institut français d'archéologie orientale, 1986.

———. *Catalogue des ostraca hiératiques littéraires de Deir el-Médineh V*. Cairo: Institut français d'archéologie orientale, 2005.

———. *Catalogue des ostraca hiératiques littéraires de Deir el-Médina*. Cairo: Institut français d'archéologie orientale, 1990.

Grandet, Pierre. *Catalogue des ostraca hiératiques littéraires de Deir el-Médina VIII–X*. Cairo: Institut français d'archéologie orientale, 2000–2006.

Häggman, Sofia. *Directing Deir el-Medina. The External Administration of the Necropolis*. Uppsala, Sweden: Uppsala University, Department of Archaeology and Ancient History, 2002.

Haring, Ben. *The Tomb of Sennedjem (TT1) in Deir el-Medina. Palaeography*. Cairo: Institut français d'archéologie orientale, 2007.

Helck, Wolfgang. *Die datierten und datierbaren Ostraka, Papyri, und Graffiti von Deir el-Medineh*. Wiesbaden, Germany: Otto Harrassowitz, 2002.

Heurtel, Chantal. *Les inscriptions coptes et gracques du temple d'Hathor à Deir al-Médîna*. Cairo: Institut français d'archéologie orientale, 2004.

Janssen, Jac. J. *Donkeys at Deir el-Medina*. Leiden: Nederlands Instituut voor het Nabije Oosten, 2005.

——. *Village Varia*. Leiden: Nederlands Instituut voor het Nabije Oosten, 1997.

Janssen, Jac. J., Elizabeth Frood, and Maren Goecke-Bauer. *Woodcutters, Potters, and Door-Keepers: Service Personnel of the Deir el-Medina Workmen*. Leiden: Nederlands Instituut voor het Nabije Oosten, 2003.

Koenig, Yvan. *Catalogue des étiquettes de jarres hiératiques de Deir el-Médineh*. 2 vols. Cairo: Institut français d'archéologie orientale, 1979–1980.

McDowell, Andrea. *Jurisdiction in the Workmen's Community of Deir el-Medina*. Leiden: Nederlands Instituut voor het Nabije Oosten, 1990.

——. *Village Life in Ancient Egypt*. Oxford, U.K., Oxford University Press, 1999.

Maystre, Charles. *Tombes de Deir el-Médineh: La tombe de Nebenmât (no. 219)*. Cairo: Institut français d'archéologie orientale, 1936.

Posener, Georges. *Catalogue des ostraca hiératiques littéraires de Deir el-Médineh*. 3 vols. Cairo: Institut français d'archéologie orientale, 1934–1980.

Schiaparelli, Ernesto. *Relazione sui lavori della missione archaeologica italiana in Egitto II: La tomba intatta dell'architetto Kha*. Turin, Italy: Ministero della Pubblica Istruzione, 1927.

Shedid, Abdel Ghaffar. *Das Grab des Sennedjem*. Mainz am Rhein, Germany: Philipp von Zabern, 1994.

Toivari-Viitala, Jaana. *Women at Deir el-Medina*. Leiden: Nederlands Instituut voor het Nabije Oosten, 2001.

Valbelle, Dominique. *La tombe de Hay à Deir el-Medineh*. Cairo: Institut français d'archéologie orientale, 1975.

Vandier, Jacques. *Tombes de Deir el-Médineh: La tombe de Nefer-abou*. Cairo: Institut français d'archéologie orientale, 1935.

Vandier, Jacques, and Geneviève Jourdain. *Deux tombes de Deir el-Médineh*. Cairo: Institut français d'archéologie orientale, 1939.

Vandier d'Abbadie, Jeanne. *Catalogue des ostraca figurés de Deir el-Médineh*. 4 fasc. Cairo: Institut français d'archéologie orientale, 1936–1959.

Wild, Henri. *La tombe de Néferhotep (I) et Neb.néfer à Deir el-Medina [No 6] et autres documents les concernant. II.* Cairo: Institut français d'archéologie orientale, 1979.

Zivie, Alain. *La tombe de Pached à Deir el-Médineh (no 3).* Cairo: Institut français d'archéologie orientale, 1979.

Deir el-Naqlun

Derda, Tomasz. *Deir el-Naqlun: The Greek Papyri.* Warsaw, Poland: Wydawnictwa Uniwersytetu Warsazawskiego, 1995.

Dendera

Castel, Georges, François Daumas, and Jean-Claude Golvin. *Les fontaines de la porte nord.* Cairo: Institut français d'archéologie orientale, 1984.

Cauville, Sylvie. *Dendera: Les chapelles osiriennes.* 3 vols. Cairo: Institut français d'archéologie orientale, 1997.

———. *Dendera: Les fêtes d'Hathor.* Louvain, Belgium: Peeters, 2002.

———. *Dendera I–VI: Traduction.* Louvain, Belgium: Peeters, 1997–2004.

———. *Le temple de Dendera.* Cairo: Institut français d'archéologie orientale, 1990.

———. *Le zodiaque d'Osiris.* Louvain, Belgium: Peeters, 1997.

Chassinat, Émile. *Le mystère d'Osiris au mois de Khoiak.* Cairo: Institut français d'archéologie orientale, 1966–1968.

Chassinat, Émile, François Daumas, and Sylvie Cauville. *Le temple de Dendera.* 10 vols. Cairo: Institut français d'archéologie orientale, 1934–1997.

Daumas, François. *Dendera et le temple d'Hathor, notice sommaire.* Cairo: Institut français d'archéologie orientale, 1969.

———. *Les Mammisis de Dendera.* Cairo: Institut français d'archéologie orientale, 1959.

Mariette, Auguste. *Denderah.* 4 vols. Paris: F. Vieweg, 1870–1880.

Petrie, W. M. Flinders. *Dendereh.* London: Egypt Exploration Fund, 1900.

Preys, René. *Les complexes de la Demure du sistre et du Trône de Rê.* Louvain, Belgium: Peeters, 2002.

Waitkus, Wolfgang. *Der Texte in den Unteren Krypten des Hathortempels von Dendera.* Mainz am Rhein, Germany: Philipp von Zabern, 1997.

Dendur

Blackman, Aylward. *The Temple of Dendur.* Cairo: Institut français d'archéologie orientale, 1911.

Derr

Blackman, Aylward. *The Temple of Derr*. Cairo: Institut français d'archéologie orientale, 1913.

Lurson, Benoit. *Osiris, Ramsès, Thot et le Nil. Les chapelles secondaires des temples de Derr et Ouadi es-Seboua*. Louvain, Belgium: Peeters, 2007.

Edfu

Cauville, Sylvie. *Edfou*. Cairo: Institut français d'archéologie orientale, 1984.

———. *Edfou VIII. Die Inschriften des Tempels von Edfu I*. Wiesbaden, Germany: Otto Harrassowitz, 1998.

———. *Edfu Temple: A Guide by an Ancient Egyptian Priest*. Cairo: American University in Cairo Press, 2004.

———. *Essai sur la théologie du temple d'Horus à Edfou*. 2 vols. Cairo: Institut français d'archéologie orientale, 1987.

———. *La théologie d'Osiris à Edfou*. Cairo: Institut français d'archéologie orientale, 1983.

Kurth, Dieter. *Edfu VII. Die Inschriften des Tempels von Edfu I, 2*. Wiesbaden, Germany: Otto Harrassowitz, 2004.

Michalowski, Kazimierz, Christiane Desroches-Noblecourt, J. de Linage, J. Manteuffel, and M. Zejmo-Zejmis. *Tell Edfou*. 4 vols. Cairo: 1937–1950.

Rochemonteix, F. J., Marquis de Maxence de Chalvet, Émile Chassinat, and Sylvie Cauville. *Le temple d'Edfou*. 15 vols. 2 rev. vols. Paris: E. Leroux, 1897; Cairo: Institut francais d'archéologie orientale, 1918–1990.

Elephantine

Arnold, Felix. *Elephantine XXX: Die Nachnutzung des Chnumtempelbezirks*. Deutsches Archäologisches Institut. Abteilung Kairo. Archäologische Veröffentlichungen 116. Mainz am Rhein, Germany: Philipp von Zabern, 2003.

Bresciani, Edda, Daniele Foraboschi, and Sergio Pernigotti. *Assuan*. Pisa, Italy: Giardini, 1978.

Dreyer, Günter. *Elephantine VIII: Der Tempel der Satet. Die Funde der Frühzeit und der Alten Reiches*. Deutsches Archäologisches Institut. Abteilung Kairo. Archäologische Veröffentlichungen 39. Mainz am Rhein, Germany: Philipp von Zabern, 1986.

Edel, Elmar. *Die Felsengräber der Qubbet el-Hawa bei Assuan*. Wiesbaden, Germany: Otto Harrassowitz, 1967–1980.

Gempeler, Robert D. *Elephantine X: Die Keramik römischer bis früharabischer Zeit*. Deutsches Archäologisches Institut. Abteilung Kairo. Archäologische

Veröffentlichungen 43. Mainz am Rhein, Germany: Philipp von Zabern, 1993.

Grossmann, Peter. *Elephantine II: Kirche und spätantike Hausanlagen im Chnumtempelhof.* Deutsches Archäologisches Institut. Abteilung Kairo. Archäologische Veröffentlichungen 25. Mainz am Rhein, Germany: Philipp von Zabern, 1980.

Habachi, Labib. *Elephantine IV: The Sanctuary of Heqaib.* Deutsches Archäologisches Institut. Abteilung Kairo. Archäologische Veröffentlichungen 33. Mainz am Rhein, Germany: Philipp von Zabern, 1985.

Jaritz, Horst. *Elephantine III: Die Terrassen vor den Tempeln des Chnum und des Satet.* Deutsches Archäologisches Institut. Abteilung Kairo. Archäologische Veröffentlichungen 32. Mainz am Rhein, Germany: Philipp von Zabern, 1980.

Jenni, Hanna. *Elephantine XVII: Die Dekoration des Chnumtempels auf Elephantine durch Nektanebos II.* Deutsches Archäologisches Institut. Abteilung Kairo. Archäologische Veröffentlichungen 90. Mainz am Rhein, Germany: Philipp von Zabern, 1998.

Junge, Friedrich. *Elephantine XI: Funde und Bauteile.* Deutsches Archäologisches Institut. Abteilung Kairo. Archäologische Veröffentlichungen 49. Mainz am Rhein, Germany: Philipp von Zabern, 1987.

Kopp, Peter. *Elephantine XXXXII: Die Siedlung der Naqadazeit.* Deutsches Archäologisches Institut. Abteilung Kairo. Archäologische Veröffentlichungen 49. Mainz am Rhein, Germany: Philipp von Zabern, 2006.

Laskowska-Kusztal, Ewa. *Elephantine XV: Die Dekorfragmente der ptolemäisch-römischen Tempel von Elephantine.* Deutsches Archäologisches Institut. Abteilung Kairo. Archäologische Veröffentlichungen 73. Mainz am Rhein, Germany: Philipp von Zabern, 1995.

Niederberger, Walter. *Elephantine XX: Der Chnumtempel Nektanebos' II.* Deutsches Archäologisches Institut. Abteilung Kairo. Archäologische Veröffentlichungen 96. Mainz am Rhein, Germany: Philipp von Zabern, 1999.

Pilgrim, Cornelius von. *Elephantine XVIII: Untersuchungen zur Stadt Elephantine im mittleren Reich under der Zweiten Zwischenzeit.* Deutsches Archäologisches Institut. Abteilung Kairo. Archäologische Veröffentlichungen 91. Mainz am Rhein, Germany: Philipp von Zabern, 1996.

Porten, Bezalel, J. Joel Farber, Cary J. Martin, Gunter Vittmann, Leslie S. B. MacCoull, Sarah Clackson, Simon Hopkins, and Ramon Katzoff. *The Elephantine Papyri in English.* Leiden, Netherlands: Brill, 1996.

Rodziewicz, Mieczyslaw. *Elephantine XXVII: Early Roman Industries on Elephantine.* Deutsches Archäologisches Institut. Abteilung Kairo. Archäologische Veröffentlichungen 107. Mainz am Rhein, Germany: Philipp von Zabern, 2005.

Ubertini, Christian. *Elephantine XXXIV: Restitution architecturale à partir des blocs et fragments épars d'époque ptolémaïque et romaine*. Deutsches Archäologisches Institut. Abteilung Kairo. Archäologische Veröffentlichungen 120. Mainz am Rhein, Germany: Philipp von Zabern, 2005.

Zierman, Martin. *Elephantine XVI: Befestigungsanlagen und Stadtentwicklung in der Frühzeit und im frühen Alten Reich*. Deutsches Archäologisches Institut. Abteilung Kairo. Archäologische Veröffentlichungen 87. Mainz am Rhein, Germany: Philipp von Zabern, 1993.

———. *Elephantine XXVIII: Die Baustrukteren der alteren Satdt (Fruhzeit und Altes Reich)*. Deutsches Archäologisches Institut. Abteilung Kairo. Archäologische Veröffentlichungen 108. Mainz am Rhein, Germany: Philipp von Zabern, 2003.

Elkab

Bingen, Jean, and Willy Clarysse. *Elkab III: Les ostraca grecs*. Brussels, Belgium: Fondation Égyptologique Reine Élisabeth, 1989.

Derchain, Philippe. *Elkab I: Les monuments religieux à l'entrée de l'Ouady Hellal*. Brussels, Belgium: Fondation Égyptologique Reine Élisabeth, 1971.

Eder, Christian. *Elkab VII: Die Barkenkapelle des Königs Sobekhotep III in Elkab*. Brussels, Belgium: Fondation Égyptologique Reine Élisabeth, 2002.

Fondation Égyptologique Reine Élisabeth. *Elkab IV: Topographie*. Brussels, Belgium: Fondation Égyptologique Reine Élisabeth, 1991.

———. *Fouilles de El Kab Documents*. Brussels, Belgium: Fondation Égyptologique Reine Élisabeth, 1940.

Hendrickx, Stan. *Elkab V: The Naqada III Cemetery*. Brussels, Belgium: Fondation Égyptologique Reine Élisabeth, 1994.

Quibell, James E. *El-Kab*. London: Egyptian Research Account, 1898.

Tylor, Joseph J. *Wall Drawings and Monuments of El Kab: The Tomb of Paheri*. London: Egypt Exploration Fund, 1895.

———. *Wall Drawings and Monuments of El Kab: The Tomb of Renni*. London: B. Quaritch, 1900.

———. *Wall Drawings and Monuments of El Kab: The Tomb of Sobeknakht*. London: B. Quaritch, 1896.

Vandekerckhove, Hans, and Renate Muller-Wollerman. *Elkab VI: Die Felinschriften des Wadi Hilaâl*. Turnhout, Belgium: Brepols: 2001.

Vermeersch, Pierre. *Elkab II: L'Elkabien, Épipalaeolithique de la Vallée du Nil Égyptien*. Brussels, Belgium: Fondation Égyptologique Reine Élisabeth, 1978.

Esna

Downes, Dorothy. *The Excavations at Esna, 1905–1906*. Warminster, G.B.: Aris & Phillips, 1974.

Meeks, Dimitri. *Les Architraves du temple d'Esna. Paléographie*. Cairo: Institut français d'archéologie orientale, 2004.

Sauneron, Serge. *Esna*. 7 vols. Cairo: Institut français d'archéologie orientale, 1959–1982.

Sauneron, Serge, and Jean Jacquet. *Les ermitages chrétiens du désert d'Esna*. 4 vols. Cairo: Institut français d'archéologie orientale, 1972.

Faras

Dzierzykray-Rogalski, Tadeusz. *Faras VIII: The Bishops of Faras. An Anthropological-Medical Study*. Warsaw, Poland: PWN-Éditions scientifiques de Pologne, 1985.

Godlewski, Wlodzimierz. *Faras VI: Les baptistères nubiens*. Warsaw, Poland: PWN-Éditions scientifiques de Pologne, 1979.

———. *Pachoras. The Cathedrals of Aetios, Paulos, and Petros*. Warsaw, Poland: Warsaw University Press, 2005.

Jakobielski, Stefan. *Faras III: A History of the Bishopric of Pachoras*. Warsaw, Poland: PWN-Éditions scientifiques de Pologne, 1972.

Karkowski, Janusz. *Faras V: The Pharaonic Inscriptions from Faras*. Warsaw, Poland: PWN-Éditions scientifiques de Pologne, 1981.

Kubinska, Jadwiga. *Faras IV: Inscriptions grecques et chrétiennes*. Warsaw, Poland: PWN-Éditions scientifiques de Pologne, 1974.

Martens-Czarnecka, Malgorzata. *Les éléments décoratifs sur les peintures de Faras*. Warsaw, Poland: PWN-Éditions scientifiques de Pologne, 1982.

Michalowski, Kazimierz. *Faras: Wall Paintings in the Collection of the National Museum in Warsaw*. Warsaw, Poland: Wydawnictwo Artystyczno-Graficzne, 1974.

———. *Faras I: Fouilles polonaises 1961*. Warsaw, Poland: PWN-Éditions scientifiques de Pologne, 1962.

———. *Faras II: Fouilles polonaises 1961–1962*. Warsaw, Poland: PWN-Éditions scientifiques de Pologne, 1965.

Vantini, John. *The Excavations at Faras*. Bologna, Italy: Editrice Nigrizia, 1970.

Fayum

See also individual sites.

Caton-Thompson, Gertrude, and Ernest W. Gardner. *The Desert Fayum*. London: Royal Anthropological Institute of Great Britain and Ireland, 1934.

Davoli, Paola. *L'Archeologia Urbana nel Fayyum di Eta Ellenistica e Romana*. Naples, Italy: Generoso Procaccini, 1998.

Griggs, C. Wilfred. *Excavations at Seila, Egypt*. Provo, Utah: Brigham Young University Press, 1988.

Vecchi, M. *Hieroglyphic Inscriptions from the Fayyum I–II*. Imola, Italy: Editrice La Mandragora, 2006.

Gebel el-Silsila

Caminos, Ricardo A., and T. G. Henry James. *Gebel es-Silsilah I*. London: Egypt Exploration Society, 1963.

Thiem, Andrea-Christina. *Speos von Gebel es-Silsileh*. Wiesbaden, Germany: Otto Harrassowitz, 2000.

Gebel el-Zeit

Castel, Georges, and Georges Soukiassian. *Gebel el-Zeit I*. Cairo: Institut français d'archéologie orientale, 1989.

Gebelein

Donadoni Roveri, Anna Maria, D'Amicone Elvira, and Leospo Enrica. *Gebelein. Il villaggio e la necropoli*. Turin, Italy: Artema, 1994.

Posener-Kriéger, Paule. *I papiri di Gebelein. Scavi G. Farina 1935*. Turin, Italy: Ministero per I Beni e le Attivitá Culturali-Sopintendenza al Museo delle Antichitá Egizie, 2004.

Gerf Hussein

Jacquet, Jean, and Hassan el-Achirie. *Gerf Hussein I*. Cairo: Centre d'Etudes et de Documentation sur l'Ancienne Égypte, 1978.

el-Tanbouli, M., H. de Meulenaere, and A. A. Sadek. *Gerf Hussein II–IV*. Cairo: Centre d'Etudes et de Documentation sur l'Ancienne Égypte, 1974–1978.

Gerzeh

Stevenson, Alice. *Gerzeh, a Cemetery Shortly before History*. London: Golden House Publications, 2006.

Giza

Abu-Bakr, Abdel-Moneim. *Excavations at Giza, 1949–1950*. Cairo: Government Press, 1953.

Badawy, Alexander. *The Tomb of Nyhetep-Ptah at Giza and the Tomb of 'Ankhm'ahor at Saqqara*. Berkeley: University of California Press, 1978.

———. *The Tombs of Iteti, Sekhem'ankh-Ptah, and Kaemnofret at Giza*. Berkeley: University of California Press, 1976.

Brovarski, Edward. *Giza Mastabas VII: The Senedjemib Complex Part I*. Boston: Museum of Fine Arts, 2002.

Brunner-Traut, Emma. *Die altägyptische Grabkammer Seschemnofers III. aus Gîsa*. Mainz am Rhein, Germany: Philipp von Zabern, 1977.

Corteggiani, Jean-Pierre. *The Pyramids of Giza: Facts, Legends, and Mysteries*. London: Thames & Hudson, 2007.

Curto, Silvio. *Gli scavi italiani a El-Ghiza (1903)*. Rome: Centro per le Antichità e la Storia dell'Arte del Vicino Oriente, 1963.

Der Manuelian, Peter. *Slab Stelae of the Giza Necropolis*. New Haven, Conn., and Philadelphia, Pa.: Peabody Museum of Natural History of Yale University and University of Pennsylvania Museum of Archaeology and Anthropology, 2003.

Dunham, Dows, and William Kelly Simpson. *Giza Mastabas 1: The Mastaba of Queen Mersyankh III, G 7530–7540*. Boston: Museum of Fine Arts, 1974.

Fisher, Clarence. *The Minor Cemetery at Giza*. Philadelphia, Pa.: University Museum, 1924.

Haase, Michael. *Eine Stätte für die Ewigkeit. Der Pyramidenkomplex des Cheops aus Baulicher, Architektonischer und Kulturhistorischer Sicht*. Mainz am Rhein, Germany: Philipp von Zabern, 2004.

Hölscher, Uvo. *Das Grabdenkmal des Königs Chephren*. Leipzig, Germany: J. C. Hinrichs, 1912.

Jenkins, Nancy. *The Boat beneath the Pyramid*. London: Thames & Hudson, 1980.

Junker, Hermann. *Giza*. 12 vols. Vienna, Austria: Österreichische Akademie der Wissenschaften, 1929–1955.

Kanawati, Naguib. *Tombs at Giza I: Kaiemankh (G4561) and Seshemnefer I (G4940)*. Warminster, G.B.: Aris & Phillips, 2001.

———. *Tombs at Giza II: Seshahetep/Heti (G5150), Nesutnefer (G4970), and Seshemnefer II (G5080)*. Warminster, G.B.: Aris & Phillips, 2002.

Kromer, Karl. *Nezlet Batran: Eine Mastaba aus dem Alten Reich bei Giseh (Ägypten)*. Vienna, Austria: Österrreichischen Akademie der Wissenschaften, 1991.

———. *Siedlungsfunde aus dem frühen Alten Reich in Giseh*. Vienna, Austria: Österreichische Akademie der Wissenschaften, 1978.

Lehner, Mark. *The Pyramid Tomb of Hetep-heres and the Satellite Pyramid of Khufu*. SDAIK 19. Mainz am Rhein, Germany: Philipp von Zabern, 1985.

Lehner, Mark, and Wilma Weterstrom, eds. *Giza Reports: The Giza Plateau Mapping Project I*. Boston: Ancient Egypt Research Associates, 2006.

Nour, Muhammd Zaki, Z. Y. Iskandar, M. S. Osman, and A.Y. Moustafa. *The Cheops Boats. Part I*. Cairo: Antiquities Department of Egypt, 1960.

Petrie, W. M. Flinders. *Gizeh and Rifeh*. London: Egyptian Research Account, 1907.

———. *The Pyramids and Temples of Gizeh*. London: Field and Tuer, 1883; reprint with update by Zahi Hawass, London: Histories and Mysteries of Man, 1990.

Reisner, George A. *A History of the Giza Necropolis I*. Cambridge, Mass.: Harvard University Press, 1942.

———. *A History of the Giza Necropolis II. The Tomb of Hetepheres the Mother of Kheops*. Cambridge, Mass.: Harvard University Press, 1955.

———. *Mycerinus: The Temples of the Third Pyramid at Giza*. Cambridge, Mass.: Harvard University Press, 1931.

Romer, John. *The Great Pyramid: Ancient Egypt Revisited*. Cambridge, U.K.: Cambridge University Press, 2007.

Rossi, Corinna. *The Pyramids and the Sphinx*. Vercelli, Italy: White Star Publications, 2005.

Roth, Anne M. *Giza Mastabas 6: A Cemetery of Palace Attendants*. Boston: Museum of Fine Arts, 1995.

el-Sadek, Wafaa. *Twenty-Sixth Dynasty Necropolis at Gizeh*. Beiträge zur Ägyptologie 5. Vienna, Austria: Institut für Africanistik und Ägyptologie Universität Wien, 1984.

Simpson, William Kelly. *Giza Mastabas 2: The Mastabas of Qar and Idu, G 7101–7102*. Boston: Museum of Fine Arts, 1976.

———. *Giza Mastabas 3: The Mastabas of Kawab, Khafkhufu I and II, G 7110–7120, 7130–7140, and 750 and Subsidiary Mastabas of Street 7100*. Boston: Museum of Fine Arts, 1978.

———. *Giza Mastabas 4: Mastabas of the Western Cemetery, Part I*. Boston: Museum of Fine Arts, 1980.

Usick, Patricia, and Deborah Manley. *The Sphinx Revealed: A Forgotten Record of Pioneering Excavations*. London: British Museum Press, 2007.

Weeks, Kent R. *Giza Mastabas 5: Mastabas of Cemetery G6000*. Boston: Museum of Fine Arts, 1994.

Zivie-Coche, Christiane. *Giza au Deuxième Millénaire*. Cairo: Institut français d'archéologie orientale, 1976.

———. *Giza au Premier Millénaire*. Boston: Museum of Fine Arts, 1991.

———. *Sphinx: History of a Monument*. Ithaca, N.Y.: Cornell University Press, 2002.

Gurob

Brunton, Guy, and Reginald Engelbach. *Gurob*. London: British School of Archaeology in Egypt, 1927.

Loat, Leonard. *Gurob*. London: British School of Archaeology in Egypt, 1905.

Petrie, W. M. Flinders. *Illahun, Kahun, and Gurob*. London: D. Nutt, 1891.

———. *Kahun, Gurob, and Hawara*. London: Kegan Paul, Trench, Trübner & Co., 1890.

Thomas, Angela. *Gurob: A New Kingdom Town*. Warminster, G.B.: Aris & Phillips, 1981.

Harageh

Engelbach, Rex. *Harageh*. London: British School of Archaeology in Egypt, 1923.

Grajetzki, Wolfram. *Harageh, an Egyptian Burial Ground for the Rich around 1800 BC*. London: Golden House Publications, 2004.

Hawara

Blom-Böer, Ingrid. *Die Tempelanlage Amenemhets III. in Hawara*. Leiden: Nederlands Instituut voor het Nabije Oosten, 2006.

Farag, Naguib, and Zaki Iskander. *The Discovery of Neferwptah*. Cairo: Antiquities Department of Egypt, 1971.

Hughes, George R., and Richard Jasnow. *Oriental Institute Hawara Papyri*. Chicago: Oriental Institute of the University of Chicago, 1997.

Petrie, W. M. Flinders. *Hawara, Biahmu, and Arsinoe*. London: Field and Tuer, 1889.

———. *The Hawara Portfolio*. London: British School of Archaeology in Egypt, 1913.

———. *Kahun, Gurob, and Hawara*. London: Kegan Paul, Trench, Trübner & Co., 1890.

Petrie, W. M. Flinders, Gerald A. Wainwright, and Ernest Mackay. *The Labyrinth, Gerzeh, and Mazguneh*. London: British School of Archaeology in Egypt, 1912.

Heliopolis

Debono, Fernand, and Bodil Mortensen. *The Predynastic Cemetery at Heliopolis*. Deutsches Archäologisches Institut. Abteilung Kairo. Archäologische Veröffentlichungen 63. Mainz am Rhein, Germany: Philipp von Zabern, 1988.

Petrie, W. M. Flinders, and Ernest Mackay. *Heliopolis, Kafr Ammar, and Shurafa*. London: British School of Archaeology in Egypt, 1915.

Saleh, Abdel-Aziz. *Excavations at Heliopolis*. 2 vols. Cairo: Cairo University, 1981–1983.

el-Sawi, Ahmad, and Farouk Gomaa. *Das Grab des Panehsi, Gottesvaters von Heliopolis in Matariya*. Wiesbaden, Germany: Otto Harrassowitz, 1993.

Helwan

Saad, Zaki. *The Excavations at Helwan*. Norman: University of Oklahoma Press, 1969.

———. *Royal Excavations at Saqqara and Helwan, 1941–1945*. Cairo: Service des Antiquités de l'Egypte, 1947.

Herakleopolis

Lopez Grande, Maria José, Fernando Quesada Sanz, and Miguel Angel Molinero. *Excavaciones en Ehnasya el Medina (Heracleopolis Magna)*. Vol. 2. Madrid, Spain: Ministerio de Cultura, 1995.

Mukhtar, Mohamed Gamal el-din. *Ihnâsya el-Medina (Herakleopolis Magna): Its Importance and Its Role in Pharaonic History*. Cairo: Institut français d'archéologie orientale, 1983.

Naville, Édouard. *Ahnas al Medineh (Heracleopolis Magna)*. London: Egypt Exploration Fund, 1894.

Padró, Josep. *Études Historico-Archéologiques sur Héracléopolis Magna. La Nécropole de la muraille méridionale*. Barcelona, Spain: Universitat de Barcelona, 1999.

Perez-Die, Maria del Carmen. *Ehnasaya El Medina. Heracleopolis Magna Egito. Excavaciones 1984–2004*. Madrid, Spain: Ministerio de Cultura, 2005.

Perez-Die, Maria del Carmen, and Pascal Vernus. *Excavaciones en Ehnasya el Medina (Heracleopolis Magna)*. Vol. 1. Madrid, Spain: Ministerio de Cultura, 1992.

Petrie, W. M. Flinders. *Ehnasya 1904*. London: Egypt Exploration Fund, 1905.

———. *Roman Ehnasya (Herakleopolis Magna) 1904*. London: Egypt Exploration Fund, 1905.

Hermopolis

Hanke, Rainer. *Amarna-reliefs aus Hermopolis*. Hildesheimer Ägyptologische Beiträge 2. Hildesheim, Germany: Gerstenberg, 1978.

Roeder, Günther. *Amarna-Reliefs aus Hermopolis*. Hildesheim, Germany: Gebrüder Gerstenberg, 1969.

———. *Hermopolis 1929–1939*. Hildesheim, Germany: Gebrüder Gerstenberg, 1959.

Snape, Steven. *A Temple of Domitian at El-Ashmunein*. British Museum Occasional Paper 68. London: British Museum Publications, 1989.

Snape, Steven, and Donald M. Bailey. *The Great Portico at Hermopolis Magna: Present State and Past Prospects*. British Museum Occasional Paper 63. London: British Museum Publications, 1988.

Spencer, A. Jeffrey, and Donald M. Bailey. *Excavations at El-Ashmunein*. 5 vols. London: British Museum Press, 1983–1998.

Hiba, el-

Wenke, Robert J. *Archaeological Investigations at el-Hibeh 1980: Preliminary Report*. Malibu, Calif.: Undena Publications, 1984.

Hierakonpolis

Adams, Barbara. *Ancient Hierakonpolis*. 2 vols. Warminster, G.B.: Aris & Phillips, 1974.

———. *Ancient Nekhen*. New Malden, G.B.: SIA Publishing, 1995.

———. *The Fort Cemetery at Hierakonpolis (Excavated by John Garstang)*. London: Kegan Paul International, 1988.

Hoffman, Michael. *The Predynastic of Hierakonpolis*. Cairo: Cairo University Herbarium, 1982.

Quibell, James E., and Frederick W. Green. *Hierakonpolis*. 2 vols. London: Egyptian Research Account, 1900–1902.

Hu

Petrie, W. M. Flinders. *Diospolis Parva*. London: British School of Archaeology, 1901.

Kalabsha

Daumas, François. *Le ouabet de Kalabscha*. Cairo: Centre d'Etudes et de Documentation sur l'Ancienne Égypte, 1970.

De Meulenare, Herman. *La chapelle ptolémaïque de Kalabcha*. Cairo: Centre d'Etudes et de Documentation sur l'Ancienne Égypte, 1964–1970.

Gauthier, Henri. *Le Temple de Kalabchah*. Cairo: Institut français d'archéologie orientale, 1911–1927.

Siegler, Karl Georg. *Kalabsha: Architektur und Baugeschichte des Tempels*. Deutsches Archäologisches Institut. Abteilung Kairo. Archäologische Veröffentlichungen 1. Berlin, Germany: Gebr. Mann, 1970.

Strouhal, Eugen. *Wadi Qitna and Kalabsha South. Vol. 1. Archaeology*. Prague, Czech Republic: Charles University, 1984.

Wright, George R. H. *Kalabsha: The Preserving of the Temple*. Deutsches Archäologisches Institut. Abteilung Kairo. Archäologische Veröffentlichungen 2. Berlin, Germany: Gebr. Mann, 1972.

———. *Kalabsha III. The Ptolemiac Sanctuary of Kalabsha*. Deutsches Archäologisches Institut. Abteilung Kairo. Archäologische Veröffentlichungen 3,1. Mainz am Rhein, Germany: Philipp von Zabern, 1987.

Karanis

Boak, Arthur E. *Karanis: The Temple, Coin Hoards, Botanical and Zoological Reports, Seasons 1924–1931*. Ann Arbor: University of Michigan, 1933.

Boak, Arthur E., and Enoch E. Peterson. *Karanis: Topographical and Architectural Report of the Excavations during Seasons 1924–1928*. Ann Arbor: University of Michigan, 1931.

Boak, Arthur E., and Herbert C. Youtie. *The Archives of Aurelius Isidorus*. Ann Arbor: University of Michigan, 1960.

Haatvedt, Rolfe A., Enoch E. Peterson, and Elinor Husselman. *Coin from Karanis*. Ann Arbor: University of Michigan, 1964.

Harden, Donald B. *Roman Glass from Karanis*. Ann Arbor: University of Michigan, 1936.

Husselman, Elinor. *Karanis: Excavations of the University of Michigan in Egypt, 1928–1935. Topography and Architecture*. Ann Arbor: University of Michigan, 1979.

———. *Papyri from Karanis*. 3rd series. London: American Philological Association, 1971.

Johnson, Barbara. *Pottery from Karanis*. Ann Arbor: University of Michigan, 1981.

Riad, Henry, and John C. Shelton. *A Tax-List from Karanis*. Bonn, Germany: Rudolf Habelt Verlag, 1975.

Shier, Louise. *Terracotta Lamps from Karanis, Egypt*. Ann Arbor: University of Michigan, 1978.

Youtie, Herbert C., John G. Winter, eds. *Papyri and Ostraca from Karanis*. 2nd series. Ann Arbor: University of Michigan, 1944–1951.

———. *Tax Rolls from Karanis*. Ann Arbor: University of Michigan, 1936–1939.

Karnak

Amer, Amin A. M. A. *The Gateway of Ramesses IX in the Temple of Amun at Karnak*. Warminster, G.B.: Aris & Philipps, 1999.

Azim, Michel, and Gérard Réveillac. *Karnak dans l'objectif de Georges Legrain*. Paris: CNRS, 2004.

Azim, Michel, Fridrik Bjarnason, Patrick Deleuze, and Patrick Dexyl. *Karnak et sa Topographie: Vol. 1. Les releves modernes du temple d'Amon-Rê*. Paris: Éditions CNRS, 1998.

Barguet, Paul. *Le Temple d'Amon-Rê á Karnak. Essai d'Exégèse*. Rev. ed. Cairo: Institut français d'archéologie orientale, 2006.

Benson, Margaret, and Janet Gourlay. *The Temple of Mut in Asher*. London: John Murray, 1899.

Blyth, Elizabeth. *Karnak: Evolution of a Temple*. London and New York: Routledge, 2006.

Burgos, Franck, and François Larché. *La chapelle Rouge. Le sanctuaire de barque d'Hatshepsout. I Facsimiles et Photographes des Scènes*. Paris: Éditions Recherche sur les civilisations, 2006.

Centre Franco-Égyptien d'Étude des Temples de Karnak. *Cahiers de Karnak V–XI*. 6 vols. Luxor, Egypt: Centre Franco-Égyptien d'Étude des Temples de Karnak, 1975–2003.

Chevrier, Henri. *Le temple reposoir de Séti II à Karnak*. Cairo: Service des Antiquités de l'Égypte, 1940.

Epigraphic Survey. *Reliefs and Inscriptions at Karnak*. 4 vols. Chicago: Oriental Institute of the University of Chicago, 1936–1986.

Gabolde, Luc. *Le "Grand Château d'Amon" de Sésostris Ier à Karnak*. Paris: Brocard, 1998.

———. *Monuments décorés en bas relief aux noms de Thoutmosis II et Hatchepsout à Karnak*. Cairo: Institut français d'archéologie orientale, 2005.

———. *The Temple of Khonsu*. 2 vols. Chicago: Oriental Institute of the University of Chicago, 1979–1981.

Gohary, Jocelyn. *Akhenaten's Sed-Festival at Karnak*. London: Kegan Paul International, 1992.

Jacquet-Gordon, Helen. *The Temple of Khonsu 3: The Graffiti on the Khonsu Temple Roof at Karnak: A Manifestation of Personal Piety*. Chicago: Oriental Institute of the University of Chicago, 2004.

Lacau, Pierre, and Henri Chevrier. *Une chapelle d'Hatshepsout à Karnak*. 2 vols. Cairo: Service des Antiquités de l'Égypte, 1977–1979.

———. *Une chapelle de Sésostris Ier à Karnak*. 2 vols. Cairo: Service des Antiquités de l'Égypte, 1956–1969.

Lauffray, Jean, Claude Traunecker, F. Le Saout, and Olivier Masson. *La chapelle d'Achôris à Karnak*. Paris: Éditions ADPF, 1981–1995.

Le Fur, Daniel. *La Conservation des peintures murales des temples de Karnak*. Paris: Éditions Recherche sur les Civilisations, 1994.

Legrain, Georges. *Les Temples du Karnak*. Brussels, Belgium: Vromant & Co., 1929.

Nelson, Harold H. *The Great Hypostyle Hall at Karnak I, Part 1. The Wall Reliefs*. Chicago: Oriental Institute of the University of Chicago, 1981.

Parker, Richard, Jean Leclant, and Jean-Claude Goyon. *The Edifice of Taharqa by the Sacred Lake of Karnak*. Providence, R.I.: Brown University Press, 1979.

Redford, Donald B. *The Akhenaten Temple Project 3: The Excavations of Kom el-Ahmar and Environs*. Toronto: University of Toronto, 1994.

Rondot, Vincent. *La grand salle hypostyle de Karnak: Les architraves*. 2 vols. Paris: Éditions Recherche sur les Civilisations, 1998.

Sauneron, Serge. *La porte ptolémaïque de l'enceinte de Mout à Karnak*. Cairo: Institut français d'archéologie orientale, 1983.

Smith, Ray W., and Donald B. Redford. *The Akhenaten Temple Project I*. Warminster, G.B.: Aris & Phillips, 1977.

Van Siclen, Charles. *The Alabaster Shrine of King Amenhotep II*. San Antonio, Tx.: Van Siclen Books, 1986.

Kerma

Bonnet, Charles. *Kerma: Territoire et métropole*. Cairo: Institut français d'archéologie orientale, 1986.

———. *Le temple principal de la ville de Kerma et son quartier religieux*. Paris: Editions Errance, 2004.

Dunham, Dows. *Excavations at Kerma. Part VI*. Boston: Museum of Fine Arts, 1982.

Reisner, George A. *Excavations at Kerma I–V.* 2 vols. Cambridge, Mass.: Peabody Museum of Harvard University, 1923.

Kharga Oasis

Barakat, Hala N., and Nathalie Baum. *La végétation antique de Douch (Oasis de Kharga).* Cairo: Institut français d'archéologie orientale, 1992.

Bousquet, Bernard. *Tell-Douch et sa région.* Cairo: Institut français d'archéologie orientale, 1996.

Caton-Thompson, Gertrude. *Kharga Oasis in Prehistory.* London: Athlone Press, 1952.

Cruz-Uribe, Eugene. *Hibis Temple Project I.* San Antonio, Tx.: Van Siclen Books, 1988.

Cuvigny, Hélène, and Guy Wagner. *Les ostraca grecs de Douch.* 5 fascs. Cairo: Institut français d'archéologie orientale, 1986–2001.

Cuvigny, Hélène, Adel Hussein, and Guy Wagner. *Les ostraca grecs d'Aïn Waqfa.* Cairo: Institut français d'archéologie orientale, 1993.

Devauchelle, Didier, and Guy Wagner. *Les graffites du Gebel Teir.* Textes démotiques et grecs. Cairo: Institut français d'archéologie orientale, 1984.

Dunand, Fernand, J. L. Heim, N. Heneim, and R. Lichtenberg. *La nécropole de Douch (Oasis de Kharga) I: Tombes à 72.* Cairo: Institut français d'archéologie orientale, 1992.

——. *La nécropole de Douch (Oasis de Kharga) II: Tombes 73 à 92.* Cairo: Institut français d'archéologie orientale, 2005.

Hussein, Adel. *Le sanctuaire rupestre de Piyris Ayn al-Labakha (Oasis de Kharga).* Cairo: Institut français d'archéologie orientale, 2000.

Reddé, Michel, ed. *Kysis. Fouilles de l'IFAO à Douch Oasis de Kharga (1985–1990).* Cairo: Institut français d'archéologie orientale, 2004.

——. *Le trésor de Douch (Oasis de Kharga).* Cairo: Institut français d'archéologie orientale, 1992.

Winlock, Herbert. *The Temple of Hibis in the el-Khargheh Oasis.* 2 vols. New York: Metropolitan Museum of Art, 1938–1941.

Kom Abu Billo

Abd el-Al, Abdel-Hafeez, Jean-Claude Grenier, and Guy Wagner. *Stèles funéraires de Kom Abu Bellou.* Paris: Éditions Recherche sur les Civilisations, 1985.

Hooper, Finley A. *Funerary Stelae from Kom Abou Billou.* Ann Arbor, Mich.: Kelsey Museum of Archaeology, 1961.

Kom el-Ahmar Sawirus

Schenkel, Wolfgang, and Farouk Gomaà. *Scharuna I. Die Grabungsplatz. Die Nekropole. Gräber aus der Alten-Reichs-Nekrople.* Mainz am Rhein, Germany: Philipp von Zabern, 2004.

Kom el-Hisn

Cagle, Anthony. *The Spatial Structure of Kom el-Hisn: An Old Kingdom Town in the Western Nile Delta, Egypt.* Oxford, U.K.: BAR, 2003.
Coulson, William D. E., and Albert Leonard. *Cities of the Delta I: Naukratis: Preliminary Report on the 1977–1978 and 1980 Seasons.* Malibu, Calif.: Undena Publications, 1981.

Kom Ombo

Gutbub, Adolphe. *Kom Ombo I.* Cairo: Institut français d'archéologie orientale, 1995.
Morgan, Jacques de, Urbain Bouriant, Georges Legrain, Gustave Jéquier, and A. Barsanti. *Kom Ombos.* 2 vols. Vienna, Austria: A. Holzhausen, 1895–1909.

Kumma

See Archaeology: Excavations and Surveys, Semna.

Lahun

Collier, Mark, and Stephen Quirke. *The UCL Lahun Papyri: Letters.* Oxford, U.K.: BAR, 2002.
——. *The UCL Lahun Papyri: Religious, Literary, Legal, Mathematical, Medical.* Oxford, U.K.: BAR, 2004.
——. *The UCL Lahun Papyri: Accounts.* Oxford, U.K.: BAR, 2006.
Luft, Ulrich. *Das Archiv von Illahun Briefe 1.* Hieratische Papyri aus den Staatlichen Museen zu Berlin I. Berlin, Germany: Akademie Verlag, 1992.
——. *Urkunden zur Chronologie der späten 12. Dynastie. Brief aus Illahun.* Vienna, Austria: Österreichische Akademie der Wissenschaften, 2005.
Petrie, W. M. Flinders. *Illahun, Kahun, and Gurob.* London: D. Nutt, 1891.
——. *Kahun, Gurob, and Hawara.* London: Kegan Paul, Trench, Trübner & Co., 1890.

Petrie, W. M. Flinders, and Guy Brunton. *Lahun I–II*. London: British School of Archaeology in Egypt, University College, 1920–1922.

Petrie, W. M. Flinders, Guy Brunton, and Margaret A. Murray. *Lahun II*. London: British School of Archaeology in Egypt, University College, 1923.

Quirke, Stephen. *Lahun. A Town in Egypt 1800 BC, and the History of Landscape*. London: Golden House Publications, 2006.

——. *Lahun Studies*. London: SIA, 1998.

Lisht

Arnold, Dieter. *Middle Kingdom Tomb Architecture at Lisht*. New Haven, Conn.: Yale University Press, 2007.

——. *The South Cemeteries of Lisht I: The Pyramid of Senwosret I*. New York: Metropolian Museum of Art, 1988.

——. *The South Cemeteries of Lisht III: The Pyramid Complex of Senwosret I*. New York: Metropolitan Museum of Art, 1992.

Arnold, Felix. *The South Cemeteries of Lisht II: The Control Notes and Team Marks*. New York: Metropolitan Museum of Art, 1990.

Goedicke, Hans. *Re-used Blocks from the Pyramid of Amenemhet I at Lisht*. New York: Metropolitan Museum of Art, 1971.

Hayes, William C. *The Texts in the Mastaba of Se'n-Wosret-'Ankh at Lisht*. New York: Metropolitan Museum of Art, 1937.

Mace, Arthur C., and Herbert Winlock. *The Tomb of Senebtisi at Lisht*. New York: Metropolitan Museum of Art, 1916.

Luxor

Abdel-Raziq, Mahmud. *Die Darstellugen und Texte des Sanktuars Alexander des Grossen im Tempel von Luxor*. Deutsches Archäologisches Institut. Abteilung Kairo. Archäologische Veröffentlichungen 16. Mainz am Rhein, Germany: Philipp von Zabern, 1984.

——. *Das Sanktuar Amenophis, III im Luxor Tempel*. Studies in Egyptian Culture 3. Tokyo: Waseda University, 1986.

Brunner, Hellmut. *Die südlichen Räume des Tempels von Luxor*. Deutsches Archäologisches Institut. Abteilung Kairo. Archäologische Veröffentlichungen 18. Mainz am Rhein, Germany: Philipp von Zabern, 1977.

Epigraphic Survey. *Reliefs and Inscriptions at Luxor Termple I: The Festival Procession of Opet in the Colonnade Hall*. Chicago: Oriental Institute of the University of Chicago, 1994.

Gayet, Albert. *Le temple de Louxor*. Paris: Ernest Leroux, 1894.

Kuentz, Charles. *La faces sud du massif est du pylone de Ramsès II à Louxor*. Cairo: Centre d'Etudes et de Documentation sur l'Ancienne Égypte, 1971.

el-Saghir, Mohammed. *Das Statuenversteck im Luxortempel*. Mainz am Rhein, Germany: Philipp von Zabern, 1992.

el-Saghir, Mohammed, Jean-Claude Golvin, Michel Ředde, E. Hegazy, and Guy Wagner. *Le camp romain de Louqsor*. Cairo: Institut français d'archéologie orientale, 1986.

Maadi

Menghin, Oswald, and Mustafa Amer. *The Excavations of the Egyptian University in the Neolithic Site at Maadi*. 2 vols. Cairo: Government Press, 1932–1936.

Rizkana, Ibrahim, and Jürgen Seeher. *Maadi*. 4 vols. Deutsches Archäologisches Institut. Abteilung Kairo. Archäologische Veröffentlichungen 64–65, 80–81. Mainz am Rhein, Germany: Philipp von Zabern, 1986–1990.

Malkata

Hope, Colin. *Excavations at Malkata and Birket Habu, 1971–1974 V*. Warminster, G.B.: Aris & Phillips, 1978.

Leahy, M. Anthony. *Excavations at Malkata and Birket Habu, 1971–1974 IV*. Warminster, G.B.: Aris & Phillips, 1978.

Tytus, Robb de P. *A Preliminary Report on the Pre-excavation of the Palace of Amenhotep III*. New York: Winthrop Press, 1903.

Waseda University, Architectural Research Mission for the Study of Ancient Egyptian Architecture. *Studies on the Palace of Malqata, 1985–1988* (in Japanese with English summary). Tokyo: Waseda University, 1992.

Waseda University Egypt Archaeological Mission. *The Excavations at Malkata-South, 1972–1980*. Studies in Egyptian Culture 1. Tokyo: Waseda University, 1985.

———. *Malkata-South* (in Japanese with English summary). 4 vols. Tokyo: Waseda University, 1983–1992.

Watanabe, Yasutada, and Kazuaki Seki. *The Architecture of Kom el Samak at Malkata South: A Study of Architectural Restoration*. Studies in Egyptian Culture 5. Tokyo: Waseda University, 1986.

Medamud

Robichon, Clément, and Alexandre Varille. *Description sommaire du temple primitif de Médamoud*. Cairo: Institut français d'archéologie orientale, 1940.

Medinet Habu

Chicago Epigraphic Survey. *Medinet Habu*. 8 vols. Chicago: Oriental Institute of the University of Chicago, 1930–1970.

Hölscher, Uvo. *The Excavation of Medinet Habu*. 5 vols. Chicago: Oriental Institute of the University of Chicago, 1934–1954.

Teeter, Emily, and Terry Wilfong. *Scarabs, Scarboid Seals, and Seal Impressions from Medinet Habu*. Chicago: Oriental Institute of the University of Chicago, 2003.

Medinet Madi

Bresciani, Edda. *Kom Madi 1977 e 1978. Le pitture murali del cenotafio di Alessandro Magno*. Pisa, Italy: Edizioni ETS, 2003.

——. *Rapporto preliminare delle campagne di scavo 1966 e 1967*. Milan, Italy: Instituto editoriale Cisalpino-La Goliardica, 1968.

——. *Rapporto preliminare delle campagne di scavo 1968 e 1969*. Milan, Italy: Instituto editoriale Cisalpino-La Goliardica, 1976.

Bresciani, Edda, Sergio Pernigotti, and Maria Carmela Betrò. *Ostraka demotici di Narmuthi*. Pisa, Italy: Giardini, 1983.

Gallo, P. *Ostraca demotici e ieratici d'all' archivio bilingue di Narmuthis*. Pisa, Italy: Giardini, 1997.

Mechetti, Angiolo. *Ostraka demotici e bilingui da Narmuthis*. Pisa, Italy: Edizioni ETS, 2005.

Pintaudi, Rosario, and Pieter J. Sijpesteijn. *Ostraka greci da Narmuthis*. Pisa, Italy: Giardini, 1993.

Vogliano, Achille. *Rapporto degli scavi condotti dalla Missione Archaeologica d'Egitto della R. Università di Milano nella zone di Medinet Maadi 1935–1936*. Milan, Italy: Università di Milano, 1936–1937.

Meidum

Harpur, Yvonne. *The Tombs of Nefermaat and Rahotep at Maidum. Discovery, Destruction, and Reconstruction*. Oxford, U.K.: Oxford Expedition to Egypt, 2001.

el-Khouli, Ali. *Meidum*. Sydney: Australian Centre for Egyptology, Macquarie University, 1991.

Petrie, W. M. Flinders. *Meydum*. London: Egypt Exploration Society, 1892.

Petrie, W. M. Flinders, Ernest Mackay, and Gerald Wainwright. *Maydum and Memphis III*. London: British School of Archaeology in Egypt, 1910.

Meir

Blackman, Aylward M. *The Rock Tombs of Meir*. 6 vols. London: Egypt Exploration Society, 1914–1953.

el-Khouli, Ali, and Naguib Kanawati. *Quseir el-Amarna*. Sydney: Australian Centre for Egyptology, Macquarie University, 1989.

Memphis

Abdulla, Said M. A. *A New Temple for Hathor at Memphis*. Warminster, G.B.: Aris & Phillips, 1978.

Anthes, Rudolf. *Mit Rahineh 1955*. Philadelphia, Pa.: University Museum, 1959.

———. *Mit Rahineh 1956*. Philadelphia, Pa.: University Museum, 1965.

Ashton, Sally-Anne. *Petrie's Ptolemaic and Roman Memphis*. London: Institute of Archaeology, UCL, 2003.

Aston, David A, and David G. Jeffreys. *The Survey of Memphis III. The Third Intermediate Period Levels*. London: Egypt Exploration Society, 2007.

Engelbach, Reginald. *Riqqeh and Memphis VI*. London: British School of Archaeology in Egypt, 1915.

Giddy, Lisa. *The Survey of Memphis I: Kom Rabi'a. The New Kingdom and Post–New Kingdom Objects*. London: Egypt Exploration Society, 1999.

Jeffreys, David G. *The Survey of Memphis*. London: Egypt Exploration Society, 1985.

———. *The Survey of Memphis V. Kom Rabia: The New Kingdom Settlement (Levels II–V)*. London: Egypt Exploration Society, 2006.

Petrie, W. M. Flinders. *Memphis I*. London: British School of Archaeology in Egypt, 1909.

———. *Palace of Apries (Memphis II)*. London: British School of Archaeology in Egypt, 1909.

———. *Roman Portraits and Memphis (IV)*. London: British School of Archaeology in Egypt, 1911.

Petrie, W. M. Flinders, Ernest Mackay, and Gerald Wainwright. *Meydum and Memphis (III)*. London: British School of Archaeology in Egypt, 1910.

Petrie, W. M. Flinders, Gerald Wainwright, and Alan H. Gardiner. *Tarkhan and Memphis V*. London: British School of Archaeology in Egypt, 1913.

Mendes

De Meulenaere, Herman, and Pierre Mackay. *Mendes II*. Warminster, G.B.: Aris & Phillips, 1976.

Hall, Emma S., and Bernard V. Bothmer. *Mendes I*. Warminster, G.B.: Aris 7 Phillips, 1977.
Redford, Donald B. *Excavations at Mendes. Vol I The Royal Necropolis*. Leiden, Netherlands: Brill, 2004.
Wilson, Karen. *Cities of the Delta, Part II. Mendes: Preliminary Report on the 1979 and 1980 Seasons*. Malibu, Calif.: Undena Publications, 1982.

Merimda Beni Salama

Eiwanger, Josef. *Merimde-Benisalâme*. 3 vols. Deutsches Archäologisches Institut. Abteilung Kairo. Archäologische Veröffentlichungen 47, 51, 59. Mainz am Rhein, Germany: Philipp von Zabern, 1984–1993.
Junker, Hermann. *Vorläufer Bericht über die Grabung der Akademie der Wissenschaften in Wien auf der neolitischen Siedlung von Merimde-Beni Salâme*. 6 vols. Vienna, Austria: 1929–1940.

Meroe

Dunham, Dows, and Suzanne Chapman. *The Royal Cemeteries of Kush III–V*. Boston: Museum of Fine Arts, 1952–1963.
Grzymski, Krzysztof. *Meroe Reports I*. Mississauga, Canada: SSEA, 2003.
Shinnie, Peter L., and Julie R. Anderson. *The Capital of Kush II. Meroe Excavations, 1973–1984*. Wiesbaden, Germany: Otto Harrasowitz, 2004.
Shinnie, Peter L., and Rebecca J. Bradley. *The Capital of Kush I. Meroe Excavations, 1965–1972. Meroitica 4*. Berlin, Germany: Akademie Verlag, 1980.
Török, László. *Meroe City: An Ancient African Capital. John Garstang's Excavations in the Sudan*. London: Egypt Exploration Society, 1997.

Minshat Abu Omar

Kroeper, Karla, and Dietrich Wildung. *Minshat Abu Omar: Münchner Ostdelta-Expedition Vorbericht 1978–1984*. Munich, Germany: Staatliche Sammlung Ägyptischer Kunst, 1985.
———. *Minshat Abu Omar: Ein vor- und frühgeschichlicher Friedhof im Nildelta I*. Mainz am Rhein, Germany: Philipp von Zabern, 1994.
———. *Minschat Abu Omar II*. Mainz am Rhein, Germany: Philipp von Zabern, 2000.

Mirgissa

Dunham, Dows. *Second Cataract Forts. Vol. II. Uronarti Shalfak Mirgissa.* Boston: Museum of Fine Arts, 1967.

Vercoutter, Jean. *Mirgissa.* 3 vols. Paris: P. Geuthner, 1970–1976.

Moalla, el-

Vandier, Jacques. *Mo'alla, la tombe d'Anktifi et la tombe de Sébekhotep.* Cairo: Institut français d'archéologie orientale, 1950.

Mons Claudianus

Bingen, Jean, Adam Bülow-Jacobsen, Walter E. H. Cockle, Hélène Cuvigny, Lene Rubinstein, and Wilfried Van Rengen. *Mons Claudianus: Ostraca Graeca et Latina. I–III.* Cairo: Institut français d'archéologie orientale, 1992–2000.

Maxfield, Valerie A., and David P. S. Peacock. *Survey and Excavation. Mons Claudianus 1987–1993 II: Excavations Part 1.* Cairo: Institut français d'archéologie orientale, 2001.

———. *Survey and Excavation. Mons Claudianus 1987–1993 III: Ceramic and Related Vessels.* Cairo: Institut français d'archéologie orientale, 2006.

Peacock, David P. S., and Valerie A. Maxfield. *Survey and Excavation. Mons Claudianus 1987–1993 I: Topography and Quarries.* Cairo: Institut français d'archéologie orientale, 1997.

Mons Porphyrites

Maxfield, Valerie A., and David P. S. Peacock. *The Roman Imperial Quarries Surrey and Excavation at Mons Porphyrites 1994–1998 I: Topography and Quarries.* London: Egypt Exploration Society, 2001.

Peacock, David P. S., and Valerie Maxfield. *The Roman Imperial Quarries. Survey and Excavations at Mons Porphyrites 1994–1998 II: The Excavations.* London: Egypt Exploration Society, 2007.

Myos Hormos

Peacock, David P. S., and Lucy Blue. *Myos Hormos-Quseir al-Khadim. Roman and Islamic ports on the Red Sea I. Survey and Excavations 1999–2003.* Oxford, U.K.: Oxbow Books, 2006.

Whitcomb, Donald S., and Janet S Johnson. *Quseir al-Khadim 1978*. Cairo: American Research Center in Egypt, 1979.
——. *Quseir al-Khadim 1980*. Malibu, Calif.: Undena Publications, 1982.

Naga el-Deir

Dunham, Dows. *Naga-ed-Dêr Stelae of the First Intermediate Period*. Oxford, U.K.: Oxford University Press, 1937.
Lythgoe, Albert M., and Dows Dunham. *The Predynastic Cemetery N7000. Nag-ed-Dêr IV*. Berkeley: University of California Press, 1965.
Podzorski, Patricia V. *Their Bones Shall Not Perish*. New Malden, G.B.: SIA Publications, 1990.
Reisner, George A. *A Provincial Cemetery of the Pyramid Age: Naga-ed-Dêr*. Oxford, U.K.: Oxford University Press, 1932.
Reisner, George A., and Arthur Mace. *The Early Dynastic Cemeteries of Naga-ed-Dêr*. Leipzig, Germany: J. C. Hinrichs, 1908–1909.
Simpson, William Kelly. *Papyrus Reisner I–IV*. Boston: Museum of Fine Arts, 1963–1986.

Nag el-Mashayikh

Ockinga, Boyo G., and Yahya al-Masri. *Two Ramesside Tombs at El Mashayikh*. Sydney: Ancient History Documentary Research Centre, Macquarie University, 1988–1990.

Napata

Dunham, Dows. *The Barkal Temples*. Boston: Museum of Fine Arts, 1970.
——. *The Royal Cemeteries of Kush*. 5 vols. Cambridge, Mass.: Harvard University Press, 1950; Boston: Museum of Fine Arts, 1955–1963.
Kendall, Timothy. *Gebel Barkal Epigraphic Survey 1986: Preliminary Report to the Visiting Committee of the Department of Egyptian Art*. Boston: Museum of Fine Arts, 1986.

Naqada

Baumgartel, Elise J. *Petrie's Naqada Excavation: A Supplement*. London: Bernard Quaritch Ltd., 1970.
Petrie, W. M. Flinders, and James E. Quibell. *Naqada and Ballas*. London: Bernard Quaritch Ltd., 1896.

Naukratis

Coulson, William D. E. *Ancient Naukratis II, Part I: The Survey at Naukratis*. Oxford, U.K.: Oxbow Books, 1996.

Coulson, William D. E., and Albert Leonard. *Cities of the Delta I: Naukratis: Preliminary Report on the 1977–1978 and 1980 Seasons*. Malibu, Calif.: Undena Publications, 1981.

Gardner, Ernest A. *Naukratis II*. London: Egypt Exploration Fund, 1888.

Möller, Astrid. *Naukratis. Trade in Archaic Greece*. Oxford, U.K.: Oxford University Press, 2000.

Petrie, W. M. Flinders, and Ernest A. Gardner. *Naukratis I*. London: Egypt Exploration Fund, 1886.

Piekarski, Dirk. *Die Keramik aus Naukratis im Akademischen Kunstmuseum Bonn*. Wiesbaden, Germany: Otto Harrassowitz, 2001.

Villing, Alexandra, and Udo Schlotzhauer. *Naukratis: Greek Diversity in Egypt*. London: British Museum Press, 2006.

Oxyrhynchus

Bowman, Alan K., R. A. Coles, N. Gonis, D. Obbink, and P. J. Parsons. *Oxyrhynchus. A City and Its Texts*. London: Egypt Exploration Society, 2007.

Egypt Exploration Society. *The Oxyrhynchus Papyri I–LXXI*. London: Egypt Exploration Society, 1898–2007.

Pelusium

Carrez-Maratray, Jean-Yves. *Péluse*. Cairo: Institut français d'archéologie orientale, 1999.

Qantir

Aston, David A. *Die Grabungen des Pelizaeus-Museums Hildesheim in Qantir-Pi-Ramesse I. Die Kermaik des Grabungsplatzes QI. I Corpus of Fabrics, Wares, and Shapes*. Mainz am Rhein, Germany: Philipp von Zabern, 1998.

Hayes, William C. *Glazed Tiles from a Palace of Ramesses II at Kantir*. New York: Metropolitan Museum of Art, 1937.

Herold, Anja. *Streitwagentechnologie in der Ramses-Stadt*. 2 vols. Mainz am Rhein, Germany: Philipp von Zabern, 1999–2006.

Qasr Ibrim

Adams, William Y. *Qasr Ibrim: The Late Medieval Period*. London: Egypt Exploration Society, 1996.
Caminos, Ricardo A. *The Shrines and Rock Inscriptions of Ibrim*. London: Egypt Exploration Society, 1968.
Hinds, Martin, and Hamdi Sakkout. *Arabic Documents from the Ottoman Period from Qasr Ibrim*. London: Egypt Exploration Society, 1986.
Hinds, Martin, and Victor Ménage. *Qasr Ibrim in the Ottoman Period: Turkish and Further Arabic Documents*. London: Egypt Exploration Society, 1991.
Mills, Anthony J. *The Cemeteries of Qasr Ibrim*. London: Egypt Exploration Society, 1982.
Plumley, J. Martin. *The Scrolls of Bishop Timotheos*. London: Egypt Exploration Society, 1975.
Plumley, J. Martin, and Gerald M. Browne. *Old Nubian Texts from Qasr Ibrim*. 3 vols. London: Egypt Exploration Society, 1988–1991.
Ray, John D. *Demotic Papyri and Ostraca from Qasr Ibrim*. London: Egypt Exploration Society, 2005.
Rose, Pamela. *The Meroitic Temple Complex at Qasr Ibrim*. London: Egypt Exploration Society, 2007.
———. *Qasr Ibrim: The Hinterland Survey*. London: Egypt Exploration Society, 1996.

Qau el-Kebir

Brunton, Guy. *Qau and Badari*. 2 vols. London: British School of Archaeology in Egypt, 1927–1928.
el-Khouli, Ali, and Naguib Kanawati. *The Old Kingdom Tombs of El-Hammamiya*. Sydney: Australian Centre for Egyptology, Macquarie University, 1990.
Mackay, Ernest, Guy Brunton, and W. M. Flinders Petrie. *Bahrein and el-Hemamieh*. London: British School of Archaeology in Egypt, 1929.
Petrie, W. M. Flinders. *Antaeopolis. The Tombs of Qau*. London: British School of Archaeology in Egypt, 1930.
Steckeweh, Hans. *Die Fürstengräber von Qau*. Leipzig, Germany: J. C. Hinrichs, 1936.

Ramesseum

Goyon, Jean-Claude, H. El-Achirie, and B. Fonquernie. *Le Ramesseum X*. 2 vols. Cairo: Centre d'Études et de Documentation sur l'Ancienne Égypte, 1976.

Goyon, Jean-Claude, and Hassan el-Achirie. *Le Ramesseum I: Hypostle N.* Cairo: Centre d'Etudes et de Documentation sur l'Ancienne Égypte, 1973.

———. *Le Ramesseum VI: La Salle des Litanies (R).* Cairo: Centre d'Etudes et de Documentation sur l'Ancienne Égypte, 1974.

Leblanc, Christian, and Ismail El-Sayed. *Le Ramesseum IX 1–2: Les piliers "Osiriaques."* 2 vols. Cairo: Organisation Égyptienne des Antiquités, 1980–1988.

Maher-Taha, Mahmoud, and A. Loyrette. *Le Ramesseum XI: Les fêtes du dieu Min.* Cairo: Organisation Égyptienne des Antiquités, 1979.

Quibell, James E., Wilhelm Spiegelberg, R. F. E. Paget, and A. A. Pirie. *The Ramesseum.* London: Bernard Quaritch Ltd., 1898.

Youssef, Ahmad A. H., Christian Leblanc, and Mahmoud Maher. *Le Ramesseum IV: Les batailles de Tounip et de Dapur.* Cairo: Centre d'Etudes et de Documentation sur l'Ancienne Égypte, 1977.

Saft el-Henna

Davoli, Paola. *Saft el-Henna. Archeologia e stroia di una città del Delta orientale.* Imola, Italy: Editrice La Mandragora, 2001.

Naville, Édouard. *The Shrine of Saft el-Henneh and the Land of Goschen.* London: Egypt Exploration Fund, 1887.

Petrie, W. M. Flinders. *Hyksos and Israelite Cities.* London: British School of Archaeology, 1906.

Sais

el-Sayed, Ramadan. *Documents relatifs à Saïs et ses divinités.* Cairo: Institut français d'archéologie orientale, 1975.

Wilson, Penelope. *The Survey of Sais (Sa el-Hagar) 1997–2002.* London: Egypt Exploration Society, 2006.

Saqqara

See also Archaeology: Excavations and Surveys, Serapeum.

Betro, Maria Carmela. *Saqqara III: I Testi Solari del Portale di Pascerientaisu (BN2).* Pisa, Italy: Giardini, 1989.

Bourriau, Janine, David Aston, Maarten J. Raven, Rene Van Walsem, and Colin Hope. *The Memphite Tomb of Horemheb III, Commander-in-Chief of Tutankahmun. The New Kingdom Pottery.* London: Egypt Exploration Society. 2005.

Bresciani, Edda, S. Pernigotti, S. El Naggar, and F. Silvano. *Saqqara I: Tomba di Boccori. La Galleria di Padineit*. Pisa, Italy: Giardini, 1980.

——. *La Tomba di Ciennehebu, Capo della Flotta del Re*. Pisa, Italy: Giardini, 1977.

Capart, Jean. *Une rue de tombeaux à Saqqarah*. Brussels, Belgium: Vromant & Co., 1947.

Davies, Sue. *The Sacred Animal Necropolis at North Saqqara: Mother of Apis and Baboon Catacombs*. London: Egypt Exploration Society, 2006.

Davies, Sue, and Henry S. Smith. *The Sacred Animal Necropolis at North Saqqara: The Falcon Complex and Catacomb. The Archaeological Report*. London: Egypt Exploration Society, 2005.

Davies, W. Vivian, Aly El-Khouli, Alan Lloyd, and A. Jeffrey Spencer. *Saqqara Tombs I–II*. 2 vols. London: Egypt Exploration Society, 1984–1990.

Emery, Walter B. *Excavations at Saqqara: Great Tombs of the First Dynasty I*. Cairo: Service des Antiquités de l'Égypte, 1949.

——. *Excavations at Saqqara: The Tomb of Hemaka*. Cairo: Service des Antiquités de l'Égypte, 1938.

——. *Excavations at Saqqara, 1937–1938: The Tomb of Hor-Aha*. Cairo: Service des Antiquités de l'Égypte, 1939.

——. *Great Tombs of the First Dynasty II–III*. London: Egypt Exploration Fund, 1954–1958.

Épron, Lucienne, François Daumas, and Henri Wild. *Le Tombeau de Ti*. Cairo: Institut français d'archéologie orientale, 1939–1966.

el-Fikey, Said A. *The Tomb of the Vizier Re'wer at Saqqara*. Warminster, G.B.: Aris & Phillips, 1980.

Firth, Cecil, and Battiscombe Gunn. *Excavations at Saqqara: Teti Pyramid Cemeteries*. Cairo: Service des Antiquités de l'Égypte, 1926.

Firth, Cecil, and James E. Quibell. *Excavations at Saqqara: The Step Pyramid*. Cairo: Service des Antiquités de l'Égypte, 1935.

Gaballa, Gabulla A. *The Memphite Tomb Chapel of Mose*. Warminster, G.B.: Aris & Phillips, 1978.

Giddy, Lisa. *The Anubieion at Saqqara II: The Cemeteries*. London: Egypt Exploration Society, 1992.

Green, Christine. I. *The Temple Furniture from the Sacred Animal Necropolis at North Saqqâra, 1964–1976*. London: Egypt Exploration Society, 1987.

Harpur, Yvonne, and Paolo Scremin. *The Chapel of Kagemni*. Reading, England: Oxford Expedition to Egypt, 2006.

Hassan, Selim. *Excavations at Saqqara 1937–1938*. 3 vols. Cairo: Government Printing Office, 1975.

Hastings, Elizabeth A. *The Sculpture from the Sacred Animal Necropolis at North Saqqara*. London: Egypt Exploration Society, 1997.

James, T. G. Henry. *The Mastaba of Khentika Called Ikheki*. London: Egypt Exploration Society, 1953.

Jécquier, Gustave. *Fouilles à Saqqarah*. 6 vols. Cairo: Service des Antiquités de l'Égypte, 1928–1938.

Jeffreys, David, and Henry S. Smith. *The Anubieion at Saqqara I: The Settlement and the Temple Precinct*. London: Egypt Exploration Society, 1988.

Kanawati, Naguib. *The Teti Cemetery at Saqqara III, V–VIII*. Australian Centre for Egyptology. Warminster, G.B.: Aris & Phillips, 1998–2006.

———. *The Unis Cemetery at Saqqara II: The Tombs of Iynefert and Ihy (Reused by Idut)*. Australian Centre for Egyptology. Oxford, U.K.: Aris & Phillips, 2003.

Kanawati, Naguib, Ali El-Khouli, Ann McFarlane, and Naguib V. Maksoud. *Excavations at Saqqara Northwest of Teti's Pyramid*. 2 vols. Sydney: Australian Centre for Egyptology, Macquarie University, 1984–1988.

Kanawati, Naguib, and Ali Hassan. *The Teti Cemetery at Saqqara I–II*. Australian Centre for Egyptology. Sydney and Warminster, G.B.: Macquarie University and Aris & Phillips, 1996–1997.

Kanawati, Naguib, and Mahmud Abder-Raziq. *Mereruka and His Family. Part I: The Tomb of Meryteti*. Sydney: Australian Centre for Egyptology, Macquarie University, 2004.

Labrousse, Audran. *L'Architecture des Pyramides à Texts*. 2 vols. Cairo: Institut français d'archéologie orientale, 1996.

Labrousse, Audran, Jean-Philippe Lauer, and Jean Leclant. *Le temple haut du complexe funéraire du roi Ounas*. Cairo: Institut français d'archéologie orientale, 1977.

Labrousse, Audran, and Ahmed Moussa. *La chaussée du complex funéraire du roi Ounas*. Cairo: Institut français d'archéologie orientale, 2002.

———. *Le temple d'accueil du complexe funéraire du roi Ounas*. Cairo: Institut français d'archéologie orientale, 1996.

Lauer, Jean-Philippe. *Les Pyramides de Saqqarah*. 6th ed. Cairo: Institut français d'archéologie orientale, 1991.

———. *Saqqara: The Royal Cemetery of Memphis: Excavations and Discoveries since 1850*. London: Thames & Hudson, 1976.

Lauer, Jean-Philippe, and Jean Leclant. *Le temple haut du complexe funéraire du roi Téti*. Cairo: Institut français d'archéologie orientale, 1972.

Lauer, Jean-Philippe, and Pierre Lacau. *Fouilles à Sakkarah: La Pyramide à degrés I–V*. Cairo: Service des Antiquités de l'Égypte, 1936–1965.

Lloyd, Alan, A. Jeffrey Spencer, and Ali el-Khouli. *Saqqara Tombs III: The Mastaba of Neferseshemptah*. London: Egypt Exploration Society, 2008.

Macfarlane, Anne. *Mastabas at Saqqara: Kaiemheset, Kaipunesut, Kaiemsenu, Sehepu, and Others*. Australian Centre for Egyptology. Oxford, U.K.: Aris & Phillips, 2003.

——. *The Unis Cemetery at Saqqara I: The Tomb of Irukaptah*. Australian Centre for Egyptology. Warminster, G.B.: Aris & Phillips, 2000.

Macramallah, Rizkallah. *Fouilles à Saqqarah: Un cimitière archaïque de la classe moyenne du peuple à Saqqarah*. Cairo: Service des Antiquités de l'Égypte, 1940.

Mariette, Auguste. *Les Mastabas de l'Ancien Empire*. Paris: F. Vieweg, 1889.

Martin, Geoffrey T. *Corpus of Reliefs of the New Kingdom from the Memphite Necropolis and Lower Egypt I*. London: Kegan Paul International, 1987.

——. *The Hidden Tombs of Memphis: New Discoveries from the Time of Tutankhamun and Ramesses the Great*. London: Thames & Hudson, 1991.

——. *The Memphite Tomb of Horemeheb, Commander-in-Chief of Tutankahmun I: The Reliefs, Inscriptions, and Commentary*. London: Egypt Exploration Society, 1989.

——. *The Sacred Animal Necropolis at North Saqqara*. London: Egypt Exploration Society, 1981.

——. *The Tomb Chapels of Paser and Ra'ia at Saqqara*. London: Egypt Exploration Society, 1985.

——. *The Tomb of Hetepka*. London: Egypt Exploration Society, 1979.

——. *The Tomb of Tia and Tia*. London: Egypt Exploration Society, 1997.

——. *The Tombs of Three Memphite Officials, Ramose, Khay, and Pabes*. London: Egypt Exploration Society, 2001.

Moussa, Ahmed, and Friedrich Junge. *Two Tombs of Craftsmen*. Deutsches Archäologisches Institut. Abteilung Kairo. Archäologische Veröffentlichungen 9. Mainz am Rhein, Germany: Philipp von Zabern, 1975.

Moussa, Ahmed M., and Hartwig Altenmüller. *Saqqara: Das Grab des Nianchchnum und Chnumhotep*. Deutsches Archäologisches Institut. Abteilung Kairo. Archäologische Veröffentlichungen 21. Mainz am Rhein, Germany: Philipp von Zabern, 1977.

——. *The Tomb of Nefer and Ka-Hay*. Deutsches Archäologisches Institut. Abteilung Kairo. Archäologische Veröffentlichungen 5. Mainz am Rhein, Germany: Philipp von Zabern, 1971.

Munro, Peter. *Der Unas-Friedhof Nordwest I*. Mainz am Rhein, Germany: Philipp von Zabern, 1993.

Mysliwiec, Karol. *Saqqara I. The Tomb of Merefnebef*. Warsaw, Poland: Editions Neriton, 2004.

Ockinga, Boyo G. *Amenemone the Chief Goldsmith: A New Kingdom Tomb in the Teti Cemetery at Saqqara*. Sydney: Australian Centre for Egyptology, Macquarie University, 2004.

Quibell, James E. *Excavations at Saqqara (1905–1906)*. Cairo: Service des Antiquités de l'Égypte, 1907.

——. *Excavations at Saqqara (1906–1907)*. Cairo: Service des Antiquités de l'Égypte, 1908.

———. *Excavations at Saqqara (1907–1908)*. Cairo: Service des Antiquités de l'Égypte, 1909.

———. *Excavations at Saqqara (1908–1909, 1909–1910): The Monastery of Apa Jeremias*. Cairo: Service des Antiquités de l'Égypte, 1912.

———. *Excavations at Saqqara (1911–1912): The Tomb of Hesy*. Cairo: Service des Antiquités de l'Égypte, 1913.

———. *Excavations at Saqqara (1912–1914): Archaic Mastabas*. Cairo: Service des Antiquités de l'Égypte, 1923.

Quibell, James E., and Angelo Hayter. *Excavations at Saqqara: Teti Pyramid North Side*. Cairo: Service des Antiquités de l'Égypte, 1927.

Raven, Maarten J. *The Tomb of Irudef*. London: Egypt Exploration Society, 1991.

———. *The Tomb of Maya and Meryt II: Objects and Skeletal Remains*. London: Egypt Exploration Society, 2001.

———. *The Tomb of Pay and Raia at Saqqara*. London: Egypt Exploration Society, 2005.

Ricke, Herbert. *Das Sonnenheiligtum des Königs Userkaf*. Beiträge für Ägyptischen Bauforschung und Altertumskunde 7–8. Cairo: Schweizerisches Institut fur Ägyptische, 1965–1969.

Rzeuska, Teodozja. *Saqqara II. Pottery of the Late Old Kingdom*. Warsaw, Poland: Editions Neriton, 2006.

Smith, Henry S., Sue Davies, and Kenneth J. Frazer. *The Sacred Animal Necropolis at North Saqqara: The Main Temple Complex. The Archaeological Report*. London: Egypt Exploration Society, 2006.

Sowada, Karin, Tracey Callaghan, and Paul Bentley. *The Teti Cemetery at Saqqara IV*. Australian Centre for Egyptology. Warminster, G.B., Aris & Phillips, 1999.

Ziegler, Christiane. *Le Mastaba d'Akhethetep*. Louvain, Belgium: Peeters, 2007.

Zivie, Alain. *Découverte à Saqqarah: Le vizier oublié*. Paris: Seuil, 1990.

Sedment

Grajetski, Wolfram. *Sedment, Burials of Egyptian Farmers and Noblemen over the Centuries*. London: Golden House Publications, 2005.

Petrie, W. M. Flinders, and Guy Brunton. *Sedment I–II*. London: British School of Archaeology in Egypt, 1924.

Semna

Caminos, Ricardo. *Semna-Kumma*. 2 vols. London: Egypt Exploration Society, 1998.

Dunham, Dows, and Jozef M. A. Janssen. *Second Cataract Forts. Vol. 1. Semna Kumma*. Boston: Museum of Fine Arts, 1960.

Serabit el-Khadim

Petrie, W. M. Flinders, and Charles T. Curelly. *Researches in Sinai*. London: J. Murray, 1906.
Valbelle, Dominique, and Charles Bonnet. *Le sanctuaire d'Hathor maîtresse de la turquoise*. Paris: Picard, 1996.

Serapeum

Lauer, Jean-Philippe, and Charles Picard. *Les statues ptolémaïques du Sérapiéion de Memphis*. Paris: Presses Universitaires de France, 1955.
Malinine, Michel, Georges Posener, and Jean Vercoutter. *Catalogue des stèles du Sérapeum de Memphis I*. Paris: Musées Nationaux, 1968.
Mariette, Auguste. *Le Sérapéum de Memphis*, ed. Gaston Maspero. Paris: F. Vieweg, 1882.

Shalfak

See Archaeology: Excavations and Surveys, Uronarti.

Shanhur

Willems, Harco, Filip Coppens, and Marleen de Meyer. *The Temple of Shanhur I: The Sanctuary, the Wabet, and the Gates of the Central Hall and the Great Vestibule (1–98)*. Louvain, Belgium: Peeters, 2003.

Siwa Oasis

Fakhry, Ahmed. *The Oases of Egypt I: Siwa Oasis*. Cairo: American University in Cairo Press, 1973.
———. *Siwa Oasis*. Cairo: Government Press, 1944.
Giddy, Lisa. *Egyptian Oases*. Warminster, G.B.: Aris & Phillips, 1987.

Soleb

Giorgini, Michela Schiff. *Soleb*. 2 vols. Florence, Italy: Sansoni, 1965–1971.

Tanis

Brissaud, Philippe. *Cahiers de Tanis I*. Paris: Éditions Recherche sur les Civilisations, 1987.

Brissaud, Philippe, and Christiane Zivie-Coche. *Tanis. Travaux Récents sur le Tell Sân el-Hagar. Mission Française des fouilles de Tanis 1987–1997*. Paris: Éditions Noêsis, 1998.

———. *Tanis. Travaux Récents sur le Tell Sân el-Hagar 2. Mission Française des fouilles de Tanis 1997–2000*. Paris: Éditions Noêsis, 2000.

Montet, Pierre. *Le lac sacré de Tanis*. Paris: C. Klincksieck, 1966.

———. *La nécropole royale de Tanis*. 3 vols. Paris, 1947–1960.

———. *Les nouvelles fouilles de Tanis*. Paris: Les Belles Lettres, 1933.

Petrie, W. M. Flinders. *Tanis*. 2 vols. London: Egypt Exploration Fund, 1885–1888.

Yoyotte, Jean, Jean Leclant, and Pascal Vernus. *Tanis: L'or des pharaons*. Paris: Ministère des Affaires Étrangères, 1987.

Zivie-Coche, Christiane. *Tanis. Travaux Récents sur le Tell Sân el-Hagar. Mission Française des fouilles de Tanis. Statues et Autobiographies de Dignitaires. Tanis a l'époque ptolémaïque*. Paris: Éditions Cybele, 2004.

Taposiris Magna

Vörös, Gyozo. *Taposiris Magna. Port of Isis*. Budapest: Egypt Exploration Society of Hungary, 2001.

Tarkhan

Grajetzki, Wolfram. *Tarkhan: A Cemetery at the Time of Egyptian State Formation*. London: Golden House Pubications, 2004.

Petrie, W. M. Flinders. *Heliopolis, Kafr Ammar, and Shurafa*. London: British School of Archaeology in Egypt, 1915.

———. *Tarkhan II*. London: British School of Archaeology in Egypt, 1914.

Petrie, W. M. Flinders, G. A. Wainwright, and A. H. Gardiner. *Tarkhan I and Memphis V*. London: British School of Archaeology in Egypt, 1913.

Tebtunis

Boak, Arthur A. *Papyri from Tebtunis*. Ann Arbor: University of Michigan Press, 1933.

Gallazzi, Claudio, and Gisèle Hadji-Minaglou. *Tebtynis I*. Cairo: Institut français d'archéologie orientale, 2000.

Grenfell, Bernard, and Arthur Hunt, and P. M. Meyer. *Tebtunis Papyris I–III*. London: Henry Frowde and Humphrey, Milford, 1902–1933.

Hadji-Minaglou, Gisèle. *Tebtynis IV: Les Habitations á l'est du Temple de Soknebtynis*. Cairo: Institut français d'archéologie orientale, 2007.

Husselman, Elinor. *Papyri from Tebtunis II*. Ann Arbor: University of Michigan Press, 1944.

Keenan, James G., and John C. Shelton. *Papyri from Tebtunis IV*. London: Egypt Exploration Society, 1976.

Lippert, Sandra, and Martin Schentuleit. *Tebtynis und Soknopaiu Nesos: Leben in römerzeitlichen Fajum*. Wiesbaden, Germany: Otto Harrassowitz, 2005.

Rondot, Vincent. *Tebtynis II: Le Temple de Sobnebtynis et son Dromos*. Cairo: Institut français d'archéologie orientale, 2004.

Tait, W. John. *Papyri from Tebtunis in Egyptian and Greek*. London: Egypt Exploration Society, 1977.

Tell Dafana

Petrie, W. M. Flinders. *Tanis II, Nebesheh (Am), and Defenneh (Tahpanhes)*. London: Egypt Exploration Fund, 1888.

Tell el-Balamun

Spencer, A. Jeffrey. *Excavations at Tell el-Balamun, 1991–1994*. London: British Museum Press, 1996.

———. *Excavations at Tell el-Balamun, 1995–1998*. London: British Museum Press, 1999.

———. *Excavations at Tell el-Balamun, 1999–2001*. London: British Museum Press, 2003.

Tell el-Farkha

Chlodnicki, Marek, and Krzysztof M. Cialowicz. *Ivory and Gold: Beginnings of Egyptian Art-Discoveries in Tell el-Farkha*. Poznan, Poland: Poznan Prehistoric Society, 2007.

Jucha, Mariuz. *Tell el-Farkha II: The Pottery of the Predynastic Settlement (Phases 2 to 5)*. Krakow/Poznan, Poland: Institute of Archaeology, Jagiiellonian University, Krakow and Archaeological Museum, Poznan, 2005.

Tell el-Maskhuta

Holladay, John S. *Cities of the Delta III: Tell el-Maskhuta*. Malibu, Calif.: Undena Publications, 1982.

Naville, Édouard. *The Store-City of Pithom and the Route of the Exodus*. London: Egypt Exploration Fund, 1885.

Tell el-Yahudiya

Naville, Édouard. *The Mound of the Jew and the City of Onias*. London: Egypt Exploration Fund, 1890.

Petrie, W. M. Flinders. *Hyksos and Israelite Cities*. London: British School of Archaeology in Egypt, 1906.

Tell Hebua

Abd el-Maksoud, Mohamed. *Tell Heboua (1981–1991)*. Paris: Ministère des Affaires Étrangères, 1998.

Thebes: Private Tombs

Arnold, Dieter. *Gräber des Alten und Mittleren Reiches in El-Tarif*. Deutsches Archäologisches Institut. Abteilung Kairo. Archäologische Veröffentlichungen 17. Mainz am Rhein, Germany: Philipp von Zabern, 1976.

———. *Grabung im Asasif 1963–1970 I. Das Grab des Jnj-jtj.f: Die Architectur*. Deutsches Archäologisches Institut. Abteilung Kairo. Archäologische Veröffentlichungen 4. Mainz am Rhein, Germany: Philipp von Zabern, 1971.

Assmann, Jan. *Das Grab des Amenemope (TT41): Theben III*. Mainz am Rhein, Germany: Philipp von Zabern, 1991.

———. *Grabung im Asasif 1963–1970 II. Das Grab des Basa (Nr. 389) in der thebanischen Nekropole*. Deutsches Archäologisches Institut. Abteilung Kairo. Archäologische Veröffentlichungen 6. Mainz am Rhein, Germany: Philipp von Zabern, 1973.

———. *Grabung im Asasif 1963–1970 VI. Das Grab des Mutirdis*. Deutsches Archäologisches Institut. Abteilung Kairo. Archäologische Veröffentlichungen 13. Mainz am Rhein, Germany: Philipp von Zabern, 1977.

———. *Sonnenhymnen in Thebanischen Gräber: Theben I*. Mainz am Rhein, Germany: Philipp von Zabern, 1983.

Bietak, Manfred, and Elfriede Reiser-Haslauer. *Das Grab des 'Anch-hor,Obersthofmeister der Gottesgemahlin Nitokris*. 2 vols. Untersuchungen der Zweigstelle Kairo des Österreichischen Archäologischen Institut IV–V. Vienna, Austria: Österreichischen Akademie der Wissenschaften, 1978–1982.

Brack, Annelies, and Artur Brack. *Das Grab des Haremheb: Theben Nr. 78.* Deutsches Archäologisches Institut. Abteilung Kairo. Archäologische Veröffentlichungen 35. Mainz am Rhein, Germany: Philipp von Zabern, 1980.

———. *Das Grab des Tjanuni: Theban Nr. 74.* Deutsches Archäologisches Institut. Abteilung Kairo. Archäologische Veröffentlichungen 19. Mainz am Rhein, Germany: Philipp von Zabern, 1977.

Burkard, Günter. *Grabung im Asasif 1963–1970 III. Die Papyrusfunde.* Deutsches Archäologisches Institut. Abteilung Kairo. Archäologische Veröffentlichungen 22. Mainz am Rhein, Germany: Philipp von Zabern, 1986.

Davies, Norman de Garis. *The Tomb of Ken-amun at Thebes.* New York: Metropolitan Museum of Art, 1930.

———. *The Tomb of Nakht at Thebes.* New York: Metropolitan Museum of Art, 1917.

———. *The Tomb of Nefer-hotep at Thebes.* New York: Metropolitan Museum of Art, 1933.

———. *The Tomb of Rekh-mi-re at Thebes.* New York: Metropolitan Museum of Art, 1943.

———. *The Tomb of Two Sculptors at Thebes.* New York: Metropolitan Museum of Art, 1925.

Dorman, Peter. *The Tombs of Senenemut.* New York: Metropolitan Museum of Art, 1991.

Dorman, Peter, and Betsy Bryan, eds. *Sacred Space and Sacred Function in Ancient Thebes.* Chicago: Oriental Institute of the University of Chicago, 2007.

Dziobek, Eberhard. *Das Grab des Ineni: Theben Nr. 81.* Deutsches Archäologisches Institut. Abteilung Kairo. Archäologisches Veröffentlichungen 68. Mainz am Rhein, Germany: Philipp von Zabern, 1991.

———. *Die Gräber des Vezirs User-Amun: Theben Nr. 61 und 131.* Deutsches Archäologisches Institut. Abteilung Kairo. Archäologische Veröffentlichungen 84. Mainz am Rhein, Germany: Philipp von Zabern, 1994.

Dziobek, Eberhard, and Mahmud Abdel Raziq. *Das Grab des Sobekhotep: Theben Nr. 63.* Deutsches Archäologisches Institut. Abteilung Kairo. Archäologische Veröffentlichungen 71. Mainz am Rhein, Germany: Philipp von Zabern, 1990.

Eigner, Dieter. *Die Monumentalen Grabbauten der Spätzeit in der Thebanischen Nekrople.* Denkschriften der Gesamtakademie VIII. Vienna, Austria: Österreichische Akademie der Wisenschaften, 1984.

Epigraphic Survey. *The Tomb of Kheruef: Theban Tomb 192.* Chicago: Oriental Institute of the University of Chicago, 1980.

Feucht, Erika. *Theben II: Das Grab des Nefersecheru (TT 296).* Mainz am Rhein, Germany: Philipp von Zabern, 1985.

———. *Theben XV: Die Gräber des Nedjemger (TT 138) und des Hori (TT 259).* Mainz am Rhein, Germany: Philipp von Zabern, 2006.

Graefe, Erhart. *Das Grab des Ibi*. Brussels, Belgium: Fondation Égyptologique Reine Élisabeth, 1990.

———. *Das Grab des Padihorresnet, Obervermögensverwalter der Gottesgemahlin des Amun (Thebanisches Grab Nr. 196)*. Turnhout, Belgium: Brepols, 2003.

Grimm, Alfred, and Hermann A. Schlögl. *Das Thebanische Grab Nr. 136 unter der Beginn der Amarnazeit*. Wiesbaden, Germany: Otto Harrassowitz, 2005.

Guksch, Heike. *Das Grab des Benja gennant Paheqamen: Theben Nr. 343*. Deutsches Archäologisches Institut. Abteilung Kairo. Archäologische Veröffentlichungen 7. Mainz am Rhein, Germany: Philipp von Zabern, 1978.

———. *Die Gräber des Nacht-Min und des Men-cheper-Ra-Seneb: Theben Nr. 87 und 79*. Deutsches Archäologisches Institut. Abteilung Kairo. Archäologische Veröffentlichungen 34. Mainz am Rhein, Germany: Philipp von Zabern, 1995.

Habachi, Labib, and Pierre Anus. *Le tombeau de Nay à Gournet Mar'ei*. Cairo: Institut français d'archéologie orientale, 1977.

Hari, Robert. *La tombe thébaine du père divin Neferhotep (TT 50)*. Geneva, Switzerland: Éditions de Belles-Lettres, 1985.

Hawass, Zahi, and Mahmoud Maher-Taha. *Le Tombeau de Menna [TT. No 69]*. Cairo: Supreme Council of Antiquities, 2002.

Hegazy, El Sayed A., and Mario Tosi. *A Theban Private Tomb no. 295*. Deutsches Archäologisches Institut. Abteilung Kairo. Archäologische Veröffentlichungen 45. Mainz am Rhein, Germany: Philipp von Zabern, 1978.

Hofmann, Eva. *Theben IX: Das Grab des Neferrenpet gen. Kenro (TT 178)*. Mainz am Rhein, Germany: Philipp von Zabern, 1995.

———. *Theben XVII: Bilder im Wandel. Die Kunst der Ramessidischen Privatgräber*. Mainz am Rhein, Germany: Philipp von Zabern, 2004.

Jaros-Deckert, Brigitte. *Grabung im Asasif 1963–1970 V. Das Grab des Jnj-jtj.f: Die Wandmalereien der XI. Dynastie*. Deutsches Archäologisches Institut. Abteilung Kairo. Archäologische Veröffentlichungen 12. Mainz am Rhein, Germany: Philipp von Zabern, 1984.

Kákosy, László, Tamás A. Bács, Zoltán Bartos, Zoltán I. Fábián, and Ernő Gaál. *The Mortuary Monument of Djehutymes (TT32)*. Budapest, Hungary: Archaeolingua Alapítvány, 2004.

Kampp, Friederike. *Theben XII: Die thebanische Nekropole*. Mainz am Rhein, Germany: Philipp von Zabern, 1993.

Kuhlmann, Klaus, and Wolfgang Schenkel. *Das Grab des Ibi, Obergutsverwalters der Gottesgemahlin des Amun (Thebanischen Grab Nr. 36) I*. Deutsches Archäologisches Institut. Abteilung Kairo. Archäologische Veröffentlichungen 15. Mainz am Rhein, Germany: Philipp von Zabern, 1983.

Manniche, Lise. *Lost Ramesside Tombs and Late Period Tombs in the Theban Necropolis.* Carsten Niebuhr Institute of Ancient Near Eastern Studies Publications 33. Copenhagen, Denmark: Museum Tusculanum Press. 2007.

———. *Lost Tombs.* London: Kegan Paul International, 1988.

———. *The Wall Decoration of Three Theban Tombs (TT 77, 175, and 249).* Carsten Niebuhr Institute of Ancient Near Eastern Studies Publications 4. Copenhagen, Denmark: Museum Tusculanum Press, 1988.

Mostafa, Maher F. *Das Grab des Neferhotep und des Meh: Theben VIII.* Mainz am Rhein, Germany: Philipp von Zabern, 1995.

Negm, Maged. *The Tomb of Simut (Kyky): Theban Tomb 409 at Qurnah.* Warminster, G.B.: Aris & Phillips, 1997.

Polz, Daniel. *Das Grab des Hui und des Kel: Theben Nr. 54.* Deutsches Archäologisches Institut. Abteilung Kairo. Archäologische Veröffentlichungen 74. Mainz am Rhein, Germany: Philipp von Zabern, 1996.

Redford, Susan, and Donald Redford. *The Akhenaten Temple Project 4: The Tomb of Reca.* Toronto: University of Toronto, 1994.

Römisch-Germanisches Museum Köln. *Sen-nefer. Die Grabkammer des Bürgermeisters von Theben.* Mainz am Rhein, Germany: Philipp von Zabern, 1986.

el-Saady, Hassan. *The Tomb of Amenhab No. 44 at Qurnah.* Warminster, G.B.: Aris & Phillips, 1997.

Saleh, Mohammed. *Three Old-Kingdom Tombs at Thebes.* Deutsches Archäologisches Institut. Abteilung Kairo. Archäologische Veröffentlichungen 14. Mainz am Rhein, Germany: Philipp von Zabern, 1977.

Säve-Söderbergh, Torgny. *Private Tombs at Thebes.* 4 vols. Oxford, U.K.: Griffith Institute, 1957–1963.

Seele, Keith. *The Tomb of Tjanefer at Thebes.* Chicago: Oriental Institute of the University of Chicago, 1959.

Seidel, Matthias, and Abdel Ghaffar Shedid. *Das Grab des Nacht.* Mainz am Rhein, Germany: Philipp von Zabern, 1992.

Seyfried, Karl-Joachim. *Das Grab des Amonmose (TT 373): Theben IV.* Mainz am Rhein, Germany: Philipp von Zabern, 1990.

———. *Das Grab des Djehutiemhab (TT 194): Theben VII.* Mainz am Rhein, Germany: Philipp von Zabern, 1995.

———. *Das Grab des Paenkhemenu (TT 68) und die Anlage TT 227: Theben VI.* Mainz am Rhein, Germany: Philipp von Zabern, 1991.

Strudwick, Nigel. *The Tombs of Amenhotep, Khnummose, and Amenmose at Thebes (Nos. 294, 253, and 254).* Oxford, U.K.: Griffith Institute, 1996.

Strudwick, Nigel, and Helen Strudwick. *Thebes in Egypt.* London: British Museum Press, 1999.

Strudwick, Nigel, and John H. Taylor. *The Theban Necropolis: Past, Present, and Future.* London: British Museum Press, 2003.

Vandier d'Abbadie, Jeanne. *Deux tombes ramessides à Gournet-Mouraï*. Cairo: Institut français d'archéologie orientale, 1954.

Thebes: Valley of the Kings

For Tutankhamun *see* History, Tutankhamun.

Bongioanni, Alessandro. *Luxor and the Valley of the Kings*. Vercelli, Italy: White Star Publications, 2004.

Dodson, Aidan. *After the Pyramids: The Valley of the Kings and Beyond*. London: Rubicon Press, 2000.

Hawass, Zaki. *The Royal Tombs of Egypt: The Art of Thebes Revealed*. London: Thames & Hudson, 2006.

Helck, Wolfgang. *Das Grab Nr 55 im Königsgräbertal*. Mainz am Rhein, Germany: Philipp von Zabern, 2001.

Hornung, Erik. *Das Grab des Haremhab im Tal der Könige*. Bern, Switzerland: Francke Verlag, 1971.

——. *The Tomb of Pharaoh Seti I*. Zurich, Switzerland: Artemis Verlag, 1991.

——. *The Valley of the Kings: Horizon of Eternity*, trans. David Warburton. New York: Timken Publishers, 1990.

——. *Zwei ramessidische Königsgräber: Ramses IV. und Ramses VII. Theben XI*. Mainz am Rhein, Germany: Philipp von Zabern, 1990.

Jenni, Hanna. *Das Grab Ramses' X (KV 18)*. Aegyptiaca Helvetica 16. Basel, Switzerland: Schwabe & Co. AG Verlag, 2000.

Reeves, C. Nicholas. *After Tutankhamun*. London: Kegan Paul International, 1992.

——. *Valley of the Kings: The Decline of a Royal Necropolis*. London: Kegan Paul International, 1990.

Reeves, C. Nicholas, and Richard H. Wilkinson. *The Complete Valley of the Kings*. London: Thames & Hudson, 1996.

Rose, John. *Tomb KV39: A Double Archaeological Enigma*. Bristol, U.K.: Western Academic and Specialist Press, 2000.

Weeks, Kent. *Atlas of the Valley of the Kings*. Cairo: American University in Cairo Press, 2000.

——. *KV5: A Preliminary Report on the Excavation of the Tomb of the Sons of Ramesses II in the Valley of the Kings*. 2nd ed. Cairo: American University in Cairo Press, 2006.

——. *The Lost Tomb*. London: Weidenfeld & Nicolson, 1998.

——, ed. *Valley of the Kings*. Vercelli, Italy: White Star Publications, 2001.

Thebes: Valley of the Queens

Hassanein, F., and M. Nelson. *La tombe du Prince Amon-(her)-khepchef*. Cairo: Centre d'Etudes et de Documentation sur l'Ancienne Égypte, 1976.

Leblanc, Christian. *Ta Set Nefrou: Une nécropole de Thèbes-Ouest et son histoire I*. Cairo: Nubar Printing House, 1989.

Lilyquist, Christine. *The Tomb of Tuthmosis III's Foreign Wives*. New York: Metropolitan Musuem of Art, 2004.

Macke, André, Christaine Macke-Ribet, and Jacques Connan. *Ta Set Nefrou: Une nécropole de Thèbes-Ouest et son histoire V*. Cairo: Dar Namatallah Press, 2002.

McDonald, John K. *House of Eternity: The Tomb of Nefertari*. London: Thames & Hudson, 1996.

Schiaparelli, Ernesto. *Esplorazione della "Valle delle Regine."* Turin, Italy: 1923.

Schmidt, Heike C., and Joachim Willeitner. *Nefertari-Gemahlin Ramses' II*. Mainz am Rhein, Germany: Philipp von Zabern, 1994.

Thausing, Gertrud, and Hans Goedicke. *Nofretari*. Graz, Austria: Akademische Druck- u. Verlagsanstalt, 1971.

Thebes: West Bank Temples

See also Archaeology: Excavations and Surveys, Medinet Habu; Archaeology: Excavations and Surveys, Ramesseum.

Barbotin, Christophe, and Christian Leblanc. *Les Monuments d'Éternité de Ramsés II: Nouvelles fouilles thébaines*. Paris: Réunion des Musées Nationaux, 1999.

Bickel, Susanne. *Untersuchungen im Totentempel des Merenptah in Theben III: Tore und andere Wiederverwendete Bauteile Amenophis' III*. Beiträge zur Ägyptischen Bauforschung und Altertumskunde 16. Stuttgart, Germany: Franz Steiner, 1997.

Guidotti, Maria Christina, and Flora Silvano. *La ceramica del tempio di Thutmosi IV a Gurna*. Pisa, Italy: Edizioni ETS, 2003.

Haeny, Gerhard. *Untersuchungen im Totentempel Amenophis' III*. Beiträge zur Ägyptischen Bauforschung und Altertumskunde 11. Wiesbaden, Germany: Franz Steiner Verlag, 1981.

Osing, Jürgen. *Der Tempel Sethos' I in Gurna: Die Reliefs und Inschriften I*. Deutsches Archäologisches Institut. Abteilung Kairo. Archäologische Veröffentlichungen 20. Mainz am Rhein, Germany: Philipp von Zabern, 1977.

Petrie, W. M. Flinders. *Six Temples at Thebes 1896*. London: Bernard Quaritch Ltd., 1897.

Polz, Daniel, and Anne Seiler. *Die Pyramidenanlage des Königs Nub-Cheper-Re Intef in Dra' Abu el-Naga*. Mainz am Rhein, Germany: Philipp von Zabern, 2003.

Vörös, Gyozo. *Temple on the Pyramid of Thebes*. Budapest, Hungary: Szazs-zorszep Kiado es Nyomda Ltd., 1998.

Timna

Rothenberg, Benno. *The Egyptian Mining Temple at Timna*. London: Institute for Archao-Metallurgical Studies, Institute of Archaeology, University College London, 1988.

———. *Timna: Valley of the Biblical Copper Mines*. London: Thames & Hudson, 1972.

Tod

Bisson de la Roque, F., G. Conteneau, and F. Chapouthier. *Le trésor de Tôd*. Cairo: Institut français d'archéologie orientale, 1953.

Grenier, Jean-Claude. *Tôd. Les Inscriptions du temple ptolémaïque et romain I*. Cairo: Institut français d'archéologie orientale, 1980.

Thiers, Christophe. *Tôd. Les Inscriptions du temple ptolémaïque et romain II–III*. Cairo: Institut français d'archéologie orientale, 2003.

Tuna el-Gebel

Boessneck, Joachim, Angela von der Dreisch, and Dieter Kessler. *Tuna el-Gebel I: Die Tiergalerien*. Hildesheimer Ägyptologische Beiträge 24. Hildesheim, Germany: Gerstenberg, 1987.

Cherpion, Nadine, Jean-Pierre Corteggiani, and Jean-François Gout. *Petosiris. Releve photographique*. Cairo: Institut français d'archéologie orientale, 2007.

Gabra, Sami, Étienne Drioton, Paul Perdrizet, and William G. Waddell. *Rapport sur les fouilles d'Hermopolis Ouest*. Cairo: Institut français d'archéologie orientale, 1941.

Kessler, Dieter. *Tuna el-Gebel II: Die Paviankultkammer G-C-C-2*. Hildesheimer Ägyptologische Beiträge 43. Hildesheim, Germany: Gerstenberg, 1998.

Lefebvre, Gustave. *Le Tombeau de Petosiris*. Cairo: Service des Antiquités de l'Égypte, 1923.

Uronarti

Dunham, Dows. *Second Cataract Forts. Vol. II. Uronarti Shalfak Mirgissa*. Boston: Museum of Fine Arts, 1967.

Wadi el-Hudi

Fakhry, Ahmed. *The Inscriptions of the Amethyst Quarries at Wadi el Hudi.* Cairo: Service des Antiquités de l'Egypte, 1952.

Sadek, Ashraf I. *The Amethyst Mining Inscriptions of Wadi el-Hudi.* 2 vols. Warminster, G.B.: Aris 7 Phillips, 1980–1985.

Wadi es-Sebua

Gauthier, Henri. *Le Temple de Ouadi es-Sebouâ.* Cairo: Institut français d'archéologie orientale, 1912.

Lurson, Benoit. *Osiris, Ramsès, Thot et le Nil. Les chapelles secondaires des temples de Derr et Ouadi es-Seboua.* Louvain, Belgium: Peeters, 2007.

Wadi Hamammat

Couyat, Jules, and Pierre Montet. *Les inscriptions hiéroglyphiques et hiératiques du Ouâdi Hammâmât.* Cairo: Institut français d'archéologie orientale, 1912.

Cuvigny, Hélène. *Ostraca de Krokodilô. La correspondance militaire et son circulation.* Cairo: Institut français d'archéologie orientale, 2003.

———, ed. *La route de Myos Hormos.* 2 vols. Cairo: Institut français d'archéologie orientale, 2003.

Zawiyet el-Aryan

Dunham, Dows. *Zawiyet el-Aryan.* Boston: Museum of Fine Arts, 1978.

Zawiyet Sultan

Osing, Jurgen. *Das Grab des Nefersecheru in Zawiyet Sultan.* Deutsches Archäologisches Institut. Abteilung Kairo. Archäologische Veröffentlichungen 88. Mainz am Rhein, Germany: Philipp von Zabern, 1992.

ART AND ARCHITECTURE

Aldred, Cyril. *Egyptian Art: In the Days of the Pharaohs, 3100–320 BC.* London: Thames & Hudson, 1980.

Arnold, Dieter. *Building in Egypt: Pharaonic Stone Masonry.* Oxford, U.K.: Oxford University Press, 1991.

——. *The Encyclopedia of Ancient Egyptian Architecture*. London: I. B. Tauris, 2002.

Aufrère, Sydney, and Jean-Claude Golvin. *L'Égypte restituée*. 3 vols. Éditions Errance, 1991–1997.

Badawy, Alexander. *A History of Egyptian Architecture*. 3 vols. Berkeley: University of California Press, 1966–1968.

Bothmer, Bernard V. *Egyptian Sculpture of the Late Period 700 BC to AD 100*. New York: Arno Press, 1969.

Davies, Nina M., and Alan H. Gardiner. *Ancient Egyptian Painting*. 3 vols. Chicago: University of Chicago Press, 1936.

Dodson, Aidan. *Egyptian Rock-cut Tombs*. Aylesbury, G.B.: Shire Publications, 1991.

Doxiadis, Euphrosyne. *The Mysterious Fayum Portraits: Faces from Ancient Egypt*. London: Thames & Hudson, 1996.

Goyon, Jean-Claude, Jean-Claude Glovin, Claire Simon Boidot, and Gilles Martinet. *La Construction Pharaonique du Moyen Empire à l'époque Gréco-romaine: Contexte et principes technologiques*. Paris: Picard, 2004.

James, T. G. Henry. *Egyptian Painting and Drawing in the British Museum*. London: British Museum Publications, 1985.

James, T. G. Henry, and W. Vivian Davies. *Egyptian Sculpture*. London: British Museum Publications, 1983.

Josephson, Jack A. *Egyptian Royal Sculpture of the Late Period, 400–246 B.C.* Mainz am Rhein, Germany: Philipp von Zabern, 1997.

Kischkewitz, Hannelore, and Werner Forman. *Egyptian Art: Drawings and Paintings*. London: Hamlyn, 1989.

Lange, Kurt, and Max Hirmer. *Egypt: Architecture, Sculpture, Painting in Three Thousand Years*. London and New York: Phaidon, 1956.

McKenzie, Judith. *The Architecture of Alexandria and Egypt, 300 BC–AD 700*. New Haven and London: Yale University Press, 2007.

Mekhitarian, Arpag. *Egyptian Painting*. Geneva, Switzerland: Skira, 1954.

Michalowski, Kazimierz. *The Art of Ancient Egypt*. London: Thames & Hudson, 1969. 2nd ed. reprinted in French, Jean-Pierre Corteggiani and Alessandro Roccati, *L'Art de l'Égypte*. Paris: Citadelles et Mazenod, 1994.

Peck, William H., and John G. Ross. *Drawings from Ancient Egypt*. London: Thames & Hudson, 1978.

Riggs, Christina. *The Beautiful Death in Roman Egypt: Art, Identity, and Funerary Religion*. Oxford, U.K.: Oxford University Press, 2006.

Robins, Gay. *The Art of Ancient Egypt*. London: British Museum Press, 1997.

——. *Egyptian Painting and Relief*. Aylesbury, G.B.: Shire Publications, 1986.

——. *Egyptian Statues*. Princes Risborough, G.B.: Shire Publications, 2001.

——. *Proportion and Style in Ancient Egyptian Art*. London: Thames & Hudson, 1994.

Rossi, Corinna. *Architecture and Mathematics in Ancient Egypt*. Cambridge, U.K.: Cambridge University Press, 2003.

Russmann, Edna R. *Egyptian Sculpture: Cairo and Luxor*. Austin: University of Texas Press, 1989.

Schäfer, Heinrich. *Principles of Egyptian Art*, ed. Emma Brunner-Traut, trans. and ed. John Baines. Oxford, U .K.: Clarendon Press, 1974.

Shore, A. F. *Portrait Painting from Roman Egypt*. London: British Museum Publications, 1972.

Smith, W. Stevenson. *The Art and Architecture of Ancient Egypt*. Rev. ed. London: Penguin Books, 1981.

Spencer, A. Jeffrey. *Brick Architecture in Ancient Egypt*. Warminster, G.B.: Aris & Phillips, 1979.

Walker, Susan, and Morris Bierbrier. *Ancient Faces*. London: British Museum Press, 1997.

PYRAMIDS AND OBELISKS

Edwards, I. Eiddon S. *The Pyramids of Egypt*. London: Penguin, 1993.

Fakhry, Ahmed. *The Pyramids*. 2nd ed. Chicago: University of Chicago Press, 1969.

Jenkins, Nancy. *The Boat beneath the Pyramid: King Cheops' Royal Ship*. London: Thames & Hudson, 1980.

Habachi, Labib. *The Obelisks of Egypt: Skyscrapers of the Past*. New York: Charles Scribner, 1977.

———. *Die Unsterblichen Obelisken Ägyptens*. Mainz am Rhein, Germany: Philipp von Zabern, 2000.

Iversen, Erik. *Obelisks in Exile*. 2 vols. Copenhagen: G. E. C. Gad, 1968–1972.

Lehner, Mark. *The Complete Pyramids*. London: Thames & Hudson, 1997.

Stadelmann, Rainer. *Die ägyptischen Pyramiden: Vom Ziegelbau zum Weltwunder*. Mainz am Rhein, Germany: Philipp von Zabern, 1985.

Verner, Miroslav. *The Pyramids: Their Archaeology and History*. New York: Grove/Atlantic, 2001.

Watson, Philip. *Egyptian Pyramids and Mastaba Tombs*. Aylesbury, G.B.: Shire Publications, 1987.

RELIGION

See also Mummification and Funerary Practices.

Allen, James P. *Genesis in Egypt: The Philosophy of Ancient Egyptian Creation Accounts*. Yale Egyptological Studies 2. New Haven, Conn.: Yale Egyptological Seminar, 1974.

Arnold, Dieter. *Temples of the Last Pharaohs*. Oxford, U.K.: Oxford University Press, 1999.

Assmann, Jan. *Egyptian Solar Religion in the New Kingdom: Re, Amun, and the Crises of Polytheismus*, trans. A. Alcock. London: KPI, 1995.

———. *Ma'at: Gerechtigkeit und Unsterblichkeit im Alten Ägypten*. Munich, Germany: C. H. Beck, 1990.

———. *The Search for God in Ancient Egypt*, trans. David Lorton. Ithaca, N.Y.: Cornell University Press, 2001.

Billing, Nils. *Nut: The Goddess of Life in Text and Iconography*. Uppsala, Sweden: Uppsala University, 2002.

Dodson, Aidan, and Salima Ikram. *The Tomb in Ancient Egypt*. London: Thames & Hudson, 2008.

Dunand, Françoise, and Christiane Zivie-Coche. *Gods and Men in Egypt, 3000 BCE to 395 CE*. Ithaca, N.Y.: Cornell University Press, 2004.

Frankfurter, David. *Religion in Roman Egypt*. Princeton, N.J.: Princeton University Press, 1998.

Hart, George. *Egyptian Myths*. London: British Museum Press, 1990.

———. *The Routledge Dictionary of Egyptian Gods and Goddesses*. London: Routledge, 2005.

Hornung, Erik. *Conceptions of God in Ancient Egypt: The One and the Many*, trans. John R. Baines. London: Routledge and Kegan Paul, 1983.

Ikram, Salima, ed. *Divine Creatures: Animal Mummies in Ancient Egypt*. Cairo: American University in Cairo Press.

Johnson, Sally B. *The Cobra Goddess of Ancient Egypt*. London and New York: Kegan Paul International. 1990.

Kaper, Olaf. *The Egyptian God Tutu: A Study of the Sphinx-God and Master of Demons with a Corpus of Monuments*. Louvain, Belgium: Peeters, 2003.

Leitz, Christian. *Lexikon der ägyptischen Götter und Götterbezeichnungen*. 8 vols. Louvain, Belgium: Peeters, 2002–2003.

McFarlane, Anne. *The God Min to the End of the Old Kingdom*. Sydney: Australian Centre for Egyptology, 1995.

Meeks, Dimitri, and Christine Meeks-Favard. *Daily Life of the Egyptian Gods*, trans. G. M. Goshgarian. Ithaca, N.Y.: Cornell University Press, 1996.

Minas-Nerpel, Martina. *Der Gott Chepri*. Louvain, Belgium: Peeters, 2006.

Mojsov, Bojana. *Osiris: Death and Afterlife of a God*. Oxford, U.K.: Blackwell, 2005.

Morenz, Siegfried. *Egyptian Religion*, trans. Ann E. Keep. London: Methuen & Co., 1973.

Otto, Eberhard. *Egyptian Art and the Cults of Osiris and Amon*. London: Thames & Hudson, 1968.

Pinch, Geraldine. *Magic in Ancient Egypt*. Rev. ed. London: British Museum Press, 2006.

———. *Votive Offerings to Hathor*. Oxford, U.K.: Griffith Institute, 1993.

Quirke, Stephen. *Ancient Egyptian Religion*. London: British Museum Press, 1992.

———. *The Cult of Ra*. London: Thames & Hudson, 2001.

———. *The Temple in Ancient Egypt*. London: British Museum Press, 1997.

Sandri, Sandra. *Har-pa-chered (Harpocrates). Die Genese eines ägyptischen Götterkindes*. Louvain, Belgium: Peeters, 2006.

Sauneron, Serge. *The Priests of Ancient Egypt*, trans. David Lorton. Ithaca, N.Y.: Cornell University Press, 2000.

Shafer, Byron E., ed. *Religion in Ancient Egypt: Gods, Myths, and Personal Practice*. Ithaca, N.Y.: Cornell University Press, 1991.

———. *Temples of Ancient Egypt*. London: I. B. Tauris, 1998.

Snape, Steven. *Egyptian Temples*. Aylesbury, G.B.: Shire Publications, 1996.

Szpakowska, Katia, ed. *Through A Glass Darkly: Magic, Dreams, and Prophecy in Ancient Egypt*. Swansea, U.K.: Classical Press of Wales, 2006.

Thomas, Angela. *Gods and Myths*. Aylesbury, G.B.: Shire Publications, 1986.

Wilkinson, Richard H. *The Complete Gods and Goddesses of Ancient Egypt*. London: Thames & Hudson, 2003.

MUMMIFICATION AND FUNERARY PRACTICES

Adams, Barbara. *Egyptian Mummies*. Aylesbury, G.B.: Shire Publications, 1984.

Andrews, Carol. *Egyptian Mummies*. London: British Museum Publications, 1984.

Assmann, Jan. *Death and Salvation in Ancient Egypt*. Ithaca, N.Y.: Cornell University Press, 2005.

Aubert, Jacques-F., and Liliane Aubert. *Statuettes égyptiennes: Chaouabtis, ouchebtis*. Paris: Adrien Maisonneuve, 1974.

Aufderheide, Arthur C. *The Scientific Study of Mummies*. Cambridge, U.K.: Cambridge University Press, 2003.

Balout, Lionel, and C. Roubet. *La Momie de Ramsès II*. Paris: Éditions Recherche sur les Civilisations, 1985.

Borghouts, Joris. *Book of the Dead (39): From Shouting to Structure*. Wiesbaden, Germany: Otto Harrassowitz, 2007.

Budge, E. A. T. Wallis. *The Mummy: A Handbook of Egyptian Funerary Archaeology*. 2nd ed. Cambridge, U.K.: Cambridge University Press, 1925.

Cockburn, Aidan, and Eve Cockburn, eds. *Mummies, Disease, and Ancient Cultures*. Cambridge, U.K.: Cambridge University Press, 1980.

Corbelli, Judith A. *The Art of Death in Graeco-Roman Egypt*. Princes Risborough, G.B.: Shire Publications, 2006.

Davies, W. Vivian, and Roxie Walker, eds. *Biological Anthropology and the Study of Ancient Egypt*. London: British Museum Press, 1993.

Dawson, D. P., S. Giles, and M. W. Ponsford, eds. *Horemkenesi: May He Live Forever. The Bristol Mummy Project*. Bristol: Bristol Museums and Art Gallery, 2002.

Dodson, Aidan. *The Canopic Equipment of the Kings of Egypt*. London: Kegan Paul International, 1994.

Dunand, Françoise, and Roger Lichtenberg. *Mummies and Death in Ancient Egypt*. Ithaca. N.Y. and London: Cornell University Press, 2006.

Faulkner, Raymond O. *The Ancient Egyptian Book of the Dead*. Rev. ed. London: British Museum Publications, 1985.

——. *The Ancient Egyptian Coffin Texts*. New ed. Oxford, U.K.: Aris & Phillips, 2004.

——. *The Ancient Egyptian Pyramid Texts*. Oxford, U.K.: Clarendon Press, 1969.

Faulkner, Raymond O., and Ogden Goelet. *The Egyptian Book of the Dead: The Papyrus of Ani*. San Francisco, Calif.: Chronicle Books, 1994.

Forman, Werner, and Stephen Quirke. *Hieroglyphs and the Afterlife in Ancient Egypt*. London: British Museum Press, 1996.

Grajetzki, Wolfram. *Burial Customs in Ancient Egypt*. London: Duckworth, 2003.

Harris, James E., and Edward F. Wente. *An X-Ray Atlas of the Royal Mummies*. London: University of Chicago Press, 1980.

Harris, James E., and Kent R. Weeks. *X-Raying the Pharaohs*. London: Macdonald & Co., 1973.

Ikram, Salima, and Aidan Dodson. *The Mummy in Ancient Egypt*. London: Thames & Hudson, 1998.

——. *Royal Mummies in the Egyptian Museum*. Cairo: American University in Cairo Press, 1997.

Kanawati, Naguib. *The Tomb and Beyond: Burial Customs of the Egyptian Officials*. Warminster, G.B.: Aris & Phillips, 2001.

Lucarelli, Rita. *The Book of the Dead of Gatseshen: Ancient Egyptian Funerary Religion in the 10th Century BC*. Leiden: Nederlands Instituut voor het Nabije Oosten, 2006.

Petrie, W. M. Flinders. *Shabtis*. 1935. Reprint, Warminster, G.B.: Aris & Phillips, 1974.

Riggs, Christina. *The Beautiful Burial in Roman Egypt*. Oxford, U.K.: Oxford University Press, 2006.

Schneider, Hans D. *Shabtis*. 3 vols. Leiden, Netherlands: Rijkmuseum van Oudheden, 1977.

Smith, G. Elliott, and Warren R. Dawson. *Egyptian Mummies*. 1924. Reprint, London: Kegan Paul International, 1991.

Spencer, A. Jeffrey. *Death in Ancient Egypt*. Harmondsworth, G.B.: Penguin Books, 1982.

Stewart, Harry M. *Egyptian Shabtis*. Aylesbury, G.B.: Shire Publications, 1995.

Taylor, John H. *Egyptian Coffins*. Aylesbury, G.B.: Shire Publications, 1989.

———. *Mummy: The Inside Story*. London: British Museum Press, 2004.

———. *Unwrapping a Mummy: The Life, Death, and Embalming of Horemkenesi*. Egyptian Bookshelf. London: British Museum Press, 1995.

Taylor, John H., and Strudwick, Nigel. *Mummies: Death and the Afterlife in Ancient Egypt. Treasures from the British Museum*. London: British Museum Press, 2005.

Whelan, Paul. *Mere Scraps of Rough Wood? 17th–18th Dynasty Stick Shabtis*. London: Golden House Publications, 2007.

Wisseman, Sarah U. *The Virtual Mummy*. Champaign: University of Illinois Press, 2003.

SCARABS AND AMULETS

Andrews, Carol. *Amulets of Ancient Egypt*. London: British Museum Press, 1994.

Bietak, Manfred, and Ernest Czerny, eds. *Scarabs of the Second Millennium BC from Egypt, Nubia, Crete, and the Levant: Chronological and Historical Implications*. Vienna, Austria: Österreichischen Akademie der Wissenschaften, 2004.

Hornung, Erik, and Elisabeth Staehelin, eds. *Skarabäen und andere Siegelamulette aus Basler Sammlungen*. Mainz am Rhein, Germany: Philipp Von Zabern, 1976.

Müller-Winkler, Claudia. *Die ägyptischen Objekt-Amulette*. Freiburg, Switzerland and Göttingen, Germany: Éditions Universitaires and Vandenhoeck & Ruprecht, 1987.

Petrie, W. M. Flinders. *Buttons and Design Scarabs*. 1925. Reprint, Warminster, G.B.: Aris & Phillips, 1974.

———. *Scarabs and Cylinders with Names*. 1925. Reprint, Warminster, G.B.: Aris & Phillips, 1974.

Tufnell, Olga, and William A. Ward. *Studies on Scarab Seals*. 2 vols. Warminster, G.B.: Aris & Phillips, 1978–1984.

DAILY LIFE

See also Archaeology: Excavations and Surveys, Deir el-Medina.

Alston, Richard. *The City in Roman and Byzantine Egypt*. London and New York: Routledge, 2002.

Brovarski, Edward, S. K. Doll, and Rita E. Freed, eds. *Egypt's Golden Age: The Art of Living in the New Kingdom, 1558–1085 BC*. Boston: Museum of Fine Arts, 1982.

Darby, William, Paul Ghalioungui, and Louis Grivetti. *Food: The Gift of Osiris*. 2 vols. London: Academic Press, 1977.

Decker, Wolfgang. *Sports and Games of Ancient Egypt*, trans. Allen Guttmann. New Haven, Conn.: Yale University Press, 1992.

Erman, Adolf. *Life in Ancient Egypt*. 1894. Reprint, New York: Dover, 1971.

Filer, Joyce. *Disease*. Egyptian Bookshelf. London: British Museum Press, 1995.

Gillam, Robyn. *Performance and Drama in Ancient Egypt*. London: Duckworth, 2005.

Hall, Rosalind. *Egyptian Textiles*. Aylesbury, G.B.: Shire Publications, 1986.

Hepper, F. Nigel. *Pharaoh's Flowers: The Botanical Treasures of Tutankhamun*. London: HMSO, 1990.

Hope, Colin. *Egyptian Pottery*. Aylesbury, G.B.: Shire Publications, 1991.

James, T. G. Henry. *Pharaoh's People: Scenes from Life in Imperial Egypt*. London: Bodley Head, 1984.

Janssen, Jac. J. *Commodity Prices from the Ramesside Period*. Leiden, Netherlands: Brill, 1975.

Janssen, Rosalind M., and Jack Janssen. *Egyptian Household Animals*. Aylesbury, G.B.: Shire Publications, 1989.

———. *Growing Up and Getting Old in Ancient Egypt*. London: Golden House, 2007.

Lewis, Naphtali. *Life in Egypt under Roman Rule*. Oxford, U.K.: Clarendon Press, 1984.

Malek, Jaromir. *The Cat in Ancient Egypt*. London: British Museum Press, 1993.

Manniche, Lise. *An Ancient Egyptian Herbal*. London: British Museum Publications, 1989.

———. *Ancient Egyptian Musical Instruments*. Münchner Ägyptologische Studien 34. Munich, Germany: Deutscher Kunstverlag, 1975.

———. *Music and Musicians in Ancient Egypt*. London: British Museum Press, 1991.

———. *Sexual Life in Ancient Egypt*. London: KPI, 1987.

Morkot, Robert G. *Historical Dictionary of Ancient Egyptian Warfare*. Lanham, Md.: Sacrecrow Press, 2003.

Nunn, John F. *Ancient Egyptian Medicine*. London: British Museum Press, 1996.

Petrie, W. M. Flinders. *Objects of Daily Use*. 1927. Reprint, Warminster, G.B.: Aris & Phillips, 1974.

Pritchard, Frances. *Clothing Culture: Dress in Egypt in the First Millennium AD*. Manchester, England: Whitworth Art Gallery, 2006.

Reeves, Carole. *Egyptian Medicine*. Aylesbury, G.B.: Shire Publications, 1992.

Robins, Gay. *Women in Ancient Egypt*. London: British Museum Press, 1993.

Scheel, Bernd. *Egyptian Metalworking and Tools*. Aylesbury, G.B.: Shire Publications, 1995.

Shaw, Ian. *Egyptian Warfare and Weapons*. Aylesbury, G.B.: Shire Publications, 1991.

Spalinger, Anthony J. *War in Ancient Egypt*. Oxford, U.K.: Blackwell, 2005.

Strouhal, Eugen. *Life in Ancient Egypt*. Cambridge, U.K.: Cambridge University Press, 1992.

Tooley, Angela. *Egyptian Models and Scenes*. Aylesbury, G.B.: Shire Publications, 1995.

Tyldesley, Joyce. *Egyptian Games and Sports*. Princes Risborough, G.B.: Shire Publications, 2007.

Vogelsang-Eastwood, Gillian. *Pharaonic Egyptian Clothing*. Leiden, Netherlands: Brill, 1993.

Wilkinson, Alix. *The Garden in Ancient Egypt*. London: Rubicon Press, 1998.

Wilkinson, Toby. *Lives of the Ancient Egyptians*. London: Thames & Hudson, 2007.

Wilson, Hilary. *Egyptian Food and Drink*. Aylesbury, G.B.: Shire Publications, 1988.

APPLIED ARTS

Aldred, Cyril. *Jewels of the Pharaohs: Egyptian Jewellery of the Dynastic Period*. London: Thames & Hudson, 1971.

Andrews, Carol A. R. *Ancient Egyptian Jewellery*. London: British Museum Publications, 1996.

Baker, Hollis S. *Furniture in the Ancient World: Origins and Evolution, 3100–475 B.C.* London: Connoisseur, 1966.

Friedman, Florence D., ed. *Gifts of the Nile: Ancient Egyptian Faience*. London: Thames & Hudson, 1998.

Grose, David Fred. *The Toledo Museum of Art: Early Ancient Glass*. New York: Hudson Hills Press, 1989.

Killen, Geoffrey. *Ancient Egyptian Furniture*. 2 vols. Warminster, G.B.: Aris & Phillips, 1980, 1994.

———. *Egyptian Woodworking and Furniture*. Aylesbury, G.B.: Shire Publications, 1994.

Nicholson, Paul T. *Egyptian Faience and Glass*. Aylesbury, G.B.: Shire Publications, 1993.

Ogden, Jack. *Jewellery of the Ancient World*. London: Trefoil Books, 1982.

Tait, Hugh, ed. *Five Thousand Years of Glass*. London: British Museum Press, 1991.

———. *Seven Thousand Years of Jewellery*. London: British Museum Publications, 1986.

Wilkinson, Alix. *Ancient Egyptian Jewellery*. London: Methuen & Co., 1971.

LANGUAGE AND LITERATURE

Allen, James P. *Middle Egyptian: An Introduction to the Language and Culture of Hieroglyphs*. Cambridge, U.K.: Cambridge University Press, 2001.

Andrews, Carol A. R. *The Rosetta Stone*. London: British Museum Publications, 1982.

Andrews, Carol A. R., and Stephen Quirke. *The Rosetta Stone: Facsimile Drawing*. London: British Museum Publications, 1988.

Baines, John. *Visual and Written Culture in Ancient Egypt*. Oxford, U.K.: Oxford University Press, 2007.

Cerny, Jaroslav. *Paper and Books in Ancient Egypt*. 1952. Reprint, Chicago: Ares Publishers, 1977.

Collier, Mark, and Bill Manley. *How to Read Egyptian Hieroglyphs*. Rev. ed. London: British Museum Press, 1998.

Davies, W. Vivian. *Egyptian Hieroglyphs*. London: British Museum Publications, 1987.

Englund, Gertie. *Middle Egyptian: An Introduction*. Uppsala, Sweden: Uppsala University Press, 1988.

Faulkner, Raymond O. *A Concise Dictionary of Middle Egyptian*. 10th reprint. Oxford, U.K.: Griffith Institute, 2006.

Fischer, Henry George. *Ancient Egyptian Calligraphy: A Beginner's Guide to Writing Hieroglyphics*. 2nd ed. New York: Metropolitan Museum of Art, 1983.

Gardiner, Alan. H. *Egyptian Grammar: Being an Introduction to the Study of Hieroglyphics*. 3rd ed. Oxford, U.K.: Oxford University Press, 1957.

Goyon, Jean-Claude. *Grammaire de l'Égyptien hiéroglyphique du Moyen Empire au début du Nouvel Empire*. Lyons: Editions ACV, 2007.

Hannig, Rainier. *Ägyptisches Wörterbuch I–II*. Mainz am Rhein, Germany: Philipp von Zabern, 2003–2006.

———. *Die Sprache der Pharaonen: Grosses Handwörterbuch Ägyptisch-Deutsch (2800 bis 950 v. Chr.)*. 4th ed. Mainz am Rhein, Germany: Philipp von Zabern 2006.

Hoffman, Friedhelm, and Joachim Quack. *Anthologie der Demotischen Literatur*. Berlin, Germany: LIT, 2007.

Junge, Friedrich. *Late Egyptian Grammar: An Introduction*. Oxford, U.K.: Griffith Institute, 2001.

Kitchen, Kenneth A. *Poetry of Ancient Egypt*. Jonsered, Sweden: Paul Åströms, 1999.

Lewis, Naphtali. *Papyrus in Classical Antiquity*. Oxford, U.K.: Clarendon Press, 1974.

Lichtheim, Miriam. *Ancient Egyptian Autobiographies Chiefly of the Middle Kingdom: A Study and an Anthology*. Orbis Biblicus et Orientalis 84. Fribourg, Switzerland: Universitätsverlag, 1988.

———. *Ancient Egyptian Literature: A Book of Readings*. 3 vols. Berkeley: University of California Press, 1973–1980.

Loprieno, Antonio. *Ancient Egyptian: A Linguistic Introduction*. Cambridge, U.K.: Cambridge University Press, 1995.

———, ed. *Ancient Egyptian Literature: History and Forms*. Leiden, Netherlands: Brill, 1996.

Malek, Jaromir. *A B C of Egyptian Hieroglyphs*. Oxford, U.K.: Ashmolean Museum, 1994.

Parkinson, Richard. *Cracking Codes: The Rosetta Stone and Decipherment*. London: British Musuem Press, 1999.

———. *Poetry and Culture in Middle Kingdom Egypt*. London and New York: Continuum, 2002.

———. *Tale of Sinuhe*. Oxford, U.K.: Oxford University Press, 1997.

———. *Voices from Ancient Egypt: An Anthology of Middle Kingdom Writings*. London: British Museum Press, 1991.

Parkinson, Richard, and Stephen Quirke. *Papyrus*. Egyptian Bookshelf. London: British Museum Press, 1995.

Quirke, Stephen. *Egyptian Literature 1800 BC: Questions and Answers*. London: Golden House Publications, 2004.

Simpson, William Kelly. *The Literature of Ancient Egypt: An Anthology of Stories, Instructions, and Poetry*, trans. Raymond O. Faulkner. 2nd ed. New Haven, Conn.: Yale University Press, 1973.

Turner, Eric. *Geek Papyri: An Introduction*. Oxford, U.K.: Clarendon Press, 1968.

Wente, Edward F. *Letters from Ancient Egypt*. Atlanta. Ga.: Scholars Press, 1990.

Zauzich, Karl-Theodor. *Discovering Egyptian Hieroglyphs: A Practical Guide*. London: Thames & Hudson, 1992.

MATHEMATICS AND ASTRONOMY

Chace, Arnold Buffum. *The Rhind Mathematical Papyrus*. 1927–1929. reprint, Reston, Va.: National Council of Teachers of Mathematics, 1979.

Gillings, Richard J. *Mathematics in the Time of the Pharaohs*. Cambridge, Mass.: MIT Press, 1972.

Neugebauer, Otto E. *The Exact Sciences in Antiquity*. Reprint of 2nd ed. New York: Harper & Brothers, 1962.

Neugebauer, Otto E., and Richard A. Parker. *Egyptian Astronomical Texts*. 3 vols. London: Brown University Press, 1960–1969.

Parker, Richard A. *The Calendars of Ancient Egypt*. Studies in Ancient Oriental Civilization 26. Chicago: University of Chicago Press, 1950.

Robins, Gay, and Charles Shute. *The Rhind Mathematical Papyrus: An Ancient Egyptian Text*. London: British Museum Publications, 1987.

SCIENCE AND TECHNOLOGY

Bowman, Sheridan. *Radiocarbon Dating*. London: British Museum Publications, 1990.

David, Rosalie A., ed. *Science in Egyptology*. Manchester, G.B.: Manchester University Press, 1986.

Hope, Colin. *Egyptian Pottery*. 2nd ed. Princes Risborough, G.B.: Shire Publications, 2001.

Nicholson, Paul T., and Ian Shaw. *Ancient Egyptian Materials and Technology*. Cambridge, U.K.: Cambridge University Press, 2000.

Singer, Charles J., E. J. Holmyard, and A. R. Hall. *A History of Technology. Vol. 1*. Oxford, U.K.: Clarendon Press, 1954.

NATURAL ENVIRONMENT

Brewer, Douglas, and Renée Friedman. *Fish and Fishing in Ancient Egypt*. Warminster, G.B.: Aris & Phillips, 1989.

Brewer, Douglas, Donald Redford, and Susan Redford. *Domestic Plants and Animals*. Warminster, G.B.: Aris & Phillips, 1994.

Germer, Renate. *Flora des pharaonischen Ägypten*. Mainz am Rhein, Germany: Philipp von Zabern, 1985.

Germond, Philippe. *Egyptian Bestiary*. London: Thames & Hudson, 2001.

Houlihan, Patrick. *The Animal World of the Pharaohs*. Cairo: American University in Cairo Press, 1996.

———. *The Birds of Ancient Egypt*. Warminster, G.B.: Aris & Phillips, 1986.

Klemm, Rosemarie, and Dietrich Klemm. *Stones and Quarries in Ancient Egypt*. London: British Museum Press, 2007.

Malek, Jaromir. *The Cat in Ancient Egypt*. London: British Museum Press, 1993.

Manniche, Lise. *An Ancient Egyptian Herbal*. London: British Museum Press, 2006.

Osburn, Dale. *Mammals of Ancient Egypt*. Warminster, G.B.: Aris & Phillips, 1998.

Vartavan, Christian de, and Victoria Asensi Amorós. *Codex of Ancient Egyptian Plant Remains*. London: Triade Exploration, 1997.

NAVIGATION

Fabre, David. *Seafaring in Ancient Egypt*. London: Periplus Publishing, 2004.

Glanville, Stephen R., and Raymond O. Faulkner. *Catalogue of Egyptian Antiquities in the British Museum II: Wooden Model Boats*. London: Trustees of the British Museum, 1972.

Jones, Dilwyn. *Boats*. Egyptian Bookshelf. London: British Museum Press, 1995.

Landström, Björn. *Ships of the Pharaohs: 4000 Years of Egyptian Shipbuilding*. London: Allen & Unwin, 1970.

Vinson, Steve. *Egyptian Boats and Ships*. Aylesbury, G.B.: Shire Publications, 1994.

MUSEUM COLLECTIONS

Australia

Potts, Daniel T., and Karin N. Sowada. *Treasures of the Nicholson Museum, The University of Sydney*. Sydney, Australia: The Nicholson Museum, 2004.

Sowada, Karin N., and Boyo G. Ockinga. *Egyptian Art in the Nicholson Museum, Sydney*. Sydney, Australia: Mediterranean Archaeology, 2006.

Austria

Vienna

Egner, Roswitha, and Elfriede Haslauer. *Kunsthistorisches Museum Wien: Ägyptisch-Orientalische Sammlung. Lieferung 10: Särge der dritten Zwischenzeit, Teil 1.* Corpus Antiquitatum Aegyptiacarum. Mainz am Rhein, Germany: Philipp von Zabern, 1994.

Hein, Irmgard, and Helmut Satzinger. *Kunsthistorisches Museum Wien: Ägyptisch-Orientalische Sammlung. Lieferung 4: Stelen des mittleren Reiches, einschliesslich der I und II Zwischenzeit, Teil 1.* Corpus Antiquitatum Aegyptiacarum. Mainz am Rhein, Germany: Philipp von Zabern, 1989.

———. *Kunsthistorisches Museum Wien: Ägyptisch-Orientalische Sammlung. Lieferung 7: Stelen des mittleren Reiches, einschliesslich der I und II Zwischenzeit, Teil 2.* Corpus Antiquitatum Aegyptiacarum. Mainz am Rhein, Germany: Philipp von Zabern, 1993.

Hölzl, Regina. *Kunsthistorisches Museum Wien: Ägyptisch-Orientalische Sammlung. Lieferung 18: Reliefs und Inschriftsteine des Alten Reiches I.* Corpus Antiquitatum Aegyptiacarum. Mainz am Rhein, Germany: Philipp von Zabern, 1999.

———. *Kunsthistorisches Museum Wien: Ägyptisch-Orientalische Sammlung. Lieferung 21: Reliefs und Inschriftsteine des Alten Reiches II.* Corpus Antiquitatum Aegyptiacarum. Mainz am Rhein, Germany: Philipp von Zabern, 2000.

Hüttner, Michaela, and Helmut Satzinger. *Kunsthistorisches Museum Wien: Ägyptisch-Orientalische Sammlung. Lieferung 16: Stelen, Inschriftsteine und Relief aus der Zeit der 18 Dynastie.* Corpus Antiquitatum Aegyptiacarum. Mainz am Rhein, Germany: Philipp von Zabern, 1999.

Jaros-Deckert, Brigitte. *Kunsthistorisches Museum Wien: Ägyptisch-Orientalische Sammlung. Lieferung 1: Statuen des mittleren Reichs und der 18 Dynastie.* Corpus Antiquitatum Aegyptiacarum. Mainz am Rhein, Germany: Philipp von Zabern, 1987.

Jaros-Deckert, Brigitte, and Eva Rogge. *Kunsthistorisches Museum Wien: Ägyptisch-Orientalische Sammlung. Lieferung 15: Statuen des alten Reiches.* Corpus Antiquitatum Aegyptiacarum. Mainz am Rhein, Germany: Philipp von Zabern, 1993.

Reiser-Haslauer, Elfriede. *Kunsthistorisches Museum Wien: Ägyptisch-Orientalische Sammlung. Lieferung 2: Die Kanopen, Teil 1.* Corpus Antiquitatum Aegyptiacarum. Mainz am Rhein, Germany: Philipp von Zabern, 1989.

———. *Kunsthistorisches Museum Wien: Ägyptisch-Orientalische Sammlung. Lieferung 3: Die Kanopen, Teil 2.* Corpus Antiquitatum Aegyptiacarum. Mainz am Rhein, Germany: Philipp von Zabern, 1989.

——. *Kunsthistorisches Museum Wien: Ägyptisch-Orientalische Sammlung. Lieferung 5: Uschebti, Teil 1.* Corpus Antiquitatum Aegyptiacarum. Mainz am Rhein, Germany: Philipp von Zabern, 1990.

——. *Kunsthistorisches Museum Wien: Ägyptisch-Orientalische Sammlung. Lieferung 8: Uschebti, Teil 2.* Corpus Antiquitatum Aegyptiacarum. Mainz am Rhein, Germany: Philipp von Zabern, 1992.

Rogge, Eva. *Kunsthistorisches Museum Wien: Ägyptisch-Orientalische Sammlung. Lieferung 6: Statuetten des neuen Reiches und der dritten Zwischenzeit.* Corpus Antiquitatum Aegyptiacarum. Mainz am Rhein, Germany: Philipp von Zabern, 1990.

——. *Kunsthistorisches Museum Wien: Ägyptisch-Orientalische Sammlung. Lieferung 9: Statuen der Spätzeit.* Corpus Antiquitatum Aegyptiacarum. Mainz am Rhein, Germany: Philipp von Zabern, 1992.

Satzinger, Helmut. *Das Kunsthistorische Museum in Wien: Die Ägyptisch-Orientalische Sammlung.* Mainz am Rhein, Germany: Philipp von Zabern, 1994.

Belgium

Antwerp

Museum Vleeshuis. *Egypte Onomwonden: Egyptische oudheden van het museum Vleeshuis.* Antwerp, Belgium: Pandora, 1995.

Brussels

Limme, Luc. *Stèles égyptiennes: Musée de Bruxelles.* Brussels, Belgium: Musées Royaux d'Art et d'Histoire, 1979.

Van de Walle, Baudoin, L. Limme, and H. De Meulenaere. *La collection égyptienne: Les étapes marquantes de son développement.* Brussels: Musées Royaux d'Art et d'Histoire, 1980.

Mariemont

Musée Royal de Mariémont. *Choix d'oeuvres, Égypte 1.* Mariémont, Belgium: Musée Royal de Mariémont, 1990.

Namur

Bruwier, Marie-Cécile. *Présence de l'Égypte dans les collections de la Bibliothèque Universitaire Moretus Plantin.* Namur, Belgium: Namur University Press, 1994.

Brazil

Kitchen, Kenneth A. *Catalogue of the Egyptian Collection in the National Museum, Rio de Janeiro*. Rio de Janeiro, Brazil, and Warminster, G.B.: Museum Nacional and Aris & Phillips, 1990.

Croatia

Monnet Saleh, Janine. *Les Antiquités Égyptiennes de Zagreb*. Paris: Mouton, 1970.

Cuba

Lipinska, Jadwiga. *Monuments de l'Égypte ancienne au Palacio de Bellas Artes à la Havane et du Museo Bacardí à Santiago de Cuba*. Corpus Antiquitatum Aegyptiacarum. Mainz am Rhein, Germany: Philipp von Zabern, 1982.

Czech Republic

Pavlasová, Sylva. *The Land of Pyramids and Pharaohs: Ancient Egypt in the Náprstek Museum Collection* (in Czech and English). Prague, Czech Republic: Národní Museum, 1997.

Verner, Miroslav. *Altägyptische Särge in den Museen und Sammlungen der Tschechoslowakei. Lieferung 1:1*. Corpus Antiquitatum Aegyptiacarum. Prague, Czech Republic: Charles University, 1982.

———. *Altägyptische Särge in den Museen und Sammlungen der Tschechoslowakei Lieferung 1:2*. Corpus Antiquitatum Aegyptiacarum. Prague, Czech Republic: Univerzita Karlova, 1982.

———. *Altägyptische Särge in den Museen und Sammlungen der Tschechoslowakei Lieferung 1:3*. Corpus Antiquitatum Aegyptiacarum. Prague, Czech Republic: Univerzita Karlova, 1982.

Denmark

Manniche, Lise. *Egyptian Art in Denmark*. Copenhagen, Denmark: Gyldendal, 2004.

Copenhagen: Carsten Niebuhr Institute

Frandsen, Paul J., and Kim Ryholt. *The Carlsberg Papyri 3: A Miscellany of Demotic Texts and Studies*. Carsten Niebuhr Institute of Ancient Near Eastern Studies Publications 22. Copenhagen, Denmark: Museum Tusculanum Press, 2000.

Osing, Jürgen. *The Carlsberg Papyri 2: Hieratische Papyri aus Tebtunis, I.* Carsten Niebuhr Institute of Ancient Near Eastern Studies Publications 17. Copenhagen, Denmark: Museum Tusculanum Press, 1998.

Ryholt, Kim. *The Carlsberg Papyri 4: The Story of Petese Son of Petetum and Seventy Other Good and Bad Stories.* Carsten Niebuhr Institute of Ancient Near Eastern Studies Publications 23. Copenhagen, Denmark: Museum Tusculanum Press, 1999.

————. *The Carlsberg Papyri 6: The Petese Stories II.* Carsten Niebuhr Institute of Ancient Near Eastern Studies Publications 29. Copenhagen, Denmark: Museum Tusculanum Press, 2006.

————, ed. *The Carlsberg Papyri 7: Hieratic Texts from the Collection.* Carsten Niebuhr Institute of Ancient Near Eastern Studies Publications 30. Copenhagen, Denmark: Museum Tusculanum Press, 2006.

Smith, Mark. *The Carlsberg Papyri 5: On the Primeval Ocean.* Carsten Niebuhr Institute of Ancient Near Eastern Studies Publications 26. Copenhagen, Denmark: Museum Tusculanum Press, 2002.

Zauzich, Karl-Theodor, W. John Tait, and Michel Chaveau. *The Carlsberg Papyri 1: Demotic Texts from the Collection.* Carsten Niebuhr Institute of Ancient Near Eastern Studies Publications 15. Copenhagen, Denmark: Museum Tusculanum Press, 1991.

Copenhagen: National Museum

Buhl, Marie-Louise. *A Hundred Masterpieces from the Ancient Near East.* Copenhagen, Denmark: National Museum of Denmark, 1974.

Mogensen, Maria. *Inscriptions hiéroglyphiques du Musée National de Copenhague.* Copenhagen, Denmark: A. F. Hörst et fils, 1918.

Copenhagen: Ny Carlsberg

Frandsen, Paul. J. *The Carlsberg Papyri I: Demotic Texts from the Collection.* Copenhagen, Denmark: Museum Tusculanum Press, 1991.

Jorgensen, Mogens. *Egypt I (3000–1550 BC): Ny Carlsberg Glyptotek.* Copenhagen, Denmark: Ny Carlsberg Glyptotek, 1996.

————. *Egypt II (1550–1080 BC): Ny Carlsberg Glyptotek.* Copenhagen, Denmark: Ny Carlsberg Glyptotek, 1996.

————. *Egypt III (1080BC–AD 400): Ny Carlsberg Glyptotek.* Copenhagen, Denmark: Ny Carlsberg Glyptotek, 1996.

Koefod-Petersen, Otto. *Catalogue des bas-reliefs et peintures égyptiens.* Copenhagen, Denmark: Ny Carlsberg Glyptotek, 1956.

———. *Catalogue des sarcophages et cercueils égyptiens.* Copenhagen, Denmark: Ny Carlsberg Glyptotek, 1951.

———. *Catalogue des statues et statuettes égyptiennnes.* Copenhagen, Denmark: Ny Carlsberg Glyptotek, 1950.

———. *Egyptian Sculpture in the Ny Carlsberg Glyptotek.* Copenhagen, Denmark: Bianco Lunos Bogtrykkeri, 1951.

———. *Recueil des inscriptions hiéroglyphiques de la Glyptothèque Ny Carlsberg.* Brussels, Belgium: Fondation Égyptologique Reine Élisabeth, 1936.

———. *Les stèles égyptiennes.* Copenhagen, Denmark: Ny Carlsberg Glyptotek, 1948.

Egypt

Alexandria

Breccia, Evaristo. *Le Musée gréco-romain d'Alexandrie, 1925–1931.* Rome: "L'Erma" di Bretschneider, 1970.

———. *La necropoli di Sciatbi (Musée d'Alexandrie).* Cairo: Service des Antiquités de l'Égypte, 1912.

Empereur, Jean-Yves. *A Short Guide to the Graeco-Roman Museum Alexandria.* Alexandria, Egypt: Sarapis Publications, 1995.

Aswan

Gaballa, Gaballa Ali. *Nubia Museum.* Aswan, Egypt: Ministry of Culture, n.d.

Cairo: Coptic Museum

Gabra, Gawdat. *Cairo: The Coptic Museum and Old Churches.* Cairo: Egyptian International Publishing Co., 1993.

Gabra, Gawdat, and Marianne Eaton-Krauss. *The Treasures of Coptic Art in the Coptic Museum and Churches of Old Cairo.* Cairo and New York: American University in Cairo Press, 2006.

Robinson, James M., ed. *The Nag Hammadi Library in English.* 4th ed. Leiden, Netherlands: Brill, 1996.

Cairo: Egyptian Museum

Abou-Ghazi, Dia, and Alexandre Moret. *Denkmäler des Alten Reiches.* Vol. 3, fascs. 1–2. Cairo: Service des Antiquités de l'Égypte, 1980.

Bénédite, Georges. *Miroirs*. Cairo: Service des Antiquités de l'Égypte, 1907.

———. *Objets de toilettes: Vol. I. Peignes, etc*. Cairo: Service des Antiquités de l'Égypte, 1911.

Bissing, Friedrich W. von. *Fayencegefässe*. Vienna, Austria: Adolf Holzhausen, 1902.

———. *Metalgefässe*. Vienna: Adolf Holzhausen, 1901.

———. *Steingefässe*. 2 vols. Vienna, Austria: Adolf Holzhausen, 1904–1907.

———. *Tongefässe: Teil I*. Vienna, Austria: Adolf Holzhausen, 1913.

Borchardt, Ludwig. *Denkmäler des Alten Reiches (ausser den Statuen)*. Vol. I. Berlin, Germany: Reichsdruckerei, 1937. Vol. II. Cairo: Service des Antiquités de l'Égypte, 1964.

———. *Statuen und Statuetten von Königen und Privatleuten*. 5 vols. Berlin, Germany: Reichsdruckerei, 1911–1936.

Carter, Henri, and Percy E. Newberry. *The Tomb of Thoutmosis IV*. London: Archibald Constable & Co., 1904.

Cerny, Jaroslav. *Ostraca hiératiques*. 2 vols. Cairo: Service des Antiquités de l'Égypte, 1930–1937.

Chassinat, Émile. *La seconde Trouvaille de Deir-el-Bahari (Sarcophages)*. Cairo: Service des Antiquités de l'Égypte, 1909.

Crum, Walter E. *Coptic Monuments*. Cairo: Service des Antiquités de l'Égypte, 1902.

Curelly, Charles T. *Stone Implements*. Cairo: Service des Antiquités de l'Égypte, 1913.

Daressy, Georges. *Cerceuils et cachettes royales*. Cairo: Service des Antiquités de l'Égypte, 1909.

———. *Fouilles de la Vallée des Rois 1898–1899*. Cairo: Service des Antiquités de l'Égypte, 1902.

———. *Ostraca*. Cairo: Service des Antiquités de l'Égypte, 1901.

———. *Statues de divinités*. Cairo: Service des Antiquités de l'Égypte, 1906.

———. *Textes et dessins magiques*. Cairo: Service des Antiquités de l'Égypte, 1903.

Edgar, Campbell C. *Graeco-Egyptian Coffins, Masks, and Portraits*. Cairo: Service des Antiquités de l'Égypte, 1905.

———. *Graeco-Egyptian Glass*. Cairo: Service des Antiquités de l'Égypte, 1905.

———. *Greek Bronzes*. Cairo: Service des Antiquités de l'Égypte, 1903.

———. *Greek Moulds*. Cairo: Service des Antiquités de l'Égypte, 1903.

———. *Greek Sculpture*. Cairo: Service des Antiquités de l'Égypte, 1903.

———. *Greek Vases*. Cairo: Service des Antiquités de l'Égypte, 1911.

———. *Sculptors' Studies and Unfinished Works*. Cairo: Service des Antiquités de l'Égypte, 1906.

Gaillard, Claude, and Georges Daressy. *La faune momifiée de l'antique Égypte*. Cairo: Service des Antiquités de l'Égypte, 1905.

Gauthier, Henri. *Cercueils anthropoides des prêtres de Montou*. Cairo: Service des Antiquités de l'Égypte, 1913.

Golenischeff, Vladimir S. *Papyrus hiératiques*. Fasc. 1. Cairo: Service des Antiquités de l'Égypte, 1927.

Grenfell, Bernard P., and Arthur S. Hunt. *Greek Papyri*. Oxford, U.K.: Oxford University Press, 1903.

Hawass, Zaki. *Hidden Treasures of the Egyptian Museum: One Hundred Masterpieces from the Centennial Exhibition*. Cairo: American University in Cairo Press, 2002.

Jansen-Winkeln, Karl. *Biographische und religiose Inschriften der Spätzeit aus dem Aegyptischen Museum Kairo*. Wiesbaden, Germany: Otto Harrassowitz, 2001.

Kamal, Ahmad. *Stèles ptolemaïques et romaines*. 2 vols. Cairo: Service des Antiquités de l'Égypte, 1904–1905.

———. *Tables d'Offrandes*. Cairo: Service des Antiquités de l'Égypte, 1906–1909.

Kuentz, Charles. *Obélisques*. Cairo: Service des Antiquités de l'Égypte, 1932.

Lacau, Pierre. *Sarcophages antérieurs au Nouvel Empire*. 2 vols. Cairo: Service des Antiquités de l'Égypte, 1904–1906.

———. *Stèles du Nouvel Empire*. 2 fascs. Cairo: Service des Antiquités de l'Égypte, 1909–1926.

Lange, Hans O., and Heinrich Schaefer. *Grab- und Denksteine des Mittel Reichs*. 4 vols. Berlin, Germany: Reichsdruckerei, 1902–1925.

Lefebvre, Gustave. *Papyrus du Ménandre*. Cairo: Service des Antiquités de l'Égypte, 1911.

Legrain, Georges. *Statues et statuettes des rois et des particuliers*. 3 vols. Cairo: Service des Antiquités de l'Égypte, 1906–1914.

Maspero, Gaston. *Sarcophages des époque persane et ptolemaïque*. 2 vols. Cairo: Service des Antiquités de l'Égypte, 1908–1914.

Maspero, Jean. *Papyrus grecs d'époque byzantine*. 3 vols. Cairo: Service des Antiquités de l'Égypte, 1911–1916.

Milne, Joseph G. *Greek Inscriptions*. Oxford, U.K.: Oxford University Press, 1905.

Moret, Alexandre. *Sarcophages de l'époque bubastite à l'époque saïte*. Cairo: Service des Antiquités de l'Égypte, 1913.

Munier, Henri. *Manuscrits coptes*. Cairo: Service des Antiquités de l'Égypte, 1916.

Munro, Irmtraut. *Die Totenbuch-Handschriften der 18. Dynastie im Ägyptischen Museum Cairo*. 2 vols. Wiesbaden, Germany: Otto Harrassowitz, 1994.

Newberry, Percy E. *Funerary Statuettes and Model Sarcophagi*. Fascs. 1–2. Cairo: Service des Antiquités de l'Égypte, 1930–1937.

———. *Scarab-Shaped Seals*. London: Archibald Constable & Co., 1907.

Quibell, James E. *Archaic Objects*. 2 vols. Cairo: Service des Antiquités de l'Égypte, 1905.

———. *The Tomb of Yuaa and Thuiu*. Cairo: Service des Antiquités de l'Égypte, 1908.

Reisner, George A. *Amulets*. Cairo: Service des Antiquités de l'Égypte, 1907.

———. *Canopics*. Cairo: Service des Antiquités de l'Égypte, 1967.

———. *Models of Ships and Boats*. Cairo: Service des Antiquités de l'Égypte, 1913.

Roeder, Günther. *Naos*. Leipzig, Germany: Breitkopf und Härtel, 1914.

Saleh, Mohamed, and Hourig Sourouzian. *The Egyptian Museum, Cairo*. Mainz am Rhein, Germany: Philipp von Zabern, 1987.

Smith, Grafton Elliot. *The Royal Mummies*. Cairo: Service des Antiquités de l'Égypte, 1913.

Spiegelberg, Wilhelm. *Demotische Denkmäler I: Inschriften*. Leipzig, Germany: W. Drugulin, 1904.

———. *Demotische Denkmäler II: Papyrus*. 2 vols. Strassburg, Germany: Elsässiche Druckerei and Dumont, Schauberg, 1906–1908.

———. *Demotische Denkmäler III. Demotische Inschriften Papyrus*. Berlin, Germany: Reichsdruckerei, 1932.

Strzygowski, Josef. *Koptische Kunst*. Vienna, Austria: Adolf Holzhausen, 1904.

Vernier, Émile. *Bijoux et Orfèveries: Text and Plates*. Cairo: Service des Antiquités de l'Égypte, 1927.

Weigall, Arthur E. P. *Weights and Balances*. Cairo: Service des Antiquités de l'Égypte, 1908.

Luxor

Romano, James F. *The Luxor Museum of Ancient Art Catalogue*. Cairo: American Research Center in Egypt, 1979.

Supreme Council of Antiquities. *Mummification Museum*. Luxor: S. C. A. Press, 1997.

France

Aix-en-Provence

Barbotin, Christophe. *Musée Granet. Collection égyptienne*. Aix en Provence, France: Musée Granet, 1995.

Aix-les-Bains

See Museum Collections, France, Annecy.

Amiens

Perdu, Olivier, and Elsa Rickal. *La collection égyptienne du Musée de Picardie.* Amiens, France: Musée de Picardie, 1994.

Angers

Affholder-Gérard, Brigitte, and Marie-Jeanne Cornic. *Angers, Musée Pincé: La collection égyptienne.* Paris: Réunion des Musées Nationaux, 1990.

Annecy

Ratié, Suzanne. *Annecy, musée-château; Chambéry, musées d'art et d'histoire; Aix-les-Bains, musée archéologique: Collections égyptiennes.* Paris: Éditions de la Réunion des Musées Nationaux, 1984.

Autun

Pinette, Mathieu. *Les collections égyptiennes dans les musées de Saône et Loire.* Autun, France: Ville d'Autun, 1988.

Avignon

Foissy-Aufrère, Marie-Pierre. *Égypte & Provence.* Avignon, France: Fondation du Muséum Calvet, 1985.

Besançon

Gasse, Annie. *Loin du sable.* Besançon, France: Ville de Besançon, 1990.

Bordeaux

Orgogozo, Chantal, Marie-Hélène Rutchowscaya, and François Villard. *Égypte et Mediterranée: Objets antiques du Musée d'Aquitaine.* Bordeaux, France: Ville de Bordeaux, 1992.

Cannes

Margaine, Anne-Marie. *L'Égypte ancienne: Petits guides des Musées de Cannes 1*. Cannes, France: Musée de la Castre, 1984.

Chalon-sur-Saône

See Museum Collections, France, Autun.

Chambéry

See Museum Collections, France, Annecy.

Cherbourg

Loffet, Henri. *Collections Égyptiennes du Museum Emmanuel Liais de Cherbourg Octeville*. Paris: Cybele, 2007.

Dijon

Laurent, Véronique. *Antiquités égyptiennes. Inventaire des collections du Musée des Beaux-Arts de Dijon*. Bourgogne, France: Ministère de la Culture et de la Communication-DRAC de Bourgogne, 1997.

Figeac

Dewachter, Michel. *La collection égyptienne du Musée Champollion*. Figeac, France: Musée Champollion, 1986.

Grenoble

Kueny, Gabrielle, and Jean Yoyotte. *Grenoble, Musée des Beaux Arts: Collection égyptienne*. Paris: Éditions de la Réunion des Musées Nationaux, 1979.

Marseilles

Cahier du Musée d'Archéologie Méditerranéenne: La collection égyptienne. Guide du visiteur. Marseilles, France: 1995.

Paris: Bibliothèque Nationale

Ledrain, Eugène. *Les monuments égyptiens de la Bibliothèque Nationale (Cabinet des médailles et antiques)*. Paris: F. Vieweg, 1879.

Lucchesi, Elisabeth. *Répertoire des manuscrits coptes (sahidiques) de la Bibliothèque Nationale, Cahiers d'orientalisme I*. Geneva, Switzerland: Patrick Cramer, 1981.

Paris: Cluny Museum

Lorquin, Alexandra. *Les tissus coptes au Musée National du Moyen Age*. Paris: Réunion des Musées Nationaux, 1992.

Paris: Louvre

Andreu, Guillemette. *La statuette d'Ahmès Nefertari*. Paris: Réunion des Musées Nationaux, 1997.

Andreu, Guillemette, Marie-Hélène Rutschowscaya, and Christiane Ziegler. *L'Égypte ancienne au Louvre*. Paris: Réunion des Musées Nationaux, 1997.

Barbotin, Christophe. *Les Statues Égyptiens du Nouvel Empire. Statues royales et divines*. Paris: Khéops-Musée du Louvre, 2007.

Bénazeth, Dominique. *L'Art du metal au début de l'ère chrétienne*. Paris: Réunion des Musées Nationaux, 1992.

Bernard, Étienne. *Inscriptions Grecques d'Égypte et de Nubie au Musée du Louvre*. Paris: Editions du Centre National de la Recherche Scientifique, 1992.

Bovot, Jean-Luc. *Les serviteurs funéraires royaux et princiers de l'Ancienne Égypte*. Paris: Réunion des Musées Nationaux, 2003.

Delange, Elisabeth. *Catalogue des statues égyptiennes du Moyen-Empire*. Paris: Réunion des Musées Nationaux, 1987.

———. *Rites et beauté: Objets de toilette égyptiens*. Paris: Réunion des Musées Nationaux, 1993.

———. *Le scribe Nebmeroutef*. Paris: Louvre Service Culturel, 1997.

Du Bourguet, Pierre. *Catalogue des étoffes coptes*. Paris: Musée National du Louvre, 1964.

Dunand, Françoise. *Terres cuites gréco-romaines d'Égypte*. Paris: Réunion des Musées Nationaux, 1990.

Malinine, Michel, Georges Posener, and Jean Vercoutter. *Catalogue des stèles du Serapeum de Memphis*. Paris: Éditions des Musées Nationaux, 1968.

Montembault, Véronique. *Catalogue des chaussures de l'Antiquité Égyptienne*. Paris: Réunion des Musées Nationaux, 2000.

Musée du Louvre. *Guide des antiquités égyptiennes.* Paris: Réunion des Musées Nationaux, 1997.

——. *Guide des antiquités égyptiennes romaines.* Paris: Réunion des Musées Nationaux, 1997.

Pierret, Paul. *Recueil d'inscriptions inédites du Musée égyptien du Louvre.* Paris: A. Franck, 1874–1878.

Rutschowscaya, Marie-Hélène. *Catalogue des bois de l'Égypte copte.* Paris: Réunion des Musées Nationaux, 1986.

——. *La peinture copte.* Paris: Réunion des Musées Nationaux, 1992.

Vandier d'Abbadie, Jeanne. *Catalogue des objets de toilette égyptiens.* Paris: Réunion des Musées Nationaux, 1972.

Ziegler, Chistiane. *Catalogue des instruments de musique égyptiens.* Paris: Réunion des Musées Nationaux, 1979.

——. *Catalogue des stèles, peintures et reliefs égyptiens del'Ancien Empire et de la Première Période Intermédiaire.* Paris: Réunion des Musées Nationaux, 1990.

——. *Egyptian Antiquities.* London: Scala Publications, 1990.

——. *Le mastaba d'Akhethetep: Une chapelle funéraire de l'Ancien Empire.* Paris: Réunion des Musées Nationaux, 1993.

——. *Statues de l'Ancien Empire au Louvre.* Paris: Réunion des Musées Nationaux, 1997.

Ziegler, Christiane, Lisa Davidson, Guillemette Andreu, and Marie-Helene Rutschowscaya. *Ancient Egypt in the Louvre.* London: I. B. Tauris, 1999.

Roanne

Moinet, Eric. *Catalogue des antiquités égyptiennes du Musée Joseph Déchelette.* Roanne, France: Musée J. Déchelette, 1990.

Rouen

Aufrère, Sydney. *Collections égyptiennes.* Rouen, France: Musées départementaux de Seine Maritime, 1987.

Sèvres

Bulté, Jeanne. *Catalogue des collections égyptiennes du Musée National de Céramique à Sèvres.* Paris: Centre National de la Recherche Scientifique, 1981.

Strasbourg

Lionnard, Marie. *Un Rêve d'Éternité. Antiquités égyptiennes de la Collection G. Schlumberger*. Strasbourg, France: Musée Strasbourg, 1998.

Bouvier, Guillaume. *Les Étiquettes de Jarres hiératiques de l'Institut d'Égyptologie de Strasbourg*. Cairo: Institut français d'archéologie orientale, 1999–2003.

Toulouse

Ramond, Pierre. *Les stèles égyptiennes du Musée G. Labit à Toulouse*. Cairo: Institut français d'archéologie orientale, 1977.

Varzy

Matoïan, Valérie, and Henri Loffet. *Les antiquités égyptiennes et assyriennes de Musée Auguste Grasset de Varzy*. Musées de la Nièvre. Études et Documents 1. Nevers, France: Conseil Général de la Nièvre, 1997.

Germany

Berlin

Priese, Karl-Heinz. *Ägyptisches Museum: Museuminsel Berlin*. Mainz am Rhein, Germany: Philipp von Zabern, 1991.

Settgast, Jürgen. *Ägyptisches Museum Berlin*. 1st ed. Mainz am Rhein, Germany: Philipp von Zabern, 1983. English translation *Egyptian Museum Berlin*, 3rd ed., 1986.

Bremen

Martin, Karl. *Übersee-Museum Bremen. Lieferung I: Die Altägyptischen Denkmäler. Teil 1*. Corpus Antiquitatum Aegyptiacarum. Mainz am Rhein, Germany: Philipp von Zabern, 1991.

Frankfurt-am-Main

Bayer-Niemeier, Eva, Birgit Schlick-Nolte, and von Droste zu Hülshoff, Vera. *Liebieghaus-Museum Alter Plastik: Ägyptische Bildwerke. Band II. Statuetten, Gefässe, und Geräte*. Melsungen, Germany: Gutenberg, 1991.

———. *Liebieghaus-Museum Alter Plastik: Ägyptische Bildwerke. Band III. Skulptur, Malerei, Papyri, und Särge.* Melsungen, Germany: Gutenberg, 1993.

Gessler-Löhr, Beatrix. *Ägyptische Kunst im Liebieghaus.* Frankfurt-am-Main: Museum Alter Plastik, 1981.

Schlick-Nolte, Birgit, and Vera von Droste zu Hülshoff. *Liebieghaus Museum Alter Plastik: Ägyptische Bildwerke. Band I. Skarabäen, Amulette, und Schmuck.* Melsungen, Germany: Gutenberg, 1990.

Hannover

Beste, Irmtraut. *Kestner-Museum Hannover. Lieferung 1: Skarabäen, Teil 1.* Corpus Antiquitatum Aegyptiacarum. Mainz am Rhein, Germany: Philipp von Zabern, 1978.

———. *Kestner-Museum Hannover. Lieferung 2: Skarabäen, Teil 2.* Corpus Antiquitatum Aegyptiacarum. Mainz am Rhein, Germany: Philipp von Zabern, 1979.

———. *Kestner-Museum Hannover. Lieferung 3: Skarabäen, Teil 3.* Corpus Antiquitatum Aegyptiacarum. Mainz am Rhein, Germany: Philipp von Zabern, 1979.

Drenkhahn, Rosemarie. *Ägyptische Reliefs im Kestner-Museum Hannover.* Hannover, Germany: Kestner-Museum, 1989.

Woldering, Irma. *Aegyptische Kunst. Bildkataloge des Kestner-Museums Hannover I: Ausgewählte Werke der Aegyptischen Sammlung.* Hannover, Germany: Kestner-Museum, 1955.

Heidelberg

Feucht, Erika. *Vom Nil zum Neckar.* Berlin, Germany: Springer, 1986.

Hildesheim

Eggebrecht, Arne, ed. *Pelizaeus-Museum Hildesheim: The Egyptian Collection.* Mainz am Rhein, Germany: Philipp von Zabern, 1996.

Eggebrecht, Eva. *Pelizaeus-Museum Hildesheim. Lieferung 2: Spätantike und Koptische Textilien, Teil 1.* Corpus Antiquitatum Aegyptiacarum. Mainz am Rhein, Germany: Philipp von Zabern, 1978.

Martin, Karl. *Pelizaeus-Museum, Hildesheim. Lieferung 3: Reliefs des Alten Reiches, Teil 1.* Corpus Antiquitatum Aegyptiacarum. Mainz am Rhein, Germany: Philipp von Zabern, 1978.

——. *Pelizaeus-Museum, Hildesheim. Lieferung 7: Reliefs des Alten Reiches, Teil 2.* Corpus Antiquitatum Aegyptiacarum. Mainz am Rhein, Germany: Philipp von Zabern, 1979.

——. *Pelizaeus-Museum, Hildesheim. Lieferung 8: Reliefs des Alten Reiches, Teil 3.* Corpus Antiquitatum Aegyptiacarum. Mainz am Rhein, Germany: Philipp von Zabern, 1980.

Martin-Pardey, Eva. *Pelizaeus-Museum, Hildesheim. Lieferung 1: Plastik des Alten Reiches, Teil 1.* Corpus Antiquitatum Aegyptiacarum. Mainz am Rhein, Germany: Philipp von Zabern, 1977.

——. *Pelizaeus-Museum, Hildesheim. Lieferung 4: Plastik des Alten Reiches, Teil 2.* Corpus Antiquitatum Aegyptiacarum. Mainz am Rhein, Germany: Philipp von Zabern, 1978.

——. *Pelizaeus-Museum, Hildesheim. Lieferung 5: Eingeweidegefässe.* Corpus Antiquitatum Aegyptiacarum. Mainz am Rhein, Germany: Philipp von Zabern, 1980.

——. *Pelizaeus-Museum, Hildesheim. Lieferung 6: Grabbeigaben, Nachträge, und Ergänzungen.* Corpus Antiquitatum Aegyptiacarum. Mainz am Rhein, Germany: Philipp von Zabern, 1991.

Leipzig

Krauspe, Renate. *Das Ägyptische Museum der Universität Leipzig.* Mainz am Rhein, Germany: Philipp von Zabern, 1997.

Munich

Schoske, Sylvia, and Alfred Grimm, eds. *Staatliche Sammlung Ägyptischer Kunst München.* Mainz am Rhein, Germany: Philipp von Zabern, 1995.

Rhine Region

von Droste zu Hülshoff, Vera, and Birgit Schlick-Nolte. *Museen der Rhein-Main-Region. Lieferung 1: Aegyptiaca Diversa, Teil 1.* Corpus Antiquitatum Aegyptiacarum. Mainz am Rhein, Germany: Philipp von Zabern, 1984.

Tübingen

Brunner-Traut, Emma, and Hellmut Brunner. *Die Ägyptische Sammlung der Universität Tübingen.* Mainz am Rhein, Germany: Philipp von Zabern, 1981.

Hungary

Nagy, István. *Museum of Fine Arts Budapest: Guide to the Egyptian Collection.* Budapest, Hungary: Museum of Fine Arts, 1999.

Török, László. *Coptic Antiquities.* 2 vols. Rome: L'Erma di Bretschneider, 1993.

Varga, Edith, and Vilmos Wessetzky. *Szépmüvészeti Múzeum. Egyiptomi Kiállítás.* Budapest, Hungary: Múzeumi Ismeretterjesztö Központ, 1964.

Italy

Asti

Leospo, Enrichetta. *Museo Archeologico di Asti: La collezione egizia.* Turin, Italy: Comune di Asti, 1986.

Bergamo

Guidotti, Maria Christina. *Civiltà egizia nel Civico Museo Archeologico di Bergamo.* Bergamo, Italy: Comune di Bergamo, 2002.

Bologna

Besciani, Edda. *Le stele egiziane del Museo Civico Archeologico di Bologna.* Bologna, Italy: Grafis Edizioni, 1985.

Pernigotti, Sergio. *La collezione egiziana: Museo Civico Archeologicodi Bologna.* Bologna, Italy: Leonardo Arte, 1994.

———. *La statuaria egiziana nel Museo Civico Archeologico di Bologna.* Bologna, Italy: Instituto per la Storia di Bologna, 1980.

Como

Guidotti, Maria Christina, and Enrichetta Leospo. *La collezione egizia del civico Museo Archeologico di Como.* Como, Italy: Comune di Como, 1994.

Cortona

Botti, Giuseppe. *Le antichità egiziane del Museo dell'Accademia di Cortona: Ordinate e descritte.* Florence, Italy: Leo S. Olschki, 1955.

Florence

Bosticco, Sergio. *Le stele egiziane.* 3 vols. Rome: Instituto Poligrafico dello Stato, 1959–1972.

Del Francia, Pier R., and Maria Christina Guidotti. *Cento Immagini Femminili nel Museo Egizio di Firenze.* Florence, Italy: XI Settimana dei Beni Culturali, 1995.

Guidotti, Maria Christina. *La Mummie del Museo Egizio di Firenze.* Florence, Italy: Giunti, 2001.

Guidotti, Maria Christina, Pier R. Del Francia, and Flora Sivano. *Gioielli e Cosmesi del Museo Egizio di Firenze.* Florence, Italy: Giunti, 2003.

Milan

Lise, Giorgio. *Museo Archeologico: Raccolta egizia.* Milan, Italy: Electa Editrice, 1979.

Naples

Borriello, Maria Rosaria, and Teresa Giove. *The Egyptian Collection of the Archaeological Museum of Naples.* Naples, Italy: Electa Napoli and Soprintendenza Archeologica di Napoli e Caserta, 2000.

Hölbl, Günther. *Le stele funerarie della collezione egizia.* Rome: Instituto Poligrafico e Zecca dello Stato, 1985.

Parma

Botti, Giuseppe. *I cimeli egizi del Museo di Antichità de Parma.* Florence, Italy: Leo S. Olschki, 1964.

Pisa

Bresciani, Edda, and F. Silvano. *La collezione Schiff Giorgini: Catalogo delle collezione egittologiche, Università di Pisa-Musei di Ateneo, 1.* Pisa, Italy: Giardini, 1992.

Rome

Careddu, Giorgio. *Museo Barracco de Scultura Antica: La collezione egizia.* Rome: Istituto Poligrafico e Zecca dello Stato, 1985.

Vittozzi, Serena E. *Musei Capitolini: La collezione egizia*. Rome: Silvana Editoriale, 1990.

Rovigo

Dolzani, *Claudia*. *La collezione Egiziana del Museo dell'Accademia dei Concordi in Rovigo*. Rome: Centro per le Antichitá e la Storia dell'Arte del Vicino Oriente, 1969.

Turin

Behlmer, Heike. *Shenute von Atripe-De Judicio*. Monumenti e Testi, 8. Turin, Italy: Ministero per I Beni e le Attivitá Culturali–Sopintendenza al Museo delle Antichitá Egizie, 1996.

Botti, Giuseppe. *L'archivio demotico da Deir el Medineh, tomo I (Testo) e II (Tavole), n. 55501–55547*. Serie I—Monumenti e Testi, Vol. I. Florence, Italy: Le Monnier, 1967.

Ciampini, E. M. *La sepoltura di Henib*. Serie I—Monumenti e Testi, Vol. 11. Turin, Italy: Ministero per I Beni e le Attivitá Culturali–Sopintendenza al Museo delle Antichitá Egizie. 2003.

Curto, Silvio. *L'antico Egitto nel Museo Egizio di Torino*. Turin, Italy: Tipografia Torinese Editrice, 1984.

———. *Storia del Museo Egizio di Torino*. Turin, Italy: Centro Studi Piemontesi, 1976.

Delorenzi, Enzo, and Renato Grilletto. *Le mummie del Museo Egizio di Torino, n. 13001–13026*. Serie II—Collezioni, Vol. VI. Milan, Italy: Cisalpino–La Goliardica, 1989.

Demichelis, Sara. *Il Calendario delle feste di Montu*. Serie I—Monumenti e Testi 10. Turin, Italy: Ministero per I Beni e le Attivitá Culturali–Sopintendenza al Museo delle Antichitá Egizie, 2002.

Dolzani, Claudia. *Vasi Canopi, n. 19001–19153*. Serie II—Collezioni, Vol. IV. Milan, Italy: Cisalpino–La Goliardica, 1982.

Donadoni Roveri, Anna Maria. *Egyptian Civilization*. 3 vols. Milan, Italy: Electa, 1988–1989.

———. *Museo Egizio*. Turin, Italy: Barisone Editore, 1996.

Habachi, Labib. *Tavole d'offerta, are e bacili da libagione, n. 22001–22067*. Serie II—Collezioni, Vol. II. Turin, Italy: Edizioni d'Arte Fratelli Pozzo, 1977.

Kákosy, László. *Egyptian Healing Statues in Three Museums in Italy*. Serie I—Monumenti e Testi 9. Turin, Italy: Ministero per I Beni e le Attivitá Culturali–Sopintendenza al Museo delle Antichitá Egizie, 1999.

Leospo, Enrichetta. *La mensa Isiaca di Torino*. Serie I—Monumenti e Testi, Vol. IV. Leiden, Netherlands: Brill, 1978.

López, Jesus. *Ostraca ieratici*. Serie II—Collezioni, Vol. III, 1–4. Milan: Cisalpino–La Goliardica, 19781984.

Niwinski, Andrzej. *Sarcofagi della XXI Dinastia (CGT 10101–10122)*. Serie II—Collezioni, Vol. IX. Turin: Ministero per I Beni e le Attivitá Culturali–Sopintendenza al Museo delle Antichitá Egizie, 2004.

Omlin, Joseph A. *Der Papyrus 55001 und Satirisch-erotische Zeichnungen und Inschriften*. Serie I—Monumenti e Testi, Vol. III. Turin, Italy: Edizioni d'Arte Fratelli Pozzo, 1970.

Pestman, Pieter W. *L'archivio di Amenothes, figlio di Horos*. Serie I–Monumenti e Testi, Vol. V. Milan, , Italy: Cisalpino-La Goliardica, 1981.

———. *Il processo di Hermias e altri documenti dell'archivio dei Choachiti*. Serie I—Monumenti e Testi, Vol. VI. Turin, Italy: Ministry of Culture, 1992.

Roccati, Alessandro. *Papiro ieratico n. 54003. Estratti magici e rituali del primo Medio Regno*. Serie I—Monumenti e Testi, Vol. II. Turin, Italy: Edizioni d'Arte Fratelli Pozzo, 1970.

Ronsecco, Paolo. *Due libri dei morti del principio del Nuovo Regno il lenzuolo funerario della principessa Ahmosi et le tele del Sa-nesu Ahmosi*. Serie I—Monumenti e Testi, Vol. VII. Turin, Italy: Ministero per i Beni Culturali e Ambientali, 1996.

Tosi, Mario, and Alessandro Roccati. *Stele e altre epigrafi di Deir el Medina, n. 50001–50262*. Serie II—Collezioni, Vol. I. Turin, Italy: Edizioni d'Arte Fratelli Pozzo, 1972.

Netherlands

Amsterdam

Van Haarlem, Willem. *Allard Pierson Museum, Fasc. I: Selection from the Collection. Vol. I*. Corpus Antiquitatum Aegyptiacarum. Mainz am Rhein, Germany: Philipp von Zabern, 1986.

———. *Allard Pierson Museum, Fasc. II, Vols. 1–2: Shabtis*. Amsterdam, Netherlands: Allard Pearson Museum, 1990.

———. *Allard Pierson Museum, Fasc. III: Stelae and Reliefs*. Corpus Antiquitatum Aegyptiacarum. Amsterdam, Netherlands: Allard Pearson Museum, 1995.

Van Haarlem, Willem, and Scheurleer, R. A. L. *Gids voor de Afdeling Egypte*. Amsterdam, Netherlands: Allard Pierson Museum, 1986.

The Hague

Spiegelberg, Wilhelm. *Die Aegyptische Sammlung des Museum-Meermanno-Westreenianum im Haag*. Strassburg, Germany: Karl J. Trübner, 1896.

Leiden

Raven, Maarten J., and Taconis, Wybren K. *Mummies: Radiological Atlas of the Collections of the National Museum of Antiquities in Leiden*. Turnhout, Belgium: Brepols, 2005.

Schneider, Hans D. *Egyptisch Kunsthandwerk*. Amsterdam, Netherlands: De Bataafsche Leeuw, 1995.

———. *De Egyptische Outheid*. Gravenhage Gravenhage: Staatsuitgeverij, 1981.

Norway

Naguib, Saphinaz Amal. *Etnografisk Museum Oslo, Fasc. I: Funerary Statuettes*. Corpus Antiquitatum Aegyptiacarum. Mainz, Germany: Philipp von Zabern, 1985.

———. *Etnografisk Museum Oslo, Fasc. 2: Predynastic Pottery*. Corpus Antiquitatum Aegyptiacarum. Oslo, Norway: Novus Forlag, 1987.

Poland

Babraj, Krzysztof, and Szymanska, Hanna. *The Gods of Ancient Egypt*. Cracow, Poland: Archaeological Museum in Cracow, 2000.

Portugal

De Araujo, Luis Manuel. *Antiquidades Egicias. Museu National de Arqueologia*. Lisbon, Portugal: Museu National de Arqueologia, 1993.

Russia

Berlev, Oleg, and Svetlana Hodjash. *Catalogue of the Monuments of Ancient Egypt from the Museums of the Russian Federation, Ukraine, Bielorussia, Caucasus, Middle Asia, and the Baltic States*. Fribourg, Switzerland: UP, 1998.

Moscow

Hodjash, Svetlana. *Ancient Egyptian Vessels in the State Pushkin Museum of Fine Art, Moscow.* Baltimore: Halgo, 2005.

———. *The Way to Immortality: Monuments of Ancient Egyptian Art from the Collection of the Pushkin State Museum of Fine Arts.* Moscow, Russia: Vostochnaya Literatura, 2002. (In Russian.)

Hodjash, Svetlana, and Oleg Berlev. *The Egyptian Reliefs and Stelae in the Pushkin Museum, Moscow.* Leningrad, Russia: Aurora Art Publishers, 1982.

St. Petersburg

Bolshakov, Andrey O. *Studies on the Old Kingdom: Reliefs and Sculpture in the Hermitage.* Wiesbaden, Germany, Otto Harrasowitz, 2005.

Bolshakov, Andrey, and Stephan Qurike. *The Middle Kingdom Stelae in the Hermitage.* Utrecht, Netherlands: Utrecht University, 1999.

Piotrovsky, Boris, ed. *Egyptian Antiquities in the Hermitage.* Leningrad, Russia: Aurora Art Publishers, 1974.

Spain

Almenara Rosales, Eduardo, and Candelaria Martín del Río Alvarez. *Colección de Vasos Egipcios del Museo Municipal de Bellas Artes de Santa Cruz de Tenerife.* Tenerife, Spain: Ayuntamiento de Santa Cruz de Tenerife, 2000.

Seco Alvarez, Myriam. *La Colección Egipcia de la Universidad Hispalense.* Seville, Spain: University of Seville, 2000.

Switzerland

Chappaz, Jean-Luc, and Sandra Poggia. *Collections égyptiennes publiques de Suisse.* Cahiers de la Société d'Égyptologie, vol. 3. Geneva, Switzerland: Société d'Egyptologie Genève, 1996.

Basel

Wiese, André. *Antikenmuseum Basel und Sammlung Ludwig: Die Ägyptische Abteilung.* Mainz am Rhein, Germany: Philipp von Zabern, 2001.

Geneva: Bibliotheca Bodmeriana

Chappaz, Jean-Luc, and Sandrine Vuilleumier. *Sortir au jour. Art égyptien de la Fondation Martin Bodmer.* Geneva, Switzerland: Bibliotheca Bodmeriana, 2001.

Geneva: Musee d'Art et d'Histoire

Castioni, Christiane, Dominique Dérobert, Robert Hari, Jocelyne Muller-Aubert, and Bérengère Stahl-Guinand. *Égypte.* Geneva, Switzerland: Musée d'Art et d'Histoire, 1977.

Chappaz, Jean-Luc. *Les figurines funéraires du Musée d'Art et d'histoire de Genève.* Geneva, Switzerland: Musée d'Art et d'Histoire Genève, 1984.

Vodoz, Irene. *Les scarabées gravés du Musée d'Art et d'Histoire de Genève.* Geneva, Switzerland: Musée d'Art et d'Histoire, 1978.

United Kingdom

Cambridge

Martin, Geoffrey T. *Stelae from Egypt and Nubia in the Fitzwilliam Museum.* Cambridge, U.K.: Cambridge University Press, 2005.

Vassilika, Eleni. *Egyptian Art: Fitzwilliam Museum Handbooks.* Cambridge, U.K.: Cambridge University Press, 1995.

Glasgow

McDowell, Andrea G. *Hieratic Ostraca in the Hunterian Museum, Glasgow.* Oxford, U.K.: Griffith Institute, 1993.

Ipswich

Plunkett, Steven. *From the Mummy's Tomb: Ancient Egyptian Treasures in Ipswich Museum.* Ipswich, U.K.: Ipswich Borough Council, 1993.

Liverpool

Bienkowski, Piotr, and Angela M. J. Tooley. *Gifts of the Nile: Ancient Egyptian Arts and Crafts in the Liverpool Museum.* London: HMSO, 1995.

Bienkowski, Piotr, and Edmund Southworth. *Egyptian Antiquities in the Liverpool Museum, Vol. I: A List of the Provenanced Objects.* Warminster, G.B.: Aris & Phillips, 1986.

London: British Museum

Anderson, Robert D. *Catalogue of Egyptian Antiquities in the British Museum, Vol. III: Musical Instruments.* London: British Museum Publications, 1976.

Andrews, Carol A. R. *Catalogue of Egyptian Antiquities in the British Museum, Vol. VI: Jewellery from the Earliest Times to the 17th Dynasty*. London: British Museum Publications, 1981.

——. *Catalogue of Demotic Papyri in the British Museum, Vol. IV: Ptolemaic Legal Texts from the Theban Area*. London: British Museum Publications, 1990.

Bierbrier, Morris L. *Hieroglyphic Texts from Egyptian Stelae in the British Museum. Part 10*. London: British Museum Publications, 1982.

——. *Hieroglyphic Texts from Egyptian Stelae in the British Museum. Part 11*. London: British Museum Publications, 1987.

——. *Hieroglyphic Texts from Egyptian Stelae in the British Museum. Part 12*. London: British Museum Press, 1993.

Birch, Samuel. *Select Papyri in the Hieratic Character from the Collections of the British Museum. Parts 1–2*. London: British Museum, 1844–1860.

British Museum. *Hieroglyphic Texts from Egyptian Stelae, etc. in the British Museum. Parts 1–12*. London: British Museum, 1911–1993.

Budge, E. A. Wallis. *Facsimiles of Egyptian Hieratic Papyri in the British Museum*. London: British Museum, 1910.

——. *Facsimiles of Egyptian Hieratic Papyri in the British Museum, 2nd Series*. London: British Museum, 1923.

Cooney, John D. *Catalogue of Egyptian Antiquities in the British Museum, Vol. IV: Glass*. London: British Museum Publications, 1976.

Davies, W. Vivian. *Catalogue of Egyptian Antiquities in the British Museum, Vol. VII: Tools and Weapons*. London: British Museum Publications, 1987.

Dawson, Warren. R., and Peter H. K. Gray. *Catalogue of Egyptian Antiquities in the British Museum, Vol. I: Mummies and Human Remains*. London: British Museum, 1968.

Demarée, Robert J. *The Bankes Late Ramesside Papyri*. London: British Museum Press, 2006.

——. *Ramesside Ostraca*. London: British Museum Press, 2003.

Edwards, I. Eiddon S. *Hieratic Papyri in the British Museum, 4th Series: Oracular Amuletic Decrees of the Late New Kingdom*. London: British Museum, 1960.

——. *Hieroglyphic Texts from Egyptian Stelae, etc. Part 8*. London: British Museum, 1939.

Gardiner, Alan H. *Hieratic Papyri in the British Museum, 3rd Series: Chester Beatty Gift*. London: British Museum, 1935.

Glanville, Stephen R. K. *Catalogue of Demotic Papyri in the British Museum, Vol. I: A Theban Archive of the Reign of Ptolemy I, Soter*. London: British Museum, 1939.

———. *Catalogue of Demotic Papyri in the British Museum, Vol. II: The Instructions of 'Onchsheshonqy (P. BM 10508)*. London: British Museum: 1955.

———. *Catalogue of Egyptian Antiquities in the British Museum, Vol. II: Wooden and Model Boats*. London: British Museum, 1972.

Hall, Henry R. *Hieroglyphic Texts from Egyptian Stelae, etc. in the British Museum*. London: British Museum, 1925.

Herbin, François. *Late Egyptian Religious Texts in the BM I: Book of Breathing and Related Texts*. London: British Museum Press, 2006.

James, T. G. Henry. *Hieroglyphic Texts from Egyptian Stelae in the British Museum. Part 9*. London: British Museum, 1970.

Janssen, Jac J. *Grain Transport in the Ramesside Period: Papyrus Baldwin and Papyrus Amiens*. London: British Museum Press, 2004.

———. *Hieratic Papyri in the British Museum VI. Late Ramesside Letters and Communications*. London: British Museum Publications, 1991.

Lapp, Günther. *Catalogue of the Books of the Dead in the British Museum, Vol. I: The Papyrus of Nu (BM EA 10477)*. London: British Museum Press, 1997.

———. *Catalogue of the Books of the Dead in the British Museum, Vol. III: The Papyrus of Nebseni (BM EA 9900)*. London: British Museum Press, 2004.

Leitz, Christian. *Catalogue of Hieratic Papyri in the British Musuem VII: Magical and Medical Papyri of the New Kingdom*. London: British Museum Press, 2000.

Mosher, Malcolm, Jr. *Catalogue of the Books of the Dead in the British Museum, Vol. II: The Papyrus of Hor*. London: British Museum Press, 2001.

Posener-Kriéger, Paule, and Jean L. de Cenival. *Hieratic Papyri in the British Museum, 5th Series: Abu Sir Papyri*. London: British Museum, 1968.

Robins, Gay, and Charles Shute. *The Rhind Mathematical Papyrus*. London: British Museum Publications, 1987.

Russman, Edna. *Eternal Egypt: Masterworks of Ancient Art from the British Museum*. London and New York: British Museum Press and American Federation of Arts, 2001.

Smith, Mark. *Catalogue of Demotic Papyri in the British Museum, Vol. III: The Mortuary Texts of P. BM 10507*. London: British Museum Publications, 1987.

Spencer, A. Jeffrey. *Catalogue of Egyptian Antiquities in the British Museum, Vol. V: Early Dynastic Objects*. London: British Museum Publications, 1980.

Spencer, Neal. *The Gayer-Anderson Cat*. London: British Museum Press, 2007.

Strudwick, Nigel. *Masterpieces of Ancient Egypt*. London: British Museum Press, 2006.

Thompson, Herbert. *A Family Archive from Siut from Papyri in the British Museum*. Oxford, U.K.: Clarendon Press, 1934.

London: Petrie Museum

Adams, Barbara. *Sculptured Pottery from Koptos*. Warminster, G.B.: Aris & Phillips, 1986.

Page, Anthea. *Ancient Egyptian Figured Ostraca from the Petrie Collection*. Warminster, G.B.: Aris & Phillips, 1983.

Picton, Jan, Stephen Quirke, and Paul Roberts. *Living Images: Egyptian Funerary Portraits in the Petrie Museum*. Walnut Creek, Calif.: Left Coast Press, 2007.

Raisman, Vivian, and Geoffrey T. Martin. *Canopic Equipment in the Petrie Museum*. Warminster, G.B.: Aris & Phillips, 1984.

Samson, Julia. *Amarna, City of Akhenaten and Nefertiti: Key Pieces from the Petrie Collection*. Warminster, G.B.: Aris & Phillips, 1979.

Stewart, Harry M. *Egyptian Stelae, Reliefs, and Paintings from the Petrie Collection*. 3 vols. Warminster, G.B.: Aris & Phillips, 1976–1983.

———. *Mummy Cases and Inscribed Funerary Cones in the Petrie Collection*. Warminster, G.B.: Aris & Phillips, 1985.

Trope, Betsy T., Stephen Quirke, and Peter Lacovara. *Excavating Egypt: Great Discoveries from the Petrie Museum of Egyptian Archaeology*. Atlanta, Ga.: Michael C. Carlos Museum, 2005.

London: Victoria and Albert Museum (now in the British Museum)

Adams, Barbara. *Egyptian Objects in the Victoria and Albert Museum*. Warminster, G.B.: Aris & Phillips, 1979.

Macclesfield

David, A. Rosalie. *The Macclesfield Collection of Egyptian Antiquities*. Warminster, G.B.: Aris & Phillips, 1980.

Oxford

Moorey, P. Roger S. *Ancient Egypt: University of Oxford, Ashmolean Museum*. Oxford, U.K.: Ashmolean Museum, 1970.

Payne, Joan Crowfoot. *Catalogue of the Predynastic Egyptian Collection in the Ashmolean Museum, Oxford*. Oxford, U.K.: Clarendon Press, 1993.

United States

Baltimore

Schulz, Regina. *Khepereru-Scarabs, Scarabs, Scarboids, and Plaques from Egypt and the Near East in the Walters Art Museum, Baltimore.* Baltimore: Halgo, 2007.
Steindorff, Georg. *Catalogue of the Egyptian Sculpture in the Walters Art Gallery.* Baltimore: Walters Art Gallery, 1946.

Boston

Brovarski, Edward. *Museum of Fine Arts, Boston. Fasc. I: Canopic Jars.* Corpus Antiquitatum Aegyptiacarum. Mainz am Rhein, Germany: Philipp von Zabern, 1978.
Dunham, Dows. *The Egyptian Department and Its Excavations.* Boston: Museum of Fine Arts, 1958.
Freed, Rita, Lawrence Berman, and Denise Doxey. *Arts of Ancient Egypt.* Boston: Museum of Fine Arts Publications, 2003.
Leprohon, Ronald J. *Museum of Fine Arts, Boston. Fasc. II: Stelae 1, The Early Dynastic Period to the Late Middle Kingdom.* Corpus Antiquitatum Aegyptiacarum. Mainz am Rhein, Germany: Philipp von Zabern, 1985.
———. *Museum of Fine Arts, Boston. Fasc. III: Stelae 2, The New Kingdom to the Coptic Period.* Corpus Antiquitatum Aegyptiacarum. Mainz am Rhein, Germany: Philipp von Zabern, 1991.

Chicago

Teeter, Emily. *Ancient Egypt: Treasures from the Collection of the Oriental Institute.* Chicago: University of Chicago Press, 2003.

Cleveland

Berman, Lawrence. *The Cleveland Museum of Art: Catalogue of Egyptian Art.* Cleveland, Ohio: Cleveland Museum of Art, 1999.

New Haven

Scott, Gerry D., III. *Ancient Egyptian Art at Yale.* New Haven, Conn.: Yale University Art Gallery, 1986.

New York: Brooklyn Museum

Fazzini, Richard A., Robert S. Bianchi, James F. Romano, and Donald B. Spanel. *Ancient Egyptian Art in The Brooklyn Museum*. Brooklyn. N.Y.: Brooklyn Museum and Thames & Hudson, 1989.
———. *Art For Eternity: Masterworks from Ancient Egypt*. Brooklyn, N.Y.: Brooklyn Museum of Art and Scala, 1999.
Hayes, William C. *A Papyrus of the Late Middle Kingdom in The Brooklyn Museum (Pap Brooklyn 35.1446)*. Brooklyn, N.Y.: Brooklyn Museum, 1955.
Hughes, George R. *Catalog of Demotic Texts in the Brooklyn Museum*. Chicago: Oriental Institute of the University of Chicago, 2005.
James, T. G. Henry. *Corpus of Hieroglyphic Inscriptions in The Brooklyn Museum I*. Brooklyn, N.Y.: Brooklyn Museum, 1974.
Jasnow, Richard. *A Late Period Hieratic Wisdom Text (P. Brooklyn 47.218.135)*. Chicago: Oriental Institute of the University of Chicago, 1992.
Meeks, Dimitri. *Mythes et Légends du Delta d'après le papyrus Brooklyn 47.218.84*. Cairo: Institut français d'archéologie orientale, 2006.
Riefstahl, Elisabeth. *Ancient Egyptian Glass and Glazes in The Brooklyn Museum*. Brooklyn, N.Y.: Brooklyn Museum, 1968.
Sauneron, Serge. *Le papyrus magique illustré de Brooklyn*. Brooklyn, N.Y.: Brooklyn Museum: 1970.
Thompson, Deborah. *Coptic Textiles in The Brooklyn Museum*. Brooklyn, N.Y.: Brooklyn Museum, 1971.

New York: Metropolitan Museum of Art

Allen, James P. *The Heqanakht Papyri*. New York: Metropolitan Museum of Art, 2002.
Metropolitan Museum of Art. *Guide to the Metropolitan Museum of Art*. New York: Metropolitan Museum of Art, 1972.
Smith, Mark. *Papyrus Harkness*. Oxford, U.K.: Griffith Institute, 2005.
Wilkinson, Charles, and Marsha Hill. *The Metropolitan Museum of Art's Collection of Facsimiles*. New York: Metropolitan Museum of Art, 1983.

Pittsburgh

Patch, Diana C. *Reflections of Greatness: Ancient Egypt at The Carnegie Museum of Natural History*. Pittsburgh, Pa.: Carnegie Museum of Natural History, 1990.

San Bernardino

Kaplan, Julius D. *Predynastic Pottery in the Collection of the Robert V. Fullerton Art Museum, California State University, San Bernardino*. San Bernardino, Calif.: Robert V. Fuller Art Museum, 2005.

Washington, D.C.

Gunter, Ann C. *A Collector's Journey: Charles Lang Freer and Egypt*. Washington: Freer Art Gallery and Scala Publishers, 2002.

Vatican City

Botti, Giuseppe, and Pietro Romanelli. *Le sculture del Museo Gregoriano Egizio*. Vatican City: Poliglotta Vaticana, 1951.
Gasse, Annie. *Les papyrus hiératiques et hiéroglyphiques du Museo Gregoriano Egizio*. Vatican City: Monumenti, Musei e Gallerie Pontificie 1993.
———. *Les sarcophages de la troisième periode intermèdiaire du Museo Gregoriano Egizio*. Vatican City: Monumenti, Musei e Gallerie Pontificie, 1996.
Grenier, Jean-Claude. *Museo Gregoriano Egizio: Guide cataloghi musei Vaticani*. Rome: L'Erma di Bretschneider, 1993.
———. *Les statuettes funéraires du Museo Gregoriano Egizio*. Vatican City: Monumenti, Musei e Gallerie Pontificie, 1996.

CLASSICAL SOURCES

Burton, Anne. *Diodorus Siculus. Book I: A Commentary*. Leiden, Netherlands: Brill, 1972.
Diodorus Siculus. *The Library of History, Book I*, trans. C. H. Oldfather. Loeb Classical Library. London: William Heinemann, 1933.
Griffiths, J. Gwyn. *Apuleius of Madauros: The Isis Book, Metamorphoses Book XI*. Leiden, Netherlands: Brill, 1975.
———. *Plutarch's De Iside et Osiride*. Cambridge, U.K.: University of Wales Press, 1970.
Herodotus. *Histories, Book II*, trans. A. D. Godley. Loeb Classical Library. London: William Heinemann, 1921.
Horapollo. *The Hieroglyphics*, trans. George Boas. Bollinger Series XXIII. New York: Pantheon Books, 1950. New edition with new foreword, Princeton, N.J.: Princeton University Press, 1993.

Lloyd, Alan B. *Herodotus Book II: Introduction and Commentary*. 3 vols. Leiden, Netherlands: Brill, 1975–1988.
Manetho. *Aegyptiaca*, trans. W. G. Wadell. Loeb Classical Library. London: William Heinemann, 1940.
Strabo. *The Geography of Strabo VIII, Book 17*, trans. H. L. Jones. Loeb Classical Library. London: William Heinemann, 1982.

HISTORY OF EGYPTOLOGY AND TRAVELERS TO EGYPT

Bednarski, Andrew. *Holding Egypt: Tracing the Reception of the Description d'Égypte in Nineteenth-Century Great Britain*. London: Golden House Publications, 2005.
Buhl, Marie-Louise. *Les dessins archéologiques et topographiques de l'Egypte ancienne faits par F. L. Norden 1737–1738*. Copenhagen: L'Académie royale des Sciences et Lettres de Denmark, 1993.
Champollion, Jean-François. *Monuments de l'Égypte et de la Nubie*. 2 vols. 1835. Reprint, Geneva: Éditions de Belles-Lettres, 1972.
Clayton, Peter A. *The Rediscovery of Ancient Egypt*. London: Thames & Hudson, 1984.
Curl, James Stevens. *The Egyptian Revival*. London: George Allen & Unwin, 1982.
Dawson, Warren R., and Eric P. Uphill. *Who Was Who in Egyptology*. 3rd ed., revised by M. L. Bierbrier. London: Egypt Exploration Society, 1995.
Dewachter, Michel, and Charles C. Gillispie. *Monuments of Egypt: The Napoleonic Expedition*. Princeton, N.J.: Princeton Architectural Press, 1987.
Donadoni, Sergio, Silvio Curto, and Anna Maria Donadoni Roveri. *Egypt from Myth to Egyptology*. Milan, Italy: Fabbri Editori, 1990.
Drower, Margaret S. *Flinders Petrie: A Life in Archaeology*. London: Victor Gollancz, 1985.
———. *Letters from the Desert: The Correspondence of Flinders and Hilda Petrie*. Oxford, U.K.: Aris & Phillips, 2004.
Greener, Leslie. *The Discovery of Egypt*. London: Cassell, 1966.
Grundon, Imogen. *The Rash Adventurer: A Life of John Pendlebury*. London: Libri, 2007.
Hankey, Julie. *A Passion for Egypt: A Biography of Arthur Weigall*. London: I. B. Tauris, 2001.
James, T. G. Henry. *Howard Carter: The Path to Tutankhamun*. London: Kegan Paul International, 1992.
Kamil, Jill. *Labib Habachi: The Life and Legacy of an Egyptologist*. Cairo: American University in Cairo Press, 2007.

Lepsius, Carl Richard. *Denkmaeler aus Aegypten und Aethiopien.* 3 vols. 1849–1859. Reprint, Geneva: Éditions de Belles-Lettres, 1975.

Manley, Deborah, and Peta Rée. *Henry Salt.* London: Libri, 2001.

Mayes, Stanley. *The Great Belzoni.* London: Putnam, 1959.

Moon, Brenda. *More Usefully Employed: Amelia B. Edwards, Writer, Traveller and Campaigner for Ancient Egypt.* London: Egypt Exploration Society, 2006.

Ray, John. *The Rosetta Stone and the Rebirth of Ancient Egypt.* London: Profile Books, 2007.

Ridley, Ronald T. *Napoleon's Proconsul in Egypt: The Life and Times of Bernardino Drovetti.* London: Rubicon Press, 1998.

Roehrig, Catherine. *Explorers and Artists in the Valley of the Kings.* Vercelli, Italy: White Star Publications, 2001.

Schneider, Hans, ed. *"Notes diverses" d'un futur grand antiquaire. Un manuscript de jeuness de J.-F. Champollion se trouvant au Musée d'Antiquités des Pays-Bas a Leyde.* Turnhout, Belgium: Brepols, 2006.

Sim, Katherine. *Desert Traveller: The Life of Jean Louis Burckhardt.* London: Victor Gollancz, 1969.

Spencer, Patricia, ed. *The Egypt Exploration Society: The Early Years.* London: Egypt Exploration Society, 2007.

Thompson, Jason. *Edward William Lane.* Oxford, U.K.: Oxbow Books, 2008.

———. *Sir Gardner Wilkinson and His Circle.* Austin: University of Texas Press, 1992.

Tillett, Selwyn. *Egypt Itself: The Career of Robert Hay, Esquire of Linplum and Nunraw, 1799–1863.* London: SD Books, 1984.

Wilson, John. *Signs and Wonders upon Pharaoh.* Chicago: University of Chicago Press, 1964.

TRAVEL

Kamil, Jill. *Aswan and Abu Simbel.* Cairo: American University in Cairo Press, 1991.

———. *Luxor: A Guide to Ancient Thebes.* Cairo: Egyptian International Publishing Co., 1996.

———. *Sakkara: A Guide to the Necropolis of Sakkara and the Site of Memphis.* Cairo: Egyptian International Publishing Co., 1996.

———. *Upper Egypt: Historical Outline and Descriptive Guide to the Ancient Sites.* Cairo: Egyptian International Publishing Co., 1996.

Morkot, Robert. *Egypt Land of the Pharaohs.* Hong Kong: Odyssey Publications, 2000.

Murnane, William J. *The Penguin Guide to Ancient Egypt*. Rev. ed. London: Penguin Books, 1996.

Richardson, Dan, and Daniel Jacobs. *The Rough Guide to Egypt*. 7th ed. New York and London: Rough Guides, 2007.

Seton-Williams, Veronica, and Peter Stocks. *Blue Guide to Egypt*. 3rd ed. London: A&C Black, 1993.

BIBLIOGRAPHIES

Beinlich-Seeber, Christine. *Bibliographie Altägypten, 1822–1946*. 3 vols. Wiesbaden, Germany: Otto Harrassowitz, 1998.

Henrickx, Stan. *Analytical Bibliography of the Prehistory and Early Dynastic Period of Egypt and Northern Sudan*. Leuven, Belgium: Leuven University Press, 1995.

Hilmy, Ibrahim. *The Literature of Egypt and the Soudan from the Earliest Times to the Year 1885 Inclusive*. 2 vols. London: Trübner & Co., 1886.

Janssen, Jozef M. A., Louis M. Zonhoven, Jac J. Janssen, and Matthieu Sybrand Huibert Gerard Heerma van Voss. *Annual Egyptological Bibliography*. Leiden, Netherlands and Warminster, G.B.: Brill, 1947–1976 and Aris & Phillips, 1977–1981 and International Association of Egyptologists, 1982–.

Kalfatovic, Martin R. *Nile Notes of a Howadji: A Bibliography of Travelers' Tales from Egypt from the Earliest Times to 1918*. Metuchen, N.J.: Scarecrow Press, 1992.

Kammerer, Wilfred. *Coptic Bibliography*. Ann Arbor: University of Michigan Press, 1950.

Malek, Jaromir. *Topographical Bibliography of Ancient Egyptian Hieroglyphic Texts, Reliefs, and Paintings, VIII: Objects of Provenance Not Known*. Oxford, U.K.: Griffith Institute, 1999–2007.

Porter, Bertha, and Rosalind L. B. Moss. *Topographical Bibliography of Ancient Egyptian Hieroglyphic Texts, Reliefs, and Paintings*. 7 vols. Oxford, U.K.: Clarendon Press, 1927–1960. New edition in progress, vols. 1–3, 1960–1981; from 1974 edited by Jaromir Malek.

Pratt, Ida A. *Ancient Egypt*. Sources for Information in the New York Public Library. 2 vols. New York: New York Public Library, 1925–1942.

Weeks, Kent R. *An Historical Bibliography of Egyptian Prehistory*. American Research Center in Egypt. Catalogs, No. 6. Winona Lake, Ind.: Eisenbrauns, 1985.

PERIODICALS

Bibliotheca Orientalis. Leiden, Netherlands, 1947– . Annually.
Bulletin Copte. Cairo, 1935– . Annually.
Bulletin de la Société d'Égyptologie Genève. Geneva, Switzerland, 1979– . Annually.
Bulletin de la Société française d'Égyptologie. Paris, 1949– . Triannually.
Bulletin de l'Institut français d'Archéologie orientale. Cairo, 1901– . Annually.
Bulletin of the Egyptological Seminar. New York, 1979– . Annually.
Cahier de recherches de l'Institut de Papyrologie et d'Égyptologie de Lille. Lille, France, 1973– . Annually.
Chronique d'Égypte. Brussels, Belgium, 1925– . Annually.
Egyptian Archaeology. London, 1991–1993. Annually. 1994– . Biannually.
Enchoria. Wiesbaden, Germany, 1971– . Annually.
Göttinger Miszellen. Göttingen, Germany, 1972– .
Journal of Egyptian Archaeology. London, 1914– . Annually.
Journal of Near Eastern Studies. Chicago, 1942– . Annually.
Journal of the American Research Center in Egypt. New York, 1962– . Annually.
Journal of the Society for the Study of Egyptian Antiquities. Toronto, 1970– .
KMT. San Francisco, Calif., 1990– . Quarterly.
Lingua Aegyptia. Göttingen, Germany, 1991– . Annually.
Mitteilungen des Deutschen Archäologischen Instituts Abteilung Kairo. Mainz am Rhein, Germany, 1930– . Annually.
Orientalia. Rome, 1920– . Annually.
Studien zur Altägyptischen Kultur. Hamburg, Germany, 1974– . Annually.
Zeitschrift für ägyptische Sprache und Altertumskunde. Berlin, Germany, 1863– . Biannually.

About the Author

Morris L. Bierbrier (B.A., McGill College, Montreal; M.A., University of Toronto; Ph.D., University of Liverpool) was assistant keeper in the Department of Egyptian Antiquities at the British Museum, London, for 25 years before his retirement. He is a fellow of the Society of Antiquaries. Bierbrier is author of *The Late New Kingdom in Egypt: A Genealogical and Chronological Investigation* (1975) and *The Tomb-Builders of the Pharaohs* (1992), which has been translated into French, Arabic, and Japanese. He has written numerous articles and reviews in professional journals and is the editor of *Who Was Who in Egyptology*.